Denver & South Park—HIGH LINE DISTRICT—Como and Leadville.

Supplement No. 1 to Time Table No. 21. August 1st, 1889.

WESTWARD (left) · EASTWARD (right)

Length of sidings in feet, and Location of Scales, Water, Fuel and Turning Stations	3d Class 417 Freight — Leave Daily Exc. Sunday	Second Class 499 Time Frt. — Leave Daily Exc. Monday	Second Class 483 Frt. & Pass. — Leave Daily Exc. Sunday	First Class 401 Mail & Ex. — Leave Daily	Distances from Denver	STATIONS	Distances from Leadville	First Class 402 Mail & Ex. — Arrive Daily	Second Class 482 Frt. & Pass. — Arrive Daily Exc. Sunday	Second Class 488 Time Frt. — Arrive Daily Exc. Sunday	3d Class 416 Freight — Arrive Daily Exc. Sunday	Minimum time for third-class trains between stations
11,863 T.F.W	7.15 am	2.05 am		1.25 pm	88.2	N—— COMO ——Mo	62.9	12.40 pm		7.40 pm	3.20 pm	.08
1,734					88.7	Coals Spur 0.5	62.4					.30
808 w	8.05	2.40*		1.50*	93.8	Half Way 5.1	57.3	12.16*		7.10	2.52	.17
665	8.30	2.57*		2.04*	96.6	Selkirk Spur 2.8	54.5	12.05* pm		6 55	2.32	.13
1,566 T. F.W	8.50	3.10		2.15	98.7	D—— Boreas ——Bo 2.1	52.4	11.55 am		6.40	{ 2.15, 2.05 }	.07
480	8.57	3.16*		2.20*	99.9	Farnham Spur 1.2	51.2	11.50*		6.29	1.50	.06
738	9.05	3.20*		2.23*	100.8	Dwyer Spur 0.9	50.3	11.48*		6.20	1.40	.08
					102.1	Bakers Tank 1.3	49.0					
814 F.W	9.25	3.32*		2.35*	103.7	Argentine 1.6	47.4	11.30*		5.55	1.10	.10
322					105.8	Washington Spur 2.1	46.8					.13
565	9.40	3.43*		2.45*	106.4	Mayo Spur 0.6	44.7	11.19*		5.35	12.40	.05
297					108.1	Suttons Spur 1.7	43.0					.08
212					108.5	Little Mountain Spur 0.4	42.6					.03
3 965 Y.F.W	10.15	4.00	3.15 pm	3.00	110.0	D—— Breckenridge ——Hd 1.5	41.1	11.00	{ 10.15, 9.40 am }	5.05	12.01 pm	.08
175	10.37				111.7	Bartholomews Spur 1.7	39.4					.08
1,072	{ 10.47, 11.05 }	4.14*	3.30	3.11*	113.3	Braddocks 1.6	37.8	10.47*	9.25	4.40	11.30 am	.07
4,383 Y.F.W	11.45 am	4.25	{ 3.40 pm, 4.25 }	3.22	116.4	D—— Dickey ——Jd 3.1	34.7	10.38	9.15 am	{ 4.25, 4.10 }	{ 11.05, 10.38, 10.28 }	.16
669	12.15 pm			3.29	118.3	Hathaways 1.9	32.8	10.31				.11
1,141	12.15 pm	4.42*		3.35*	119.9	Frisco 1.6	31.2	10.25*		3.52	10.05	.09
728	12.30	4.53*		3 42	122.0	Curtin 2.1	29.1	10.18*		{ 3.42, 3.32 }	9.50	.13
1,355 w	1.00	5.18*		3.57*	126.1	Wheeler 4.1	25.0	10.05*		3.05	9.30	.20
281					130.5	Wilders Spur 4.4	20.6					.22
w					132.2	Kokomo Tank 1.7	18.9					.09
1,214	1.55	5.45*		4.20	132.9	D—— Kokomo ——Ko 0.7	18.2	9.45		2.30	8.55	
1,175	{ 2.10, 2.20 }	5.55*		4.27	134.6	D—— Robinson ——Rb 1.7	16.5	9.38		2.20	8.45	
1,854 T.F.	2.40	6.10*		4.39	137.4	D—— Climax ——Ak 2.8	13.7	9.29		2.05	8.30	
733	2.48	6.16*		4.44*	138.9	Alicante 1.5	12.2	9.23*		1.55	8.20	
297					142.3	French Gulch Spur 3.4	8.8					
217					143.1	English Gulch Spur 0.8	8.0					
532 w	3.15	6.37*		5.00*	144.8	Birds Eye Spur 1.7	6.3	9.05*		1.20	7.40	
					147.5	Three Mile Tank 1.7	3.6					
					150.4	D. & R. G. R. R. Crossing 2.9						
12,840 S.T. F.W	3.50 pm	7.00 am		5.20 pm	151.1	D—— LEADVILLE ——Vi 0.7	0.7	8.45 am		12.40 pm	7.00 am	

Westward footings: Arrive Daily Exc. Sunday (417) — Arrive Daily Exc. Monday (499) — Arrive Daily Exc. Sunday (483) — Arrive Daily (401). (8.35) (4.55) (0.25) (3.55)

Eastward footings: Leave Daily (402) — Leave Daily Exc. Sunday (482) — Leave Daily Exc. Sunday (488) — Leave Daily Exc. Sunday (416). (3.55) (0.25) (7.00) (3.30) (8.30)

(62.9) (18 C)

West-bound trains will have absolute right to the track over East-bound trains of the same or inferior class. See Rule 62.

When any train becomes 12 hours late it loses all Time Table rights. See Rule 63.   No Train or Engine will leave Como or Leadville without Special Order or Release Ticket.

1994.8.41

MEMORIAL EDITION

DENVER SOUTH PARK & PACIFIC

In Memory of
M. C. "Mac" Poor

June 28th, 1901 -- April 17th, 1973

MEMORIAL EDITION

DENVER SOUTH PARK & PACIFIC

M. C. POOR

Printed by the World Press
Denver, Colorado, U.S.A.

PUBLISHED BY

THE

ROCKY MOUNTAIN

RAILROAD CLUB

P. O. BOX 2391
DENVER, COLORADO
80201

TO THE READER

During the time this history was being written, it was thought that, upon completion, it would be published by the Railway & Locomotive Historical Society of Boston, Mass.

However, when the work was completed, it was found that the history, with its accompanying maps, charts, and illustrations, was too large a project for the Society to handle unless a considerable proportion of the material was cut out. The elimination of any material was rejected by the author.

This volume, published by the Rocky Mountain Railroad Club of Denver, Colorado, includes the entire original manuscript. The author wishes to sincerely thank this organization for all their efforts in the publication and distribution of this historical book.

M. C. POOR.

EDITORS' NOTE

Over twenty-five years ago, in 1948, the Rocky Mountain Railroad Club, then a small organization of 223 members, embarked on its first, and most perilous publishing venture. Officers and directors of the club voted to undertake the publication of DENVER SOUTH PARK & PACIFIC for club member M. C. (Mac) Poor, using the prepublication subscription method to provide the necessary funding. Almost $7,000 were raised and although this was over $2,000 short of the amount required, we voted to proceed and typesetting and printing began. Thousands of pounds of lead were involved, and halfway through the printing, World Press began melting type slugs from the initial chapters to use in setting type for the final chapters. When the book came from the binders and was distributed it was an instant success and every available copy left from the 1,000 copies printed was sold shortly thereafter. With the type having been melted down, there was no way to order additional copies printed and the book became a collector's item. What copies were resold brought premium prices. Through the years the club has been berated by people who were unable to obtain a copy of this book at a reasonable price. Our organization steadfastly refused to put out a reproduction that we would have been ashamed of as had happened in similar situations with which we were familiar. This situation existed until 1971 when World Press did some sample reprinting work for the club, and Mac Poor and the club's officers and directors agreed that a reprint of sufficient quality to ensure no damage to the club's reputation could be reproduced for a price low enough to be available to the average railroad historian.

No action was taken until a few months after Mac Poor's death on April 17th, 1973, when club officials decided to proceed with the republication as a Memorial Edition dedicated to the memory of our dear friend and fellow historian and in honor of his years of ardent labor in this field.

We are deeply indebted to Mike Koch for the use of the painting "Night Train to Gunnison" and to Philip Ronfor and the Colorado Railroad Museum for the loan of the painting "Meet at Little Mountain Spur". These paintings, both by Ronfor, and a color photo of Mac Poor have been reproduced in full color for the book. Our thanks

also to Charles Ryland for loaning us his original 1883 Colorado Central Railroad, Colorado Division Timetable reproduced on page 85. We were most fortunate in being able to locate almost 100% of the maps, charts, and pictures used in the original book and to be able to add some very rare and interesting historical photographs to many of the blank pages in the original publication. Only four of the original photos could not be obtained and these were replaced with almost duplicate photographs. The only changes made were the correction of a few minor typographical errors, enlarging and relocating a few of the photos, printing the entire 1883 timetable, adding to the index, and using the Colorado Central and Denver South Park & Pacific locomotive rosters from the Pictorial Supplement to Denver South Park & Pacific, 1959, which in turn were revised somewhat to provide additional information and make minor corrections.

In conclusion, our sincere thanks to all our fellow members for their valuable assistance and support in this endeavor. Thanks also to Lou Doughty, owner and manager of World Press, Incorporated, and to Bob Schreiner of the Capitol Engraving Company, whose technical knowledge and cooperation in all phases of this publication were invaluable. And last but not least, we salute cameraman Kenneth N. Ferguson and pressman William A. Ervin, whose skill and exacting labor have made this printing of DENVER SOUTH PARK & PACIFIC far superior in quality to the original 1949 edition.

E. J. Haley

R. H. Kindig

viii

TABLE OF CONTENTS

PART I

REVIEW OF EARLY COLORADO RAILROAD HISTORY UP TO THE TIME OF THE ORGANIZATION OF THE DENVER SOUTH PARK & PACIFIC RAILWAY COMPANY

PART II

THE HISTORY OF THE COLORADO CENTRAL R. R. CO.

PART III

HISTORY OF THE DENVER GEORGETOWN & UTAH RAILWAY COMPANY

PART IV

HISTORY OF THE DENVER SOUTH PARK & PACIFIC RAILROAD COMPANY

MAP AND CHART LIST

IN POCKET AT REAR OF BOOK

PAINTINGS

A HISTORY

of the

DENVER SOUTH PARK & PACIFIC RAILROAD

and

ALLIED NARROW GAUGE LINES

of the

COLORADO & SOUTHERN RAILWAY COMPANY

PREFACE

A man should have an avocation to keep him from growing old when the twilight years draw nigh, lest he have no pleasure in them. In this respect, my principal interest is the history of early Colorado railroads, and heading the list is the great old Denver South Park & Pacific, more commonly known as the "South Park."

I have spent ten years gathering and arranging the material used in writing this history of the narrow gauge divisions of the Colorado & Southern Railway.

Most worthwhile railroad history contains much matter not only tiresome, but difficult to read and rather mischievous to remember. It is often the unprofitable task of the historian to busy himself in searching out and saving from oblivion some uninteresting but vital pieces of knowledge necessary to present a well-rounded treatise.

It is possible that some criticism of this book may be offered because of the amount of additional Colorado history, not directly related to the principal subject itself, which is incorporated within these pages. This criticism I will accept for the reason that when this project was first begun it was my intention to limit the work to the history of the Denver South Park & Pacific exclusively. However, the search for material which was required to write a few opening paragraphs relative to the underlying causes that brought about the organization of the South Park road, disclosed so much additional interesting information pertaining to this subject that I finally concluded it was impossible to incorporate it all in a few opening paragraphs. Consequently, I could not reconcile myself to eliminating so much vitally important early Colorado history, both directly and indirectly related to the organization and construction of the South Park.

Therefore, I retained a considerable proportion of this material and developed it into a complete section, calling it Part I. This section includes a brief geographical outline of the early Territory of Colorado wherein our story lies, along with a description of the physical, economic and political conditions existing in Colorado in the early '70's, especially those conditions which concerned the railroad situation; followed by a resumé of early Colorado railroad history preliminary to the date of the organization of the Denver South Park & Pacific Railway.

By the same token, more material than was anticipated came to light concerning both the narrow gauge Clear Creek Canon line of the Colorado Central, and the Denver, Georgetown & Utah, a forerunner of the South Park. I have set up these two sections independently of the South Park, and called them Parts II and III, respectively.

The last section, Part IV, deals with the history proper of the Denver South Park & Pacific, which, together with the Clear Creek section of the Colorado Central, eventually became a part of the Colorado & Southern Railway.

The difficulty of compiling and presenting a complete and well-rounded manuscript on the origin, construction, and management of a railroad should be recognized. To produce such a history, one needs the services of a Philadelphia lawyer to interpret the legal aspects of the road's corporate history; a Certified Public Accountant to untangle and explain all the financial ramifications; a statistician to count ties, spikes, telegraph poles, bridges, etc.; an engineer to report on curvature, grades, and weight of rail; a motive power man who never looks at equipment behind the locomotive and tender; a rolling stock addict who never looks at a train until the engine has passed; a draftsman to draw fine maps; a combination detective and photographer to ferret out old photographs and take new ones; a "boomer" who has worked himself up from brakeman to Night Yardmaster at Como (apologies to Pocatello) to season it with a few old timer's tales; not to mention a college professor with a degree as long as a whistle cord to assemble the material properly, correct misspelling, and put all the periods, commas, hyphens, and paragraphs in their proper places. Not being able to afford such a retinue of assistants, amateur railroad historians, as well as many professional writers, are handicapped in their efforts. As a result, it is not surprising that the general concept of railroad history is replete with inaccuracies, incomplete or partially explained details, misunderstandings, and in many cases, unjustifiable bias.

It must be frankly admitted that this situation is not altogether the fault of the historian, as many railroads have been (and, in a few cases, continue to be) reluctant to permit the use of their old records, even by qualified historians. On the other hand, most railroads have neither the inclination, the time, nor the help to dig into musty, dust-covered boxes of ancient records to assist some distant struggling amateur historian who cannot afford the time nor the money to journey hither and yon in search of material. Thus, to a great extent, the historical student is forced to rely on old newspapers, magazines, publicly recorded reports and documents, the oft-time unreliable memory of mortals, and other similar sources, for his information.

Quite often the writer becomes either a critic or an advocate of his subject. In this respect I must admit that I am an advocate of the South Park railroad. Furthermore, I am of that school which has a definite dislike for diesels and trucks, and I sincerely believe that, with few exceptions, good old American railroading lost its interest and died between the turn of the century and World War I.

I do not pretend to exhaust the historical possibilities of my subject. Unquestionably, there remains additional information and interesting and valuable data yet to be uncovered. For example, further information relative to the following subjects, picked at random from this book, would be welcomed by the author:

1. The Soda Lakes and Garfield spurs built out of Morrison.

2. The construction of the main line down Trout Creek.

3. The London South Park & Leadville line, built between Alma Junction and the London Mine.

4. James Evans' choice of a right of way between St. Elmo and Alpine Tunnel.

5. The Union Pacific's choice of the High Line as their entry into Leadville.

6. The general conniving and friction between the Union Pacific and the Denver & Rio Grande during the '80's.

7. Colorado & Southern and Colorado Midland relations.

8. The proposed Colorado & Southern line up the South Fork of the South Platte toward Cripple Creek.

9. Early C.B.&Q. and C.&S. activity in Colorado, followed by the Burlington's acquisition of the latter road.

It would be entirely too much to hope that this volume is free from error. In this connection I trust that the reader will excuse any shortcomings of mine and accept this history in the spirit in which it was written—the work of an amateur.

Without the valued assistance of many persons I would have been unable to complete my task. Principally among those to whom I am greatly indebted is Professor Samuel D. Mock, whose thesis "Railroad Development in the Colorado Region to 1880," more or less formed the framework around which I assembled the greater portion of the first three parts of this book. I am deeply obligated to Mr. Robert R. Hicks of the Colorado & Southern for the very great amount of material which he furnished. I am also greatly indebted to Mr. E. J. Haley for his help—most especially for the group of fine maps which he has prepared; and to Mr. R. H. Kindig for his assistance in proof reading and captioning illustrations. I want to express my appreciation to Mr. J. C. Thode for all his help. I want to acknowledge the assistance and courtesies extended to me by Miss Ina T. Aulls of the Denver Public Library; many informative and valuable old newspaper reports and other items were dug out of the archives by this kind lady for my use. Especially do I want to thank Messrs. George A. Trout, Librarian of the Colorado Supreme Court; Charles C. Squires; H. L. Curtiss; William Wendell; William Cairns; F. O. Kelley; Roy Morton; and J. M. Cuenin for all the material they furnished. A word of appreciation is due Mr. H. E. Mose of the Crerar Library in Chicago, and to Dr. LeRoy Hafen, Executive Director of the State Historical Society of Colorado. Mr. H. O. Brayer, State Archivist of Colorado, has made available many of the original W. H. Jackson photos which are used in this book. Mr. George Root of the Kansas State Historical Society, Mrs. Pearle Casey of Gunnison, and Mr. A. T. Million of the Colorado & Southern Railway were also of assistance. The timetable from which the end sheets were reproduced was loaned by Mr. Robert LeMassena. I wish to express my sincere gratitude to my fellow members of the Rocky Mountain Railroad Club, who have contributed countless hours of labor in preparing this book for publication: I. E. August, Morris Cafky, Les Logue, Ed Mahoney, John W. Maxwell, Otto Perry, Francis Rizzari, Phil Ronfor, and Charles Ryland. And to all others who have rendered assistance, I want to express my thanks; their help was greatly appreciated. Lastly, I desire to thank Misses Verna Larsen and Helen Grimm for retyping the manuscript, following its completion.

November, 1949   M. C. POOR.

MEMORIAL EDITION

DENVER SOUTH PARK & PACIFIC

PART I

REVIEW OF EARLY COLORADO RAILROAD HISTORY UP TO THE TIME
OF THE ORGANIZATION OF THE
DENVER SOUTH PARK & PACIFIC RAILWAY COMPANY

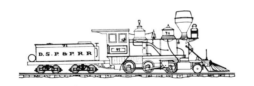

CHAPTER I

EARLY SETTLEMENT

COLORADO! An inspiring name when railroads in the Rocky Mountain area are mentioned. Within this vast mountainous region of Colorado, completely isolated in a veil of formidable mystery was, and is still, to be found some of the most rugged and surface-broken area, much of which is without equal magnitude on the continent. The rocky faces of the mountains often presented impassable barriers, even to pedestrian travel, and precipitous slopes rendered direct routes utterly impossible. There was only one pass on the Continental Divide within the State, "Muddy Creek Pass", that was less than 10,000 feet high.[1] There were no navigable streams.

Into this mountainous region that had been pierced only here and there by some adventuresome explorer whose reports were entirely inadequate to convey any idea of its geography, came the railroads and their engineers in an effort to lay their steel trail over almost inaccessible passes and through deep canons[2] in order that man might have transportation.

The story of Colorado's early railroad development centered around Denver, but as it is a long and, nevertheless, an exceedingly interesting story, we will cover it only with a brief review. This will enable the reader to gain a clear conception of what took place and what the conditions were at the time of the organization of The Denver South Park & Pacific Railway Company.

Colorado territory was first explored by the Spanish under Coronado around 1542. Later, in 1806, Lt. Zebulon M. Pike explored various streams, valleys, and mountain passes. Following Pike, came Major Long, who was directed by the Government, in 1820, to locate the source of the South Platte River. It is recorded, on a map now on file in Denver, that in 1845 William Gilpin, who later became the first Governor of Colorado Territory, traversed the entire length of the Grand River country. The present Gunnison River, which was named after Captain Gunnison, was known as the South Fork of the Grand River in the early days of Rocky Mountain exploration, while the present Colorado River, prior to 1921, was known as the Grand River. Gilpin's exploration trip was followed by Captain James W. Gunnison, who set out from Westport, now Kansas City,

Missouri, on June 23, 1853, with instructions from the War Department to make the "Gunnison Survey".[1] The idea of this survey was one of the preliminary efforts on the part of the Government to determine the best transcontinental railroad route across the plains and mountains. Gunnison's orders were to proceed up the Huerfano River into the San Luis Valley, and thence through the most eligible pass to the valley of the Grand River and westwardly into Utah. Captain Gunnison and seven of his men were brutally murdered by Indians near Sevier Lake, Utah, on October 26, 1853.[1] His aide, Lieutenant E. G. Beckwith, carried out the task, and reported on the thirty-eighth and thirty-ninth parallel route for the Pacific Railroad, the objective being Salt Lake City, Utah, there to connect with a survey to California said to be in progress by the Mormons.

Other early Colorado explorers included such men as Jim Bridger, and Jim Beckwourth. The reports of the various explorers soon brought the trapper and the fur trader, who naturally penetrated the heart of the mountain country and, who, in turn, were followed by miners and prospectors.

1858 marked the first gold rush to Colorado, known then as Pikes Peak Territory. For more than ten years the busy trails to Santa Fe and Oregon had carried their thousands past the regions of Colorado to the coast; but now the cry of "gold in them thar hills" was heard far and wide. The movement changed and the westward tide of gold seekers and homesteaders turned to the mountains of Colorado. Active life sprang into existence at the forks of Cherry Creek and the South Platte, while a restless population, hungry from the panic of 1857, filled the new mining camps of Colorado. By the latter part of 1858, a group of these settlers had already built some cabins near the junction of these two streams, and by November 1st the settlement had grown in population until there were about 200 persons living there.

They laid out a small townsite and on November 4th, the place was given the name of Auraria, (a Latin name meaning "Gold Town") now West Denver. In December, 1858, the town of St. Charles was laid out where lower downtown Denver is now located, and in

1. "History of Colorado", J. H. Baker & L. R. Hafen.
2. This spelling of the word "canon", found in much Colorado history, is of Spanish origin.

1. Colorado State Normal School Bulletin, June 1, 1916.

the following spring the two settlements combined and were given the name Denver. It was named after General James W. Denver, the first Governor of Kansas Territory, of which the present state of Colorado was, at one time, a part.

It may interest students of early western history to know that among those early Denver citizens were two famous characters, Uncle Dick (Richens) Wootton, of Raton Pass fame, and Horace A. W. Tabor, of Leadville fame, of whom we shall hear more later.

In the meantime, the miners and prospectors out in the mountains had not been wasting their time. Gold and silver, in paying quantities, were being discovered in many different locations. Among the more prominent of these earlier discoveries were those in the Clear Creek territory. Gold was discovered along both the north and south forks of Clear Creek in 1859, and soon the rush was on. During that summer the hordes of fortune hunters in this vicinity increased by the hundreds. These prospectors soon ventured beyond the first range and in a short time a booming mining camp was in full sway on Tarryall Creek near Hamilton, in what is now Park County, east of Leadville. This place was known as "The Tarryall Diggings".

By the spring of 1860 these miners and prospectors had found their way into California Gulch, later known as Leadville, where many rich discoveries of gold were made. Before the fall of that year the news had spread like wildfire, and over 10,000 people had emigrated into the upper reaches of the Arkansas River in this vicinity. By November of that year over $2,500,000 in gold had been washed out by the miners in that territory. However, the rise of Leadville is another story, and we will leave that until later.

Numerous gold camps and boom towns sprang up in the canons and on the mountain sides. The population of a town would double and even quadruple in a fortnight as word of a "strike" spread throughout the surrounding camps and adjacent areas. Similarly, and in the space of a few short days, a roaring camp could become a deserted ghost town when the ore "petered out".[1] It was during this hectic but colorful era that such camps as Black Hawk, Central City, Spanish Bar or Payne's Bar, later known as Idaho Springs, Hamilton, Fairplay, Gold Run, Buckskin Joe, Breckenridge, Ten Mile, and many others too numerous to mention, were founded. These new camps, with their stampede of gold-crazy newcomers, naturally called for some sort of transportation. As a result, every kind of burden-bearing draft animal and every sort of conveyance possible was pressed into service in the wild scramble to the hills. Stories of great riches spread fast and thousands of people headed west. By 1859, organized stage, express, and freight lines were swamped with traffic, and many

new outfits sprang into existence. Hawbert's History states that from 60,000 to 70,000 people left the East for the Rocky Mountains in the year 1860, and that during the warmer months of that year there was almost a steady stream of wagon trains extending from the Missouri River to the mountains. These hardy western pioneers traveled west in search of adventure, freedom, and fortune, with the expectation of later returning to their eastern homes, but practically all of them remained to create the great Rocky Mountain empire. The first commercial transportation company directly serving Colorado from the east was The Leavenworth & Pikes Peak Express between Leavenworth, Kansas, and Denver. The first stage coach arrived in Denver in May, 1859,[1] making the trip of 687 miles in 19 days.

With all this feverish activity going on in the territory, the reader can well understand how the stage was being set for a new era of transportation in the west. People were needing food, clothing, and other miscellaneous supplies. The mail and express business was gaining in volume rapidly. The cry of a mushrooming mining industry for better transportation began to be heard. As a result, and in order to furnish this transportation, a network of wagon and toll roads soon began to find their way west and southwest from Denver.

And thus it came about that, with the advance of civilization into this almost trackless area where the rugged Rockies formed an apparently insurmountable barrier across the path of progress, transportation became a problem that challenged the courage, energy, and resourcefulness of our first pioneers.

To provide for the need for some sort of a Government in the gold region, the illegitimate Commonwealth, or Territory of Jefferson, was then organized in 1858, and in November of that year one Hiram J. Graham left for Washington, via horseback, to petition the National Congress for its official blessing.[2] History records that as a result of these and other efforts, the Territory of Colorado was created by an Act of the Congress of the United States entitled "An Act to provide a temporary Government for the Territory of Colorado", and that it was approved February 28, 1861. Abraham Lincoln then appointed William Gilpin first Territorial Governor. From the time of the organization of the Territory until January, 1868, all corporations of the Territory of Colorado were created by special Acts of the Territorial Legislature, and therefore the charters of the early railroad companies were Acts of the Territorial Legislative Assembly of the Territory of Colorado.

After January, 1868, all railroad corporations in the Territory were organized under a General Law as set forth in the Revised Statutes. On August 1, 1876, President Grant issued the proclamation whereby Colo-

1. McMechen, "The Moffat Tunnel of Colorado". p. 28.
2. "The Brand Book" (The Westerners). Dr. L. J. Hafen, November 1, 1945.

1. Swan, Henry, "Early Transportation in Colorado". The Newcomen Society, 1944.

rado was admitted as a State into the Union, and after the first meeting of the State Legislature in 1877, "An Act to provide for the formation of Corporations" was approved on March 14, 1877, whereby all railroad companies were organized in accordance with this law.

An examination of the records of the first Session of the Legislative Assembly, held in 1861, shows that the question of transportation between the mining districts in the mountains and the larger settlements on the plains took up considerable time of the law makers.

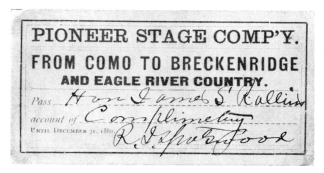

At first, these efforts were directed toward the incorporation and construction of wagon and toll roads to render the mining districts accessible to the towns at the foot of the mountains and at the mouths of the canons. These wagon roads, constructed at first for stages and wagons, in many cases afterwards became the partially constructed roadbeds of the future railroads, and the rights possessed by the toll road companies were often purchased and became part of the right of way of the newly organized railroad companies.

The first wagon and toll road to open up was built between Denver and Central City in the spring of 1860. It was owned and operated by Castro & Sheppard, who hauled passengers, mail and express. A stage coach, with Billy Updike as driver, made the first trip in June of that year. During the same year the Denver Auraria & Colorado Wagon Road Co. and The Denver & South Park Stage Co. were organized and built southwest into the South Park district to serve Fairplay, the Tarryall Dig-

gings, Buckskin Joe, Breckenridge, California Gulch, and adjacent territory.

In August, 1862, the Tarryall & Arkansas River Wagon Road Co. was organized. By 1865, the mountain territory west and southwest of Denver was well supplied with these toll roads, over which freighters, stage coaches and private individuals were doing a land office business. It was with much interest that the author ran across some of the rules, regulations and miscellaneous rates charged on these toll roads.

Tolls varied from 50c to $1.00 for each vehicle drawn by a single span of animals. This charge also depended on the distance one traveled over the road. A charge of 25c was made for each additional team. Standard rates for persons on horseback were 10c, cattle 5c per head, and sheep driven along the road 1c per head. Religious and funeral trips, generally speaking, were free. Freight rates in 1865 were as follows: flour, 9c per pound; sugar, 13½c per pound; bacon and dry goods, 15c per pound; whiskey 18c per gallon. No stage coach fares were found in this source of material; however, it would have been interesting to learn what they were in order that they might be compared with rail fares of a later date.

A view of the remains of one of these old wagon and toll roads can be seen in the photograph of the Palisades, found elsewhere. This particular road was the route of The Alpine and South Park Toll Road Company that ran west from Heywood Springs over Williams Pass, to Gunnison and points in the Gunnison valley. Williams Pass, sometimes called Hancock Pass, is located on the Continental Divide, about one mile due southeast of the Alpine Tunnel. Another section of one of these old toll roads may be seen when driving over highway number 285 just above Webster on the east slope of Kenosha Hill. At this particular spot, just opposite mile post 75 on the South Park right of way, the old toll road crossed a low, swampy spot, or marsh, and the logs laid crosswise to form a more solid roadbed are still there. Both sections of these old toll roads, as described, are still plainly visible to this day.

CHAPTER II

INTRODUCTION OF PROMINENT CHARACTERS

Before proceeding further with this book, we will introduce some of the leading characters. First, and foremost, comes Dr. John Evans, who played a very prominent part in this early railroad history of Colorado and a role of major importance later on in the history of the Denver South Park & Pacific. In McMechen's "Life of Gov. John Evans", we read:

GOV. JOHN EVANS.

"John Evans was born in Waynesville, Ohio on March 9th, 1814. He studied for the medical profession, which he completed, and started practicing in the rural communities of Indiana and Illinois. In 1840 he went to Chicago and became associated with the Rush Medical School, which was at that time, and still is, a very famous medical center. While in Chicago, he became interested in the founding of Northwestern University, which is located in Evanston, a suburb to the north of the city. The city of Evanston was named after Dr. John Evans. Eventually, he began to take an interest in politics and real estate, gradually dropping from the medical profession. His first interest in railroad promotion work manifested itself in his connection with the old Ft. Wayne & Chicago R. R., now a part of the Pennsylvania System. Under his influence and direction, the west end of the line and the terminal at Chicago were constructed. Later, in 1861, he was instrumental in organizing the Chicago & Evanston R. R., now a part of the Milwaukee road.

"His interest in politics developed to the point where he became a good friend of Abraham Lincoln. The office of the Gov. of the Territory of Colorado was going to be vacant, and Mr. Lincoln asked Dr. Evans if he would accept the honor. After a journey by stagecoach from Chicago to look the Territory over, Dr. Evans agreed, and as a result he was appointed as the second Territorial Governor of the Territory of Colorado on March 26th, 1861, replacing Gov. Wm. Gilpin. He arrived in Denver on April 19th, 1862 to assume his duties."

It has already been told how the mining and transportation industry was rapidly developing in this territory, and such activities being directly in Dr. Evans' line, he took over his new duties with a great deal of vigor and genuine interest. Gov. Evans had a great deal of faith in the future of Denver and took a very active part in the city's development. The rivalry between Denver and Golden resulted in the springing up of two political factions within the state. Gov. Evans immediately arrayed himself on Denver's side, which included such well known citizens as J. B. Chaffee, David H. Moffat, Jr., B. M. Hughes, Chas. B. Kountze, W. F. Johnson, Jos. E. Bates, F. M. Case, Wm. N. Clayton, John Pierce, John W. Smith, L. H. Eicholtz, F. Z. Solomon, J. M. Palmer, and others. It will be well for the reader to remember the names of these men mentioned here, for they are to play an important part in the development of Colorado's railroads within the next few years.

Governor Evans' work and efforts in the interest of Denver brought him a great deal of respect, and he gradually became one of the city's most influential citizens. He belonged to the Masonic Fraternity, and was a member of the Methodist Church. However, politics deals out some strange hands at times; for various political reasons, he resigned as Governor of the Territory on August 1, 1865. The citizens' faith in him was renewed a short time later, when he was appointed Senator from Colorado on December 18, 1865. The organization of The Denver Pacific Railway & Telegraph Company, under his expert guidance, and how it saved Denver, and his organization and construction of The Denver South Park & Pacific Railroad will be fully taken up elsewhere. Together with John Iliff, early Colorado cattleman, he also organized and established the University of Denver. Always Denver's development and growth were uppermost in his mind. He died very quietly in Denver on July 2, 1897, shortly after his 83rd birthday, respected by the community as one of its greatest citizens.

Another prominent pioneer citizen of Colorado who played an important part in the early-day railroad history of the state was W. A. H. Loveland. Due to the many railroad activities on his part, we will include a short review of his life's history.

W. A. H. LOVELAND.

William Austin Hamilton Loveland was born in Chatham, Mass., May 30, 1826. In 1837, his parents moved west to Illinois, where young Loveland grew up and finished his education. After finishing school, he went with the American Army into old Mexico, where he was severely wounded at Chapultepec. In 1848, he returned to his Illinois home, and in the spring of 1849 crossed the plains to California, where he engaged in the mining business in Grass Valley. This turned out to be an unprofitable venture, so he went to South America and thence, in 1851, back to Illinois, where he engaged in the mercantile business for several years.

In the spring of 1859, he crossed the plains to the Rocky Mountains, with an ox-train laden with a stock of general merchandise, and settled on the site of a little camp known as Golden City. Golden City was named after Thomas Golden,[1] an early Colorado pioneer in that immediate territory. Loveland was one of the founders of this town, becoming a leader in the community, and his store was its headquarters.

In his determination to make Golden the Colorado metropolis, he personally influenced its selection, in 1862, as the seat of the Territorial Government. Golden remained the capital, despite several attempts to have it removed, until the latter part of 1867, when it was moved to Denver. He made a sizeable fortune in the mercantile business and became a man of great force of character, possessing extraordinary energy and executive ability. He had a great deal of faith in this Colorado country, kept faith with his friends and was a tireless antagonist to his opponents. In his later years he became a citizen of Denver, and purchased control of the Rocky Mountain News. In 1888, he was nominated as his party's candidate for Governor of Colorado on the Democratic ticket, but lost the election, along with the rest of his party. Mr. Loveland died December 17, 1894, at Lakewood, where he had established his residence in 1888.

Another leader in the Golden crowd, and associated with Loveland, was Henry M. Teller, a young Central City attorney who was later to become one of the leading lights in early Colorado political affairs, being elected to the United States Senate.

1. Smiley, "History of Denver".

Looking over the Colorado Central roundhouse at Golden. Note the Golden City & South Platte trestle across Clear Creek, in central background.

Colorado Central roundhouse at Golden during the 1870's. Numbers of the narrow gauge engines at left are not known but standard gauge engines at right are 3, 2, and 1. Note the Master Mechanic's Prince Albert coat and stovepipe hat.

CHAPTER III

THE TRANSCONTINENTAL RAILROAD ROUTE AND PRELIMINARY ATTEMPTS BY VARIOUS FACTIONS TO GAIN THE INITIATIVE

By 1860 almost everyone in the territory was aware of the fact that the Union Pacific Railroad, with the help of the Federal Government, was making plans and preliminary surveys for their proposed route across the continent to meet the oncoming Central Pacific, which was at that time in the process of being organized preparatory to building their line east. The formative period of most new regions is characterized by a confusing welter of conflicting rivalries. Before lines are firmly drawn, and before the political and economic destinies of the several component sections are clearly apparent, a slight advantage at one point may bring in its train tremendous consequences at another.

Such was the case in the history of Colorado. Every little hamlet thought itself the future metropolis of the Rocky Mountain region. And because of the inevitable uncertainty at this early stage, every hamlet was mutually jealous of every other, lest indeed its rivals' claims should eventually prove to be founded in fact. Each point of the slightest strategic importance was therefore emphasized vigorously. But one of the most important phases of this rivalry was exemplified in the efforts of the several localities to make the Pacific Railroad, or at least its Colorado branch, its own private monopoly.

For the honor of thus inducting the Pacific Railroad into Colorado there were two outstanding claimants— Denver and Golden. In a sense, their rivalry was inherent in their respective locations. Both of them, though the latter especially, were commercial appendages of the mountain mining region. Reduced to its simplest denominators, the rivalry between the two towns could be stated in the single question: to which should all passing in or coming out of that mining hinterland pay toll?[1]

Each had certain advantages of location. Thus Denver, by virtue of its position out on the plains, was able to intercept trade and travel between the mountains and the plains; and it was not—like Golden—tied definitely to one region. Golden, on the other hand, was the true gateway to the Clear Creek mining region.

Prominent among a number of U. S. Army Engineers

that the Government had working in the mountains during the year 1861, in an effort to discover a favorable route across the Continental Divide, was Captain Edward L. Berthoud. Captain Berthoud was born in Geneva, Switzerland in 1828, and came to America when a young man. Being born in the mountainous country of Switzerland, it is easy to understand how a man of his engineering ability would gravitate to a country like Colorado.

It so happened that during that same summer, The Central Overland California & Pikes Peak Express Company was seeking a shorter route for their stage line through Colorado to Utah and California. Golden City, being an ambitious little community, joined forces with the Central Overland outfit and with the help of a number of citizens residing in Spanish Bar, Gregory Gulch and other of the small canon towns, fitted out an expedition to explore and survey a route for a wagon road from Golden to Salt Lake City. This group, in turn, joined forces with Captain Berthoud, making him the leader of the expedition. The Captain went to work assembling his crew at Empire City on May 6, 1861. In the meantime, Wm. H. Russell, president of the Central Overland Co., accompanied by the old scout, Jim Bridger, had arrived in Denver. Russell directed Bridger to join the expedition and work with Captain Berthoud in locating a route across the Snowy Range.

On May 10, 1861, the party of ten men set out from Empire City.[1] The party divided and Bridger, accompanied by two men, left the main group and branched off south toward the Tarryall district to search for a suitable pass in that particular locality. Captain Berthoud and his party continued up the West Fork of Clear Creek toward the Continental Divide.[1] Five days later, on May 15, 1861, he discovered the famous pass which bears his name.[2] Berthoud Pass, 11,314 feet above sea level, is located 13 miles due west of Central City, at the headwaters of Hoop Creek.

Both Berthoud and Bridger then returned to Denver and reported their discoveries. On July 6th following,

1. Mock.

1. Colorado Magazine, March, 1926.
2. McMechen, "The Moffat Tunnel of Colorado." Vol. 1, page 29.

another expedition under the leadership of these two men started out and explored over 1,100 miles of country between the Clear Creek territory and Salt Lake City, locating and marking out a proposed route between the two points.

Upon their return, Berthoud reported that a satisfactory wagon road route could be built through, and that although the first section of the road through Clear Creek Canon and over the main range at Berthoud Pass would present the greatest difficulties; the balance of the proposed route west of the main range via Hot Sulphur Springs and up the Yampa River to Salt Lake City was not quite so mountainous, and construction should not prove too difficult. However, due to political quarrels, nothing further was done for the time being toward getting the proposed wagon road established.

In June, 1862, another exploration party (financed by popular subscription) headed by Gov. Evans, F. M. Case, a Civil Engineer, and Wm. N. Byers, Editor of the Rocky Mountain News, set out to explore this territory to determine what they thought the possibilities were for a railroad through this section and over Berthoud Pass. The party returned shortly and reported that, although the grade was admittedly a bit steep, they thought it would be practicable. After much discussion of the idea, Engineer Case volunteered to survey the route to determine just what the true conditions were. His party left on July 24, 1862, the same day Congress passed the Pacific Railroad Bill providing for the first transcontinental railroad. Denver was jubilant over this glorious piece of news.

In due time Case and his party returned with rather a disappointing report. The grade was found to be over the maximum, which was 116 feet per mile, as set by Congress. Case had determined the altitude of the pass at 11,495 feet above sea level; however, this was officially set later as 11,314 feet. Another obstacle, he reported, was the presence of a great amount of snow he had found on the pass, even in the summer time. Thus Case's report was: that the grade was prohibitive and that any railroad that proposed to follow this route would have to tunnel under the pass, on account of the steep grades and the heavy winter snows. This report put a sort of a temporary chill, for the time being, on the idea of constructing a railroad over Berthoud Pass.

Due to political maneuvers, The Colorado & Pacific Wagon Telegraph & Railroad Company, which was formed in 1861, had the grant of a right of way over this pass incorporated in their charter, but they did nothing toward developing the route; consequently, this grant was repealed by the Territorial Legislature on February 10, 1865.[1] The Overland Stage Company was then authorized to build a road over the pass; however, this company did not do anything either. At this point, it may be of some interest to the reader to learn that it

1. McMechen, "The Moffat Tunnel of Colorado", p. 33.

was not until 1874 that a company organized by one William Cushman of Georgetown, built a wagon road over the pass.

Among those who realized the great need for better transportation in the territory was W. A. H. Loveland. Mr. Loveland was an adventuresome character, and had not been in Golden very long before he became seriously interested in this scheme of building a railroad up Clear Creek Canon and over Berthoud Pass. His first move was made in 1863, when he and a few citizens of Golden, and Henry M. Teller, organized a wagon road company to build up Clear Creek. Later on, in 1865, this corporation was reorganized as The Colorado & Clear Creek Railroad Company. Included in this expanded organization of Loveland's were seven Coloradoans, three Union Pacific officials, and a group of eastern capitalists.

Their charter provided for the construction of a railroad west from Denver, up Clear Creek and its branches to Black Hawk, Central City, Idaho Springs and other mining camps. It also provided for a line to be built northeast from Golden toward the Cache la Poudre River territory. Captain Berthoud, who was Secretary and Chief Engineer of the road, made some preliminary surveys up Clear Creek Canon to the Forks of the Creek, and thence up the North Fork to Black Hawk and Central City. This work was carried on in the fall of 1865 and the spring of 1866.

In 1866, Loveland again reorganized his road under the name of The Colorado Central & Pacific Railroad Company, and had his charter amended, giving him authority to extend his line west from Golden by way of Clear Creek to the west boundary line of the State, and from Golden east to the east boundary line of the State. The inference was, first, that if the Union Pacific did not come through Colorado with its main line, it would connect with his Cache la Poudre branch in northern Colorado, and second, that the Kansas Pacific, then building west from Kansas City, Missouri, would connect with his proposed railroad, to be built eastward from Golden. It can easily be seen that Loveland's plan was to make his railroad a part of either the Union Pacific or Kansas Pacific transcontinental line, with Golden as the center of all railroad transportation in Colorado. It was Loveland's idea that if these plans could be carried through, Denver would be completely isolated as a future railroad center. As the territory of Colorado gradually developed, these bitter feelings between the two towns constantly grew and played an important part in Colorado's early railroad history.

Loveland failed to obtain the necessary capital he required, and, as a result, turned to the Union Pacific for help. The Union Pacific officials figured that it would be good business to keep a finger in the pie, so to speak; for, regardless of how things turned out, they had nothing much to lose, but instead, stood a chance to gain. John A. Dix, himself, looked upon Loveland's plan with much favor, and apparently Loveland was led to believe that his ideas and plans were accepted, but he either deceived himself or was deceived, for all fell through and the Union Pacific chose the northern route, as will be explained later.

By this time, there was considerable activity on the part of both the Government and the Union Pacific as to the final choice of a route for this great transcontinental railroad. In 1866, the Engineering Department of the Union Pacific prepared a very extensive report for the United States Government, dealing with the preliminary surveys covering the proposed routes that the Union Pacific might possibly use in building their line west across the Rocky Mountains. This report consisted of a full description of each of the ten different routes that the engineers had lined up for consideration. All points in favor or against each of the ten routes were incorporated in this report, prepared by Mr. J. L. Williams, a Government Director of the Union Pacific Railroad Co., under the date of November 23, 1866. Following is an outline of the ten different routes:

Route No. 1. Over Hoosier Pass at the head waters of the South Platte River.

Route No. 2. Over Tarryall Pass via the South Platte River.

Route No. 3. Through the North Fork of the South Platte River.

Route No. 4. The Berthoud Pass route.

Route No. 5. The Boulder Pass route. A six mile tunnel at an altitude of 11,700 feet would be required, if this route were chosen.

Route No. 6. The Cache la Poudre and Dale Creek route over Antelope Pass.

Route No. 7. The Lodge Pole, Crow, and Lone Tree Creeks route over Evans Pass.

Route No. 8. The Lodge Pole, Camp Walbach, and Crow Creek route.

Route No. 9. The Lodge Pole Creek, Cheyenne Pass and Bridger's Pass route.

Route No. 10. The Laramie Canon Route.

Inasmuch as number four, the Berthoud Pass route, is of particular interest to this book, the author will include the full report of the engineer as regards this route.

NUMBER 4—THE BERTHOUD PASS ROUTE

"From the beginning of these investigations this route has attracted much interest as well from the general belief of mountaineers that it was the most favorable pass through the Snowy Range, as from its locality, being in the direct course from Denver to Salt Lake City, the two chief points on the route, both of which it is important to pass. In the summer of 1862, Mr. F. M. Case, at the instance of the Union Pacific incorporators, and with some financial assistance from Colorado friends, made what he called an instrumental reconnaissance of this route. His rather disappointing report, addressed to Hon. John Evans, then Governor of Colorado Territory, was embodied in his subsequent official report of December 15th, 1864. Subsequently, in 1866, by direction of this board, a second and more careful survey of this route was made by Mr. P. T. Brown, one of the Union Pacific engineers. In the general topographical facts, the two surveys agree. First: J. L. Williams passed over this route as far as the summit of the range, accompanied by Colonel S. Semour (Union Pacific Consulting Engineer) and Mr. Brown. The line from the South Platte River at Denver to the summit of Berthoud Pass is 60 miles in length. The Survey was extended west into the Middle Park 78 miles from Denver, in the direction of Salt Lake City. For general description, it naturally divides as follows:

"First: Denver to Golden City, 14½ miles. This is over a rolling and rapidly rising plain, falling into Clear Creek valley, 6 miles east of the mountains and meeting the foot of the range 12 miles from Denver. Ruling grade, 116 feet per mile, of which there is about 3 miles. Construction not very expensive.

"Second: Golden City to upper end of Clear Creek canon, 15¾ miles. Golden City is at the transition point from the sedimentary to the granite formation. Here the line enters Clear Creek canon, which extends 15¾ miles, rising in this direction 1,544 feet. Through a portion of the canon the valley rises faster than the maximum grade, but with careful location and heavy cost, Mr. Brown thinks the grade need not exceed 116 feet per mile, approximately 2.19%, at any point. Two-thirds of the distance will be curved, much of it sharp. The greater part of the distance may be called close canon, and a part narrow, open canon with abrupt slopes.

"Third: From the head of the canon to the east portal of Berthoud Tunnel—28½ miles—the line follows the narrow mountain valley of Clear Creek through the midst of the gold mining developments, passing many quartz mills; ruling grade 116 feet per mile, of which there will be about 13 miles. For 7 or 8 miles of the upper portion, the fall of the valley greatly exceeds the maximum grade, reaching in places over 300 feet per mile. Using the maximum grade of 116 feet per mile from the tunnel eastward, the line is necessarily thrown on the steep, rocky, and, in places, precipitous mountain sides, at an elevation of 100 to 400 feet above the creek, involving, of course, very heavy construction. In the whole district from the base of the mountain to the tunnel, Clear Creek, as Mr. Brown supposes, would be bridged perhaps 20 times, with probably two to three miles of tunneling through sharp points. To give greater length of line for the purpose of reducing the grade to the maximum prescribed by law, the surveyed route in ascending, turns up South Clear Creek for 2½ miles, thence by a short tunnel through a ridge into Bard's

Creek valley, which it follows down, reaching the main valley at Empire City.

"Fourth: Berthoud Tunnel would be 3.1 miles long, and pierce the mountain 1,364 feet below the summit of the pass. Solid granite is expected to be encountered throughout the entire length of the bore. (Evans and Case thought there might be a possibility of finding some gold.) Grade line in tunnel at highest point is 10,100 feet, and summit of pass is 11,426 feet[1] above sea-level.

"Fifth: West portal of the tunnel to end of the survey, 16½ miles. Descending westward, the slope of the mountain is followed for some distance until reaching the valley of Moses Creek, a tributary of the Colorado River, and thence through this valley to the Middle Park. Grade 116 feet per mile, for the first 11½ miles. I did not pass over this portion of the route."

In the final comparison of these ten routes, Mr. Williams grouped them into two classes; five of them crossed the Snowy Range, while the remaining five crossed the Black Hills Range. Of those in the Snowy Range, the Berthoud Pass route was considered the most feasible, while number nine, the Lodge Pole Creek route via Bridger's Pass at an altitude of 7,534 feet, was considered the most feasible of the northern group.

Bailey's history of the Union Pacific states that the road's officials considered it very essential that their line of railroad go by way of Denver, and that it would be with considerable reluctance, if they were forced to abandon the Snowy Range or southern route, that would take them through Denver. Just how much sincerity is incorporated in this last statement is a debatable question.

Be that as it may, the Union Pacific's choice of a route west was the basis for the great economic issue of the day. Should the Union Pacific build their main line through the canons of Clear Creek and over Berthoud Pass, and if they did decide on this route through the mountains, would the line south come directly to Denver or Golden? The rivalry between the two groups representing both Denver and Golden over this most important decision was running high.

After due consideration and comparison of the two most practical routes, General Grenville M. Dodge, the Chief Engineer of the Union Pacific, turned thumbs down on the Berthoud Pass route and announced that the road had selected as the line of its route, the one that followed up Lodge Pole Creek to Cheyenne Pass, through the Black Hills and over Bridger's Pass, thus eliminating Colorado entirely.[2] However, he did recommend that if arrangements could be made at all, a branch line

---

1. F. M. Case, in 1862, had reported the altitude of Berthoud Pass as 11,495 feet.
   P. T. Brown, in 1866, reported the altitude as 11,426 feet. The U. S. Geological Map shows the altitude as 11,316 feet. The present historical marker, as erected by the Colorado State Historical Society, says 11,314 feet.

2. Dodge, "How We Built the Union Pacific Railway".

should be laid down to Denver. This famous decision left Denver about 100 miles south of the main line.

In the meantime Denver was struggling for her very existence. Pessimistic stories to the effect that the mines were beginning to play out, cropped up. The basis for these rumors is explained by Mock, who states:

"The chief difficulty was that the supply of easily handled gold and silver ores had given out and the technical knowledge for the handling of the more refractory ores was lacking. Paying placer bars and the beds of decomposed quartz which could be treated by the crude stamp mills were almost exhausted. (The stamp mill was very wasteful, and in many instances, saved only an insignificant fraction of the gold content of the ore.—Hollister.) Literally, mountains of gold still remained, but if the mining industry was to provide a base for the economy of the region it would be necessary to discover some process which would solve the tough problem of the sulphuret ores".

The Civil War had divided the people, a bad fire and flood had visited the little town and numerous Indian wars of late had tended to cut off much of their supplies and communications from the east.

Then along came this official announcement by the Union Pacific of their decision to build along the northern route. It drained the population toward Cheyenne, and diverted the city's commerce. The citizens were just about ready to throw in the sponge. This was the crushing blow; Denver was pronounced as "too dead to bury".[1]

Denver was not alone in her misery; the whole territory was involved. With Colorado thus at the bottom of an economic depression of such proportions as to cast doubt on the region's future it can be understood why the Union Pacific was none too anxious, for the time being, to promote a branch to accommodate the gold region. Therefore, any initiative on the construction of a branch road into the territory would have to come from Colorado.

Loveland had been east early in 1867, and is supposed to have made some sort of a tentative arrangement with the Union Pacific relative to the building of a line north to Wyoming. The Union Pacific officials had proposed that if Loveland's road, the Colorado Central & Pacific, in which they now had a financial interest, would grade a roadbed and furnish the ties for a line north to Cheyenne, the Union Pacific would iron, equip, and operate the line under a traffic contract in direct connection to their main line.

The next step was a survey by Captain Berthoud of possible routes on which the line might be built. Two lines were surveyed, both from Golden. One line ran along the base of the foothills on a route which would have entirely avoided Denver. The other ran down Clear Creek to the junction with the South Platte, and thence northward along the west side of this stream and Lone Tree Creek to a junction with the Union Pacific. A branch to Denver, seven miles long, was included in the

---

1. Bailey, "The First Transcontinental Railroad".

plan. This fact caused the Daily Colorado Tribune to observe sarcastically that Denver was "honored" by "this branch of a branch road".

At this point, Mock gives us a description of one phase of railroad manipulation that existed at this particular period.

"These local capitalists, who have surveyed the potentialities of the region and staked out their claims, are now—because of the local funds—compelled to dicker with outsiders for the all-essential financial assistance they can offer. Naturally, they would surrender no more of their equities than necessary, but since each was a necessary supplement to the other, a 'modus vivendi' usually could be arranged whereby the local and outside managers could go forth arm in arm to exploit—and incidentally, to benefit—the economy of the new region.

"The favorite device of local promoters seeking home funds was the exchange of County Bonds for railroad stocks. The latter were notoriously worthless, while the County Bonds were at least salable. Thus, in an exchange of equal amounts of bonds for stocks, the railroad stood to gain the difference. The game, therefore, was to stimulate railroad interest within a County, after which—with the public sufficiently 'softened'—the railroads at first did not find it too difficult to persuade the voters to consent to the exchange. The Colorado Central was the first Colorado railroad to utilize this scheme of money raising."

At a large railroad booster meeting held in Denver in 1867, both Union Pacific and Colorado Central representatives suggested that county bond issues be voted to partially defray the cost of constructing a railroad into Denver. By the time the bond elections were actually held, however, mutual suspicion among the sections concerned was shown in the reservations attached to some of the bond issues. Boulder stipulated that its bonds would be issued only if the Colorado Central & Pacific were built on the west side of the South Platte River; Gilpin County's bonds would be available only for use in grading to Central City; and Denver offered the Arapahoe County bonds upon the condition that the railroad stay east of the South Platte River and come directly to Denver, then it could be built west to Golden and Central City.

Details of Loveland's additional efforts to advance the cause of the Colorado Central & Pacific will appear later in the chapter dealing with the history of the Colorado Central.

Meanwhile, the Union Pacific had been completed and opened for business between Omaha and the confluence of the North and South Platte Rivers, a distance of 295 miles, and advance construction work was bearing in a direction that left no possible hope of its diversion to Colorado, much less Denver. Therefore, it appeared that the proposition the Union Pacific had offered the Central, together with Gov. Evans' special bond provision (if accepted by the Loveland-Teller group) was opening the way toward providing Denver with a railroad connection with the great transcontinental line.

The stipulations that had been attached to the various county bond issues killed the Colorado Central & Pacific's scheme of building a railroad to the Union Pacific line. The only means the road had for the grading of its line were these county bonds, and now they were tied up or were unacceptable to the Loveland group. The only real source of income which the Central possessed and could use toward the construction of a railroad was the $100,000 of Jefferson County bonds. They were voted in August, 1867. Apparently, Weld and Larimer counties had refused to issue bonds. The Arapahoe bonds especially were useless, inasmuch as Loveland absolutely refused to build his railroad down the east side of the Platte River. The reason for this refusal was very obvious—how could Golden become the center of Colorado's railway transportation system, if Denver's terms were abided by? In Loveland, Gov. Evans found his most stubborn individual opponent. They were bitter rivals throughout their active careers. As each opportunity presented itself, Loveland exhausted every resource at his command to defeat and isolate the town of Denver.

This refusal to accept the Arapahoe bonds caused the Denver people to declare against any further cooperation with the Colorado Central & Pacific plans. All interest in the Loveland road was discarded and the bonds that had been voted were never issued.

In September, Oliver Ames, a Union Pacific official, let it be known in Denver that his road had no agreement with the Loveland road on the construction of any lines; apparently, the Union Pacific was not interested in assisting a railroad project which had no valuable considerations to offer it.

The Colorado Central had been shunted onto a siding, and the track was now clear for any group of promoters who could raise the money for grading and tieing a roadbed to the Union Pacific. It was Denver's turn to try its hand at securing the "iron horse".

During that summer of 1867, there had been numerous rumors afloat that the Kansas Pacific,[1] which was working its way across Kansas, intended to follow the southern route and branch off toward the southeastern part of the state, thus passing up Denver entirely. Loveland and Thomas J. Carter, in their intercourse with the Denver people, had carefully done all they could to confirm these beliefs. After the proceedings of the July railroad meeting in Denver were made public, Isaac E. Newton, representing the Kansas Pacific, announced in the newspapers that Loveland and Carter had misrepresented the intentions of the Kansas Pacific and that he was authorized to state that his road would be built into Denver. This announcement caused much excitement in Denver, and brought about a division of sentiment, raising the question of whether Denver should try to cooperate with Loveland and Carter and the Union Pacific-Colorado Central scheme, or pin their hopes on a railroad connection with the Kansas Pacific.

1. Poor's Manual of R. R., 1870.

Colorado Central engine 8 at the Brooks Locomotive Works. In the early days the railroads usually furnished their own headlights.

Colorado Central engine 7 at the Georgetown depot on August 17, 1878.

After Loveland's efforts had failed that fall to get the much desired rail connection, Denver began to look toward the Kansas Pacific as the medium for getting it out of the transportation wilderness.

The Union Pacific (Eastern Division) was changed to Kansas Pacific by Congress on March 3, 1869.

In the meantime, the Kansas Pacific had been gradually working its way west. At the moment, it was temporarily stranded in the prairies of western Kansas for lack of finances. In the face of this situation, which was unknown to the citizens of Denver, Colonel James Archer, a representative of the Kansas Pacific, visited Denver in November of 1867 and announced their proposed plans for continuing the road's construction on west to the city without any outside financial assistance. Many Denver citizens were now ready to anchor their hopes in the Kansas Pacific, favoring this road as the town's eastern railroad connection, over that of the proposed line north to the Union Pacific at Cheyenne.

However, it developed that the Kansas Pacific *would* need help, and asked the citizens of Denver and Arapahoe County for a bonus of $2,000,000 in order that the road might be continued on into Denver. The Kansas Pacific even intimated that unless the citizens complied, the railroad might never be built to Denver. Colonel Archer might as well have asked for ten million dollars for all the difference it made. This amount of money was absolutely out of the question.

The fact that the Union Pacific offer was not accepted by the Colorado Central group, for reasons already explained, combined with the Kansas Pacific's demand for a bonus of two million dollars before they could continue west, placed Denver's railroad plight in a critical situation. Denver's railroad leaders realized that the time had come for some quick action on their part if serious disaster to the city was to be avoided. Accordingly, they proceeded at once to organize a Board of Trade, something through which the people could act as a unit. A meeting of citizens was held at Cole's Hall on Larimer Street, November 13, 1867, at which time the Board was organized. The Board's Directors consisted of such prominent citizens as W. M. Clayton, H. C. Leach, General John Pierce, Frank Palmer, Isaac Brinker, D. H. Moffat, Jr., J. W. Smith, F. Z. Solomon, etc. The Directors organized by electing J. W. Smith, President; General John Pierce, Vice-President; Frank Palmer, Treasurer; and H. C. Leach, Secretary.

At that time the Chicago & North Western Railroad was represented in Denver by Colonel D. C. Dodge. As the reader will have seen, something closely akin to a crisis in Denver's career was then impending, and an incident, for which Col. Dodge was chiefly responsible, demonstrated in a striking way how great consequences may develop from a simple but timely act.[1]

The day the Kansas Pacific representative, Col. Archer, arrived, Col. Dodge had telegraphed General Grenville M. Dodge, the Union Pacific Engineer, notifying him of Archer's visit, of its purposes, and of the certain failure of the mission, and asking that someone be sent to Denver to take up the railroad question with the people on some basis within their reach. Promptly came a reply that George Francis Train would come to Denver immediately. Train was not liked very well in Denver and when the people learned who was coming to lead them out of the wilderness, they were inclined to resent the appearance of such a guide and counsellor.

The new Board of Trade called a general meeting of citizens at Cole's Hall for the evening of November 14th, which was very well attended. General Bela M. Hughes addressed the audience in his characteristic manner, urging the imperative necessity for heartily supporting the new organization of business men, and the even greater necessity for immediate action upon the railroad question if the supremacy of Denver in Colorado was to be maintained and the city's very existence was to be continued. Col. Archer then spoke briefly. He told them of the Kansas Pacific's condition, what it could do and what it could not do, and repeated his proposition that if the people of Denver would provide a bonus of two million dollars, the Kansas Pacific would be built to the city; otherwise, it would not.

George F. Train had arrived in Denver that morning and was present at the meeting. He had busied himself through the day in gathering information, and when Col. Archer concluded his remarks, Train began his famous speech which proved so potent and notable in Denver's railroad annals. He urged the people to no longer look to others for help but to remember and act upon the fact that "God helps those who help themselves"; to abandon all thought of subsidizing the Kansas Pacific, and let it end in the Kansas prairies or go in any direction its owners desired; that the valley of the Platte River afforded an easy and direct route for a railroad that could be cheaply built to connect with the line of the Union Pacific; to organize a company within themselves and build a railroad of their own, either down the Platte or on the shorter route to the Union Pacific directly north to Cheyenne; to own and operate it, and if there were any money to be made in the business, to make it for themselves. After entering into some explanatory details, Train concluded by urging the people, as competent and sensible business men, to carefully consider his advice and suggestions, and then immediately act upon them. This proved to be the turning point in Denver's history.

1. Mock.

Examples of early South Park and Colorado Central passes, issued to P. F. Barr, location and construction engineer during the building of Alpine Tunnel.

CHAPTER IV

COLORADO'S FIRST RAILROADS

The citizens of Denver resolved that if the railroad would not come to them, they would go to it. It was then that Gov. Evans and his associates decided that they would accept the Union Pacific's proposition, and would build their own railroad. As a result of this important decision, The Denver Pacific Railway & Telegraph Company was duly organized on November 18, 1867. One wonders what might have happened to Denver if Col. Dodge had not sent his message and if George Francis Train had not come to Denver in response to its request.

Arrangements were made for incorporating the road with a capital stock of $2,000,000 by the following Board of Directors: Joseph E. Bates, Wm. M. Clayton, John Evans, Bela M. Hughes, Wm. F. Johnson, Luther Kountze, David H. Moffat, Jr., John Pierce, and John W. Smith. The first officers of the road were: Bela M. Hughes, President; Luther Kountze, Vice-President; David H. Moffat, Jr., Treasurer; W. F. Johnson, Secretary; and F. M. Case, Chief Engineer. (Mr. Case was later succeeded by Mr. L. H. Eicholtz.)

On January 20, 1868, Arapahoe county, by a large majority, voted a bond issue of $500,000 in behalf of the Denver Pacific. Thus, the first definite steps were taken toward building what proved to be the first railroad into Denver, Colorado. In commenting on this procedure Mock states:

"Under the circumstances, there was little choice; it was railroads at such costs or none at all. Coloradoans elected the former; they could pay the piper later."

Now that the town had made a definite move toward getting their long desired railroad connection, a feeling of optimism began to prevail, bringing with it a period of pipe dreams. Denver newspaper readers were treated to a steady diet of railroad articles, hopefully painting Denver as the great railroad center of the future. A crop of proposed railroads developed, chief among which were the Denver & Georgetown Railroad, the Denver South Park & Rio Grande Railway, and the Denver & Santa Fe Railroad. The Denver & Georgetown road was designed to be the connecting line between the Denver Pacific and the mountains, and thus kill off the Golden-inspired Colorado Central. Later in the 1870's, under other names, this road proved to be a troublesome factor in the tangled railroad setup in the mining region.

Other proposed lines included such roads as the Rocky Mountain Railway & Telegraph Co., planned to run into the mountains and on to a connection with the Union Pacific west of Cheyenne; the Denver Boulder & Cache la Poudre, planned to fill the gap caused by the proposed routing of the Denver Pacific so far out on the plains east of the mountains; and the Arapahoe Jefferson & South Park—a tram line into the mountains, which would reduce the cost of wood and stone in Denver.

Also in December of that year, 1867, the capital had been removed from Golden to Denver,[1] all of which combined to inspire new hope and confidence in the city's future. The details as to how Golden lost out may well be left to sink into oblivion. Late in January, 1868, the Union Pacific officials informed the Denver Pacific that the same proposition that they had previously made to the Colorado Central regarding the construction and operation of a line north to their main line was still open, and that if the Denver Pacific officials were still interested, the Union Pacific was ready to carry out any negotiations to that end. As a result, Gov. Evans and General John Pierce went east and made all the necessary arrangements covering the construction of their line. The contract for the actual construction work was made with Thomas Durant and Sidney Dillon, both of the Union Pacific. This was followed by a great amount of dickering and negotiating between the Denver Pacific, the Kansas Pacific, and the Government at Washington, which resulted in the granting of a right of way and the making of the necessary financial arrangements, so that the Denver Pacific might get started on the construction of their road.

These negotiations and the various agreements between the Denver and the Kansas Pacific were the beginning of a long period of close cooperative understanding between the two roads.

Meanwhile, in December, 1867, Engineer Case and a party set out in zero weather to locate a line. On this trip, Case ran 67 miles of located line and 75 miles of preliminary location. Due to the great amount of ill-feeling Denver had for Cheyenne, this first line was run to a point on the Union Pacific near Pine Bluffs, Wyoming, 43 miles east of Cheyenne, but due to Union Pa-

1. Smiley, "History of Denver".

cific influence Cheyenne eventually became the connecting point.

All this activity added confusion to the already muddled railroad situation in Colorado, and efforts on the part of the Union Pacific and others to smooth out the differences, especially between Denver and Golden, were attempted. The point of issue was whether Colorado's railroad connection to the Union Pacific would be built by the Colorado Central or the Denver Pacific. The Central insisted that it alone enjoyed Union Pacific support; however, the Denver Pacific continued its surveys as if it fully expected to build the line. Loveland and Teller concluded that they must make some sort of a pretense toward construction of the Colorado Central; consequently, on New Year's Day, 1868, amid speeches and cheers, some 200 feet of roadbed was built within the city limits of Golden. However, this constituted all constructional activities on the Central for quite some time.

In the meantime, arrangements were made to commence construction of the Denver Pacific at the northern end of the line; however, it was considered more appropriate to have the opening ceremonies at the Denver end. This they did.

The Rocky Mountain News reported that about one thousand people were present when the Denver Band, promptly at 11:15 A.M., struck up the "St. Louis Quickstep". The first ground was then broken for the earliest Colorado railroad, The Denver Pacific Railway & Telegraph Company on Monday, May 13, 1868,[1] near the old Denver Fairgrounds. This was followed by the opening of a few kegs of lager and the inevitable speechmaking. The Brass Band then struck up the "Railroad Gallop" and everyone pitched in and turned his few shovels of dirt. Although the exact spot is not known, it was near what is known today as the intersection of Blake Street and 40th Avenue in northern Denver.

Construction work on the northern end proceeded very slowly; meanwhile, the work of grading the roadbed on the Denver end was commenced in earnest and went forward in good shape, and by that winter practically all grading was completed north to the Platte River, crossing at a place called Evans, 48 miles north of Denver. At this point, the Union Pacific backed down on their agreement, giving the reason that financial difficulties prevented them from carrying out their part of the bargain, and the Denver Pacific bogged down badly. However, it was strongly suspected that the real reasons were: first, that the Union Pacific, being financially interested to a certain extent, was still toying with the Colorado Central scheme; second, they did not agree with the Denver Pacific as to the correct location of the northern half of the road; third, the Union Pacific was too busy with their own main line construction to bother with the Denver Pacific; and fourth, although the Union

1. Daily Colorado Tribune, June 3, 1870.

Pacific had promoted various financial schemes to gain control of the Denver Pacific, they did not consider their control of the road, at this time, as absolute. Whatever the reasons were, the Denver Pacific could get no satisfaction at all out of the Union Pacific officials. This was quite a blow and resulted in the contract being cancelled and all relations with the Union Pacific more or less suspended.

Gov. Evans came to the rescue, took over the contract himself, and persuaded the Union Pacific to sell him the necessary iron and some rolling stock, and the Denver Pacific would finish the road themselves. Then he disposed of the contract for building the Denver Pacific to a construction company in which he, Walter Cheesman, and Dave Moffat, of the Denver Pacific, held a one-half interest, and General Robert Carr, of the Kansas Pacific, the other half interest. For thus participating, Carr received one-half of the remaining Denver Pacific stock and other considerations. It was in this manner, then, that the Kansas Pacific became one of the two largest stockholders in the Denver road, thus aligning the two together very closely.

After considerable trouble in raising the necessary finances, construction work started on the northern end in September, 1869, and was completed to the Platte River, crossing at Evans, and the first train reached this point on December 16th of that year. The road was standard gauge and was completed through from Cheyenne to Denver, a distance of 106 miles, by June, 1870.

Every railroad has to have a great celebration over the driving of the last spike, and the Denver Pacific was no exception. In this case, the last spike was a silver one, donated by the miners of Georgetown. On one side was engraved "Georgetown to the Denver Pacific Railway". On the opposite side, "John Evans, President. June 24, 1870". A number of conflicting stories relating to this silver spike and the attending ceremony have been told; however, the author prefers to accept the word of the State Historical Society of Colorado as being far more authentic than the others. The November, 1945, Colorado Magazine, published by the Society, states:

"When Denver's first railroad, the Denver Pacific, was to be dedicated, and the last spike driven, June 24th, 1870, Billy Barton, the proprietor of the Barton House of Georgetown, and the miners here sent word that Georgetown would furnish a spike of pure silver for the ceremony. It was welded out of ores from the Georgetown mines. Billy Barton and his miners, who took the spike to present it, got drunk, pawned the spike and slept through the ceremony. Governor John Evans made his speech at noon. The first train had come down the track, the band was playing and all of Denver was gathered around the platform to see the Governor drive the silver spike. At the moment the spike was to be presented there was silence, no Billy Barton. The attorney general of the territory, General Sam E. Browne, being quick witted, stooped down unobserved, picked up an ordinary iron spike and tearing a sheet of white paper from his notebook, he quickly wrapped it tightly around the spike and handed it to the Governor, saying in a loud voice, 'Here's the silver spike from Georgetown, with the compliments of the people of Clear Creek County'. Governor Evans held the spike in such a way that the white paper passed for silver."

Note: Governor Evans later redeemed the spike from the pawn shop and it is still held to this day as a valuable possession by the Evans family in Denver.

The FIRST passenger train on The Denver Pacific Railway & Telegraph Company's line arrived in Denver on Wednesday, about seven o'clock P.M, June 22, 1870, and this was the FIRST passenger train in the state of Colorado to reach Denver. (The first actual railroad trackage in the Territory of Colorado was at Julesburg in the northeast corner of the state. The Union Pacific's main line, in following the valley of the South Platte River, dipped down into the state for a few miles at this point.)

The following newspaper item was copied from The Daily Colorado Tribune under the date of Thursday, June 23, 1870.

ARRIVAL OF FIRST TRAIN

"The first train over the Denver Pacific Railway arrived in Denver last evening, June 22, 1870, about seven o'clock, bringing Chicago papers of the 20th, and Omaha papers of the 21st. A large number of people were at the depot to witness the incoming of the train. Trains will leave regularly hereafter, each morning at 6:10, Denver time, and arrive at 7:00 P.M. Time on the road, 5 hours; fare $10.00.

"The track has been entirely completed with the exception of laying two or three rails and the driving of the silver spike, which will take place on Friday morning.

"After the completion of the laying of the track, Mr. L. H. Eicholtz, the efficient Chief Engineer of the Company, and Superintendent of construction, was invited to the general office of the Company and presented with an elegant gold watch and chain by the officers of the road. Gov. Evans made a short speech complimenting Mr. Eicholtz on his energy, ability and gentlemanly bearing and assuring him of the high appreciation the officers of the road had of his services. Mr. Eicholtz replied in a few words, expressing his opinion that his services had been overrated, and his gratitude for the compliment paid him."

The Rocky Mountain News, under date of June 23, 1870, had the following word for word report on the arrival of this first train, which occurred on Wednesday, June 22, 1870.

"The first through passenger train over the Denver Pacific arrived shortly after seven o'clock last evening, bringing about 40 passengers. The train consisted of two elegant passenger coaches and a baggage car and was drawn by engine number 30. Despite the rain, a large number of citizens were at the depot to witness the train's arrival".

No doubt many of the crowd present to witness the arrival of the first train in Denver felt as did the editor of the Daily Miner's Register, when he said:

"As the railroad approaches we seem to be drawn closer and closer to the borders of that ancient civilization which we left seven or eight years ago to build up a new empire."

A description of the Denver Pacific coaches, taken from the "Cheyenne Leader" was given in the Daily Colorado Tribune, May 18, 1870. It stated:

"The new cars are the most beautiful and elegant we have ever seen. The lady's coaches are finished inside with Hungarian Ash and Black Walnut set in elegant panels, showing the natural grain of these beautiful woods. The doors are finished with rosewood. Between each window is a small oval mirror surmounted with elaborate carved designs. The seats are lined with fine silk plush; the fronts of a beautiful Solferino color, and the backs a rich green. The cushions are of the most approved material, and are fixed upon delicate springs, which altogether makes the most luxurious seat we ever occupied. Equal to a stuffed Elizabeth chair. The entire interior is of unsurpassed beauty and magnificence. The smoking or second class cars are finished in a plain but very neat style with cushioned seats."

The territorial press carried jubilant accounts of the event. "GLORY HALLELUJURUM" shouted the Daily Central City Register of June 23rd. The Boulder County News chimed in with:

"Farewell to the long—sometimes dreary—and yet the pleasant rides across the plains. We leave (all that) with fond affection but no tears."

And the Daily Colorado Tribune headed its account as follows:

ARRIVAL OF THE IRON HORSE IN DENVER
VELVET CUSHIONED SEATS AND SILVER PALACE CARS
STAGE COACHES AND ACHING BONES DISCOUNTED
WHAT DENVER HAS ACCOMPLISHED FOR COLORADO
THE REWARD OF PLUCK AND PERSISTENCY
ARAPAHOE COUNTY HAS A SOLID INVESTMENT
ALL HAIL THE DENVER PACIFIC RAILWAY

In the meantime, the Kansas Pacific had realized the error of their shortsighted policy of demanding $2,-000,000 bonus from Denver and awoke to the fact that upon the completion of the Denver Pacific to the Union Pacific line, all the Denver business would go east over the latter road. Denver was satisfied that once the Denver Pacific was built, the Kansas Pacific had no other alternative but to come their way. This was borne out by the fact that the Kansas Pacific soon gave up any thoughts of building their line into any other part of Colorado and turned the construction of their road toward the general direction of Denver.

Meanwhile, Loveland was leaving no stone unturned. He still had the idea that he could make a "way-station" out of Denver. When he realized that he could not block construction of the Denver Pacific, he and his associates took Jefferson County's $100,000 that had been voted in favor of his road and, with some assistance from the Union Pacific, started construction of the first division of the Colorado Central east from Golden to a point north of Denver, known as Jersey. By building to Jersey, he had hoped to intercept the line of the Denver Pacific and divert the bulk of that road's traffic to Golden. Construction of the Colorado Central commenced in May of 1868, but due to lack of sufficient finances, it dragged along very slowly.

During this time, Loveland carried on extensive negotiations with the Kansas Pacific and did everything in his power to get that road to build to Jersey, connect with his Colorado Central line for Golden, and thus avoid Denver entirely. This was a good idea, too, but once again he had underestimated the strength of the opposition. Upon completion of the Denver Pacific, Governor Evans immediately transferred his construction forces to the building of the terminal end of the Kansas Pacific—as Denver would prefer it. His grading crews commenced from a point on Denver Pacific rails within the city limits of Denver and continued east to meet the oncoming Kansas Pacific. Thousands of pine and spruce ties were cut in Platte Canon and floated down the river to Denver, where booms caught them for delivery to the railroad contractors. By the middle of August, the gap was closed 40 miles east of Denver and the Kansas Pacific completed construction of their standard gauge line of railroad into Denver, two months after the arrival of the Denver Pacific. The first Kansas Pacific train pulled into the little town on August 15, 1870, and this was the SECOND railroad to reach Denver.

At this time, the construction of a depot by the Denver Pacific was nearing completion. The depot, an elegant brick affair, was erected at the foot of 22nd Street. The corner stone was laid on June 24, 1870, with the Masonic Fraternity conducting the ceremonies.[1] This was Denver's first depot.

Governor Evans and his associates, together with the citizens of Denver, were quite jubilant over the arrival of both the Denver Pacific and the Kansas Pacific. Everyone was happy but Golden. So far Denver was playing a winning hand; first, she became the southern terminus of the Denver Pacific and then the western terminus of the Kansas Pacific. Loveland's scheme of building his line to Jersey proved to be a rather expensive proposition, for, as things turned out, the Colorado Central was forced to pay a heavy fee for trackage rights, in order to operate their trains from Jersey Junction into Denver over the Denver Pacific. These victories over Loveland, Teller and their associates, greatly increased Denver's strength over her opponent, Golden. Loveland had made a desperate effort to divert this traffic to Golden, and although he had lost this first round, he refused to go down for the count. He was still looking for another opportunity to put Denver in the back yard as far as Colorado railroad transportation was concerned.

During 1869 and 1870, construction was continued on the Central until it was completed through to Jersey Junction, about three miles north of Denver on the Denver Pacific. This first section of the Colorado Central

1. Vickers, "History of Colorado".

20

was a standard gauge line of road and was approximately 14.9 miles in length. It was completed and opened to traffic on September 24, 1870, and with the exception of the Union Pacific trackage across the northeast corner of the state, this was the THIRD railroad to be built and operated within the State of Colorado. This 14.9 miles of trackage constituted the sum total of line built by the Colorado Central up to this time, and although surveys were completed for the first portion of the Central's narrow gauge line up Clear Creek Canon west of Golden, no actual construction work had been done.

The fourth railroad in the state was the Boulder Valley Railroad. This was strictly a Colorado road. It was organized and constructed by Governor Evans and his associates, as a counter move against Loveland, and also, to insure a coal supply for the locomotives of both the Denver Pacific and the Kansas Pacific. The road was originally intended to be a branch of the Denver Pacific, and that company guaranteed $300,000 of its bonds to provide for construction. The road ran west from Hughes Station (now the town of Brighton) 19.4 miles north of Denver on the Denver Pacific, through the Erie and Marshall coal fields to Boulder, a distance of 27 miles. The Boulder Valley, a standard gauge line, was chartered October 1, 1870. Construction began at Hughes Station on October the 24th following, and a line some 15 miles long was completed to the Erie coal fields in Boulder County and opened for business on January 24, 1871. All rolling stock was furnished by the Denver Pacific. Its proprietary interests organized the Boulder Valley Coal Company and established the coal mining village of Erie at the terminus of the road. The citizens of Boulder were vitally interested in having the road extended to their town, and by subscriptions, provided means for preparing the roadbed for the rails, the railroad company agreeing to put down the track and operate the road. The Boulder people began grading in March, 1871, and completed the work within a few months, but the railroad company failed to carry out their part of the agreement.

In June, 1872, the franchise, the 15 miles of line between Hughes Station and Erie, together with the extension grade, were all taken over by the Boulder interests, who reorganized the road as the Denver & Boulder Valley Railroad Company. The unfinished part of the line was then completed to Boulder, being opened throughout on September 2, 1873. Inasmuch as the Colorado Central's line to Longmont, which was by way of Boulder, had just been completed that spring, Boulder could now boast of two railroads. Strange as it may seem, the complete line of the Denver & Boulder Valley Railroad Company was then leased back to, and operated by, the Denver Pacific interests.

The Boulder Valley line eventually passed into control of the Union Pacific where it remains to this day. After it was taken over by the Union Pacific, all rolling stock was furnished by the Colorado Central.

The fifth and largest of all Colorado railroads was General William J. Palmer's Denver & Rio Grande. Even a brief history of the Rio Grande would fill many pages; however, we shall attempt to present a thumbnail sketch of the road's early history.

The Denver Pacific had been completed. The Kansas Pacific had finished its line to Denver. Even the Colorado Central, after years of promising much and doing little, had finally managed to complete the first section of its proposed mountain railroad system. Coloradoans had worked hard to secure these results and it is not strange that, in celebrating these triumphs, they almost completely overlooked the initiation of still another railroad scheme—the Denver & Rio Grande. And yet, within a few years of its inauspicious beginning, that road was destined to become one of the most important factors in the development of the Colorado mining region. The soundness of the project, as conceived by General Palmer, can, under the circumstances, hardly be open to question.

General Palmer, like Governor Evans—one of his sharpest rivals—was a practical railroad man. He had been associated with John Edgar Thompson, President of the Pennsylvania Railroad System, and at the outbreak of the Civil War, had enlisted with the Union Forces. After a brilliant career in the Army, he returned to private life and, following the lead of his former associates, interested himself in the fortunes of the young and struggling Kansas Pacific Railroad. As Chief Engineer of the Kansas Pacific, his most important services to that road came through his surveys in 1867-68 of the 32nd and 35th parallel routes to the Pacific. In conducting these early transcontinental surveys, General Palmer came to the conclusion that between the Overland Trail through Wyoming on the North, and the Santa Fe Trail in New Mexico on the South, there extended from the margin of the great plains for several hundred miles westward, an unsurveyed and little explored mountainous area full of mystery and natural resources of unknown magnitude. The first transcontinental railroad had veered to the north, passing up Colorado and this great mountainous area. Therefore, in General Palmer's opinion, this was the territory and the time was ripe for a large railway system such as he envisioned.

The general idea of Palmer and his associates was to build a trunk line along the eastern foothills of the Continental Divide, and the Sangre de Cristo Range, beginning at Denver and terminating in Mexico City, the capital of old Mexico. Branches were contemplated from points on this trunk line wherever found promising, extending into the canons of the mountainous territory lying adjacent on the west, even as far as Salt Lake City.

The Denver & Rio Grande Railway was chartered on October 27, 1870, and was to be of narrow gauge construction. Construction commenced in January, 1871.[1] The reader might be interested to learn that the first switch engine was a mule, and that the first timecard was written on a piece of letter paper by the Superintendent. The road's first locomotive, the Montezuma, was a 2-4-0 built by Baldwin. The running of the first train, over a distance of some 4 miles, occurred on August 14, 1871. This train consisted of two baggage cars, two smoking cars, and two passenger cars named the "Denver" and the "El Paso". This train was pulled by locomotive number 2, the "Tabi Wachi", a 2-6-0.

The road was opened for business to Colorado Springs, a distance of 76 miles, on October 27, 1871.[2] Passenger fare was ten cents per mile straight, and freight was sixty cents per hundred. On June 15, 1872,[2] the line reached Pueblo, and by November 1st,[2] of the same year, the tracks had been extended to the Labran Coal Fields (Florence). At this time, the panic of 1873 curtailed construction, and aside from pushing westward to Canon City in July of 1874,[2] no further mileage was added until 1876,[2] when the road reached La Veta and El Moro in the southern part of the state. After the controversy with the Santa Fe over the Royal Gorge route up the Arkansas River to Leadville was settled, expansion took place rapidly, and by 1884, the Rio Grande had some 1,600 miles of narrow gauge railroad in operation, covering the greater part of the south and west part of the state, and reaching out into New Mexico and Utah.

1. Anderson, "Gen. Wm. J. Palmer".
2. D. & R. G. Annual Reports.

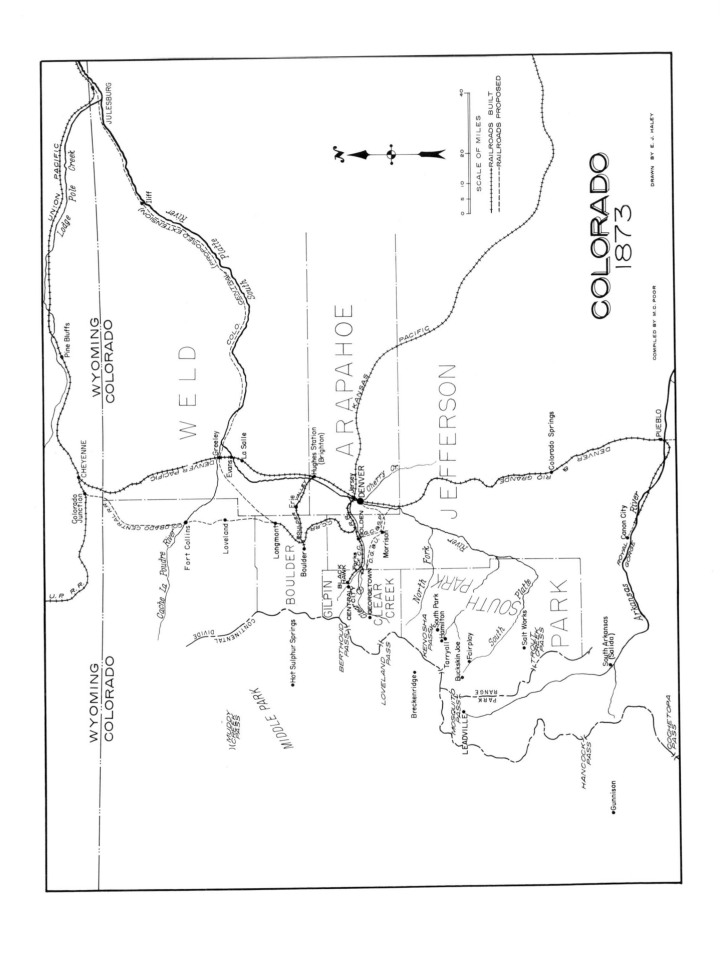

COLORADO
1873

DRAWN BY E. J. HALEY

COMPILED BY M. C. POOR

SCALE OF MILES

RAILROADS BUILT
RAILROADS PROPOSED

CHAPTER V

PERIOD OF RIVALRY AND FRICTION IN COLORADO

During the next few years following 1870, there developed in the Colorado region a great deal of friction between rival railroad builders, their roads, and their projects. No sooner had the Kansas Pacific been completed, than it was placed in competition with the Union Pacific line from Omaha to Cheyenne. Trouble arose immediately over the division of rates and business between the Missouri valley and the mining region of Colorado. This friction between these two roads continued unabated for over a period of ten years, until such time as the Kansas Pacific was absorbed into the famous Union Pacific consolidation of 1880.

Besides its continual friction with the Kansas Pacific, the Union Pacific began having its troubles with the Colorado Central. Ever since the Loveland road had been fairly well organized, the Union Pacific had made sporadic attempts to cooperate with the Central, largely to insure themselves of a share of the Colorado traffic and to protect their own personal interests more than anything else.

During 1871, the Union Pacific interests were divided amongst themselves as to the proper steps to take in this Colorado traffic squabble. One group contended that the logical way out of the whole muddle would be to purchase the Denver Pacific outright; while another group argued that the company should come to some sort of a permanent agreement with the Central, and extend its line to the Union Pacific in Wyoming. An effort to purchase the Denver Pacific failed, but the Union Pacific did secure a traffic agreement with the Denver road which would have made any Wyoming extension of the Central unnecessary; however, the contract was abrogated shortly afterward.

The possibility of extending the Colorado Central to the Union Pacific line in Wyoming was very closely related to the latter's feud with the Kansas Pacific. In the Kansas Pacific's efforts to secure concessions from the Union Pacific, its most effective weapon was its control, through the Denver Pacific, of the Colorado traffic. By threatening to secure that traffic for itself, independently of the Denver Pacific, the Union Pacific would be depriving the Kansas road of its chief bargaining weapon.

An agreement between the Colorado Central and the Union Pacific for the extension of the Central's line to the Union Pacific was reported to have been made even before the completion of the Denver Pacific in 1870. Preliminary surveys for the route of the proposed line to Pine Bluffs on the Union Pacific were actually made in the fall of that year. But the Colorado Central was not in any financial position to build the line, and the Union Pacific did not advance the necessary funds, for at that time they themselves were in a rather precarious financial position.

Due to the Union Pacific's failure to purchase the Denver Pacific, combined with their continued dispute with the Kansas Pacific, steps were once again taken to divert this Colorado traffic to their system. Accordingly, a new line known as the Golden-Julesburg line was projected. This proposed line of standard gauge railroad ran from Golden northeast to a connection with the main line of the Union Pacific at Julesburg, Colorado. The completion of such a project would please both the Central and the Union Pacific. To Loveland and his Colorado group, it meant that all this mountain traffic would be diverted through Golden and thus pass up Denver entirely. To the Union Pacific, it meant traffic for their road instead of the Kansas Pacific. This Golden-Julesburg line, in connection with Loveland's proposed narrow gauge line up the Canon of Clear Creek, was also designed to defeat construction of the Denver Georgetown & Utah road, the history of which will be taken up in full later on.

Meanwhile, there developed a considerable amount of squabbling and dickering between internal groups of both the Colorado Central and the Union Pacific and between both roads themselves, as to certain management policies, financial arrangements, construction, etc. While all this dissension was in progress, the Kansas Pacific strengthened themselves greatly in their fight with the Union Pacific by securing complete control of the Denver Pacific. The Union Pacific realized what this meant and revised their tactics immediately. Control of the Colorado Central was regained at once and the various troubles between the two interests were supposedly smoothed over and forgotten for the time being. Following this, a construction company known as The Colorado Improvement Company was organized in 1872 to build the proposed line. Amid much political mudslinging, Boulder County voted a $200,000 bond issue to help finance the construction of the line. During the melee, certain Denver interests, among other things, even threatened to organize a road known as The Denver & Platte Valley Railroad, a standard gauge line from Denver to Fort Morgan,[1] in an attempt to kill the proposed Julesburg extension; however, the Denver & Platte Valley never advanced beyond the threat stage. Finally, work got under way on the Golden-Julesburg line in the fall of 1872, and the rails had just reached Longmont the following April when the panic of 1873 hit, which put a stop to practically all railroad construction.

Another monument to the vaulting ambitions of Loveland and the Boston managers of the Colorado Central-Union Pacific organization is the decaying grade of the Golden City & South Platte Ry. Palmer's Denver & Rio Grande road, which had been organized in 1870 and upon which construction had been commenced during 1871, gave Loveland another brilliant idea. It occurred to Loveland that this construction of the Grande, due south out of Denver, would afford him another opportunity to take a slap at his old opponent, Governor Evans.

Loveland proposed to take advantage of this Rio Grande development and intercept Palmer's new road south of Denver, just as he had planned to connect with the Denver Pacific by means of his line between Golden and Jersey Junction, and later by means of his proposed Golden-Julesburg project. He believed that if he could tap Denver's southern transportation artery at a point somewhere below the city, the line would serve as a feeder to the Colorado Central by diverting north bound traffic by way of Golden and thus isolate Denver as a transportation center.

Accordingly, the Golden City & South Platte Railway & Telegraph Company was incorporated on January 18, 1872, with the following officers: Charles C. Welch, President, and Edward L. Berthoud, Secretary. The original incorporation papers do not show Loveland as an officer of the road; nevertheless, he was listed as one of the incorporators and was in reality "the power behind the throne". This proposed line of railroad, approximately 17 miles in length, commenced at Golden, followed the hogbacks south and east of that point, turned east along Bear Creek in the vicinity of Morrison, and thence to a connection with the Denver & Rio Grande road about ten miles south of Denver near Littleton, or near the confluence of Plum Creek and the South Platte River, whichever was the most feasible. It was to be of narrow gauge construction.

Concerning any actual construction of this projected railroad, there seems to be some difference of opinion as to just how much of the line was ever built. A few individuals contend that the line was completed and placed in operation as far as Morrison. In a fancy travel advertising booklet published by the Passenger Traffic Department of the Union Pacific during this period was

1. Rocky Mountain News. September 25, 1872.

found the statement that the proposed extension of the Colorado Central R. R. from Golden to Littleton would soon be opened to the traveling public. Charles Ryland reports that C. C. Rogers, an old-time Colorado Central employee living in Golden, possesses a newspaper clipping dated June 27, 1880, which tells of a train crashing through the G. C. & S. P. bridge across Clear Creek at Golden. According to the news item this bridge, which shows clearly in a photograph owned by Mr. Ryland, was weakened by flood waters coming down Clear Creek.

Apparently the entire line was graded and about three miles completed. Confirmation of this is based on the following: The Rocky Mountain News of July 27, 1873, states:

"The Golden City & South Platte Railway, backed by the Union Pacific, is making the dirt fly along their whole line, and are doing their best to reach Platte Canon. . . ."

A book, "The History of Clear Creek and Boulder Valley"[1] published in 1880, states (under the heading "Colorado Central Railroad"):

"Fifteen miles of the Golden City & South Platte were graded when work was suspended due to the panic of 1873. Work was recommenced in 1880 and three miles of the line are now in operation."

Smiley, in his "History of Denver" states:

"The roadway of about eighteen miles of the Golden City & South Platte was graded in the spring and summer of 1873. . . ."

Most important of all, however, is a letter written by Captain Edward L. Berthoud, then Chief Engineer of the Colorado Central and Secretary of the G. C. & S. P., and published in the Railway Age of January 15, 1880. We quote in part:

"The Golden City & South Platte is to run from Golden City south-east by south twenty miles to Plum Creek on the Denver & Rio Grande. . . . It is three-foot gauge. . . . thirty pound rail is being used. At Bear Creek, ten miles south of Golden, the line intersects the Morrison branch of the Denver South Park & Pacific. At Plum Creek, eight miles farther, it intersects the main line of the D. S. P. & P. Two miles beyond Plum Creek it connects with the main line of the Denver & Rio Grande. During 1879, the company completed three miles with all bridges, 550 feet of side track and connections with the Colorado Central at Golden".

From the above information and in view of the fact that no map or schedule has been located showing the line as having been in operation, the writer is of the opinion that this railroad was never completed beyond the three miles mentioned by Berthoud.

But to return to our story. Denver's strength was not all that helped defeat this idea. The panic of 1873 hit and the Boston interests, who had been backing Loveland in this scheme, deserted his organization, sacrificing most of the investments they had made up to this time rather than risk any further losses in any future devel-

1. Courtesy E. J. Haley.

*W. H. Jackson photo,
from the State Historical Society of Colorado.*

This general view of the Georgetown Loop region looks northeast and shows the numerous loops and bridges required to gain altitude between Georgetown and Silver Plume. (See the Georgetown Loop map in pocket at back of book.) Colorado Central engine 8 is in the foreground with the big fill above its domes, a westbound four-car passenger train crosses Clear Creek near the center of the photo, and dimly seen at the base of the hill on the left, another train crosses the high bridge.

opment of the idea;[1] and in common with the Golden-Julesburg enterprise, the Golden-Littleton project suddenly went down in the financial gale of that year and, with the exception of the small amount of work done during 1879, was never revived.[2]

Had Loveland been able to complete these two plans of his, he would have been in a position to carry out his idea of making Golden the apex of a great transportation "V", with Denver isolated between its arms, and dependent entirely upon Golden's good will. Had not the panic intervened, he might have curtailed, or at least embarrassed, Denver's future; for his scheme was bold, and not without logic, while his ability and persistence were well recognized. However, Denver's superior location and extensive room for any conceivable future growth would have overcome, in time, any possible obstacle that Loveland might have been able to erect.

These disputes over a Union Pacific connection to the mining region of Colorado, and whether Denver or Golden was to be the transportation center of this new empire, constituted only a portion of the territory's troubles. Another major problem was the construction of a railroad up the Canon of Clear Creek, the story of which will follow later. Continued threats from the Denver and Kansas Pacific interests to build a line of railroad west from Denver to the Georgetown mining region kept the Colorado Central interests in "hot water". Due to a weak financial position, the Central could not afford to build the line; neither, at the same time, could it afford not to build. Neither could the Union Pacific fail to protect their interests in the mining region by their failure to support the Central. It was a bad situation for the Loveland road. As a result of this situation, construction of the Clear Creek line progressed very slowly. Continued friction between the Loveland and the Union Pacific interests did not help matters in the least. Indeed, these were troublesome times for Colorado. Eventually, the Central, with Union Pacific help, completed the Clear Creek line through to Forks Creek by September of 1872, but it was like pulling teeth to gain this Union Pacific assistance. From Forks Creek, a line up the North Fork was completed to Black Hawk by December of that year, while another branch up the South Fork from Forks Creek was completed to Floyd Hill by March, 1873.

The building of this narrow gauge line west from Golden up Clear Creek precipitated another long period of dissension between Denver and Golden railroad interests. Inasmuch as that portion of the Central's line between Denver and Golden was standard gauge, while that portion west of Golden into the mining region was narrow gauge, the Denver and Kansas Pacific interests, realizing what the completion of the proposed Golden-Julesburg line would mean, wanted a third narrow gauge rail laid between Denver and Golden. This would eliminate the expensive transfer of freight at Golden and enable Denver to compete with Golden and the Colorado Central for the mountain trade. Under normal conditions, only one unloading would be necessary on all freight destined to or from the mountains through the Denver mercantile houses. But a second transfer at Golden, necessary only so long as Loveland kept his line between the two towns standard gauge, added to the cost of freight charges, which, of course, all shippers desired to avoid. Such a condition would interfere with Denver's commercial prosperity. One of the reasons for the organization of the Denver Georgetown & Utah was that it might force Loveland to lay this third rail, but Mr. Loveland refused to be inveigled into any such action. Indeed, the situation was a thorn in Denver's side. Once it was Loveland and his Colorado Central who were in trouble over the Clear Creek line—now the tables were turned—it was Denver and the Denver and Kansas Pacific interests who were on the "wrong end of the stick". This third rail wrangling and bickering, accompanied by threats and counterthreats from both Golden and Denver, continued unabated for six years, or until all interests concerned were liquidated in favor of the Union Pacific monopoly, at which time the third rail was laid.

In the early '70's, Jay Gould appeared on the Colorado scene. He gradually gained control of the Kansas Pacific and began paving the way for his forced consolidation of the Kansas Pacific and Union Pacific, which occurred in 1880. The story of how the nefarious Gould gained control of the northern Colorado railroad system and settled the region's transportation problems to his own personal and financial satisfaction, is a long and most interesting story, but the inclusion of these events are irrelevant to this review; therefore, we will have to pass them by.

By the latter part of 1871, there were five railroads partially or totally completed and in actual operation in the Denver region. Following this date was a period of Colorado railroad history characterized by individualism, localism, and chaos—a period of trial and error, of feeling out the territory and its possibilities. However, interwoven with all this uncertainty were the foundation stones of a great future for Denver. The financial and commercial success which was to come to the little town was not gained by merely standing by and hoping for the best.

Had it not been for Gov. Evans and his efforts behind the Denver Pacific at the time related, Denver today might have been just another average mountain town. Denver owes its gratitude and sincere thanks to this man for saving the city from disaster, and the success that she was to enjoy in the future may be summed up in the following brief review of events:

1. Vickers, "History of Colorado".
2. Smiley, "History of Denver".

1st. The completion of the Denver Pacific gave Denver rail connection with the outside world after the Union Pacific had turned "thumbs down" upon the city and backed out of their agreement.

2nd. It thwarted efforts of the Loveland-Golden-Union Pacific coalition, when it became apparent that a branch road must be built into Colorado from the north, to make Golden the front door of the Territory with Denver as the back yard.

3rd. It enabled Denver to maintain her position as the main distribution point for the great mining industry which was developing rapidly at this time, despite rumors to the contrary a short time back, and which enabled it to grow from a population of 4,760 in 1870 to over 35,000 in 1880.

4th. It enabled the city to develop into the political and commercial capital of a vast and rich empire embraced within the State of Colorado and surrounding territory.

The completion of five of Colorado's first six railroads into the city of Denver, more especially the Denver Pacific, actually changed the course of this empire in the west. Seldom has such a short road as the Denver Pacific had such momentous effect upon the development of a city. The few years start, afforded by this railroad, sufficed to give Denver an impetus that was too great to be overcome by any man or interest. The site of the town was unquestionably located on natural highways of commerce; only the Continental Divide offered any sort of a barrier to her commercial growth, and this obstacle was soon overcome by the railroads and their engineers.

Record of railroads built in the State of Colorado, in the order of their appearance:

1. Denver Pacific, June 22, 1870, reached Denver.

2. Kansas Pacific, August 15, 1870, reached Denver.

3. Colorado Central, Sept. 24, 1870, line open between Golden and Jersey.

4. Boulder Valley, January 24, 1871, line west of Hughes Station opened.

5. Denver & Rio Grande, August 14, 1871, line opened south of Denver.

6. Denver South Park & Pacific, June 18, 1874, line between Denver and Morrison opened.

By 1885, some 285 different railroads were projected within the state and had filed their papers with the Secretary of State. It appears that they were limited only by man's imagination and his ability to think up a name for his railroad and some place to build to. For example, there were over seventeen different companies organized, whose Articles of Incorporation stated that their intentions were to build a railroad between Denver and the Clear Creek territory. Obviously, the greater percentage of them never got any further than the paper they were written on. Paper roads, they were called. The beginning and the end of their histories appear in the written records of the Secretary of State. However, from these many dreams there emerged a few sound projects, brilliantly executed and amazingly successful. Chief among these were Gov. Evans' Denver South Park & Pacific and General Palmer's Denver & Rio Grande. It has ever been an inspiration to contemplate the daring spirit and cool courage that animated the early builders of Colorado, who raised millions of dollars within frontier Denver, and gambled splendidly against the Railroad Kings of the nation. This dauntless spirit must remain Denver's proudest heritage from the past.

THOSE WERE THE GOLDEN YEARS OF RAILROAD CONSTRUCTION, with no restrictive Interstate Commerce Commission and no antitrust laws to hamper the roads and their managers in their expansion programs. The general policy was that known as the "Survival of the Fittest", an age of ruthless competition, with all the elemental tactics that the phrases imply. Each railroad had its list of preferred shippers, who in return for rebates, gave their entire business to the secret parent. Ex-U. S. Senator Hill, an early-day Solon of Denver, testified before the Pacific Railway Commission that "Denver was a good place to establish a business, providing you were able to get on the inside track with the Union Pacific or some of the other large roads operating in the territory".

Under this system, the city of Denver became one of the largest distribution points between the Missouri River and the Pacific Coast. Great fortunes were made in mercantile pursuits within the compass of a few years. Some of the old established houses that had prospered under the wagon-transit method were unable to make the proper connections with the right railroads and quickly went to the wall, because new and favored establishments were able to ship goods into the mining camps and sell at less than their unfortunate rivals could sell the merchandise for in Denver. It was a cruel and merciless mode of doing business, but thus have empires been born.

Colorado Central 150 at Morrison, Colorado about 1890. This engine was built by the Brooks Locomotive Works in March 1880 as Colorado Central 8.

Denver Public Library Western Collection.

PART II

THE HISTORY OF THE
COLORADO CENTRAL R. R. CO.

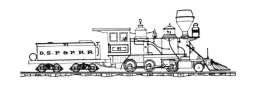

W. H. Jackson photo,
from J. C. Thode Collection.

Colorado Central 30, with one coach and crew stands beneath the high bridge of the Georgetown Loop. This locomotive was scrapped in 1889. It was built in 1873 by Porter-Bell as Colorado Central 4.

J. C. Thode Collection.

Union Pacific Denver & Gulf 107 was photographed at the Silver Plume, Colorado station on April 12, 1893, with an eastbound passenger train.

INTRODUCTION

In compiling the review of the early Colorado railroads up to the time of the organization of the Denver South Park & Pacific, it was necessary that many highlights of the Colorado Central be brought out for the reason that this road played an important role during this early period. For reasons of clarity and continuity, these previously mentioned points will be covered again, only more thoroughly, in this history of the Colorado Central. Inasmuch as we are concerned with only the narrow gauge lines of the Central, the portion that eventually became a part of the narrow gauge division of the Colorado & Southern Ry., as incorporated in this book, the standard gauge lines will be mentioned only where essential. This particular section will cover the Colorado Central from its beginning up to April 1, 1890, at which time it was absorbed by the Union Pacific Denver & Gulf consolidation. The balance of the road's history will then be included in that part of this book dealing with the 1890 consolidation and its eventual inclusion in the Colorado & Southern organization.

The history of the Colorado Central is a story of one of the most colorful little narrow gauge roads that went to make up a part of the Colorado & Southern system. Similar to the South Park Division, it was strictly a mineral road, born with the mining industry in Colorado and died with it, so to speak. The Clear Creek region, through which the little railroad was built and operated, rose to great prominence and fame as a gold producing area, which had its inception in 1859, when the first discovery of this precious metal was made in the canons of Clear Creek, first known as Vasquez Fork of the South Platte.

George A. Jackson, a prospector from Missouri, discovered rich placer ground near Spanish Bar, also known as Payne's Bar, near the mouth of Chicago Creek in Clear Creek County on January 7, 1859. The spot is now marked by a monument. Nearby, on Gregory Hill between Black Hawk and Central City, John H. Gregory, a prospector from Georgia, discovered the first gold lode on May 6, 1859.[1] His claims were known as the "Gregory Diggings". History also tells us that during this same year, George M. Pullman, of Pullman car fame, made a rich strike for himself in nearby Russell Gulch. During that summer, the stampede of goldseekers commenced in earnest and the mountains were overrun with miners and prospectors. The rush was on; they roamed

1. The Colorado Magazine, July, 1943.

the hills in every direction and penetrated every gulch. Each new day brought in reports of rich placer diggings and quartz discoveries. By the fall of 1859, the population of this area was estimated to be over 15,000 persons. Even "Haw" Tabor, of Leadville fame, was on hand. Accompanied by his wife, he spent three weeks during July and August of 1859, driving the first wagon from Golden up Clear Creek Canon to Russell Gulch.

A few years later, on September 14, 1864, the first silver in this area of Colorado was discovered by James Huff about 8 miles north of Georgetown. New mining camps such as Central City, Mountain City, Eureka, Spanish Bar, Empire City, Nevada, Black Hawk, Georgetown, and many others, sprang into existence along Clear Creek and in adjacent territory. The first steam quartz mill was erected near the Gregory Diggings on September 17, 1859. The boom had started, and soon the quartz mills were numerous in and around Black Hawk and Central City, and the rattling of their descending stamps, night and day, spoke of the tremendous wealth of this mountain country.

The first successful smelter was erected at Black Hawk in 1865; it was known as The Rocky Mountain Smelter and was operated by James Lyons. George M. Pullman was also interested in this venture. The best known of the early day smelters erected here was The Boston & Colorado Smelter built in Black Hawk in 1867-68 by the late Senator N. P. Hill. In 1878, this smelter was moved to Argo, near Denver. Slag from this and other smelters went into the construction of many miles of roadbed for early Colorado railroads.

These mining camps needed food, clothing, hardware, and many other miscellaneous supplies, along with a great amount of mining machinery and mining supplies. It was at this point that the first wagon and toll road companies were organized in the territory. It will be interesting to note that the rights possessed by some of these toll road companies, together with their roads that had been constructed at first for stages and wagons, were later purchased and became part of the right of way of The Colorado Central R. R. Co. One of the early wagon and toll roads built into this territory passed through a gap north of the mouth of Clear Creek Canon, called "Golden Gate". Through this gap and canon went a steady stream of mail, express, stages, freight teams, miners, prospectors, etc. Until the railroad was completed, this toll road company enjoyed a very lucrative business, the tolls at this point amounting to $16,000 to $24,000 per year.

At this time, almost everyone was aware of the fact that the Union Pacific Railroad, with the help of the Federal Government, was making plans and preliminary surveys for their proposed route across the continent to meet the oncoming Central Pacific, which, at that time, was building its line east. It has already been told in a previous chapter how an exploration party under the direction of Captain Edward L. Berthoud had explored and laid out, during 1861, a proposed route for a wagon road between the Clear Creek district and Salt Lake City, via Berthoud Pass. The expedition reported that the most difficult construction problems to be encountered would be found in the first ten miles of Clear Creek Canon, and the main range at Berthoud Pass; and that the proposed route west of the main range, via Hot Sulphur Springs and up the Yampa River to Salt Lake City, was not quite so mountainous and that construction should not prove too difficult.

In July 1862, another exploration party, financed by popular subscription, made a few preliminary surveys for a possible railroad route through this section and over Berthoud Pass. Upon their return, they reported that the grade was prohibitive, and that any railroad that proposed to follow this route would have to tunnel under the pass, on account of the steep grades and heavy winter snows. (See full account of this report in the description of the Berthoud Pass route in the first section of this book.)

In the meantime, business between the mining camps and the outside world had increased to a point where the need for some sort of transportation, other than that furnished by wagon teams, began to manifest itself very strongly. Citizens were clamoring for the road over the pass to be opened, arguing that the telegraph and railroad were bound to follow. A great number of persons thought that perhaps this proposed Union Pacific main line might, by some miracle, cross the mountains through this particular locality, and the idea sud-denly dawned upon a few farsighted individuals that any railroad that they might build through this Clear Creek territory might well tie in very conveniently with the plans of this transcontinental line.

Among the many persons who were seriously interested in getting a railroad organized and built in this territory, and who eventually saw his idea partly carried out, was William A. H. Loveland. The story of his early life and his final decision to establish himself in Golden in 1859 has already been told. Loveland, above all others, had a pretty good idea of what the situation was and what was going on as far as transportation activites were concerned. He was also well aware of what it would mean to Golden and a Clear Creek railroad should the Union Pacific be persuaded to build their main line through this territory. As Union Pacific construction work advanced west, this mountain crossing point became of vital importance. Loveland refused to give up hope and sincerely believed that a railroad could be constructed west from Golden across the mountains. Some way, some how, it could be accomplished. The fact that he was succeessful financially in the mercantile business enabled him to take a serious and active interest in the transportation problems confronting the Clear Creek district and surrounding territory. Even as early as 1861, Loveland, in cooperation with a Mr. F. J. Ebert of Denver, made the first actual survey for a railroad in the Colorado Territory. In the spring of that year, under the direction of these two men, a line was surveyed from Denver to Golden City, thence up Clear Creek to the vicinity of Black Hawk and Central City.[1] It is interesting to note that later on the main line of the Central closely followed that old survey.

Before commencing with the corporate setup of the Colorado Central Railroad, the author suggests that the reader follow all maps and diagrams in order that a more comprehensive understanding may be had of the road as this history unfolds itself.

1. Smiley, "History of Denver".

CHAPTER I

ORGANIZATION OF THE FIRST TRANSPORTATION COMPANIES

The first of these companies to be organized was The Apex & Gregory Wagon Road Company. An Act to incorporate this company was approved by the First Legislative Assembly of the Territory of Colorado on October 11, 1861. The route of this wagon road company, over which the owners had certain rights, was from Cold Springs Ranch, about 10 miles from Denver, via Amos Gulch, Gregory Road, Big Hill, Forks of the Creek, and thence up North Clear Creek to Gregory Gulch, with a branch from the mouth of Russell's Gulch via Lake Gulch to Missouri City in Gilpin County. The rights owned by this company between the Forks of the Creek and Black Hawk, were afterwards used by the Colorado Central Railroad between these two points.

During this same year another company, known as The Colorado & Pacific Wagon, Telegraph & Railroad Company, was organized by Henry M. Teller and John Turk of Central City, and C. C. Welch of Golden. Henry Teller, of whom we shall hear considerable, was, at that time, a young lawyer living in Central City.

The Act to incorporate this company was approved by the First Legislative Assembly on November 6, 1861. This company had certain rights commencing on the south bank of Clear Creek opposite the village of Arapahoe[1] in the county of Jefferson, thence up Clear Creek via Golden City to the junction of Guy Gulch and Clear Creek, a distance of 7 miles. History also tells us that through political maneuvers of the Territorial Courts, the grant to this company also included the route over Berthoud Pass, as previously laid out by Captain Berthoud. However, nothing was done at the time toward getting any actual construction started.

As previously mentioned, Loveland refused to believe that a railroad could not be constructed west from Golden across the mountains via Berthoud Pass. He continued to nurse this idea along, and in 1862 he and a group of Golden citizens composed of A. C. Hunt, Andrew Sagendorf, Captain Berthoud, E. B. Smith and Nelson K. Smith, secured a charter, ostensibly for a wagon road up Clear Creek to the mines, and went quietly about formulating their plans. The name of this or-

ganization was The Clear Creek & Guy Gulch Wagon Road Co. The Act to incorporate this company was approved by the Second Legislative Assembly on November 10, 1862. Nine days later, on November the 19th, the wagon road rights only (no railroad rights) of The Colorado & Pacific Wagon, Telegraph & Railroad Co., which had been organized about a year previously, were leased to Loveland and his Clear Creek & Guy Gulch Wagon Road Co.

Loveland's idea was to go ahead and complete the construction of this wagon road up Clear Creek following Berthoud's original survey over the pass. Considerable work, including an expenditure of about $50,000, was done on this road, with the firm idea in mind that any effort put forth in the building of such a road would not be wasted, because sooner or later his railroad would occupy the route, and he would be just that much farther along in the realization of his ambitions.

Soon after this, Loveland took his first steps toward getting his railroad company organized and set up. Accordingly, The Colorado & Clear Creek Railroad Company was incorporated by an Act of the Legislative Assembly on February 9, 1865, and this was the beginning of what was to be the Colorado Central Railroad.

The charter is interesting in its details and in its implications. Eight of the incorporators were Coloradoans, and fourteen were easterners. The Colorado group included the following: Messrs. Wm. A. H. Loveland, Henry M. Teller, John T. Lynch, John A. Nye, Thomas Mason, Milo Lee, Albert Gilbert, and Enos Baxter. The fourteen easterners included three Union Pacific officials, Messrs. John A. Dix (president of the Union Pacific from October, 1863, to June, 1868), James M. Mills, and George Hoyt. The remaining eleven gentlemen were a miscellaneous group of eastern capitalists.

The second section of the charter enumerated the routes upon which the company might construct and operate railroads, which were as follows: the company was authorized and empowered to survey, locate, construct, complete, maintain and operate a standard gauge railroad with one or more tracks, commencing at or near the western boundary line of Golden City in Jef-

1. Arapahoe was east of Golden on Clear Creek, three or four miles east of the gap between North and South Table Mountains. The place had 50 houses at one time.

ferson County, Colorado Territory, thence running in a westerly direction up the stream of Clear Creek to the junction of the north and south forks of said stream, and from the junction of said forks up the north fork to the cities of Black Hawk and Central City in the county of Gilpin; also, from the junction of said forks up the south fork of said stream to Idaho Springs and Empire City in Clear Creek County.

Also commencing at the aforesaid starting point at or near the western boundary line of Golden City and thence running in a southeast direction over the most feasible route to Denver City, thence to the Kiowa and Bijou basin. Also, commencing at same western boundary line of Golden City and running in a northeast direction by the most practical route to the coal beds on Coal Creek, Boulder City, St. Vrains, Big Thompson and Cache la Poudre Rivers in Colorado Territory. This Act, as granted, included a right of way 100 feet in width over public lands.

As indicated by the name—The Colorado & Clear Creek Railroad—these were local points that laid within a radius of 75 miles of Golden. The road was purely local in scope; and a local road without any lines to other railroads would obviously be of small utility. This fact implies that either Loveland and his fellow incorporators expected the Union Pacific to adopt a route through central Colorado, or, failing that, they intended to use one of the lines mentioned in the charter as a connection with the Union Pacific.

The capital stock of the corporation was set at $5,-000,000, with the proviso that it might be increased as needed and actually expended on the road. Shares were to be valued at $500 each. Control was vested in a board of eleven directors, "five of whom at least shall be residents of Colorado". The railroad was to be free of territorial or state taxes during the period of its construction. Permission was also granted incorporated cities and towns, as well as counties, to subscribe to the capital stock of the railroad company, such stock to be paid for in the bonds of the political division voting the aid. The company was also given the right to issue bonds, with no limitations imposed except that they should not be issued in smaller units than $500.

Curiously enough, coupled with the provision that the railroad should have full control over its rates, was the added provision that after 25 years the legislature might examine and set rates, and at every 20 year period thereafter as well. Probably the 20 year periods need not be taken too seriously. In a speculative venture of this sort, the investors would expect to make their profit within the first 25 years. Had none been realized by then, there probably never would have been any profits forthcoming. And so the provision that the company should enjoy a 25 year immunity in the fixing of its rates is probably more important than the provision that

the state should regulate and supervise rate making thereafter.

It was provided in the charter that the line to Central City should be surveyed within four months of the passage of the Act, and the remainder of the lines within the year. The line to Central City should be completed within three and one-half years; to Empire City in four years; the Cache la Poudre branch in five years; and the others (i.e., to Denver and Kiowa) in six years. That Denver should have been obliged to wait until the other points had secured railroad communications is typical of the rivalry that was fast growing between Golden and Denver for the mountain trade. No doubt Loveland felt that with the advantage thus provided, Golden would be amply protected against any possibility of Denver hegemony over the trade of the Clear Creek district.

With the charter secured, Loveland proceeded with the location of the Clear Creek line. The Colorado & Clear Creek Railroad made some preliminary surveys between Denver and Golden, up Clear Creek to the forks of the creek and thence to Black Hawk and Central City. However, no information appears as to just the exact time these surveys were actually made.

Captain Berthoud's engineering reports were optimistic; the gradients on this particular section would be within the requirements stipulated in the Pacific Railroad Act. (116 feet to the mile or a maximum grade of about 2.19%.) This was all very satisfactory indeed. By holding the engineering specifications to the Government's requirements, Loveland figured that the results could be used to great advantage toward influencing the Government interests in their forthcoming decision in the choice of the transcontinental railroad route; and if by chance, such a favorable decision was decided upon, he would be in a strategic position to make his railroad a part of this great route. Such a decision would also greatly advance Golden's chances of becoming Colorado's most important metropolis. It was the opportunity he had long sought.

In the fall of 1865, Loveland went East to complete arrangements for the building of the railroad, and to secure funds with which to erect iron works and rail mills at Golden. In connection with William P. Laman, the first president of the Central, an attempt was made to obtain some capital from foreign sources, but this failed so Loveland turned to the Union Pacific for assistance. John A. Dix, the Union Pacific president, appeared to look upon his plan with much favor, and Loveland was led to believe that his ideas and plans were accepted, but in this either he deceived himself or he was deceived, for before the year 1866 was over, everything fell through as will be explained shortly.

Apparently, however, Loveland must have had some sort of an understanding with the Union Pacific, for when the Colorado Legislature reconvened in January, 1866, the Colorado & Clear Creek road was on the ground with some highly significant amendments to its 1865 charter.

Four changes were made in the original charter. The first was a change in the corporate name, while the last three had to do with the revision of the proposed lines. On January 20, 1866, the corporate name of the road was changed to The Colorado Central & Pacific Railroad Company. This Second Act, in addition to the provision for the change of name, also amended the original Act by extending the Idaho Springs and Empire City line, "and from thence over the Berthoud Pass or by the most feasible route to the western boundary of said Territory in the direction of Provost City, in the Territory of Utah" and also extending the Kiowa and Bijou basin line "in a southeasterly direction to a point on the east line of said Territory, where the Kansas Pacific R. R. intersects said east boundary line". The amendment also provided for an additional line "commencing at the initial point aforesaid and running in a northeasterly direction over the most practical route to the east boundary line of said Territory at a point where the northern branch of the Pacific R. R. intersects said east boundary line". In other words, Loveland's idea here was to build to the east boundary line of the Territory and meet either the oncoming Union Pacific or Kansas Pacific and thus make his proposed road a part of either the Union Pacific or Kansas Pacific transcontinental line by way of Golden, Clear Creek and Berthoud Pass. No doubt it was a clever move on Loveland's part as the reader will observe here that this scheme was of paramount importance to him, in his determined effort to sidetrack Denver and thus make Golden the transportation center of Colorado.

In the meantime, Captain Berthoud's reports of his discovery of a pass over the main range had sounded interesting to the officials of the Union Pacific. Therefore, in the month of August, 1866, the Union Pacific directed their engineers to accompany Captain Berthoud, the Secretary and Chief Engineer of The Colorado Central & Pacific R. R., over its surveyed line up Clear Creek and across the pass for an investigation. This investigation by the Union Pacific people was with the idea of examining this territory and route, as surveyed by Captain Berthoud, as a possible route for the construction of their main line west over the main range. This was the basis for the great economic issue of the day. Should the Union Pacific build their main line through the canons of Clear Creek and over Berthoud Pass, and if they did decide on this route through the mountains, would the line come south directly to Denver or to Golden? The rivalry over this proposed transcontinental route between the Denver and Golden groups was running high.

As a result of this investigation, General Grenville M. Dodge, the Chief Engineer of the Union Pacific, turned thumbs down on the Clear Creek and Berthoud Pass route and announced in November, 1866, following, that his railroad had selected as the line of its route the one that followed up Lodge Pole Creek to Cheyenne Pass, through the Black Hills and Bridger Pass, thus passing up Colorado entirely.

This Union Pacific decision was a serious blow to William Loveland and his well-planned scheme for making his Clear Creek railroad a part of a great transportation line and, at the same time, for putting Denver in the back yard, so to speak, so far as its becoming Colorado's railway center was concerned. But the man refused to be defeated.

In Loveland's opinion there was still a ray of hope. At the time the Union Pacific had made this decision to adopt the northern route, General Dodge had recommended, that if suitable arrangement could be made, a branch road to Denver and the mining district of Colorado, both for the general traffic it would develop and for the coal supply it would afford the Union Pacific, should be constructed. The Union Pacific did not feel very much inclined, for the moment, to lend much assistance toward this project, but felt that they should keep a finger in the pie, so to speak, just in case something profitable should develop. The officials of the Union Pacific figured that they had nothing to lose and perhaps there might be much to gain. Any initiative, on the construction of a branch road into the territory, would have to come from Colorado.

On the strength of the Union Pacific's recommendation of a branch road into the territory, Loveland's next move was in the form of an effort to procure the co-operative assistance of its officers in making the Central, a system of roads in Colorado, tributary to the Union Pacific. Apparently the Union Pacific approved of his idea, for in January, 1867, a committee was appointed to investigate these Colorado resources and report upon the advisability of assisting in the construction of a system of Colorado roads as a tributary to the Union Pacific. This committee made a favorable report advocating the construction of a road from some point on the Union Pacific *to Denver*, thence to Golden and up Clear Creek to the forks of the creek and up both north and south branches, as well as a line to Boulder, with a view of making Boulder the beginning of a north and south line along the base of the mountains with branches into the mountains as future development might require.

Following this committee's report, Loveland went east early in 1867 and is supposed to have made some sort of a tentative agreement with the Union Pacific officials relative to the building of a line north to Wyoming. The Union Pacific proposed that if Loveland's road, The Colorado Central & Pacific, would grade a roadbed and furnish the ties for a line north to Cheyenne, the Union Pacific would iron, equip, and operate the line under a traffic contract in direct connection with their main line.

Consequently, Loveland returned to Colorado and set about at once to get the ball rolling toward carrying out these proposed plans.

Accordingly, the Colorado Central & Pacific was reorganized in June of that year, 1867, with the Union Pacific interests practically in control. The next step was a survey, by the Central's engineer, Captain Berthoud, of possible routes on which the line might be built. At this point Loveland's policy of "Golden first", entered the picture again, and as a result, Berthoud's survey differed slightly from the Union Pacific's suggested plan of a Colorado branch road centering at Denver. Two lines were surveyed, both from Golden. One ran along the base of the foothills, north, on a line which avoided Denver entirely. The other ran down Clear Creek to the junction with the South Platte, and thence northward along the west side of the latter and Lone Tree Creek to a junction with the Union Pacific. Just in order to carry out the Union Pacific's idea of including Denver, a 7-mile long branch road to the town was included in the plan. This, incidentally, seemed to amuse the citizens of Denver, inasmuch as they looked with scorn on Loveland's various schemes.

Joseph M. Collier photo,
from the State Historical Society of Colorado.

The eastbound morning passenger train from Silver Plume halts at Forks Creek to pick up passengers from the Central City connection, standing in the background.

CHAPTER II

EARLY FINANCING PLANS

The general theme of all concerned in Colorado that summer was the possibility of getting some sort of a railroad connection into the territory. Accordingly, a large railroad meeting was scheduled to be held in Denver, to ascertain just what could be done.

On July 11, 1867, Colonel Thomas J. Carter, who was the United States Government's representative on the Union Pacific Board of Directors, came to Denver to ascertain just what the people of Denver and the surrounding territory could and would do toward aiding the construction of the contemplated Colorado tributary system of the Union Pacific, the basis for which he proposed using the Colorado Central & Pacific organization. A public meeting of citizens was held at Cole's Hall on the evening of the 12th, to consider any proposition Col. Carter might submit. The meeting was presided over by Gov. A. C. Hunt. Col. Carter's plan was to begin the Colorado Central & Pacific by constructing a road from the Union Pacific to Denver, thence to Golden and on up Clear Creek, with a branch line from the main line to Boulder; and that the people along the route should, as stockholders in the road, prepare the roadbed for the iron and furnish the ties, and upon that being done, the Union Pacific interests would iron, equip, and, if found best to do so, lease and operate the road in direct connection with their main line. To make the proposition as attractive as possible, he explained that all the Coloradoans would have to do would be to furnish the roadbed and ties and that the Union Pacific would do the rest; thus, three-fourths of the cost would be met by funds raised in the east, and only one-fourth would have to be met by Colorado money. That one-fourth, he estimated, would amount to about $600,000—a suspiciously small sum, considering the great amount of mountain construction work that would have to be done.

Col. Carter was followed by General B. M. Hughes, Governor John Evans, and Governor Hunt who urged the assembled citizens to carefully consider Col. Carter's proposition, and prepare to act promptly, SHOULD the plan be accepted. Loveland also spoke, backing up all of Carter's remarks. He was also careful to assure Denver of his road's good will and mentioned that all the Central wanted was the City's endorsement of the proposition, and the use of an Arapahoe County bond issue. However, Loveland himself well knew that he did not propose to let any such railroad as was planned come by way of Denver, and that he would leave no stone unturned in an effort to see that no railroad did, either. In agreeing with Carter's remarks that the road should come by way of Denver, Loveland made a hypocritical statement, but he paid for it later. Similar railroad booster meetings were held elsewhere in the territory and at the first hearing, the proposition to aid the Colorado Central by county bond issues was enthusiastically received.

To provide means with which to prepare the roadbed for the rails in the most equitable manner, it was proposed that Arapahoe, Jefferson, Gilpin, Boulder, Weld and Larimer Counties should issue bonds totalling this $600,000, which was given as the approximate amount of Colorado's share. Among the different amounts each county was to raise, Jefferson County, of which Golden was the County Seat, was to vote a $100,000 bond issue, and Arapahoe County, in which Denver was located, was to vote a $200,000 bond issue. The balance, $300,000, was divided proportionately between the other four counties. After various topics were discussed, the meeting was closed with a general feeling that Colorado was on her way toward obtaining the much desired railroad connection.

Practically all counties concerned voted their respective bond issues, but it was mostly a case of each fellow looking out after his own community's interest, instead of the interest of the territory as a whole. For example, Boulder County stipulated that its bonds would be issued only on condition that the proposed road be built on the north and west side of the Platte; Gilpin County added that her bonds would be available only for the construction of a line to Central City. With a certain amount of suspicion of Loveland and his railroad associates, Denver offered the Arapahoe bonds; however, Gov. Evans had attached a provision to the Arapahoe bonds that specifically stated that this proposed line *MUST* follow down the east side of the Platte River direct to Denver, thence west to Golden and the Clear Creek mining towns, or said bonds would not be available. This provision was necessary to Denver because if this proposed line of railroad was constructed down the west side of the Platte, it meant only isolation for Denver, as far as railway transportation was concerned.

The amendments that had been attached to these various county bond issues killed Loveland's plans of building his Colorado Central & Pacific road north to the Union Pacific. The only means the road had for the grading of its line were these county bonds, and now they were tied up or were unacceptable for reasons stated. The only real source of income which Loveland possessed, and which he could use toward the construction of a railroad, was the $100,000 of Jefferson County bonds which had been voted in August, 1867. The Arapahoe bonds were useless, inasmuch as Loveland absolutely refused to build his railroad down the east side of the Platte. It was another manifestation of the bitterness and ill-feeling that was growing between Loveland and Evans. The reason for this refusal was very obvious; Golden could not become the center of Colorado's transportation system if Evans' terms were abided by.

With Loveland's visions of a railroad line to Wyoming quashed, the Central was back where it started—nowhere—and with no particular financial backing. The Union Pacific, for the time being, lost interest in the Loveland road. Such was the condition of the Colorado Central & Pacific in the fall of 1867.

In the meantime, Denver, in an effort to get a railroad connection, had organized The Denver Pacific Railway & Telegraph Company in November, 1867, and with the help of a $500,000 bond issue, voted in the road's favor by Arapahoe County, started preparations for the building of their road. The Denver Pacific signed a construction contract with two Union Pacific officials and had hopes of getting construction started as soon as possible.

The fall and winter of 1867-68 was a great period of pseudo-prosperity in the Denver region as far as railroad construction and transportation was concerned. The Denver railroad promoters were planning great things. As evidence, the Daily Colorado Tribune came out with a map in their November 22nd issue showing six main line railroads and numerous branches radiating from Denver. Most of them were projected in connection with the Denver Pacific. Some of them were soundly conceived and later built, but the majority never progressed any further than the paper stage. There was, for example, The Denver & Georgetown R. R. & Telegraph Company which proposed to build up Clear Creek canon and kill the Golden-inspired Colorado Central & Pacific. In the early 1870's, this road, under other names, proved to be a troublesome factor in the tangled railroad setup of the mining region. The Denver South Park & Rio Grande Ry. was later to be represented by the lines of the Denver South Park & Pacific and of the Denver & Rio Grande railroads. Other of these proposed lines included the Denver & Santa Fe, the Rocky Mountain Railway & Telegraph Co., the Denver Boulder & Cache la Poudre, and the Arapahoe Jefferson & South Park.

In December, the Denver Pacific had begun surveys for its line north to the Union Pacific. All this activity only added confusion to the already muddled railroad situation in Colorado. This was especially true of the Colorado Central and the railroad plans of the mining regions. Efforts were made to smooth out the differences between Denver and Golden, and peace meetings were held and petitions signed in an attempt to have the rival railroad projects consolidate their activities. The mountain regions, dubious of the Central's ability to give them a railroad outlet, were in back of these moves.

According to articles appearing at various times during the first part of 1868 in the Colorado Transcript, there were reports of three-cornered conferences between the Union Pacific, the Central, and the Denver Pacific. The point at issue seems to have been whether the branch to the Union Pacific should be built on the Denver Pacific or on the Colorado Central charter. The Union Pacific was reported to have informed the Denver Pacific that it would have to settle its quarrel with the Central and suggested that the Denver Pacific be the connecting road and to let the Central have free sway in the mountains. The Union Pacific, however, avoided a decision in the matter, and the whole outlook remained as uncertain as ever. The Denver Pacific continued with its surveys, just as if it were going to build the line; and the Colorado Central continued to insist that it alone enjoyed Union Pacific support.

In the meanwhile, Loveland had received another blow that was hard to take. The fact that Golden was the Capital of the Territory had not only been a humiliation to Denver, but had given the smaller town great prestige abroad and appeared to justify its claims that it was and always would be the metropolis of Colorado. By some sort of political maneuver, which is of no consequence here, Golden lost the Capital in December of that year, 1867. The measure was bitterly opposed by Loveland and other Golden citizens, but to no avail. The enactment was a fatal blow to the ambitions of the little town, and though the future looked very gloomy, they refused to give up.

CHAPTER III

FIRST CONSTRUCTION

Loveland had persisted in his endeavors to advance his Colorado Central & Pacific enterprise, yet really had accomplished little beyond making surveys. However, in the face of all the Denver Pacific activity, it was thought a good idea to have a demonstration of progress. Consequently, a formal beginning of construction work was made at Golden on New Year's Day (January 1, 1868), when the first ground was broken on the Colorado Central & Pacific Railroad.[1] With much ceremony, the citizens of the town assembled and proceeded to the site, officers for the occasion were elected, speeches and promises were made and, amid cheers, some two hundred feet of roadbed was graded in an easy place. The gala affair apparently came as a surprise to Golden and considerably revived its flagging spirits. On January the 8th, following, the Colorado Transcript came out with an article headed "Surprise New Year!!" The article took a jubilant "We told you so" attitude toward the scoffers who had derided the Central as a "paper road" only.

At this time the Central was reorganized for the third time. On January 14, 1868, at the annual meeting of stockholders of the Colorado Central & Pacific Railroad Company, a resolution was passed whereby the corporate name of the road was changed to the Colorado Central Railroad Company, this being recorded on that date with the Secretary of the Territory of Colorado.

As previously stated, the Central had made a nominal beginning on January 1, 1868, and by the following May, Loveland was making preparations for further construction on the road. On the strength of the $100,000 in bonds which Jefferson County had voted the Central, the road issued a call for bids on grading the line. It seemed as if the project, almost dormant for some years, was about to take on new life. Although it had been originally planned that the Central's first line of railroad to be built would be in the general direction of the Union Pacific in Wyoming, the exact line of the route had not yet been definitely established. Meanwhile, the Denver Pacific had started grading on their line. Loveland kept himself well posted on the plans and progress of both the Denver Pacific and the Kansas Pacific, and as the situation appeared to him, reasoned that the first part of his line to be actually constructed should

1. Colorado Transcript, January 8, 1868.

be east along Clear Creek in the general direction of Denver. His strategy will be explained later. Just what the definite route would be at the other end, as the line proceeded east, had not been fully determined as yet. By midsummer of that year, the Central had contracted for about six miles of grading and masonry work on the right of way east from Golden. Shortly afterward additional contracts were let, and by the close of November about 11 miles of line had been graded, bridges completed and ties delivered on the ground. Up to this point about $87,000 had been spent, with the result that further construction was halted due to the lack of finances.

As soon as it appeared that the Colorado Central was in earnest, the Denver interests opened an attack on that road. Their chief criticism was that the line was poorly located on unnecessarily steep grades, that it led into a "blind alley" at Golden, and so could not possibly serve as a practical route to the mountains, and—most important to Denver—that its line was so indirect as to make the distance between Denver and Golden approximately 22 miles instead of the logical 12 miles.

The attack was undoubtedly inspired by the fact that the Denver interests had incorporated, in 1868, their own line—The Denver & Georgetown R. R.—to build into the mountains. It appears that at the time the Denver Pacific had signed their construction contract with the Union Pacific, one of the clauses in the agreement stated that a railroad should be built west from Denver to Central City and Georgetown. This accounts for the organization of the Denver & Georgetown R. R. Denver at that point was flushed with high hopes; work had begun on its Denver Pacific project and many other projects only waited the proper moment. It could afford to indulge in a bit of bullying at the expense of the less successful Colorado Central.

Unfortunately for the Colorado Central, the mountain towns tended to agree with the Denver analysis of the situation, and the Colorado Transcript was kept busy repelling the charges levelled at the Central by the papers of the mining towns. Their fear that Golden was interested merely in becoming the mountain terminus of the road, with all the business advantages which would accrue to the point of trans-shipment, fitted well into the Denver attack. The fact that the Central was doing nothing to complete its grade from Golden to Central

City also lent credence to the charge that the Central was primarily interested in building up Golden as a mercantile center.

The Denver Pacific, on the other hand, could well commend itself to the mining regions, for it possessed two all-essential items which the Colorado Central did not have: the backing of the powerful Union Pacific (for the moment); and a valuable land grant from Congress. The Golden press might taunt Denver on its hoggishness, but that would neither inspire confidence of the mining towns nor build the Colorado Central line. Indeed, it was almost two years from the time the grading contracts on the Central were let until the road was even able to announce that it had secured funds to grade its line from Golden to its eastern terminus. Obviously, until it had completed that section of its line, there would be no possibility of its holding out any hope of railroad facilities for the mining regions of Central City and Georgetown.

Meanwhile, on January 11, 1869, the Colorado Central held its annual election of Directors. Six of the eleven members chosen to constitute the Board were Union Pacific men, sometimes known as "the Boston Managers" of the Union Pacific. These men were: T. J. Carter, F. G. Dexter, John Duff, A. Lambert, J. B. Taft, and J. G. Tappan. The other five were: W. A. H. Loveland of Jefferson County, John Turk of Clear Creek County, and Henry M. Teller, Truman Whitcomb and E. K. Baxter of Gilpin County.

During 1869, Denver Pacific and Kansas Pacific railroad construction was slowly going ahead and Denver was eagerly looking forward to their completion. Everyone was more or less happy but Golden and the Colorado Central. Some additional construction work had been done during 1869, but the project had been lagging so long that even its most enthusiastic boosters must have despaired. According to the road's annual report for 1869, $103,647.17 had been expended on construction and no rails had as yet been laid.

For this delay, there had been several reasons. One was the uncertainty of the Colorado railroad situation during the years 1868, '69 and '70. The uncertainty in regard to the construction of the Union Pacific's connecting line into Colorado from the north, and of the Kansas Pacific's line into Colorado from the east, and the nearest point at which either or both of these lines of railway might be connected with the Colorado Central, occasioned numerous negotiations between the Colorado company and these other companies, in an effort to determine the best course for the Central to follow. Another was the lack of finances. The road had suffered from a lack of funds from its inception, and although the Central was largely under control of the Union Pacific interests, they failed to provide any money for its construction. Loveland experienced some of the same difficulties in getting active assistance from the Union Pacific that

Denver and the Denver Pacific were encountering. About all the funds it had on which to operate were the proceeds from the sale of the $100,000 in county bonds which Jefferson County had voted the road. There were possibly a few advances from private sources, such as the approximately $30,000 advanced the road by its president, T. J. Carter, but these must have been entirely inadequate. Outside aid, therefore, was essential.

Meanwhile, much delay and trouble developed between the Union Pacific and the Denver Pacific over getting the latter's construction work started. For various reasons, as explained elsewhere, the Union Pacific refused to carry out their part of the bargain with the Denver road, and as a result, all contracts between the two roads were cancelled and it is a well known story that Governor Evans and the people of Denver took over the contracts and built the Denver Pacific themselves.

Although it had become rather thin at times, Loveland had retained his alliance with the Union Pacific through the several years of his endeavors to inaugurate construction of the Central; in fact, the relationship got to a point which, as previously stated, resulted in a partial reorganization of the company in June, 1867, leaving the Union Pacific interests practically in control; yet they failed to provide any money for the Central's advancement. This was due to a certain amount of friction between some of the officers of each road and between the two roads themselves. Meanwhile, the Kansas Pacific had strengthened themselves considerably in their fight with the Union Pacific by securing control of the Denver Pacific. This compelled the Union Pacific to reverse its policy once more. First, it had abandoned the Colorado Central, and then it had abandoned the Denver Pacific. Now, as a result, the Kansas Pacific had scooped up the Denver Pacific and was threatening to exclude the Union Pacific from the Colorado traffic. The Union Pacific then faced the realization that they would have no Colorado connection, principally because the Denver Pacific, which they had planned on to be their connecting line to Denver and the Colorado mining regions, had come under Kansas Pacific control. This meant that the latter road would then be in a position to manipulate rates on the Denver road so as to shut the Union Pacific out of Colorado and force all the mountain trade to go by Kansas Pacific east to St. Louis.

In view of this situation, it is understandable why Oliver Ames and other Union Pacific promoters came to the active support of the Colorado Central (the Denver Pacific's local rival) in 1870. Just what the nature of this agreement was cannot be definitely ascertained but it is clear that financial help of the Union Pacific alone made it possible to complete construction of the Central east from Golden. Later developments made it clear that just as the Denver Pacific, in return for financial assistance from the Kansas Pacific, had become the creature of that road, so the Colorado Central, in return for financial assistance from the Union Pacific, became the creature of that road. This Union Pacific support was made with just one paramount view in mind: to gain complete control of the Loveland road and make it a "feeder" to the main line of the Union Pacific, and that is just what materialized.

Now that the powerful Union Pacific was in back of the Colorado Central, the picture took on a different hue. An ambitious campaign was planned and opened. The prime requisite at the moment was to get the Central's construction forces in action as soon as possible. Loveland realized that it was too late to block construction of the Denver Pacific, and he was also aware of the fact that the Kansas Pacific was headed toward Denver in such a direction that their line of railway would come in at a point a few miles north of the city. In a desperate effort to achieve success for his railroad, he came to the conclusion that the first line of railway to be built should be due east of Golden to a point where the Kansas Pacific was expected to come in just north of Denver, and make a junction with the Denver Pacific. He concluded that if he could get his road built through to this predetermined point and successfully connect with the Kansas Pacific, it would shunt Denver on to a mere branch of the Colorado railroad system, and all Kansas Pacific traffic would therefore flow straight through to Golden, thus passing up Denver entirely. In addition to this, it would also tend to divert Denver Pacific traffic over the Central, and thus give supremacy to his railroad and to his ambitious little city of Golden. It was an ambitious scheme if only his plan would succeed.

Therefore, in 1870, when the Denver Pacific and the Kansas Pacific were approaching completion, active construction work was resumed on the Central and was continued without interruption until the line was completed through to a junction with these two roads, slightly north of Denver. This line was ironed and equipped by the Union Pacific. This connection, known as "Jersey Junction" (sometimes called Denver Junction) was located about three miles north of what was then the center of the city of Denver. The line of railroad, therefore, first constructed was between Golden City and Jersey Junction, a distance of 14.97 miles and was STANDARD GAUGE.

There seems to be a difference of opinion as to just the exact date that the line was completed. Quoting from the Rocky Mountain News of September 25, 1870:

"The road was completed to Golden City at about 10 o'clock yesterday morning."

That makes the date September the 24th; however, Mock states:

"The first engine came into Golden City over the Colorado Central on September 23rd, 1870, but the celebration of the completion of the road, scheduled for that date (as per a letter of invitation to the festivities sent out by the Colorado Central Railroad, in the Berthoud Scrap-Book C.S.H.S.) had to be

postponed until the 26th (as per the Colorado Transcript of September the 27th). On that day, however, Golden celebrated. There were free rides on the Colorado Central, free eats, fireworks, a free dance, two brass bands, the driving of a gold and silver spike, and the inevitable speeches. . . ."

It appears that the first official run carrying passengers occurred on September the 24th, when a train left Golden for Denver via Jersey Junction and the Denver Pacific. The following word for word newspaper story of this event was published in the Rocky Mountain News under the date of September 25, 1870.

"COMPLETION OF THE COLORADO CENTRAL
"Excursion of Golden Citizens to Denver

"At three o'clock, yesterday afternoon, the first train over the Colorado Central railroad arrived at the depot of the Denver Pacific, having on board a large number of ladies and gentlemen from Golden City, among whom we recognized the following:

"T. J. Carter, President of the road; W. A. H. Loveland and wife; Judge Johnson and wife; John Turk; Arthur C. Harris; Wm. Jennison; Miss Baird; Miss Jennison; George West of the Transcript; David Barnes and wife; Dr. Anderson and wife; Mrs. Woodberry; Mrs. Schram; Rev. C. Whitehead and wife; Mrs. Adams; Mrs. Everett; John Bush; Judge Mann; C. C. Welch; C. B. Clements; Mr. Learned and wife; Mr. Burrell; and Captain Edward L. Berthoud and wife.

"Upon arriving the party were conveyed in the elegant omnibuses of the Denver Transfer Company to the American House. At five o'clock the party started upon their return, all apparently highly pleased with their visit. The road was completed to Golden City at about 10 o'clock yesterday morning, and as has already been announced, its completion will be celebrated at that place tomorrow by the driving of gold and silver spikes, speeches, toasts, dancing, etc. Large delegations will be present from Denver, the mountains and surrounding country. We heartily congratulate our neighbors of Golden upon the completion of the Colorado Central, and trust that their fondest hopes as to the prosperity that the completion of this road is to bring them may be more than realized."

On the next day, the 26th, a great celebration was had at Golden in honor of this occasion, and the following newspaper account describing the festivities appeared in the Rocky Mountain News under the date of September 27, 1870.

"THE COLORADO CENTRAL
"Grand Celebration in honor of its Completion to Golden City
"Excursion trains—A big crowd—Music—Speeches—
and the driving of the Gold and Silver Spikes.

"The completion of the Colorado Central railway to Golden City was an event which gave pleasure and satisfaction to all portions of Colorado. To Denver it gave another railway, it being the third road which centers at our city. To Golden it was the fulfillment of years of hope, the promise of new days of prosperity, and the certain evidence that they were connected by iron rail with the commercial centers of the territory and of the nation. The mountains rejoiced that a railway was nearer, and all Colorado was pleased to know that there was twelve miles more of railroad within the boundaries of the territory.

"This is the event which was very appropriately celebrated at Golden yesterday. Denver joined heartily in the festivities, many were present from mountains and various portions of Colorado, and all were pleased to congratulate the joyful inhabitants of Golden, and to rejoice with them on the completion of the road to their city.

Colorado & Southern engine 44 in Clear Creek Canon near Roscoe.

"There were three excursion trains left Denver during the day, the ride being free to all. The crowd went on the 12 o'clock train, which was accompanied by the G.A.R. band, the cornet band having gone up in the mountains. It was composed of six cars, drawn by the engine 'GOLDEN', which was decorated most handsomely with flags and wreaths of evergreen. Mr. H. A. Pratt was conductor, George Wilkins, engineer, and A. Willock, fireman. There were not less than 700 persons on the train. After a rapid run and pleasant ride, the train arrived at Golden, and rolled up to the depot amid loud cheers, the firing of cannon, and the sweet strains of music.

"The exercises began about half-past two by the driving of the gold and silver spikes by the President of the company, Mr. T. J. Carter. The gold spike was engraved as follows: 'Presented to the C.C.R.R. Co. by Gilpin County, September 26th, 1870'. The silver spike bore the following description: 'Presented to the C.C.R.R. Co. by J. W. Watson, September 26th, 1870' The two spikes were presented by Hon. W. A. H. Loveland, President of the day, to the President of the road, who proceeded to drive them down, amid loud cheers.

"The audience then adjourned to the large depot where Mr. Loveland presented Mr. Carter with a handsome gold watch and chain in behalf of the citizens of Golden. Appropriate speeches were made by both gentlemen. Among the sentiments read were: The President of the United States; the President of the Colorado Central; Denver; The Denver Pacific; Gilpin and Clear Creek Counties; The Colorado Stage Company; Omaha; Chicago; the pioneers; The United States officials; Hon. W. A. H. Loveland; the ladies; Southern Colorado; The Union Pacific Railroad; Mike Guilford; and the Press. Among the speakers were Judge Eyster; Mr. Carter; D. C. Collier, of *The Register;* Hon. J. B. Chaffee; Hon. W. A. H. Loveland; General Chamberlain; Col. Craig; Gov. McCook; Mr. J. J. T. Ball; Gov. Patterson; and others. Many of the speeches were eloquent, humorous and appropriate. The exercises were interspersed with music, and it was after five o'clock when they closed.

"The train on which our reporter left departed shortly after, and landed its load of living freight safely in Denver. In the evening there was a grand ball and a display of fireworks.

"Most favorable mention must be made of the excellent collation which was prepared, and to which full justice was done. There were not less than 2,000 people present during the day.

"We regret that we have not more space to devote to this affair, which did so much credit to the citizens of Golden, and afforded all so much pleasure. We wish, however, to acknowledge the kindness, courtesy and hospitalities which were extended to the citizens of Denver, and the evident desire on the part of all to render the celebration, one which the citizens of both towns could unite and enjoy. Especially, let praise be rendered to Hon. W. A. H. Loveland, who, as President of the day, did so much toward rendering the affair a success. Let us also add that to his untiring energy and enterprise are the people of Denver and Golden indebted for the iron road which now unites the two cities. The day, in conclusion, was a pleasant success, one which will bind more closely Denver and Golden, marred by no accident, and an occasion which will be long remembered by all who participated."

The author notes with considerable interest that the owner and editor of the Rocky Mountain News, the Denver newspaper which published this very complimentary and diplomatic story, was Mr. Wm. N. Byers, a true friend and supporter of the city of Denver, Governor Evans, the Denver Pacific, and the Kansas Pacific, during all their bitter quarrels with Loveland, Golden City, and the Colorado Central railroad. Throughout this period of friction between the two factions, Byers spared no ink when he dipped his pen to write what villainous characters, in his opinion, Loveland, Teller and other cohorts of these men were.

But to return to our story. As previously stated, Loveland had hoped that the construction of his line from Golden to Jersey would intercept the line of the Denver Pacific and divert the bulk of that road's traffic to Golden. Along with this plan, he left no stone unturned in his effort to make Denver a way station on the Kansas Pacific. To this end, he carried on extensive negotiations with this road urging its builders to continue on through Jersey Junction to Golden and avoid Denver entirely. But Governor Evans beat him to the draw, and, as related elsewhere, succeeded in getting the Kansas Pacific rails laid direct into Denver. Loveland's ideas were good and his schemes were clever, but they proved ineffective. Thus, for the second time, he had underestimated the strength of the Denver opposition. The construction of 17 miles of road, which made 5 miles of additional line to construct, operate and maintain, together with the large fee of $6,000 per year for trackage rights over the Denver Pacific into Denver, was the price Loveland had to pay for his miscalculation. This arrangement continued until 1874, when he built his own direct line into the Denver station.

Colorado now had three railroads. The Denver Pacific had been completed from Cheyenne to Denver on June 22nd; the Kansas Pacific, Kansas City to Denver on August 15th; and the Colorado Central, Golden to Denver (via Jersey Junction) on September 24th. As far as railroads were concerned, the year 1870 had done well by Colorado.

CHAPTER IV

BRIEF HISTORY OF THE STANDARD GAUGE DIVISION
OF THE COLORADO CENTRAL RAILROAD

One of the major problems after the completion of the line to Jersey was the promotion of the Colorado Central's extension to the main line of the Union Pacific.

In order that the reader might be familiar with this standard gauge division of the Central, sometimes called the "Valley Lines", and its relation to the narrow gauge division, we will give a brief review of that part here.

Part of this campaign on the part of the Union Pacific in the promotion of the Central was the construction of the standard gauge division of that road, as defined in its charter, so as to compete with the Denver-Kansas Pacific combination, which was competitive and antagonistic to the Union Pacific.

An agreement between the Colorado Central and the Union Pacific for the extension of the Central's line to the Union Pacific was reported to have been made, even before the completion of the Denver Pacific in 1870. Preliminary surveys for the route of the proposed line from Golden to a point known as Pine Bluffs on the Union Pacific were actually made in the fall of that year. But the Colorado Central was not in a financial position to build the line, and it is highly improbable that the Union Pacific would have advanced the necessary funds just then for they themselves were in a rather precarious financial position.

Now that competition for this Colorado traffic had developed to a point which forced the Union Pacific's hand, definite steps were taken to divert this traffic to the Union Pacific. Accordingly, a line of railroad known as the Golden-Julesburg extension was projected. This proposed extension, in connection with the Central's narrow gauge line up the canon of Clear Creek, was also designed to defeat construction of The Denver Georgetown & Utah. This road, which was originally known as The Denver & Georgetown R. R., had been projected by Evans and Carr of the Denver and Kansas Pacific roads, to be built directly west from Denver across the mountains.

If the completion of this Golden-Julesburg extension could be carried out, it would be to the mutual satisfaction of both the Colorado Central and the Union Pacific. To Loveland, it meant that all this mountain traffic would be diverted through Golden and not Den-

ver; to the Union Pacific, it meant traffic for their road instead of the Kansas Pacific.

As these various developments unfold, one can very readily see how the rivalry and hard feelings between the two leaders represented by John Evans and the Denver railroad interests, and Loveland and his Colorado Central-Union Pacific combine together with the Golden interests, were growing.

Meanwhile, rumors were heard quite frequently that the building of this Julesburg extension would commence at any time. But matters continued in this uncertain fashion throughout 1871, with no attempt made to get construction started. This delay was largely due to internal troubles, management policies, and financial and construction problems. Finally, their differences were temporarily smoothed over and plans for getting underway with the building of the extension were commenced.

It had been decided that this second proposed line should connect with the Union Pacific at Julesburg, known at one time as Denver Junction,[1] instead of Pine Bluffs. Julesburg was located on the main line of the Union Pacific where the road makes a short dip down into Colorado at the northeast corner of the state. Accordingly, a standard gauge road was surveyed in 1872,[2] from a point called Golden Junction, about two and one-half miles east of Golden on the Golden-Denver line, down the valley of the Platte River to Julesburg. The line was located by way of Golden Junction, the Marshall coal fields, Longmont, Greeley, Iliff and Julesburg, and was intended to be the main line of the Colorado Central, thus leaving Denver off to one side to be reached only by the branch road from Golden to the Denver Pacific junction at Jersey. After the surveys were completed, a company known as The Colorado Improvement Company was organized in 1872 by the Colorado Central and the Union Pacific interests to build the proposed line. The first contract was let for the construction of that part of the road between Golden Junction and Longmont. This contract, at first, pro-

---

1. Jersey Junction, just north of Denver, was also known at times as Denver Junction.
2. Rocky Mountain News, September 18, 1872.

vided for a line direct to Longmont with a branch to Boulder City, but afterward, it was modified so that the main line made a detour to a point near Boulder (later known as Boulder Junction) and thence to Longmont. Thus, the route was from Golden Junction by way of the Marshall Coal Fields, Boulder Junction, Longmont, Greeley, and Julesburg. In July 1872, Boulder County voted the railroad $200,000 in bonds, and Weld County voted $150,000. Work on the road began in September, 1872. Construction was pushed quite rapidly and by April 17, 1873, the track had been completed from Golden Junction to Longmont, a distance of 39.15 miles, and opened to traffic. At this time, further work on the line was discontinued and was never resumed by Loveland. The strategic value of the Julesburg extension to the Union Pacific was practically nil as long as it stopped at Longmont; but there it did stop—a victim, it was reported, of the Panic of 1873. Longmont remained the terminus of the road until 1877. At this time, the plans were altered and the extension was not to be built over the logical cutoff to Julesburg, as previously planned, but to Colorado Junction, sometimes known as Hazard, just west of Cheyenne on the main line of the Union Pacific. It was simply to be the cheapest line which would open Colorado to the Union Pacific. This Longmont-Colorado Junction line, including switches and 72 miles[1] of track, was laid in 67 days. At the state line, the Colorado Central track connected with a railroad in the Territory of Wyoming built under the name of The Colorado Central Railroad of Wyoming, which in turn connected with the Union Pacific 6 miles west of Cheyenne at Colorado Junction. This made a complete railroad from Denver via Golden Junction, Boulder Junction, Longmont, Berthoud, Loveland, Ft. Collins and Colorado Junction to Cheyenne. The line was opened for business on November 7, 1877.

In view of the great demand for coal in the Clear Creek mining regions, the Colorado Central, in 1877, built a three-rail line north out of Golden for a distance of 7.80 miles to reach the Marshall Coal Fields, located along the standard gauge line to Longmont. This was to accomodate the narrow gauge cars and thus eliminate the troublesome transfer at Golden. The new line connected with the Longmont line at a point then known as Ralston.[2] The following year, that portion of the old standard gauge line between Golden Junction and Ralston, a distance of 4.72 miles, was abandoned and the track removed. This left the main line of the road from Denver to Ft. Collins and Cheyenne by way of Golden.

1. Longmont to State line—63.90 miles.
   State line to Colorado Jct.—8.62 miles.
2. Corporate History, C. & S. Ry. (Author's note: Indisputable evidence shows that this junction was not at the place designated as Ralston on 1888 U. S. Gov't. Survey Maps, but was located some three miles north near Leyden Gulch.)

In the year 1881, as a result of the Burlington & Colorado Railroad (later Chicago Burlington & Quincy) extension from the state of Nebraska to Denver, the company proceeded with the construction of what was then known as the Julesburg branch, or cutoff. This line connected with the Union Pacific at Julesburg, Colorado, at one end, and with the line of the same company (that company at this time having acquired the old Denver Pacific Railway) at La Salle at the other end. As the Union Pacific interests, at this time, also controlled the Colorado Central, that portion of the surveyed, located and partially constructed line of the latter company between Longmont and the Cache la Poudre River at or near Greeley was abandoned, the connection being made with the line of the Denver Pacific branch of the Union Pacific rather than with the Colorado Central road proper, although the Julesburg branch was built under the name of, and as a part of, the Colorado Central.

The portion of the line from Julesburg to Iliff, a distance of 45.83 miles, was completed in 1881, and the remainder, from Iliff to La Salle, 105.65 miles, was completed in 1882. This line remained as part of the Colorado Central until sold to the Union Pacific Denver & Gulf Railway.

At this time, the Union Pacific, being the owner and in control of the Colorado Central, and having a line of its own from Denver to Cheyenne, the old Denver Pacific, considered it unnecessary to further operate that portion of the line of the Colorado Central between Ft. Collins and the Colorado-Wyoming line, and therefore in 1888-89 abandoned and took up the track upon this portion of the road, a distance of 33.05 miles.[1]

The Union Pacific, at this time, obtained control of the old line of the Denver Western & Pacific Ry., and reorganized that company as the Denver Marshall & Boulder Ry., and completed the line between Denver and Boulder via Marshall. It was considered unnecessary and inadvisable to further operate that portion of the old line of the Colorado Central between Louisville Junction, and a point near Ralston, a distance of 14.72 miles, and therefore they abandoned and took up this portion of the track in 1888-89.

As nearly as can be determined, all of the standard gauge line between Golden and Ralston, a distance of 7.80 miles (built in 1877), was removed about 1889. This left only 1.70 miles of narrow gauge line between Golden and the brick yard. The balance of the standard gauge section passed into control of The Union Pacific Denver & Gulf Railway Company on April 1, 1890, later becoming a part of The Colorado & Southern Railway system on December 28, 1898.

1. A second Ft. Collins—Cheyenne connection was rebuilt by the C. & S. Ry. Co. in 1911. (Corporate History, C. & S. Ry.)

CHAPTER V

THE PERIOD FOLLOWING THE COMPLETION OF
THE GOLDEN-JERSEY JUNCTION LINE

During the next two or three years following the completion of the Golden-Jersey Jct. line by the Colorado Central, there developed a great deal of friction between rival railroad builders, their roads and their projects, in the Denver region, much of it revolving around Loveland and his Colorado Central. Loveland's road was no exception; much internal friction developed among the Colorado Central's officials themselves. During this period, when construction was first commenced on the narrow gauge division of the Colorado Central, a considerable amount of Colorado railroad history, which concerned the road both directly and indirectly, was unfolded.

As already stated in the section covering the proposed Julesburg extension, the Union Pacific was attempting to cooperate with the Colorado Central in the promotion of that road, largely to insure themselves of a share of the Colorado traffic, and to protect their own personal interests, more than anything else. Rumors regarding various plans of the two railroads continued to appear, but outside of the completion of the road to Jersey Junction in 1870, nothing developed for the time being. Matters continued in this fashion, and as a result, 1871 was a comparatively quiet year in Colorado railroad history, as far as actual construction was concerned.

Much of the inactivity on the part of the Colorado Central was due to the uncertainty within the corporate setup of both roads. While various changes were taking place among the Union Pacific officials, the Colorado Central was undergoing a change of directors at the same time. T. J. Carter, the ex-government director of the Pacific railroad, had been president of the Colorado Central almost from its inception. But at the annual stockholders' meeting held in the spring of 1871, he was ousted in favor of a locally controlled board. Henry M. Teller, the young Central City lawyer, and W. A. H. Loveland, the Golden politician and merchant, were made president and vice-president, respectively. John B. Taft, of Boston, who had thrown in with the Colorado party, was elected secretary and treasurer.

The move must have been a surprise coup which took the Union Pacific parties completely off their guard. Just before being ousted, President Carter was cham-

pioning the Colorado Central at a Georgetown railroad meeting; and just after being ousted, he was in Boston berating the Colorado Central and attempting to regain the control he had lost. A drastic housecleaning of the corporate setup followed. In spite of protests from the Boston crowd, the Carter personnel was turned out of the Colorado Central in wholesale lots.

Just what had occasioned this sudden outburst is rather difficult to determine, but some highly interesting sidelights on the matter have been brought to light by the historian, Mock. There is, first of all, the question of Carter's relation to the Colorado Central. Teller's action in firing the Carter-employed personnel, and his statement that

"When I took the position as president of the company, Carter had selected *all* the employees of the road. *No* man was in the employ of the company who had been appointed on the recommendation of any of the Colorado directors."

indicates quite definitely that there was a good deal of friction between what may be called the Colorado and the eastern parties in the Colorado Central. The inference, then, is that Carter represented the eastern group and was, for that reason (and possibly for others), ousted from control.

There is also the fact that Carter had differences with the new group over financial matters. "T. J. Carter & Co." seems to have been the construction company by which the road had been built. As a result of the common practice of paying the contractor in the securities of the road he was building, certain securities were claimed by T. J. Carter & Co. as still owing—a claim the new control refused to recognize. The company also owed Carter some money—possibly arising out of personal advances he may have made the road—and Carter, because of the company's failure to reimburse him, in retaliation held a considerable amount of Colorado Central property. Historical documents show this amount was $23,804.60.

But that was not the full extent of the differences between the two parties. The Colorado group definitely felt aggrieved by the course pursued by the eastern group, in their road. In one letter, under the date of

November 13, 1871, which Taft wrote to Teller, he stated:

"It does seem to me that the Union Pacific R. R. Co. occupy the position of a set of down-right plunderers as far as their acts go toward your road."

In another letter, under date of March 8, 1872:

"You are quite correct that we are dealing with sharpers, and not only so, but some of them try to be of the first water."

That same letter Taft wound up with the exhortation:

"Let us proceed so as not to get cheated this time."

Some financial deal had apparently been highly displeasing to the group which executed the coup, and while it cannot be proven by records brought to light so far that this deal had to do with the construction contract which Carter and his eastern associates had secured while the road was under their control, still something of that sort may well have been the case. Building a railroad was often the only lucrative side to railroading in the early west, and the Colorado party may have felt that Carter had prevented them from participating in that little game.

It is known, for instance, that the Colorado party was not averse to profiting at the expense of what the eastern party put into the road. In fact, the entire history of the Colorado Central Railroad is the story of one double cross of the double crosser after another. The classic example of such dealings revolves around the securing of the right of way, by the Union Pacific, for the Colorado Central up the canon of Clear Creek, the only practical entryway into the Gilpin and Clear Creek mining territory west of Golden. This right of way had been secured by Loveland, Teller, and a few more of their cohorts for a wagon road into that region. When the Union Pacific attempted to secure title to this right of way up the canon, this group was not disposed to let their opportunity go undeveloped. The Union Pacific had no choice if it wished to see the road built to the mines but to accept the terms proposed by this group of worthies. When the Omaha road offered them $75,000 in Colorado Central bonds for their right of way, the offer was refused. Only after the Union Pacific, which was paying for the construction of this clique's *own* railroad, raised their offer from an additional $25,000 in stocks to $100,000 in bonds, would they permit these outsiders (the Union Pacific) to build *their* own local railroad over *their* own right of way. The little deal was reported to have netted the conspirators a neat profit of $60,000!

The second instance illustrating the willingness of the Colorado group to profit at the expense of the eastern interests is bound up with the Kansas Pacific-Union Pacific feud. Almost the first concern the Union Pacific showed after receiving the news of the Colorado coup was that the Colorado Central line would now be leased to the rival Kansas Pacific. It was this, no doubt, which explains in a considerable measure why the Union Pacific was so upset by the coup.

Actually, the fear was far from groundless. The Kansas Pacific was seriously interested in securing control of the Colorado Central, and once threatened to build its own line to the mines if it were thwarted in this attempt. Naturally, the interest of the Colorado Central was to forestall such an invasion of their territory and under the circumstances—if the Union Pacific failed to support them—the Colorado Central might have been expected to string along with the railroad interest which could afford them the greatest amount of protection and financial advantage. As brought out in letters written between Taft, Loveland and Teller in March 1872, this is exactly what the Colorado party proposed to do.

The Union Pacific was clearly aware of all this, and every effort, fair or foul, was therefore made to regain control of the Colorado Central, even threatening to seize the Central's books. They approached Taft (who was in the East) to ascertain under what condition he would join the eastern group, which he refused to do. At this same time, it was reported in the Colorado Miner, under date of March 28, 1872, that the Union Pacific had threatened to abandon the Colorado Central unless it was given complete control of the road.

The fact that the Colorado Central failed to live up to expectations as a money maker only intensified the breach. Teller might write Oliver Ames that the road was not only paying operating expenses, but was also paying the Denver Pacific $500 monthly for trackage rights between Jersey Junction and Denver, and $450 per month to the Union Pacific for the use of its equipment, but the fact remains that at the outset the Colorado Central showed a decided deficit. Only piecemeal reports are available, but they reveal such facts as the following: a deficit of $1,579.93 for the operating department of the road during the month of February 1871; a deficit of $3,995.01 during the month of April 1871; and a deficit of $5,421.05 for September 1871.

The Union Pacific was split wide open on the question as to what its attitude toward the new management of the Colorado Central should be. One group would have cheerfully kicked out Loveland, Teller and the rest of their party, if it could have done so; the other defended the new management. One group wished to purchase the Denver Pacific as the logical way out of the whole muddle; the other wished to come to terms with the Colorado Central and extend its line to the Union Pacific in Wyoming. In brief, those who were on the inside as a result of the Teller coup opposed any recession from their position (such as would have entailed from the proposed purchase of, or settlement with, the Denver Pacific) while the "outs" were anxious to thwart the new management, no matter at what cost.

The actual effort to purchase the Denver Pacific failed, but the Union Pacific did secure a traffic contract with the Denver Pacific which would have made the Julesburg extension unnecessary. The contract was abrogated shortly thereafter, but meanwhile, rumors that the Union Pacific had given up its plans to extend the Colorado Central were circulating in Colorado.

Apparently, the Union Pacific had seen to it that there was more than one string to its bow; for a visit to Colorado of J. B. Duff, Bushnell, Grenville Dodge and T. E. Sickles, in the fall of 1871 had resulted in a temporary settlement of the disputes between the two companies. While the purpose of the visit may well have been the purchase of the Denver Pacific, and while it was probably on this visit that the agreement with the Denver Pacific heretofore alluded to was made, the Union Pacific parties also took the opportunity to set the Colorado Central house in order. According to Teller, the Union Pacific at that time agreed to:

". . . .go on with the road, pay off the indebtedness of the company and fix the right-of-way up the canon of Clear Creek, etc., and to look after the company generally."

It was at this time that the Kansas Pacific secured control of the Denver Pacific thus forcing the Union Pacific to revise its tactics immediately.

The first step was to regain control of the Colorado Central. This was accomplished at the next election in the spring of 1872, when the Omaha group took over control on May 14th. Just how it was done does not appear, but since Teller was maintained as president of the road, even though at least some of his associates were turned out, including J. B. Taft, who was replaced by E. H. Rollins; and since the Union Pacific had already set the wheels in motion to extend the Colorado Central to its line north of Colorado, it would appear that some sort of a deal was made whereby in return for these considerations, Teller agreed to sell out his former allies, and throw his lot in with the eastern group. Teller had a reputation for going back on his friends after they had served their purpose.

Alex Martin photo,
from E. J. Haley Collection.

Colorado Central 3 with one coach on a trestle above Black Hawk in the late 1870's.

CHAPTER VI

THE FIGHT FOR THE MOUNTAINS

That the Colorado trade was a prize well worth striving for has already been brought out. But merely building lines to the distributing point for this Colorado trade would have been to neglect one of the most valuable phases of this traffic. The mountain mining regions (i.e., chiefly Gilpin and Clear Creek Counties) were the real reason for the existence of any such distributing point as Denver, and the railroad which could command the channels up and down which produce flowed between the distributing point and the real producing areas would be in entire control of the situation. Not only would it have the extensive mountain haul at remunerative rates, but it would also be able to direct such shipments over its own trunk line system. It is therefore not strange that both the Kansas Pacific and the Union Pacific attempted to corral this mountain traffic each for itself.

This they attempted to do by means of subsidiaries building from three points at the base of the mountains—Denver, Golden and Boulder—to two main objectives in the mountains—Central City and Georgetown, and to some extent the South Park region. In the case of the Union Pacific, the local subsidiary utilized for this purpose was the Colorado Central. For the Kansas Pacific, three subsidiaries were projected: the Denver & Boulder Valley Railroad (this road was taken up in a previous chapter) to run to Boulder and on into the mountains from that point; the Denver Georgetown & Utah Railway (this road, under its various names, will be taken up in full detail later on) to run from Denver to Georgetown; and the Denver, South Park & Pacific Railway, from Denver to the South Park country, the major theme of this entire book, and whose story will follow later on.

Central City, after a brief period of courting by the Denver-Kansas Pacific crowd, came to be regarded as lying undisputedly within the Colorado Central's sphere of influence. The question of which of the two rival railroad interests should build to Georgetown was bitterly disputed.

This saga of "The Fight for the Mountain Trade" is a rather complicated, but highly interesting story, and could be more easily understood if viewed from four main angles, namely:

First: The possibility of utilizing the Denver &

Boulder Valley to make Boulder the gateway to the mountain traffic.

Second: The extension of the Colorado Central to Central City.

Third: The fight to monopolize the Georgetown traffic.

Fourth: The inception and construction of the Denver South Park & Pacific Railway.

Inasmuch as we are concerned ONLY with the histories of the railroads that are directly connected with the history of the Denver South Park & Pacific, namely, the Colorado Central and the Denver Georgetown & Utah, only the histories of these two roads will be taken up. For an exceptionally complete treatise on this subject of the fight for the mountain trade, the reader is referred to Mock's *"Railroad Development in the Colorado Region to 1880"*.

After the Colorado Central had announced that their line west of Golden was going to be of narrow gauge construction, the Denver interests, headed by Gov. Evans, who represented the city as far as the railroad situation was concerned, realized at once what a disadvantage it would be to Denver's commercial position as a distributing point for the mining regions if part of the Clear Creek line was narrow gauge and part standard gauge. It was Evans' earnest desire that any road built between the mountain district and Denver should be of uniform gauge all the way through. Accordingly, he urged Loveland to lay a third rail along his line between Golden and Denver, and thus eliminate the breaking of gauge on any through traffic between the mountains and Denver, but Loveland refused, which was, of course, no surprise to Evans.

Shortly after the completion of the Denver Pacific and the Kansas Pacific into Denver, a violent war broke out between the Union Pacific and the Kansas Pacific over the division of business and the matter of rates. The Kansas Pacific, being the weaker of the two roads, began to lose out in the long haul traffic business and soon realized that something would have to be done to relieve the situation. The need for an independent and friendly outlet from Denver to the west became of extreme importance to the Kansas Pacific, if they intended to hold their share of traffic. Another important point was that such an outlet to the mountains would

A view on the Union Pacific-controlled Greeley Salt Lake & Pacific Railroad, at Sunset, Colorado, showing Colorado Central engine 10. Fireman Sam Specs in gangway and engineer Squire 1. Thorne in cab. The "U" on cab denotes Union Pacific ownership.

also tend to bring a large portion of the mountain traffic to their road via Denver, thus strengthening both the Kansas Pacific and Denver against their opponents.

In an effort to cope with this situation and to enable the Kansas Pacific to be in a better condition to meet its adversary, John Evans resigned the presidency of the Denver Pacific, in 1872, and was succeeded by Robert E. Carr, who was also president of the Kansas Pacific. This move gave Carr complete control of the route from Kansas City through to Cheyenne, thus making the Kansas Pacific one route. This was followed immediately by the organization of the Denver Georgetown & Utah Ry. by John Evans and the Denver and Kansas Pacific interests. They proposed to build this road from Denver directly west across the mountains, via Georgetown, to a connection with the Central Pacific in Utah. The completion of such a line would make the Kansas

Pacific independent of the Colorado Central-Union Pacific combination. Evans also believed that perhaps the organization of the Denver Georgetown & Utah might force the Colorado Central to lay the third rail between Denver and Golden. However, Loveland and Teller did not propose to lay any such third rail, relying on the fact that the completion of the Julesburg extension would counteract any such moves as contemplated by Evans and Carr. Their proposed main line to Julesburg, in connection with the narrow gauge line up Clear Creek, was Loveland and Teller's answer to Governor Evans and his Kansas Pacific-Denver Georgetown & Utah combination. We shall first take up the construction of the narrow gauge division of the Colorado Central, after which will follow the history of the Denver Georgetown & Utah Railway Company.

An 1875 Porter-Bell, Colorado Central 2, pauses during switching operations in the Black Hawk yards circa 1880.

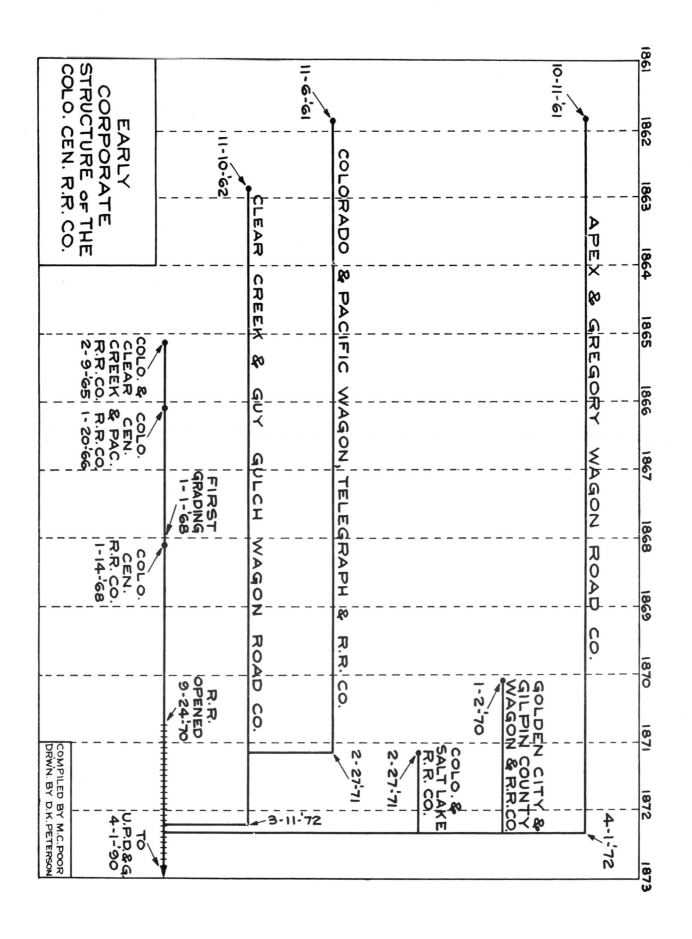

EARLY
CORPORATE
STRUCTURE of THE
COLO. CEN. R.R. CO.

APEX & GREGORY WAGON ROAD CO.

10-11-'61

COLORADO & PACIFIC WAGON, TELEGRAPH & R.R. CO.

11-6-'61

CLEAR CREEK & GUY GULCH WAGON ROAD CO.

11-10-'62

COLO. & COLO.
CLEAR CEN.
CREEK & PAC.
R.R. CO. R.R. CO.
2-9-'65 1-20-'66

FIRST
GRADING
1-1-'68

COLO.
CEN.
R.R. CO.
1-14-'68

R.R.
OPENED
9-24-'70

TO
U.P.D.&G.
4-1-'90

GOLDEN CITY &
GILPIN COUNTY
WAGON & R.R. CO.

1-2-'70

COLO. &
SALT LAKE
R.R. CO.

2-27-'71

2-27-'71

3-11-'72

4-1-'72

COMPILED BY M.C. POOR
DRWN. BY D.K. PETERSON

1861 1862 1863 1864 1865 1866 1867 1868 1869 1870 1871 1872 1873

CHAPTER VII

CONSTRUCTION OF THE NARROW GAUGE
LINE UP CLEAR CREEK CANON

After the Colorado Central's line between Golden and Jersey Junction had been completed and opened to traffic, Loveland set about making his plans for the building of the railroad up to the mines in the Gilpin and Clear Creek mining regions. To reach this territory it would be necessary to build up the pathway carved out by Clear Creek and on through its rugged defiles up into the mountains. At the time it may not have been fully realized, but Clear Creek afforded the only really practicable route into the rich central mining region.

Even so, the route, at times, seemed unlikely to accomodate a railroad except at well-nigh prohibitive costs of construction. When the Union Pacific had sent survey parties into Colorado looking for possible lines to the Pacific, the usual verdict on the route up Clear Creek had been something akin to "possible, but not favorable".

At that time, however, Clear Creek Canon was occupied by wagon roads of various toll road companies which had obtained certain privileges and right of way by virtue of special Acts of the Territorial Legislature that had been granted in the first years of the existence of the Territory. The organization of three of these toll road companies, namely: The Apex & Gregory Wagon Road Company, The Colorado & Pacific Wagon Telegraph & Railroad Company, and The Clear Creek & Guy Gulch Wagon Road Company, has already been related. The reader will also remember that immediately after the organization of the last named road by Loveland and some if his associates, they leased the wagon road rights only of The Colorado & Pacific Wagon Telegraph & R. R. Company. The Clear Creek & Guy Gulch Company then completed about 6 or 7 miles of wagon road up Clear Creek canon to the vicinity of Guy Gulch, at a cost of about $50,000. Then, on February 27, 1871, Loveland and his Clear Creek & Guy Gulch Company took over The Colorado & Pacific Wagon Telegraph & R. R. Company completely, with all their wagon, railroad and miscellaneous rights, franchises, etc. This was followed by the Colorado Central R. R. Company's purchase, on March 11, 1872, of Loveland and Teller's Clear Creek & Guy Gulch

Wagon Road Company, for which the Colorado Central paid $100,000.

In the meantime, there had been organized another company, known as the Golden City & Gilpin County Wagon & Railroad Company. This company was incorporated on January 12, 1870. It possessed, or claimed to possess, certain rights of way, located and surveyed in Clear Creek canon which were more or less in conflict with the rights of The Colorado Central Railroad Company. This company's rights, etc., were acquired by the Central on April 1, 1872. About the same time, there was in existence a railroad company which also claimed to possess certain rights of way in the canon, and which conflicted with the rights claimed by the Central. This company was known as the Colorado & Salt Lake Railroad Company. It was incorporated on February 27, 1871. The property and corporate rights of this company were acquired by the Colorado Central on April 1, 1872. A study of the accompanying chart will show the reader at a glance what the complete setup was from the time of the organization of the first wagon road company in that district up to the point where the Colorado Central had acquired all of them, along with their miscellaneous claims and rights, and was ready to commence construction without interference.

The entire Colorado Central Railroad, including the Clear Creek Canon line, had been originally projected and surveyed as a standard gauge railroad. The engineering plans and specifications of the Clear Creek line, as originally laid out under the direction of Captain Berthoud of the Colorado Central, and Mr. T. E. Sickels, Chief Engineer of the Union Pacific, called for several tunnels and a large amount of expensive rock work.

Narrow gauge railroads were then almost unknown and their special fitness for mountain defiles was still undemonstrated. To Captain Edward L. Berthoud, it is believed, belongs the honor of first suggesting a narrow gauge road for the Clear Creek, or Western Division of the Colorado Central.[1] Loveland caught the idea at

1. Hall's "History of Colorado" states: Captain Berthoud first suggested narrow gauge construction for the Colorado Central in 1866.

once, but his associates did not fully share his confidence in the success of the new idea.[1] As a result of Berthoud's suggestion, further investigation was made and it was finally decided in May and June of 1870 (see Captain Berthoud's letter following) that the great, if not prohibitive, cost of constructing a standard gauge railroad in that winding canon made it imperative to adopt the narrow gauge as the more suitable track. Relative to the estimated cost of grading the Clear Creek line, we read in *"Narrow Gauge Railways of America,"* by Fleming,[2] the following:

"Mr. T. E. Sickles writing of the section of the Colorado Central Rwy. that passes through Clear Creek Canon says: 'On this 13½ miles, the creek falls 1,700 feet. The cost of grading a road bed through the canon for a four foot eight and one-half inch track was estimated to be $90,000 per mile. The *actual cost* of grading a road bed for a three foot track, has not exceeded $20,000 per mile. This large difference resulting from the fact that the location of the two lines occupy different ground. On the broad gauge location, the minimum radius of curvature adopted was 955 feet, and on the narrow gauge it is 220 feet. The canon is so tortuous that the broad gauge location would have required, in construction, numerous tunnels and bridges across the stream, with high embankments, and deep, open rock cuttings. The adoption of the narrow gauge admitted of an alignment conforming approximately to the windings of the canon, enabling a graded road bed to be obtained for less than one-quarter of the estimated cost of a broad gauge road bed, with the additional advantage that increase of distance secured more favorable grades.' "

Many persons have regarded General Palmer as the progenitor of the narrow gauge solution to the western mountain railroad question. However, evidence found by the writer seems to refute that claim. Paul Stewart Logan, in his history of the Denver & Rio Grande Railway, 1871-81, writes:

"The Rio Grande was NOT the first in the field with the narrow gauge track. Before the Grande was started, the Colorado Central had decided on a narrow gauge line. The credit which goes to the D. & R. G. is that it was the first railroad in the west to put into actual operation, a narrow gauge line."

Author's note: This statement is correct. The first run on the D. & R. G. was made August 14, 1871. The first run made on the (n. g.) Colorado Central was made September 1, 1872.

Additional information regarding this subject is found in a letter written by Captain Berthoud to the Railway Age and published in that periodical of April 15, 1880. Captain Berthoud's letter is as follows:

"Golden, Colo.
April 8th, 1880.

"Editor Railway Age:
"In your paper of March 25, 1880, I notice a communication from Mr. A. W. Wright who justly claims that the credit of the success of the D. & R. G. R. R. is due to Mr. Howard Schuyler and that he advanced the adoption of the three-foot gauge.
"The Colorado Central R. R., Western Division, was the first narrow gauge railway built, after the example and success of some Pennsylvania railroads that years ago adopted gauges less than four feet, eight and one-half inches.

1. Vickers, "History of Colorado".
2. Courtesy Owen Davies.

"In April 1870[1], the location of the Colorado Central R. R. (narrow gauge) was begun and two and one-fourth miles were graded and 14 miles located that year. In May and June, 1870, three feet was established as its normal gauge and its construction was resumed upon that basis. The D. & R. G. R. R. was organized and chartered after the Colorado Central was begun and its width established as a narrow gauge railroad of three feet.
"Early in 1871, General T. E. Sickels, Chief Engineer of the Union Pacific R. R., and General G. M. Dodge were consulted and the three-foot gauge received their unqualified commendation as practicable and proper.
E. L. Berthoud.

Chief Engineer,
Colorado Central R. R."

Jerome C. Smiley, in his *"History of Denver,"* states:

"It has been made to appear in bygone times that the D. & R. G. was the pioneer in preparing for the introduction of the three-foot gauge system of roads here in the west; but that was an error."

On the other hand, the Colorado Central is itself the authority for the statement found in their 1873 Annual Report that:

"The introduction for the narrow gauge system into Colorado by The Denver & Rio Grande Ry. Co. solved the difficulty of cost of construction of a road to these mining districts by bringing it within reasonable limits. . . ."

In view of this statement, an explanation will have to be sought in the surmise that this report referred to the fact that General Palmer's narrow gauge Rio Grande, completed to Pueblo (June 1872) before the Colorado Central had even made a serious start on its own Clear Creek line, afforded the Central a working model for their own experiment in narrow gauge railroading. When all the evidence is considered, it is believed, therefore, that credit for the establishment of narrow gauge railroad construction in the Colorado mountain territory belongs to the Colorado Central.

Up to this period, we have discussed the construction of Colorado's first five railroads: the Denver Pacific, Kansas Pacific, Colorado Central, Boulder Valley, and the Denver & Rio Grande. Of these five, note that all the lines constructed on the plains east of the mountains were standard gauge, while those lines constructed in the mountainous district (the Clear Creek division of the Colorado Central and the Denver & Rio Grande) were of narrow gauge construction. This fact bears out Captain Berthoud's idea that the narrow gauge road was the more adaptable track to build in the mountains. This theory held for a great many years.

The mountain mining towns did not permit the Colorado railroads which were completed in 1870 to rest upon their laurels very long. Hardly were the initial lines built before these communities were declaring impatiently, through their newspapers such as the Daily Central City Register and the Colorado Miner, that they were tired of waiting for the Colorado Central,

1. The first surveys for a railroad line up the canon were made in 1869 by Berthoud.

54

and would look elsewhere for a railroad if the Colorado Central did not immediately and forthwith build to their towns.

The agitation for a railroad came to a head in a convention which was called by a Georgetown railroad meeting. It convened at Golden in April, 1871. Delegates were invited from the five counties concerned: Arapahoe, Jefferson, Gilpin, Clear Creek and Summit. Nothing of tremendous significance was accomplished but neither, it was reported, was there the customary bitterness in evidence. Loveland introduced a resolution that since circumstances demanded a railroad to Central City and Georgetown, the Colorado Central would do all it could to secure and hasten the completion of a road to the mining regions. After appointing an executive committee of four members, one from each of the four counties (Summit county failed to send any delegates), the meeting adjourned. The committee met in Denver the next day and appointed John Evans their spokesman in the negotiations for the building of the line.

It is easy to say who had dominated the whole affair, and his purpose is likewise far from opaque. John Evans had suggested the calling of the Golden railroad convention when, in addressing a meeting concerning railroads, in Georgetown, he had assured his listeners that if the Colorado Central failed to build to their town "within the year" he and his friends would stand willing to see it done. At the convention, he had stressed the necessity for an independent line to the mountains. According to the Colorado Transcript of May 3, 1871, Evans succeeded in sidetracking Engineer Greenwood when he raised the embarrassing question as to routes, for he (Evans) realized that the Colorado Central had prior rights to the only really practicable route to Central City and Georgetown, and did not wish to have that issue placed before the convention. Evans closed the meeting with "three cheers for the railroad in the mountains in one year", thereby again stressing the road's immediate construction, and winning for himself the appointment as sole agent for securing the objective of a railroad to the mountains.

Behind all this, Evans' purpose seems to stand out rather clearly. Undoubtedly, he knew about internal difficulties between the Colorado Central and the Union Pacific and was making the most of his opportunities. He must have realized that the Colorado Central was in no position to build a railroad to the mountains "within the year", and so he had maneuvered them into a bad spot: the mountains were so impatient for a railroad that if the Colorado Central did not give it to them "within the year" they would be likely to abandon the Central and turn to the Evans group for their railroad. Thus, while the Colorado Central could not afford *to build* the line, neither at the same time could it afford *not* to build. It was a bad situation for the Loveland road.

As a matter of fact, the Denver-Kansas Pacific interests were in the mountains sounding out the mining towns on the likelihood of securing aid for their own line even before the Golden convention. Indeed, one of the early railroad projects pushed by Denver was the promotion of the previously mentioned Denver & Georgetown, to be built to Central City and Georgetown. Under such active competition, the surface harmony of the Golden meeting could not be expected to last very long. The Colorado Central would be forced to fight back.

It did fight back. In July, 1871, it proposed that Gilpin county should vote on an issue of $300,000 in county bonds for the Colorado Central. These bonds carried a clause stipulating that to insure delivery, the road must be completed through to Black Hawk by May 1, 1872, to Central City by June 1, and to Nevada by November 1. Evidently, the road also intended building on to Caribou, for an advertising booklet put out by the Union Pacific at that time went on to state, in glowing terms, how the line would soon be completed through to Caribou. The Kansas Pacific then retaliated with a proposal, no doubt intended to embarrass the Colorado Central proposition, in which it asked that $150,000 in bonds be given to the railroad which reached Central City first. The election took place on August 31st, and the Colorado Central proposition was victorious.

The fat was in the fire. The Kansas Pacific had succeeded in forcing the Colorado Central's hand. How things stood in the Colorado Central camp is rather clearly revealed by a letter from Teller to Oliver Ames dated November 22, 1871. Ames had apparently reproved Teller for making excessive promises in the bond campaign at Central City, just completed, and warning him that the Union Pacific would not be likely to push the Colorado Central's tracks beyond the Forks of Clear Creek, 13 miles west of Golden. To this, Teller replied somewhat warmly. The Colorado Central, he said, had been forced to promise to build to Central City and Nevada "because other parties were offering to build to Nevada and were thus likely to defeat our bonds". Furthermore, he pointed out, if the road were only built to Forks Creek, it would not do "one-fourth of the business" it would do if extended all the way to Central City and Nevada. And finally, he pleaded:

"I trust your people will not entertain the idea of having the work stop at Forks Creek. . . . because I fear if we do not obtain the $300,000 of Gilpin County bonds, an effort will be made to build a rival road here and get bonds from the county. . . ."

Ames' question, answered in this same letter, as to whether the bonds could be gotten at a later election if the Colorado Central was not built as stipulated in the present agreement, is also indicative of the Union

Chas. Weitfle photo,
from Francis Rizzari Collection.
Colorado Central train, headed by an 0-6-0 locomotive, in
Clear Creek Canon.

Alex Martin photo,
from Francis Rizzari Collection.
Colorado Central mixed train at Beaver Brook station, in Clear
Creek Canon.

Alex Martin photo,
from Charles Ryland Collection.
Colorado Central engine 4 on the original wooden trestle at
Forks Creek.

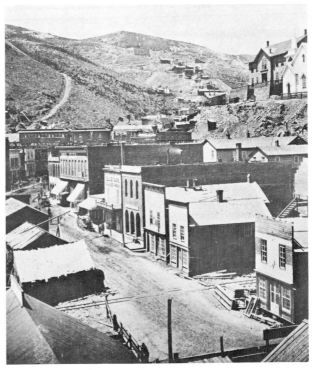

Chas. Weitfle photo,
from Denver Public Library Western Collection.
Colorado Central train on the trestle which crossed Selak and
Gregory Streets in Black Hawk.

Pacific's attitude toward the Central. It had agreed in the fall of 1871 "to go on with the road", but evidently was far from anxious to do so. Again the interests of the two roads were divergent: the Union Pacific, not too strong financially, wanted to build only as little as absolute necessity required; and the Colorado Central, hard pressed by the rival Denver-Kansas Pacific combination, and interested in getting as much railroad as the Union Pacific would build for them, wished the road extended into the heart of the Gilpin county mining region.

In the final analysis, the decision rested with the Union Pacific, which, by its control of the purse strings, could dictate both the speed and extent of construction. Finally, as we have read in Captain Berthoud's letter, grading got under way in April of 1870. But the Union Pacific was very sparing with assistance with the result that construction proceeded rather slowly. However, the building of this railroad up the canon was, without a doubt, a very difficult piece of railroad construction. In the face of such engineering difficulties, together with a minimum of Union Pacific assistance, only 8 miles out of the 24 miles between Golden and Central City was graded by the end of March, 1872. Since the agreement was that the road was to be completed to Black Hawk by May 1, 1872, the Gilpin bonds were already hopelessly lost. For this delay, the Union Pacific had blamed "the severity of the winter". But Central City, mightily irked, had another explanation for the delay, and when the Union Pacific asked for a new bond issue (the old one having been definitely lost) they thought they were correct in their suspicions.

Already in the preceeding March there had been rumors that the Union Pacific would terminate the road at Forks Creek, demand the bonds it had been voted for building all the way to Central City and Nevada, and if they were not forthcoming, leave the road permanently at that point. This definitely looked like that sort of a game to some in Central City; unless the new bonds were voted, the road would be abandoned entirely, and Central City's hopes of getting a railroad would be shattered for years to come. Frank Hall, editor of The Daily Central City Register, wrote a stinging letter to Teller, mentioning the report as having come from one to whom Teller was reported to have said that:

". . . . the track would never be laid to Forks Creek until the bonds were voted; that you intended if they were defeated to make a toll road of the grade, and make the rates high enough to make them pay the full amount of interest expected from the bonds. . . . It struck me that if true, the declaration was entirely unwarrantable, unfair, and unjust to the people whose good faith you have no reason to doubt.

"I . . . . will continue to maintain that the construction of the road to Forks Creek with all possible dispatch would insure not only the acceptance of your proposition but a certain relief from our embarrassment."

Probably these suspicions were shared by many others, but Central City really had little choice in the matter.

It was the Colorado Central or nothing. Times had been hard, and Sickles had blandly promised Central City all sorts of relief from the heavy tolls of the freighters. As an example of these promises, Frank Hall claimed that Sickles told him personally . . . "that a maximum charge of $2.00 per ton on freight from the valley to Black Hawk would be ample, affording the road satisfactory profits. . . ." And, Hall added, "on this basis Central City began wondrous dreams of future glories, but, as Mark Twain said: 'They danced blithely out to enjoy a rainbow, and got struck by lightning'". The whole matter was brought to a head in June, 1872, when Sickles appeared in Central City and affably secured the consent of the County Commissioners to call another election on a new bond issue of $250,000, with the provision that the Colorado Central should be completed to Forks Creek by September 1, 1872; Black Hawk by January 1, 1873; and to Central City within one year, or January 1, 1874. The new bond issue was approved.

In the meantime, some of the differences between the Colorado Central and the Union Pacific had been ironed out. This factor, together with an increased activity on the part of the Denver Pacific-Kansas Pacific interests and their Denver Central & Georgetown project, caused the Union Pacific to speed up their construction program in the canon. By the time stipulated in the new bond agreement, September 1, 1872, the road had been completed through to Forks Creek, 13.11 miles west of Golden.

On that day, September 1, 1872, an excursion was run over the line which the Colorado Transcript termed "A Stupendous Railroad Enterprise", and marked an "Era in Colorado History". The paper reported that there "was no accident to mar the trip", but in commenting on the Sunday excusion, the paper stated:

"The engine 'Phil Sheridan' walked off on his ear twice, but the first time the male passengers and the crew succeeded in lifting 'Phil' back on the tracks."

And in the next breath, the paper boasted of the safety of the road. They did not mention just what difficulties were encountered in getting "Phil" back on the tracks the second time he went off.

Relative to the first freight shipment to move down the canon we read in the Rocky Mountain News of September 25, 1872:

"The first load of freight came down Clear Creek Canon Saturday September the 21st. It was a load of machinery shipped by Hendrie Brothers from their Eureka foundry."[1]

From Forks Creek the road made a steady rate of progress. Some construction and grading work had already been done in June and July of 1871. The construction gangs made good time and reached Black Hawk two weeks ahead of the time stipulated in the

1. This was the Eureka Foundry & Machine Shop located in Central City.

bond agreement. The Rocky Mountain News of November 26, 1872, carries a very informative article relative to the railroad's progress beyond Forks Creek, some of its first rolling stock, details of construction, scenery, etc. We quote the article in full.

"DENVER TO CENTRAL
"The Narrow Gauge Road—Its Equipment—A Success
"The Scenery—A Grand Ride

"Central City, November 22. We rode today for the first time over the narrow gauge division of the Colorado Central Railroad. The run from Golden to 'End-of-Track' was made in about two hours and one-half, being at the rate of eight miles per hour. The train consisted, of one locomotive and tender, baggage car, and passenger coach. The latter is a very handsome and elegant car, from the Omaha car shops of the Union Pacific Co. It is the same size and very much like the coaches of the Rio Grande. Today it was crowded full of passengers. The baggage car is almost new, but considerably smaller and not so well-finished as those of the Rio Grande road. The engine is not quite adequate to its work; being one of the machines built for, and used in grading the approaches to the Omaha bridge over the Missouri. It is a rude, roughly made engine, and its power was taxed to the utmost on the steeper grades. Three of these engines are in use, but much of their time is necessarily employed in bringing forward construction material. Better engines are expected before long. Probably they have not been procured sooner because the company wanted first to experiment and determine what power it would be necessary to get. Certainly, they must be satisfied by this time that motive power greatly in excess of the common proportion will be necessary to operate the road successfully. Either trains will have to be short and light; the locomotive very strong and heavy, or else used in twos and threes. The grade is very steep—in some places exceeding two hundred feet to the mile for short distances. The difficulty of surmounting it is greatly augmented by the almost constant curvature of the track. Very little is straight. Reverse curves succeed one another as continuous as the track of a snake.

"Generally speaking, the road bed is first class. In a few places very high water may encroach upon it, but there cannot be much damage from that source. Almost continuously it is supported on the side toward the stream by a retaining wall of stone laid up without mortar, and varying from five to thirty feet in height. In the beginning, some of these were built too near perpendicular. Most such have been rebuilt, and all are now very substantial. It is the best tied railroad we ever saw. The surface is fully half covered with them, and the rails are very securely fastened. The track is yet rough, every energy having been bent to its extension. Very little has been done at aligning or leveling the track up since the tracklayers left it.

"Passengers were carried today to a point within two miles of the city limits of Black Hawk. Tomorrow, the transfer will be at the mouth of Smith Hill Gulch. Graders are scattered all along from that point to Black Hawk. Probably they number 200—blasting rocks, digging and wheeling dirt. The railway destroys the wagon road, following in it most of the way. A bridge to be built just below Black Hawk will probably delay the track somewhat, but it will be in the town before the date stipulated in the contract for County Bonds, January 1, 1873.

"Altogether, this section of the road is a great accomplishment; great in the fact itself, but greater as the first and successful experiment in building over ground that, until this trial, would have been considered totally impracticable as a railway route, for the double reason of its steepness and tortuous pathway. Properly finished and with rolling stock adapted to its requirements, there is no reason why it may not be operated with entire success, though a competing line over more favorable ground would, of course, have an advantage over it. Of course,

with age, it will have many improvements. The heavy grades will be cut down and the curves lengthened.

"The scenery from Golden to Central is without comparison in railway travel. For stupendous heights and wild grandeur, the railroad world cannot produce its like. In the spring and summer seasons, when Vasquez River (later known as Clear Creek) will be at the flood, and its tributaries are pouring in cascades down the mountain sides, it will alone be worth a journey across the continent to see."

The Rocky Mountain News tells us that the tracks were laid to the old "Quartz Mill Depot" in lower Black Hawk, on Sunday, December 17, 1872.

The following newspaper clipping was found in the effects of the late Col. D. C. Dodge, pioneer Colorado railroad builder. We quote in part:

"The Central had managed to reach Black Hawk on time and the local citizenry felt that their territory's prayer for a railroad was at last answered. However, there was one serious draw-back; there was no terminal depot nor was there any room for one in the narrow gulch on the water grade along which the road had poked its winding way up the canon of Clear Creek. Bill Loveland, the builder of the Colorado Central, was in despair until one day he discovered that the very thing that blocked the way was a big hulk of a stamp mill in the lower end of Black Hawk, which had never been occupied. It was an over-large stone building for such a small community, and was, therefore, a worthless appendage to the town. It had been built by General Fitz John Porter, of Civil War fame, for a defunct concern known as The New York Mining & Milling Company, and had cost the trifling sum of $125,000.

"The company had a group of mine prospects up in the hills, but the outfit went broke before the machinery had been placed in the big mill building, and there it stood, as a monument to somebody's mistake in accepting too much for granted. The big barn, therefore, became just the very institution for the Colorado Central terminus and Bill Loveland commandeered it pronto. They had to run the railroad right through the blamed thing, as there was no room to get around it.

"To accomplish this, they broke out a great hole in each end of the building, and built large doors. The track was then laid right through the middle from stem to gudgeon and thus transformed the nuisance into a practical utility which covered an entire passenger train, and afforded a grand central station of metropolitan dignity and proportions. Black Hawk's great stone depot remained on the job and served as the Central's local terminus until the track was built up over the hill to Central City, in 1878, at which time a new depot was erected in the upper end of the town."

Because of the extreme mountainous conditions encountered between Forks Creek and Black Hawk, the right of way followed along the banks of the north fork of Clear Creek very closely. Since the original construction of the railroad through this section of the canon, both the tracks and the bed of Clear Creek have been shifted numerous times, due to mining activities along the stream. However, in order to give the reader some idea of the curves and grades encountered here, a profile chart as drawn from 1935 engineering figures, and which is typical of this stretch of track since its original construction, shows the following figures.

Within the 7.10 miles of right of way, the track negotiated twenty-five curves of 20 degrees or over. Some of the sharper ones included a 30, a 34, and a 36 degree curve; the 36 degree curve being located just below milepost 32 on a 3.96% grade. Among some of the steeper grades encountered, there were twenty-six sections of track of a 3% grade or over, with a high of 3.96% located on a 36 degree curve as previously explained. Relative to the numerous curves encountered in this piece of track, the Rocky Mountain News of October 6, 1880, stated:

"Engineers have been out over the Central and report that many of the kinks in the line are to be taken out. It seems to have been the ambition of the original locaters to make this railroad the crookedest in the world."

Construction up the heavy incline from Black Hawk to Central City was interrupted at that time by considerable engineering difficulties, and before a satisfactory solution could be found, the panic of 1873 hit and brought a stop to any further work on this line for the time being. For the next few years, Black Hawk remained the terminus of this north fork branch, and it was not until 1878 that the line was completed, utilizing the switchback method to reach Central City.

Because the road was not completed through to Central City as stipulated, the historian, Hall, states that $50,000 of the $250,000 bonds voted were withheld. But according to the Colorado Central's Annual Report of 1873, the Colorado Central received only $100,000 of the Gilpin bonds. In a letter written by Teller to J. W. Gannett, he mentions that the Central derived only $84,000 from the Gilpin bonds, a figure which would seem to indicate that only $100,000 of the bonds had been received.

Meanwhile, during 1872, the quarrel between the Colorado Central and the Denver, Georgetown & Utah as to who was going to build a railroad to Georgetown took place. Although Georgetown had voted a bond issue to the latter road, that road, for reasons explained elsewhere, failed to carry through with their plans. The Colorado Central then stepped in and offered to complete their road to Georgetown within fifteen months, if provided with bond aid. Accordingly, Georgetown and Clear Creek county held an election in the latter part of November, 1872, and voted the Central a $200,000 bond issue. But alas! The gentlemen of Clear Creek county little realized that it would be a number of years before they would ever see an engine and cars in Georgetown.

Now that the Colorado Central interests had the Clear Creek territory pretty well sewed up—so to speak— they were inclined to be a bit independent, and from all appearances, were not overexerting themselves in getting their line extended to Georgetown. Meanwhile, construction had proceeded up the South Fork of Clear Creek very slowly. Finally, on March 1, 1873, the end-of-track reached Floyd Hill, 3.3 miles beyond Forks Creek. By this time, the Panic of 1873 appeared on the scene, and the Colorado Central bogged down financially, cutting short any possibilities that the road

R. B. Jackson.

Ruins of mill which was used as original Black Hawk depot. Photographed in 1937.

W. A. Gibson.

The second Black Hawk depot, photographed in 1939.

S. L. Logue Collection.

Buffalo depot in 1898.

O. C. Perry.

London Junction (Alma) depot in 1937.

would be completed to Georgetown, for the time being. Railroad construction had come to a halt in Colorado. For a number of years, Floyd Hill and Black Hawk remained the termini of these two branches of the Clear Creek line. Meanwhile, vague rumors that the road would be completed kept the silver camp hopeful, but in the interim, Georgetown simply had to make the best of the situation. However, the community was not left entirely unprovided for. In the spring of 1873, the railroad had instituted a through service to Georgetown, which utilized wagons between the end-of-track at Floyd Hill and the town. This arrangement was far from satisfactory, but still, it was better than nothing. In fact, some old Colorado Central reports furnish us with the following figures: the Floyd Hill station at the end-of-line on the Georgetown branch of the Colorado Central, in April of 1873, handled 1,047,470 pounds of freight. Another report found in the same collection, reported a business of 16,747,870 pounds of freight for the Floyd Hill station for the year 1875, and in 1876, the Central moved 33,000 tons of freight into Georgetown and Central City.

As far as can be determined, there was but one effort after the panic broke to extend the road to the silver capital. In October of 1874, a party of Union Pacific officials paid a brief visit to Georgetown to talk over the railroad situation. The Union Pacific suggested that Clear Creek county finance that part of the line between Georgetown and Idaho Springs, but Georgetown felt that under the circumstances, this was more than the county could handle, but did offer "to tender some aid to the Union Pacific company", and expressed hope that the abandonment of the Julesburg project might "serve to materially modify their demands on the county". Sometime after this interview between the two parties was over, Oliver Ames directed a letter to Teller, under date of February 12, 1875, in which he stated:

"Our interview with them last fall showed they had but very little public spirit and love of their town. If we build the road, they will seek the first opportunity to pass some Granger law to force us to run it without profit. I want to see them put their money in the road and then they will be interested to make it pay."

Nothing resulted from the negotiations, for the offers of the two parties were too far apart to make any agreement possible. Thus, the situation remained unchanged until the completion of the Kansas Pacific-Union Pacific negotiations of 1875, one of the results of which was the transfer of control of the Colorado Central road to the Kansas Pacific. It was then anticipated that this change would lead to the completion of the Central to Georgetown, but since this Kansas Pacific control of the Clear Creek line was of short duration, the silver camp did not secure the much coveted railroad. Here matters rested, until the Central completed their new arrangements with the Union Pacific following Loveland's famous coup of May, 1876.

The panic of 1873 entailed very grave circumstances in and around Denver. It brought about a serious shrinkage of local business and much unemployment among railroad construction workers. So far as the struggle between the Union Pacific and the Kansas Pacific and their respective allies was concerned, the panic left the Union Pacific rather in the lead, with the Kansas Pacific in a seriously crippled condition and more or less helpless and at the mercy of its great rival, the Union Pacific. There was no more railroad construction of any great amount around Denver for several years.

The Colorado Central managed to establish itself fairly well in the canons of Clear Creek, and the returns on this Western Division were gratifying. A statement of freight shipped to and from Black Hawk in April, 1873, showed more than 700 tons handled at that point alone during this period. And the Annual Report of the Colorado Central for the year 1873 stated that the Western Division grossed $70,043.49 in the three-month period ending July 31st of that year. Since expenses totaled only $33,450.16, the net return on this line for its three-month period was $36,593.33, certainly a very fair showing.

There can be little doubt of the value of the extension of the railroad to the economic development of the territory. The line served a number of important functions. The inbound freight trains carried a multitude of various supplies for both the population and the mines, while the outbound trains were loaded with ore. The opening of the road was also a boon to both the mountains and the Boulder Valley area, as it afforded that area a great market for its agricultural products. It was estimated that approximately 75 tons of merchandise, hay, and grain, were carried up the canon daily. The transportation of coal into the mining districts to be used as fuel, both in the smelters and for domestic purposes, replacing the rapidly diminishing wood supply, was another important feature. And last, but not least, was the improved transportation facilities the road afforded the travelling public.

Not much information has been found regarding the Colorado Central's narrow gauge rolling stock. By 1880, the road owned nine passenger cars, and two combination mail, express and baggage cars. For the transportation of freight, the road had 30 box cars, 26 flat cars, and 62 gondolas for hauling coal and ore.[1] By 1885, this rolling stock had increased to 19 passenger cars, 5 combination mail, express and baggage cars, 100 box cars, 8 stock cars, 41 flat cars, 57 gondolas, 20 dump cars, and 2 cabooses. From this date until the time the Clear Creek line was absorbed by the Colorado & Southern in 1899, no particular change was noted in the number of passenger and freight cars.

The line had been built at a rather reasonable figure for a mountain road; however, Oliver Ames, of the

1. Poor's Manual of Railroads, 1880.

60

Union Pacific, complained of the costs, and wrote Teller inquiring as to "what could be the cause of such a large excess of expenditures over and above the estimates". The books of the Colorado Central, in 1874, placed the cost of the Western Division (lines West of Golden) at $886,221.39, which, making due allowance for the short branch up the south fork of Clear Creek to Floyd Hill, which was included in that figure, amounted to an average cost of about $36,900 per mile.

The following figures were taken from a letter written by Teller to J. W. Gannett, and represent the cost of the entire Colorado Central system as it stood at this point.[1]

Denver to Golden, about 17 miles............$ 396,025.24
Eastern Division:
  Golden to Longmont, about 40 miles...... 774,000.00
  Grading, 110 of 167 miles between
    Longmont and Julesburg.................. 110,000.00

1. Mock, "Railroad Development in the Colorado Region".

Western Division:
  Golden to Black Hawk, about 20 miles,
    and branch from Forks Creek to
    Floyd Hill, about 4 miles............... 886,221.39
                                            _____
    Total about 86 miles $2,166,246.63

Bond Aid from the Counties reduced the
  cost to the Company as follows:
Jefferson County Bonds—
  $100,000.00—Yielded .... $ 65,000.00
Boulder County Bonds—
  $200,000.00—Yielded 200,000.00
Gilpin County Bonds—
  $100,000.00—Yielded 84,000.00
                                        _____
    Total ....$ 349,000.00

Chas. Weitfle photo,
from Denver Public Library Western Collection.

A Colorado Central passenger train near Mountain City.

Chas. Weitfle photo,
from Francis Rizzari Collection.

Colorado Central 6 headed downgrade beside Clear Creek, a short distance below Idaho Springs.

CHAPTER VIII

THE FIGHT FOR COLORADO CENTRAL CONTROL

Shortly after the completion of the Denver Pacific and Kansas Pacific into Denver, and while the Colorado Central was busy extending their narrow gauge line up Clear Creek Canon, a rate war of considerable proportions broke out between the Union Pacific and Kansas Pacific roads. In their effort to settle the dispute, the Union Pacific, in the fall of 1871, instituted a move to purchase the Denver Pacific. This forced the hand of the Kansas Pacific, who seized control of the Denver road, thus blocking the Union Pacific's move. Failing in this, the Union Pacific began, in earnest, to make plans for the extension of the Colorado Central's line to Julesburg. They figured that if Colorado traffic could not be obtained in one way, they would try another.

Thus, both roads continued to discriminate against each other. The Kansas Pacific tried every expedient to force the Union Pacific to prorate, and the Union Pacific retaliated by pushing work on the Colorado Central. The whole prorate question was dragged through one court after another. The rate war gradually weakened the Kansas Pacific, and the road finally went into receivership in 1874. They offered to sell out to the Union Pacific, who refused, and the dog fight was on once more. Finally, in April 1875, representatives of the two roads met in Philadelphia to discuss "a general consolidation of interests". A settlement was reached and one of the principal agreements was as follows: the Kansas Pacific and the Colorado Central were to be consolidated into one new corporation known as the Kansas Pacific Railway Company. The new company was to be capitalized for $20,000,000, with one-half of the new corporation's stock to be held in control by the Union Pacific. The date of the agreement was May 6, 1875. Part of the agreement read as follows:

". . . . if the arrangements for consolidation of the Kansas Pacific Railway Co. and the Colorado Central Ry. Co. now pending be carried out, the Union Pacific R. R. Company will abandon to the consolidated company all the local traffic in Colorado, and will not interfere therewith, and that the consolidated company will abandon to the Union Pacific Company all claims to pro-rate on traffic west of Cheyenne."

The Kansas Pacific would then finish the long-uncompleted Mountain Division of the Colorado Central. The Julesburg extension and the Littleton cutoff threats to Denver would also be abandoned. And best of all, the Kansas Pacific entered into an agreement with Denver whereby it agreed to lay the THIRD NARROW GAUGE RAIL from Denver to Golden, and to remove that road's shops from Golden to Denver. In return, Denver would exempt all Kansas Pacific lands from taxation.

The agreement was a bombshell in Colorado railroad circles! Upon receipt of the news, Denver was jubilant. The people of Golden, who regarded it as a sellout, were very much downcast.

The Colorado Central stockholders approved the agreement by a vote of 9,300 to 4,343. Opposing the move were the counties (Boulder, Gilpin and Jefferson) which held Colorado Central stock as a result of bonds voted in aid of the road, and other local stockholders. The local parties were united in their opposition to the move, and the defeat at that one point did not end the matter. Stockholder's meetings were held in August and September, to consider the further matter of actual consolidation, but no decision was reached, and Carr took the stump in the counties concerned to convince them they should vote their county stocks for consolidation.

One of his strongest arguments was the disclosure of a floating debt of over a million dollars in the Colorado Central. This surprise he bolstered with figures to show that the road was losing money in its operations. A convenient creditor's dun, by two concerns, threatening foreclosure unless consolidation went through, was also effective.

The local parties were fighting a losing fight. By December, the Colorado Transcript, archenemy of consolidation, admitted defeat and counselled united action to secure the best possible terms. Henry M. Teller was retained as president of the road, while Carr made himself General Manager. Other important posts were also filled with Kansas Pacific men. Carr's plans were to move the general offices to Kansas City, and completely revamp operations of the road. The two roads had been consolidated in everything except name.

After revealing the dire financial plight of the Colorado Central, Carr sprang the trap; an offer of twenty cents on the dollar to the counties for their holdings of Colorado Central stock. This meant the loss of four-fifths of the nominal value of their stock if accepted. Boulder and Jefferson counties were disposed to accept the offer, but Gilpin taxpayers, in a meeting assembled by the call of the county commissioners, instructed their representatives to vote against the consolidation.

A further session of the adjourned meetings of the Central's stockholders was held on December the 8th. There Teller's resolution that Carr's offer of twenty cents on the dollar for the railroad stock held by the counties was fair and liberal and ought to be accepted, received approval from all except Gilpin's 1000 votes. The Gilpin delegates had been instructed to hold out for twenty-five cents on the dollar. Next, Teller proposed a resolution ratifying the contract of consolidation, and this too passed muster, but only by a vote of 9,350 to 4,270. Apparently, the counties were willing to accept the Kansas Pacific offer without feeling bound thereby to vote for consolidation. The lease went into effect at once; the Kansas Pacific took possession of the Colorado Central, and thought it had reached the end of most of its troubles.

Then followed a muddled period of uncertainty. Boulder county rejected the action of its representatives in accepting the Kansas Pacific offer. Next, the Kansas Pacific withdrew its offer, to the intense disgust of those who had wished to sell. And finally, although consolidation had not yet been definitely approved, the articles of consolidation were discovered to have already been filed in the office of the Secretary of State. Apparently, the game was to get the consolidation through by subterfuge without having to pay the counties for their holdings of Colorado Central stocks.

But at the annual meeting held in Golden on May 18th and 19th, 1876, a surprise was in store for the Kansas Pacific. Whether by design or not, President Teller was absent, and Vice President Loveland, who had been merely biding his time, took the chair. He selected the proper men for the committee on inspection of the elections, and they, on a technicality, promptly threw out E. W. Rollins' proxy to vote 7,200 shares of stock. Since Rollins was voting the Union Pacific's controlling interest in the road, this meant the Colorado group had secured control.

The meeting then utterly repudiated the action of the company's directors in the previous December, and elected a board opposed to the consolidation of the roads. The only Union Pacific representative chosen on this new board was Oliver Ames. The new board then elected Loveland president of the company in place of Teller, and then, to undo the consolidation proceedings, the following resolution was proposed:

"That all and every vote resolution, contract or agreement heretofore made. . . . in relation to and in favor of consolidation. . . . with the Kansas Pacific Railway Co. and all or every contract or agreement . . . . looking to a consolidation of said two companies is hereby rescinded, revoked, and declared null and void."

It was passed by a vote of 4,253 to 2,130, the rump voting for it unanimously. To complete the destruction

of the consolidation agreement, it was also agreed that Loveland should be empowered to:

"take immediate possession and supervision. . . . and to assume the general management of the business of the Company until otherwise ordered by the board."

and that:

"The office of the Company in Golden. . . . is hereby declared to be the permanent General Headquarters."

This audacious coup was then followed by the forcible seizure of the railroad by the Loveland forces on May 21, 1876. The consolidation scheme had aroused the indignation of the people of Boulder, Jefferson, and Gilpin counties to a high pitch, and they were ready, if necessary, to support Loveland by force of arms. Loveland and Colonel Fisher, the General Manager of the Kansas Pacific and the Colorado Central, issued broadsides; telegraph wires were cut; some track was torn up; new men hired; and a show of force used to secure possession of the railroad's property at Denver and at Golden. The Denver Times reported that the Central's men "slept in the shops on their guns".

The Loveland group was in the saddle, but it was not seated very firmly. There were numerous rumors that the whole coup had not been displeasing to the Union Pacific, which was unwilling to see control of the Colorado Central pass into the hands of the Kansas Pacific. It is impossible to go behind all the scheming and say just how far such rumors were accurate, but it is certain that the Union Pacific was greatly chagrined by the turn of events.

Immediately after Loveland's forces took possession of the road, the Union Pacific went into court at Boulder and entered a suit against the Colorado Central for $1,500,000 for materials, rolling stock, etc., alleged to be due it from the Central and enjoined the Loveland management from doing a great variety of things. The Union Pacific also asked for, and received, an injunction against the issue of any further stocks or bonds by the Central, or the lease of the road to any parties. A civil suit for the repayment of the $800,000 floating debt was also instituted in the district courts of the territory. Attorney Poppleton was sent out by the Union Pacific to "effect some amicable settlement . . . which would restore possession to the true owners, and failing in that to apply for a receiver".

The settlement proposed, apparently, was an effort to buy the County stock at thirty cents on the dollar, payable in Union Pacific funds at par. The offer was refused, and Poppleton moved for the appointment of a Receiver for the Colorado Central. After protracted hearings, the request was approved, and in August Judge A. W. Stone, of the Second Judicial District, was scheduled to appoint David H. Moffat as Receiver for the road. This precipitated a series of events that made for a great time all 'round.

The mountain regions were indignant. "Judicial

venality" was scored and more than hints of bribery were broadcast. Moffat, interested and influential in the Kansas Pacific (which would stand to profit by the move), was denounced as a "hand picked" party to the whole proceedings. Talk of refusing to turn the property over to the Court's appointee was even heard.

The unfaltering Loveland was not dismayed by these proceedings, and held a firm grip on his railroad. A group of men, apparently unknown to Loveland or anyone else at the time, but who were sympathetic with the Colorado Central, decided to take matters into their own hands. As the term of court at Boulder would end August 15th, this group concluded that the receivership proceedings could be interrupted by capturing Judge Stone and holding him until after the limit of the term. The identity of these men remained a secret for many years and only recently was it disclosed[1] that this group consisted of fourteen men under the leadership of Matt Johnson and C. W. Lake of Golden and surrounding territory.

The affair had all the melodramatic aspects of the best western tales. Inasmuch as Judge Stone had heard the petition for the receivership, it became his solemn duty to travel to Boulder to complete the formalities and qualify Receiver Moffat. So—while the unsuspecting Judge was merrily on his way from Denver to Boulder—his train was stopped by a pile of ties on the track near Kenneer's Lake, about half way between Denver and Boulder. Two masked men then boarded the train, inquiring for the Judge, and when asked for their authority for causing such an unusual disturbance, answered with a flourish of their "shootin' irons" explaining "this is our authority". The Judge was then forcibly taken from the train. Before leaving, they cut the telegraph wires and then, taking the Judge with them, the entire group of armed and masked men galloped off into the hills. The abductors had expected to capture Receiver Moffat on the train also, but he had taken the other road to Boulder, and so escaped.

When this remarkable news reached Denver, it created a tremendous sensation. Loveland telegraphed Governor Routt, explaining what had happened, and asked authority to organize a posse to pursue and capture the bold kidnappers of the good Judge. Governor Routt referred him to the Sheriff of Boulder County, urged immediate action by that peace officer, and solicited Loveland's cooperation. But matters were so managed at the Boulder end of the line that Judge Stone's hosts were given plenty of time to get well up into the foothills. News of this delay reached Denver late in the afternoon and added fresh fuel to the public excitement. Rumors that the Sheriff of Arapahoe County was preparing to lead a force of men in pursuit of the brigands caused all sorts of men with a large array of "shootin' irons and artillery" to congregate at the rail-

1. Colorado Magazine, January, 1940.

road depot to board the special train that had been made up to take them to the hunting grounds. However, they did not get to go.

In the evening of that day, the Governor peremptorily extended the term of court and assigned Judge A. W. Brazee to go to Boulder to open Court and remain there until disposition was made of the judicial business on hand. The Governor's Guard was mobilized under Arapahoe County Sheriff Dan J. Cook, who was also a Brigadier General of the Militia, and the military-judicial expedition, the Governor accompanying it, reached Boulder about 10 o'clock that night, where Court was immediately opened.

In the meantime, Judge Stone's captors had kept him moving. He had been put into a carriage, driven up in the foothills to a ranch house, where a supper was obtained. After night, the party proceeded on horseback to a point near Golden, the brigand escort of 14 men wearing their masks all the while. There, the Judge was put into another carriage, and with two of his masked captors, was driven to Denver, where, with just the proper touch of mystery, he was dumped out in front of the Alvord House late at night—or early in the morning—none the worse for his adventure; his brigand friends having treated him with great courtesy and consideration while he had been in their custody.

Accompanied by a military escort, Judge Stone then went to Boulder, approved Receiver Moffat's bond, and ordered the Colorado Central surrendered to him. Sarcastically, the Colorado Transcript agreed the guard was not sent along to overawe the people, but to . . . "see that the room was properly lighted and that the spittoons were ready for judicial expectoration". The Receiver's demand for possession was refused, and a writ from Judge Stone on August 21st failed to accomplish that end. Loveland managed to retain his hold, and in November, Colorado having become a State in the meantime, the judicial proceedings were transferred to the higher United States Courts. There they seesawed back and forth, and in February 1877, the Union Pacific began another suit against the Colorado Central for $2,000,000 for rolling stock, track materials, and damages. The resourceful Loveland met and parried this attack, and then the Union Pacific capitulated. Loveland then went east to attend the annual meeting of the Union Pacific and make the necessary arrangements for a settlement.

In its surrender, the Union Pacific agreed to stop all litigation and to retain Loveland at the head and in command of the Central. They also agreed to assist in the completion of the partially built extensions to Georgetown and Central City, and to complete the proposed Longmont connection between the Colorado Central system and the Union Pacific's main line at Colorado Junction. Loveland then returned from Boston and announced the formal truce and plans between his road and the Union Pacific, in the Colorado Transcript of March 28, 1877. Loveland, by fair means or foul, had scored a direct hit for the Colorado Central Railroad. Golden and northern Colorado were well pleased with the results. The people of Boulder, Jefferson, and Gilpin Counties had heartily approved Loveland's actions. The Central ran through these counties, and since many of the local citizens had helped the road financially, naturally they preferred home management. While public opinion in that area sustained Loveland and his daring methods, it was bitterly against him in Denver. Loveland's railroad operations had, from the beginning, been a menace to Denver, and while the people of Denver could not refuse recognition of his remarkable ability as a leader, they had long, and with reason regarded him as inimical to the city's progress.

W. H. Jackson photo,
from the State Historical Society of Colorado.
Colorado Central 32 eastbound at Inspiration Point.

CHAPTER IX

FINAL COMPLETION OF ALL COLORADO CENTRAL
CONSTRUCTION

With the improvement of general economic conditions and these new arrangements for Union Pacific co-operation and financial assistance, construction of the line west of Floyd Hill up the South Fork was resumed early in 1877. By the middle of June the railhead had been pushed 5.3 miles west of Floyd Hill to Idaho Springs where, according to the Colorado Miner of June 16, 1877, a big celebration took place in honor of the occasion. The Railroad Gazette of June 29, 1877, tells us that by the latter part of June, trains were running one mile west of Idaho Springs and that the remaining 11.33 miles to Georgetown through Fall River, Dumont, Lawson and Empire were graded and ready for ties and rails. The entire line between Floyd Hill and Georgetown, a distance of 17.63 miles, was completed and opened to traffic on August 14, 1877. It was a great day for the silver mining region.

There was no further construction on this branch by the Colorado Central Railroad. Georgetown remained the terminus of the road until 1884, at which time it was extended farther west to Graymont under the name of the Georgetown Breckenridge & Leadville Railway Co., the details of which will follow shortly. The same conditions that made possible the continuation of the Georgetown branch also applied to the Central City branch. Accordingly, on July 1, 1877, work was resumed on the line beyond Black Hawk and continued without interruption until it was completed through to Central City, a distance of 3.91 miles (new Black Hawk depot to end-of-track at Central City). The Railroad Gazette tells us that the roadbed was ready for the rails by January 25th and that the job was completed on the following May 20th, but the line was not opened to traffic until May 31, 1878.

The physical obstacles encountered on this Central City extension beyond Black Hawk prevented the engineers from building a continuous line of railroad between the two points. The air-line distance between the two depots in these respective towns lacked about 1,000 feet of being an exact mile and a quarter; while the altitude at the Black Hawk depot is 8,035 feet, the altitude of the Central City depot is 8,517 feet, or a difference of 482 feet. Black Hawk proper is situated down in the canon of Clear Creek, while Central City lies back up on the mountain side, practically due west. With these engineering figures in mind, the reader can readily understand or visualize the difficulties encountered in the building of this one and a quarter miles of railroad, and at the same time climbing up the side of the mountain in an effort to gain 482 feet of altitude. After considerable preliminary surveying and engineering work, the engineers decided to use the switchback method in order to get their railroad tracks up to Central City. In the construction of this piece of track, the engineers were forced to use two switchbacks and a total of 3.91 miles of trackage, in order to negotiate this mile and a quarter distance between the two towns.

Due to the extremely rough and mountainous terrain encountered along the two levels of the double switchback, a considerable amount of bridge and trestle construction was necessary. Immediately after leaving the main line in the north end of Black Hawk, the track of the first switchback crossed over two streets, Selak and Gregory, in Black Hawk's business district, on a 7-span, 229-foot steel and wood trestle. The engineering records of 1885 describe this combination bridge and trestle as a lattice deck, girder type, consisting of three 55-foot steel spans supported by iron columns, and four 16-foot wooden spans with timber supports. The total length of the trestle was 229 feet, while the height above the street level was given as 20 feet. Later on after the structure was rebuilt and strengthened, it consisted of 6 steel spans of various lengths, totalling 175 feet, and 4 wooden spans totalling 57 feet, with a combined length of 232 feet. In both cases, the wood spans were located at the upper end of the trestle. The grade over the steel structure was 1.8%, while the grade over the wooden part of the structure was 1.23%.

Between this trestle in Black Hawk and the end of the first switchback, the track crossed over two deep dry gulches. The first was bridged with a 7-span, 112-foot wooden structure, 32 feet in height, while the second gulch was bridged with a 13-span, 218-foot wooden structure 45 feet in height. On the second switchback, there was only one structure of any importance. This was an 8-span, 132-foot wooden structure over

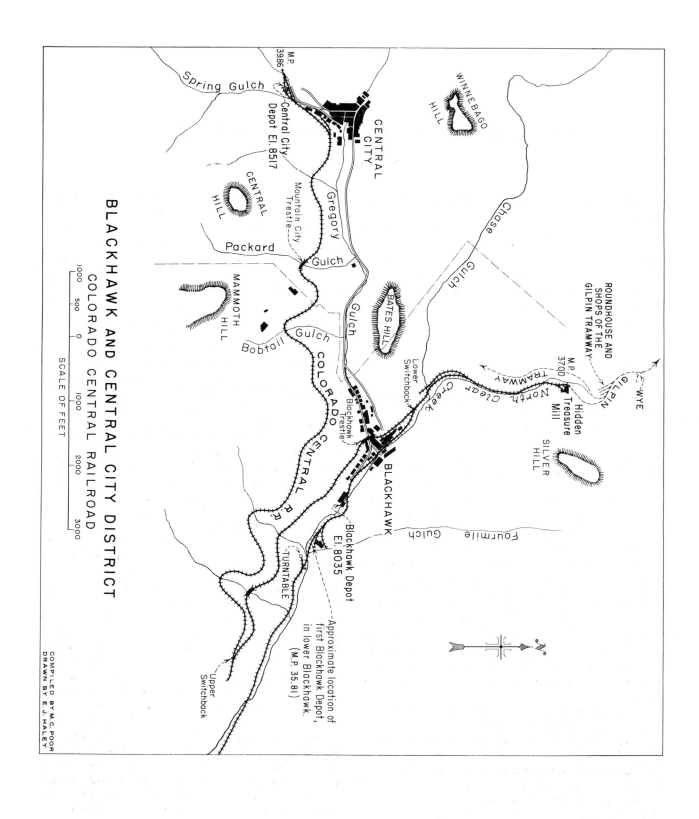

BLACKHAWK AND CENTRAL CITY DISTRICT

COLORADO CENTRAL RAILROAD

SCALE OF FEET

1000 500 0   1000   2000   3000

COMPILED BY M.C. POOR
DRAWN BY E.J. HALEY

Spring Gulch

M.P.
3986

Central City
Depot El. 8517

CENTRAL
CITY

WINNEBAGO
HILL

CENTRAL
HILL

Packard

Mountain City
Trestle

Gregory

Gulch

Chase
Gulch

ROUNDHOUSE AND
SHOPS OF THE
GILPIN TRAMWAY

MAMMOTH
HILL

Bobtail Gulch

Gulch

BATES HILL

Lower
Switchback

North Clear Creek

M.P.
3700

Hidden
Treasure
Mill

GILPIN

WYE

TRAMWAY

SILVER
HILL

COLORADO CENTRAL R.R.

Blackhawk
Trestle

BLACKHAWK

Fourmile Gulch

Blackhawk Depot
El. 8035

Approximate location of
first Blackhawk Depot,
in lower Blackhawk.
(M.P. 35.81)

TURNTABLE

Upper
Switchback

Packard Gulch. Its height was 39 feet. From the time of the original construction of these trestles up to their abandonment, certain repairs and minor changes were made; however, the original dimensions remained about the same.

When the switchback was originally built, the engineers followed the usual early day Colorado railroad construction methods; rough hewn ties, no tie plates, and a dirt road bed. Forty and forty-five pound rail was used throughout; however, around the turn of the century, a greater portion of the line was relaid with 50-pound rail, with some 52 and 56 scattered here and there, with the usual added improvements in the track and roadbed. Some of the old 40-pound rail was left in, near the end of the track beyond the Central City depot.

A study of the map and profile of this switchback is a complete and interesting story within itself. Within this 3.91 miles of right of way, the track negotiated 30 curves whose curvature was of 20 degrees or over. Among the sharper ones to be found were six 30 degree, one 33 degree, two 34 degree, one 36 degree, and three 40 degree curves. The 36 degree curve was encountered just after crossing the third and last bridge on the first switchback on a 2.14% grade. The three 40 degree curves were the sharpest curves to be found on the whole Colorado Central system. Two of them, one immediately following the other, formed a reverse curve slightly beyond milepost 39 just before crossing the eleven span, 160-foot wood trestle over Packard Gulch. The third, and sharpest, a 40 degree and 30 minute curve, was encountered just as the track approached the Central City depot on a 2.50% grade.

Among some of the steeper grades encountered were 12 sections of track of 2.50% or better, while there were 4 sections of 3% or over. The grade approaching the Selak and Gregory Streets bridge in Black Hawk was 3.24% and included a 24 degree and 30 minute right curve, and a 20 degree and 45 minute left curve. The steepest grade encountered was 3.68%, located just beyond the Central City depot near the end-of-track.[1]

The complete line between Black Hawk and Central City was opened to traffic on May 31, 1878, thus completing the through line of the Colorado Central from Denver to Central City. The first train to arrive in Central City consisted of a dummy engine and an old remodeled street car, and was welcomed with the usual celebration. The author found the following old newspaper clipping (name of paper not known) describing an excursion over the line to Central City:

"On September the 6th, (1878) the initial excursion of the

1. Some 4.15% and 4.20% grade was to be found along the extension of the main line up Clear Creek Canon above Black Hawk which served the Hidden Treasure Mill and also as a connection with the Gilpin County Tramway.

newly organized State Editorial Association was to Central City. While going up over the 'Shoofly' beyond Black Hawk, the track spread, causing a passenger car to topple over. Only damage was the frightful screech let out by one Miss Patience Thornton, who was soon picked up and promptly remedied."

With the completion of this line to Central City, the Colorado Central may be said to have achieved a well-integrated, if not yet complete, railroad system. There was the line from Golden to Denver, over which much produce was shipped; the line from the agricultural and coal producing region of Boulder County; and now this line directly into the heart of the famous Gilpin mining region. Each line complemented the other. And what is even more important, each of them served legitimate needs of the regions traversed.

Meanwhile, Loveland had concluded that the railroad and economic situation in the Denver area had developed to a point where the Colorado Central's eastern connection at Jersey, with the Denver Pacific, was becoming a hindrance to the road's progress. As the situation now appeared, there were no advantages to be gained by the Central in the continuation of their policy of avoiding Denver. It must have grieved the man's soul to admit defeat on this one point; however, it was deemed advisable by the Colorado Central interests to construct a more direct line or route into Denver proper. Accordingly, in October 1874, a line of standard gauge railroad from Cutoff Junction (near what was later known as Utah Junction) was completed south into Denver, a distance of 3.44 miles. Although at that time this line was considered a branch road, it afterwards became the main line of the Colorado Central into Denver, and the original line from Cutoff Junction to Jersey Junction was known as the Jersey Cutoff. The construction of this direct line brought an end to the payment of $6,000 per year to the Denver Pacific for trackage rights into Denver.

The reader will recall that one of the agreements reached in 1877 between Loveland and the U. P. was that the proposed extension between the Colorado Central and Union Pacific lines be completed. In this new agreement, the connecting road was not to be built over the original cutoff line to Julesburg, as under former plans, but to Colorado Junction (later known as Hazard) six miles west of Cheyenne. It was simply to be the cheapest line which would open Colorado to the Union Pacific. While still in the east, Loveland had dispatched orders to his engineering department that surveys for the line should begin at once. Denver took alarm, for the line, if built, would completely wreck its Denver Pacific and might even mean the downfall of its trade supremacy. On July 21, 1877, the first rail was laid at Longmont and by November the road was completed. A bad snow storm held up the excursion celebration for six hours, but the train finally bucked its way through to Cheyenne.

From this point on, the railroad situation in north-

Note the Colorado Central track in the foreground of this early day photo of Central City.

Colorado Central engine 1 at the upper switchback on the Central City extension.

Colorado Central engine 2 on Mountain City trestle over Packard Gulch near Central City.

ern Colorado began to quiet down somewhat. The completion of the Hazard extension permitted the Union Pacific to route its Colorado business over a company controlled line. This meant leaner business for the Denver Pacific, and the Kansas Pacific, and placed both these roads at the mercy of the more powerful Union Pacific. After Loveland had ousted the Kansas Pacific from their brief possession of the Colorado Central (December 1875 to May 1876), the Kansas Pacific came to the conclusion that the Union Pacific's scheme to dump the Central into their nearly empty hopper was a hopeless proposition, and it left the road in a generally dejected state of mind. Loveland's seizure of his Colorado Central had destroyed the Union Pacific-Kansas Pacific settlement, and whether with or without the connivance of the Union Pacific, he had dealt the Kansas Pacific a hard blow.

The Kansas Pacific continued its prorate fight with the Union Pacific for a time. Meanwhile, Jay Gould appeared on the scene, and by 1880, had gained control of the whole setup; the Union Pacific, the Kansas Pacific, the Denver Pacific, and the Colorado Central, and thus, with one sweep, brought the northern Colorado railroad quarreling to an end. Gould's name reeked, but he was King.

Prior to the spring of 1876, the Colorado Central had been using the Denver Pacific depot for the arrival and departure of its Denver trains. However, shortly after the road had withdrawn from its brief association with the Kansas Pacific, they had built a small wooden passenger station on the east side of 16th street, on a part of the present site of the Union Passenger station. This arrangement continued until the autumn of 1879, when the Denver & Rio Grande, the Denver South Park & Pacific, and the Colorado Central made an agreement under which the three narrow gauge roads were to use the Central's station at the foot of 16th street. The Rio Grande and the South Park then bridged Cherry Creek, and ran their trains to this small depot of the Central. A short time later, The Union Depot & Railway Company was organized, and a new and larger station was built between 16th and 18th streets, partly on the site of the old Colorado Central station. This new passenger station was opened in June 1881 (see complete details in Denver South Park & Pacific section) and the Central continued to operate all their trains in and out of this station from that time on.

Chas. Weitfle photo,
from Denver Public Library Western Collection.
A westbound passenger train on brand new track near Central City.

Chas. Weitfle photo,
from Francis Rizzari Collection.
Loading gravel ballast on flatcars at the end of Beaver Brook Spur.

CHAPTER X

THE GEORGETOWN BRECKENRIDGE & LEADVILLE RAILWAY

From the time the very first railroad lines were ever proposed or surveyed in the regions west of Denver near the headwaters of Clear Creek, it was the ambitious dream of innumerable railroad men and engineers to find some feasible route over this section of the Continental Divide whereby they might lay a track that would safely and economically carry the iron horse to the other side. Early attempts to even locate a suitable route for a wagon and toll road seemed almost futile at first. Men were able to build their wagon roads up the canon following the south fork of Clear Creek past Georgetown, Silver Plume and Bakerville, or south out of Georgetown and up Leavenworth Canon, but from there on, they faced a mountain barrier that seemed to defy all attempts to negotiate its passes. Finally in 1878, a wagon and toll road, the remains of which may be plainly seen to this day from the new highway, was built over Loveland Pass at an altitude of 11,992 feet.

Many plans were submitted by the disciples of the rod and chain, proposing the use of tunnels or some mountain pass, but the ruggedness and high altitude of the main range in this particular vicinity proved too great an obstacle for the railroad engineer, and successfully defied all his attempts to locate a satisfactory route that would not involve too huge an outlay of money.

The plan of the Gould-Loveland-Union Pacific interests to extend the track of the Colorado Central or some subsidiary road over the range beyond Georgetown and thereby gain a short and direct route between Denver and the Leadville and Arkansas Valley regions was a part of the struggle between the Union Pacific, Atchison Topeka & Santa Fe, and Rio Grande during 1878-79-80. This conflict was an attempt to gain control of the Denver South Park & Pacific and Colorado's great ore traffic, especially that of the Leadville district. Inasmuch as the details of this struggle are related elsewhere in this book, we shall not repeat them here.

Prominent among some of the early projected, and Union Pacific sponsored, railroad lines across the range in this locality were the Georgetown, Leadville & San Juan R. R., the Gray's Peak Snake River & Leadville R. R., and the Loveland Pass Mining & R. R. Tunnel Co. Two other projected railroads over this section were the Atlantic-Pacific Tunnel & Gray's Peak Railway, and the Atlantic-Pacific Railway Tunnel Co. These last two projects were organized by one M. M. Pomeroy. Due to the interest of a great number of readers relative to proposed routes and other details regarding projected railroads over the Continental Divide in this vicinity, we shall include the miscellaneous data that has come to light.

1. Georgetown Leadville & San Juan R. R. (Narrow gauge.) Route: Georgetown, Silver Plume, Loveland Pass, Snake River, Tenmile Creek, Fremont Pass, and Leadville. The road was organized and incorporated by Jay Gould, Sidney Dillon, Russel Sage, and other Union Pacific interests who owned all the stock. One of the first references, relative to the projected route of this railroad, is found in a letter written by Captain E. L. Berthoud to the Railway Age and published in that periodical June 5, 1879.

"To The Editors of Railway Age:

"Inclosed I send you a reproduction of a newly surveyed route for a narrow gauge railroad from Georgetown to Leadville. The line of railway is designed to cross the main range of the Rocky Mountains a few miles west of Gray's Peak, where a favorable location has been found by which we can pierce through the mountain range by a tunnel not over 1,600 feet long. This takes us to near the head of Snake River, a branch of the Blue River. This is followed for several miles in a southwesterly direction, until we reach the valley of Tenmile Creek. We follow up this stream until we reach its headwaters, and recross the range to reach Leadville, giving us a line but little over 62 miles long from Georgetown to Leadville.

"The tunnel will have an altitude where we enter it of about 11,725 feet above sea-level. The whole line from Georgetown will be at an altitude but little less than 9,000 feet above sea-level, and in crossing the Snowy Range the altitude will even exceed Meiggs' Andean railways. We expect to begin work upon it soon . . . The tunnel is fully 200 feet above timber line.

"We are here about 4 miles northwest of Gray's Peak, and at the farthest headwaters of the west fork of Clear Creek. The railway line of 3-foot gauge is located from Georgetown, southwest through what are believed to be the richest mining regions of the whole U. S. From Georgetown we pass over a continued succession of rich silver bearing veins, and through the wealthy mining towns of Silver Plume and Brownville, and two miles north of the Stevens Mine near Gray's Peak. We pass in Snake River Valley, some three miles below St. John and Montezuma, two rich mining centers, and on Tenmile Creek to Leadville pass through Frisco, Kokomo, and Carbonateville, all populous mining towns, with hundreds of newly discovered mines to supply the railway with freight. The distance to Leadville by this route from Denver is 110 miles.

E. L. Berthoud, Secretary"

In the Colorado Miner (Georgetown) July 26, 1879, we read:

"Union Pacific surveyors under direction of Captain E. L. Berthoud pass Tabor City on their survey for the Georgetown-Leadville line. (Note: Tabor City, named after H. A. W. Tabor, was a mining camp located in the vicinity of Fremont Pass. In 1881, the place was supposed to have had one store and twelve buildings.) 'Private Information' warrants that the U. P. will build their line immediately, i.e., as soon as the road can be practically and profitably built. The route follows up the Arkansas to Tabor City, to Kokomo, down Tenmile Creek, across the Blue River near its junction with Snake River, up Snake River to Loveland Pass, and down to Georgetown by the usual route. This is a new survey and passes over the range 1,300 feet lower than Captain Berthoud's line of some years back via Argentine Pass. . . . Engineers Hudnutt and Bleckensderfer proclaim the route entirely practicable, and recommend it. The Union Pacific could have cars in Leadville in three months."

In the Railway World of January 24, 1880, we read:

"This projected line crosses the Continental Range twice and will have a length of 70 miles. The surveyors have worked in the snow since October 14th, and in November the thermometer touched ten degrees below zero. The Range is crossed at Loveland and Tenmile Pass. They went about 1,000 feet above the timber line where nothing was found in the shape of vegetation but mosses."

2. Gray's Peak Snake River & Leadville R. R. (Narrow gauge.) Incorporated December 19, 1878, by W. A. H. Loveland and associates. Stock owned by the Union Pacific. Route copied from Incorporation Papers.

"The said Railroad shall commence at or near Georgetown . . . and shall run thence up Clear Creek to the mouth of Sabine Gulch, and thence up said Gulch by the most feasible route to the foot of Loveland Pass, thence by tunnel or otherwise, through or over said Pass, to the north fork of Snake River, thence to the mouth of Peru Gulch, thence down Snake River to Tenmile Creek, thence up Tenmile Creek, thence through or over Tenmile Pass to Leadville."
(Note: Tenmile Pass was an early name for Fremont Pass.)

In the Railway Age of February 6, 1879, we read:

"W. A. H. Loveland states that construction of the Gray's Peak route is to proceed this spring, and build from a point near the Mt. of Holy Cross, to the Gunnison River, to Lake City, Ouray, the San Juan, and to Arizona to connect with the Southern Pacific."

3. Loveland Pass Mining & Railroad Tunnel Co. (Narrow gauge.) Incorporated July 15, 1881, by W. A. H. Loveland and associates. Stock owned by the Union Pacific. Route copied from Incorporation Papers.

"Miscellaneous mining activities, etc. . . . and to drive, construct, maintain, and operate a tunnel under what is known as Loveland Pass, and on the line of the Gray's Peak Snake River & Leadville R. R. Co., and of such depth and width with necessary approaches thereto, as will admit passage of railroad cars and locomotives."

In the Railway Age of May 18, 1882, we read:

"It is stated that the Union Pacific has just made arrangements to lease the tunnel of the Loveland Pass Mining & R. R. Tunnel Co., paying therefore, $2.00 for each railroad car passing through each way, and guaranteeing the interest on the $400,000 bonds at 7%. The Eastern Portal is about 15 miles southwest of Georgetown, and the Western Portal is 12 miles from Dillon. A contract has been made for completion of the Tunnel." (Author's note: They even had "Rackets" in those days.)

4. Atlantic-Pacific Tunnel & Gray's Peak Ry. (Thought to be narrow gauge.) Incorporated October 23, 1882, by M. M. Pomeroy and associates. Route copied from Incorporation Papers.

"To build and operate a railway from a point at or near Bakerville and thence up the Valley of Quail Creek via the east end of the Atlantic-Pacific Tunnel, and thence up the Valley of said Quail Creek to the Continental Divide near Gray's Peak, thence into the Valley of the Snake River to the west of the Atlantic-Pacific Tunnel in the County of Summit, with a branch from the said main line near the head of Quail Creek to the summit of Gray's Peak . . ."

5. Atlantic-Pacific Railway Tunnel Company. Incorporated February 14, 1884, by M. M. Pomeroy and associates. Object, copied from Incorporation Papers.

"Running a tunnel from Atlantic City in Clear Creek County to Pacific City in Summit County . . ."
Author's note: With the incorporation date of the tunnel two years later than his railroad, it is a little difficult to understand Pomeroy's reference to the Atlantic-Pacific Tunnel in his first organization.

Further information regarding Pomeroy's tunnel venture is found in the Denver Post under date of November 30, 1941. This news article concerned a highway tunnel which the Colorado State Highway Commission was contemplating building under Loveland Pass at the time. We quote in part:

"As work was getting under way Saturday on the mile-long highway tunnel under Loveland Pass, the ghost of Marcus M. (Brick) Pomeroy, fiery, ill-starred pioneer Colorado tunnel builder, rose to suggest that modern engineers may be overlooking a bet by ignoring the famous railroad bore he started to drive under the same pass more than fifty years ago.

"Announcement this week that the state highway department has awarded the contract for the pioneer bore of a new highway tunnel under the pass reminded John T. Jones of Golden of Pomeroy's costly venture.

"Jones, who for eighteen years has been employed as a stationary engineer at the Colorado School of Mines, grew up in the Silver Plume district, and knows the Loveland Pass region intimately. He went to Prof. Robert Baxter of the School of Mines, and to W. R. Coyle, editor of the Jefferson County Republican, with the suggestion that Pomeroy's old tunnel, now almost forgotten but still intact, might save the time, expense and effort of driving a new bore under the pass at a higher level.

"PANIC OF 1893 HALTED PROJECT.

"Jones recalled, according to Coyle, that the old Atlantic & Pacific railroad tunnel had been driven in several thousand feet from the east and several hundred feet from the west at a cost of at least one million dollars in private funds when the panic of 1893 put the project on the rocks.

"Pomeroy's financing methods of the 80's would turn the members of the modern securities and exchange commission indigo with indignation, but in those days the blue sky was the limit. He organized a seven million dollar company, sold bonds at 8 per cent all over the United States and even in Europe, to anyone willing to take a flyer with him. When the panic struck and creditors swooped down to cart off rails, machinery and all other tangible assets, a bore twelve feet high by twelve feet wide, had been driven far in from the east portal, not far from the present Loveland Pass highway beyond Silver Plume, and starting at an altitude of 10,200 feet in forest country, well below timberline.

"GEORGETOWN MAN NOW OWNS BORE.

"Friday, according to Coyle, Jones went to the east portal of Pomeroy's old tunnel and found it securely barred by an iron gate. O. B. Willmarth, a Georgetown mining man, now owns the tunnel. Its title long was the subject of litigation. Pomeroy died in 1896, and the tunnel, which even then was reputed to have tapped gold, silver, and lead veins, occasioned a dispute among his heirs, it is said. In 1931, Willmarth discovered that the tunnel property was, in fact, ownerless, and obtained title to it by the simple process of filing a mining claim.

" 'Willmarth tells me,' Coyle said Saturday, 'that the bore from the east end, in hard, solid granite, goes back about 4,000 feet, and has been cleared of all debris.

" 'Sunday, with his permission granted, a party from Golden, including Jones, Professor Baxter, O. A. Nelson, president of the Golden Chamber of Commerce, and myself, are going up to the old tunnel and look into it thoroly.

"WEST PORTAL DRILLED FOR 800 FEET.

" 'W. A. Gray, engineer for the state highway department in charge of the Loveland Pass district, tells me one of his men was sent up to look into the possibilities of the old A. & P. tunnel months ago, when the highway department was seeking to locate a route for the highway bore. He told me his man reported the old A. & P. bore was in only 300 feet. Jones told me, however, that the mountains there are dotted with holes, and that a bore only 300 feet deep could not be the old Pomeroy railroad diggings, which Jones recalled to be in about 5,000 feet, and which Willmarth says is 4,000 feet long. I understand the west portal bore is only about 800 feet inside the mountain . . .' "

In the Railway Age of July 3, 1884, we find an article concerning the proposed construction of another tunnel under Gray's Peak. No details such as the name of the railroad or company promoting the project were given. This article went on to tell that the tunnel was supposed to be 4 and ¾ miles long at an elevation of 10,000 feet, and could be easily reached at both portals. We quote:

"The east portal is located just about one and one-half miles from Bakerville and the west portal, known as Decatur, was near the head of Snake Creek. The tunnel is 10 feet wide and 9 feet high. 1,600 feet of the east end and about 1,000 feet at the west end are already completed".

Another mysterious article regarding a tunnel in this vicinity is found in the Colorado Magazine of January, 1943. This article states that the Atlantic & Pacific Tunnel, projected by Baron Walter B. von Richthofen, has its beginning near Georgetown and was to pierce the Continental Divide, thus cutting through and disclosing all the various treasure veins, the gold and silver, and the hidden riches of the mountains. After being dug some distance, the tunnel was declared a failure.

With so many projected tunnels and railroads between Bakerville and the Snake River, the surveyors and engineers probably had well-worn paths going up and down Loveland Pass, and stumbled over each other's survey stakes.

How much seriousness was attached to some of these earlier proposed Union Pacific extensions beyond Georgetown, is not known. None of them ever advanced any further than the surveying stage. However, as the struggle with the Rio Grande progressed, developments soon reached the point where the management deemed it necessary to commence actual construction of a railroad between Georgetown and Leadville. Accordingly, in the early part of 1881, the Union Pacific announced their decision to build a railroad from the end of the Colorado Central track at Georgetown to Leadville and beyond. Because the Colorado Central's principal indebtedness was a closed mortgage, and in order to obtain necessary financial assistance for the construction of additional railroad mileage, it was considered necessary and advisable to build the extension under the name of a new company instead of the Colorado Central. For some unknown reason, none of the previously organized railroad companies were used; instead, the Union Pacific organized a new road known as the Georgetown Breckenridge & Leadville Railway Company. The new line was to be built in the interest of the Union Pacific who owned all the securities. The Certificate of Incorporation was dated February 23, 1881. The company was capitalized for $200,000. The incorporators were: Cyrus W. Fisher, Virgil M. Came, Willard Teller, Edwin A. Madgett, and Frank W. Baldwin. The directors were: Augustus A. Egbert, Cyrus W. Fisher, Willard Teller, Virgil M. Came, Sidney Dillon, Jay Gould, and Jay W. Gannett. The object of the corporation was to:

"Construct, operate, and maintain a line of narrow gauge railroad commencing in Georgetown, Colorado, at or near the end of the present line of the Colorado Central R. R. . . . and shall run thence up the Middle Fork of Clear Creek to Silver Plume, and thence up said Creek to Sabine Gulch, and thence up said Gulch by the most practicable route to the foot of what is sometimes known as Loveland Pass, thence by tunnel through, or otherwise over said pass to the North Fork of Snake River; thence down said Fork to the main Snake River; thence down said Snake River to its junction with the Blue River; thence by a branch up the said Blue River to Breckenridge . . . Also from said junction of the Snake River with the Blue River to the mouth of Tenmile Creek, thence up said Tenmile Creek to Kokomo, thence by the most practicable route over, or through the Tenmile Pass to Leadville in Lake County, Colorado. Also a branch commencing on the Blue River at the mouth of said Tenmile Creek, thence down the said Blue River to the mouth of the Grand River, thence up the Grand River by the most practicable route to the Hot Sulphur Springs, from thence up the Grand River to Grand Lake by the most practicable route up the tributary of the Grand River, thence by the most feasible route to the Rabbit Ear Mountains at the foot of the Rabbit Ear Range. Also a branch from the said Grand River at or near the Hot Sulphur Springs by the most practicable route by some tributary of the Grand River on the north into Egeria Park and from thence westerly by the most practicable route to Salt Lake City".

The route was located and laid out by Robert Blickensderfer, a civil engineer employed by the Union

Pacific.[1] Robert B. Stanton was Chief Engineer of the G.B.&L., known as the "High Line". Working under Stanton was Frank A. Maxwell, who did the actual field engineering, and E. J. Milner, location and construction engineer. Chester W. Collins was the general contractor.[1] Construction began in January of 1882, and by October of that year the grading was completed through to Bakerville at which time all further work was temporarily suspended. As nearly as can be determined from data found on a revised copy (owned by the writer) of the original map filed with the U. S. Government Land Office, this was due to a change in the route. Information on this map indicates that between September 26, 1881, and December 14, 1882, Stanton made a new survey on the steep slopes of Loveland Pass whereby the line was to be built in such a manner as to connect with the track of the Denver South Park & Pacific R. R. on the waters of Little Snake River, a distance of 11.05 miles from the summit. The new route was adopted by the Board of Directors on December 20, 1882. This map contains no information relative to the various extensions to Breckenridge, Leadville, or Hot Sulphur Springs. Work on the railroad was resumed in the summer of 1883. In the Railway Age of June 30, 1883, we read:

"Grading on the Georgetown Breckenridge & Leadville is completed from Georgetown to Bakerville and track laying has commenced".

But due to the many difficulties encountered in the construction of the loop and bridge, it was not until the spring of 1884 that the end-of-track reached Silver Plume. In the Rocky Mountain News of March 13, 1884, we read:

"The railroad reached the city limits of Silver Plume Saturday night, March the 8th. The following Monday the track was completed to the center of the town. The citizens had waited so long for the railroad to reach them that there was little enthusiasm and no demonstration".

The line was completed through to Bakerville, or Graymont as it was later known, 4.00 miles beyond Silver Plume. The first regular passenger train over the high line to Silver Plume was run March 31, 1884, it being the regular night train from Denver. Regular passenger service started April 1st, the train arriving thereafter at Silver Plume every evening at 7:25 and leaving every morning at 6:50. The fare between Georgetown and Silver Plume was 35 cents and the running time was 25 minutes. The Union Pacific officials spent April 1, 1884, with Photographer William Henry Jackson of Denver taking pictures of the loop bridge and surroundings. One picture was of four trains bound for Silver Plume with pilots pointing the four directions—north, east, south, and west.[2]

A few individuals contend that by the time the Union

Pacific had extended their rails about a mile beyond Silver Plume they had given up the idea of building the road over the mountains to Leadville and ceased all further construction. It is their contention that a mine located at Graymont wanted rail service to facilitate the shipment of ore into Denver. Therefore, in order to get a railroad connection, the mine owners laid about three miles of track from the end of the Union Pacific's rails to Graymont, whereupon the railroad company agreed to transport their ore for them. When the mine was worked out and abandoned in 1898, the mine owners took up their three miles of rail and sold it along with their mining machinery.

Others contend that the Union Pacific themselves completed the construction of the track through to Graymont. The official corporate history of the Georgetown Breckenridge & Leadville road definitely states that the Union Pacific completed the construction of the road through to Graymont. The records also disclose that on February 14, 1884, just two months before the rails reached Silver Plume, the original capital stock of the road was increased from $200,000 to $2,500,000, evidence that the Union Pacific probably planned on carrying out their original construction program. The Union Pacific annual report for the year ending December 31, 1884, states:

". . . the line was completed from Georgetown through to Graymont in the spring of 1884, 6.52 miles of track having been laid this year . . . should this line ever be completed across the range, it will shorten the distance between Denver and Leadville from 277 miles via the D. & R. G. and 151 miles via the D. S. P. & P. to 127 miles via Georgetown."

The fact that the Union Pacific ran regularly scheduled passenger trains to Graymont also lends further strength to the theory that the railroad company built the entire line. The author, after weighing all the evidence that has come to light, is inclined to believe the entire Georgetown-Graymont line was constructed by and for Union Pacific interests.

The distance from Georgetown to Graymont was 8.47 miles and, together with the Colorado Central, made a total track distance of 58.10 miles from Denver to Graymont. As history records, Graymont remained the end-of-track and no further construction of any kind was ever attempted.

By 1884, the Union Pacific had completed the extension of the Denver South Park & Pacific high line via Boreas and Climax into Leadville, thus controlling their own entryway into the great mining camp. By this time, the battle for Leadville had quieted down somewhat and the railroad picture in this section of Colorado took on a slightly different aspect. Completion of the gap between Graymont and Keystone, the end of the South Park's Snake River branch, would have afforded the Union Pacific a much shorter and more direct route between Denver and Leadville, but after

1. Rocky Mountain News, February 23, 1881.
2. Colorado Magazine, September, 1947.

This photo, taken April 1, 1884, at the high bridge of the Georgetown Loop, shows four trains, headed north, south, east and west. Two, in the distance, may be seen through the central span of the bridge.

W. H. Jackson photo, from the State Historical Society of Colorado.

The end of the Georgetown Breckenridge & Leadville Railway
at Graymont (Bakerville).

considerable ballyhoo and spending of money, the officials suddenly decided to stop all further construction on the basis that the initial cost and heavy maintenance of such a line would not justify its completion. There is also the great probability that the proposed Loveland Pass project had served its purpose during their struggle for Leadville with the Denver & Rio Grande, and that any further extension of the Georgetown line, in the face of existing economic and financial conditions, would be useless. For a few years following the completion of the Silver Plume line, a news item would appear now and then announcing the survey for a new route beyond Georgetown; e.g., a report published in the Railway Review of September 24, 1887, stated that a new standard gauge line between Georgetown and Keystone was being surveyed, but beyond the usual announcement, nothing in the way of actual construction ever occurred.

To merely state that the Union Pacific extended the Colorado Central's tracks 8.47 miles beyond Georgetown to Graymont under the name of the Georgetown Breckenridge & Leadville would not ordinarily raise a great deal of interest. However, this eight miles of mountain line was far from being just an ordinary piece of railroad construction. Between these two points, there was to be found one of the most difficult mountain railroad construction problems that had faced the engineers up to this time. This marvel of early-day railroad construction was the famous "Georgetown Loop and Bridge", and was one of the greatest engineering feats to be found on any Colorado railroad. Quoting from the 1884 Union Pacific Annual Report, we read the following:

"This Georgetown Breckenridge & Leadville line was the most difficult piece of mountain construction in the whole Union Pacific system; an ascent of 638 feet above Georgetown being overcome in 4.47 miles, or an average of approximately 143 feet per mile".

The loop and bridge were located between Georgetown and Silver Plume; in fact, by the time a train had finished negotiating the complete loop, it was practically at the Silver Plume depot. The bridge itself was about two miles west of Georgetown by rail. The Georgetown depot is 8,476 feet above sea level; Silver Plume is 9,114, a difference of 638 feet. The actual distance between the two stations was 4.47 miles while the air-line distance between the two points was slightly over two miles. In order to overcome this two mile distance, and at the same time gain an altitude of 638 feet, the engineers utilized the "loop or railroad spiral" in connection with numerous sharp curves and steep grades. Examination of the map and profile of this loop makes a very interesting study. Within this 4.47 miles of line between the two stations, the track negotiated 14 curves whose curvature was 18 degrees or over. Among some of the sharper curves to be found were four 20 degree, two 24 degree, one 28 degree, one 29 degree, and one 30 degree curve. This 30 degree curve was located near the upper end of the loop on a big fill, and was on a 4.13% grade. Among some of the steeper grades encountered were nine sections of 3.5% or more. The steepest grade was 4.20%, located just beyond milepost 50 on the western edge of Georgetown.

Construction of the bridge, under the general supervision of Robert Blickensderfer, Chief Engineer of the Union Pacific at that time, was begun during 1882. The Phoenix Bridge Company of Phoenixville, Penna., contracted to furnish the iron for the bridge and erect it. The iron arrived in Denver on standard gauge cars on September 20, 1883. It was then transferred to narrow gauge cars for shipment up the canon and the first car arrived at Georgetown Friday night, October 5, 1883. Twenty-three cars were retained at Golden where they were held until needed.[1] The Rocky Mountain News of October 14, 1883, states the timber scaffolding used in the construction of the bridge was a mountain of lumber. The granite masonry piers were completed on October 4th and the first steel girder was placed in position October 15th. The construction gang started laying rail on the bridge January 29th, and on February 28, 1884, the first locomotive, driven by Mr. George Cooper of Idaho Springs, crossed over the great bridge. On March 5th, Superintendent Pat Touhy and Roadmaster Chas. Burgdorf (of the Denver Pacific Division) inspected the structure and one week later the bridge was completed.[1] In the Denver News of March 13, 1884, we read:

"The Georgetown Loop Bridge was tested yesterday by running several trains over it and was found OK".

A peculiar story has cropped up to the effect that the loop bridge was erected backward and had to be reconstructed before the railroad would accept it. The story, which appeared in the Colorado Magazine under date of September, 1947, was credited to a news item in the Rocky Mountain News of November 29, 1883. We quote in part:

"On November 25, 1883, the great bridge was completed— or so it was thought.
"Then, owing to defective riveting and to the fact that the bridge was built wrong end foremost, Chief Engineer Stanton would not accept it. The columns placed on the north end of the structure should have been on the south end. The entire bridge had to be taken down and rebuilt. The bridge builders must have become dizzy and lost their directions coming up the serpentine trail. The poor riveting was charged to the frequent change of mechanics. They would work a short time on the 90 foot structure over roaring Clear Creek and then head back to Denver that night.
"The bridge builders, who had been discharged and left November 25th, were recalled and the work of turning the bridge around was started. On January 20, 1884, it was reported that the big viaduct over the Devil's Gate would again

be completed in a week and be ready for inspection. Chief Engineer Stanton went to Georgetown and accepted the bridge".

The writer is inclined to take issue with this story. History tells us that the contractor building the bridge had many inexperienced men on the job. It is quite possible that the workmen might have put a girder or two in backward and some news reporter, hearing about it, concluded it would form the basis for a good newspaper story.

First, the entire bridge was built on an 18 degree curve, the radius of which was 311 feet, which fact in itself alone discounts the story considerably. Second, Mr. Robert B. Stanton, Chief Engineer, and Mr. F. J. Milner, Construction Engineer, were on the job more or less constantly during the erection of the bridge. Such a major error, if allowed to occur, would not only have been a reflection on the ability of these two men, but also on the entire engineering department of the Union Pacific, which in reality built the structure as they owned and controlled the G.B.&L. Third, following the completion of the bridge, Mr. Adolphus Bonzano, Chief Engineer of the Phoenix Bridge Company, which fabricated the bridge, issued a detailed report on the bridge and its erection. The writer has a copy of this report and no mention is made of such an error. Fourth, the Annual Reports of the Georgetown Breckenridge & Leadville Ry. for the years 1883, 1884, and 1885, make no mention of such an error. Neither were there any references to such a blunder found in any of the trade publications of these dates. In view of the above facts, the writer doubts the veracity of this story.

An excellent description of the bridge and some of its constructional details was found in an early issue of the Railroad Gazette. The article was written by Mr. Adolphus Bonzano, Vice President and Chief Engineer of Clarke Reeves & Company, later known as the Phoenix Bridge Company of Pennsylvania. (See page 70 in the 1884 issue of Poor's Manual of Railroads for one of their interesting old time advertisements.) Mr. Bonzano states:

"Inasmuch as this particular section of the Georgetown Breckenridge & Leadville track was built in the form of a spiral, it became known as the loop or 'Georgetown Loop'. A railroad spiral is a device for gaining distance on heavy grades on which the line, in climbing, is turned back upon itself and crosses over itself at a higher elevation. It is a rare feature in railroad location. The simpler term 'loop' is quite frequently used. The Georgetown 'bridge spiral' is the only spiral of this type known to exist at this time. There are two kinds of spirals; bridge spirals and tunnel spirals.
"This section of the railroad was first located in the summer of 1879 by Mr. Jacob B. Blickensderfer,[1] later Chief Engineer of the Union Pacific Railroad, at the time when that railroad expected to build a short line into Leadville from Denver, and is on the extension of the Colorado Central Railroad from

1. Colorado Magazine, September, 1947.

1. The Rocky Mountain News of February 23, 1881, states that the line was located by Robert Blickensderfer (son of Jacob Blickensderfer). In view of other evidence the name Jacob here is thought to be in error.

Denver to Georgetown. Nothing, however, was done towards construction until the winter of 1881-82. The general contract for construction of the first 8½ miles was then let to Messrs. Laughorn & Ballard. The grading contract was sublet to Robert Given of Denver. Mr. Robert B. Stanton, the road's Chief Engineer, took charge of the work. Mr. E. J. Milner was location and construction engineer. Stanton made a complete revision of the location, and while the idea of a spiral, or loop, is just as it was, the details of the alignment have been greatly modified. The gradient or rise of track on, and in the vicinity of, the spiral is almost continous at 185 feet to the mile (3½%) for the first four miles, being equated 0.03 per 100 feet per degree of curvature. The maximum curvature, found on the big fill, sometimes known as Horseshoe Curve, is 30 degrees, or 193.2 foot radius. In one instance, there are 210 degrees in one curve. The spiral will be seen to be laid out with very sharp 28 degree curves, and the line is a good illustration of the fact that the use of sharp curves in difficult country not only effects a direct saving, but makes possible lines and grades which would otherwise be wholly out of the question.

"To convey an idea of the great amount of work necessary to complete this 8½ miles of track, including the spiral, the following figures are given: earth work, 243,000 cubic yards; loose rock, 44,000 cubic yards; hard rock, 55,000 cubic yards; masonry, 8,500 cubic yards. Native granite quarried in the vicinity was used in building the piers.[1] Construction of the road included the usual plain dirt roadbed, cedar ties, no tie plates, and 40 pound rail. (Author's note: About 1905 a considerable portion of the line was relaid with 50-52 pound rail.) The total cost for the 8½ miles of grading and masonry work was $225,000, or $26,500 per mile, while the total cost of the entire line from Georgetown to Graymont was $432,597.60, or $51,074 per mile.[2]

"The bridge proper is on an 18 degree, 30 minute curve (311 foot radius) and was built by Clarke Reeves & Company. The erection of the 'Devil's Gate Viaduct' was attended by many difficulties. The snow was more than a foot deep in August when we commenced the erection of the bridge. The workmen employed in the erection were, for the most, roving miners who would leave their work on the bridge whenever any news concerning some rich ore discovery was circulated around. We had to pay $5.00 per day for such unskilled and unreliable labor."

ENGINEERING DATA ON THE GEORGETOWN LOOP BRIDGE

The high bridge is on a curve, the radius of which ....311.0 Ft.
Degree of curvature on bridge proper ....18° 30'
Top of bridge above sea level ....8,715.0 Ft.
Elevation of lower track above sea level ... 8,640.4 Ft.
Distance between tracks at the point of crossing ....74.6 Ft.
Height of track on top of bridge above channel of Clear Creek ....95.6 Ft.
Height of lower track above channel of Clear Creek ....21.0 Ft.
Length of the loop track between point of crossing ....3,812.0 Ft.
Weight of rail on bridge ....40.0 Lb.

1. The masonry piers were built under the supervision of Mr. W. P. Jones, a resident Union Pacific construction engineer. —Rocky Mountain News, February 23, 1881.
2. The 1885 Report of the Colorado Railroad Commission gives the cost as $428,380.81.

Grade of track directly over the bridge 2.0%
Length of bridge ....300.0 Ft.
Spans: Number of 30 foot iron plate girders .... 8.
      Number of 60 foot lattice girders (iron) ..... 1.
Weight of iron spans..157,482.0 Lbs.
Granite masonry in piers and abutments ... 735 Cu. Yds.
Timber in deck of bridge including ties ... 36.136 M.B.F.

The bridge was strengthened in 1921 by adding 42,000 lbs. of steel bracing, and the old rail on the bridge was replaced with 75 lb. rail at the same time. There is no record of any other changes being made on the bridge since its original construction.

The bridge was first known as "The Devil's Gate Viaduct" and, as a mecca for the Colorado tourist and sightseer, it had few equals. A very interesting description of a railroad trip up the canon, from the tourist's viewpoint, is published in Brent's "Empire of the West". Here we find a somewhat flowery but interesting story of a train ride up Clear Creek and over the famous loop and bridge. We quote in part:

"There is nothing like Clear Creek Canon in America. The wild rugged scenery simply cannot be described. You may throw a mass of gorgeous words together but they are puny and inadequate. As you proceed up the Canon, the restless mountain torrent of Clear Creek rushes past you. Clear Creek is clear in name only, being greatly discolored because of the sluice-mining operation throughout the canon. The walls are close enough to touch at times, and then again the canon widens out into a few brief acres, green, shady, inviting, and you are allowed a few glimpses of dazzling snow-covered mountain peaks far off in the upper sky. A thing of beauty, which cannot be taken away from its mountain home, and can never be reproduced by man with either paint brush or mere words. Gashed, seamed and rent, are the mountains in every direction, but a beautiful plateau of ten or fifteen acres is left here and there for a small hamlet or town. Most famous of all Clear Creek Canon towns is Georgetown.

"The bright sunshine, the pure atmosphere, the mountain breeze, the cool dewless nights render life in this section of the Rockies a pleasurable and inspiring existance. During the winter the temperature is even less severe and more bearable than the winters in Denver. The snowfall is usually so light that sleighing and winter sports are almost unknown, while the winter season by no means interferes with the mining industry.

"The railway follows the water level of Clear Creek into the heart of the mountains and, at the virtual head of the canon where Georgetown is situated, every part of the range is reached without undue exertion, but with comfort and pleasure. Perched above Georgetown is the famous 'Georgetown Loop and Bridge', a wonderful piece of engineering skill, now world famous.

"Passing above West Clear Creek, with just a glimpse of the picturesque bridge that spans Devil's Gate, the road runs under the great viaduct, and rises and rises until you have left the city hundreds of feet below; and to the north, but with a sudden turn, it is seen again, with the train this time rolling towards the city and still climbing; again a turn to the east; now 75 feet below is the track we just passed.

"Away again on the further side of the mountain; again crossing to west side, suddenly turning to the east until the 'Big Fill', 76 feet high—too sharp a curve for a bridge—has given another circle to the track, then with a turn to the west around the slope of Mt. McClellan; still another view of Georgetown with all the tracks in view, each seeming to have

W. H. Jackson photo

from Denver Public Library Western Collection.

Colorado Central engine 8 on the big fill of the Georgetown Loop, near Silver Plume

tains discloses the little town of Silver Plume, the close ally no relation to its neighbor, until another valley in the mountains and best friend of Georgetown. But the 'Loop' is a railway on a 'Bender'; it is the apotheosis of gyration, the supreme luxury of entanglement — yet all wisely, clearly, skillfully planned—a wondrous monument to human genius and engineering skill."

Not much information has come to light regarding early-day operation of this road. Although owned by the Union Pacific, the line was operated under its real name in connection with the Colorado Central, which furnished all rolling stock and motive power. From the opening of the road up to around 1925, time table schedules list two daily passenger trains. However, during the summer tourist season, especially in the early days of the road, this passenger service was increased considerably. In its heyday, as many as seven special trains per day were required to carry the tourists and sightseers up Clear Creek Canon to see and ride over the highly advertised "Scenic Wonder of the West— the great Georgetown Loop and Bridge".

Evidently, there was never much of a demand for passenger service beyond Silver Plume. Of the numerous time tables consulted, many listed Graymont but only a very few showed passenger service to the end of the line. Information found in an April, 1892, Official Guide shows two regular passenger trains running all the way to Graymont. An 1893 Rocky Mountain Railway Guide, which listed one daily train, was the last information found by the author showing service to Graymont.

Some interesting material was found in the old Union Pacific Annual Reports. It appears that the greater percentage of the road's business was its passenger traffic. The 1884 report states that 21,631 revenue passengers

were carried that year, and that the average passenger fare (on the G. B. & L.) was 4.1 cents per mile. What little freight traffic the road had, consisted mostly of ore, lumber, coal and mining supplies.[1] It seems that the only really profitable source of operation was derived from a contract the road had for carrying the United States Mail. During the six year period following its completion, through which time the road was under Union Pacific control, the financial side of the story was not very good. The following profit and loss figures, as disclosed by the Union Pacific Annual Reports for that period, show these results:

The 1884 loss was $ 4,016.00
The 1885 loss was $19,741.00
The 1886 loss was $13,007.00
The 1887 loss was $13,604.00
The 1888 loss was $14,190.00
The 1889 loss was $11,226.00

Although these reports show an annual loss for each year, they failed to state just what advantages had accrued to the Colorado Central in the way of a percentage increase in business, due to the road acting as a feeder line. Inasmuch as the Union Pacific controlled both roads, they could perhaps afford to operate the loop line at a loss.

The operation of the Georgetown Breckenridge & Leadville continued until April 1, 1890, when, in connection with certain other railroad properties as hereinafter stated, it was merged with the Union Pacific Denver & Gulf Railway Company.

1. The 1885 Colorado Railroad Commission Reports state that the average freight rate per ton per mile on the G.B.&L. was 25.65 cents.

Colorado Central narrow gauge engine 4, built by Porter-Bell in 1875.

This scene of the Georgetown Loop area, photographed from the big fill, shows an eastbound Colorado Central passenger train and a single engine on the high bridge.

W. H. Jackson photo,
from the State Historical Society of Colorado.

CHAPTER XI

CONSOLIDATION AND THE THIRD RAIL

During the few years' period following the intended Union Pacific-Kansas Pacific settlement in 1875, Denver had stood by, the helpless victim of all the wrangling between these two roads. First, she blamed the Union Pacific for her troubles due to rate discriminations, and later she blamed the Kansas Pacific. Then Loveland's successful coup in the Colorado Central, already detailed, took place. When the situation had cleared sufficiently to show Coloradoans the turn which events were likely to take, Denver was panic-stricken. Few events caused so great an uproar in Colorado railroad circles as Loveland's proposal to build his competing Colorado Central extension to Hazard.

The reason for the intensity of the reaction is not difficult to understand. If built, the line would completely ruin the Denver Pacific. With the Union Pacific charging almost prohibitive rates on outgoing shipments over its lines, and with the Kansas Pacific forcing the Denver Pacific to charge similar rates on business coming to it from the Union Pacific, it had little enough business already. A new connecting line, run in cooperation with the Union Pacific, would be able to charge such rates as to secure practically all haulage into and out of northern Colorado. But even that was not the full extent of the threat. This proposed Colorado Central line to Hazard would avoid Denver altogether. With practically all northern trade moving by the new line, Denver, as the distributing center of the territory, would be doomed.[1]

All this, Denver realized perfectly. The trouble was, the Kansas Pacific did nothing about it. What angered Denver most was the way in which the Kansas Pacific, looking out for its own interests only, had by its bunglesome strategy defeated every move which would have made the building of the Hazard extension unnecessary. The old war-cry—Denver's "community of interests" with the Kansas Pacific—was forcibly exposed for the fraud it really was. The Kansas Pacific wanted prorate privileges from the Union Pacific; Denver wanted cheap rates. The two interests were far from harmonious.

Denver, seeing it could expect little help from its erstwhile ally, proceeded to try for its own relief from the proposed Hazard extension. Three separate moves

1. Mock.

were noted. First was a renewed effort to induce the Colorado Central to lay the third narrow gauge rail between Golden and Denver. The second was to make suitable traffic arrangements with the Union Pacific, independently of the Kansas Pacific. The third, and most drastic solution, was to divorce the Denver Pacific from the Kansas Pacific by having it placed in receivership.

It will be remembered that the Denver railroad interests had organized the Denver Georgetown & Utah in 1872, with the possible hope that it might force Loveland and Teller to lay this third rail. This, of course, they refused to do and so the matter rested for some time. But the Hazard extension revived the issue. Only if the third rail were laid, thus completing a narrow gauge railroad from Denver through to the mountains, which would eliminate the expensive rehandling of freight at Golden, could Denver hope to compete at all with Golden and the Colorado Central for the mountain trade. That is, under normal conditions the transfer would follow at Denver. But a transfer at Golden, necessary only as long as the Colorado Central from Denver to Golden was standard gauge and from Golden to the mountains was narrow gauge, added the cost of rehandling to the freight charges. This additional charge (over the ordinary two cent per mile wheel-toll) was reported to have added an average cost of $1.24 per carload on freight to Black Hawk. Hiding behind the advantage afforded by the lack of this third rail, and making full use of the rate differentials which the Union Pacific was willing to give the Colorado Central, Golden was making great plans to monopolize the mountain trade for itself.

The standard gauge Hazard extension was completed in 1877, and gave the Union Pacific access to Denver and the Clear Creek mining districts over lines directly under its control. Thus, one of the Union Pacific's long cherished ambitions had now come to pass—the Colorado Central Railroad had been made what they intended it to be—a mountain feeder to the great Union Pacific system.

How Golden and the Colorado Central were using the third rail situation to their advantage can be seen in the discussion centering around the proposed construction of a new railroad projected by Nathaniel P. Hill to afford relief for his Boston & Colorado Smelting Works from Colorado Central rate policies. This new road was known as The Denver & Rocky Mountain Railway Company, and was actually incorporated on November 27, 1877. N. P. Hill's smelter, then located at Black Hawk, was entirely dependent on the Colorado Central for both its coal and ore. The Central's traffic rates on ores were exorbitant; for example, the road charged $5.00 per ton for the 28 mile haul from Georgetown to Black Hawk, while the rate from the mountains to Kansas City was only $6.50 per ton. At the same time, Hill's plant was virtually compelled to use coal from mines in which the Colorado Central had at least indirect interest. The rich Marshall coal fields near Boulder (Denver Pacific controlled) were naturally closed to the mountain regions by means of prohibitory Colorado Central tariffs. Furthermore, a great deal of ore was prevented from coming from other parts of the territory, especially from regions tapped by the Denver & Rio Grande and the Denver South Park & Pacific, because of the plant's location away from the Denver terminus of such feeder lines. Therefore, to better his situation, Hill threatened to build his own railroad and even to move his smelting works from Black Hawk to Denver unless the third rail was laid or the ore rates reduced. Had he made this latter move, he undoubtedly would have had to build his own railroad to the mining camps, for otherwise, the Colorado Central would have diverted ores eastward over the Union Pacific to the Omaha smelters. The Denver Daily Times of February 4, 1878, stated that the Central was already reported to have been doing that very thing by increasing the rates between Golden and Denver. The increase was regarded as a threat to Hill not to move his smelter to Denver. Truly, in the case of railroad management, those were the "golden years of railroading".

During the winter of 1877-78 the press was replete with articles on the road and how the third rail would now have to be laid. The newspapers of the several mining towns in the mountains generally favored the project also, but the Colorado Transcript, true to form, stoutly defended the Colorado Central and its actions. Hill's Denver & Rocky Mountain Ry. was never built and as yet Denver was still without the third rail. Hill moved his smelter to Argo, just north of Denver, in 1878.

Denver then tried to negotiate directly with the Union Pacific, in an effort to see what could be done about some sort of rate adjustment, but nothing materialized. Steps were then taken toward placing the Denver Pacific in receivership, but this move failed; the Kansas Pacific maintaining a firm control over the Denver road. The usual wrangling between the three roads continued with the result that they were getting nowhere, fast.

At this point, affairs took a very sharp turn. In 1879, three events of far-reaching significance took place in rapid succession; Jay Gould, who had for several years

been the dominant figure in the Union Pacific, now secured control of the Kansas Pacific; a settlement was agreed upon between the Kansas Pacific and the Union Pacific; and the Denver Pacific was placed in the hands of receivers. Probably Jay Gould can be regarded as the common denominator of all three occurrences.

The details of how Gould appeared on the Colorado scene and brought about the consolidation of the Union Pacific, the Colorado Central, the Kansas Pacific, and the Denver Pacific, thus bringing peace to the northern Colorado railroad tangle, is a long and interesting story. However, the details are irrelevant to this history. The only point of significance is that Gould's manipulations had finally led to the placing of all northern Colorado railroad lines under control of the Union Pacific. This merger took place January 24, 1880, and was known as the great Union Pacific Consolidation of 1880.

The Kansas Pacific prorate fight with the Union Pacific was definitely ended. The rivalry between Denver and Golden was liquidated in favor of the Union Pacific monopoly. The third rail situation, the thorn in Denver's side for some ten years, was now remedied. Inasmuch as Gould's consolidation had placed the two quarreling neighbors, the Denver and Golden interests, all under one head, there was no further excuse for their continued wrangling; they were just one big happy family now—or at least they were supposed to be as far as the railroad situation was concerned.

The job of laying the third narrow gauge rail was not much of a construction problem. Announcement was made in the Railroad Gazette in October, 1879, that the rail was being laid. The Rocky Mountain News of November 5, 1879, stated that it was laid for a distance of six miles east of Golden, but that a lack of iron had caused a temporary halt. The job was completed in December.

In the Rocky Mountain News under date of November 29, 1879, we find the following article:

"THE THIRD RAIL COMPLETED

"Thursday noon, November the 27th, the first train moved smoothly into Argo over the third rail on the Colorado Central between Golden and that point. This train was in charge of Conductor Carpenter and embraced six car-loads of ore. Captain P. S. Reed, roadmaster of the Colorado Central, was the only passenger. A third rail from Argo to Denver has been in use for some time. Hence, narrow gauge connection with the mountain cities is now complete."

In the Rocky Mountain News under the date of December 5, 1879, we find the following article:

"THIRD RAIL IN DENVER

"Yesterday, December the 4th, the new third rail on the Colorado Central was extended to the passenger depot at the foot of sixteenth street, and Captain Reed and his men are now busy in pushing the desired improvement out to the freight depot, rolling mills and stock yards near the eastern line of the city. The work is costly in many respects, involving some four miles of rail and not less than one hundred 'frogs' costing from $50 to $75 each. The Elliott Double-pointed steel 'frog', a

UNION PACIFIC RAILWAY.

COLORADO DIVISION

COLORADO CENTRAL RAILROAD.

TIME SCHEDULE No. 10.

TO TAKE EFFECT MONDAY, OCTOBER 1st, 1883, AT 5:45 A. M.

For the Government and Information of Employes Only.   The Company Reserves the Right to Vary Therefrom at Pleasure.

WESTWARD AND NORTHWARD. / NAMES OF STATIONS. / EASTWARD AND SOUTHWARD.

BROAD GAUGE.

No. 253 Argo Freight.	No. 251 Argo Freight.	No. 245 Freight.	No. 243 Freight.	No. 241 Passenger.	No. 235 Passenger.	No. 233 Passenger and Mail.	No. 231 Freight.	No. 229 Passenger.	No. 227 Passenger.	No. 225 Passenger & Mail	DIST. FROM DENVER	STATIONS	DIST. FROM CHEYENNE	No. 226 Passenger & Mail.	No. 228 Passenger.	No. 230 Freight.	No. 232 Freight.	No. 234 Passenger & Mail.	No. 236 Passenger.	No. 242 Passenger.	No. 244 Freight.	No. 246 Freight.	No. 252 Argo Freight.	No. 254 Argo Freight.
2 50 pm.lv	10 20am.lv	5 45am.lv	11 55am.lv	6 15pm.lv	2 25pm.lv	8 30am.lv		8 50 am.lv		7 00am lv	157.7	Denver	137.7	6 15pm.ar		4 45pm.ar		6 05pm.ar	11 10am.ar	8 50am.ar	3 45pm.ar	5 50pm.ar	9 35am.ar	2 05pm.lv
3 10 pm.ar	10 40am.ar	6 00	12 10	6 27	2 37	8 40		9 05		7 10	2.0	Argo 2.0	155.7	6 05		4 30		5 53	10 58	8 40	3 30	5 35	9 15am.lv	1 45pm.lv
		6 35	12 43	6 45	2 55	8 58		9 35		7 25	7.6	Arvada 5.6	130.1	5 50		4 00		5 35	10 40	8 20	2 55	5 00		
		7 20am.ar	1 30 pm.ar	7 10pm.ar	3 20pm.ar	9 20am.ar		10 15 ar 10 30 lv		7 45	15.6	Golden 1.5	122.1	5 30		3 20 lv 2 45 ar		5 10pm.lv	10 15am.lv	7 55am.lv	2 10pm.lv	4 20pm.lv		
								10 45		7 55	17.1	Jones' Siding 2.4	120.6	5 20		2 30								
								11 00		8 05	19.5	Ralston 8.7	118.2	5 10		2 15								
								11 45		8 25	28.2	Church's 9.1	109.5	4 52		1 30								
							7 00 pm.lv	12 35 ar 1 00 lv		8 47	37.3	Louisville 8.9	100.4	4 30		12 35 lv 12 00 ar		7 00am.ar						
							8 00pm.ar	1 45 ar 2 10 lv	7 20pm lv	9 20	45.8	Boulder 7.3	92.4	4 00		11 15 lv 10 30 ar	7 35am.ar	6 00am lv						
								2 50	7 45	9 42	52.6	Niwot 5.2	85.1	3 35		7 30		9 42						
								3 22	8 00pm.ar	10 00	57.8	Longmont 5.0	79.9	3 22		7 15pm.lv		9 10						
								3 50		10 15	62.8	Highland 3.6	74.9	3 10				8 40						
								4 10		10 25	66.4	Berthoud 8.4	71.3	3 00				8 20						
								5 00		10 45	74.8	Loveland 13.8	62.9	2 40				7 35						
								6 10pm.ar		11 15am.ar	88.6	Fort Collins 16.8	49.1	2 10pm.lv		6 25am.lv								
											105.4	Bristol 8.2	32.3											
											113.6	Taylors 11.6	24.1											
											125.2	Lone Tree 6.8	12.5											
											132.0	Colorado Junction 5.7	5.7											
											137.7	Cheyenne												

Three Rails.

WESTWARD. / NARROW GAUGE. / EASTWARD.

No. 249 Freight.	No. 247 Freight.	No. 245 Freight.	No. 239 Freight.	No. 237 Passenger and Mail.	No. 235 Passenger.	No. 233 Passenger and Mail.	DIST. FROM GOLDEN	STATIONS	DIST. FROM CENTRAL AND GEORGETOWN	No. 234 Passenger and Mail.	No. 236 Passenger.	No. 238 Passenger and Mail.	No. 240 Passenger.	No. 246 Freight.	No. 248 Freight.	No. 250 Freight.
2 40pm.lv	6 35am.lv	7 45am.lv	3 30pm.lv	9 35am.lv	9 25pm.lv	9 30am.lv		Golden	24.1	5 05pm.ar	10 05am.ar	5 00pm.ar	10 10am.ar	4 10pm.ar	12 30pm.ar	8 30pm.ar
3 00	6 55	8 07	3 48	9 50 ar 9 55 lv	3 43	9 45 lv 9 50 lv	3.1	Chimney Gulch 3.1	21.0	4 52	9 50 lv 9 45 ar	4 47	9 55 lv 9 50 lv	3 48 lv 3 43 lv	12 10	8 10
3 22	7 15	8 25	4 06	10 07	4 00	10 02	6.2	Guy Gulch 1.4	17.9	4 40	9 33	4 35	9 38	3 22	11 53	7 53
3 30	7 25	8 35	4 15	10 15	4 10	10 10	7.6	Beaver Brook 1.1	16.5	4 30	9 25	4 25	9 30	3 12	11 43	7 43
3 37	7 32	8 48	4 20 ar 4 25 lv	10 20	4 15 lv 4 20 lv	10 15	8.7	Elk Creek 3.4	15.4	4 25 lv 4 20 ar	9 20	4 20 lv 4 15 ar	9 25	3 05	11 35	7 35
3 58 ar 4 03 lv	7 53	9 05 lv 9 10 lv	4 45	10 35	4 40	10 30	12.1	Big Hill 0.9	12.0	4 03	9 05	3 58	9 10	2 47	11 13 pm	7 13
4 10	8 00	9 20am.ar	4 55	10 46	4 50pm.ar	10 35am.ar	13.0	Forks Creek 2.1	11.1	3 55 pm.lv	9 00 am.lv	3 50	9 05	2 40 pm.lv	11 05	7 05
4 30	8 20		5 10	10 50			15.1	Cottonwood 2.6	9.0			3 40	8 55		10 50	6 45
4 50	8 40		5 25	11 10			17.7	Smith Hill 2.7	6.4			3 25	8 40		10 30	6 25
5 15pm.ar	9 05am.ar		5 45	11 28			20.4	Black Hawk 3.7	3.7			3 10	8 20		10 00 am.lv	6 00pm.lv
			6 15pm.ar	11 55am.ar			24.1	Central City				2 40pm.lv	7 50 am.lv			

			9 20am.lv		4 55pm.lv	10 40am.lv	13.0	Forks Creek 3.4	21.2			3 55pm.lv	9 00 am.ar		2 40pm.ar	
			9 45		5 15	10 55	16.4	Floyd Hill 5.3	17.8			3 40	8 42		2 22	
			10 20		5 40	11 20	21.7	Idaho Springs 1.9	12.5			3 20	8 20		1 50	
			10 32		5 55	11 30	23.6	Fall River 3.1	10.6			3 10	8 10		1 35	
			10 50		6 18	11 45	26.7	Dumont 1.8	7.5			2 55	7 55		1 12	
			11 03		6 35	11 58	28.5	Lawson 1.5	5.7			2 45	7 42		1 02	
			11 15		6 33	12 02	30.0	Empire 4.2	4.2			2 37	7 35		12 50	
			11 40am.ar		6 55pm.ar	12 20pm.ar	34.2	Georgetown				2 20 pm.lv	7 15 am.lv		12 25 pm.lv	

WESTWARD. / G. S. L. & P. R'Y. / EASTWARD.

No. 255 Mixed.	DIST. FROM BOULDER	NARROW GAUGE. STATIONS	DIST. FROM PENN. GULCH	No. 256 Mixed.
9 30am.lv		Boulder	13.0	3 50pm ar
9 55	3.0	Oredel 3.0	10.0	3 25
10 20	6.0	Crisman 2.6	7.0	3 00
10 40	8.6	Sugar Loaf 4.4	4.4	2 40
11 15am.ar	13.0	Penn. Gulch		2 05pm.lv

J. BLAIR, Train Dispatcher.   A. A. EGBERT, Gen'l Sup't.   S. H. H. CLARK, Gen'l Manager.

P. TOUHY, Div. Sup't.   THOS. L. KIMBALL, Asst. Gen'l Manager.

TRAINS 229, 230, 231, 232, 235, 236, 239, 240, 243, 244, 245, 246, 247, 248, 249, 250, 251, 252, 253 and 254, RUN DAILY EXCEPT SUNDAY.   OTHER TRAINS DAILY.

NOTE IMPORTANT CHANGES IN RULES AND NUMBERS OF TRAINS.

Special Rule No. 1.—Full Face Figures indicate Meeting and Passing points.

Special Rule No. 2.—Freight Trains, when behind time, will not exceed their card time except by special order.

Special Rule No. 3.—Study Rules Well, and Know that you Understand them.

Special Rule No. 4.—The standard time for this division is Denver time, which is 35 minutes slower than Omaha time.

Special Rule No. 5.—Narrow Gauge Freight Trains will not carry passengers, or employes with passes, without special order.

Special Rule No. 6.—Train No. 255, when late, will run to Penn. Gulch regardless of Train 256.

Special Rule No. 7.—Trains No. 231 and 232 will not carry passengers.

TIMES PRINTING CO., DENVER.

satisfactory piece of mechanism, is largely used. Superintendent Egbert favors the best in everything."

Inasmuch as the Denver Pacific would serve as the connecting line for all the Colorado traffic flowing north, there was no further need for the once strategic Hazard extension; consequently that part of the extension north of Ft. Collins was subsequently abandoned.

Truly as stated in the Union Pacific's Annual Report for the year 1879, the consolidation disposed of "many questions of a vexatious and disturbing nature . . .". Not the least of these was the problem of the tangled railroad situation in northern Colorado. Gould had temporarily cleaned the slate with a single sweep. Hereafter local interests, thus far manipulated to serve their own ends, were to be subordinated to the interests of the combined Union Pacific, Kansas Pacific, Denver Pacific and Colorado Central lines in Colorado—the powerful "northern Colorado pool".

The traffic contract and agreement that had been in existence between the Colorado Central and the Union Pacific changed into a lease. Accordingly, in November, 1879, the Union Pacific leased the Colorado Central Railroad for a period of 50 years; and until the organization of the Union Pacific Denver & Gulf Railway Company in 1890, operated it as a part of the Union Pacific system.

Shortly after this lease was signed, Loveland, who had been retained as the head of the Central, was displaced and forced out of the great railroad system of which he had been the life and soul from its conception in early territorial times, by those who were most indebted to his energy and ability. But in the lexicon of Jay Gould and his associates, such considerations had no place. With the exception of his interest in the building of a line of railroad over Loveland Pass to Leadville, William A. H. Loveland did not participate in any further extensive railroad construction. He made his exit with very little to show after 20 years of tireless effort in behalf of the system of roads he had planned in pioneer times; only a part of the great system he had in view was ever constructed. Mr. Loveland had purchased The Rocky Mountain News in 1878, and his subsequent acquisition of other interests in Denver, including the Denver Circle Railroad, a local suburban steam line, identified him with that city during the remainder of his life, which terminated December 17, 1894.

When one reads of the many troubles and difficulties this man encountered in his effort to carry out his life's ambition of seeing the Colorado Central railroad built as he had planned it, and of his sincere effort to do something for his home town of Golden, a feeling of sympathy goes out for him. However, in those days, it was a "dog-eat-dog" policy, and although it was a cruel and merciless method of doing business, it boiled down to a case of survival of the fittest.

After Wm. A. H. Loveland was ousted from the

Colorado Central, S. H. H. Clark, a Union Pacific Director, was elected president of the road, and from that time until 1890 the management of the Colorado Central was vested in various Union Pacific officials. Clark held the position of president during the years 1881 and 1882. He, in turn, was followed by Sidney Dillon, who headed the Central during 1883 and 1884, and from then until 1890, Charles Francis Adams, Jr., the president of the Union Pacific, was also president of the Colorado Central.

During this period the Central was wholly owned and operated by the Union Pacific and was officially known as the Colorado Central Branch of the Union Pacific Railway. The road continued to operate under the name of The Colorado Central Railroad Company, thus retaining its original identity, until April 1, 1890, when, with other railroad companies, it entered into Articles of Consolidation and Agreement and formed the Union Pacific Denver & Gulf Railway Company, as hereafter will appear.

Chronological inventory of narrow gauge Colorado Central mileage on April 1, 1890:

	Miles
DENVER TO GOLDEN. Three-rail. Completed December 4, 1879	15.60

The original standard gauge line between Golden and Jersey Junction, a distance of 14.97 miles, was completed September 24, 1870.

GOLDEN TO FORKS CREEK. Completed September 1, 1872	13.11
FORKS CREEK TO BLACK HAWK. Completed December 17, 1872	7.24

This includes the later extension of the line to the site of the new depot in upper Black Hawk.

FORKS CREEK TO FLOYD HILL. Completed March 1, 1873	3.29
GOLDEN TO CHURCH'S BRICK YARD. Completed in 1877	1.70

This was originally a part of the old three-rail line to Ralston on the Longmont Branch.

FLOYD HILL TO GEORGETOWN. Completed August 14, 1877	17.63
EXTENSION of line in upper Black Hawk to mill in north end of canon in 1878	.51
BLACK HAWK TO CENTRAL CITY. Completed May 31, 1878	3.91
GEORGETOWN TO GRAYMONT. Completed April 1, 1884	8.47

This was the Georgetown Breckenridge & Leadville Ry.

MILES	71.46

CHAPTER XII

DESCRIPTION OF THE CLEAR CREEK LINE

There were few stretches of track in America that contained as many interesting railroad construction problems from an engineering standpoint as were found in the 70-odd miles of narrow gauge line between Denver, Graymont and Central City. The main line had a track distance of approximately 58 miles between Denver and Graymont, overcoming an elevation of 4,585 feet by the time it reached the latter point. This was an average grade of 79 feet per mile, which was the equivalent of a continuous grade of 1.49% or better. From Denver to Central City, the track overcame an elevation of 3,341 feet. The Loveland road followed many tortuous paths to reach its destinations. Beyond Golden the road consisted of a continuous succession of curves as it twisted its way along the banks of Clear Creek, which flows through a great, contracted, water-worn chasm. The right of way was literally chiseled out of the granite walls of the canon, and the blasted and fallen rock that tumbled down into Clear Creek turned the stream and threw its current into a thousand cataracts and eddies.

In order to convey to the reader some idea of the many sharp curves and steep grades encountered on the Denver-Graymont line, the following figures have been compiled. The air-line distance between these two points is approximately 44 miles, while the rail distance was 58 miles. Within this 58 miles the track negotiated twenty-five 20 degree curves, eighteen 24 degree curves, ten 26 degree curves, four 30 degree curves, two 32 degree curves, and one 33 degree curve. This last, and sharpest "bend" was located between Floyd Hill and Idaho Springs just beyond M.P. 35. In addition to all these curves, there were thirty-two of from 21 to 29 degrees each. Among some of the steeper grades encountered, there were 39 sections of track with a 3% grade or over, with a high of 4.20% found at two locations; one between M.P. 23 and 24 near Elk Creek, and the second just beyond M.P. 50 where the track approached the Georgetown Loop. As a matter of fact, a greater percentage of these steep grades were found beyond Georgetown.

Between Denver and Graymont there were innumerable small bridges of less than 10 feet in length; however, there were 93 bridges and trestles varying in length all the way from 10 feet to 480 feet. The tracks crossed Clear Creek 18 times between these two points over bridges from 51 feet in length to the great 300-foot loop bridge. These 18 crossings also included a 296-foot trestle 4½ miles west of Denver, a 102-foot span west of Chimney Rock, a 101-foot span between Beaver Brook and Elk Creek, and four 100-foot spans between Forks Creek and Floyd Hill. Additional larger spans, other than the ones over Clear Creek, included a 480-foot trestle over the Platte River within the City of Denver, followed by a 220-foot trestle located one-half mile farther on, a 98-foot trestle over Ralston Creek, a 64-foot trestle over Empire Creek near Empire station, and a 54-foot bridge over South Clear Creek at Georgetown. With the exception of the Georgetown Loop Bridge, practically all of the above bridges were variously described as "Howe Truss", "Pony Howe Truss", and "Beam Truss" structures with stone abutments, and varied in height from 10 to 35 feet above the water.

Obviously, the most interesting of all bridges on this line was the famous Georgetown Loop Bridge. By rail, this bridge was 2 miles west of Georgetown and 51.83 miles west of Denver.

For an interesting early-day description of a trip taken over the Colorado Central's lines up the canon, and a brief description of the communities and mining settlements enroute, we shall quote the following article from a very early Colorado railroad guide published in 1881, known as "Crofutt's Grip-Sack Guide of Colorado".

"There are two passenger trains daily, operating on the narrow gauge division of the Colorado Central Railroad, between Denver and the mountain cities up Clear Creek canon. When first built, that part of the line between Denver and Golden was standard gauge, but in 1879 a third rail was laid between the two points, thus it can be said that the narrow gauge division starts in Denver.

"After purchasing our transportation, we climb aboard and take a seat in the elegant observation car that is run on all trains during the summer tourist season. It is not long before we hear the shrill whistle of the locomotive, and our train pulls out from the new and commodious Depot that the railroad has just finished building, and we are off on an adventuresome journey. Our first stop is at a place called Argo. This is a comparatively new town, having only been founded in 1878, as the new site for The Boston & Colorado Smelting Works after the concern decided to leave Black Hawk and locate near Denver. The smelter employs about 200 men, and the furnaces are going night and day, reducing the ore to gold and silver

*J. B. Sturtevant photo,
from M. R. Parsons Collection.*

Colorado Central engine 59 and train at the Crisman depot, on the Boulder Canon branch of the Union Pacific.

*J. B. Sturtevant photo,
from M. R. Parsons Collection.*

Denver South Park & Pacific engine 160 on bridge at Sunset, Colorado, on the Boulder Canon branch of the Union Pacific.

bricks. After leaving Argo, our train turns to the left and far ahead of us can be seen the snowy peaks of the mountains. After crossing Ralston Creek, we pass through the little settlement of Arvada. This place was known in earlier days as Ralston Point or Ralston Station. The rising foothills of the mountains are coming into view now and soon we reach Golden.

"Golden is a very pretty little town; it is located on the south bank of Clear Creek, about 15 miles west of Denver in Jefferson county. The town was named after Thomas Golden, an early pioneer in this particular locality. The site was first settled in 1858-59 due to a small amount of mining activity; however, with the exception of some coal mining in the immediate vicinity, the mining industry was of short duration. At one time Golden was the Capitol of the Colorado Territory, but soon lost out in favor of Denver. The place is now noted for its extensive manufacturing business, the chief products of which are fire-brick, tile and pottery, due to the close proximity of some fine clay deposits.

"The shops and general offices of the Colorado Central Railroad are located here. The railroad also builds most of its freight cars here.

"At Golden the train is divided into two sections, one goes to Central City and the other to Georgetown; however, they run over the same track until they reach the Forks of Clear Creek, 13 miles from Golden.

"The Georgetown train is the first to leave. While waiting for the train to leave, there is much speculation on the part of the passengers as to just what point we would take to enter into the mountains, and the possibility of getting over and around them; they looked like impenetrable barriers. All were eager, and all eyes were on the alert.

" 'All-aboard' was heard and in the throng we noticed a little old man, who, from his appearance, was evidently an Irishman just over from the 'auld sod'. He had no idea the direction the train would go, and when it gently started directly for the high mountains, he thought surely something was wrong. He wanted to know if the 'guard' knew which way the thing is heading. Presently, the 200 pound conductor came along and assured him that 'the thing' was going all right and that the train would easily get over the mountains. The little old man quieted down, but we could easily see by his flashing eyes what he thought of that conductor. Entering the mouth of the canon, we follow the creek in its tortuous course—in places far above—and then on a level with its banks, beside perpendicular cliffs and beneath overhanging walls a thousand feet or more in height. Some of these perpendicular walls are so close to the track and car windows that they can almost be touched by hand from the car windows. The whole scene changes with every revolution of the wheels, and to be sure that we do not miss any of the grand views, one must keep alert and watchful at all times.

"Chimney Gulch is passed in three miles and Guy Gulch in another three. Between these two gulches are many old placer claims, but little has been done on them since the early sixties when this was a busy camp. Two miles further we come to Beaver Brook, the first stopping place since leaving Golden. At Beaver Brook, a small stream comes in on the left down a narrow canon, up which six miles distant is located a saw mill in a perfect forest of timber. Near the station, away up on the projecting point of the mountain, 300 feet above the track, and almost overhanging it, is located a pavillion with a stairway leading to it from near the platform below. The spot is a great place for picnic parties in the summer time, and the railroad runs special excursions out to this point.

"The scenery at this point is magnificent; the mountains are fully one thousand feet high above the track on either hand, and covered in places with a dense growth of young pine and spruce trees, presenting an appearance as wild, picturesque and romantic as any one could wish for. Many interesting rock formations are given such names as Hanging Rock, Mother Grundy and Inspiration Point.

"Leaving Beaver Brook, the railroad makes a very sharp curve to the right, up a grade of 272 feet to the mile, under a projecting spur of the mountain which rises 1,500 feet above the train, while the creek which is close, but far below, is thundering along down its rocky bed.

"The little old Irishman on the train who had said nothing up to reaching this point, but had scanned the route with an eager eye, now exclaimed 'The mon that picked out this route must have been a perfect devil wid wings'. When told it was Mr. Loveland, President of the Colorado Central Railroad, who selected the route, he declared, 'He was a bold chap—no bit of a fool'. To the last proposition, all the passengers agreed.

"Elk Creek, a side track for passing trains, is reached one mile above Beaver Brook, and we continue climbing up, between towering mountain cliffs, in places clothed with evergreen pines, cedar and spruce trees, with shrubs of various kinds until we reach a point 3 miles above Elk Creek, where the walls on the west side of the Creek slope away, and our train rolls past a place called Big Hill.

"Here the old Mt. Vernon wagon road comes down the mountain from the left, the grade of which, in places, is 34 feet to the 100 feet. (34%). This road leaves the valley from about 2 miles south of Golden City, and after climbing the mountains via Mt. Vernon canon, to an altitude of 8,000 feet, descends this 'hill', and runs up the north branch of Clear Creek to Black Hawk. Most of the stamp mill and mining machinery used in these mountains in the early days, before the railroad, was hauled over this old wagon road; and where the grades were the steepest, the wagons were eased down by ropes secured by a turn or two around the trunk of a huge pine tree, and at this time, the marks of the ropes are still to be seen on the stumps where they have peeled the bark, so taut were the lines. We know—of our own personal knowledge—where it took ten men, besides their teams, nine days to lower down this hill, one steam boiler which weighed a little over seven tons. Those who grumble at railroad charges, please take notice; the wagon road is still there.

"Forks Creek, one mile further on, is the junction of the North and South Clear Creek. Here the route for Georgetown turns to the left, across the bridge, while that for Black Hawk and Central City keeps to the right. We shall keep to the right and proceed up the canon to Black Hawk which is seven miles up the north fork. From Forks Creek to Black Hawk and from Floyd Hill to Georgetown (on the south fork) nearly every foot of the creek bed has been gone over, and dug over time and time again, by miners in search of the elusive gold. Dams, in many places, have turned the waters of the creek through flumes, first on one side of the creek bed and then on the other, and the greater portion of the earth and sand, from surface to bed-rock, and from one side of the gulch to the other, have been dug and washed over by white men, and when given up by them have been jumped by the Chinese Companies. Many of these Chinese can be seen daily, washing and working these old placer diggings over again.

"Cottonwood, which is just a passing track, is two miles up the creek from the Forks, and the same below Smith Hill. Just at this station comes in the old wagon road built in 1862; it is a branch of the old Golden Gate wagon road which is built over the famous 'Guy Hill', one of the most notorious mining camps in this part of the mountains.

"Nearly opposite this station, comes down Russell Gulch up which are located the old placer mines that were so famous around 1859.

"Proceeding onward and upward, about one mile above Cottonwood, we pass on the left the old Excelsior and Whipple

A Colorado & Southern excursion train, headed by engine 7, rounds Inspiration Point, 23 miles from Denver, in Clear Creek Canon about 1900.

L. C. McClure.

Mills, now abandoned except as a shelter for a few Chinese miners who work along the creek. As we ride along, we pass several quartz mills; across the creek to the west bank, and along the road on the right, is the site and ruins of the first reduction works of the Boston & Colorado Co., whose present works, as previously stated, are located at Argo.

"By looking away up on the mountain side on the left, westward, can be seen the railroad track where it runs along on a switch-back, first to the south, then back to the north, gaining altitude all the while, in order to overcome the heavy grade and allow our train to reach Central City. Three miles above Smith Hill is located Black Hawk.

"As we come into Black Hawk the train passes through a great stone building which the railroad uses as a depot. It was an old abandoned mill and when the railroad reached Black Hawk they just cut out large holes in each end of the big building and appropriated it as their depot. The railroad track runs right on through, in at one end and out the other.

"Black Hawk, a city of about 2,000 population, practically all of whom are engaged in the mining business, is located in Gilpin county. The town derived its name from an early mining concern, Lee, Judd & Lee. The story is recorded that, in 1860, this group of men brought some mining machinery into these mountains and established themselves at the upper end of the gulch where the town is now located. One of their quartz mills had, as a trade-mark, the name of the famous Indian Chief 'Black Hawk', so they decided to give the settlement this name. Black Hawk, seven miles up the north branch of Clear Creek from Forks Creek, is sandwiched in between gulches, ravines, rocks and projecting mountain crags in a most peculiar and irregular manner. Gold in paying quantities was discovered in the immediate vicinity by John H. Gregory on May 6th, 1859, and is the principal mining industry in this locality.

"Our next and last place to visit on this particular branch of the railroad will be Central City located at the end of the line up on the mountain west of Black Hawk. The difference in altitude between the two towns is something like 470 feet, and in order to negotiate such an excessively steep grade, the railroad had to build a double switchback. After pulling out from the depot in Black Hawk, our train chugs its way on up the canon through the town for about one-half mile. The wagon road between the two towns can be seen on our left, as it winds its way up Gregory Gulch west through old Mountain City, and past several quartz mills. The distance by wagon road is a little over one mile, while by railroad it is about four miles. Near the Eagle Mill our train comes to a halt, while one of the crew throws the switch for the first switch back. While traveling up the first switch back, we will be riding backwards. Leaving the bottom of the canon, the track runs up the left, or south side of the gulch among the numerous mills and open mouths of mining tunnels. Reaching Bates Hill, our little train quickly twists around a sharp curve and gradually crawls out over Selak and Gregory Streets on a long trestle. We now find ourselves high above Black Hawk's busy streets, busy mills, and busy mines. From the amount of smoke and cinders being sent skyward, we know our little engine is working hard as we continue to climb steadily up the steep grade along the sides of the mountain. Twisting in and around numerous sharp curves, we cross over two immense dry gulches and are afforded an excellent open view, for the moment, of the surrounding mountain sides, and of Clear Creek canon stretched out far below and the railroad up which we came to reach Black Hawk. One gives a slight sigh of relief as we reach the end of some trestle and start through a cut in some protruding shoulder of the mountain side.

"Soon we reach the end of the first switch back, one of the crew throws the switch and once again we start rolling, engine first, as is natural. We cross the famous Gregory, Briggs, and Bob Tail Mines, now producing over $50,000 per month in gold. In passing these and many other busy mining properties, we slowly wind our way around numerous sharp curves, climbing steadily while crossing Bob Tail and Packard Gulches. Clinging to the side of Mammoth Hill overlooking the entire gulch, we soon get our first view of Central City and the snowy peaks far beyond. Shortly after going around one of the sharpest curves on the entire line, as is plainly evident from the familiar screeching of the car wheels, our train pulls up to the little Central City Depot."

Continuing from Crofutt's Guide, we read his description of Central City.

"Central City was one of the earliest mining camps established in this territory. The name of the settlement was suggested by Wm. N. Byers, Editor of The Rocky Mountain News at that time. During the Civil War period the camp reached its peak in population—10,000—as the mines were gradually worked out the population declined until the town only boasted of about 2,500 people in the early '70's. The mining camp known as Mountain City, which was located between Black Hawk and Central City, was absorbed by the latter. Central City is the county seat of Gilpin county, and at one time was surrounded by many small villages, camps and diggings, some of which numbered five or six hundred persons. The first man legally hung in Colorado was hung in Central City in January, 1864. The altitude of the city is about 470 feet higher than Black Hawk. The city is the commercial center of Gilpin county, one of the oldest and perhaps best developed mining sections in Colorado. The veins are all true fissures, and there are many shafts down to a depth of 700 to 1,200 feet. Practically the whole population is more or less engaged in the mining business, purchasing the greater portion of their daily needs at Central City. The town is the terminus of the north fork branch of the Colorado Central and is about 39 miles west of Denver.

"We will now return to Forks Creek and take the Georgetown train. Upon leaving Forks Creek, our train crosses the bridge over Clear Creek and follows up the South branch towards Floyd Hill. Soon after this, our train arrives at a narrow gorge and a sharp curve in the track, where a huge spur of the mountain projects out within 200 feet of its tall brother on the opposite side of the creek; and as the train passes under this overhanging cliff, we enter one of the grandest natural amphitheatres of the world. The mountain rises over 2,000 feet above the stream which is here compressed to a rapid torrent thundering at its very base. The space between the mountain cliffs is just sufficient for the creek and the railroad tracks; in others, the road bed had to be blasted out from the mountain side. The scenery for the next two miles is unusually impressive. In places small pine and cedar trees can be seen in the gorges and crevices, which add additional beauty to the scene.

"About three miles above the junction, the track curves to the right, opposite the base of Floyd Hill, down which comes the old Floyd Hill wagon road from Bergen's township to the southeast, and follows up the west bank crossing the creek at Floyd Hill Station. From this point up to Georgetown, about 18 miles, the creek shows many evidences of 'placer mining'. As we proceed, the creek bottom widens out and the mountains are not quite so high. Several old deserted mills and the remains of old placer diggings along the creek bed are to be seen. Five miles more brings us to Idaho Springs, known in the early days as Spanish Bar. It was here, near where Chicago Creek flows into Clear Creek, that George Jackson, in January, 1859, discovered the first gold lode in this region. The elevation at this point is 7,541 feet above sea-level. Idaho Springs is noted for its hot and cold mineral springs, and has become quite a summer resort. The average population of the town is about 1,300. Leaving Idaho Springs and continuing on up the north side of the creek, we come to Trail Creek which comes in from the southwest; up this creek are located some good quartz mines and extensive forests of timber. Here is located the Freeland Mills, while nearby are the famous Freeland and Hukill Lodes.

"Fall River is two miles above Idaho Springs. Here comes in from the north a small creek known as Fall River, about 8 miles in length, along which are located hundreds of quartz claims and several mills.

"Above Fall River about one-half mile, Turkey Run comes down from the south, where are located the Stevens mining properties and the Stevens Mill. A little further on we come to Spring Gulch; up the gulch are located numerous mills and valuable mines. Dumont, once known as Mill City, is four miles above Fall River, at the mouth of Mill Creek, which comes in from the north. Up this creek are located several valuable mines and mills. As our train passes by the mouths of these various gulches and canons, many extensive mining improvements, including some placer mining, are to be observed, and all of these many mines and mills are furnishing considerable traffic for the railroad. Two miles above Dumont we come to Lawson located at the base of Red Elephant Mountain. Nearby are located many valuable quartz mines; the opening or 'dump' of many of these mines can be seen away up near the top of the mountain, marked by a white deposit line extending down towards the valley below.

"Empire, the station for Empire City (originally known as Valley City), is about one and one-half miles above Lawson. It is impossible to get a view of Empire City, as the town is located a little over a mile to the westward, up the West Fork of Clear Creek.

"The road over the range to Middle Park, via Berthoud Pass, runs through Empire, and is one of the most beautiful mountain roads for variety of ever-changing panoramic views to be had in the world, of which more hereafter. After crossing the West Fork, our course is almost due south, running along the base of Douglas Mountain, which rises above the road almost perpendicular, 1,100 feet, while on the east Saxon Mountain raises its crest over 3,000 feet above the level of Clear Creek. On the sides of these mountains can be seen shafts, tunnels, and prospect holes in great numbers.

"A little farther on the Union Pass wagon road can be seen away up the side of the mountain to the right. This road is built through a depression between Douglas and Democrat Mountains, and is bordered on both sides with tremendous precipices affording an excellent view, from the summit, of the valleys of Clear Creek and Bard Creek with Georgetown and Empire in plain sight. Soon we are approaching the base of Republican Mountain where Georgetown is located. This is the end-of-track. Beyond Georgetown are located a number of small towns and mining camps, chief of which are Silver Plume, Brownville, Silverdale, and Graymont.

"At this time the tracks of the Colorado Central have not been extended beyond Georgetown so we will stay in this busy little city for awhile and enjoy some of the beautiful mountain scenery which surrounds the town. Georgetown, first known as Elizabeth Town, is approximately 50 miles west of Denver. The town has a population of 3,210 and is the County Seat of Clear Creek County. The altitude here is 8,476 feet (railroad depot) above sea-level. The city is located at the base of the Snowy Range, and is the center of one of the oldest and richest silver mining regions in the state. The first silver discovered in Colorado was found about eight miles above Georgetown by James Huff on September 14th, 1864. The town is also noted as quite a summer and winter resort".

With the conclusion of this narrative from "Crofutt's Guide" we will take leave of Colorado Central history. We shall pick it up again when the Clear Creek road becomes a part of the Union Pacific Denver & Gulf consolidation in April, 1890.

Dow Helmers Collection.

Denver South Park & Pacific 141, a Dawson & Bailey locomotive, built in 1879, stands in front of the superintendent's office at Como in the late 1880's.

PART III

HISTORY OF THE
DENVER GEORGETOWN & UTAH RAILWAY COMPANY

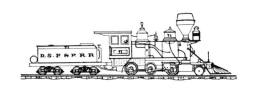

One of the Colorado Central Moguls stands on the high bridge of the Georgetown Loop in 1884.

CHAPTER I

BACKGROUND AND ORGANIZATION

Before taking up the history proper of THE DENVER SOUTH PARK & PACIFIC RAILROAD, we must first take up the history of a railroad that not only exerted considerable influence on Denver's railroad history at this time, but also one that figured most prominently in the organization of the Denver South Park & Pacific, namely: THE DENVER GEORGETOWN & UTAH RAILWAY COMPANY. In the struggle for supremacy in which the region's principal early railroad promoters sought to gain control of that coveted prize— the Colorado mountain trade together with control of the channels over which this valuable commerce would flow—the Denver Georgetown & Utah, like Gould's Georgetown Leadville & San Juan, became one of Colorado's famous paper railroads.

During the brief interval just after the completion of both the Denver Pacific and the Kansas Pacific, Governor Evans decided to take a much deserved vacation and rest. Accordingly, in 1871, he took his family and sailed for Europe. Upon his return late that year, the Governor found the Colorado railroad situation in a very unsettled condition. The years 1872 and 1873 were, as we have mentioned, times of great turmoil between rival railroads, rival railroad projects, and rival railroad builders in the Denver region. It will be necessary to review briefly this tangled railroad situation in the territory in order to find the explanation for the existence of the Denver Georgetown & Utah—the story of a railroad that was never built.

Central City has already been pointed out as the capital of the gold producing region of Colorado, but the silver mining region had its own capital—Georgetown. Of course, this is not to say that each region produced one metal only, but these two metals were the predominating ores found in the respective territories. Between the two capitals a considerable degree of rivalry had developed, based largely on their respective positions in the two great branches of the mining industry.

The railroad question tended to accentuate this rivalry. Both centers needed the railroad for the development of their mines; without railroads neither region would have been able to continue the profitable working of the mines upon which they had to depend for their prosperity. As a matter of fact, they regarded the question of transportation as a panacea for all their economic problems. The natural inlets to the mountainous regions around Central City and Georgetown were so located that when a railroad was constructed to tap the mining centers, it would have to choose between building its line first to Central City and in due season to Georgetown, or *vice versa*. That is, the only practical route into the mining interior was up Clear Creek to its forks and thence up its north fork to Central City and the gold region, and up the south fork to Georgetown and the silver region. Thus, both regions vied with each other to secure the first railroad connections with the markets on the plains.

How the Colorado Central, the railroad which had secured control of the Clear Creek route, had decided the issue as to its prime destination has already been related in the history of that road. Central City was selected and Georgetown was left to await the construction of a Colorado Central branch in such season as might be pleasing to the railroad company. To make matters worse, the Colorado Central had such a record of dilatory tactics, and was so seriously embarrassed because of a chronic lack of funds, except when aided by the Union Pacific, that Georgetown could hardly hope for action from the Central, even when it had completed its line a short distance up the south branch beyond Forks Creek to Floyd Hill.

But Georgetown's efforts to secure a railroad from some source other than the Colorado Central dated back to a point considerably before that road had made its choice of destination. The fact that the two highest officials of the Colorado Central, Loveland and Teller, had come from Golden and Central City, respectively, had, to a certain extent, caused Georgetown to turn toward Denver for railroad assistance.

This early affinity of interests between Georgetown and Denver goes back a number of years to the time when Gov. John Evans and his Denver associates were first dickering with the Union Pacific in 1868 regarding the construction of the Denver Pacific. One of the agreements between Denver and the Union Pacific officials was that a branch road should be organized to build west from Denver to the mining regions in the mountains. Accordingly, the Denver & Georgetown Railroad & Telegraph Company was duly organized.

Colorado & Southern 70 approaching the station at Golden on January 1, 1941.

Colorado & Southern 8 with a regular passenger train in Clear Creek Canon.

The Articles of Incorporation of this road were dated January 7, 1868, and filed with the Secretary of the Territory of Colorado on February 25, 1868. The incorporators were as follows: Wm. F. Johnson, John W. Smith, Joseph E. Bates, Wm. M. Clayton, F. M. Case, and David H. Moffat, Jr. The articles stated that the object of the company was:

". . . to locate, construct, operate, and maintain a railroad and telegraph line from the City of Denver in Arapahoe County by the most feasible route to Idaho (Idaho Springs), and thence up Clear Creek Valley to Georgetown, in Clear Creek County, with a Branch from the most feasible point on said route to Black Hawk, Central City, and Nevada, in Gilpin County, Colorado Territory."

The company was capitalized for $2,000,000 consisting of 20,000 shares at $100 each. The Trustees of the road were as follows: Wm. F. Johnson, John W. Smith, Joseph E. Bates, Wm. M. Clayton, F. M. Case, David H. Moffat, Jr., and John Pierce. The principal office of the railroad was to be in Denver and business was to be carried on in Denver, Georgetown, and Central City.

The omission of Central City (the other important mining center of the region) from the title was rectified later on that year when the road was reorganized as the Denver Central & Georgetown Railway Company. The Articles of Incorporation of this second road were dated and filed with the Secretary of the Territory on November 25, 1868. The incorporation papers give the following information:

Incorporators: John Evans, John W. Smith, John Pierce, Wm. M. Clayton, David H. Moffat, Jr., and Bela M. Hughes.

Object:

". . . to construct, maintain, and operate a railroad from Denver City in Arapahoe County by the most feasible route to Idaho Springs, and thence up Clear Creek Valley to Georgetown, in Clear Creek County, with a Branch from the most feasible point on said route to Black Hawk, Central City and Nevada, in Gilpin County, Colorado Territory."

Capital: $2,000,000, consisting of 20,000 shares at $100 each. Trustees were as follows: John Evans, John Pierce, John W. Smith, Wm. M. Clayton, David H. Moffat, Jr., Bela M. Hughes, Jerome B. Chaffee, John T. Nunck, and Joseph M. Marshall.

Principal office was to be in Denver, and business was to be carried on in Denver, Georgetown, and Central City.

The records further reveal that this road was again reorganized as the Denver Central & Georgetown Railroad Company on March 5, 1870, with the following changes noted: The capital had been reduced from $2,000,000 to $500,000. The name of John Evans appeared in the original papers as one of the incorporators and trustees, but had been ruled out. The object of the company was not altered. With the exception of Evans' name, the incorporators were the same. Concerning the new trustees, Evans, Hughes and Nunck were replaced by Charles Burleigh, Joseph W. Watson and H. A. Gray.

The Denver & Georgetown Railroad & Telegraph Company was one of John Evans' earliest railroad schemes, and although it was overshadowed by the more important necessity of getting the Denver Pacific built, he did see to it that surveys of routes to Georgetown and Central City were initiated by the road. When the railroad's surveyors were locating a line south of Golden 500 to 600 feet above the bed of Clear Creek, the Colorado Transcript (issue of May 18, 1870) called the projectors "Crazy" but wished them "God-speed" anyway—it was Denver's money that was being thrown away. In a letter written by Evans to Henry M. Teller under date of October 2, 1872, we read the following:

". . . a careful survey of the route has been made 'at large expense' by that line."

There were even some negotiations in 1870 between Loveland and Evans toward having their two railroad companies join hands in the prosecution of the work, but nothing ever materialized.

With the completion of the Denver Pacific, the Denver-Kansas Pacific crowd began to lay plans for lines into the mountain mining regions, a movement which culminated in the Georgetown railroad convention held in Golden in April, 1871. It need only be recalled at this point that the convention placed John Evans in the position he wished, that of agent for securing a railroad for Georgetown. The way in which he attempted to utilize this commission in the promotion and protection of Denver's commercial and railroad interests forms an interesting chapter in the railroad history of the territory, but before it can be told a slight deviation must be made in order to make subsequent events meaningful.

Denver, at the outset of the railroad period, enjoyed a predominant role in the territory's economic system as its distribution center. In fact, that was to all intents and purposes the justification for Denver's very existence; and its future prosperity would depend on whether it would be able to continue to hold that trade hegemony. Since the early railroad development had continued Denver as the focal center around which the economic life of the territory revolved, there seemed to be but little question as to the city's future. That is, there would have been little question but for two disturbing factors: first, there was the possibility of the Union Pacific's proposal to tap Colorado by means of the Colorado Central's Julesburg extension and thus build up a rival trade center; and second, was the seemingly harmless factor of a railroad gauge that revolved around Loveland's proposed narrow gauge line west of Golden into the mountains.

All three of the first roads built in Colorado were standard gauge, but when the Colorado Central built up Clear Creek toward the mining regions, it adopted the narrow gauge for its line from Golden into the mountains. This change of gauge at Golden necessitated a break of bulk at that point. Such transfer meant an advantage to Golden, but did no harm to Denver as long as it remained the through billing point for mountain bound freight. That is, the Kansas Pacific gave through rates to shipments from points on its line to Denver; freight destined for the mountains would then be consigned to Denver wholesalers and reshipped by them over the Colorado Central, at the local rates of that road. As long as this method continued to be the practice, no harm would be occasioned Denver wholesale business by the necessity of a second transhipment at the break of gauges in Golden. The only parties to suffer would be the consumers who would have to pay higher rates as a result of the double transfer.

However, if this practice should be changed, there was a real threat to Denver's wholesale business. The more economic process would be to do away with the first transhipment at Denver by through billing mountain freight to Golden, where the change in gauges made one transfer inevitable. Ordinarily, the inertia of business practices might continue the uneconomic double transfer; but if the pressure of competition, or of popular clamor, or of producers seeking a cheap market, should become too great, the unnecessary and purely customary transfer at Denver—in the interests only of Denver's mercantile houses—would have to give way. Something of this sort seems to have taken place, for the Colorado Miner of March 28, 1872, carried the following statement:

"We take pleasure in announcing that the Colorado Central has made arrangements with the Kansas Pacific to have all shipments of freight over the Kansas Pacific for Georgetown, Central City, and Golden billed through from Kansas City, thus avoiding transfer and delay at Denver."

In view of the supposedly close cooperation between the Denver interests and the Kansas Pacific, it seems strange that any such agreement as this might be made; however, as has been shown, these supposedly close ties never carried much weight when an opportunity to take advantage of the other party presented itself. This threatened agreement was not carried out and the double transfer of freight continued to exist for some years, but the potential threat to Denver's trade supremacy, contained in the matter of gauges, had materialized.

As a result, something of the following faced John Evans as he prepared to carry out the plans of the Georgetown railroad convention to provide that town with a railroad.

Fear of the Union Pacific's next move was a serious threat to Denver's monopoly of the double transfer racket. Although the Union Pacific had failed, in the fall of 1871, to gain control of the Denver Pacific—the existing link between their main line and the Colorado Central—it was still possible that control of the Denver road might slip out of the hands of the Kansas Pacific into those of the rival Union Pacific; or, in the event of the failure of this move, the Union Pacific would proceed with the construction of the Julesburg branch. If the former move materialized, the Kansas Pacific would be between the hammer and the anvil; and if the latter came to pass, then Denver would occupy the unenviable position. But this was not all; to add fuel to the fire, there was the constant wrangling and quarreling between the Union Pacific and the Kansas Pacific over the division of business and the matter of rates, and as previously stated, these relations were going from bad to worse.

As matters now stood, the trio (Denver, the Denver Pacific, and the Kansas Pacific) faced serious consequences if something was not done to relieve the situation. Denver feared the narrow gauge Clear Creek Canon line, the Denver Pacific feared the Union Pacific might gain control of it or else build into Colorado, and the Kansas Pacific saw starvation ahead if something was not done to bring about an equal division of traffic with the Union Pacific on a satisfactory rate basis.

It was a most unhappy situation for John Evans, for he was interested in all three—Denver, the Denver Pacific, and the Kansas Pacific—and the security of any one of the three would have to be gained at the expense of the other two. Finally, the dilemma was solved by sacrificing the Denver Pacific to the Kansas Pacific, leaving Denver entirely dependent upon the latter road.

Therefore, to enable the trio to be in a better position to meet their adversaries, John Evans resigned the presidency of the Denver Pacific early in March, 1872, an office he had been elected to in January, 1870, and was succeeded by General Robert E. Carr, who was also president of the Kansas Pacific. This move gave Carr absolute control of the route from Kansas City through to Cheyenne and made the Kansas Pacific one route in fact, although the Denver Pacific remained nominally a separate corporation.

The next step was to organize a railroad company to build a line directly west from Denver to be operated in connection with the Kansas Pacific road. Accordingly, John Evans and his associates reorganized the Denver Central & Georgetown Railroad Company as THE DENVER GEORGETOWN & UTAH RAILWAY COMPANY. It was announced that the purpose of the road was to secure for the Kansas Pacific a friendly and independent outlet from Denver, west across the mountains, to connect with the Central Pacific and the Pacific Coast trade. Just how true this statement was, is not known. The road might possibly have been designed as a threat to force the Union Pacific to prorate with the Kansas Pacific or to force the Colorado Central to lay the third rail, or both. Further discussion of this subject will be taken up later on.

The articles of incorporation of the Denver Georgetown & Utah Railway Company were dated March 9, 1872, and filed with the Secretary of the Territory of Colorado on the same day. The papers were signed by the following: Bela M. Hughes, Walter S. Cheesman, Horace A. Gray, Wm. M. Clayton, John Evans, and John D. Perry. The trustees for the first year of its existence were: Robert E. Carr, John Evans, John Hughes, John D. Perry, David H. Moffat, Jr., Joseph E. Bates, Thomas A. Scott, Alfred Sayer, and Wm. H. Clark. The road was capitalized for $5,000,000. For further information relative to the object of the company, its officers, etc., we will quote directly from the Rocky Mountain News of Sunday, March 10, 1872.

"The railroad conferences of the past week have resulted in decided action on the part of railroad men in the section. Only yesterday, the Denver Georgetown & Utah Railway Company filed its articles of incorporation in the office of the Secretary of the Territory. The objects of the company, as set forth in the second section of the articles, are as follows:

" 'That the object of the said company is to locate, construct, operate, and maintain a narrow gauge railway with branches and telegraph lines along the same, which are hereafter named and described, and to acquire, improve, and dispose of lands and mines, or any interest therein, in whole or in part, either absolutely or on condition, for the purpose of aiding in any manner in the construction and maintenance of said railway, its branches and telegraph lines, which are named and the routes thereof that are described as follows, viz:

" 'Commencing at Denver, Colorado Territory, thence in a southwesterly direction in Arapahoe County, thence in a westerly direction by the way of Bear Creek canon and Mt. Vernon canon in Jefferson County, Idaho Springs, and Georgetown in Clear Creek County, to the west boundary line of said Territory; thence to a railroad connection in Utah Territory that shall secure the best practicable trans-continental line from the Atlantic to the Pacific ocean, with a branch road from the line by the most convenient and practicable route to Black Hawk,

Central City, or Nevada in Gilpin County, with branches or spurs from the line of said railway to the mines adjacent or in the vicinity of said railway and branch above described. The line of said railway and branch above described to be constructed and operated through and across the counties of Arapahoe, Jefferson, Clear Creek, Gilpin and Summit.'[1]

"A meeting of the incorporators of the above company was held in this city, in the old rooms of the Denver Pacific Railway Company, in the First National Bank block, yesterday afternoon at 1 o'clock. The meeting was called to order and John D. Perry, esq., assumed the chair upon request of the members present. This gentleman explained the objects of the meeting. Governor Evans drew up and presented temporary by-laws providing for the election of officers, etc. On motion the election by ballot of permanent officers was then had, resulting as follows: Robert E. Carr, president; John D. Perry, vice president; R. R. McCormick, secretary; and David H. Moffat, Jr., treasurer, Governor John Evans acting as advisor and in charge of promoting the enterprise.

"John D. Perry, esq., was then commissioned by the company to act as a committee, with full powers to confer with and arrange terms with the citizens of Clear Creek county, for the railway from Denver to Georgetown, and the voting of $200,000 of bonds of Clear Creek county. After sundry other preliminaries of organization, etc., a deputation was decided upon to proceed to Georgetown forthwith to conclude arrangements and accomplish the objects of the company in carrying their intentions to a successful termination."

1. In addition to these projected lines enumerated by the Rocky Mountain News, McMechen, in his "Life of Governor Evans" states: "A branch was to go by way of South Park and Buena Vista to the Anthracite fields of Gunnison County". NOTE: It is the writer's thought that McMechen, in referring to Buena Vista as an intermediate point enroute to Gunnison County, probably meant "the mouth of Trout Creek", inasmuch as Buena Vista (originally known as Cotton Wood) was not organized until November, 1879. (May, 1940, Colorado Magazine.)

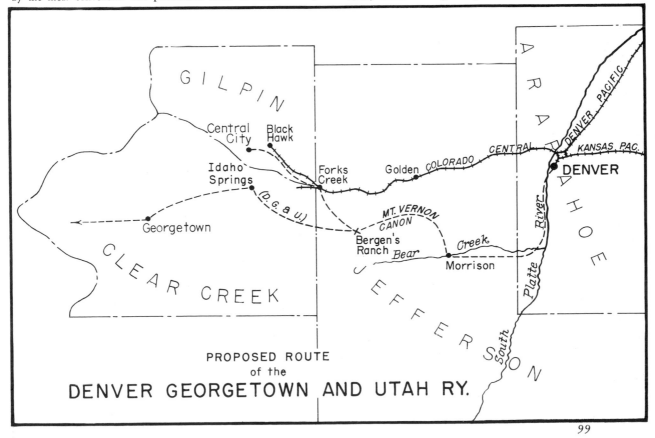

PROPOSED ROUTE
of the
DENVER GEORGETOWN AND UTAH RY.

99

E. J. Haley.

Multiple flash photo of the interior of Alpine Tunnel. This photo, taken August 21, 1944, shows the remarkable preservation of the redwood timbering west of the apex.

CHAPTER II

FRICTION AND FINANCE

Mere incorporation itself was not enough to prove serious intentions. Accordingly, Georgetown and Clear Creek County were asked to vote a bond issue of $200,000 to aid in the construction of the Denver Georgetown & Utah Railroad. No trouble was experienced in getting this request granted, for the citizens of both Georgetown and Clear Creek County had more or less lost faith in the many promises, and apparent slowness, on the part of the Colorado Central toward building a railroad to Georgetown. The county commissioners acceded to the request and the date of the election was set for April 15, 1872.

Under the terms of the contract between the county and the railroad, the bonds were to be issued to the company only when:

". . . the cars are running on said railway over the Colorado Central Railroad, from Denver to Georgetown, by the first of December next (December 1, 1872), or in case a favorable arrangement cannot be made with said Colorado Central Railroad for running cars over said railroad, then as soon as the cars run from Denver to Georgetown over the Denver Georgetown & Utah Railway, all the way from Denver on a line that shall pass either down the valley of Clear Creek or over the so-called 'high line route' south of said Clear Creek, to Denver aforesaid, within *eighteen months* (October 15, 1873) from the time said bonds shall be voted."

Another clause attached to the bond issue stated that any road constructed with the aid of said bonds must be of uniform gauge all the way between Denver and Georgetown, or be denied the use of said bonds. An additional clause stated that the Clear Creek bond issue for the D. G. & U. could be used only in building in Clear Creek County.

The proposition carried both the big stick and an olive branch. In essence the proposition simply meant that the Colorado Central would be given the opportunity to offer the Denver Georgetown & Utah trackage rights upon its Mountain Division; but if it refused to make such an offer, the Denver group threatened to go ahead and build their own line to Georgetown in competition with the Colorado Central.

John Evans had again succeeded in placing the Colorado Central behind the proverbial eight-ball; it was an embarrassing situation for Loveland and Teller. Naturally, the Central had no enthusiasm for the former alternative, and since its relations with the Union Pacific at that particular time were rather unsettled, it could offer little opposition if the Denver Georgetown & Utah made good its threat and actually built the line. Certainly the Colorado Central was not in a financial position to put a quietus upon Georgetown's demands for a railroad by actually building the line itself. As far as the Colorado Central was concerned, John Evans' neat little scheme could hardly have come at a more inopportune moment.

Nevertheless, the Colorado Central decided to fight the bond issue. It submitted its own proposition which Teller claimed as "similar in terms to the one the company had intended to make at an early date", thereby doing his best to imply that the Central had planned to take that course regardless of the pressure applied by the Denver group. But the proposition was not put up to the voters as a direct choice. Instead, it was so phrased as to make it applicable only if the Denver Georgetown & Utah proposition was rejected. More accurately: if the Denver Georgetown & Utah proposition was defeated, an election was to be called immediately to consider a proposition the Colorado Central would then make. Undoubtedly, this procedure was adopted in an effort to defeat the rival proposition and stall for time.

The pressure campaign got under way immediately. Teller secured the usual telegram from high Union Pacific officials guaranteeing the building of the road to Georgetown if the county voted aid to the Colorado Central.

Many arguments, both pro and con, were brought out regarding the two propositions. As usual in most Colorado railroad elections, this particular election was contested vigorously and probably none too cleanly with the usual amount of tangle-leg whiskey disappearing. However, April 15th soon rolled around and when the final votes were counted, it was found that the Denver Georgetown & Utah proposition had carried by quite a sizeable margin.

But the auspicious beginning went no further than that. For some reason, in spite of a provision in the bond issue that work should begin immediately upon the voting of the bonds, no actual construction work was started. Georgetown was irked by the turn of events and charged Denver with bad faith. The Colorado Miner, a mountain newspaper, was asking "Gentlemen —when shall ground be broken in Clear Creek County?"

Denver passed the blame on to its Kansas Pacific associates who, they explained, were not providing the necessary funds to begin the work.

All this very agreeably played into the hands of the Colorado Central. The Denver victory in the recent Georgetown election had released the Central from building the road at a time when they did not have the means to build, and the Denver failure to follow up gave them an opportunity to reopen the matter at their own good leisure. Furthermore, Georgetown resentment against Denver now assured the Central of a ready welcome whenever they wished. The balance of strategic power had now definitely reverted to the Colorado Central. John Evans lost this round.

At this point Governor Evans changed his policy somewhat, from the idea of getting a line built to Georgetown, to that of securing the third rail. This new policy was embodied in a letter from Evans to Teller dated September 11, 1872, in which he strongly urged the Colorado Central to lay the third rail and complete their narrow gauge line on west. He offered the franchise and all rights of the Denver Georgetown & Utah along with Denver's help and cooperation in completing a railroad of uniform gauge through to the Georgetown territory. Although this was a tacit admission on Evans' part of his failure to break up the Colorado Central's monopoly of the mountain trade, he was due credit for his efforts in attempting to promote Denver's commercial interests.

Mr. Teller replied on September 26th following, notifying Evans in a most positive manner that the Colorado Central would refuse to entertain any sort of a proposition that tended toward the construction of a uniform gauge road with through cars between Denver and the mountain towns; neither would they lay any third rail between Denver and Golden. Continuing, he added that Georgetown was without a railroad simply because of the Denver crowd's machinations; and that at the time the Denver Georgetown & Utah first entered the picture, the Colorado Central was preparing to build to Georgetown but that the provisions attached to the Georgetown bond issue prevented his road from carrying out its plans. (Teller failed to say *when* they were going to build, or what they were going to use for money.) Relative to Evans' proposal that his company would turn over to the Colorado Central rights and franchises if the former would build to Georgetown and lay the third rail, Teller remarked:

"Inasmuch as your company has failed to comply with the conditions of your proposition to commence work at once and as your company has been to no expense of any kind I do not see why you should make it a condition to the transfer of the rights and franchises of your company to the C. C. R. R. Co. that the company should run its cars from Denver to Georgetown.

"I am not able to see that your company has any rights, privileges, or franchises of any value whatever to the C. C. R. R. Co. . . ."

102

Teller's letter, although astutely worded, was open to an unfavorable interpretation. Evans maneuvered accordingly. Replying under date of October 2nd, Evans wrote:

"And especially do I regret the announcement of the main reason assigned for the rejection of the proposition which as I understand your letter, is that you object to allowing the cars to run through to Denver on your line . . .

"This will compel a break of bulk and changes of cars at or near Golden City which will be a serious obstruction to the public business. (This) is a matter of sufficient importance to the people to entitle them to ask it (i.e., the laying of the third rail) in consideration of the surrender of the whole matter into your hands."

His closing paragraph was a warning:

"A railroad from Denver to Georgetown and Central City that will run through without a change of cars is imperatively demanded by the exigencies of the case. And since your company declines a fair and equitable proposition to meet the wants of the people of both Denver and the mountains they must rely upon their own efforts and the aid they may obtain elsewhere to protect and conserve their interests."

This shot would, of course, have been more to the point had not the Denver Georgetown & Utah already been so embarrassed by a lack of funds as to make its threat lack significance.

Teller returned the compliment on October 10th following, in a letter containing little new except the statement:

"The peculiar location of the Colorado Central Railroad Company occupying as it does, the only feasible route for a railroad from mining regions of Clear Creek and Gilpin Counties to the plains is a guarantee of a large profitable business. With the extension of its branches in the South Park from Idaho Springs and from Central City and Caribou there will be (undecipherable)—(author's note: probably "carried") on this line the transportation of the mineral wealth of Colorado . . ."

Taken in conjunction with his statement in his letter of September 26th that the Colorado Central planned to place a proposition for bond aid before the voters of Clear Creek County as soon as the Denver Georgetown & Utah encumbrance was removed, this could only mean that the company planned to force the issue on the Georgetown front. Once again threats and wrangling between John Evans and the Central failed to secure for Denver the third rail or the railroad for Georgetown.

But John Evans was not through yet. He carried his fight for the third rail to the Colorado Central's superior, the Union Pacific. Apparently, that company merely turned the matter over to Teller for handling, consequently, there was cold comfort to be expected from that angle. He also moved for action through the Denver Board of Trade, inquiring in their behalf, in a letter to Teller under date of October 19th, on what basis the Colorado Central *would* lay the third rail. Teller replied that his company would be glad to lay the third rail if Denver saw fit to pay for it. On this basis, Evans suggested that the Denver Board of Trade sponsor a campaign for a county bond vote of $50,000 to bring an end to this troublesome matter. But, according to the Rocky Mountain News of November the 6th, although the suggestion was approved by the Board, no further action was ever taken on the matter. Just why this idea, after being approved by the Board, was sidetracked, is not known—it would be interesting to know the real facts.

The correspondence just mentioned had apparently convinced John Evans at last that he could not expect the Colorado Central to give his company trackage rights over its line into the mountains, and therefore it would be necessary for the Denver Georgetown & Utah to secure funds to build its own line.

It will be remembered that one of the stipulations attached to the Georgetown issue was that their bonds could be used only for construction of that part of the Denver Georgetown & Utah which was to be located in Clear Creek County. Also, due to the Kansas Pacific's failure to come forth with any financial assistance in the construction of the road, Evans and his associates realized that it was up to Denver to raise the money necessary to carry out their part of the project. Accordingly, it was proposed that Arapahoe County vote a $200,000 bond issue to aid in the construction of the eastern end of the Denver Georgetown & Utah. The date for the election was set for November the 11th. The Denver press furnished the necessary publicity and the campaign got under way immediately.

It was the same old story over again; the story of John Evans and Denver arrayed against their old enemies, Loveland and Teller and the Golden group. The campaign was pushed vigorously and the Denver citizens were well posted as to just what faced them and their city if the issue failed to pass. There are meager reports that Teller visited Denver during the campaign in the latter part of September and made a speech urging defeat of the bond issue; however, it is not definitely known just what the theme of his talk was.

In order that the reader might have an exceptionally clear picture of the situation in Denver at this time, we will quote one of Wm. N. Byers' famous editorials as published in his Rocky Mountain News on October 19, 1872.

"LET DENVER NOT BE DECEIVED.

"Divested of all side issues and stripped of other matters, the question before our people is simply this: Shall Denver remain the commercial center and the point of distribution for the trade of Colorado? Clearly and undeniably this is the real proposition involved in the ratification or rejection of Georgetown bonds. Let Denver not be deceived in this matter. It is the old fight she has so often fought. We must win again, or lose all we have gained in the past. Reviewing the history of the Colorado Central management, from its inception to the present time, it has been one determined and continuous effort to run the trade of Gilpin and Clear Creek counties around Denver, and build up a rival railway center. It was to protect herself against this policy that the condition was put into the $200,000 bonds voted to the Colorado Central in

1867, that their line should be located on the east side of the Platte; on account of which condition the bonds were refused. The Denver Pacific was located upon this line which public opinion dictated as the most conducive to our interests, and was consequently opposed by the Colorado Central managers. When Governor Evans, General Pierce, and others of Denver's representatives appeared before the Union Pacific directory, at various times, to complete the negotiations which were afterwards violated by that company, they found Teller and Loveland and Carter, their most active opponents. These men were there, in Boston and New York, fighting Denver's representatives and Denver's interests; and that the Union Pacific at a later day violated its pledges, and failed to perform its written contracts, was most probably due in no small measure to the false representations and malign influence of these gentlemen. The Denver Pacific was built, however; and then the Colorado Central started to find some eastern connection other than at Denver; building, in 1870, seventeen miles of railroad to go twelve, and finally being compelled to pay $6,000 a year to the Denver Pacific to get into Denver. Five miles of additional road to construct, to operate, and to maintain, with $6,000 a year for trackage rights is the price now being paid by the Colorado Central Company for their efforts to run around Denver. Later it became necessary for the Union Pacific to project the Julesburg extension in order to obtain a chance at our trade, and to pay the penalty for having violated their contracts of 1868, leaving Denver to shift for itself.

"In the negotiations which ensued between the Union Pacific and Colorado representatives in the directory of the Colorado Central, it was expressly stipulated that the Julesburg line should not come to Denver, but be run direct to Golden; Teller, Loveland and other of Denver's opponents making this the ultimatum, viz.: the construction of a line by which the trade of Gilpin and Clear Creek counties can avoid Denver.

"This is the history of a management which Mr. Teller asserts is not hostile to Denver and does not propose to build up any rival interest to Denver. When the Golden-Julesburg line is completed, this mountain trade *can* pass to the north of us and avoid Denver. Knowing this, and confident of the inability of our city to avert the blow that has been levelled at our prosperity, Mr. Teller, on the 26th of September, in the most positive manner, refused to lay a 'third rail' between Denver and Golden, or to accept any proposition which required a uniform gauge and through cars between Denver and the mountain towns. The Georgetown 'Pool' was made, and then came Mr. Teller, with a tumble never equalled by a circus performer, and a bow worthy of a French dancing master, and offered the 'third rail', no discrimination, etc., mingled with assurances of distinguished consideration, and a friendly regard for our interests. If Mr. Teller and his Colorado Central associates were not hostile to Denver, and actuated by no intense hatred of her prosperity, why did they compel the agreement for the Julesburg line to run to Golden and not Denver? If they had always been desirous of friendly relations with Denver, why did they not accept the propositions made them on September 11th, and refused on the 26th? It is now within the power of these men to run the traffic of the mines around our city—who does not believe they intend to use it? The whole history of their management is a guarantee that they will. There is but one way in which Denver can again make itself master of the situation, and that is by building the Denver Georgetown & Utah road. The Colorado Central managers know this fact, and hence their extreme readiness to comply with anything we may ask at the present. Mark the fact however, they still have it in their power to run their business around our city,[1] which point they do not propose to yield; and it is just this point that Denver is now called upon to dispute or concede. We re-

1. Reference is made here to the Golden City & South Platte by way of Golden, Morrison and the Rio Grande which the Loveland group were promoting at this time.

gain our mastery of the situation, and retain our position of railway eminence by building the Georgetown line; we place ourselves in the hands of our enemies by failing to do so. Therefore—let no one be deceived. Let not the real matter at issue be covered by fair words and deceptive promises. We never have had anything from this management but what we have forced from it; we never can expect anything but what we compel it to grant. Shall the Colorado Central remain in the power of Denver, or shall Denver put herself in the power of the Colorado Central. This is the question to decide. The NEWS proposes that Denver retain all she has, and points to the building of the Denver Georgetown & Utah road as the only safe and sure method of so doing."

Finally November the 11th rolled around and it was time for the citizens of Arapahoe County to have their say. The campaign had not been as exciting as the usual Colorado railroad bond election. The Denver Georgetown & Utah bond issue carried, but the small vote (686 to 105), in the words of the Rocky Mountain News showed a "disgraceful apathy". Mock summarizes the situation by writing that "possibly Denver was becoming just a trifle bored with all the railroad hocuspocus of its railroad capitalists".

The only other attempt to raise money in behalf of the Georgetown line, other than the Clear Creek and Arapahoe County bond issues, was during the Colorado Central's campaign for the Clear Creek bond vote. The Colorado Miner, Nov. 21, 1872, and the Denver Daily Times, Jan. 24, 1873, reported that Governor Evans appeared in Georgetown during the above campaign apparently to push private subscriptions to the stock of the Denver Georgetown & Utah. According to these papers, Governor Evans was offering the following inducement to any investors: for each $1,000 of cash subscribed, the subscriber was to receive $1,000 in first mortgage bonds of the road, $444.44 of county bonds, $555.56 in income bonds of the road, and $2,000 in the stock of the road—a grand total of $4,000! The results of his visit to Georgetown are not known.

At this point, the story shifts back to the Colorado Central. The Central, as promised by Teller in his correspondence with Evans relative to the third rail, had offered to complete the building of their railroad to Georgetown in fifteen months, if Clear Creek County would vote bond aid of $200,000. The Georgetown and Clear Creek citizens apparently were interested in the Central's proposition and accepted their offer, with the result that the campaign for the bond issue got under way at once. The date for the election was set for November 27, 1872. This time with public opinion

in back of the Colorado Central, the Denver group was the opposition party and as usual, a lively time was had by all. There are reasons to believe that the Denver group exercised a bit of strategy by setting the date for the Arapahoe election on November the 11th. Thus, the Denver vote took place some two weeks before the vote in Georgetown on the Colorado Central proposition and certainly, possibly intentionally, confused the issue. The Clear Creek County voters were not certain that their county would not still be legally held for the $200,000 it had already voted the Denver project in the preceeding April. The Colorado Central attempted to parry this propoganda by recording an agreement under the terms of which it would not demand delivery of the county bonds (if they were voted) should the courts rule the county liable for the Denver Georgetown & Utah bonds. With this assurance, the proposition for bond aid to the Colorado Central carried in Clear Creek County by a small margin of 39 votes.

At this point in the history of the Denver Georgetown & Utah, it becomes necessary to stop and take into account the extent of its influence on the Colorado Central organization.

As the summer and fall of 1872 drew on, the Colorado Central officials could not help but note a certain amount of progress which the Denver interests were gradually making with their Georgetown project. First —there was the Clear Creek County bond issue that had been voted them. The next item to command their attention was the fact that all the surveys between Denver and Georgetown, via the "high line route" were completed. Next was the proposal that Arapahoe County vote a bond issue in favor of the Georgetown road, the results of which have already been told. Thus, it began to appear that the Denver interests were serious regarding their proposed construction of the Denver Georgetown & Utah.

Loveland and Teller were well aware of the gradual progress of the Georgetown project and were not standing idly by doing nothing about it. To some extent, the Denver Georgetown & Utah was partially fulfilling its mission in life. This is reflected in the Colorado Central's and Union Pacific's increased activity in the Clear Creek Canon that fall. Although the Denver Georgetown & Utah was not wholly responsible for the completion of the Colorado Central between Golden and Black Hawk by December of that year, it was apparent that its influence was strongly present.

CHAPTER III

FADE OUT OF THE DENVER GEORGETOWN & UTAH

Although the Denver Georgetown & Utah had made a certain amount of progress, the situation was not as rosy as it appeared on the surface. As the summer and fall of 1872 drew on, the situation in the Denver region was gradually developing to a point where any hopes of success for the Georgetown project were slowly fading. In lieu of all this, we began to form the opinion that John Evans was becoming just a bit tired and weary of the continual wrangling and fruitless attempts to gain any satisfaction from the Colorado Central interests. Added to this was the disappointment brought about by the miserable failure on the part of the Kansas Pacific to furnish their portion of financial assistance in carrying out the original plans of the Denver Georgetown & Utah project. With the Black Hawk extension near completion, it began to appear that the Central was partially serious in their halfhearted promises and threats to eventually push their line through to Georgetown. With these facts in mind, it can be clearly understood why Evans was becoming discouraged with the progress of the third rail plans and the Georgetown project; and yet, they could not be cast off like so much chaff—too much effort had been expended in the road's behalf.

In short, John Evans was slowly coming to the conclusion that sooner or later he might possibly be forced to look to other fields in which he might continue his railroad activities; while at the same time continue to carry on with the Denver Georgetown & Utah in the hope of saving it, and if not, utilizing what he could of the project in order that past efforts might not be wasted altogether.

The new field of operations which had begun to draw the interest and attention of John Evans was the great South Park country, located southwest of the Denver region. He was aware of the future possibilities in this territory and believed that a railroad built into that region could be developed into a successful and profitable venture, and at the same time greatly aid in the promotion of Denver's commercial trade.

Consequently, as the future of the Denver Georgetown & Utah grew less hopeful, this idea of a new railroad in a new territory grew more and more significant in the mind of John Evans. Eventually, he came to a final decision—his new railroad would build into the

South Park country and its name would be THE DENVER SOUTH PARK & PACIFIC RAILWAY COMPANY. The exact date on which he made this eventful decision is not known, but after considerable study and taking all things concerned into consideration, it must have been sometime during June or July of 1872. As this new railroad project of John Evans was, to a certain degree, the successor or offspring of the Denver Georgetown & Utah; his plans would tie into that road's organization very nicely. The reader will remember that the Articles of Association of the Georgetown road contained the statement that the object of said company is to locate, and construct . . . a narrow gauge railway with BRANCHES and telegraph lines along the same. In line with this same thought McMechen states: "A branch of the Denver Georgetown & Utah was to go by way of the South Park and Buena Vista to the anthracite fields of Gunnison County". Therefore, Evans' *first* plans for his new road were to follow the proposed route of the Denver Georgetown & Utah west to the vicinity of Georgetown, and thence south into the South Park country.

Inasmuch as the Denver South Park & Pacific, now in its embryo stage and not yet fully organized, was to be backed by practically the same interests as was the Denver Georgetown & Utah, it becomes necessary that we take up the relationship that existed between these two roads.

According to numerous declarations, the purpose of the Denver Georgetown & Utah was to secure for the Kansas Pacific an independent and friendly outlet from Denver to the west and to the Central Pacific and the Pacific Coast. Rocky Mountain News, March 10, 1872; Railroad Gazette, March 23, 1872; and McMechen, all state that this was the original intention of the company. This attempt would have been entirely in line with the previous desires of the Kansas Pacific Company to secure its own line to the coast, independent of the Union Pacific, but whether they ever seriously contemplated the project is open to doubt. Probably it was merely designed as a threat to force the Union Pacific to prorate.

On the other hand, there can be little question that the immediate objectives were entirely local. In fact, this threat to build a Denver-Kansas Pacific road into the mountains was itself the big stick whereby Evans hoped to force the Colorado Central both into providing Georgetown with the railroad he had promised them and into furnishing Denver with the narrow gauge third rail between that city and Golden. In fact, Teller insisted in a letter to Evans on September 26, 1872, that the Denver Georgetown & Utah had been organized in order to force the laying of the third rail and to embarrass the efforts of the Colorado Central in the prosecution of their mountain objectives. When one considers the topography of the mountainous area along the proposed route of the D. G. & U. between Denver and Georgetown, it can readily be observed that the construction of any railroad through this section, especially the western end, would incur a tremendous expense. It is truly admitted that the Colorado Central possessed the only practical route into this mountainous region, and that was the canon of Clear Creek.

Therefore, from the meager information available, it cannot be definitely stated that the Denver and Kansas Pacific interests fully intended to build the Georgetown road. From all intents and purposes this *was* the original intention, but circumstances and subsequent events lead one to wonder.

Whatever the motives (original or later) of the Denver Georgetown & Utah, either as a western outlet for the Kansas Pacific; as a threat to force the Union Pacific to prorate with the Kansas Pacific; or as a threat to force the Colorado Central to lay the third rail, it was gradually becoming apparent to Evans and his associates that from all indications the Georgetown road's chances for success were growing less and less. As previously explained, this situation brought about the preliminary organization of the Denver South Park & Pacific Railway Company, which furnishes the grounds for strongly suspecting that the Denver group had other motives in mind beyond the mere building of the Denver Georgetown & Utah when the details of that road's Arapahoe County bond issue were first drawn up. Shortly after this, at the height of the agitation over the third rail and a line to Georgetown, John Evans brought forth and publicly announced in the Rocky Mountain News under date of October 2, 1872, the organization of the Denver South Park & Pacific Railway Company.

As evidence of the close relationship between these two roads, we find the following notice as published in the Rocky Mountain News under date of November 7, 1872, four days before the election. It was a special election notice which read as follows:

". . . one-half of said bonds ($100,000) to be delivered to The Denver Georgetown & Utah Railway Company as soon as the road-bed is graded from Denver to Georgetown, or from the point of its junction with The Denver South Park & Pacific Railway Company to Georgetown . . . and the other one-half to be delivered as soon as cars shall run all the way from Denver to Georgetown."

Further evidence of this close relationship between the two roads appeared in the same newspaper the following day, November 8, 1872. This notice read as follows:

"The Denver Georgetown & Utah will operate their trains into Denver over the track of the Denver South Park & Pacific, from their junction, at or near Bear Creek canon. The road will also use the depot facilities of the South Park line in Denver. The two enterprises are, therefore, closely identified, and will be controlled each for the benefit of the other. While they will open up two leading mining districts centering their trade in Denver, these roads, or rather this road to Bear Creek canon will also be of great benefit to the stone and lime business of that section."

The results of the election on November the 11th, in which the Denver Georgetown & Utah bonds were voted, has already been told. In commenting on this election, Mock states: "It was with the understanding that the Arapahoe bond vote would aid, simultaneously, in the furthering of both lines that Denver had voted the $200,000 to the Denver Georgetown & Utah." Thus, it can be clearly understood how the Denver group was fostering the development of both new projects.

Inasmuch as all the necessary bond issues were now voted, and the preliminary surveys completed, further action was planned so as to get under way with the actual construction. In line with this, the following advertisement was placed in the Rocky Mountain News under date of January 1, 1873:

"TO CONTRACTORS—Sealed proposals will be received at the office of Governor John Evans until the 10th of January, 1873, for grading the first division of the Denver Georgetown & Utah Ry. between Denver and Bear Creek canon, also for furnishing 40,000 ties for same. Profiles and specifications can be seen at the engineer's office of the company at No. 6 Evans Block. F. M. Case, Chief Engineer."

From what can be learned, with one exception—the time the Santa Fe and the South Park railroad interests attempted to form an alliance in 1878 and proposed to extend the old high line to Georgetown—this was the last gasp of the Denver Georgetown & Utah.

In the meantime, the successful campaign on the part of John Evans and his associates in promoting the Denver bond issue had aroused the Colorado Central people to considerable activity in the Clear Creek Canon district and to a certain extent was responsible for that road being completed to Forks Creek by September and to Black Hawk by December of that year. The completion of the Colorado Central into the upper forks of Clear Creek that fall and winter of 1872, together with the fact that the Central's bond issue had been voted in Georgetown, had an exceptionally strong influence on the future plans of the Denver Georgetown & Utah. While it did not withdraw from the scene immediately, it did mark an important change in the road's plans.

The idea of building the road began to subside and within the next year or so plans for this independent

W. H. Jackson photo,
from the State Historical Society of Colorado.

Colorado Central engine 30 and Denver South Park & Pacific coach 9, specially outfitted as W. H. Jackson's photographic car, wait on the upper leg of the Black Hawk-Central City switchback while Jackson photographs the two levels of track just west of the upper switchback, which is hidden behind the hill sloping through the center of the picture. Crossing the trestle on the lower leg is Colorado Central engine 33, pushing a baggage car and Colorado Central coach 186 toward Black Hawk.

mountain enterprise were completely abandoned. In the meantime, Georgetown was drifting away from its Denver moorings, and since the route for the Denver South Park & Pacific road was now located on a line different from the one which the Georgetown line would take, and since the Colorado Central had apparently won out in the Georgetown field, Denver began plans to sever its connection with Georgetown.

On May 1, 1873, the Rocky Mountain News threatened Georgetown that unless it cooperated with Denver, Denver would take its $200,000 subscription to the Denver Georgetown & Utah and build a line elsewhere. On June the 14th following, the Denver Board of Trade advocated making good the threat, and two days later, June 16th, the Denver South Park & Pacific Railroad Company was duly incorporated. Shortly after this, the campaign for the promotion of the "South Park" road was taken up by the Denver press and Denver very suddenly lost its ardor for securing a railroad for its mountain friends at Georgetown. With its interests now focused elsewhere, Denver abandoned Georgetown to the tender mercies of the Colorado Central. Finally, five years later, with the financial assistance of the Union Pacific, the Colorado Central managed to build its tracks to Georgetown.

The Clear Creek bonds that were voted to the Denver Georgetown & Utah road were never issued, and the subsequent disposal of the $200,000 Arapahoe County bond issue will be taken up in the following portion of this book.

Although the idea of building the Denver Georgetown & Utah line remained in the minds of a few persons for some time, the road was never built. The articles of incorporation remained on the Secretary of State's books until September 3, 1913, at which time they were declared defunct and inoperative for failure to pay their license tax. The reason for this action being carried over so long a period is that all corporation laws of the State of Colorado were amended by the Legislature in 1911, thus automatically throwing out any defunct organizations.

As a sort of eulogy in behalf of the Denver Georgetown & Utah we might sum up its short-lived existence as follows: After the Kansas Pacific's failure to assist in its promotion, the project seemed to have developed to a point where it was nothing more than an organization which Evans had sincerely hoped might be utilized to force Loveland and Teller to complete their railroad to Georgetown and to lay the third rail between Denver and Golden. The project, to a certain extent, tended to hasten Colorado Central construction up Clear Creek, but as to forcing the laying of the third rail, the scheme failed in its mission. The Loveland interests refused to be coerced, and Denver went without its much coveted third rail until the latter part of 1879 when it was finally laid. When it was realized that the Georgetown project might possibly fail in its purpose and that no actual construction would ever materialize, Evans moved to salvage all efforts he had put into the road and organized a successor. This successor, the Denver South Park & Pacific, was organized to replace the Georgetown road to a certain extent but was projected in a different direction.

As a parting word in behalf of our old friend, the Kansas Pacific, we might add that in view of the failure of the Denver Georgetown & Utah and its subsequent reorganization as the Denver South Park & Pacific, together with the failure of the Union Pacific scheme to give it the Colorado Central, all augmented by the Panic of 1873, the road was permanently denied its coveted outlet from Denver, west across the mountains. In such a weakened condition, it soon became enmeshed in the hungry tentacles of Jay Gould, eventually winding up as a part of its powerful rival, the Union Pacific, in the consolidation that Gould maneuvered in January, 1880.

PART IV

HISTORY OF THE DENVER SOUTH PARK &
PACIFIC RAILROAD COMPANY

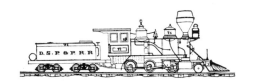

W. G. Chamberlain photo,
from Alex Rooney Collection.

Denver South Park & Pacific 1, the "Fairplay", leaves Morrison, Colorado enroute to Denver with the morning mixed train in the late 1870's.

CHAPTER I

EARLY HISTORY AND ORGANIZATION

The history of the "South Park", as the name is so familiarly known to everyone, is a story of one of the most colorful narrow gauge railroads in the state of Colorado. It is a frontier epic. Although the road was beset with financial difficulties at its inception and headed toward the rainbow's foot, as many believed, it was the supreme achievement of Governor John Evans' economic genius, reflecting his shrewdness, patience, tenacity, and brimming optimism. It paralleled, as nearly as an industry can parallel human experience, the progress of the fortunate prospector, who, living for a few years in a squalid shanty, half starved and wholly desperate, the next year stepped from his palatial home into an upholstered carriage, and grinned with simple pride as he glanced at the massive watch chain of gold nuggets that stretched across his ample paunch. Then, as often happens to individuals, misfortune overtakes him and he spends his declining years amid waning circumstances; soon his alloted time draws nigh and he is gone, but not forgotten—by his faithful friends.

The South Park was often spoken of, especially in the early days, as a mineral road. This was an appropriate title. The road was conceived and born along with Colorado's early day mining industry and, with the exception of certain other factors and influences, the decline of this mining industry brought about its end.

The old South Park is rapidly fading into that forgotten limbo of the past.

All the narrow gauge lines have been abandoned, sold, or converted to standard gauge. The road's memory is kept alive only in the minds of a few amateur railroad historians and some of the older employees who are still living. Mute evidences of its one-time existence disclose themselves in the scattered sections of the old right of way, usually covered with decaying cedar ties, which are to be found to this day here and there along some splashing mountain stream deep in a canon, or on a 10,000 foot high pass, or hanging perilously along some mountain side.

It was the largest narrow gauge railroad system wholly contained within the state. When the road was at the height of its glory and all divisions operating, the system consisted of some 335 miles of track, and its right of way passed through a country that possessed an assortment of scenery that had few equals within the confines of the state. Leaving Denver, the road plunged almost immediately into the famous Platte River Canon and thence across Kenosha Pass at an altitude of almost 10,000 feet. From this point, the track sprawled across the great South Park, from whence the road derived its famous name, entered the Arkansas River Valley through a gap in the mountains whence flowed Trout Creek, climbed up Chalk Creek Canon to find its way through the great Alpine Tunnel under the Continental Divide, from which it dropped down into Quartz Creek Valley and on into Gunnison, the western terminus of the road. At Como, a branch line turned back north, crossing the Continental Divide in the Park Range twice, at heights of over 11,000 feet, to find its way through the canons of Blue River and Tenmile Creek into Leadville.

But the clanking side rods, accompanied by the shrill whistle of the little engines wailing for a crossing, are heard no more. In its opulent years, two ornate narrow gauge Pullman trains travelled to and from the "diggings" every day, while millions of dollars in ore rumbled over the high passes and through the deep canons, destined for the smelters. All this is gone now; you can no longer ride behind a little 20-ton diamond stack in a stove-heated wooden coach and enjoy these magnificent scenes—so the next best thing to do is to read the written story of this railroad and look at a few reproductions of some highly prized photographs.

But to return to the inception of this new project. As previously stated, this new field of operations which had begun to draw the interest and attention of Gov. John Evans was the great South Park country located southwest of the Denver region.

From the time Denver's first railroad was completed from Cheyenne in June, 1870, plans began to be considered for railroad lines south and west of Denver into the mountain country. In February, 1868, Gov. A. C. Hunt had organized The Denver South Park & Rio Grande Railroad Co. and surveyed a route for this road from Denver to Santa Fe, via the Platte Canon, the South Park, Trout Creek Pass, Arkansas River, Poncha Pass, the Rio Grande, and on south.[1]

That same year, Dick Irwin, a noted prospector of the period, had penetrated the San Juan country and

1. Colorado Magazine, October, 1928.

brought back glowing reports of its mineral wealth, supported by samples of rich surface ore from the "Great San Juan Triangle" which is to this day a constant producer of gold, silver and other valuable ores.[1] From the very beginning of his administration in 1862, Gov. John Evans began a systematic study of the natural resources of Colorado, especially of the territory in the southwestern part of the state. From visiting scouts, hunters and trappers, he learned much of this southwestern territory. Friendly Ute Indian Chieftains had told him of the broad valleys and large streams in a country they had occupied for many generations.

The Governor had frequently ridden over the country southwest of Denver on horseback, exploring the territory from Bear Creek Canon to Kenosha Pass. During these journeys he noted the almost endless stands of fine virgin timber that stretched in every direction as far as the eye could see. This great expanse of timber filled nearly every canon and extended far up the mountain sides. He also noted the rich agricultural country up Bear Creek toward the little settlement that was soon to be known as Morrison. Also located here were some excellent stone quarries and valuable mineral springs. He was impressed by the broad fertile valley between the mouth of Bear Creek and the point where the Platte River flows out of the mountains. He was enthusiastic about the future of Geneva Gulch, which debouches into the Platte Canon at Grant, and believed the region to be highly mineralized. From Kenosha Pass, the north rim of the great South Park, John Evans looked out across one of the finest views in the west. Here, spread out below him in all its beauty, was the valley of the South Park, some fifty miles in length and ten to twenty miles in width. Gandy, in his "Life of H. A. W. Tabor", sums it up as follows: "To anyone who sees it for the first time on a spring morning, in all its pristine loveliness, South Park seems like an earthly paradise." The park is bordered on the east by the Tarryall Mountains and the west slopes of the Frontal Range, and on the west by the Park Range. In this latter range, and in plain view, are some of the highest mountain peaks in Colorado, among which are Mt. Democrat, Cameron, Lincoln, Bross, and others. The broad valley of the park itself is a very rich agricultural region. The view from Kenosha Pass is a vision that would stir any man's emotions and ambitions. It must be seen to be appreciated; no photograph can do it justice.

Far to the west end and to the right, in the Park Range, were the famous gold camps of Hamilton, Tarryall, Buckskin Joe, Horseshoe, and others. Production of placer gold, silver, and other valuable metals at these camps was no idle dream or hearsay. The U. S. Government official records on mining in Colorado report that from 1858 to 1872, inclusive, Park County had produced over $2,961,500 worth of these metals and Chaffee

1. Colorado Magazine, October, 1928.

County over $490,000 worth. Also, on the west slope of the Park Range, was the famous Leadville camp which had produced over $5,775,600 in precious metals within the same period. (The reader must remember, however, that Leadville's glorious rise to fame and fortune had not burst forth just yet, for her mines, which later poured out their millions in rich treasures, were still undiscovered.) In the far distance, across and beyond South Park, lay the famous San Juan country where mining activities were increasing rapidly.

As a result of these various trips through the Platte Canon and into adjacent regions, John Evans became well aware of the territory's future possibilities. It is no small wonder then that he firmly resolved that this was the territory in which to build his railroad. He sincerely believed that a railroad built into this part of Colorado could be developed into a successful and profitable venture, and that a systematic development of these regions with their large belts of timber, stone quarries, limestone ledges, gypsum beds, mineral and agricultural resources, would furnish ample traffic for his railroad, while at the same time it would tend greatly to strengthen and perpetuate the rise of Denver's commercial trade.

On the other hand, regardless of Evans' great faith in the South Park project, it was hard to convince people that it was possible to construct a railroad along a mountain canon in many parts of which a trail was impossible, and the possibility of a wagon road a myth. It was urged in opposition to the road, that for a great part of the route the mountains would have to be tunnelled at enormous expense, and where the track could be laid along the water line, the torrents that swept through the canon every spring would toss away the embankments like so much straw, and cause the entire receipts of the road to be absorbed in repairs. Other objectors claimed a great part of the route lay in sections where the snow was on the ground seven months of the year, and opinions as to the wealth in a country like this differed. Only a few insisted on the wealth of the mountains. Others argued that excessive grades were impractical and expensive beyond all computation. They contended that the treasury of any company that might undertake such a task would be subject to a constant drain to meet expenses.

As a result of these contentions, many were inclined to call the South Park project a wild dream; however, they were restrained by a wholesome respect for the abilities of John Evans and his associates. Evans' faith in himself and his belief in a successful future for the South Park regions, overcame these puny voices of the opposition. His decision had been made and he fully intended to see it through. The Denver South Park & Pacific would be built.

Before taking up the formal organization of the South Park railroad, let us deal briefly with the group of men who were associated with Governor Evans and his South Park enterprise. This group consisted of some of the leading business men of Denver, most of whom had been conspicuously instrumental in the building of the Denver Pacific. They were men of sound business judgment and broad vision who foresaw that the future of Denver depended upon the development of surrounding territory by rail communication and upon the construction of adequate public utilities and works. Among the leaders of this group, other than Governor Evans, were such men as David H. Moffat, Jr., a young banker who was destined to take an important part in the financial and railroad life of the territory; Bela M. Hughes, a prominent attorney and one of Colorado's greatest legal minds; and Jerome Chaffee, a political figure. Others included such prominent men as Henry Crow, Joseph E. Bates, Charles B. Kountze, Frederick A. Clark, Walter S. Cheesman, F. Z. Salomon, John Hughes, J. C. Reiff, and Leonard H. Eicholtz. Mr. Eicholtz was formerly a construction engineer for both the Denver Pacific and Kansas Pacific roads before he became associated with the South Park enterprises as that road's Chief Engineer.

The South Park road was organized in accordance with the general laws of the Territory of Colorado by Governor John Evans and his Denver associates, and was first known as "THE DENVER SOUTH PARK & PACIFIC RAILWAY COMPANY". It was John Evans' third railroad project and Colorado's sixth railroad to be built. As can plainly be seen, the name of the railroad was simply derived from its proposed termini and Colorado's mountain park, known as South Park, through which the road was to be built. It was from this park that the road received its well known nickname.

Attorney George A. Trout, of Denver, Colorado, has dug deep into the old records stored away in the archives of the office of the Secretary of the State of Colorado, for the following data relative to the first organization of the road and the various amendments attached to the road's Articles of Association. The early laws of Colorado provided that all Articles of Incorporation or Association, be prepared in duplicate, the original to be filed with the Secretary of the Territory and the duplicate copy with the Clerk and Recorder of the county in which the company had its principal office and place of business.

Accordingly, the records reveal that the Denver South Park & Pacific Railway Company's Articles of Association, which are dated September 30, 1872, were filed in the office of the Secretary of the Territory of Colorado on October 1, 1872, recorded in Book D, page 547, and are known as file number 732. They were also filed in the office of the Arapahoe County Clerk and recorded in Book 42, page 153. The following is an exact quotation from the Articles of Association, and

constitutes the first organization of The Denver South Park & Pacific Railway Co.

Articles of Association
of the
Denver South Park & Pacific Railway Company

The undersigned subscribers, Henry Crow, Bela M. Hughes, Joseph E. Bates, John Evans, Charles B. Kountze, David H. Moffat, Jr., Frederick A. Clark, F. Z. Salomon, and Walter S. Cheesman, do hereby agree and declare their intentions to create a company under the statutes of Colorado Territory for the purpose of constructing, owning, maintaining and operating a Narrow Gauge Rail Road and Telegraph Line from Denver in the County of Arapahoe in the Territory of Colorado, by the most feasible route thence to a point in the South Park in Park County in said Territory, such point to be determined by the Board of Trustees of said company after careful surveys are made, with extensions and branches of said Rail Road and Telegraph Line to be constructed, however, under new companies or organizations.

It is further declared that said company shall be called and designated as DENVER SOUTH PARK & PACIFIC RAILWAY COMPANY, that the amount of the Capital Stock of said company shall be two millions and five hundred thousand dollars, that the term of its existence shall be fifty years from the date of these Articles and that the number of shares of which the said stock shall consist shall be twenty-five thousand of one hundred dollars each.

It is further declared that the number of Trustees who shall manage the concerns of said company for the first year ensuing after the date hereof shall be nine—and the Trustees shall be John Evans, Henry Crow, Walter S. Cheesman, David Moffat, Jr., Frederick A. Clark, John Hughes, Leonard H. Eicholtz, J. C. Reiff, and Charles B. Kountze.

It is further declared that the operation of said company shall be carried on and its principal office and place of business shall be in the City of Denver, in the County of Arapahoe and Territory of Colorado.

It is also further declared that the Trustees of said company shall have power to make such prudential By-Laws as they shall deem proper for the management and disposition of the stock and business affairs of said company not inconsistent with the Laws of Colorado Territory, to prescribe therein the duties of Officers, Artificers, and servants that may be employed, to regulate the appointment of all officers of said company and the carrying on all kinds of business within the objects and purposes of said company.

In testimony whereof the undersigned subscribers have hereunto subscribed their several names at Denver, Colorado Territory on the thirtieth day of September, A. D. 1872.

> Bela M. Hughes
> Jos. E. Bates
> Charles B. Kountze
> David H. Moffat, Jr.
> Frederick A. Clark
> F. Z. Salomon
> Henry Crow
> W. S. Cheesman
> John Evans

Territory of Colorado ⎫
⎬ ss
County of Arapahoe ⎭

I, S. G. Collins a Notary Public within and for the County of Arapahoe and Territory of Colorado, do hereby certify that on this 30th day of September, A. D. 1872, personally appeared before me the foregoing named persons who are also personally well known to me to be the persons whose names are subscribed to the foregoing Articles of Association, namely: John Evans, Henry Crow, Walter S. Cheesman, David H. Moffat, Jr., Frederick A. Clark, Bela M. Hughes, Joseph E. Bates, F. Z. Salomon, Charles B. Kountze, and they and each of them acknowledged that they had signed the foregoing Articles of Association for the use and purposes therein set forth and stated.

In Testimony whereof I have hereunto set my hand and affixed my Notarial Seal the day and year aforesaid.

S. G. Collins

SEAL

Notary Public

DOMESTIC No. 732
Articles of Association of
Denver South Park & Pacific Railway Company.
Secy's. Office.
Filed for record Oct. 1st, 1872, at 12:30 P.M.
Recorded in Book D, page 547.   No. 1.

The following newspaper item reporting further information relative to the South Park's officials, the road's preliminary activities, etc., appeared in the Rocky Mountain News on Wednesday, October 2, 1872:

"A few days ago a number of our prominent capitalists met for the purpose of discussing the feasibility of constructing a railway line into the South Park, and formed an organization with this object in view. The proposed line is to extend to Georgetown or so far as the track of the 'Denver Georgetown & Utah' railroad will permit, and then deflect into the South Park, touching Fairplay and the adjoining mining districts.[1] A branch to Central City is, we believe, also contemplated. The enterprise is headed by some of the leading men of Denver, who will, beyond doubt, push the matter to a successful issue.

"Yesterday afternoon the first meeting of the Board of Trustees of the Denver South Park & Pacific Railway Co.—the title

1. This Fairplay branch is also supposed to include a further extension of the line across the Main Range to the anthracite fields near Gunnison. See section covering D. G. & U. history.

of the new organization—was held in this city. There were present the following trustees: Charles B. Kountze, John Evans, John Hughes, Walter S. Cheesman, David H. Moffat, Jr., Frederick A. Clark, Henry Crow, and Leonard H. Eicholtz.

"W. S. Cheesman, esq., was requested to act as chairman, and B. M. Hughes, secretary.

"On motion of Hon. John Evans, a book for subscription to stock of the company was ordered to be opened at once, under the supervision of the Board of Trustees. Subscriptions of one share each were made by the following named gentlemen: B. M. Hughes, John Evans, W. S. Cheesman, Henry Crow, F. A. Clark, D. H. Moffat, Jr., John Hughes, and L. H. Eicholtz.

"An election of officers of the company was then held with the following result:

> President: John Evans
> Vice-President: D. H. Moffat, Jr.
> Secretary: George W. Kassler
> Treasurer: Charles B. Kountze

"The following named persons were then chosen a committee on by-laws and ordered to report at an early day: D. H. Moffat, Jr., Henry M. Crow, and L. H. Eicholtz.

"The meeting then adjourned to meet at the call of the president of the company."

The company had decided that its railroad should be of the narrow (three foot) gauge. The theoretical popularity of narrow gauge railroads was then at a high stage all over the country, and many believed narrow gauge lines were destined to permanently displace all other types of railroad. The advantages of the narrow gauge for mountainous districts had begun to attract attention, chiefly because of the economy, both in construction and operation, on heavy grades and sharp curves.

As stated in the incorporation papers, the original route proposed for the South Park line was by way of Bear Creek into the mountains and thence by the most practical route to and across the South Park; yet the entire region through which it was projected was practically uninhabited, and with the exception of a few scattered mining camps, had yet to acquire a population that would need and support railroad service. There were a few houses at Morrison's stone quarry but beyond that point, with the exception of a few scattered ranches, there was not even a hamlet this side of the Tarryall mining district. Beyond the Tarryall, the only localities containing any population or activity, were the mining camps along the Middle Fork of the South Platte River, such as Buckskin Joe and Fairplay. It was originally planned that the route across South Park was to go by way of Fairplay.

To improve this condition, and to afford a division point on the railroad, the proprietary interests of the South Park, on October 24, 1872, organized the Morrison Stone, Lime & Townsite Company. The townsite was laid out that month by Joseph F. Castro, and a post office was established shortly afterward. According to the Denver Tribune of July 7, 1881, the settlement was named after George M. Morrison, an early settler. Governor Evans and his associates had built the first wagon road into Bear Creek Canon, to make available for railroad ties the valuable timber resources on the upper tributaries of that stream.[1] It was constructed as a toll road, but after a cloudburst which destroyed the wooden bridges, the Governor deeded a half interest to Morrison, on the condition that the town would replace these bridges. A second cloudburst some years later caused the remainder of the road to be given to Morrison under similar conditions. It is interesting to note that when the Denver Mountain Parks road system was constructed between 1913 and 1915, the old right of way was acquired, and is now occupied by a beautiful mountain boulevard over which thousands of people pass annually in automobiles.

The company did no construction work during the winter of 1872 and 1873 for a number of reasons. First, the necessary financial arrangements had not been completed, and second, and far more important, was the fact that a major change in the route of the road had been worked out.

As stated in the first Articles of Incorporation, the original intentions of the company had been to construct the main line from Denver to some unspecified point in South Park. The proposed route, which would, in part, utilize the tracks of the Denver Georgetown & Utah, was by way of Bear Creek Canon to some point west of Morrison, and then was to turn south to South Park. One of the earlier proposed routes of the South Park road was by way of the Canon of the South Platte River; however, the engineers, in their preliminary surveys, had pronounced the route as impractical. However, as it had been definitely decided that the Denver Georgetown & Utah was not to be built, the engineers once again headed for that conspicuous cleft in the Front Range where the South Platte emerges from its mountain fastness into the open plains. Here the engineers tackled the seemingly impossible task of locating a route through the narrow and rugged gorge of the canon. After considerable difficulty, their efforts were rewarded and a satisfactory survey for the South Park's right of way through the canon was established.

In connection with the Platte Canon survey, we quote the following item from the Rocky Mountain News of April 2, 1873:

"The engineering party under the direction of Colonel L. H. Eicholtz, now locating the line of the Denver South Park & Pacific Railway, at last advices had run the line up the river, some nine miles above the mouth of the canon, and by the end of this week they will be as far as the mouth of Buffalo Creek. They will then be able to compare this with the route via Bear Creek canon, which has been thoroughly examined as far as the Omaha Ranch." Note: The writer has been unable to determine the location of Omaha Ranch.

An official engineering report of one of the preliminary Platte Canon surveys, including estimated construction costs, is found in the company's Annual Report for 1874. We quote in part:

1. McMechen, "Life of Gov. Evans".

Denver, Dec. 26th, 1873.

Hon. John Evans,
President, Denver South Park & Pacific R. R.
Dear Sir:

I have the honor to report that according to instructions received from you I commenced a reconnaissance of the Platte Canon, at its mouth, and examined it carefully to Estabrook's Park, a distance of 31 miles, arriving at that point on the 21st inst. I was accompanied by Mr. Thomas Withers, and our outfit for transportation of provisions, etc., consisted of one man with two burros. The sides of the stream in the Canon were frozen for nearly the whole distance, and at frequent intervals across the stream, which enabled us to walk up the Canon, all the way on the ice, and to obtain a clearer idea of the character of the work than we otherwise could do, climbing along the sides of the Canon. We also had the maps and profiles of Mr. Pugh's approximate location which assisted us materially in forming our estimates of what can actually be done. . . .

The average cost of graduation and bridging from the mouth of the Canon to Estabrook's Park, 31 miles, is $9,000 per mile. The line should be located as nearly as possible just above high water mark, say from one and a half to two feet above and conforming as nearly as practical to the contour lines of the canon.

The points of the Canon should be cut as lightly as possible on account of the hard material of which they are composed (mostly granite) and the road built of the loose rock on the sides. The maximum grade will be 185 feet to the mile (and this only in Deer Creek Canon) and the sharpest curves necessary 30 degrees. A very practical line and route for a narrow gauge railway. The annexed table will show more in detail the estimated cost of the work.

From Mouth of Canon to Forks, 8½ miles.

Graduation and Bridging, $11,600 per mile	$110,500
Cross Ties, 3,000 per mile	8,625
Iron, 30 lbs. per yard, 47 tons per mile at $100	39,950
Spikes and fishplates, $560 per mile	4,760
Track laying, $500 per mile	4,250
Engineering	5,000
Water Station	600
Total	**$173,685**

From Forks to Buffalo Creek, 9½ miles.

Graduation and Bridging, $6,000 per mile	$ 57,000
Cross Ties	7,125
Iron	47,000
Spikes and Splices, $560 per mile	5,320
Track Laying at $500 per mile	4,750
Engineering	5,000
Water Stations and Buildings	4,000
Total	**$130,195**

George E. Mellen photo,
from Morris W. Abbott Collection.

Denver South Park & Pacific engine 42 and coach 9 near Cathedral Rocks in Platte Canon in the late 1880's.

From Buffalo Creek to Estabrook's Park, 13 miles.

Graduation and Bridging, $8,000 per mile	$104,000
Cross Ties, 3,000 per mile	9,750
Iron, 30 lb., 47 tons per mile, at $100	61,100
Spikes and Splices, $560 per mile	7,280
Track Laying at $500 per mile	6,500
Engineering	6,000
Water Stations and Buildings	3,000
Total	$197,630

Total Cost from Mouth of Canon
  to Estabrook's Park $501,510
  Average Cost $16,180 per mile.

Respectfully,

H. R. Holbrook, Engineer in Charge.

On January 14, 1874, Engineer Holbrook handed in a similar report covering the estimated cost of line from Estabrook's Park to Fairplay, in which his final figures were as follows:

Estabrook's Park to Hall's Valley, 18 miles.
Total Cost, $276,560; average per mile, $13,346.
Hall's Valley to Kenosha Pass, 6 miles.
Total Cost, $386,620; average per mile, $18,343.
Kenosha Pass to Fairplay, 26 miles.
Total Cost, $271,960; average per mile, $10,460.

Total estimated cost of road from Denver to Fairplay, 101 miles. $1,354,090. Average per mile, $13,405.82.

In the meantime, during the spring of 1873, the South Park interests conceived the idea of reorganizing the road on a larger scale. A number of reasons were responsible for this reorganization and change. Apparently, one of the best reasons to support the change revolved around the old Denver Georgetown & Utah organization. In view of the fact that this proposed Georgetown road was becoming more and more a dead issue, the South Park interests deemed it advisable to divorce themselves from certain declarations contained in their first Articles of Association that, to some extent, tied in with the Georgetown railroad project. Furthermore, the original proposed route into the South Park country utilizing a part of the Denver Georgetown & Utah route west of Morrison had been abandoned and a route through the Canon of the South Platte River adopted. The line west of Bear Creek Junction was thereafter to be known as the Morrison branch. Other reasons, such as increasing the capital stock so that further outside financial aid could be enlisted, which would enable the company to transact a larger business, also justified the proposed change. In due time, the reorganization plans were worked out and a new and larger railroad company emerged, fully incorporated in a new Articles of Association. Even on paper the road was growing. As in the case of the first Articles of Association, the following is the exact wording of the papers of the new DENVER SOUTH PARK & PACIFIC RAILROAD COMPANY. Note the only difference is that in the name of the new organization the word "railroad" supplants the word "railway".

Articles of Association
of the
Denver South Park & Pacific Railroad Company

The undersigned subscribers, Henry Crow, C. B. Kountze, B. M. Hughes, John Hughes, John Evans, D. H. Moffat, Jr., and S. H. Elbert do hereby agree and declare their intentions to create a Company under the Statutes of Colorado Territory for the purpose of locating, constructing, owning, maintaining, and operating a single or double track narrow gauge railroad and a Telegraph line from the City of Denver to Morrison at the Bear Creek Canon and also to and through the Platte Canon and on the most feasible route to the South Park and thence to or near the town of South Park[1] and to the Salt Springs—thence across the valley of the Arkansas River and through the Poncha Pass and across the San Luis Valley to or near the Town of Del-Norte and thence by the most feasible route to the San Juan mining districts in South Western Colorado—to be extended thence to the Pacific Ocean—with branches to Morrison—also to Summit County to be extended via the Middle Park to the Pacific Ocean—also to Dudley, and Horse Shoe, and to the head of the Arkansas Valley in Lake County in said Territory—to be located in divisions, after careful survey.

It is further declared that said Company shall be called and designated "the Denver South Park & Pacific Railroad Company"; that the Capital Stock of said Company shall be three million five hundred thousand dollars; that the term of its existence shall be fifty years from the date of these articles and that the number of shares of which the said stock shall consist shall be thirty-five thousand of one hundred dollars each.

It is further declared that the number of Trustees who shall manage the concerns of said Company for the first year ensuing after the date hereof shall be nine and the Trustees shall be John Evans, Henry Crow, Walter S. Cheesman, David H. Moffat, Jr., Frederick A. Clark, John Hughes, Leonard H. Eicholtz, J. C. Reiff, and Charles B. Kountze.

It is further declared that the operations of said Company shall be carried on and its principal office and place of business shall be in the City of Denver in the County of Arapahoe and Territory of Colorado.

It is further declared that the Trustees of said Company shall have power to make such prudential By-Laws as they shall deem proper and to alter the same at pleasure for the management and disposition of the stock and business affairs of said Company—not inconsistent with

1. This was an early stage station located at the foot of the west slope of Kenosha Pass.

the laws of Colorado Territory, to prescribe therein the duties of Officers, Artificers, and servants that may be employed, to regulate the appointment of all Officers of said Company and the carrying on all kinds of business within the objects and purposes of said Company.

In testimony whereof the undersigned subscribers have hereunto subscribed their several names at Denver, Colorado Territory, on the Fourteenth Day of June, A. D. 1873.

> John Hughes
> Samuel H. Elbert
> Charles B. Kountze
> David H. Moffat, Jr.
> Bela M. Hughes
> Henry Crow
> John Evans

Territory of Colorado ⎱
                      ⎰ ss
County of Arapahoe ⎰

I, A. B. Robbins, a Notary Public within and for the County of Arapahoe and Territory of Colorado, do hereby certify that on the fourteenth day of June, A. D. 1873, personally appeared before me the foregoing named persons who are also personally well known to me to be the persons whose names are subscribed to the Articles of Association namely, Samuel H. Elbert, Charles B. Kountze, David H. Moffat, Jr., Bela M. Hughes, Henry Crow, John Hughes, and John Evans, and they each of them acknowledged that they had signed the foregoing Articles of Association for the uses and purposes therein set forth and stated.

In testimony whereof I have hereunto set my hand and affixed my Official Seal this day and year aforesaid.

SEAL

> A. B. Robbins
> Notary Public

DOMESTIC No. 845.
Articles of Association of
The Denver South Park & Pacific Railroad Company.
June 14, 1873.
Filed for record June 16, 1873, at 9:30 o'clock A.M., and record in Book "E", page 90.   No. 2

In the reorganization of the road the same executive officers were continued, namely:

> President: John Evans
> Vice-President: David H. Moffat, Jr.
> Secretary: George W. Kassler
> Treasurer: Charles B. Kountze

At a meeting of the Directors of the Railroad Company held on July 25, 1873, a resolution was presented and adopted by which the Denver South Park & Pacific Railway Company offered to transfer and turn over to the new company, the Denver South Park & Pacific Railroad Company, all of its property, rights and privileges on condition that the latter company should assume all of the obligations of the former. And at the first meeting of the Board of Directors of the Denver South Park & Pacific Railroad Company, (the new company) held on the same day, that company accepted the transfer of the rights and assumed all obligations of the old company.

At this point, it might be well to incorporate into our history a few simple facts governing the legal rights and privileges which were to be accorded the South Park company by both the Territory, later the State of Colorado, and the Federal Government.

From the time of the organization of the Territory of Colorado until January, 1868, all corporations of the Territory of Colorado were created by special acts of the Territorial Legislature, and therefore the charters of the early railroad corporations were Acts of the Legislative Assembly of the Territory of Colorado.

After January, 1868, in pursuance of the provisions of the Revised Statutes of Colorado of the year 1868, all railroad corporations in the Territory thereafter formed were organized under a General Law set forth in such Revised Statutes, which applied not only to corporations thereafter formed, but by the provisions of the Act, all corporations then in existence which might desire any of the additional privileges contained therein were obliged to accept the entire Act in order to obtain such additional privileges.

After the admission of Colorado as a State into the Union, on August 1, 1876, the first Legislature of the State of Colorado, held in the year 1877, passed a General Corporation Act being "An Act to provide for the formation of Corporations" approved March 14, 1877, and this appears in the General Laws of Colorado. All railroad companies and other corporations organized within these various periods described were organized in accordance with the rulings, provisions or general laws as set forth during these said periods.

Accordingly, the Denver South Park & Pacific Railroad Company was a duly organized corporation under the laws of the Territory of Colorado, and by virtue of these General Laws of the Territory of Colorado was entitled to survey, locate, construct, maintain, use and operate a railroad between Denver and the Arkansas Valley in Lake County with a branch line, sixteen and one-half miles long, to Morrison in Jefferson County, and later, by an Act of Congress approved March 4, 1875, "Granting to Railroads the right of way over public lands of the United States" was entitled to its right of way, depot grounds, and material for its construction, free of charge, over, on and from said lands. In this connection, the South Park was authorized by the Territory of Colorado (later the State of Colorado) to borrow money, securing same by first mortgage on its railroad.

A study of the reorganized South Park road brings out some interesting comparisons. In the first place, note the "single track" idea has been changed to include either "single or double track". The most significant change is, of course, contained in the matter of routes. Whereas the original intentions of the company had been to construct the main line by way of Bear Creek Canon and Morrison, a part of the old Denver Georgetown & Utah route, this was now changed in favor of the Platte Canon route. The new charter stipulated that the line to Morrison was to be a branch, while the newly designated main line was definitely laid out via Platte Canon, across the South Park, the Arkansas Valley, the San Luis Valley to Del Norte, and thence westward toward the San Juan mining region, eventually expanding until it reached Fort Yuma, Arizona, and then the Pacific Coast through connections with the Southern Pacific Railroad. Branches were proposed to such points as Dudley, Horseshoe, Lake and Summit Counties, the Middle Park and westward toward the Pacific. It seems the ambitions of the new South Park organization were limited only by the Pacific Coast.

The reader will note here that there was no mention made in the new "Articles" regarding any projected extension to the Gunnison territory. Why this extension was not included is not known, as it was considered in Evans' earlier plans. However, amendments to the charter covering the construction of this line came later. Further comparison discloses the fact that the capital stock of the company was increased from $2,500,000 to $3,500,000. Also, four of the original nine subscribers, Bates, Clark, Salomon, and Cheesman, were dropped; however, two new ones, John Hughes and Governor S. H. Elbert, were added. The original nine Trustees remain intact in the reorganization.

The reader will recall that Georgetown and Clear Creek County had voted a bond issue to aid in the construction of the Denver Georgetown & Utah road, also that it had been expected that the South Park road would in part utilize the Denver Georgetown & Utah tracks. But, in view of the fact that this bond issue had expired without the road having been built, a proposal by John Evans, which was in turn supported by a resolution of the Denver Board of Trade, was made that the $200,000 in Arapahoe County bonds that had been voted in aid of that project be transferred to the Denver South Park and Pacific. With the reorganization of the South Park enterprise, which incorporated a much larger construction program, it was clearly apparent that for a project of such ambitious scope, a bond issue of $200,000 would be entirely inadequate, and while $300,000 in county bonds would be but little better, it was nevertheless proposed that Arapahoe County should raise its subscription in the new company to that figure. Thus, the South Park would be asking for $300,000; but of this amount, $200,000 having already been voted, the proposition resolved itself into a case of transfer, an additional $100,000 only being called for.

The voting of this bond issue by the people meant that the County Commissioners would be duly authorized to issue $300,000 of County Bonds in exchange for an equal nominal amount, or $300,000 of the South Park railroad's $3,500,000 of capital stock.

The date for the election was set for July 28, 1873. Almost at once, the invariable hue and cry which attends such plebiscites was underway.

This time, the opposition was engineered by General Wm. J. Palmer of the Denver & Rio Grande. That road was naturally not interested in seeing its own line to the mining interior flanked by this new project. Several exchanges of long letters to the public appeared in the Denver press over the signatures of both General Palmer and Governor Evans. Palmer attacked the idea of giving bonds before the road was built, and suggested as an alternative that Denver vote the bonds in aid of the Rio Grande road instead. Palmer stated that the D. & R. G. already had a line to Acequia and offered to construct twenty-two miles of railroad through the Platte Canon without asking a cent in bonds until the line was completed; and offered, in the event of his failure to do so, to permit the South Park road to use the Grande's tracks south from Denver to some convenient junction point where the proposed South Park line would commence construction at the entrance of Platte Canon. The offer was fair enough, but the joker in it was that in either event the Rio Grande would have protected itself from being flanked by a rival road; if the Grande built the line, the Grande would control the route; if it failed to build the line because of construction difficulties encountered in the canon, then it would be safe to assume that the South Park road would also fail to build through the canon, and there would be no need to offer the Rio Grande trackage to the South Park line.[1]

Evans, on the other hand, was plagued by the fact that his company (contrary to all precedent) was asking for the bonds before the line was built. Even the Denver Board of Trade, usually so compliant to the Governor's wishes, at first refused to support the project because of that fact. Just before the vote was taken, forty Denver business men suggested that the proposition be changed so that the bonds would not be delivered until the road was completed. John Evans acknowledged the propriety of the suggestion, but claimed that was impossible under the circumstances. He did, however, recede so far as to substitute a personal guarantee that the road would be built to specific points by specific times, for the former stipulation that the road would be built "as soon as possible". According to the Rocky Mountain News of July 23, 1873, this compromise satisfied the City Council of Denver, who then endorsed the project.

Against these charges that the road was asking for

1. Samuel D. Mock.

money before construction was completed, John Evans had some equally effective arguments. He charged that the Rio Grande was motivated in their offer by a desire to choke off some very dangerous competition. Since this "very dangerous competition" (the South Park road) was controlled by, and in the interest of, Denver, the inference was obvious: vote yourself a railroad in your own interests.[1]

Evans also charged that Palmer was interested in tapping the South Park mining region by a route which would favor some city on the Rio Grande's line other than Denver. This charge Palmer denied, but Evans had the better evidence to substantiate his charges. There was the survey made by the Rio Grande from Canon City in 1872; there was the statement of Engineer Greenwood of the Rio Grande that the Canon City route to the South Park was superior to the Platte Canon route; and, had Evans known of it, he might have cited some of Palmer's written statements in letters and documents wherein it was Palmer's contention that one of the most important of six proposed branch lines to the Denver & Rio Grande system was "The South Park Railway". This proposed railroad was from the mouth of Plum Creek (near Acequia) via the Platte Canon to Fairplay, thence via Hoosier, Hamilton, or other suitable pass to the Valley of the Blue River and to the western border of Colorado and Salt Lake City.

Quoting, in part, a portion of one of Governor Evans' letters to the public, as published in the Rocky Mountain News of July 26, 1873,[1] we read:

"The proposition of Palmer, when stripped of all its data to confuse and divert attention from the real issue involved in the case is this—Vote down your own enterprise (the South Park road) in the coming election, and the Rio Grande will have the field, and they graciously assure us they will look over the ground and see if they will not build you a road through the Platte canon to the South Park. This is all the assurance they offer except that they will build to the canon from Acequia and then push the line as far into the canon as you furnish the means to build. . . . The Denver & Rio Grande realizes that if the bonds are voted, the branch to Morrison will divert all trade off their Colorado Springs route. Hence their effort to defeat our bonds. Colonel Spotswood, of Spotswood & McClellan, the stage route owners, assures me that as soon as our cars run to Morrison, the Stage Company will run passengers on through to Fairplay by daylight. This will center all the South Park business in Denver. . . . The Morrison branch will also form a part of the route of the Denver Georgetown & Utah line, which it will be to the interest of the Kansas Pacific to extend to Georgetown at an early day. This is certainly to the interest of Arapahoe county, and she will do as much to favor it by transferring the $200,000 in bonds to the Denver South Park & Pacific as by leaving them to hang over the county until the Kansas Pacific completes that line and claims them, which they certainly can do, for they were voted unconditionally as to time."

It seems that Denver was continually faced with a struggle to maintain her position as the commercial capital of the mountain regions. During the late '60's and very early '70's, the great issue was—"shall Denver

1. Samuel D. Mock.

120

or Golden be the objective point of the Eastern railroad connections?" Byers, in his Rocky Mountain News, July 7, 1873, summed the present situation up when he stated—"Denver faces her second crisis"—"Shall Denver or Colorado Springs be the objective point of this great South Western Colorado commerce?" Continuing, he reminded the Denver citizenry that construction of the Denver South Park & Pacific road would give Denver a trunk line direct into southwest Colorado, thus heading off any schemes adverse to the city's future success.

As ever before, John Evans found his old opponent, Wm. A. H. Loveland of Golden, in the midst of the controversy, hitting for all he was worth. As previously stated in the first chapter, Loveland's plan was to take advantage of the Rio Grande's development and intercept this new road south of Denver, just as he had planned to connect with the Denver Pacific by means of his line between Golden and Jersey Junction and later by means of his proposed Golden-Julesburg project.

Accordingly, the Golden City & South Platte Railway & Telegraph Company was incorporated on January 18, 1872. The original incorporation papers did not show Loveland as an officer of the road; nevertheless, he was listed as one of the three incorporators and was in reality "the power behind the throne". This proposed line of railroad, approximately 17 miles in length, commenced at Golden, followed the hogbacks south and east of that point, turned east along Bear Creek in the vicinity of Morrison and thence to a connection with the Denver & Rio Grande road about ten miles south of Denver near Littleton, or near the confluence of Plum Creek and the South Platte River, whichever was the most feasible. Thus, by tapping Denver's southern transportation artery at some convenient point below the city, Loveland could divert traffic from that line, from Denver to Golden. General Palmer bestowed his blessings upon the project and lent his moral support when and where necessary.

As a further scheme to block Evans and Denver in their plans, Loveland on July 24, 1873, four days before the election, organized the Turkey Creek Railway Company. The three directors were W. A. H. Loveland, C. C. Welch and E. L. Berthoud. The line of this proposed road as stated in the incorporation papers commenced at a point on the Golden City & South Platte road near the junction of Bear Creek and Turkey Creek, and thence south and west following the Canon of Turkey Creek and thence by the most feasible route to the South Park territory.

This proposed Turkey Creek line was organized so that in the event the Denver South Park & Pacific project failed, Loveland would be prepared to build into the South Park region himself, and thus extend the Colorado Central-Union Pacific monopoly into that territory. What traffic this road would command would then, of course, avoid Denver by flowing through Golden via the Golden City & South Platte road. The strength and success of the Denver South Park & Pacific enterprise and that of the Denver opposition together with the panic of 1873, buried the Golden City & South Platte and the Turkey Creek railroads completely, and little more was ever heard of these two projects.

There was also some local opposition to the new project, and especially to that part of the project which looked to the granting of the bonds first and the building of the railroad "as soon as possible". When the South Park promoters changed over from the "as soon as possible" stipulation to the Evans personal guarantee, the Denver Mirror, a local paper which took the lead in this opposition, sent the statement to an attorney for his opinion of its validity at law. The attorney reported: "The requisite agreement and obligation is entirely wanting. . . . The guarantee being therefore in-operative, and creating no obligation . . . there would be no remedy for its violation." The Denver Mirror fulminated against the "railroad ring", the "monied aristocracy", and the manipulations of those who wanted Denver taxpayers to advance them the money so that they might develop their stone quarries, townsite, and other interests at Morrison. There was some basis for these allegations since the South Park promoters did have valuable interests at Morrison in the name of "The Morrison Stone, Lime, and Townsite Company".

On July 27th, the day before the election, Byers wrote in one of his editorials:

"The Golden City & South Platte road, backed by the Union Pacific, is making the dirt fly along their whole line, and are doing their best to reach the Platte as soon as possible. What means this Littleton cut-off, if it is not a combination between the Denver & Rio Grande and the Union Pacific railroads to avoid Denver? . . . If Golden don't best us and get to the Platte first, General Palmer is willing to lock it up and be its keeper until he builds his road from Colorado Springs to Fairplay."[1]

On this same day, Evans, in reply to Palmer's denial of any plans for a proposed line of railroad west from some point along the D. & R. G. into the South Park country, published in the News a map, purported to have been drawn up by the Rio Grande. This map, which Evans had secured, clearly showed the Rio Grande's plans for their proposed line west from Colorado Springs. The road was known as the Pikes Peak

1. This is thought to be The Pikes Peak & Salt Lake R. R.

& Salt Lake Railroad. Further proof of these contentions was brought to light when the old files of the Secretary of State's office disclosed that Palmer's road, the Pikes Peak & Salt Lake Railroad Company, was duly incorporated on February 25, 1873, five months before the date of the election. Briefly, the route of this proposed railroad was as follows:

"Commencing at a point not to extend one mile from the junction of Cascade and Pikes Peak Avenues in the town of Colorado Springs, and running from thence up the valley of Fountain Creek, thence in a generally westerly direction to the Platte River, thence up the valley of the Platte to the town of Fairplay, thence through Hamilton or other suitable pass and across the Snowy Range to the headwaters of the Blue River, etc. . . ."

As further proof of the apparent close teamwork between the Palmer and Loveland groups, Evans also exposed another of their maps intending to show Golden as the future railroad center of Colorado. These two maps were reproduced in the Rocky Mountain News of July 27, 1873.

But all this clamor was to no avail. Amid charges of bribery, ballot box stuffing, and subsidizing of the press, the bonds carried. The results were 1,867 for and 588 against. For the interest of the reader, some post-election comments are quoted. The Rocky Mountain News of July 29th:

"The character of the men behind the South Park enterprise carried the bonds. They had saved Denver in the past and the people still believed in them."

Rocky Mountain News of July 30th:

"We rejoice at the magnificent victory, and claim that the 500 who voted against the bonds did so under a mistaken opinion."

In the same issue, Governor Evans explained the victory in the light of poor Denver & Rio Grande strategy, so that the South Park was able to rally the people against permitting Colorado Springs to dictate to Denver.

The Denver Mirror of August 3rd:

"Talk no more of Tammany! Boast not again of the purity of the Denver ballot box. . . ."

However, regardless of the actions on the part of either faction, the Denver South Park & Pacific had achieved status. The next job confronting the promoters was to get underway with the actual construction of the railroad.

CHAPTER II

FIRST CONSTRUCTION — DENVER TO KENOSHA

Sometime prior to the voting of the bond issue July 28, 1873, the South Park interests had deemed it advisable to organize some sort of a subordinate construction company through which the actual building of the railroad could be carried on. It seemed to be the custom in early day western railroad building to set up such construction companies for this purpose. Mock states: "Building a railroad was often the only lucrative side to early day railroading in the west." Whether this was the motive in this particular case is not known, but it seems that the real factor behind this and similar movements was the desire by John Evans and his associates to maintain control over the road.

Accordingly, the South Park interests took steps to set up the usual construction company, and a private association of the parties interested, known among themselves as THE DENVER RAILWAY ASSOCIATION, was duly organized but not incorporated. Later on, during the early spring of 1874, this "Association" was incorporated and a regular contract drawn up and signed between the railroad company and the construction company covering its specific duties. Further information concerning this reorganized construction company, the contract and its contents, will be taken up shortly.

All preliminary engineering work, including surveying of terminal grounds and right of way, construction of all buildings and the equipment of the road, was to be paid for by this Denver Railway Association. In payment for all this, it was agreed that the construction company was to receive a specified amount of bonds and stocks per mile of road completed and equipped. The South Park company further agreed to issue its first mortgage bonds to the amount of $20,000 per mile of road completed. These bonds were to be secured by a mortgage on the first 150 miles of railroad and all other property of the company. In order to lend further assistance to the construction company, the South Park company agreed to have inserted upon said bonds traffic contracts which had been agreed upon with the Kansas Pacific, the North Missouri,[1] and Chicago & Alton railroad companies, for a drawback of ten percent, of all receipts of said companies from business to and from

the South Park road. The proceeds of this ten percent was to be a sinking fund to buy up and cancel said bonds. This very advantageous traffic arrangement failed on account of the default of the Kansas Pacific on its own interest before it was consummated.

The construction company was granted the use and benefit of all proceeds that might be realized, either through the sale of said capital stock or exchanged for other bonds that might be procured from Park or Lake Counties. The value of this capital stock was to be created by the building of a railroad for the South Park company, without which the county bonds (not applicable to any other purpose) were valueless.

Because it had been considered unnecessary at that particular time, the Association was not incorporated. However, due to the apparent progress of the South Park project in the meantime, Evans and his associates concluded that in order to properly transact business, and for the purpose of enlisting the aid of others and adding to the capital, this Association, or construction company, should be reorganized. Accordingly, sometime during February, 1874, the Denver Railway Association was incorporated and all construction thereafter was carried on under the direction of this, or subsequent construction companies. Inasmuch as there are no legal records concerning this particular organization, or its incorporation, on file in either the County of Denver, which possess all the old records of Arapahoe County (of which Denver was originally a part) or with the State of Colorado, it is impossible to state the exact date of its incorporation, its capitalization, or who the trustees or officers were. In his report to the Arapahoe County Commissioners, made on February 25, 1879, Evans stated: "The construction companies and contractors have always been separate and distinct from the railroad company, with different persons for officers." However, when all known information concerning the early financial operations of the South Park organization is considered, it is a foregone conclusion that the same group of men who headed the South Park road also held the purse strings of this and all succeeding construction companies.

On March 1st, following the incorporation of this construction company, a contract was drawn up and signed between the Denver South Park & Pacific Rail-

1. The North Missouri R. R. was chartered in 1857 to build northwest from St. Louis toward Iowa and Omaha, Nebr. Later, it became a part of the St. Louis Kansas City & Northern, and is now a part of the Wabash system.

road and the Denver Railway Association covering all details pertaining to the construction of the various proposed lines of railroad.

This contract between the South Park road and the Denver Railway Association is a very long affair and contains much dry and uninteresting legal matter. Eliminating a considerable portion of this legal material, which seems so unnecessary to our story, the body of this first contract incorporated the following main features:

1. The Denver South Park & Pacific Railroad Company, being a duly organized corporation under the laws of the Territory of Colorado, was the party of the first part.

2. The Denver Railway Association, being a duly organized corporation under the laws of the Territory of Colorado, was the party of the second part.

3. The Denver South Park & Pacific Railroad Company, by virtue of the laws of the Territory of Colorado, was entitled to survey, locate, construct, maintain, use, and operate a railroad between Denver and the Arkansas Valley in Lake County and points beyond, with a branch to Morrison in Jefferson County.

4. The contract provided that the Denver Railway Association, known as the construction company, was to survey the above line of railroad as described, and to construct upon said right of way, a first class three-foot gauge railroad with all the necessary equipment, in sections, as follows:

1st. From Denver to Morrison _____17 miles
2nd. From Morrison Junction (also known
        as Bear Creek Junction) at the mouth
        of Bear Creek, to the mouth of
        Buffalo Creek _____30 miles
3rd. From the mouth of Buffalo Creek to
        to Hall's Gulch (also known as Hall's
        Valley, near Webster) _____32 miles
4th. From Hall's Gulch to Fairplay _____32 miles
5th. From Fairplay to the vicinity of
        the Salt Works _____14 miles
6th. From the Salt Works to the mouth of
        Trout Creek in the valley of the
        Arkansas River _____25 miles
                                              _____
        Total _____150 miles

As the extension of the road proceeded, the construction company was to turn over each section, upon completion, to the railroad company.

5. The contract further provided that the construction company procure suitable terminal and depot grounds in Denver and at other designated locations along the line of the railroad. They were to complete all grading, tieing, bridge construction, and track laying. They were to erect all buildings such as depots, freight houses, machine shops, and other buildings necessary

for the successful operation of the railroad. They were to furnish all tools, equipment, engines, cars, and other necessary rolling stock and to defray all expenses incident to the securing of such equipment.

6. The contract further provided that the construction company was to pay the railroad company for the transportation of all iron, bridge materials, and all other miscellaneous track and building supplies required for the construction of the railroad beyond its terminus.

7. The Denver Railway Association, in assuming this contract, was to build a complete railroad as described and equip same, in a manner acceptable to both the president and chief engineer of the Denver South Park & Pacific R. R.

The time at which each section was to be completed was prescribed and provision for payment, in fully paid capital stock, was as follows:

Upon completion of 1st division—17 miles—and after cars are running—$200,000.
2nd—30 miles—$1,000,000
3rd—32 miles—$ 200,000
4th—32 miles—$ 200,000
6th—39 miles—$ 300,000
(The 5th and 6th divisions were combined for some reason.)

Meanwhile, during the spring, prior to the voting of the bond issue in July, preliminary steps were taken toward getting started with the construction of the road. One of the first moves made was an application to the City Council of the City of Denver for a franchise ordinance by which the railroad would be enabled to enter the City of Denver, along and across certain streets, alleys and public ways. Such ordinance was passed by the City Council and is known as ordinance number 67 of the series of 1873 passed and approved by the Mayor, April 24, 1873. And at a meeting of the Board of Directors of the railroad company, held on May 3rd following, a resolution was passed accepting the privileges of such ordinance and adopting the route contained therein as the designated route of the Denver South Park & Pacific R. R. Co. in the City of Denver.

Following this action, preliminary surveys, both within the city and out along the line south toward Bear Creek, together with other miscellaneous and additional preparations, were made. The voting of the bond issue on July 28, 1873, was the "go-signal" which permitted the company to make further extensive preparations toward getting started with actual construction. One of the conditions attached to the bond issue was that the railroad should be completed through from Denver to Morrison within a period of nine months from date of issue. Consequently, the promoters were anxious to get started.

In this connection, we read in the Rocky Mountain

News of July 30th following, that Colonel Eicholtz and his corps of engineers, who were at the time engaged in some preliminary engineering and survey work in Platte Canon, were notified to return to Denver immediately in order that he might organize his forces and commence construction. Inasmuch as the line of survey had already been run, Colonel Eicholtz started setting the stakes for the graders, and making other necessary arrangements to supervise the preparation of the road-bed for the laying of the rails.

Thus, it came about that sometime during the middle of August, 1873, the Denver Railway Association undertook the job of grading the first section of the South Park road between Denver and Morrison.[1] Where, or who, turned the first shovel full of dirt is not known; however, it is probably a safe bet that Governor John Evans, attended by the usual ceremonies connected with such a significant event, wielded the first spade full of earth; and whether an accompanying band played the "St. Louis Quick Step" (apologies to the Denver Pacific's opening ceremonies) or the "South Park Blues", the event did mark the beginning of one of Colorado's great narrow gauge railroad systems.

Apparently, the work of grading the line was distributed along the right of way at a number of points, for an item in the Rocky Mountain News of August 19th states:

"Tom Field, the Contractor, will put his force to work on the Denver South Park & Pacific Railroad on Wednesday, a few miles this side of Bear Creek. By the middle of next month several grading parties will be at work."[2]

At this point, the author would like to insert a newspaper story written about the South Park road and published in the Rocky Mountain News under the date of August 24, 1873, when the construction was first getting underway. Although the article paints a rather exaggerated but colorful picture of the territory through which the proposed lines of the railroad were to be built, and incorporated the usual amount of rosy predictions for a great and successful future, nevertheless it is a very interesting and informative article concerning the little railroad.

"THE DENVER SOUTH PARK & "PACIFIC RAILROAD

"This important enterprise is now fairly inaugurated, and its rapid construction may be regarded as a fixed fact. One grading force is now at work in the Platte Canon; another on the main line between Denver and the canon; while a third is at work on the Morrison branch, and other forces will be at work, at other points in a few days. Contracts for the ties, piles, and timbers will be let on the first of September. It is confidently believed that the cars will be running on fifteen miles of the road, to Morrison, in three months from the pres-

ent time. And by this time next year they will reach the mouth of Buffalo Creek, which point will be forty miles on the road to Fairplay. The company has determined to push the construction of that part of the line to Buffalo Creek as rapidly as the work can be done. They have the principal part of the means at command to do it with, independent of the sale of their first mortgage bonds. They have $300,000 cash subscription subject to draft with twenty per cent already paid in. The liberal arrangements with railroads extending from Denver to the East for a traffic contract to make a large sinking fund for its first mortgage bonds will doubtless make them the very best railroad bonds in the market, and secure their ready sale. These were the first important steps. And the $300,000 in bonds voted to the company by Arapahoe County definitely settled the question that Denver is to have a railroad direct to the South Park mines, and in fact to all the southwestern mines, for it will doubtless be extended through the Poncha Pass to Loma and Del Norte, and thence to the San Juan mines, in the southwestern corner of Colorado. The surveys of the Denver and South Park company (and they are the only actual surveys that have been made of a located line) have dispelled the delusion of the impracticability of the Platte Canon route for a narrow gauge railroad. They have proved that it is actually a much better and less expensive route, with less curvatures and lighter grades, than that in the Clear Creek Canon, through which, at a moderate expense, a railroad has been built, and is now in successful operation.

"Another merit of the route is that it diverges soon after leaving Denver from all other present railroads, and thus avoids competition. At Fairplay, ninety miles, it will have diverged from the line of the Denver & Rio Grande road on the east so that it will be about as far west of the nearest point on that road at Colorado Springs as it is from Denver. This fact demonstrates the absurdity of any claim of the Rio Grande company to the business of the South Park, as its line runs in a different direction, and its route will be separated from that of the Colorado Central up the valley of Clear Creek to the north of it by a very high and almost impassable range of mountains. Another merit of this line is that it has its starting point from Denver, the acknowledged commercial metropolis of the Rocky Mountains; a city from which five railroads now in operation diverge and this will make the sixth—a city which has more than trebled its population, trade, and wealth in three years, and which, at the same rate of increase will, in five years, have a population of not less than 50,000 inhabitants— a city to which the trade and travel of the vast mining country which will be traversed by this railroad will naturally tend, and which, of course, give it the lion's share of the business, even if another railroad should be built from another point into the South Park.

1. Corporate History, Colorado & Southern Ry.
2. Contract prices for grading were 14 cents per yard; ties 25 cents each delivered. Denver Daily Times, August 21, 1873.

Another merit of this railroad is the very heavy local business it will secure. At Morrison, fifteen miles out, it will doubtless command the stone and lime trade of Denver, as the quarries are of best quality and the greatest variety of building stone and lime, and will be the most convenient for shipment of any in the vicinity. Here, too, the extensive lumber mills of Turkey Creek will be accessible. This part of the line also passes immediately under a valuable coal bank controlled by the company two miles this side of Morrison. And as soon as the cars run to this point the road will have the travel and trade of the South Park. The stages will then run so as to carry the travel through from Denver to Fairplay by daylight. Morrison is one of the most romantic spots in Colorado, surrounded by a rich agricultural country, and has some of the most valuable mineral springs in the territory and is destined to become one of the most attractive watering places. All the way to the Platte Canon, nineteen miles, the line passes through one of the best agricultural districts in the territory. At the canon, it enters a heavily timbered country, through which the line passes for fifty miles. This is undoubtedly the best and most extensive forest in Colorado. As soon as the road reaches the mouth of Buffalo Creek, eighteen miles within the canon, to which point the company have determined to build it at once, it will be in the very midst of a forest of timber, capable of supplying the demands of the lumber, tie and wood market of Colorado for many years. And the cheapness with which these important articles can be placed on the cars at this point will doubtless enable this road to control the market for them at Denver. The vast magnitude of the lumber market, and the fact that for renewals alone the Kansas and Denver Pacific roads require annually two hundred thousand ties, will give some idea of the extensive and profitable business the road will do soon as it reaches this point. Here, too, the railroad will be reached by the wagons and stages from the South Park. The facilities it will here offer to the trade and travel of Lake, Park, and Summit Counties will not only secure all of it but vastly increase its amount. Ores that now lie on the dumps for the want of a market will, in vast quantities, be shipped from the extensive mines of these counties as soon as the railroad reaches Buffalo Creek. And the travel to the South Park will be also very largely increased. Thirty miles beyond Buffalo Creek the road reaches Hall's Gulch, having passed up the beautiful valley via Bailey's, Slaght's, and Hepburn's ranches, and through forests of excellent timber all the way. Here are the most valuable and extensive silver and lead mines, many of which are being actively worked at the present time. Here, too, the line will be within a few miles of the vast mineral regions of Snake River, across the range at and around Montezuma, from which a wagon road is now being constructed. From this point, the shipment of ores will be an immense traffic as to a large ex-

tent the mines are of argentiferous galena, which will give heavy freights in the shape of base bullion or pig lead. And from this point, for sixty miles, the route of the road passes near to the base of the mountains; abounding all the way in the richest mineral deposits. At Hamilton, twenty miles beyond Hall's Gulch, the road from Breckenridge, sixteen miles distant across the range, will be reached. Here, too, are the Tarryall mines and an excellent mine of coal near to the route which is now being worked. At Fairplay, twelve miles beyond Hamilton, the road will be in the immediate vicinity of the Mount Lincoln and Mount Bross silver mines; also, the mining districts of Montgomery, Hoosier Gulch, Buckskin Joe, Mosquito, and Horse Shoe, and it is estimated that from this point alone, a train load of ores will be shipped daily as soon as the railroad reaches it. From this place, which is destined to become a city of great importance, the line runs twenty miles south to the great salt springs. Here are already extensive works which will again assume their former importance as the principal source of the supply of salt for Colorado as soon as the road reaches them. They only suspended operations on account of the great expense of transportation by ox team ruling them out of the market upon the completion of railroads to Denver. The great quantity of salt used in the reduction of silver ores in Colorado, as well as for domestic purposes, will make this a very important traffic for the railroad as soon as it reaches this point. From the salt works to the beautiful and fertile valley of the Arkansas below Mayol's ranch, at the mouth of Trout Creek, will be twenty miles. At this point the road will command the trade of the extensive and rich mining districts of Lake County. It will be but a few miles below Granite Cache Creek and Twin Lakes, and will be accessible by good wagon roads down the Arkansas Valley from Red Mountain, California, Tennessee, Iowa, McNulty, Colorado and other mining districts around the head of the Arkansas, to which a branch will be easily extended. Here, too, it will command the San Juan mining trade and travel through the Poncha Pass by wagon road, until such time as the road shall be extended on that line. But it is the object of the company at first to build the main line to this point with its Morrison branch, and as soon as it may be found advisable, to extend the branch across the range into Summit County and down the Blue River to the Middle Park and thence to Utah, and also to extend its main line through the Poncha Pass to and up the Del Norte to the San Juan mines. This portion of the line now proposed to be built will, doubtless, form a main trunk line for the business of an immense country, connecting it all by the only feasible, direct route with Denver. The route for its entire distance of one hundred and fifty miles abounds in the most romantic scenery, and at numerous places will pass near mineral springs, along beautiful streams abounding in trout, in the vicinity of mountain lakes and through extensive forests, so that its attractions for tourists' travel will be unsurpassed by any railroad route in the world.

"That the main line of the Denver South Park & Pacific Railroad will be built, and that without delay, is now no longer a question; and that it will be one of the best paying roads in the country, when completed, there cannot be a doubt."

Prior to the voting of the bond issue, all expenses incurred in the initial preparations were paid for by the South Park interests under the name of their newly organized Denver Railway Association. However, now that the company was officially "on its way", it was imperative that necessary steps be taken to finance the construction company and supply it with funds. As an initial move toward building the Denver terminal and the 16 miles of road to Morrison, the railroad company turned over to the railway association practically all of its assets, namely the $300,000 of Arapahoe County bonds and $300,000 of railroad stock. Relative to the county bonds, Mock states:

"In spite of the fact that the eastern bond market was 'flat', the construction company realized $211,400 from the sale of the Arapahoe bonds it had received . . . the proceeds from the sale of these bonds were used to finance the building of the Morrison branch."

Although a considerable portion of the right of way had been graded along the line toward the vicinity of Bear Creek during the fall and winter of 1873-74, very little work of any other consequence seems to have been done until the following spring. However, the arrival of early spring in 1874 found much activity around our little road. First, we read in the Rocky Mountain News of February 28th where 800 tons of 30-pound iron rail had been ordered from the rolling mills. As it required approximately 47 tons of this rail per mile of track, this first shipment would be sufficient to complete the line to Morrison and take care of the miscellaneous terminal facilities in Denver. During February, terminal grounds in Denver were purchased, and in April, construction of the depot, shops, storehouses, etc., was commenced.[1] These terminal grounds were located at Lawrence Street, 6th Street, and Larimer Street. The depot, which was shared with the Denver & Rio Grande until 1879, was located on the northwest corner of 6th and Larimer. The shops and roundhouse were located on the northeast corner of 5th and Lawrence.

But a railroad must have engines and cars to operate; regarding the first cars, we read in the Rocky Mountain News of March 19, 1874, where Hallack Brothers of Denver were building 51 cars for the South Park railroad. But the building of these first 51 cars for the road is of minor importance as compared with the first locomotive. After considerable effort to locate some information relative to the South Park's first engine, the au-

1. Albert B. Sandford, Colorado Magazine. October, 1928.

126

thor had almost given up in despair when suddenly one day in the Denver Library (thanks to Miss Ina T. Aulls) we discovered, with much pleasure, the following news items, all published in the Denver Daily Times. The items are dated in order of their publication.

March 17, 1874.
"LOCOMOTIVE COMING!

"The first engine for the Denver South Park & Pacific R. R. will be shipped next week from the manufacturer at Connelsville, Penna. The builders, Dawson & Bailey, proprietors of the National Locomotive Works, claim it to be the finest narrow gauge locomotive ever built. The company has paid particular attention to this class of engine, and we have no doubt it will be first class in every respect.

"It is named 'FAIRPLAY', thus denoting the destination of the road. Thus another step is about accomplished towards the early opening of the first division of the Denver South Park & Pacific Railroad."
March 28, 1874.

"The 'FAIRPLAY' engine for the Denver South Park & Pacific, which was shipped a week ago from Pennsylvania, was being transferred yesterday at Kansas City to the Kansas Pacific track. It will probably reach this city tomorrow or the next day."

March 30, 1874.
"The engine 'FAIRPLAY' arrived via the Kansas Pacific last night. The tender is marked D S P & P R. The locomotive looks similar to those on the Denver & Rio Grande and is about the same weight. The wheels forward are smaller, however, being only 20 inches in diameter. It is besmeared with tallow to prevent rusting, and of course looks anything but handsome. A few hours work will make her look pretty as a picture."

March 31, 1874.
"The first engine for the Denver South Park & Pacific arrived here in charge of Mr. G. B. Mortimer, the travelling engineer of its builders, the National Locomotive Works of Connelsville, Penna. The engine has 34 inch drive wheels,[1] a 16 inch stroke, and its bow rests on a single pair of trucks. The furnace is five feet long, two and one-half feet high, 26 inches wide at the top, and 17 inches wide at the bottom; hence the grate surface is remarkably small. The boiler has 88 one and one-half inch tubes. The cab is of black walnut and ash. The tender sets upon six wheels, and is painted to correspond with the cab."

April 4, 1874.
"The new engine for the Denver & South Park has been 'switching' for the Denver & Rio Grande road, and is found to work admirably."

We mentioned that 800 tons of rail had been ordered in February. The March 28th Denver Daily Times states:

"The rails for the South Park are being shipped from Cincinnati, Ohio, as fast as they can be manufactured. About 300 tons are on the way."

On April 4th, the same paper stated:
"The iron for the Denver & South Park has commenced arriving in Denver, and track laying will be begun shortly."

And the News of May 3rd carried the following notice:
"All iron rail purchased by Evans in Cincinnati, Ohio, except 14 car-loads, has arrived. The balance is expected to reach here the 15th. It is 30 pounds per yard. Fish plates, bolts, and long spikes have arrived OK. The ties are 7 feet long and will be laid 3,000 to the mile, or 18 inches apart, center to center."

1. Note: 1885 U. P. records state that this engine was a 2-6-0 (mogul) with 11 x 16 cylinders, 36 inch drivers, and weighed 18 tons.

Meanwhile, the contractors had been busily engaged in making the roadbed ready for the ties and rails. The initial track laying started at the Denver Terminal grounds on April 18, 1874.[1] The track layers made good progress and by June 13th they had reached the mouth of Turkey Creek near Mt. Carbon, 14 miles from Denver. On June 24, 1874, the Rocky Mountain News carried the following item:

"The Denver South Park & Pacific's track is now completed to Morrison. The last switches were laid yesterday, June the 23rd."

The historian, Sandford, states that the South Park's first train was run into Morrison on Wednesday, June 24th, and that the event was fittingly celebrated by a grand free excursion train made up largely with passenger cars generously loaned by the Rio Grande. However, a newspaper item published in the Rocky Mountain News under the date of June 27th definitely states that the *South Park was opened* on Friday, June 26th, with a church excursion. This article also contains a statement by the newspaper reporter that "he, along with the president of the road . . . *purchased* their tickets for the benefit of the church", thus refuting the statement that the excursion was free. The newspaper story referred to is as follows:

"THE SOUTH PARK RAILROAD
"It Is Opened by a Church Excursion
"How It Was Enjoyed and What Is Thought of Morrison
"The New Road and Observations on Its
"Route, Construction, etc.

"The excursion of the Lawrence Street Methodist Episcopal Church to Morrison, yesterday, was one of the most delightful of the season. The great number of points of attraction near the depot, at Morrison, were all visited by various parties. Some went to the sulphur and chalybeate springs; some to the various groves; some to the grand red rocks; some climbed to the summits to view the picturesque scenery, and others took carriages and drove up to view the rocky cliffs in Turkey Creek Canon, but two miles away, while others still went trouting along the stream and up the canon.

"The ladies opened up their refreshment stands in the grove near the depot, on the bank of the creek, and plied the thirsty with lemonade and ice cream; while around, on tables provided for the purpose, the picnic baskets of the various parties were spread for the noon repast. All hands, our reporter and even the president of the railroad and his family, purchased their tickets for the benefit of the church; and everybody returned pleased and satisfied that they had got the worth of their money. Morrison will be the rage for picnic excursions for a long time, if not permanently, with the citizens of Denver.

"We understand an excursion train will go up on Sunday morning, leaving the depot at the crossing of

1. Albert B. Sandford, Colorado Magazine. October, 1928.

Larimer Street and the Rio Grande railroad track at 8 o'clock, and returning, arrive at 6 o'clock, P.M. Fare for round trip, $1.50. Tickets are on sale at Wells, Fargo & Co.'s office, Larimer Street, and on the train. The road will be opened for regular business on Wednesday, July 1st.

"As this is the opening of a road about which there has been much comment, we desire to say that we paid especial attention to its construction and equipment, as well as to the route over which it passes, and also to Morrison, and its future promise as a watering place. It was remarked by all the numerous people of the excursion, and especially by old railroad men, of whom there were a number, that they had never seen so smooth a track on a new road, nor a road more permanently and substantially built and equipped. The 'Dolly Varden' excursion cars are very nice, and only need an apron over the platforms to keep off the sparks, and bars at the end of the seats, to prevent accidents, to make them the most perfect cheap excursion arrangements we have seen. We understand these will be at once provided.

"The route of the road is an extremely pleasant one. Leaving the city it runs direct to the valley of the Platte, following up that stream to Bear Creek. On either hand are fine old cottonwood groves, with well cultivated farms, grain fields and gardens. Turning up Bear Creek Valley, the road for a short distance runs close to the stream, which is lined with trees, and rises on to the second bottom, leaving the valley to the right, and affording a view of one of the best cultivated and most productive agricultural valleys in Colorado. The material for the roadbed is unsurpassed, being mostly gravel; the ties are laid close, the rails fully spiked, and the track, new as it is, both smooth and solid. There is not and never has been a more thoroughly constructed road in the west. Of the prospective business and extension of the road we may speak hereafter, and here only congratulate our people upon the opening of Denver's sixth railway, and one which is destined to exercise so marked an influence upon her commercial future."

The Denver & South Park was officially opened for business on Wednesday, July 1, 1874. At this time, the system consisted of some seventeen miles of narrow gauge track, sidings, spurs, and yards. The rolling stock was limited to a pair of small locomotives, a few flat cars, a few box cars, and four passenger coaches. Two of these passenger coaches were designated as "smokers" and the other two as "ladies cars".[1] The first locomotive was a little 18-ton mogul built by Dawson & Bailey. The second engine was a 20-ton 4-4-0, also built by Dawson & Bailey, and was purchased secondhand from the narrow gauge Kansas Central Railroad. These two small engines served as the road's only motive power until number 3 arrived in 1878. From information available, it appears that the first freight and passenger

1. Albert B. Sandford, Colorado Magazine. October, 1928.

Union Pacific Denver & Gulf 108 with a derailed freight train beside Bear Creek in Morrison during the 1890's.

A view of Morrison in the 1880's, showing railroad facilities and a South Park mixed train.

cars were built by Hallack Brothers in Denver. The company's Annual Report for 1874 states that sufficient equipment to operate the Morrison Division and a portion of the second division had been provided at an expense of $47,190.75.

Freight traffic consisted largely of building stone, some marble, lime rock, and fence posts, with numerous cars of rough lumber from the saw mills scattered up and down Bear Creek.[1] At Mt. Carbon, just east of Morrison, was located a coal mine which, when the railroad was first opened, was able to supply the road with all the coal it needed.[2] In fact, the passenger business grew to such proportions that an order for six new flat cars was rushed which enabled the management to reconstruct them into excursion cars. Passengers were protected from the weather by a light roof supported by strong uprights. Seats were of common lumber, smoothed and painted, though not of the reversible type. Usually, ample time was available to turn the train on a wye near the depot at Morrison, but as that part of the track was sometimes used for the loading of freight, the cars often returned to Denver with the excursionists admiring the beauties of Bear Creek Canon riding backward.

Albert Sandford writes in Colorado Magazine, October, 1928:

". . . a pavillion was constructed, and while the younger set danced to the music of the best band Denver could furnish, the old folks rested in the shade of the trees along the clear waters of Bear Creek and talked of the wonderful progress being made in the territory, and visualized the future."

The Morrison Sulphur Springs, the large hotel, and other attractions were widely advertised by the railroad company who proposed to build up an extensive summer resort. To the people of Denver and surrounding area, Morrison remained a popular summer resort and picnic spot for years.

Apparently, the passenger business soon grew large enough to warrant two round trips per day between Denver and Morrison, for in an 1875 Official Guide we find the following published schedule:

"Trains leave Denver at 8:00 AM and 3:00 PM, arriving in Morrison (16 miles) at 9:15 AM and 4:30 PM. Returning: Leave Morrison at 9:45 AM and 5:00 PM, arriving in Denver at 11:15 AM and 6:00 PM. Connections with all diverging railroads out of Denver."

In the summer time, the passenger business was materially increased by excursions of the various Denver Sunday Schools, until the road was frequently referred to as "The Sunday School Route".

In addition to the Morrison resort business, the company also attempted to secure a more substantial source of traffic by promoting and building up the Bear Creek line both from the agricultural standpoint and as a suburban residential community for Denver. In advertis-

1. Albert B. Sandford, Colorado Magazine, October, 1928.
2. D. S. P. & P., Annual Report, 1874.

ing and promoting this potential source of traffic, the 1874 Annual Report stated:

"Besides these sources of local traffic, this division of the road passes all the way through a well settled farming country affording attractive sites for suburban villages for the residence of business men of the metropolis, and persons desiring to enjoy country air, and have fine gardens."

Very little information pertaining to the first track construction has come to light except that the grade, or roadbed, was primitive and unfinished. The track itself was constructed with 30-pound iron rail and "Fisher rail-joints" which, contrary to newspaper reports, was laid on 2,800 pine ties per mile. The rails were spiked directly to the ties, as was the early day custom in that region and as many old time photographs will bear out. Tie plates were improvements that were not to be found that far west at this period. According to the South Park's Annual Report for January 1, 1875, the 16-mile Morrison branch, or first division, cost $163,391, or an average of $10,212 per mile.

A report of earnings and expenses for the third quarter for the year 1874, by Chas. Wheeler, the railroad's auditor, shows the following results:

EARNINGS

1874	From Freight	From Passengers	From Express	From Mail	Total
July	$ 633.98	$1,300.25	$14.93	$ 50.00	$1,999.16
Aug.	881.90	1,326.00	12.57	50.00	2,270.47
Sept.	784.70	866.40	12.00	50.00	1,713.10
	$2,300.58	$3,492.65	$39.50	$150.00	$5,982.73

EXPENSES

	General Expenses	Conducting Transportation	Motive Power
July	$100.00	$ 645.12	$ 395.50
August	118.90	595.77	494.85
September	101.50	639.64	491.27
	$320.40	$1,880.53	$1,381.62

	Maintenance of Cars	Maintenance of Way	Total
	$ 26.25	$ 275.00	$1,441.87
	87.00	150.00	1,446.52
	157.11	193.00	1,582.52
	$270.36	$ 618.00	$4,470.91

Net earnings _____ $1,511.82
Average receipts per day for three months ___ 65.03
Average expenses per day for three months _ 48.60
Showing expenses to be about 75 per cent of earnings.

John W. Maxwell.

An example of the harp type switch stand commonly used on the South Park and the Colorado Central.

John W. Maxwell.

This photo shows a Fisher rail-joint in use on the South Park's track. The rail in the foreground is supported by one of these joints and a detached example is laid between the rails for comparison.

SODA LAKES AND GARFIELD QUARRY SPURS

Before taking leave of the Morrison area, mention should be made of two short spur lines built on the Morrison Branch. Very little information has come to light regarding either spur. One of them was known as Soda Lakes Spur. This track took off the Morrison line at milepost 16.9 and was built in a southerly direction for a distance of about one-quarter mile in 1878. W. E. Mahony states that some soda salts, or sodium, was secured in this vicinity in the early days but that the supply eventually played out. Jess Frazier states that there was also a fine marble quarry located here; after the quarry was abandoned, it filled up with water and that to this day a small building constructed of marble can be seen through the clear water at the bottom of the pit. The spur was abandoned in 1919.

The second spur was known as the Garfield Quarry or Satanic Mine Spur. This track branched off the Morrison line at milepost 17.6, and was built in a northerly direction for a distance of some 2¾ miles in 1878. The spur served to haul coal from a small mine known as the Satanic Coal Mine, together with limestone used by the smelters in Denver, from the quarry. From what can be learned, both the coal mine and the quarry played out and the entire line, with the exception of the wye where it branched off the main line, was abandoned in 1919. The old grade coming up from Morrison, as well as the quarry pit and the mine, can be plainly seen to this day from the Alameda Highway, which runs southwest from Denver.

Colorado's sixth railroad was now in operation; however, few persons realized the trying situations that had been involved. At the very outset the company met the most discouraging obstacle that a young railroad might encounter—the great financial panic of 1873. This financial crash, which wiped out stocks and bonds valued at millions and wholly checked railroad ventures, had its inception on September 19, 1873. Prices of securities fell, runs on banks began, and an abnormal commercial condition existed throughout the country. Colorado was no exception. It was a fateful period for railroads and their builders. Being hit harder than most lines of business, the railroads were the heaviest sufferers thereby. The depressed condition of business and a want of faith and capital in all enterprises requiring heavy outlays of money had very much retarded the progress of the Morrison line.

As previously stated in the contract between the South Park company and the Denver Railway Association, the railroad company was to issue its bonds to the extent of $20,000 per mile to the construction company. Evans spent some time in the east, including a protracted trip to Europe, in an unsuccessful attempt to dispose of the railroad's bonds. On the other hand, the capital stock was also practically valueless. Those, who in the summer of 1873, had been willing to extend aid to the South Park enterprise, refused to contribute further; and those who had declined to assist were steadfast in their refusal. Stock in the South Park company went begging at fifty cents on the dollar. The only saving factor was the optimism of John Evans, who prevented dissolution time after time by his cheering words: "Gentlemen, hold onto your stock; it is the best investment you ever made, for beyond these dark clouds I can see the bright sunlight of success which will soon burst upon us." In the due course of time, those gentlemen saw John Evans' prediction come to pass. But in view of the money stringency caused by such existing conditions, it can be easily understood why he encountered so much difficulty in attempting to obtain additional funds in order to continue with the building of the railroad.

As far as business was concerned, the little railroad experienced some dark days and tough sledding for a few years. Curious as it seems, one of the prominent factors that made it possible for the railroad to maintain its spark of life was its competitor, the stage lines. At that time, one of the largest stage lines operating southwest out of Denver into the South Park country was the Spotswood & McClellan organization. Although they were competitors from the transportation standpoint, Robert J. Spotswood and John Evans were very great friends. Spotswood's ability as a stage line manager ranked with the best of the Overland Executives. As the railhead of the South Park road continued to advance, Spotswood's stages made these points their new, though temporary, termini. How this stage business developed into tremendous proportions within the next few years due to the close cooperation between the Evans and Spotswood enterprises will be seen as the end-of-track advances west.

Soon after the completion of the South Park to Morrison, that point became the terminal of the Spotswood & McClellan stage line that had previously operated directly into Denver. Spotswood's Concord stages made connections with the South Park's morning passenger train at Morrison and delivered the passengers at Fairplay that night, a distance of approximately sixty miles via the stage road. As evidence of this cooperation between the two corporations, we quote the following notice as published in the Rocky Mountain News under date of January 1, 1875:

"Trains leave from the Denver depot of the Denver South Park & Pacific at 6th and Larimer Streets daily except Sunday. Connections at Morrison with the Spotswood & McClellan Stage Lines for Fairplay and all points in southwest Colorado."

The combined business furnished by the stage line and wagon roads out of Morrison, together with the traffic derived from the vicinity of Morrison, barely enabled the South Park to pay its operating expenses. As a further attempt to help make ends meet, the company adopted the policy of affording every facility for developing and fostering the local business and settlements

Denver & South Park Stage Company

Daily Line of Four and Six Horse Concord Coaches,

Carrying the United States Mail and Express. Connecting with the Denver and South Park railroad at Morrison, for Fairplay, Alma and all points in Park, Summit and Lake counties. The only Direct Route from Denver to Fairplay, Leadville, Oro City, and all points in California Gulch and the southwestern mines. Train connecting with the coach leaves foot of Larimer street daily at 7 a. m., and connects with coach at Morrison at 8:10 a. m. Through to Fairplay in ONE DAY.

W. C. McClellan & R. J. Spotswood, Proprietors.

From Rocky Mountain News, May 2, 1878.

along its line, relying more on the increased amount of business thus created than upon exorbitant rates. In pursuance of this policy, the company issued special tickets at exceptionally low rates for this part of the country. They also issued annual passes for a limited period to parties who would settle, build and reside in the towns and villages along its line. They also granted concessions on freight rates to persons who would establish their enterprises along the line, which would in turn increase the business of the communities. But with all this, the original estimate that the extension of the South Park road would be financed from the earnings of the completed sections failed to materialize. Throughout the depression, there was a continuous effort on the part of the South Park management to raise money on subscriptions to capital stock in order to continue construction, but they enjoyed little success. Thus lacking the necessary finances, the Denver Railway Association was unable to proceed any farther south from Bear Creek Junction with their projected main line. The panic had put an end to all railroad construction everywhere. In view of such circumstances, further prosecution of work was suspended, the South Park made no further progress to speak of, and Morrison remained the terminus of the

road for several years. They were experiencing some dark days.

In 1875, another move was made in an effort to renew construction. Meanwhile, the Denver Railway Association had been reorganized as the Denver Railway & Enterprise Company, with a capital stock of $500,000. This Denver Railway & Enterprise Company was incorporated on October 12, 1874. As was the case of the Denver Railway Association, this new organization was controlled by the officers of the South Park road. The Trustees were as follows: John Evans, David H. Moffat, Jr., Chas. B. Kountze, Henry Crow, Walter S. Cheesman, J. Sidney Brown, A. B. Daniels, John Hughes, and John W. Morrison. The old incorporation papers state that the object of the company was:

"To open and work quarries, prepare stone, make lime from the rock and plaster of paris from the gypsum, market coal, make plank, lath, shingles, and lumber. Undertake the grading, construction and equipment of The Denver South Park & Pacific R. R. or any part thereof as well as furnishing or procuring the Right-of-Way and Depot grounds therefor and the furnishing and erection of all buildings, bridges, tanks and other things necessary and applicable to such Railroad in the creation of business for the same, including the laying out of Towns at Stations on the Line thereof and promoting the set-

Colorado & Southern 70 and 69 passing the register station at Sheridan Jct. on a late winter afternoon in 1941.

Colorado & Southern 69 and 70 arriving at Denver with a train from South Platte, which was the remnant of the Platte Canon line in 1940.

tlement and improvement and the Sale of Lots or other disposition of same."

Author's note: There are no records on file pertaining to the incorporation papers of the first construction company, the Denver Railway Association; however, they must have been very similar to the papers of this second construction company as it was nothing more than a reorganization of the old company.

All securities and funds the original construction company had received for construction purposes were turned over to this new organization. Arrangements were then made for the Denver Railway & Enterprise Company to take over the original contract held by its predecessor. The contract was signed on May 8, 1875. But with the exception of a little grading work south of Bear Creek Junction, this was as far as matters progressed. Isaac W. Chatfield was the principal contractor building the line through this section. This second construction company soon became financially embarrassed and no further construction work of any importance was entered into throughout the remainder of the year. Early in 1876, there began to be raised a hue and cry for a continuation of the South Park road, and a drive was started in an effort to secure further public subscriptions to the stock of the new construction company.

During February and March, the Denver Board of Trade, through the Denver Daily Times, urged the public to lend their aid, stating that funds would have to be raised at once in order to revive Denver's "drooping advantages". This was the period when Kansas Pacific and Santa Fe activities in southern Colorado were seriously curtailing Denver's trade importance in that region. However, in spite of campaign pleas, public support was greatly lacking; in fact, notwithstanding the well known financial conditions in consequence of the panic, Governor Evans and his associates were bitterly assailed in Denver because they did not go ahead and build the road to which Arapahoe County had voted $300,000 in bonds. The burden of unreasonable criticism and faultfinding fell upon Evans, and by April of 1876, public clamor for continuation of the road had become so pressing and so much criticism was being directed against him for his failure to get results, that he offered to resign as President of the South Park, but the Directors would not even consider the idea. As a matter of fact, no one else wished to assume such responsibility.

Again a shuffling of the securities followed and a third construction company, the Denver & San Juan Construction Company, was organized with a capital stock of $350,000. The incorporation papers of the San Juan Company are dated July 6, 1876, and state that the object of the company was:

"To promote the industrial interests of the Territory of Colorado by the construction and equipment of the uncompleted portion of The Denver South Park & Pacific Rail Road Company with all its necessary Buildings, Depots, Tanks and other incidents thereto by contract and if necessary to operate the same, to procure Rights-of-way, subscriptions to the Stock of said Road, donations of property or money, and to acquire the Title by gift or purchase of lands, town-sites, lots, coal or other mines, timber, and other things for this company or The Denver South Park & Pacific Rail Road Company."

With considerable difficulty, the $350,000 was finally subscribed after which the subscribers elected a board of Trustees consisting of nine members; four were from the old company and five were of a new group. This new board consisted of John Evans, David H. Moffat, Jr., Walter S. Cheesman, and Charles B. Kountze of the old group, and John W. Smith, William Barth, Frederick J. Ebert, George Tritch, and J. Sidney Brown of the new group. John W. Smith was elected President; David Moffat, Treasurer, was the only officer from the old group. Apparently, the holders of securities in the former company were paid off with the bonds of the road, so that control was left in the hands of the new managers. Such at least must be inferred from Evans' statement: "We agreed to close out the stock and bonds and let the new people have the benefit of the enterprise."

As all previous construction companies had done before, the San Juan company took over the original construction contract and began preparations for the continuation of the South Park road. President Smith proposed to raise $150,000 with which to complete construction of the road to Bailey's Ranch, some 55 miles from Denver. He also proposed that the San Juan Construction Company take its pay in the form of the railroad company's first mortgage bonds.

It was not until 1876-77 that the financial clouds which had spread like a pall of blackness over the entire country began to lighten somewhat, and a sufficient amount of money was raised to enable the company to once again take up construction of their road. Although not on a large scale at first, construction was resumed by the San Juan Company during October, 1876, and by June of the following year they had 300 men at work in Platte Canon. However, blasting out a right of way through this mountainous defile required heavy financing and as the Morrison branch was the only part of the railroad in operation up to this time, the revenue realized from the operation of that 16-mile section was not a drop in the bucket as compared to the money necessary to combat such heavy railroad construction as was being encountered in Platte Canon. In spite of the difficulties though, the San Juan company made some fair progress and completed the grade slightly beyond milepost 26 near Stevens Gulch, with some additional partially completed grade beyond, when funds began to run low. Apparently, the old difficulty was cropping up again; it was one thing to secure subscriptions, but it was another to collect installments into which payments on stock subscriptions were divided. Thus, the Denver & San Juan Construction Company went the way of its predecessors.

At this point in our story, we shall insert a very interesting and descriptive newspaper article which covered the progress of the South Park road up to this time and explained some of the difficult construction problems which the engineers and contractors encountered in Platte Canon. This story was published in the Rocky Mountain News of October 12, 1877.

"Open the Way for the
Denver South Park & Pacific Railroad
"Progress of a Great Enterprise—Work That Tells and Work That Conquers—Autumn Days in the Mountains

"Given a quick stepping team, pleasant companions, and one of Colorado's glorious autumn days, and the ride from Denver to Platte Canon is a most enjoyable one. Such was the combination on Monday, when at less than thirty minutes notice, the writer found himself whirling along the Broadway road toward the great canon through which the South Platte finds its way to the plains, and to the Missouri—seven hundred miles to the eastward. The broad, cultivated and fertile valley of the upper Platte needs no description. The numerous stacks of hay and grain upon each farm demonstrates the wealth of its soil and the industry of its inhabitants. Its general thrift and prosperity was bespoken in the somewhat unmusical notes of the threshing machines, and the rumblings of the 'Harvest Queen' and 'Rough and Ready' mills. We pass Petersburgh, named after Peter Magnes, a Swedish pioneer of local celebrity; and Littleton, a quiet, inviting village, also named in honor of a gentleman whose enterprise and industry, and strong faith in the future of Colorado, and the Platte Valley in particular, have never been Little, although that is his honored name; we ride swiftly by the splendid ranches of Brown and Skelton and Hussey and Lilley and Shallabarger and Archer and Strong and Lehow, and, at a few moments before one, stop at Gallager's for dinner, just at the mouth of the great canon.

"All along the route from Littleton we have been travelling by the side of the South Park grade, with the ties distributed and everything in readiness for the finishing gang and the iron. And now, after an hour's rest, our team is once more in readiness, and for our road up the canon we take the railway grade, the future pathway for the Denver South Park & Pacific itself. Six miles bring our party to the end of the finished work, and we draw rein at the tie camp of Mr. C. A. Deane, of this city, where hospitable entertainment for the night is provided, and time afforded to examine into the details of the great work which is in progress there.

"WHAT HAS BEEN DONE

"The distance from the mouth of Platte Canon to the forks, where the stream divides, is eight and one-half miles, and the work upon this section of the route is under the charge and direction of Mr. Frank Bartlett, as locating engineer. Six miles of the grade are com-pleted and ready for the iron, with the exception of one or two unimportant bridges or culverts. One mile is nearly completed, and on the remaining one and one-half miles, work is just being begun. Two contractor's gangs are at work: I. W. Chatfield, with sixty men, and Robert Woods, with sixty-five men. The cost and estimated cost of the work has been as follows: For one mile, $4,000; for three miles at the rate of $8,000; for one mile, $15,000; for one mile, $17,000; and for the remaining two and one-half miles at the rate of $18,000 per mile. The highest grade is 137 feet to the mile, while the average grade is only 60 feet to the mile. The greatest curvation is 24 degrees, or a radius of 240½ feet. The distance is made with only two bridges. The first three and one-half miles skirt the north bank of the river, where a crossing is made by a fine iron bridge, something less than one hundred feet long. Thence the route follows the south bank for about three and one-half miles more, where a second iron bridge will carry the road again to the north side, which it follows for the remaining distance to the forks. Above the forks, the only information I have relative to the progress of the work is that Kennedy and Madge are grading with a force of thirty-five men, and that between there and Bailey's, five gangs are at work. The engineer in charge is Mr. Thomas Withers.

"A FINE PIECE OF ENGINEERING

"Commenting on these facts—which speak largely for themselves—it must be remarked that the work now finished has been done in the most substantial manner. Iron rails were never laid upon a firmer, safer, or more excellent grade that this one is, or will be, to the end of the canon. The location of the route is beyond criticism, and as a piece of construction engineering, must be pronounced the best it has yet been our good fortune to inspect. It is doubtful if, in the history of Rocky Mountain engineering, greater difficulties have ever confronted a locating engineer; but admitting that they have, it is certain that none have ever been overcome in a more scientific or successful manner. Mr. Bartlett seems to have studied with care the entire canon, and to have adopted a line which has been constructed with lighter grades, and at the same time with a more uniform one than upon any similar route in the country, and at a cost of less than one-half of what it was estimated at four years ago, when at that late date, even, some engineers pronounced it both impassable and impracticable.

"THE DIFFICULTIES OF THE WORK

"When the work of location ceased, the labors of the contractors began. What they have accomplished can be better seen than described. In many places they have been obliged to let their men down with ropes secured to overhanging masses of rock. A drill hole would be made with great difficulty, and the drill left within; then another a few feet away; then a tie would be lowered upon the projecting drills, and a footing was thus

L. C. McClure.

An example of the rugged terrain encountered in lower Platte Canon by the South Park construction crews.

*Chas. Weitfle photo,
from Francis Rizzari Collection.*

Above. Mason bogie 6, "Ten Mile", with a mixed train in Platte Canon.

L. C. McClure.

Right. Colorado & Southern 46 and 8 climbing Platte Canon with the daily passenger train, about 1905.

secured for the men to put in the first blast. Thus they worked down through many feet of the hardest granite, the powder and glycerine and dynamite rending away the rocks, and thus half tearing from the solid mountain wall, half stealing from the river's bed, a pathway for the iron horse. Thus for weeks and months have these fearless and energetic men labored within a few miles of our city. The ringing of the steel upon their anvils, the clinking of the drills, the steady stroke of the hammer, the sharp bang and sullen roar of the blast have not indeed been heard; but their results are to be seen all along the great mountain gorge, and the work has so far progressed that its chief difficulties may be said to have been overcome, and that which remains to be accomplished is but a small part of what has already been completed. 'The back-bone of the canon is broken', complacently remarked Mr. Bartlett, as he stood looking at one of Chatfield's sixty-foot rock cuttings, and pointed up the canon to where some of Wood's gang were hanging by their eyelids to a precipitous cliff. Progressing thus satisfactorily, it may be added that the contractor's work will not be completed until about the first of January coming.

"TIEING THE ROAD

"No mention of the constructive work of the South Park road would be complete without a reference to the work of obtaining and distributing ties, which Mr. C. A. Deane, of this city, has so successfully managed. To transport supplies to the almost inaccessible camps of the tie cutters, to construct roads for their delivery on the grade, or at the river bank to be floated down to the vast booms below, has required an amount of energy, judgment and perseverance that would tax the capacities of many men; and yet Mr. Deane has cut, drawn, floated, and delivered on grade, and at designated points, 60,000 ties at a minimum cost to the company, and at a fair profit to himself. There are yet 40,000 to be delivered, and they are being pushed forward at as fast a rate as possible, and even faster than the requirements of the company demand. The ties are six and a half, and seven feet long—seven inches face—and cut from young and thrifty pine and spruce timber, and all of the best possible quality. They will be laid at the rate of 2,800 to the mile.

"LIFE IN THE CAMPS

"Deane's tie camp is situated on the south side of the river, just where a little stream comes down from the mountains, and opens a roadway to his large timber tract not far distant. Here he proposes to build a store and hotel, for which he is now moulding brick, as well as a saw mill. A post office has been applied for. Chatfield's camp is directly opposite, on the north bank. A little farther up the gulch—known as Wolfert's—is the engineer's camp, over which Mrs. Bartlett presides with much grace and hospitality. Up the canon three-fourths of a mile, on a shelf of the rocks, are the white tents of

Wood's graders, and to which supplies have to be transported by a circuitous, if not a dangerous, trail. The men are quiet and well behaved. Few accidents, and still fewer deaths, have occurred. On few public works have the lives and comfort of the men been more carefully protected or provided for. The food furnished is excellent, and is well served. 'Boston', the cook at the tie camp, is a famous caterer, and dishes up on tin a most palatable meal, of boiled beef and potatoes, pork and beans, rice, pickles, bread and butter, pie, tea and coffee —which we must admit would be all the more inviting, even to a hungry, tramping editor, if served with the civilizing china, and silverware, napkins, table cloths, etc. Custom is by no means the least powerful of tyrants.

"AUTUMN DAYS IN THE CANON

"To describe the wild and rugged grandeur of the Platte Canon is not necessary in this connection. The granite walls rise on either side of the stream to heights varying from 500 to 1,500 feet; at times they are but forty feet apart, while the stream at the bottom of the gorge spans only twenty-three feet. The ride through the canon will not be surpassed in interest or in wealth of scenery by any on the continent. At this season the cold-gray and dark-green of the mountain slopes are relieved by rich tints of gold and crimson and brown. Following up the little streams and gulches which run into the main canon, the brightest and most varied leaves can be gathered—the coloring of the landscape lacking perhaps in New England's variety, but making up in richness and brilliancy of hue. Autumn leaves gathered here retain their tints more tenaciously than do those from eastern woods. In the more shady nooks and beneath overhanging banks and rocks can be gathered many mosses and plume-like ferns. Little do the city readers of THE NEWS know of the interest and pleasure and beauty which await the wanderers along the mountains and reward them for hard climbing and long rambles from the camp with autumn bouquets of glowing colors.

"'ALL ABOARD FOR BAILEY'S'

"The late winter or early spring is certain to see the South Park road completed to Bailey's on the north fork of the Platte. Thence it will have comparatively few difficulties to overcome to reach the South Park and upper Arkansas country, and thence to the golden region of the San Juan. Its completion, section by section, will open new industries in the state, develop new resources, quicken the commerce of our city, and lay tributary to Denver a country unsurpassed in timber, agricultural, and mineral wealth. It will build up at once a local as well as a through traffic, which will not fail to be remunerative, and which will place the Denver South Park & Pacific among the chief feeders to Denver's growth and prosperity. A Denver road, built by Denver money, owned by Denver men, and to be controlled for

W. H. Jackson photo,
from the State Historical Society of Colorado.

L. C. McClure.

Deansbury, later known as Strontia Springs, a summer resort in Platte Canon. The top photo, looking upgrade, shows the hotel in 1884; and the lower photo, looking downgrade, shows the same building about 1905.

the commercial welfare of our city—this enterprise cannot be too strongly encouraged, or too kindly fostered by our citizens. And next season, and ever thereafter, as in an elegant car, the tourist shall roll up this canon of the Platte River upon iron rails, gazing upon its scenery, and finding no words to express his wonder and admiration, let him remember the liberal enterprise and nerve of the men whose money was subscribed and paid for the road; the skill and perseverance and scientific ability of the engineers who planned and directed the work; and last, but not least, the muscular energy; and heroic endurance of the laborers who wrought long and well, and mastered at last the granite walls of the mountains and laid them down as a pathway for his train."

LEADVILLE

It was during this period while the South Park was tediously laboring its way through the canon of the South Platte, headed for Kenosha, that the first faint rumblings of the great carbonate[1] camp of Leadville were heard; rumblings that soon broke into a raucous thunder and were destined to be heard throughout the length and breadth of the land. The sudden rise of this new "El Dorado" gave the railroad a definite objective and the tremendous effect which it exerted on the future life of the Denver South Park & Pacific is a major item of first importance in its history.

The discovery of the valuable carbonate deposits at Leadville was almost providential for the road. In the fall of 1876, upon the renewal of active construction, Leadville was unheard of, and carbonates were an unknown quantity. The railroad was to be pushed forward upon the general principle, steadfastly adhered to by the original projectors, that there was wealth in the mountains, and that it would be found. Almost before the contractors had their forces fairly well trained —certainly before they had succeeded in pushing the end-of-track through Platte Canon—Leadville burst into prominence as a great mining center, amply justifying the anticipation of John Evans and his officials.

The camp first came into existence around the latter part of 1859 and early 1860, hence it dates back to the state's pioneer days. It was then that prospectors were roaming this wild rough part of the Rockies, seeking gold in the alluvial sands. Once the first strikes were made, new discoveries occurred in rapid succession from east to west across the mountainous country. The whole domain, now included in the State of Colorado, was commonly spoken of in those days as the "Pikes Peak Region", there being little idea in the minds of the eastern citizens as to the real geography of the west, except that it contained this famous mountain. The hardy prospectors who worked their way overland and discovered the rich placer diggings at Gregory Gulch and

1. So called because the principal ore was lead carbonate ($PbCO_3$) rich in silver.

Payne's Bar, subsequently known as Black Hawk and Idaho Springs, soon paved the way for more and more of these easterners, and the overflow began.

It was not long before the first range of mountains had been explored and the famous South Park country came in for its share of investigation. The gulches along the western sde of the park soon disclosed their valuable contents, and the search continued over the adjacent ranges—the Park Range and the Saguache Range in the Continental Divide. The discoveries of gold in these western portions of Colorado followed as a natural consequence in due time. The discoveries of placer gold in such districts as Tarryall, Fairplay, Buckskin Joe, Breckenridge, and California Gulch occurred during this general free-for-all prospecting indulged in by persons from eastern states, and it is a noteworthy fact that many of the greatest finds were made by men who had never before had any experience in such lines.

Some historians write that the discoveries thus made in Colorado were by men who were working their way overland to the California fields, which had come into prominence a decade before. The gulches of Colorado afforded splendid opportunity to these pioneers for experimenting in this new line of occupation. They further relate that California Gulch was given its name for the simple reason that the discoverers of gold in this gulch were satisfied to call off their proposed journey to the west coast; for they had found an "El Dorado" here—why go farther? However, the most plausible explanation of the origin of the name is found in Lewis Gandy's life of H. A. W. Tabor. According to Gandy, the gulch was discovered by five prospectors, namely, Lee, Slater, Stevens, Rafferty, and Currier. These five men had been placer mining in the vicinity of Black Hawk and, apparently dissatisfied with their luck at this camp, crossed the Park Range through Mosquito Pass during the early spring of 1860 in search of richer placer workings. The first week of April found these men prospecting in one of the many gulches at the headwaters of the Arkansas River. It seems that one of the party, Abe Lee, upon washing out a pan of gravel, let out a yell with the remark—"I've got all of Californy right in this here pan!" Thus the name "California Gulch".

The gulch proper was some four miles long and lay in an east to west direction somewhat near the center of Lake County. California Gulch, as it was duly called, was destined to enjoy a brief season of notoriety as a gold producing camp and then lapse back into obscurity for a number of years, only to awaken to a newer and mor famous period, as one of the richest mining camps in the world.

The rich placer diggings in this gulch yielded an immense quantity of the precious metal. Before fall the news had spread like chaff before the wind and over 10,000 people had emigrated into the upper reaches of the Arkansas River and the famous gulch and the im-

L. C. McClure photo,
from Denver Public Library Western Collection.

Mount Massive, Colorado's second highest peak, looms majestically to the west of Leadville, across the Arkansas Valley. The South Park station is directly over the timber trestle in the foreground, and the Colorado Midland roundhouse can be seen behind the church steeple.

mediate area was jammed with prospectors from one end to the other. Among the early fortune hunters to arrive was our friend "Haw" Tabor and his wife and child. Tabor had left Denver travelling by wagon via Ute Pass, South Park, Trout Creek Pass, and up the Arkansas to reach the new bonanza. Oro City, located at the eastern end and known for a time as Boughtown, was the main camp. The gulch was just one long street —if one could call it that.

Before November of that year 1860, over $2,500,000 in gold had been taken out of the district by these miners. The limited water supply together with a short working season due to the severe cold weather (because of the high altitude, which was in the neighborhood of 10,500 feet above sea level) was a great drawback to the development of claims. This resulted in a majority of the miners leaving the camp for Denver or other parts to return again the following spring. However, it was not long before the surface gold of the rich placer diggings had been extracted and the camp's importance dwindled. Consequently, the miners gradually abandoned the district. By 1866 only about 150 miners were left in the gulch and the glory of Oro City faded. During this period, close to $5,000,000 had been panned out of the streams and pebbles of California Gulch. The hills surrounding this famous camp were full of treasure, but men's eyes were sealed. The story is told that one of the last acts of the miners before leaving was to tear down the old log gambling hall. Upon taking up the flooring, over $2,000 was panned from the dirt directly under it. Gold dust was money here and no money except this had been used.

During the time that the early prospectors had been working the many placer bars up and down California Gulch, one striking feature had impressed itself upon all the miners. In the bottom of their pans and rockers, at each washing, there accumulated a black sand, so heavy that it interfered with the proper settling of the gold, and so abundant that it clogged the riffles in their sluice boxes. In addition, they were obliged to move numerous large boulders that interfered with their mining operations. They had no idea what this heavy black sand was, nor what the components of the many boulders were—and they did not stop to investigate.

Who first detected that this heavy black sand might be carbonate of lead is uncertain. In 1873, one A. B. Wood, together with Wm. H. Stevens, tested some of this mysterious black sand and succeeded in extracting a large portion of silver. The two metallurgists then began a systematic search for the source of this sand drift. Their experiences and difficulties, followed by the eventual discovery of the immense carbonate beds of lead and silver bearing ore, is another story, and although very interesting, cannot be included here.

Soon rumors began to spread concerning new riches in the hills surrounding old California Gulch, and by the spring of 1878, the camp's newly discovered fame was spreading like a prairie fire before the wind. In March, 1878, the first sale of mining property was made that aroused the attention of the outside world, when four mining claims were sold for something like a quarter of a million dollars. From this time on, the finger of destiny pointed toward Leadville. The thousands who had abandoned the district a few years back were now returning. The nucleus of the new camp consisted of a group of log cabins located at the western end of California Gulch. In 1877, a petition for a post office was drawn up by Messrs. Henderson, Wood and Meyer, which necessitated the adoption of a name for the new town. Mr. Wood proposed "Lead City". Mr. Henderson objected because it might be confused with a place located in the Black Hills known as Lead City. So as a compromise, the name "Leadville" was chosen.[1] The place was duly organized as a town on January 14, 1878, and "Haw" Tabor was chosen Mayor, an honor he well deserved.[2] He was also the town's Postmaster for a time.

Thus a rejuvenated mining camp was again on its way, destined to rise as Colorado's most famous and richest mining town. The Denver newspapers took up the cry, the railroads advertised it all over the east; to get to Leadville was the ambition of thousands of souls. A motley crew poured into the place. Miners, prospectors, border ruffians, pimps, con-men, bull whackers, mule skinners, cow hands, pilgrims, horse thieves, tinhorn gamblers, saloon keepers, capitalists, lawyers, bankers, doctors, merchants—all who were able to cut loose— not to forget the "Filles de Joie" and their Madams who were to comprise the tenderloin section of Leadville. They turned their footsteps toward the new El Dorado with all possible speed; even "Soapy" Smith with his mysterious little cubes of soap showed up. Human life was endangered and mule and horse flesh recklessly sacrificed. Stage companies organized and put on six-horse Concord Stages from Denver, Morrison, Colorado Springs, Canon City, and other convenient places in an effort to furnish some sort of transportation to those trying to reach the new camp. Private conveyances hauled their share and hundreds walked. There was almost a continuous procession of freighters with their mule and ox teams hauling food, machinery, and other necessary supplies which the new camp needed so badly. The spring and summer of 1879 was the same story. An average of over 200 persons a day were arriving in Leadville. Log huts, board shanties, canvas tents, and even caves dug in the sides of the hills, failed to provide enough shelter for all that came. Men were even glad to pay for the privilege of spreading their blanket on the sawdust of some barroom floor for a place to sleep or to spread out on some bales of hay in an alley. Every-

1. U. S. Geological Survey Bulletin No.'s 148-149.
2. "The Tabors" by Lewis Gandy.

141

L. C. McClure.

Looking up Platte Canon at the tiny hamlet of Bailey. Both track and station can be seen at the edge of the meandering river.

L. C. McClure.

On a sunny summer afternoon in 1903, the Denver-bound train pauses at Shawnee while the passengers scramble aboard.

where was rush and excitement. All the rough life of the earliest camps was revived, but on a larger scale. Those were boom days with their gambling hells, stock sales, and gilded glamour. There arose a motto at Leadville which ran: "We are here for dollars—not for health". Leadville by daylight was a sight to behold, but Leadville by gas light was still more wonderful, and far more suggestive. The streets were fairly alive with excitement. The miners would swarm into the town after their day's work to partake of Leadville's hospitality, wine, women, and song. Notorious State Street was a bedlam from dark to dawn. For a time the camp was called the "slaughterhouse of morals". It was no place for a weakling. As a mining town, Leadville probably had no superior on the civilized globe. Wm. S. Jackson quotes an entry from Chas. F. Adams' dairy:[1]

"Wednesday, September 22, 1886. Leadville: Left Gunnison at 7:00 sharp and ran over Alpine Pass to Leadville. Drove around town in afternoon. . . . In evening we all saw Leadville by gas light—an awful spectacle of low vice."

Fortunes were being made overnight. The beggar or tenderfoot of today became the rich man of tomorrow. Money for investment poured into the camp from New York, Chicago, and other eastern financial centers. Scanty grubstakes multiplied into hundreds of thousands of dollars within a year's time. An example of this was that of our friend, "Haw" Tabor, who was operating a small grocery store at the time, and one of his mines, the famous "Little Pittsburg" which made him many times a millionaire. History relates that Tabor grubstaked two poor boys by the name of August Rische and George Hook to the amount of something like $17.00. The two boys struck a vein of silver bearing ore at a 25-foot depth. Following this contact, they encountered an exceedingly rich vein of ore. The Little Pittsburg mine contained walls of silver- and lead-bearing ore. A short time later, Hook sold out for $98,000 and shortly afterward, Rische sold his share for $262,000. Many other famous mines were discovered such as the Winnemuc, the Soda Springs, the Adelaid, the New Discovery, the Matchless, and the Robert E. Lee. In the Matchless, which Tabor owned, were veins of ore from 3 to 20 inches thick assaying as high as 2,500 ounces of silver per ton with 30% lead. Silver was then selling at $1.11 per ounce. The reader can figure out Tabor's profit here. The Robert E. Lee, another Leadville bonanza, established some sort of a record when it produced $118,500 in silver and lead in the 17-hour period of January 13, 1880.

According to U. S. Gov't. statistics, the annual production, or combined value in dollars, of all minerals such as gold, silver, lead, copper, and zinc that were pro-

duced during this particular period in Lake County was as follows:

1858 to 1867	$ 5,322,000
1868	60,600
1869	90,900
1870	65,600
1871	101,500
1872	135,000
1873	228,800
1874	217,000
1875	63,800
1876	87,800
1877	670,600
1878	2,490,000
1879	11,285,200
1880	14,910,900
	$35,720,700

In the fall of 1877, the population of Leadville numbered something like 300 persons and the town consisted of just a few stores and saloons. We are told that within two years, it grew to be the second city in the State, with 15,000 population, only to see this figure doubled in a few more years; today, there are about 3,800 people living in the town. It was one of those extraordinary productions peculiar to a mining country; one of those places that from a lone cabin became a village in a night, a town in a week, a city within a month, and a booming metropolis the first year. In commenting on the place, the editor of the Colorado Springs Gazette called Leadville a "city"—through a violent stretch of courtesy. By 1880, Leadville had 28 miles of streets, which were, in part, lighted by gas at an expense of $5,000 per year. A critic of the town, writing in an early Colorado newspaper, stated:

"Leadville, the Colorado yearling, has announced its intentions of putting in a street car system. The place has scarcely learned to walk before it wants to ride."

The rapid growth of the camp and its mining industry brought about a tremendous need for supplies and created a transportation problem that was growing more acute every day. Since the wagon and stage coach were the only means of transportation between Leadville and the outside world, the freighters and stage line operators were taxed to the utmost. Previous to the arrival of the railroad, a large portion of this wagon and stage traffic was distributed over four principal routes. The first was from Georgetown by way of Argentine Pass (13,738 feet), thence down the Snake River, through Dillon, up Tenmile Creek past Kokomo and over Fremont Pass (11,320 feet). Stage fare was $10.00. In July, 1878, a new road was completed over Loveland Pass (11,992 feet), some 1,746 feet lower than the Argentine route. Cook & Wasson ran this stage line, also carrying the mail. The stage left Georgetown at 5:00 A.M., arriving in Leadville at 7:00 P.M. Fare was $7.00 to Kokomo and $10.00 to Leadville. Because of excessive snow, this route was later abandoned in favor of the Argentine route.

1. "Railroad Conflicts in Colorado in the 'Eighties", Colorado Magazine, January, 1946, by Justice William S. Jackson of the Colorado Supreme Court (not to be confused with the photographer William H. Jackson).

A second route, operated by Spotswood & McClellan, ran between Leadville and the railhead of the South Park railroad, the temporary stage stations moving west as the railroad advanced. This route was by way of Fairplay, Alma, thence up Mosquito Gulch and over Mosquito Pass, another hump with an elevation of 13,188 feet. From this pass, the road dropped down the west slope of the Park Range into Leadville. At the time the South Park station of Jefferson was the start of the stage run, the fare was $17.00, and the trip required two days.

The third wagon road was built up Ute Pass from Colorado Springs, west across South Park and over the Park Range via Weston Pass (11,900 feet). Crofutt's 1881 Guide states: ". . . and what a villainous pass it was." The fourth route, or southern entry, was up the Arkansas River from Canon City, by way of Buena Vista. This route was approximately 100 miles long and the stage fare was $17.00. However, with the Rio Grande reaching Leadville in August, 1880, and the South Park's railhead advancing ever closer, the camp's transportation situation was relieved considerably.

Truly, Leadville was the great carbonate city of Colorado and was reported to be the richest mining district in the world. The mineral deposits extended over a vast area more than 60 miles in length by 10 miles in width, and yielded from approximately $40 to $2,500 per ton in silver and lead. By July, 1880, it was estimated that the production of ore in the district was over 750 tons per week. Shafts and tunnels from mining operations extended under the city's streets. The entire town was cluttered up with miner's shacks, mine shafts, and ore dumps. These ore dumps grew up within the city blocks so high that many a cribbed-up waste heap stood in a back yard or side by side with dwellings. The disposal of mine tailings became a serious problem, for an ore dump could not be extended beyond the limits of the surface property of the mine. Fourteen smelters and a number of reduction works were eventually constructed to take care of the great quantities of ore that were dug out of the nearby gulches and mountain sides.

By 1881, Leadville began to develop into a fairly well governed town, becoming the County Seat of Lake County. A glance at the sides of the hills overlooking the town, where hundreds of little mine buildings all spouted ceaseless jets of steam from their ever laboring engines, and the hundreds of dumps of earth and ore brought to sudden daylight from their beds in the heart of the earth, told the story of Leadville's growth and prosperity. But today, Leadville rests, a ghost of its former glory—brooding over its fabulous gold and silver past.

The reader can readily understand how the rich Leadville traffic award, which sprang into being right before their very eyes, had such a profound effect upon the South Park road. With their principal competitor, the Denver & Rio Grande, involved in a bitter controversy with the Santa Fe for possession of the Royal Gorge and a Leadville entry, the Evans road stood well to achieve success if they could only solve their financial difficulties and get going. Their new objective was a goal well worth striving for. Therefore, it was imperative that some means or method be found whereby the extension of the Platte Canon line could be continued.

Although the Denver & San Juan company had collapsed, the South Park interests refused to admit defeat. Once again a new and fourth construction company was organized with a capital stock of $120,000. This new company was known as the Denver & South Park Railroad Construction & Land Company. With the exception of Alvin B. Daniels, who replaced Frederick J. Ebert, the new company's Board of Directors consisted of the same group who had headed its predecessor. They were John Evans, David H. Moffat, Jr., J. Sidney Brown, Walter S. Cheesman, William Barth, George Tritch, Charles B. Kountze, John W. Smith, and Alvin B. Daniels. The new officers were John W. Smith, President; George Tritch, Vice-President; Leonard H. Eicholtz, Secretary; D. H. Moffat, Treasurer; and Chas. Wheeler, Auditor.

The old incorporation papers of this fourth construction company are dated November 24, 1877, and state that the object of the newly formed company was:

"To locate, construct, and equip the uncompleted parts of the Denver South Park & Pacific Railroad, with all the appurtenances pertaining thereto, to procure right-of-way and depot grounds, to buy and sell lots and land along or near the route of said road, and to any and all acts pertaining to the building of said road, and also to the buying, selling, and disposing of such lots and lands."

Two days later, on November 26th, the new company accepted and signed the original construction contract, which had passed down through the hands of its predecessors. Although certain minor changes had been made from time to time in order to suit changing conditions and situations, the body of the original contract remained the same.

Again there was a reshuffling of the securities, holders of securities in the old company being given the option of receiving forty per cent of their subscriptions in either Denver South Park & Pacific bonds or securities of the new company. However, this point is not definitely established. According to Mock, John Evans, in an interview with Bancroft, stated that the stockholders received railroad bonds. But the Auditor of the South Park, Charles Wheeler, testified in the Pacific Railway Commission case that they all had the option of taking stock in the new company if they so desired. The capital stock of this last construction company was limited to $120,000. Evans' explanation for this move is difficult to follow. According to Mock, Evans, in an interview with Bancroft, stated: "We had to organize and get more money out of ourselves to go on through the canon, be-

Denver South Park & Pacific engine 112 at Buffalo, Colorado, about 1887. Built by Cooke in 1884 as D. S. P. & P. 70, it later became Colorado & Southern 7.

Colorado & Southern engine 9 at the Bailey station with the westbound passenger train on a summer morning in 1908.

cause we were satisfied it would pay then. We organized another construction company, and in that way we reduced our capital to raise the money we needed to go on through the canon."

Just what was implied by all these kaleidoscopic changes is difficult to say. However, it does seem that a part of this scheme was the gradual centering of control in the hands of the "insiders". It will be recalled that in the several shifts, it seems to have been a steady policy to pay off holders of stock in the former company with railroad bonds, leaving control of the new stock issue in the hands of those in back of the new company. The stockholders controlled the road, not the bond holders. Possibly, there may have been exceptions made in connection with certain parties; e.g., the Kansas Pacific was given stock in the new company pro rata for its stock in the former construction company; however, it is likely that no such differentiation would have to be made. Most stock holders would have been glad to accept bonds in exchange for stocks—especially in as dubious a venture as the South Park was considered to be at that moment.

There is also another point to be noted. Stockholders in the construction companies received a bonus of stock in the railroad. The proportion between the stocks of the two companies had varied. Thus, in the first construction company, Arapahoe County had received an amount of construction company stock equal to its subscription to the railroad stock, or one-half of the total securities issued by the construction company. In the case of the last construction company, holders of construction company stock received twenty-five times as many shares of railroad stocks as they held of construction company stocks. Thus, the Kansas Pacific held $12,000 of the new construction company's stock and $300,000 of Denver South Park & Pacific Railroad stock.

This control of $12,000 worth of Denver & South Park R. R. Construction & Land Company stock by the Kansas Pacific is more fully explained as follows: What construction had been carried out by the San Juan Construction Company had been financed by Denver capital. However, ready cash was a pretty scarce article during this period and in order to continue with the building of the road, the South Park interests entered into an agreement with the Kansas Pacific whereby that road agreed to freight in the South Park's construction and building supplies, taking construction company stock in exchange for their services.

Thus, it came about that the Kansas Pacific interests gained control of $30,000 worth of Denver & San Juan Construction Co. stock. When the San Juan company was superseded by the Denver & South Park R. R. Construction & Land Company in 1877, the Kansas Pacific took up its option on the basis of exchanging its stock in the old company for 40% of the amount in stock of the new company. This amounted to $12,000, or one-tenth of the total capital stock of the new construction company. Each share of this new construction company stock was worth 25 shares of railroad stock; consequently the Kansas Pacific came into control of $300,000 of Denver South Park & Pacific railroad stock.

Inasmuch as practically all the outstanding Denver & South Park stock was in the hands of those who had invested in the construction companies, it soon developed that those controlling the construction company also controlled the South Park road. And when, as Evans stated: ". . . we were satisfied it would pay then", there was a very real object in controlling the construction company. How true this was can be seen from the interest of the several railroads in securing control of the construction company.

As this history of the South Park road progresses, the various financial ramifications of the company continue to become more and more involved, and less easily understood. Financial information is also lacking, which makes it more difficult to explain clearly the progress of these various financial steps; in fact, the fiscal side of the South Park saga, like almost any railroad history, has become so entangled in the web of finance, that the writer has made little attempt, outside of a few highlights here and there, to further explain these intricacies of the road, and feels that the very great majority of readers are not particularly interested in this phase of the road's history.

The difficulties brought upon the country at large by the 1873 panic had begun to disappear by 1877-78. After bogging down in the latter part of 1877, the defunct Denver & San Juan company was replaced by a new construction company. Governor Evans and his associates were determined to carry on; a golden opportunity awaited the South Park railroad on the western horizon, and it behooved these men to make the most of it. At this time, the grade had been completed south of Bear Creek Junction and up the canon some six miles to near the site of Deansbury, but there were no rails on hand with which to continue construction.

Accordingly, Governor Evans went east to canvass the banking interests for some credit with which to purchase these badly needed rails. Here he encountered some bitter opposition from rival interests. The result of the trip was that the eastern bankers did not consider the South Park's financial condition sound enough to warrant any such credit, and flatly refused to help. Evans returned to Denver and made his report.

McMechen tells us that John Evans then quietly disappeared from Denver, leaving his associates to contemplate, with gloomy thought, the tremendous amount of lucrative traffic the road was losing, and perhaps, the probable loss of their investments. No one knew where he had gone; no one had seen him leave the city. Because of the tension, his inexplicable absence during the crisis created considerable excitement. Then, as suddenly

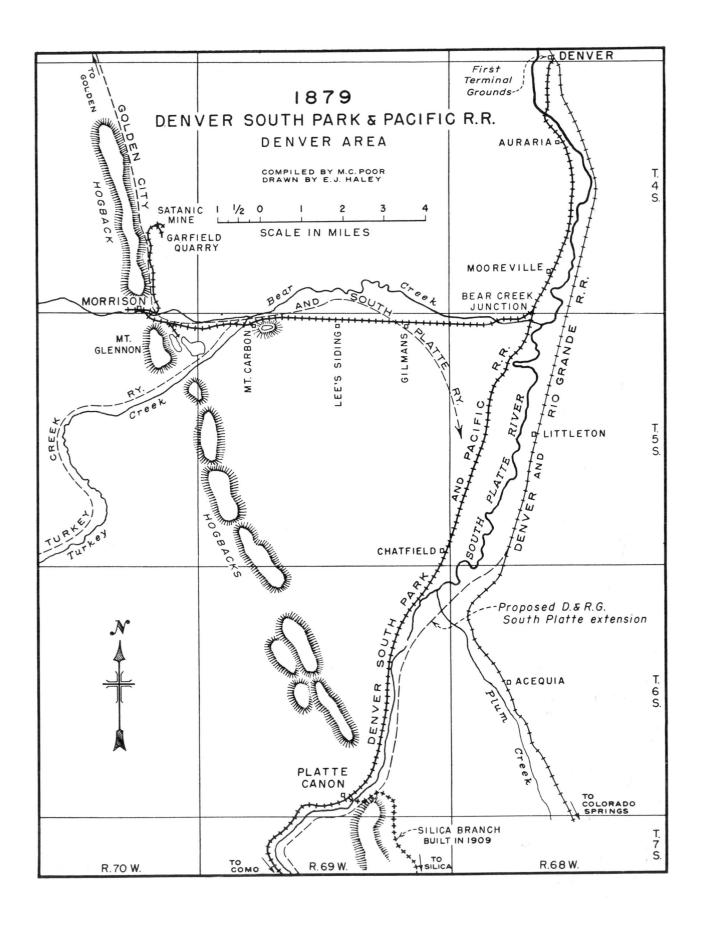

as he had gone, he reappeared a few weeks later, and calmly announced that a consignment of rails was on its way to Denver.

Accomplishments of this nature, performed at times when his foes thought him thoroughly whipped, kept them in wholesome fear of his next move, for the Governor was never so dangerous to an opponent as when he seemed at the end of his resources. From many a seeming defeat, he wrung a startling and overwhelming victory.

The Governor, in this instance, had taken a train to Cincinnati and enlisted the aid of his brother, Seth Evans, then one of the most influential bankers and meat packers of the Ohio city. From his brother he had secured the necessary credit to cover this shipment of rails so badly needed, and thus saved the day.[1] Mock reports that the Denver Daily Times of November 26, 1877, published an item stating that the South Park's backers had negotiated a much needed loan of $300,000 at this time. As to whether this was the credit to cover the purchase of the above rails, or an additional sum of money, the writer does not know.

Meanwhile, economic conditions continued to improve. Further efforts on the part of the South Park interests to dispose of their stock began to bear fruit, with the result that some of their financial troubles began to disappear. Active construction was again resumed. With rail on hand, the track layers went to work laying iron south of the junction, and the contractors again got their camps established and their gangs organized and at work at advanced locations up the canon. Some good progress was made. By May 20th, the end-of-track was completed to South Platte station —so, in honor of the occasion, the "Brass Hats" concluded that it was about time to go see how things were progressing. They would have a tour of inspection. The report of this trip, with a good sprinkling of publicity thrown in, was published in the Railway World of June, 1878. We quote in part.

"A correspondent of the Philadelphia Press, writing from Denver, Colo., on May 22, 1878, says:

"On May 20th, the writer was the guest of some railroad officials who ran their first train on a tour of inspection. This was the Denver South Park & Pacific R. R. This road was completed to Morrison in June, 1874, and preliminary lines were projected to several objective points, but the march of events directed the principal objective course of the road towards the new and vastly rich mineral district of Leadville. At present the ore from this camp is hauled out by wagon and teams to Colorado Springs, a distance of 107 miles. Mr. D. D. Streeter, the principal freighter, is running 290 head of mules and about 75 wagons. After some unavoidable delays, construction of the railroad was resumed in October, 1876. Fifty-three miles have been

1. McMechen, "Life of Governor Evans."

148

graded and 30 miles completed, and they are laying track at the rate of about a mile a day. Our pioneer train of open cars left the junction seven miles below Denver and struck out across the valley of grass and spring wheat of dark blue green and luxuriant from irrigation, to the foot hills; which, towering, seem to say, 'So far shalt thou come'. But the little locomotive wound by their base and with a shrill whistle of either welcome or defiance, curved into the main canon of the South Platte River. The engine then wound and climbed, following the tortuous course of the river through narrow canons, which opened out here and there into small parks walled in and around by peaks, singly and in groups, on all sides. The changing views presented from a front seat on the 'cowcatcher', are impressive in their rugged grandeur to the highest degree and the public, to whom the railroad will be opened in the beginning of June, have a territory before them to prospect, not surpassed, if equalled, for magnificent scenery by any railroad in the region. The cost of construction and equipment has not averaged more than from $10,000 to $11,000 per mile. This is a remarkable showing as the road is a local organization; the stock being owned and all monies paid in by gentlemen in and about Denver. All of its officers from the chief engineer to the contractors and builders are stockholders and contributors, and therefore directly interested in the economical contruction of the road. Its President is the veteran John Evans, second Governor of Colorado. Its chief engineer is also a veteran, Col. L. H. Eicholtz, of Philadelphia, whose name is connected with some of the principal engineering of the Pennsylvania, the Union Pacific, Kansas Pacific, and other roads. John W. Smith, President of the construction company, is also a Pennsylvanian. W. S. Cheesman is a prominent young banker in Denver and is Vice President of this railroad. These names, with that of the superintendent, A. S. Hughes, comprise a management of comprehensiveness and energy. . . ."

The section of the railroad through Platte Canon presented some of the most difficult track construction that faced the road's engineers and contractors. The canon had been pronounced impassable, not alone by non-professionals, but by experienced civil engineers. Few persons, except those who have actually seen this section of the track or who have ridden over it, can form any reasonable idea of the physical difficulties that presented themselves to Eicholtz and his assistants. So difficult was the preliminary work of surveying that ordinary methods were abandoned, and new means, adapted to the purpose, were employed. Every foot of the road gives evidence that the way was hard fought for— a right of way literally hewn from eternal granite.

Long stretches of track were built upon benches blasted out of the canon walls. In many places these walls of perpendicular rock descended sheer to the water's

A view at Pine Grove, Colorado, showing Denver South Park & Pacific 46 (originally D. S. P. & P. 11, built by Mason in 1879). Baldwin Consolidation 191 on the wye in background. Photo taken in the late '80's.

Denver Leadville & Gunnison 194 on the head end of an 8-car excursion train at Morrison on June 14, 1892.

edge, presenting a smooth unbroken surface worn by the action of the water until it was impossible to obtain a foothold for the workmen. By the use of long ropes, men were hung over cliffs of a dizzy height in order to do the preliminary blasting work. Suspended by these ropes, they would drill holes in the rock walls, insert pins in the holes and lay boards upon these pins. This gave them a platform on which to stand and carry on their further work of drilling and blasting. Where fills were impossible, it was necessary to construct long rock retaining walls or cribs to support the grade. To build some sections of these retaining walls, it was necessary for some of the workmen to stand waist-deep in the cold water, fresh from melting snows, flowing past at the rate of six miles per hour, a pressure against which it was exceedingly difficult for them to maintain their footing. Other portions of the route presented equally difficult problems; the confining of the torrent within narrower limits, or the turning of the river in order to avoid an impossible curve, with all the attendant risks of a freshet which would sweep away thousands of dollars worth of labor in a very short period. At some points, a shovel full of earth would be swept and torn away by the rushing stream as soon as it was thrown into the spot it was intended to occupy, and all the embankments built in the water required nearly four times the amount of labor that would be needed to do the same work on land.

During the summer of 1878, the rail-head steadily advanced up the canon, with the result that a portion of the line could be opened to the public in June. Conditions on the South Park were beginning to improve; the road had earned $157,534 for the year ending May 31, 1878. Apparently, their financial difficulties were becoming a thing of the past. By July 8th, the track had reached Pine Grove, and October found the rails laid as far as Bailey's Ranch, 56 miles from Denver.

While searching for material, the writer ran across an interesting story in the Colorado Magazine concerning Mr. William Bailey, after whom the town was named. The story relates that for some reason or other Mr. Bailey had a great dislike for civilization and railroads, especially the latter. Leaving civilization apparently behind him, he hied himself off to the mountains in 1864 and established a ranch on a choice location along the banks of the South Platte beyond the first mountain range through which the river flowed. In settling here, Bailey concluded that the Platte River Canon was so precipitous, and the mountains so high that no railroad would ever be able to reach him; thus, he would be free of his pet aversion. To his utter amazement, the South Park railroad not only came right through the canon and continued up the valley, but constructed their right of way directly through his ranch. In fact, the track was located in such a manner that it went directly between his house and the barn. The article failed to state

his reactions, but in all probability he was rather unhappy about the whole matter and put up a vigorous protest. As far as is known, the only satisfaction that came out of the incident was that the station was called Bailey's Ranch and later on just plain Baileys.

After the railhead had reached the vicinity of Baileys, the going was bit easier. The backbone of the range was now broken and the worst was behind them, thus allowing the engineering and construction crews to enjoy a sort of breathing spell for a few miles. During the fall of 1878, as the track was gradually pushed up the valley through Fairville (later known as Slaghts), and Grant, the right of way still followed the North Fork of the Platte; in fact, the line practically paralleled the stream's banks until the track reached the foot of Kenosha Hill. According to the Rocky Mountain News of January 18, 1879, the South Park's trains commenced running into Hall's Valley (later known as Webster), 69 miles from Denver on Friday, January 17th. Thus, we find the South Park's railhead at the foot of the east slope of Kenosha Pass. For the next few miles, progress was going to be difficult.

During the interval while the construction forces were preparing their assault to conquer Kenosha, Webster was the terminus of the line and developed into quite a busy station. Being the jumping-off place, Webster served as the temporary station for the stage lines and wagon freighters serving the Montezuma, Leadville, Fairplay, Alma, and Gunnison regions. The Railway Age stated that with eight stage lines running into Webster, supplemented by the Kansas Pacific selling through tickets from the east directly into Leadville via the South Park, business was booming. With such a huge volume of traffic at the road's disposal, prosperity and dame fortune were now copartners of the South Park company. The Rocky Mountain News of March 5, 1879, tells us that the little road was harvesting over $1,000 a day. According to early accounts, Webster developed into a rather tough place; in fact, their boot hill cemetery, which every well conducted cow camp or mining camp boasted of in those early days, may still be seen on top of a small hill near the foot of Kenosha Pass.

During the latter part of 1878, while construction was proceeding up the Platte toward Hall's Valley, it became apparent that perhaps the South Park might possibly locate a shorter route to Leadville than had been planned. If the engineers could locate some feasible route that would lie in a westerly course from the vicinity of Kenosha Pass, much time might possibly be saved in reaching the Leadville region.

Two new routes were taken into consideration and the South Park, momentarily, was uncertain of its next move. Should it build across the mountains from the north end of Hall's Valley and come into Leadville from the north by way of Keystone and Tenmile Creek, or should it cross the mountains farther to the south in

A passenger train arriving at Webster when it was the end of the track in 1879.

An eastbound Denver South Park & Pacific mixed train pauses in Platte Canon near the mouth of Deer Creek.

the vicinity of the Park Range and proceed up the Arkansas Valley to Leadville?

In view of this uncertainty, two new railroads were therefore organized. The first was the "Denver South Park & Ten Mile R. R. Co." which incorporated the northern route, and the second was the "Denver South Park & Leadville Railroad" which incorporated the southern route. Both roads were incorporated on December 13, 1878, with John Evans and his associates as the road's officers. The line of the Denver South Park & Ten Mile is given in that road's incorporation papers as follows:

"OBJECTS: To locate, construct, own, operate, and maintain a single or double track narrow gauge railroad and a telegraph line from the most feasible point of connection with the Denver South Park & Pacific Railroad in Park County, Colorado, by way of the confluence of Ten Mile Creek with Blue River in Summit County in said State, through the Ten Mile Canon, Summit County aforesaid and along the valley of the Arkansas River, by way of Leadville to Twin Lakes."

The line of the Denver South Park & Leadville is given in that road's incorporation papers as follows:

"OBJECTS: To locate, construct, own, operate, and maintain a single or double track narrow gauge railroad and a telegraph line from the most feasible point of connection with the Denver South Park & Pacific Railroad on Trout Creek in Lake County, Colorado, through and along the Valley and Canons of the Arkansas River, by way of, or near Leadville to the mines of its vicinity in the same County."

The northern route would continue from Hall's Valley (Webster) across the Continental Divide, and thence down French Gulch along the Swan River to the Valley of the Blue River near the site of Breckenridge. This route called for a one and a quarter mile tunnel under the Divide. The southern route would require a tunnel under the Park Range. Therefore, either route would require an excessive outlay of money, and much valuable time. Both of the new projected routes are supposed to have been surveyed. The merits of these two routes, along with the original surveyed line of the South Park were carefully weighed and given serious thought.

The fact that the South Park's plans at that time definitely called for the construction of a line into the San Juan region evidently was a strong point in favor of this route. Consequently, it was decided to follow the line of the original survey across South Park toward the confluence of Trout Creek and the Arkansas. From this point, it would be a fairly easy task to construct a branch line north up the Arkansas Valley to Leadville.

Since it had been decided to adopt the Trout Creek route, construction toward Kenosha Summit was pushed as rapidly as possible. The formal adoption of the plan to continue along the original route and abandon the two proposed short cuts was not taken care of until the following spring. In the records of the Denver South Park & Pacific Railroad, on April 15, 1879, the following motion was made by Mr. Cheesman and adopted:

"RESOLVED: That the location of the line of the road of this company from Section 33 in Township 7 South, Range 75 West (at the foot of Kenosha Hill) Park County to Section 21 in Township 14 South, of Range 78 West (near the mouth of Trout Creek) in Chaffee County, Colorado, as surveyed by Major James A. Evans, under direction of the Chief Engineer of this Company, be and the same is hereby approved and adopted as the location of that part of the line of the road of this company, and the President and Chief Engineer are directed to file certificates and plats of the same according to law."

Following this, on May 24, 1879, the records show the following motion made by Mr. Brown and adopted:

"RESOLVED: That the line of road surveyed by Major Evans and the Chief Engineer of this Company from the mouth of Trout Creek up the Arkansas Valley to or near Malta,[1] be and the same is hereby adopted as the location of the line of that part of the branch of the road of this Company and extending up said Valley, and the President and Chief Engineer are hereby directed to file plats and profiles of said location as required by law to secure the right-of-way for the same."

It would be interesting to know what passed through the minds of the road's engineers and surveyors, when they stood at the head of Hall's Valley and looked up the east slope of Kenosha Hill, wondering where they would ever locate a railroad right of way on that mountainside that would safely support an engine and cars until they could reach the summit. To achieve success at their appointed task, much deliberation and careful thought was called for. The railroad must reach the top—so they went to work. A final line of survey was at last agreed upon and the contractors were given their instructions. The powder men, and the rock men, and the graders went to work.

Leaving Webster, the grade was constructed up the northeast side of the Platte River exactly one mile beyond the Webster station. Here, on a 55-foot wooden trestle and a 30-degree left curve, on a 3.6% grade, they crossed the Platte for the 13th and last time, and began the difficult feat of surmounting Kenosha Pass. Benches were blasted out of solid rock, cuts were dug through extending arms of the mountain side, and large fills were built across gulches as the rails were pushed toward the top of the pass. The Railway World of March 29, 1879, tells us that 350 men were at work on Kenosha Hill.

In their struggle to reach the summit, the engineers encountered their most difficult construction at the lower end or base of the mountain due to the large number of gulches and extending mountain shoulders which had to be crossed. After this section of the mountain had been passed and the tracks extended up to the vicinity of Hoosier near milepost 74, which was slightly more than half way up, the approach to the summit became came a bit easier. There was a slight decrease in the number and the sharpness of the curves required; however, the right of way was still negotiating grades of 3% or more, even to within a quarter of a mile of the summit. The longest tangent from the Platte River

crossing at the foot of the mountain to the summit, a distance of 5.8 miles, was about 1,650 feet long.

Webster is a little over 9,000 feet above sea level. Kenosha Pass is 9 feet less than 10,000 feet, or 9,991 feet. The airline distance between the two points is about 4.2 miles. The rail distance is 6.8 miles. With grades ranging up to 3.9% and no small amount of both right and left 20, 25 and even 30 degree curves, the Denver South Park & Pacific R. R. was completed to the top of Kenosha Pass on May 19, 1879, a distance of 76.19 miles from Denver.

In announcing the completion of the South Park's track as far as Kenosha, we find the following newspaper item as published in one of the Denver newspapers, on May 19, 1879:

"At 1:00 o'clock this afternoon, the Denver South Park & Pacific Railroad reached Kenosha Summit with its track, and at 3:30 P.M. the first passenger train reached the summit, 10,140 feet above sea-level, the highest point attained by any railroad in North America.[1] All the most difficult construction of this road is now passed and track laying will continue down through the South Park at about the rate of one mile per day, until the road reaches Leadville. Passengers leaving Leadville then will arrive in Denver before midnight of the same day."

In order to give some sort of an idea as to what Eicholtz's engineers encountered in building the South Park's line as far as Kenosha Pass, the following data relative to curves, grades, bridges, etc., has been compiled. With the exception of the bridge data, this will include only the difficult Platte River section between Platte Canon, mile post 20.43—and Kenosha Station, mile post 76.19—a distance of 55.7 miles. In commenting on this particular section, the Railway World of July 26, 1879, stated:

"The South Park has zig-zagged up the South Platte Canon to reach Kenosha Pass, on grades that no engineer could have dared to suggest ten years ago."

The following table gives an idea of the large number of sharp curves encountered.

Degree of curvature:	22	23	24	25	26	27	28	30	31	32
Number of curves:	19	8	36	11	7	1	4	5	1	1

Within this 55-mile section there were 30.4 miles of curving track as compared to 25.3 miles of tangent track. And here is one for Ripley's "Believe it or not" column. Within this 55 miles there were 560 curves which altogether totalled 19,911 degrees, or 55.3 complete circles—practically one complete circle for each mile of track. The sharpest curve was a 32-degree left curve located just beyond Strontia Springs near milepost 29. A westbound train in travelling from mile-

1. Malta is about 4 miles west of Leadville. Any railroad coming up the Arkansas from the south would have to turn east at this point in order to reach the new mining camp.

1. The engineering department of the C. & S. Ry. gives the official height of Kenosha Summit as 9,991 feet above sea level. This honor previously belonged to the Rio Grande's famous "LaVeta Pass Line", completed in 1877, at an altitude of 9,242 feet above sea level.

W. H. Jackson photo,
from the State Historical Society of Colorado.

Denver South Park & Pacific 42 rounding the curve from Hall's Valley on its climb to the summit of Kenosha Pass.
In the distance, the town of Webster, with its station and tank, may be seen.

post 46.33 to 47.60, (an approximate distance of one and a quarter miles, a section just east of Crossons), negotiated the following curved track: first, a 25-degree right, then a 21 left, 23 right, 4 left, 26 right, 13 left, 25 left, 25 left, 28 right, 24 left, 23 right, 24 right, and a 25 left, all on a continuous grade of from 2.5% to 2.63%.

With the exception of one level and three downhill sections, each less than 800 feet long, the westbound grade from Platte Canon station to Kenosha was one continuous climb, gaining altitude every foot of the way. After passing South Platte station, the profile discloses a very heavy rate of increase in climb, encountering numerous grades of from 2.75% to a maximum of 4%. From Grant to the summit of Kenosha, it was a continuous climb of from 1.64% to 4%, with an average of 2.93%. This 4% grade, which was the maximum between Denver and Kenosha, was located about a half mile east of Webster. Another interesting segment

was found near Crystal Lake where the track encountered a continuous grade of 3.10% for over three-quarters of a mile and included a 15 degree, two 19 degree, and one 23 degree curves. Further information relative to these grades and curves may be found in the profile chart.

Between Denver and Kenosha, the South Park's track crossed the South Platte River 13 times. Some of these bridges were of iron truss and beam construction, while others were just plain wooden trestles. They varied in length from 48 to 372 feet. The following table lists the more important crossings.

Approximate Location	Length in Feet	Type
West Denver	372	Wood trestle.
Deansbury	95	Iron truss.
Buffalo	95	Iron truss.
Crossons	110	Combination truss.
Grant	112	Wood trestle.

Richard B. Jackson.

C. B. & Q. 537 (leased to C. & S.) on a special passenger train at Bailey in August, 1932.

CHAPTER III

THE LEADVILLE BOOM AND ITS EFFECT ON THE
COLORADO RAILROAD SITUATION

At this point in our history we will have to stop and take up the discussion of a very hectic, but important, period of Colorado railroad history, and its effects and relations as they concern the Denver South Park & Pacific Railroad. The particular period in question covers the rise of the Leadville mining boom and the great conflict it created between rival railroad interests for the control of the tremendous amount of traffic to and from the mining regions.

The business of constructing and operating railroads in Colorado was full of surprises and excitement. No one could tell from day to day just what group of money manipulators controlled what roads or what their relations were to each other. It seems the region was building up a national reputation as the locale of railway wars.

By 1878, railroad expansion in Colorado had developed to a point where the fierce competition between the leading transportation systems had become quite pronounced. The greatest cause of all the friction at this particular period was Leadville, the turbulent mining camp—that great traffic prize which had suddenly sprung up in the interior. "Leadville or Bust" seemed to be the maxim of the day, not only to the gold miners and prospectors, but to the railroad entrepreneurs themselves. There were four principal rivals for this transportation plum. They were:

1. The Atchison Topeka & Santa Fe Railroad.
2. The Denver & Rio Grande Railway.
3. The Denver South Park & Pacific Railroad.
4. Jay Gould and W. A. H. Loveland with their proposed Georgetown Leadville & San Juan road.

There was a pot of gold awaiting the first railroad to reach the spot and the rivalry between the four interests, for this tremendous Leadville haul, played a major role in early Colorado railroad history.

It seems that the first two, the Santa Fe and the Rio Grande, had decided to build to Leadville at about the same time. Apparently, the Rio Grande was the first to consider building a railroad up the Arkansas River to Leadville, but by the time they got around to the point of actual construction the Santa Fe was also imbued with the same idea. Due to the Rio Grande's failure to file the necessary claims with the Government, both were on an equal footing as far as priority rights in the

canon were concerned. As it so happened, these two roads could reach Leadville only through the Royal Gorge of the Arkansas, but sad to relate, there was room for only one railroad track through the narrow defile of this famous canon. General Palmer strongly contended that there was nothing more certain in the early history of the Rio Grande than the fact that its promoters had planned from the very first to construct a railroad west from Pueblo through Canon City and up the Arkansas River to the headwaters of that stream in the vicinity of Leadville. Palmer further contended that this fact stood, even though the company had failed to file the necessary maps and profiles with the U. S. General Land Office, as required by law. The rivalry of the Santa Fe and the South Park loomed large in his eyes and he stated, "This line would tend to keep both the Santa Fe and the South Park roads out of our territory".

The ensuing battle between the Santa Fe and the Rio Grande for the possession of this gorge route created a situation unparalleled in the annals of American railroads. The details of the conflict, which are fairly well known, are irrelevant to this narrative; therefore, only such facts as pertain to the history of the South Park will be incorporated in this book.

The third rival in the field for this Leadville traffic was John Evans' Denver South Park & Pacific. It will be remembered that prior to the Leadville boom, the South Park, although beset with many financial difficulties in its recuperation from the 1873 panic, had managed to carry forward with some construction work on the main line south of Bear Creek Junction toward Platte Canon. The reader will also remember that in the reorganization of the South Park in June, 1873, the Articles of Association stated that the main line was to be built through the Platte Canon, across South Park, across the valley of the Arkansas, and through Poncha Pass to the San Juan. In compiling these Articles, John Evans, not knowing what the future might have in store for the South Park road, had been foresighted enough to incorporate therein a number of branches, one of which specifically designated that it was to extend to the headwaters of the Arkansas in Lake County. As events came to pass, they proved the wisdom of John Evans' foresightedness. At the time construction was being carried out on the main line south from Bear Creek Junction toward the canon, the South Park interests naturally assumed that the main line would be directed toward the San Juan region as specified. However, it turned out to be a case of starting for a certain destination and finally winding up somewhere else. It was during the latter part of 1877 and early 1878, while the South Park was laboriously working its way through the defiles of Platte Canon, that Leadville's fame as a new and rich mining camp began to spread far and wide. Therefore, as a perfectly natural sequence, the Leadville boom suddenly gave the South Park another point of destination. John Evans' clause in the road's Articles of Association which read: "with a branch to the head of the Arkansas Valley in Lake County" gave them the legal right to follow such course.

The road which had been out of the news for some time was now quickly resurrected by the Denver press as a crying necessity. Throughout the spring of 1878 the Denver Daily Times was strongly urging that Denver would have to extend the South Park road to Leadville or it would lose an opportunity to secure a portion of the new trade which they felt belonged to them. As a matter of fact, with the Santa Fe completed between the Missouri Valley and Pueblo, and with a line from Pueblo up the Arkansas Valley by the Santa Fe or the Rio Grande a certainty, either road would have been in a definite position to secure the lion's share of the haul. Both the Kansas Pacific and the Union Pacific, depended on the Rio Grande for their Pueblo traffic, and would have been at a considerable disadvantage.

As now planned, the South Park with its 170-mile line would have a considerable advantage over the 280-mile Rio Grande's Arkansas Valley line between Denver and Leadville. The road would afford Denver, as well as both the Union Pacific and Kansas Pacific, a very efficient entryway into Leadville. With the superiority already enjoyed by Denver as a trade center, the lion's share of the business was expected to go to that point. In the light of this situation, Denver was desirous that control of the South Park remain independent or be held by either the Union Pacific or Kansas Pacific.

At the outset of the Leadville excitement, the South Park was not yet in a position to offer much competition for the traffic. As previously described, 1877 found the road just entering Platte Canon. During 1878 the end-of-track was being gradually extended through the canon of the Platte River, reaching Webster at the end of that year. Construction up the canon and valley had been held up to some extent due to the road's difficult financial situation. As the railhead gradually progressed up the valley beyond Bailey's Ranch, new connections were in turn made with the wagon road to Leadville. According to Government maps prepared by

the Hayden Survey, this main wagon road from Denver went by way of Morrison, Junction House, Bailey's Ranch, Hall Valley, Kenosha, Fairplay, and Alma. From Alma, the wagon road wound its way up Mosquito Gulch, skirted around the north side of London Mountain, crossed the Continental Divide over Mosquito Pass, and dropped down the west slope into California Gulch and Leadville.

It was not until May, 1879, that the track was finally extended to the summit of Kenosha Pass. From this point, it was still almost 50 miles by stage and wagon road to Leadville; nevertheless, the result of this advanced connection with the Mosquito Pass wagon road was that the South Park began to draw more and more of the lucrative traffic which had formerly been routed via either the Argentine-Loveland Pass-Georgetown route and thence the Colorado Central, or over the Ute Pass route via Colorado Springs and the Rio Grande.

The Denver Daily Times, under date of September 3, 1878, stated that President John Evans reported a constantly enlarging share of business was being carried by the fortuitously located South Park, and that the net earnings should be sufficient to extend the line to Fairplay and Leadville.

Once the road had successfully accomplished the difficult feat of building through the canon of the Platte to Kenosha, the Kansas Pacific, the Santa Fe, the Rio Grande, and Jay Gould himself, were up in the front office at various times with offers to buy stock in the company at highly profitable figures to the owners. These miscellaneous railroad interests were after the South Park enterprise like a pack of hounds after a fox.

The fourth rival for this Leadville traffic was Jay Gould, who saw speculative opportunities in the tumultuous railroad situation that had suddenly unfolded in the Colorado region. Gould's whole interest in railroads lay in the manipulation of the securities of his various railroad holdings. Sound development and sound operation were of no interest to this man. Control of a railroad by Gould meant only deterioration and ruin, and became a synonym for bad management and poor equipment. Of the four rivals, all except the Santa Fe were at one time or another the vehicles which Gould utilized in his bid for the Leadville haul. Here again, as will be told, Gould was the dominating figure in the solution of this Colorado railroad problem just as he had been the dominating figure in the solution of the northern Colorado tangle which involved the Union Pacific, Kansas Pacific, Denver Pacific, and Colorado Central, now known for a time as the powerful northern Colorado pool. At this time, the Gould camp, representing the northern pool, included among its various cohorts W. A. H. Loveland and the much vaunted Georgetown Leadville & San Juan project. The reader will recall mention of this projected railroad earlier in this book, the organization of which was a piece of strategy, aimed at the Union Pacific, in forcing Gould's consolidation plans upon that road.

Having now been introduced to the four rivals for this Leadville traffic, we can proceed with our story. The leading threat to the South Park had been the possibility that the Gould lines in Denver (the Union Pacific and Kansas Pacific) might make arrangements with the Rio Grande to extend its line to Leadville. Such a community of interests would have given the South Park no outlet, and would have placed it entirely at Gould's mercy. In fact, Gould seems to have been making such plans during the summer of 1878, for he was reported to have agreed to finance the Rio Grande extension to Leadville. Since earlier disputes between Gould and the Santa Fe over the division of the Colorado traffic had already caused bad blood, this only accentuated the animosity. The two interests waged a spirited fight for control of the Rio Grande, which if won by Gould would also permit him to invade the Santa Fe's southern territory.

As circumstances would have it, the fight was a three-cornered affair. The Santa Fe and the Rio Grande were fighting each other for control of the Royal Gorge route to Leadville, while at the same time the Santa Fe and Gould were fighting each other over control of the Rio Grande. After considerable court action and legal controversy, the Santa Fe gained control of the situation by leasing the Rio Grande for a period of 30 years. This lease was signed October 19, 1878,[1] and the Santa Fe took possession two months later, on December 14th. This new arrangement naturally broke off any agreements Gould may have made to extend the Rio Grande and the South Park was saved, momentarily at least, from this Rio Grande threat.

Shortly after taking control, Wm. B. Strong, Vice President and General Manager of the Santa Fe, moved to raise the rates on the Rio Grande between Denver and Pueblo in order to shut out the northern Colorado pool lines. The old game played by the Kansas Pacific in raising rates on the Denver Pacific in order to keep the Union Pacific out of Colorado was now being repeated in the south. Denver was indignant, but it was powerless to prevent the discrimination. The northern Colorado pool retaliated by refusing to permit the Santa Fe entry into their part of the state.

In view of this situation, the Santa Fe then instituted a movement to form an alliance with the South Park, which was then making a determined bid for the Leadville haul. The Santa Fe felt confident that if such a plan could be successfully carried through, it would serve a twofold purpose; first, the completion of the South Park would give the Santa Fe access to Leadville from the northeast; second, it would effectively block Gould

1. Anderson, "General William J. Palmer", Colorado College Publication.

and his northern Colorado pool from getting into Leadville by any route, except possibly over the proposed Georgetown Leadville & San Juan. After numerous negotiations over a period of time, a satisfactory arrangement between the South Park and the Santa Fe was reached. As a major step leading to the formation of this alliance with the South Park, the Santa Fe proposed to purchase outright the first mortgage bonds of the South Park, which indebtedness amounted to $700,-000. Mock further explains that the Santa Fe, according to Governor Evans' explanation, was also to receive $700,000 of South Park stocks (7,000 shares) as something of a bonus. He also states that Evans was very careful to explain that these stocks represented only a minority interest and that the South Park project was, therefore, still an "exclusively Denver road". The Santa Fe would then hold a one-fifth interest in the 35,000 shares outstanding. Strangely enough, every one of those 35,000 shares was voted in connection with the decision to accept the Santa Fe offer.

As a further discussion of this affair, we quote in part from the Denver Daily Tribune under date of December 29, 1878, the following:

"A NEW ALLIANCE
"The South Park and the Santa Fe strike hands
"The cry is 'On to Leadville'

"The South Park railroad problem which has consumed a large share of public attention of late, and which has claimed the undivided attention of its directory for months, has been solved, and to the proud satisfaction of the company, and with every indication that it will be satisfactory to Denver.

"There have been a great many rumors running wild around town in regard to negotiations pending, some of which now prove to have been baseless, and others which have come pretty near the facts. The interviews which General Manager Strong and Governor Evans had several weeks ago resulted in the laying before the capitalists controlling the Atchison Topeka & Santa Fe railroad a proposition looking to an alliance between the Denver South Park and Pacific and the Santa Fe lines. Several days ago, in pursuance of these negotiations, Thomas Nickerson and F. H. Peabody, President and Vice-President of the Atchison Topeka & Santa Fe railroad, arrived in Denver, and since their arrival have been in constant intercourse with the South Park management in relation to the alliance measures. At 11 o'clock last night, after an eight hour conference, the papers were signed by both parties to the negotiations. At that hour it was impossible to get at the details of the arrangement, but the contracts were closed by the Board of Trustees of the South Park Company for all of the means necessary to complete their road to Leadville, as quick as men and money can build it. And this, it is said, on the most advantageous terms to the city of Denver and the stockholders of the company. The absolute control of the road is secured to its present management for an indefinite but long period, if not in perpetuity.

'. . . Among the major proposals incorporated in this alliance, were the following: First and foremost, the completion of the main line of the South Park to Leadville as soon as possible. Second, the completion of the proposed extensions to the Gunnison and San Juan mines region. Third, the extension of the Morrison branch, by the old high-line route (the Denver Georgetown & Utah) to Idaho Springs, Georgetown, and Central City. . . .'

"As stated, the terms of the alliance are not public, but it is said that the Santa Fe has purchased at par $700,000 of the first mortgage bonds of the South Park road, in consideration of certain operating and construction conditions. This money is to be forthcoming within thirty days, and in the meantime the South Park will contract for building fifty miles of extension.

"The track from the mouth of Trout Creek on the old located line of the South Park railroad, to Leadville, and also to the San Juan mining country, is to be used in common by the South Park and the Atchison Topeka & Santa Fe companies, under fair traffic arrangements and equal privileges.

". . . It will be the aim of the South Park to reach Trout Creek in advance of the Santa Fe,[1] in which event, as it is understood, the South Park will become the owner instead of the lessee of the thirty-five miles to Leadville. It is believed now that the South Park will reach this point of conjunction by July first, in which event Leadville will be gained by August 1st.

"This secures the completion of the South Park as far as has ever been contemplated, and the citizens of Denver, and in fact all the country, to which its lines extend have reason to rejoice over the arrangement.

"That the management is to be and remain in Denver, indicates that the Atchison Topeka & Santa Fe Company (from the leading capitalists of which company the money is to come) is not likely long to occupy an unfriendly relation to the business of Denver. In fact this act of aid and the explanations of Mr. Goodman, General Freight Agent, if sustained by future events, will soon put that company in high favor with our people, notwithstanding the unfriendly comments with which their increase of tariffs over the Rio Grande road were at first received."

At this time (December, 1878), the South Park's track had reached the foot of Kenosha Hill, and the sum of $700,00 could certainly be put to good use.

It so happened that the lease by which the Santa Fe held control of the Rio Grande contained a clause to the effect that any traffic agreements made with competitive lines would have to be approved first by the Rio Grande. The Santa Fe-South Park deal had been arranged in absolute good faith, therefore, it was subject to approval by the Rio Grande stockholders. The Rio Grande stockholders, headed by Wm. J. Palmer, availed themselves of this clause in their lease with the Santa Fe and refused to sanction this proposed Santa Fe alliance with the South Park, on the grounds that it would have been prejudicial to the Rio Grande's interests in regard to the Leadville traffic. Inasmuch as Gould was also anxious to gain control of the South Park, he was not disposed to stand by and see his rival, the Santa Fe, secure partial control of the road. It is therefore strongly suspected that Gould brought plenty of pressure to bear behind the scenes, in an effort to have the Rio Grande interests turn the offer down.

According to the Denver Daily Times of January 24, 1879, this move was not expected by Evans, who stated that the deal would probably go through unless the Legislative Assembly passed unfriendly legislation concerning such alliances. It also happened that when this Santa Fe proposal was announced, many excitable per-

1. At this time the Santa Fe road fully expected to be in control of the Arkansas valley line to Leadville.

158

sons were opposed to the alliance, fearing that the $300,000 Arapahoe County bond aid which had been voted in favor of the South Park in July, 1873, would be hopelessly lost. As a result of this opposition, the negotiations fell through and the idea was dropped. About six months later Palmer went to court and accused the Santa Fe of giving secret aid to the South Park interests. With the exception of this affair, the details of which will be taken up in due time, this ended all interest the Santa Fe ever had in the South Park.

The leasing of the Rio Grande by the Santa Fe in October, 1878, deprived Gould of the control of that road and an entryway into Leadville, and caused him to move against the South Park. As near as can be ascertained, Gould made his first major attempt to gain a controlling interest in the Evans road during November or December of 1878. Evidently he made a very strong effort to obtain possession of the South Park, as shown by his offer. He made his proposition through a third party, offering to pay $450,000 cash, the approximate amount already spent on construction of the road. In exchange he wanted half of the capital stock, less the $300,000 owned by Arapahoe County, and half of the bonds that pertained to that portion of the road between Denver and the vicinity of Webster. The other half of the bonds was to remain in the possession of the construction company. He also proposed, in case his offer was accepted, to continue construction of the road on to Leadville and into the San Juan country, taking bonds on that portion of the road at the rate of $16,666.67 per mile. The reader will recall that in his fight with the Union Pacific, Gould had gained control of enough Kansas Pacific stock to get himself elected to that road's board of directors in May, 1878. Control of the Kansas Pacific then gave Gould control of the $12,000 of construction stock and the $300,000 of railway stock of the South Park which the Kansas Pacific held.

Gould's offer was submitted to the South Park's board of directors and rejected, since the amount of stock he wanted, plus the South Park stock which he already had under his control through the Kansas Pacific, would give him the balance of power. Governor Evans stated that the South Park interests fully believed that they were able to complete the road themselves, and therefore were not desirous of Mr. Gould's assistance.

Had Gould's offer been accepted, it would have proved very advantageous to his interests. His plans called for the routing of all inbound and outbound Leadville traffic over his various roads, which included the Union Pacific, the Kansas Pacific, the Colorado Central, and even the Golden City and South Platte cutoff.

Mr. Gould then sent his attorneys to call on the South Park. One was no less a personage than the Honorable John P. Usher, former Secretary of the Interior in Lincoln's Cabinet. Usher submitted another offer, not much different from the first. This offer was also refused, whereupon Gould's lawyers threatened to prepare a bill for discovery and relief to be filed in court for the purpose of embarrassing the South Park company and forcing them to terms. In fact, the lawyers did file a bill for receivership; however, the South Park interests, headed by Bela M. Hughes, called their bluff. Gould's attorneys withdrew their suit against the South Park, but efforts to embarrass its operation and owners were continued. In his efforts thus far to corral the Leadville traffic, Gould had lost the first two rounds, but he was not to be defeated so easily and soon we shall hear from him again.

Shortly after Gould failed in this attempt to gain control of the South Park, a certain amount of criticism began to spring up regarding the progress of the road, and its management. This criticism, and efforts to embarrass the management, can be well understood when it is explained that the attacks were led by the Rocky Mountain News, which in the previous year, 1878, had been purchased by none other than Evan's long-time opponent and one of Gould's cohorts, Wm. A. H. Loveland.

Public clamor for an investigation grew until it became necessary for Governor Evans to issue a public statement to the Arapahoe County Commissioners in defense of the South Park's affairs. This report was published in the Denver Daily Times on February 26, 1879. It was a rather long article and included, among other things, a detailed report covering the early construction of the road and the financial difficulties encountered; however, inasmuch as this material has already been incorporated in this book, we will eliminate that section and include only that part dealing more or less with the defense of the road's affairs. The article, in part, is as follows:

"THE SOUTH PARK ROAD
"Gov. Evans' Report to the County
"Commissioners

"Yesterday, Gov. Evans submitted to the Board of County Commissioners a full and explicit report of the organization, progress, past and present condition of the Denver South Park & Pacific Railroad, of which he is President, and which we condense. The opening paragraphs were devoted to a recital of the particulars of the original organization, and subsequent elections of directors from 1873 to the present time, and references to the voting of bonds and subscriptions to the stock of the road by the County of Arapahoe, with which the public is already familiar, and need not, therefore, be repeated here.

". . . the 'Denver Railway Association' was incorporated for the convenience of transacting a large business, and reorganized for the purpose of enlisting others and adding to the capital. These companies have successively assumed all the obligations and responsibilities of their predecessors, and taken an assignment of said

contract to build. The association has been at all times on a sound basis, paying all obligations in good faith, and their integrity has never been questioned. The construction companies and contractors have always been separate and distinct from the railroad company, with different persons for officers. The contract provides that the contractors shall . . . construct the road . . . furnish all equipment . . . defray all expenses incident to such work, and build the road in a manner acceptable to the President and Chief Engineer. The agreement with the railroad company provides that the contractors shall comply with all the above obligations, and are to receive in consideration all the assets of the company. The subjoined verbatim extract shows the character of the assets and agreements made.

"These assets at the time consisted alone in the capital stock of the company, and the use and benefit of all the proceeds from the same, i.e., the Arapahoe County bonds and such bonds as might be procured from Park and Lake Counties to aid in building the road, and all or any sales of said stock. All the values in said stock were to be created by building a railroad for the company, without which the county bonds, not applicable to any other purpose, were valueless. The railroad company also agreed to issue first mortgage bonds, in the amount of twenty thousand dollars per mile, on such road when it should be built by the contractors, and to have inserted upon the bonds, traffic contracts which had been agreed upon with the Kansas Pacific, North Missouri,[1] and Chicago & Alton railroad companies, for a drawback of ten per cent of all receipts of said companies from business to and from the South Park road. The proceeds of this ten per cent were to be a sinking fund to buy up and cancel said bonds. This very advantageous traffic arrangement failed, because of the default of the Kansas Pacific on its own interest before it was consumated. The amount of the bonds was subsequently reduced, by agreement, from $20,000 to $16,666 per mile.

"The contract with the Atchison Topeka & Santa Fe company provided for a still further reduction of bonds to $12,000 per mile. The vote of county aid was made to enable the railroad company to raise the means, by contract or otherwise, to build the road, and not for a stock investment. In fact, it was to induce parties to undertake the construction of a railroad for the benefit of the city and county, through and over the difficult and expensive and only feasible direct route from Denver to the South Park, as determined by the surveys referred to, that the county voted its aid. And it is certain, that without such aid, the means could not have been procured to have had a railroad through the canon of the Platte in time to prevent the diversion of the enormous traffic and travel of Lake, Park, and Summit Counties

1. North Missouri Railroad was chartered in 1857. The line eventually became a part of the St. Louis Kansas City & Northern, now a part of the Wabash main line between St. Louis and Kansas City, Mo.

away from our city and county at the present time. With the aid in County bonds, which, in payments for grading, bridging and tieing the roadbed, in the purchase of iron and rolling stock, and in sales for cash—all of which was faithfully applied by the contractors to the construction of the road, and realized $211,400 (from the sale of the Arapahoe County bonds)—the company obtained responsible contractors, who agreed to build the road. To prove that this contract has not been regarded as a desirable investment, I need only refer to the fact that it has been with the utmost difficulty that the contracting companies could raise money by disposing of their construction company's stock at par. In fact, after repeated efforts to induce investment in it, both in the East and in Europe, the company has every time been obliged to return to Denver and make appeals to her people to raise money. And even here, where all the advantages of the road and benefits of the contract were understood, it has only been by appeals to the patriotic devotion of the people, and to their interest in the city and county, that subscriptions to this construction company stock could be secured. And it is a further fact that until quite recently such construction company stock has been on the market at much less than its par value. The county is a stockholder in the railroad company by virtue of its subscription *to aid the enterprise* as made under the law. The bond of the railroad company made to the county sets forth the objects and benefits that were to be secured by the county in giving such aid, and enumerates the obligations of the company. With the profits and losses of the contractors the county has nothing to do. It could not legally be a party to such a contract, or to any contract for building any railroad whatever. The construction company does all the work, borrows the money, buys iron, does the grading, tieing, bridging, tracklaying, equipping, and in fact bears all the expenses of building and completing the road. As the road is extended it is turned over, section by section, to the railroad company, according to contract. The construction company even pays the railroad company for the transportation of the iron and other materials for building the railroad beyond its terminus. The first mortgage bonds can only be delivered to the construction company, or in fact issued at all after the road is finished in sections as you may see by the terms of the mortgage. . . . It is from its securities (i.e., stocks and bonds) the contractors must derive all of the means to build the road as provided for in the contract, and also in the bond given the county, in which the work is done as rapidly as practicable—that is to say, as rapidly as it can sell its securities (stocks and bonds) to raise the means to pay the same. The construction company has so far performed its work honestly, well and faithfully. It has built for the company and the public a first class railroad. In 1874, it completed and turned over the main line to Bear Creek, and the branch to

Morrison. In 1878 it turned over the road from Bear Creek Junction to Grant, and in January, 1879, it turned over the road from Grant to Webster in Hall's Valley, making in all, seventy-nine miles now in successful operation. The construction company is now pushing the work of extending the road into the South Park, twenty miles beyond Webster, as rapidly as it can get laborers and material with which to prosecute the work, and I have no doubt that in less than three months the cars will be running into the Park. And I beg to call your attention to the fact that this will be a compliance with the provisions of the bond given to the County, upon the conditions of which the County of Arapahoe extended its aid to the company. The contract goes farther—even across the Park. In the work of construction, the company has already expended over a million dollars in cash, and now the company is negotiating for the means with which to complete its contract and to extend the road to Leadville.

"In conclusion, the Governor says that the interests of the County have not been threatened in any way or form. The question in regard to the late agreement with the Atchison Topeka & Santa Fe, is not answered except by the submission of the document itself, which is of no force, since the contract has since been nullified by the failure of that company to fulfill its provisions. He calls special attention to the fact that under the terms of this agreement, the contract of the road was in no way lost to our citizens, nor was the interest of the County in any way jeopardized. On the other hand the trade of Denver would have been very materially benefitted, had it been carried out. The report concludes as follows:

"That proper provision shall be made by the railroad company for the carrying out of the conditions of its obligation to the County, as set forth in its penal bonds of five hundred thousand dollars, is a matter of concern to the County Commissioners, and to the public; and that the contractors charged with the responsibility are reliable, and are working in good faith for the railroad company to carry out its contracts, is important to all parties concerned. But that either the railroad company, the County, or the public has any right to inquire in what manner the construction company procures the means with which to build the road, how much interest it pays on its loans, from whom it borrows money, stocks or bonds, or both, to carry on its operations and comply with its contracts, is emphatically denied. The County only has relations with the railroad company, and has no claim upon it, except that it shall live up to its agreements, for which it holds said bond. The railroad company had a right to make a contract for building its railroad as it did, and must see to the compliance with the terms of its contract by the construction company; but has no right to say how much or how little the road shall cost the contractors in cash or in the stocks and bonds paid it for building the road. As a stockholder in the railroad company, the County has the right to vote its stock for the election of trustees or directors to manage the affairs of the company, and the Board of Commissioners, at its last meeting, exercised that right, but stockholders have no voice or responsibility in the management of business affairs of corporations under the law. As to the question of the stock of the railroad company having been watered or increased, I repeat my statement that no change whatever has been made in it since the company was organized. The relation of the County stock to the other stock of the company is precisely the same as it was when the stock was issued to the County; it all stands precisely alike, and no person has any authority to interfere with the County stock without the action of the Board of County Commissioners. Nor is it possible to water or increase the stock without a meeting of the stockholders for the purpose, notice of which would have to be published as required by law. In reply to your inquiries I make this full and fair statement of the affairs of the company in the hope it may prove satisfactory to you and the board you represent. I have the honor to be very respectfully, your obedient servant,

John Evans, President."

Following is the Arapahoe County Commissioner's answer to Evans' report, as published in the Railway World of March 29, 1879:

"It seems to this committee that the road is being constructed as soon as possible. There has been completed about 70 miles of railroad through the most difficult part of Platte Canon. It is now completed and in operation to Webster. About 350 men are at work grading the right of way near Kenosha Hill and the road will be constructed on into the South Park district within the next 60 days. From thence to Trout Creek the work will be comparatively easy and we are assured that the road will be constructed to Leadville by August 1st. This committee is decidedly of the opinion that the rapid and early completion of this railroad into Leadville is a matter of utmost importance at this time. The relations of Arapahoe County to the railroad company are the same now as they have always been. It is simply that of a stockholder owning and holding $300,000 of stock for which it has issued bonds to that amount. The railroad is earning about $1,200 per day while its operating expenses are about $480 per day, leaving a net profit of $720 per day. And this is done with 79 miles of railroad in operation. As the work progresses, the earnings must necessarily be increased and when the road is fully completed it seems to us that its business must make its earnings sufficient to pay dividends upon its stocks.

"The Denver Times states that the company has made arrangements for the money necessary to complete the line to Leadville through private sources and that the leading stockholders will put up the largest share

of it. They are determined that there shall be no further obstructions in the way of its rapid construction to its destination and the work will be pushed at the greatest speed."

Gould's failure to compel the South Park to join his northern Colorado pool had again thwarted his plans, thereby adding additional burdens to his woes. He now had three problems on his hands. First: gain control of the South Park, whereby he might corral the Leadville traffic; second: force the Union Pacific to agree to a consolidation with his Denver Pacific and Kansas Pacific roads; and third: his friction with the Santa Fe over their attempted expansion into the Colorado territory, and also their projected route to the Pacific Coast. Then followed a move, the significance of which is rather uncertain. Gould planned a little strategy to use against his adversaries. He had his henchman, Loveland, incorporate the Georgetown Leadville & San Juan Railroad Company. The date of incorporation was December 5, 1878, with Jay Gould, Sidney Dillon, and Russel Sage among the incorporators. The road was a direct subsidiary of the Colorado Central with practically the same officers as the parent company. The route of this proposed railroad from Georgetown followed the same pattern as myriads of its colleagues; Clear Creek, Silver Plume, Loveland Pass, Snake River, Dillon, Tenmile Creek, Fremont Pass, and Leadville. From this point, the line was projected down the Arkansas Valley and thence to the southwestern corner of the state, where it would be in a position to build to either Arizona and the Southern Pacific, or to Utah and the Central Pacific.

About a year previous to this time, during October, 1877, Gould had met Loveland in Colorado, apparently to discuss the possibility of extending the Colorado Central in a southwesterly direction. For some years, Loveland had planned a railroad into the South Park, or the region southwest from Georgetown, and felt certain that this was the opportunity he had long sought. Shortly after this preliminary discussion, Loveland made plans to survey a line into that area. As was customary, for propaganda purposes, the usual announcement appeared in print. In the Railroad Gazette of January 25, 1878, we read:

"As soon as the weather permits, surveys from Georgetown to South Park will be completed."

Denver understood the motive behind this move. At this time, midwinter of 1878, the third rail had not yet been laid between Denver and Golden, and if such a road as an extension of the Colorado Central, or the Georgetown Leadville & San Juan were built, all the traffic from the mines in this southern and western territory would flow over the Central by way of Golden direct to Omaha and the east, thus by-passing Denver entirely.

Shortly after the incorporation of the San Juan project, Loveland went east, seeking to complete arrangements for the construction of the line. The Colorado Miner under date of January 18, 1879, boasted:

". . . that the region would have the shortest, cheapest, quickest and most romantic route that can be selected to insure success to northern Colorado, increased prosperity to Denver, and a steady influx of ores to the smelting and reduction works of the valley."

Inasmuch as the ore traffic that would originate on this Georgetown line would flow by way of Golden to Omaha and the east, it is hard to understand just how Denver would realize any great increase in prosperity.

Georgetown was congratulating herself on her prospective importance. However, when Loveland returned from the east in March he had "nothing to report", except that he was "almost certain" that work on the new line would be undertaken very shortly, and that the line would be built "whether the Denver & South Park joins the northern pool or not". He also passed a few hints that the purchase of the South Park by Gould was a "high probability".

Loveland was unsuccessful in his efforts to persuade Gould to launch the Georgetown Leadville & San Juan. What had happened to cause the change in plans is not apparent, and none of the conjectures are entirely satisfactory. There had been a good deal of ridicule of the "High Line", and the impracticability of the route, even though it was a fairly direct line, may have caused Gould to decide against it. The story is told that George Tritch, one of the "Denver crowd", later explained that his cartoon of Loveland flinging freight across the Snowy Range by means of a strange contraption, half ferris wheel and half derrick, which was published in one of the opposition newspapers at that time, gave Gould a hearty laugh. Gould, seeing the absurdity of the idea, refused to advance Loveland the necessary funds for the construction of the line.[1]

However, there were more important factors to be considered by Gould, than any fulfillment of Loveland's hopes and desires. The important thing to Gould was that he was close to forcing his consolidation plans upon the Union Pacific, uniting that road with his Denver Pacific and Kansas Pacific roads. It is also possible that by this time Gould felt rather confident that he would be able to gain control of the South Park and thus eliminate any need for the Georgetown "High Line". Very possibly this San Juan project may have been part of a Gould plan to flank the Santa Fe, in order to thwart its transcontinental aspirations. But whatever the reasons may have been, this phantom railroad had already served whatever purpose Gould may have had, and any evidence, one way or the other, is very scanty; the issue here is not Gould's strategy in the southwest, but the bearing the road had upon the Leadville situation. There is little doubt that if a practical route across the range could have been found, the line would have been more

direct than even the South Park line. The Colorado Transcript of July 26, 1879, reported that the distance from Leadville to Georgetown by this route was approximately 65 miles, which, together with the 50 miles between Georgetown and Denver made a total of 115 miles. This would have been approximately 10 miles shorter than the combination South Park line and Mosquito Pass wagon road.

The project did not collapse immediately. Wagon roads between Georgetown and Leadville were utilized to compete with the South Park-Mosquito Pass route and other lines for the Leadville haul. Later, Union Pacific surveyors attempted to discover a more feasible route over this particular section of the Snowy Range and reports were published in local mining camp newspapers that they had succeeded in locating an "entirely practicable" line over which the Union Pacific would construct a railroad and have cars in Leadville within a short time. Regardless of how accurate this information may have been, subsequent developments rendered the road unnecessary.

Consequently, with the Santa Fe and the Rio Grande still carrying their troubles from one court to another in attempting to settle the "Royal Gorge War"; the apparent collapse of the Georgetown Leadville and San Juan project; and with the South Park railroad still continuing as a free agent after unsuccessful attempts by the Santa Fe and the Gould interests to secure control of it, the Leadville situation, by the spring of 1879, was as muddled as ever.

In the meantime, another dispute arose between the Palmer and Evans roads regarding certain agreements in the Rio Grande's lease to the Santa Fe. Palmer charged that the Santa Fe had given secret aid to the South Park interests through Kidder Peabody & Company, an investment banking house in Boston. Palmer contended that this financial aid was extended in order to enable the South Park to complete its line to Kenosha Pass. He further contended that this was a plain violation of the lease, because the Evans road was a competing line and agreements in the lease strictly prohibited such aid.

Anderson, in his "Gen. Wm. J. Palmer", states: "After the Rio Grande interests had refused to sanction the Santa Fe's proposal to purchase $700,000 worth of South Park bonds, there is strong reason to believe that a plan for indirect aid to the Evans road was developed through Kidder Peabody & Company. Thomas Nickerson of the Santa Fe did not deny that Mr. Peabody and his banking house, of which he (Nickerson) was a member had aided the South Park, but he did deny that such aid constituted a violation of the lease. To this statement Palmer replied indirectly on July 19, 1879: 'Why the devil, then, did he allow a banking firm, of which his Vice President is chief partner, to lend the South Park money to cross the Kenosha Range?' The evidence seems to be in favor of Palmer; and inasmuch as the

1. Mock, "Railroad Development in Colorado".

aid thus extended continued over a period of 90 days, it is reasonable to suppose that it furnished sufficient justification for repossession of the road."

Palmer took his troubles to court. The court directed that the Rio Grande lease to the Santa Fe be terminated and the Rio Grande system be returned to its owners. Palmer regained possession of his road on August 14, 1879; however, the decision as to who controlled the canon route to Leadville was still unsettled. In view of this, the Rio Grande's claim to priority in the upper Arkansas Valley was of doubtful validity, with the result that the road was still very far from uncontested supremacy in the matter of the Leadville route.

Shortly after Palmer had regained control of his road a rumor was spread that the Rio Grande was going to court in an effort to halt construction of the South Park's line into the Arkansas Valley and up to Leadville. In this connection we quote from the "Financial Chronicle" under date of September 27, 1879, as follows:

"It is rumored in Denver that the Denver & Rio Grande managers intend to file a writ of injunction to prevent the Denver & South Park from going into the Arkansas valley. The rumor has been investigated and there is little doubt of its truth. That such a proposition has been broached by the Denver & Rio Grande managers is positive. Whether they will dare to carry it into effect is a question which will be decided in a few days. The aim of the plan is clear. The Denver & Rio Grande claims the right-of-way along the Arkansas river and they desire to prevent the South Park from continuing its construction, just as they did the Santa Fe. The construction of the line is of such great importance, both to the South Park and the people of Leadville, that any sum the Grande may claim may be raised to prevent stoppage of construction. The South Park managers have the Santa Fe experience as a guide and they know how effective the Canon litigation was in stopping the Grande's Leadville extension from Canon City. Whether the fear of similar obstacles may move them to pay the Rio Grande managers into letting them alone, time will settle. If the writ is served, it is safe to say that Leadville will have no railroad this year and perhaps next."

This threat was never carried out for it was not many days, as will be explained, before Gould gained sufficient control of the situation to put a quietus to all friction between the two roads. The return of the Rio Grande to Palmer's control, due to the termination of the road's lease to the Santa Fe, fitted in with Gould's plans very nicely. In spite of the Rio Grande's uncertain legal status in the Arkansas Valley, Gould moved to purchase a half interest in the road with an offer of $5,500,000. Palmer and his associates accepted the offer and by September the transaction was completed. Shortly thereafter Gould and one of his associates, Russell Sage, were elected to the Rio Grande's board of directors.

The new Rio Grande control then attempted to secure a compromise with the Santa Fe and end the Royal Gorge route controversy but the Santa Fe refused to negotiate with them. However, a short time later, due to strong threats by both Palmer and Gould, to parallel certain Santa Fe lines, the latter evinced a willingness to settle some of the differences. Although the final decision as to control of the upper Arkansas Valley route had not been settled officially, Gould took advantage of this favorable situation and proceeded with his plans for the continuation of the Rio Grande toward Leadville.

Gould's success in gaining this half interest in the Rio Grande was an important step in his scheme of gaining complete control of the Colorado railroad situation. At the time he had been negotiating for this Rio Grande stock, he was also bringing pressure to bear on Evans and the South Park officials for control of that road. He wanted control of the South Park for two specific reasons: first, it would enable him to bring about a consolidation of interests between the Palmer and Evans roads and give him an entryway into Leadville; second, the road would be extremely useful to him in his carefully laid plans to force his consolidation scheme on the Union Pacific. The strategic value and location of the South Park in connection with the vast increase and excellent outlook of the mining industry in western Colorado was well known to Gould. Therefore, in order that these advantages might work to his benefit, Gould set about in earnest to gain control of the South Park. Although he failed to obtain actual control just at this time, he did bring pressure to bear to the extent that he was permitted to outline the future policies and route of the road. In view of the fact that he had only succeeded in garnering a small amount of South Park stock by the late summer of 1879, it is rather difficult to understand how he could exert such a strong influence over the South Park owners. The only clear explanation of this situation is that Gould must have had some sort of an understanding or agreement with the South Park interests that he was to have control of the road in the very near future.

Thus, we come to the end of another difficult period of Colorado railroad history, a period characterized by a series of broken traffic agreements, rate wars and wrangling, all accompanied by the usual quota of threats and counterthreats. With the Arkansas Valley and the Southwestern Colorado transportation situation now fairly well under control and on a presumably peaceful basis for the time being, awaiting the will and pleasure of the master manipulator, Jay Gould, we will now leave these miscellaneous financial and traffic problems with the attorneys and managers and get out along the line and see what the construction engineers are doing. The change of atmosphere will no doubt be refreshing.

Denver South Park & Pacific engine 4, the "San Juan", at the Mason Locomotive Works, Taunton, Mass., in 1879.

Another of the "Mason Bogies", number 13, the "Ruby", photographed about 1884.

CHAPTER IV

CONSTRUCTION FROM KENOSHA SUMMIT TO TROUT CREEK PASS AND THE KING MINES

In 1879, the general offices of the Denver South Park & Pacific were located at number 360 Lawrence Street in Denver. Here, the following officers and others entrusted with the responsibility of successfully operating the railroad held sway.

The Directors were: John Evans, Walter S. Cheesman, C. B. Kountze, David H. Moffat, Jr., Leonard H. Eicholtz, J. W. Smith, G. W. Clayton, and E. F. Hallack, all of Denver. The officers and department heads were:

John Evans	President
W. S. Cheesman	Vice President
C. B. Kountze	Treasurer
G. W. Kassler	Secretary
C. W. Fisher	General Superintendent[1]
L. H. Eicholtz	Chief Engineer
W. B. Rundle	Supt. of Telegraph
J. A. Huntington	Chief Dispatcher
J. P. Pringle	Store Keeper and Fuel Agent
Charles Bradley	Road Master
John Grenslib	Supt. of Bridges
J. H. Kirk	Master of Machinery
A. J. Cleveland	Master of Car Repairs
A. S. Hughes	Freight and Passenger Agent
Charles Wheeler	Purchasing Agent

At this time the South Park's rolling stock consisted of the following:

- 6—Locomotives
- 6—Passenger Cars
- 2—Baggage, Mail and Express Cars
- 45—Box Cars
- 109—Flat Cars
- 16—Construction and Service Cars

The first locomotive owned by the road, the "Fairplay", was a little 18-ton mogul (2-6-0) purchased new from Dawson & Bailey. This engine had 11 x 16-inch cylinders and 34-inch drivers. The South Park's second engine, the "Platte Canon", was a 20-ton American type, also called a standard (4-4-0) and was built by Dawson & Bailey. However, this engine was purchased second-

1. The first General Supt. was B. M. Gillman. He was replaced by J. W. Nesmith (date not known) who in turn resigned Jan. 31, 1879, and was succeeded by C. W. Fisher. Mr. Fisher came from the Kansas Pacific where he was a Division Superintendent.

hand from the narrow gauge Kansas Central Railroad. The third locomotive was a 21-ton, 2-6-6 Tank engine built by Mason, and was the first of quite a series of Mason engines purchased by the road. Number 3 was named the "Oro City", and was delivered to the road in May of 1878. In November of that year No. 4, the "San Juan", was received. The following February, No. 5, the "Leadville", was delivered, and in April, No. 6, the "Ten Mile", made her appearance. These locomotives, as well as those that were to follow for quite a period, were all given names symbolic of the territory through which the South Park had built, or proposed to build.

There has been very little information available regarding the origin of the first passenger and freight cars, and other miscellaneous rolling stock. From the meager data which has come to light, we find that the first cars used by the road in 1874, when it was opened to Morrison, were built by Halleck Brothers in Denver. Some of the later passenger cars were purchased secondhand from the New York elevated system.

Standard equipment of that day and age was also to be found on our South Park. Such equipment included diamond stacks and oil burning headlights on the locomotives, link and pin couplers, and open platform passenger coaches, illuminated with kerosene lamps and heated by potbellied coal stoves.

The spring of 1879 saw the curtain rising on a period in which events were to move faster than at any previous time in the history of the road. The Leadville discoveries had quickened the pulse of industry all over the state, with its effects reaching far beyond in many cases. This revived confidence had brought thousands of immigrants into the region. The completion of the South Park's track to Kenosha station gave the road the most direct route to the new carbonate camp, and thus placed it in a definitely advantageous position with respect to the camp's rapidly increasing freight and passenger traffic. It seems almost like an "Act of Providence" that such a coincidence as the arrival of Governor Evans' railroad in the South Park territory and the birth of the Leadville mining boom should occur together as they did.

The connecting link between the Leadville mining district and Kenosha was the old Mosquito Pass wagon road, and the freighters, with their wagons fully loaded, were doing a land-office business hauling the new camp's much needed mining machinery, mine supplies, foodstuffs, etc. On the return trips, their wagons were loaded down with ore and bullion. It was a paying proposition both ways. The freight business was growing by leaps and bounds and the amount of traffic was more than the railroad could handle. Concerning this great amount of traffic, Wm. B. Vickers, in his "History of Colorado" states:

". . . the travel and freight began to crowd the road to its utmost capacity. Day after day the stream of Leadville travel increased and day after day the railroad company's platforms at end-of-track were crowded with sacks of ore and pigs of base bullion that had to be left behind on account of the lack of transportation facilities. Nothing in the history of this wonderful discovery, rivalling in the splendor of its settings and results the most extravagant dreams of a dope fiend, conveys the idea of the reality of the great richness of Leadville and its outlying camps more perfectly than this brilliant achievement in railroading—that of paying the construction expenses for a mountain railroad from the receipts brought about by this never-ending stream of traffic."

On top of this was the added passenger business between Denver and Leadville and the surrounding and intermediate camps. In view of the circumstances, however, the railroad, in connection with Spotswood & McClellan and their four-horse Concord stages, were doing a noble job in taking care of the rapidly growing passenger traffic. As the railroad had gradually advanced up Platte Canon, the Spotswood & McClellan stage lines in turn established new stations and abandoned the old ones.

Leadville and the scenic wonders of the new South Park railroad were being well advertised all over the East with excellent results. The excitement and interest were so great that some eastern newspapers even sent their reporters out to the "wild and woolly west" to get a firsthand picture of the situation. The reports these fellows carried back with them serve to illustrate the picture very well. A New York newspaper man made a trip over the South Park and reports in the Railway World of June 14, 1879, as follows:

"In travelling to Leadville, the South Park was chosen because it was the shortest route. The distance from Denver to Leadville via the South Park route is about 125 miles, 75 of which the railroad has already completed. The remaining 50 miles have to be travelled by stage coach. The train connecting with the stage leaves Denver at 9:30 P.M. and is scheduled to reach the end of the track at Kenosha Summit at 4 A.M. the next morning. The night we came up the train lost two hours in getting up the mountains, and unless some means are found to increase the speed on the steep grades and sharp curves, the company will have to allow about eight hours for passenger trains to reach the entrance to South Park.

"A few miles from Denver the railroad strikes into the canon of the Platte River which it follows up through a narrow gorge between the mountains for about 50 miles, gaining an altitude at the summit of 10,040 feet[1] or about 5,000 feet above Denver. The scenery through this canon is grand beyond description. At no place is it much more than a stone's throw in width, and most of the way, the railroad has been excavated out of the solid rock. Although we passed over the road in the night, and, as we ascended the mountain, the cold wind swept through the canon as through a funnel, chilling us to the bone, many of the party could not resist the temptation to ride on the platform of the cars in order to enjoy the grand and impressive scenery. On one side of the track the Platte River, a wild mountain stream, dashed down through the canon over an almost unbroken succession of rapids and cataracts. Here and there a deep pool of clear water was provokingly suggestive of trout fishing and sportsmen of the party divided their attention between these tempting spots and the rocks that rose hundreds of feet on either side, worn by the river into all sorts of fantastic shapes and sometimes appearing almost too close over the river and the railroad

"At present this ride over the South Park is by no means a comfortable one. Travellers who have been accustomed to Palace Sleeping Cars for night travel find an all night ride in a narrow gauge car with low backed cushionless seats not a little fatiguing and hardly a good preparation for 15 hours of stage coaching over the roughest of mountain roads.

"The scenes at the end of the track, even at 5 or 6 o'clock in the morning, were extremely interesting and suggestive of our destination. The end of the track of an unfinished railroad is always a busy place; but at the summit, besides the shanties of the workmen, the heaps of construction material, and the temporary station, there were piles of base bullion, looking like pig lead and car loads of high class silver ore in small sacks, waiting for transportation to Denver, besides groceries and merchandise of every description, machinery, household goods, hay, grain, and almost every other necessity of modern civilization all ready to start through the park and over the range to Leadville on wagon trains. A short distance from the station were the camps and corrals of the wagon trains. A few were loaded ready to start, and the teamsters were hitching up their mules, each team consisting of 6 or 8 mules which pull two wagons, one chained behind the other."

In the Railway World, October 18, 1879, a Philadelphia newspaper man who made a trip over the Denver South Park & Pacific line reports:

"The battle with the natural impediments, by the engineers who constructed this railroad, was a stubborn contest at every step. Colonel Eicholtz, the Chief En-

1. Correct figure is 9,991 feet.

gineer of the road, accompanied us over the entire route. At various places, he pointed out where the engineering corps had been lowered from the high cliffs above, with ropes attached to their bodies until they could get a footing to construct platforms upon which to level their instruments. This railroad crosses Kenosha Pass at an altitude of 10,200 feet, being, with a single exception in Mexico, the highest railroad in the world. It has on it several horseshoe curves, which, as engineering, makes us cease to wonder about anything on the Pennsylvania R. R. mountain division in Pennsylvania, while the 'Muleshoe Curve' above Webster, as we reverse direction in Hall's Valley, adds awe to admiration at the boldness of this feat of modern railroad engineering. Through the canyon it has a grade varying from 137 to 158 feet to the mile, and its curves run in many places to 28 degrees. Though it is a narrow gauge railroad, there are many miles of it which cost $25,000 each. The splendid equipment of the road, the panorama of wonders that it unfolds at each turn in its curious windings, the sudden transition as you drop without warning into South Park—an aerial plateau, 9,000 feet above sea level, dotted with small lakes, stretching off for many miles in an unbroken expanse of mountain verdure to the snowy peaks of the higher 'Rockies',—make a ride on it an event never to be forgotten. It is the impunity with which man rolls along in a Palace Car, journeying over trails where the Indian and his pony scarcely dared to venture, that makes all this thing like an eastern fiction. And what else is it but those 1001 nights crystalized in realities? Here are the jewels hidden in the mountains; here are the cities at their slopes that have sprung up in the night by the conjuring wand of avarice; here is the ride through the air with the magician—steam.''

The completion of the South Park's track to Kenosha Summit had been a hard job, but this was no time for rest and reflection. Any delay in construction at this paramount hour of the road's history would be a costly proposition. With their rival for this great Leadville traffic prize, the Rio Grande, involved in the legal battle with the Santa Fe for the Royal Gorge, there was no time to be lost. It was imperative that the steel be laid toward the silver camp just as quickly as possible. The vast improvement in economic conditions during the past winter and spring had brought unlimited capital to the aid of the road. A bulging treasury thus eliminated all the rocks heretofore found in their path. The order board was "clear".

In their first surveys beyond Kenosha, the engineers had projected the original main line down across South Park by way of Hamilton and Fairplay,[1] but this route was to be altered in favor of a more direct line across the Park. The writer has been unable to ascertain just why this change was made; however, a study of the question brings out at least two logical reasons. First

1. D.S.P.&P. Annual Report for 1875.

and foremost was the all important necessity of reaching Leadville as soon as was humanly possible. The second reason, in all probability, was the somewhat rough nature of the terrain just northeast of Fairplay. Evidence of this is borne out in the fact that when the Alma branch was eventually built, the engineers chose Garos, a southerly point in the Park and considerably below Fairplay, as the most feasible point of connection from whence to build this Fairplay-Alma branch. The official resolution relative to the new route was adopted by the company's board of directors on April 15, 1879.

With the new survey completed, plans for continuing construction across the Park were quickly put into action. Meanwhile, contracts for the grading and track-laying between Kenosha and the mouth of Trout Creek had been awarded. Also, great quantities of supplies and construction materials had been assembled at Kenosha station preparatory to the advance across the Park. Without wasting a day's time, the contractors and their crews, under the direction of Colonel Eicholtz and Major Evans, were underway with the actual work even before the end-of-track had reached the summit.

We read in the Railway Age of June 5, 1879:

"The Denver Daily Times states that Carlisle Orman & Company, the contractors for grading, have finished the South Park's grade to Jefferson Creek. Track should reach the town of Jefferson by May 20th. Some 300 men are working, pushing the railhead forward about one-half to three-quarters of a mile per day."

In the various preliminary engineering and surveying operations at this time, Col. Eicholtz, the Chief Engineer, was ably assisted by Major James A. Evans, who had recently joined the South Park organization. Major Evans had previously been connected with the Union Pacific where he had charge of locating the Union Pacific's main line between Laramie and Green River, Wyoming, proving himself to be an engineer of great ability. The South Park and Col. Eicholtz were fortunate to have such a man working with them. Within a short period, Major Evans was to replace Col. Eicholtz as Chief Engineer of the South Park system.

Building a railroad across the Park was going to be a picnic to the engineering and construction forces, compared to what they had encountered since leaving Denver. The South Park region was an area some 50 miles long and about 10 miles wide, and, with the exception of the entrance to and exit from the Park, the territory was for the most part a fairly level region and did not present any great difficulties to the engineers. The few difficulties they did encounter were not extraordinary for a mountain railroad such as the South Park.

It required two and three-quarters miles of track to reach the bottom of the west slope of Kenosha, a drop of approximately 440 feet, before the right of way leveled out. This section included a few steep grades of 3.40 to 4.20 per cent, and some 20 to 28.30 degree curves. The stretch of 4.20 per cent grade, with a 26 degree

M. C. Poor photo,
from David S. Digerness Collection.

The Jefferson station in 1937. The main line extends in a southwesterly direction across South Park toward the Park Range.

M. C. Poor photo,
from Denver Public Library Western Collection.

Jefferson tank, with the Tarryall Mountains in the background, and Kenosha Pass at the right.
Note the harp type switch stand and stub switch, still in use in 1937.

curve at the foot of it, incidentally, was the steepest section of track to be found between Denver and Como. From this point on, construction across the Park proceeded quite rapidly. Practically the only labor involved consisted of scooping up enough earth to build the necessary roadbed, with a few culverts and bridges here and there. It is reported that construction work proceeded 24 hours a day, with long processions of torches to light up the grade and enable the "graveyard crew" to work all night long.

After reaching Jefferson, the right of way ran up-grade a bit to Como station, whose altitude was 9,796 feet. Soon the end-of-track reached Como, 88 miles from Denver, and the first South Park train entered the town on June 21, 1879.[1]

At that time, Como was not much more than a flag stop, but in a few years this station was to become one of the largest division points on the South Park road. From Como it was a gradual drop to the South Platte River crossing, at which point the line struck its lowest elevation in the Park—8,944 feet. The graders were kept well ahead of the tie and rail gang, and as the laying of the rail went forward, the little Masons continued to bring up additional materials. Good progress was made in those summer months. We read in the Railway World of August 16, 1879, the following news item:

"A Denver paper states that the rails are being laid at the rate of one mile per day. From Como the road will run southeast through the valley of the red sand ridge, 10 miles below Fairplay, from which point a branch will run back to that town and possibly to Alma. From the Fairplay branch on the sand ridge the road will be pushed on down the valley to Platte Station, and to the mouth of Trout Creek on the Arkansas River, where the town of Buena Vista has been plotted and surveyed. The contract has been let and the ties and rails are on the ground to build the road to this point. In less than six weeks, trains should be operating into Buena Vista. The railroad has on order 160 coal cars, 4 sleepers, and 6 engines. The grading has been completed to within three miles of the mouth of Trout Creek, and should be completed to this point by August 1st. The railroad anticipates reaching Leadville by October 1st."

Gov. Evans announced, in the Railway Age, that on September 1st slightly over 92 miles of track were in operation. This would put the railhead very close to Red Hill. Upon reaching the station of Red Hill, it must have grieved the souls of the South Park interests to realize that they were so close to their goal, and yet so far away. By air-line it was about 20 miles due west of this station to Leadville, but alas—within those 20 miles lay the impenetrable Park Range, a mountain barrier that defied all efforts of man ever to build a railroad over or under it. They were forced to take the long way around, by way of Buena Vista, a distance of some 77 miles.

The Denver newsman must have been in an optimistic frame of mind when he reported to the Railway World that trains would be operating into Buena Vista within

six weeks, for in reality, it was to be something like six months before the first South Park train would reach that point. A more truthful report on the road's progress is to be found in an advertising circular which was released from the Denver office on October 30, 1879, and which read, in part, as follows:

"The Denver South Park & Pacific Railroad Company is pleased to announce that their line of railroad is now completed to Weston, 107 miles west of Denver. . . . New stations of the road are being opened for traffic as fast as the railroad is completed."

In its exit from the Park, after crossing the South Fork of the Platte River, the line encountered a series of low-lying sand ridges and foothills, necessitating some fairly steep grades and a few sharp curves in its gradual climb to the summit of Trout Creek Pass. The altitude of the pass at the point where the railroad went through was 9,482 feet. Seven years later the Colorado Midland crossed over the South Park tracks at this point. In the section between Como and Trout Creek Pass, the grades ran from .89 per cent to 2.80 per cent, with 20 and 24 degree curves encountered just before the summit was reached.

Although it had been planned originally to build the line by way of the Salt Works in this vicinity, this point was passed up, due to the failure of the project. As near as can be determined, the rails were laid as far as the vicinity of the Salt Works by the latter part of December, 1879. Louisa Ward's book "Chalk Creek" states: "The first South Park train pulled into Chubbs Ranch (later known as Divide, 123 miles from Denver) on Christmas Day, 1879." However, the Railway World of March 13, 1880, tells that the track was only extended to a point 116 miles from Denver on December 31, 1879. This would be about midway between Platte River station and Bath, the top of the pass.

In view of numerous early historical references to the Salt Works located at the southern end of South Park, we shall include a few facts relative to its history. The project and its location played a minor role during the early surveys and plans, not only of the South Park railroad, but also of other roads projected through that region. The place is situated on the McQuaid Ranch, about three miles south of the point where the railroad crosses the South Fork of the Platte River, and a bit southwest of the Antero Reservoir in a locality surrounded by marshy ground and a few small lakes and springs of salt water. Two early settlers, John Q. A. Rollins and Charles Hall,[1] made an attempt to use the output of the salt springs commercially. They invested approximately $50,000 and erected the first and only salt works in Colorado. Their equipment consisted of some large evaporating pans, kettles, tanks, etc., with a reported capacity of approximately two tons of salt per day.[2]

1. The Brand Book (The Westerners) August, 1947.

1. Fairplay Flume, May 17, 1928.
2. Lipsey, John J., The Brand Book, Feb., 1947.

James Harvey, of the Colorado State Museum, possesses an old photograph of the Salt Works showing it to be an L-shaped wooden structure, some 50 feet wide with one wing about 100 feet long and the other about 70 feet long. Both the old square stone chimney, which was about 60 feet high, and the building are still standing. Mr. Harvey says there were about 16 to 20 kettles used at the time the place was in operation. One of these old kettles is on display at the State Museum in Denver.

When the Salt Works were erected in 1864, all the salt used in this whole western country had to be freighted in wagons from the Missouri River, a distance of 700 miles, at a cost, for freight alone, of from four to twenty cents per pound.[1] When these springs and salt lakes were discovered, they were considered as being very valuable. Due to the large amount of salt required in the reduction of silver ore, as well as that needed for domestic purposes, it was thought that these salt works would furnish a considerable amount of traffic to the South Park railroad when it reached that point. However, a great deal of friction arose between the owners and operators and the legal quarrels between these parties, plus the fact that advancing railroad lines from the east brought in cheaper salt, soon put an end to Colorado's supposedly great salt industry. The South Park track was never built directly to the works, but passed about a quarter of a mile to the west.

THE COMO AND KING MINES BRANCHES

In distributing her assets, Mother Nature not only favored Park County with gold and silver, but she also added in some valuable semibituminous coal deposits. History tells us that the first discovery of coal in this region was a five- to six-foot vein found by George W. Leckner, about 1876 or 1877. The location of his mine was about one-half mile northwest of the present site of Como. History also tells us that Leckner hauled his coal by wagon to Fairplay where he sold it for $10.00 a ton.

About the same time that Leckner had found his coal deposit, George Boyd discovered and opened up another coal mine about four miles southeast of Leckner's mine.[2] The settlement at this mine was first known as Como. It soon developed that Boyd had discovered quite a large coal deposit. As a result of these discoveries, Governor Evans and his associates organized The South Park Coal Company with the intention of developing the Park County coal deposits on a large scale. In this connection, we read in the Railway Age under date of November 11, 1880, the following news item:

"The Denver South Park & Pacific Railroad owns about 87½% of the stock of The South Park Coal Company. The coal company controls about 2,000 acres of coal lands near Como on which are located two mines."

The Denver South Park & Pacific's annual report of

December 31, 1880, lists their holdings in The South Park Coal Company as an asset valued at $85,283.43. A good supply of coal for locomotive fuel was a vital necessity, therefore, the development of the field was of major importance to the South Park management. With this idea in mind, the South Park built branch lines to both the Leckner and Boyd Mines.

Upon completion of the South Park's main line to this vicinity, a station was established near the Leckner Mine and given the name of Como. The Boyd Mine settlement was then given the name King, after W. H. King who was, at that time, County Clerk, Postmaster, and manager of the company store there. However, the settlement was often referred to as the Lower Como Mine. During 1880, after the railroad was extended through South Park, the company built a short spur, about one mile long, from Como to the Leckner Mine. Later, part of this spur was to serve as the initial construction of the high line over Boreas Pass to Leadville. The Leckner Mine, later known as the Upper Como Mine, was short-lived and was abandoned in 1883. At last report in 1908, the mine had caved in and was filled with water.

The King Mine spur branched off the main line at a point known as Coal Branch Junction, located about three-quarters of a mile northeast of Como at milepost 87.4. This branch, which was constructed during the latter part of 1879, prior to Union Pacific control, was 3.32 miles in length.[1] No information is available as to the curvature found on this particular stretch of track. The elevation at the end-of-track at the King Mines was approximately 9,500 feet. Using this figure in connection with the profile map of the main line, we find that the average grade west from King was 1.53%.

The following interesting history of the King Mines was found in the book "History of the Union Pacific Coal Mines". From the time of their opening, until January 9, 1883, the Como or King Mines, in connection with the Baldwin Mines, were owned and worked by the South Park, and later the Union Pacific's coal department. The Union Coal Company, which was a consolidation on January 9, 1883, of The Welch Coal Company, The South Park Coal Company, The Gunnison Land Mining & Tunnel Company, Colorado Coal Company, and the St. Louis & Denver Land & Mining Company, was succeeded in 1890 by the Union Pacific Coal Company which took over the operation and management of the railroad's coal properties. The history continues: "Como was the site of the most extensive and most dangerous workings of the company in Colorado, because of the presence of great quantities of explosive gas". There were, in all, five mines at King. The early records are not clear as to the opening date of each of these five mines; however, a later report published in

1. Crofutt's "Grip Sack Guide," 1881.
2. Fairplay Flume, May 17, 1928.

1. The Pacific Railway Commission Reports state that the cost of this branch averaged $8,000 per mile.

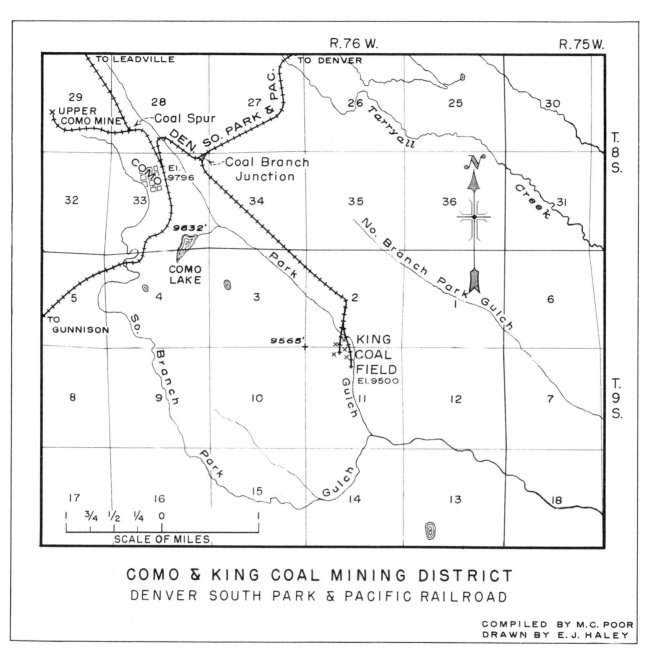

COMO & KING COAL MINING DISTRICT
DENVER SOUTH PARK & PACIFIC RAILROAD

COMPILED BY M.C. POOR
DRAWN BY E.J. HALEY

1902 states that all five were in operation by 1883, when the Union Coal Company took over their management. Of these five mines, the first four had been abandoned before The Union Pacific Coal Company assumed control in 1890. Early records state that the reason for their abandonment was not known except in the case of mine Number One, which was closed in 1889 because of a bad fire. A clue to the final closing of the King Mines is given by Mr. Robert Muir, who worked at Como in 1886. Mr. Muir recalls that the roofs of all five mines were of soft, granulated, sandy shale, and that even with the use of crossbars, lagging, and mine supports, the wet sand would seep into the mine shafts.

As previously mentioned, the presence of explosive gas resulted in numerous serious fires and explosions. One explosion, on January 10, 1893, killed 25 men. Tom Quealy, one of the famous Quealy brothers who made coal mining history in the early days of Colorado, was killed at King while serving as mine superintendent. Caveins were quite frequent and caused the death of many miners from time to time.

Despite the fact that the King Mines were operated at a loss of several thousand dollars annually, the last mine, Number Five, was not abandoned until August, 1894, when the railroad serving the mine passed out of Union Pacific control. Early records show the following production figures for the King Mines. The figures represent tons mined.

Year	Tons
1883	60,140
1884	62,471
1885	43,702
1886	24,207
1887	23,198
1888	37,240
1889	39,939
1890	49,594
1891	47,403
1892	58,979
1893	38,769
1894	25,715
Total	511,357 tons

Another bit of interesting history regarding the King Mines, found in Poor's Manual of Railroads, states that the Company Store at King made a profit of $4,402.10 for the year 1892 and $8,820.88 for the year 1893.

Mr. William Wendell, an old time South Park engineer, tells that for years engine number 29, later number 156, a Brooks mogul, was kept at Como to work between that station and the King Mines. We are also indebted to Jess Frazier for the following story as told to him by H. H. Whitney, another old time runner on the South Park.

"The main shaft into the King Mine sloped gently allowing one to walk up and down it. The little cars were lowered by gravity but were hoisted to the surface by a steam engine and cable. The slope at the main mine went down for over a thousand feet. Lighted candles used by the miners would ignite the gas and caused many fires and bad explosions. This gas condition finally got so bad that it caused the mines to close down. The coal from the King Mines was the finest steaming coal ever burned in a locomotive, and an engine that would not steam on King coal would not steam on anything. However, this coal caused working engines to throw great brilliant showers of burning sparks from their stacks and when working up a hill at night would resemble a gala Fourth of July celebration. For this reason King coal was directly responsible for the large cumbersome special spark arrestors peculiar to early South Park engines."

Another bit of interesting material concerning the King Mines is found in an old Union Pacific Building and Bridge record published in 1886. A perusal of the list of company property at these mines discloses the following noteworthy items:

60 two- and three-room wooden tenement houses.
Tenement house number 7 was listed as a saloon.
Four stables, a blacksmith shop, powder house, school house, carpenter shop, and a scale house equipped with Fairbanks track scales.
A 17,960-gallon wooden water tank.

From all available data, coal mining at King ceased around 1894-96. The records show that .35 mile of the King Mine branch was taken up in 1884, and in 1889, another 2.71 miles of track were removed. This left .26 mile of track which formed one leg of a wye at Coal Branch Junction and which remained in use until the very last, in order that trains from Denver could head into it, and back into Como, then head out for Boreas Pass.

R. H. Kindig Collection.

Denver South Park & Pacific 35, the "Dillon" at Pitkin, Colorado in the early 1880's.

CHAPTER V

THE JOINT OPERATING AGREEMENT

Events were moving along rapidly and much was happening in Colorado railroad circles concerning the South Park at this time. Therefore, in order to preserve some semblance of continuity in our story, it will be necessary for us to leave the scene of construction for a bit and return to Denver. It has already been told how Gould, in order to carry out his Colorado program, made two important moves during the early fall of 1879. The first was the half interest in the Rio Grande which he had obtained, and the second was the controlling influence he had gained in the South Park. Although he did not hold sufficient South Park stock at this time, from the standpoint of actual dollars and cents, to have control of the road, he did manage to promote some sort of an understanding with the South Park officials whereby he was permitted to dictate all future traffic arrangements and construction plans of the road.

Gould's moves at this time were very complex and his strategy is not clearly understood. His desire to build up a single system of feeder lines in the mining southwest evidently dovetailed with his efforts to thwart the westward construction of the Santa Fe. It was during this period that Gould was also maneuvering the Kansas Pacific and Union Pacific interests into such a position that he might, through his forced consolidation of the two roads, make a huge profit on his speculative investment in Kansas Pacific securities. Gould usually acted with such celerity and secrecy that the motives for his complex actions were probably understood by few except himself. Such was the case in this instance. It is quite possible to advance reasons for the sudden acquisition of control of the Rio Grande and his attempt to gain control of the South Park other than the obvious one—control of the Leadville traffic—but to do so would serve no purpose here. Any explanations brought out may or may not be a correct analysis of Gould's motives. Whatever the answer may be, Gould moved immediately to integrate the functions of the Rio Grande and the South Park roads. He outlined an entirely new policy which included both a traffic agreement and a construction program in the Arkansas Valley and southwestern Colorado regions which was supposedly designed for the common good of both roads. It was to be known as a Joint Operating Agreement.

In order that the reader might have a clear picture of the situation at this moment as far as actual railroad construction was concerned in the Arkansas Valley around October, 1879, it might be well to review a few brief details.

The South Park's plans, as outlined in their Articles of Association, and subsequent amendments attached thereto, called for the construction of their main line via the mouth of Trout Creek, Poncha Pass and the San Juan, with an extension to the Gunnison country and a branch line to Leadville. The Gunnison and Leadville extensions were to branch off the main line near the vicinity of the mouth of Trout Creek. By October, the South Park had pushed the end of their track some 107 miles southwest of Denver to the vicinity of Weston, and were proceeding down Trout Creek with their grading, headed for the Arkansas Valley. Because of the skyrocketing Leadville mining boom, this point became the immediate objective, taking precedence for the time being over the San Juan and Gunnison lines. Therefore, all energy was to be directed toward the completion of this Leadville branch as fast as conditions would permit.

The Rio Grande's plans called for the completion of their line from Pueblo through to Leadville, following the Arkansas River all the way. However, the end of their track had only reached the vicinity of Canon City and work on the balance of the line was at a halt temporarily, due to their legal controversy with the Santa Fe. Since neither of the railroads had reached the vicinity of Buena Vista by October 1st, the date of the Joint Operating Agreement, it was possible for Gould to arrange all details just as he desired them. With Gould dictating to the Rio Grande and exerting a controlling influence over the South Park officials, it did not take him long to cast aside all their carefully planned projects and rearrange the various plans of both roads, especially those of the South Park. The result of his ultimatum was that the Rio Grande build through to Leadville, and the South Park build through to the Gunnison country. Both roads were to have equal traffic rights and other privileges, under certain stipulated conditions, over the other's tracks from the point of crossover, namely, Buena Vista, Colorado.

Nothing more is ever heard of the South Park's original plans to extend their line by way of Poncha Pass to the San Juan country. This projected extension was

173

shelved in favor of another proposed route to southwestern Colorado via Gunnison, the details of which will be related later. The South Park's destination—the Gunnison country and regions beyond — was now mapped out.

The setup which Gould arranged for the two roads was incorporated in a contract titled a Joint Operating Agreement. This agreement, dated October 1, 1879, included all details, both as to further construction and the division of all traffic for both railroads, was as follows.[1]

JOINT OPERATING AGREEMENT

THIS AGREEMENT, between THE DENVER SOUTH PARK & PACIFIC RAILROAD COMPANY, party of the first part, and THE DENVER & RIO GRANDE RAILWAY COMPANY, party of the second part, WITNESSETH:

That for the purpose of harmony and mutual profit it is agreed that the party of the second part shall build from the point of junction of the lines of their respective roads at Buena Vista, in the Arkansas Valley, to Leadville or Malta, on which the party of the first part shall have equal rights and privileges in perpetuity, for which it is to pay eight per cent per annum, payable monthly, on one-half of the cash cost thereof, and pay one-half of the expenses of maintenance and repairs.

In case of the further extension of main line or branches of the line between Buena Vista and Leadville, the party of the second part shall build the same, and the party of the first part shall have like rights thereon on the like terms as above set forth.

2nd: The party of the first part shall build its line by way of Chalk Creek and Alpine Pass to and through the country drained by the Gunnison and its tributaries, and the party of the second part shall have like rights on the like terms with the Leadville line and with any branches and extensions that may be built from the main line thereof.

3rd: Should the party of the first part wish to go south of its line to Buena Vista to start its Chalk Creek line, it shall have the right to occupy the track of the road of the party of the second part on joint trackage as aforesaid to the most eligible point of departure from the same, or should it desire to extend its line to the valley of the Gunnison from any point further south, the party of the second part shall build so much of its line promptly to such point, and give trackage to the party of the first part with like rights and on like conditions as provided for in the line to Leadville. PROVIDED: the point of divergence and pass over the mountains to be used shall be mutually agreed upon.

The points of junction shall be mutually agreed upon, the lands and depot grounds at and around each shall be purchased and enjoyed equally, except that at Buena Vista, which is already located. At Buena Vista all land

for railroad purposes shall be owned and enjoyed equally.

The rates on all traffic between all points on the lines of joint trackage and said junction and Pueblo and Denver to be mutually agreed upon and to be the same.

All receipts from business passing to and from Denver and Pueblo and from and to all points on said joint trackage shall be pooled, and the gross amount thereof shall be equally divided between the parties hereto after deducting fifty per cent for expenses by the party over whose line it is carried; but either party may have an equitable readjustment of the percentage for operating expenses and the division of earnings by giving thirty days notice after six months after completion of line from Canon City to Leadville and annually thereafter. And in case of a failure to agree the question shall be referred to disinterested experts selected in the usual mode of arbitration, whose decision shall be final and binding for the ensuing year.

The Leadville extension from the junction shall be built by the Denver & Rio Grande Railway Company as soon as the South Park line reaches Buena Vista, or as soon thereafter as practicable. The Denver South Park & Pacific Company to carry material and equipment for the Leadville line at cost to be determined by Messrs. D. C. Dodge and C. W. Fisher, and in case of difference, by Mr. S. H. H. Clarke. And from the time it reaches Leadville it shall be operated by the party of the first part, who shall receive all earnings until the line reaches Trout Creek from Canon City and pay monthly to the Denver & Rio Grande Railway Company the gross earnings, less expenses of operating and fuel, repair and maintenance reckoned on the average of their expenses between Leadville and Denver. The earnings of the Gunnison extension to be pooled to Denver as provided for above from the time a point of business is opened. But in case the line from Canon City to the Junction is not completed within four months thereafter, such pooling to cease until such completion is made. At all times when said pooling occurs on any of the lines, the trackage rental of eight per cent on the half of the cash cost and half of the maintenance and repairs shall be paid, but in all other cases it shall be omitted.

All questions on which differences occur shall be settled by arbitration, each party choosing one disinterested expert, and, in case the two fail to agree, the two selecting one umpire, and in case either party fails or refuses to select an arbitrator the decision of the one selected by the other shall be the award, and the award of such arbitrator shall be final and binding on both parties. The roads of the two parties are to be consolidated as soon as practicable on a mutual beneficial and equitable basis.

IN WITNESS WHEREOF, the parties hereunto have caused these presents to be signed by their respective Presidents and affixed their seals the first day of October, one thousand eight hundred and seventy-nine.

1. Courtesy Herbert O. Brayer.

DENVER & RIO GRANDE RAILWAY
    COMPANY
By Jay Gould
DENVER SOUTH PARK & PACIFIC
    R. R. CO.
By John Evans, President
DENVER & RIO GRANDE RAILWAY
    COMPANY
By William J. Palmer, President.

Stripped of its legal phrases and condensed into short form, the agreement was as follows:

Regarding construction, the Rio Grande was to build to Leadville and beyond giving the South Park equal trackage rights from the point of junction at Buena Vista, north to Leadville in perpetuity. As a rental for the use of this part of the Rio Grande line, the South Park was to pay 8 per cent interest annually, on one-half of the construction costs, plus one-half of the maintenance expense and repairs. Pending the settlement of the Rio Grande-Santa Fe controversy, the Rio Grande, upon completion of the South Park into Buena Vista, was to commence construction from Buena Vista to Leadville; the South Park to transport and deliver at cost, all rails and other necessary construction materials, until such time as the Rio Grande could complete their line through from Canon City. Upon completion of the Buena Vista-Leadville line, and until the Rio Grande could be completed through from Canon City to Buena Vista, the South Park was to operate the line, and turn all gross earnings, less operation expense incurred, over to the Rio Grande.

Likewise, the South Park was to build up Chalk Creek into the Gunnison country, granting the Rio Grande equal trackage rights in perpetuity on a rental basis of 8 per cent annually on one-half of the construction costs, plus one-half of the maintenance expense and repairs.

Inasmuch as it was fairly well conceded that the South Park would arrive at the mouth of Trout Creek first and could continue the construction of the Gunnison line themselves, no stipulations regarding any construction of the Gunnison line by the Rio Grande were incorporated in the agreement.

Regarding the traffic agreements, all receipts from traffic passing in either direction between Denver and Pueblo and all points on the joint trackage concerned, were to be pooled and the gross amount divided equally between the two roads, after deducting 50% for expenses by the road over which said traffic had been carried. Traffic rates on both roads between the above points were to be on an equal basis. It was agreed that each road could operate two passenger trains per day between Denver and Leadville providing morning and evening arrivals. The Rio Grande trains were scheduled to make the run in 15 hours as compared to the South Park's 11 hours.

Finally, it was incorporated in the agreement that the two railroads be consolidated as soon as practical.

Inasmuch as Mock furnishes one of the best discussions regarding the merits of this much discussed contract, we will quote him directly.

"The contract, unique in several respects, was one which no two independent lines would have been likely to make. Considerations in equity were either lacking or uncertain. The provision that the Rio Grande should build the line although its rival should have equal rights in using it, seems to indicate a compromise, for if the Rio Grande had had clear title to the route it is improbable that it would have voluntarily signed away its advantage. The Evans road also claimed priority in the valley of the upper Arkansas, therefore the same can be said of them, when it came to signing away its advantages.

"The same can be said concerning the traffic pool; having sole access to Leadville there would have been little point in agreeing to permit a competitor to compete with it on equal terms. But both roads anticipated securing the bulk of the business at the common point, Buena Vista, and each had certain factors favoring it. The South Park, though a good hundred miles the shorter line between Leadville and Denver, was the more expensive line to operate. The Rio Grande, on the other hand, could offset its longer line by insisting on a break of the bulk at the common point on all freight going or coming via the South Park. It could also set the rates between the common point and Leadville at whatever level it wished. The traffic contract was almost certainly no more than a temporary accommodation to secure harmonious operations for the time being.

"The agreement that each road should be permitted to run its cars on the extensions of the other—uncertain as to equity though it may have been for both roads—was nevertheless of considerable significance. Gould very obviously was parcelling off to each its particular sphere of influence; the Rio Grande should be permitted a free hand around and west of Leadville, as well as southward into New Mexico; the South Park should be permitted a free hand in the southwest beyond Gunnison. Such an arrangement would permit the South Park to save its funds for the building of its line to the Gunnison country and beyond towards Arizona, which to all purposes, would be to Gould's advantage. He probably intended that the lines of both companies should form an integrated system of cooperating roads. It would seem to be rather evident that for the moment, at least, Gould was more interested in the southwest than in a competing through line to the Central Pacific in Utah."

CHAPTER VI

CONSTRUCTION FROM TROUT CREEK PASS TO BUENA VISTA

With their future program now laid out for them, the South Park interests went ahead with the construction of their line toward Buena Vista.

From Trout Creek Pass, also known at various times as Bath, Summit, or Hill Top, the route down to the valley of the Arkansas River is a slightly different story from the one we have just read concerning construction across the South Park. The air-line distance from the summit of the pass to the river is approximately twelve miles, while the drop in altitude is about 1,460 feet. When Mother Nature was distributing and laying out her mountains and valleys, she did not take into account the fact that some day mere man would like to build a railroad between certain points, so the railroad engineer just had to do the best he could under the circumstances.

The choice of the best route between the summit and the floor of the Arkansas Valley, at the time of the original survey, must have presented quite a problem to Colonel Eicholtz and the South Park company. For some unknown reason they selected a route directly down the line of Trout Creek Canon. The head of this creek is to be found about one-half mile southwest of the summit of the pass. This innocent appearing little stream, which empties into the Arkansas River, is not more than 17 or 18 miles long, but it furnishes a drainage or outlet to quite an extensive watershed in this particular section of the Park Range. By following down this canon, the engineers had a smooth and gradual drop from the pass down to the river with a minimum of curvature, steep grades, length of line, construction time, and expense; however, on the other hand, the right of way would be subject to possible floods and washouts. Not knowing all the facts of the case, it is hard to explain just why the South Park chose such a route. The author put this question to Mr. Wm. J. Coogan, an old time locomotive engineer on the road who lived in the Arkansas Valley between Nathrop and Buena Vista since 1883. Mr. Coogan replied:

"Regarding the line down Trout Creek. During the 80's and 90's Trout Creek was a fairly peaceable stream, and there had not been any heavy floods. The creek ran near the surface and there were little meadows, beaver dams, and lots of willows all along the route. A person seeing it now cannot realize what it looked like then. At that time no one ever expected that the creek would wash away as it has."

The author will vouch for Mr. Coogan's statement that today Trout Creek does not have the appearance of a peaceable stream. It seems that for a number of years after the South Park was built down through the canon, the stream behaved itself very well, and then around the turn of the century the railroad gradually began to have trouble with flood waters. Today, Trout Creek is what one in the southwest might call an arroyo or dry gulch. This implies a wet weather stream.

During the summer season in recent years, the author has followed the course or bed of this stream for practically its entire length, and the insignificant amount of water meandering aimlessly along the creek bed, sometimes disappearing here and there in the gravel and sand, gives the appearance of a perfectly harmless small creek. However, various members of old time South Park train crews tell that during the rainy seasons in this region in later years, Trout Creek really put on a show at times, filled up from bank to bank and went on a rampage that did considerable damage to the track and grading. A view of the many cleanly washed rocks and boulders lying haphazardly here and there in the creek bed, and the washed banks, tell the story of numerous floods. It is thought that this condition was brought about by the destruction of the forests in the Trout Creek drainage basin. The hillsides were completely denuded by firms making charcoal from the timber; the charcoal being used by smelters in the vicinity. With the timber gone, there was nothing to slow down the runoff and serious erosion resulted. This condition still exists and a huge delta has been built up at the mouth of Trout Creek in the Arkansas Valley.

In an effort to explain the company's choice of this route, a careful study of the subject, in connection with a few known facts, was made and the following conclusion has been reached.

To begin with, the original route of the road, as specified in the Articles of Association, was projected across the South Park by way of the Salt Works, thence across the Valley of the Arkansas, "near the mouth of Trout Creek in Chaffee County", and through Poncha Pass to the San Juan country. This idea continued to prevail as late as May, 1879.

At a meeting of the Board on May 24, 1879, we find

the following resolution made by Mr. Cheesman, and adopted.

RESOLVED, that the line located by the Chief Engineer from the Mouth of Trout Creek in the Arkansas Valley to and through the Poncha Pass on the main line of the road of this company . . . be and the same is hereby adopted as the road of this company and the President and Chief Engineer are directed to file plats and profiles as directed by law to secure the right of way over the same.

At the same meeting, the following resolution was made by J. S. Brown, and adopted.

RESOLVED, that the line of road surveyed by Major Evans and the Chief Engineer of this company from the Mouth of Trout Creek up the Arkansas Valley to or near Malta (Leadville) be and the same is hereby adopted as the location of the line of that part of the branch of the road of this company and extending up said valley and the President and Chief Engineer are hereby directed to file plats and profiles of said location as required by law to secure right of way for the same.

From these adopted resolutions it can be clearly seen that the main line was to be constructed by way of the Salt Works, thence to the mouth of Trout Creek continuing directly south via Poncha Pass to the San Juan country, with a branch line from the mouth of Trout Creek running back up to Malta. Malta is four miles southwest of Leadville, being a sort of "fork in the road," where railroad lines destined for Leadville turned east from the Arkansas River to enter the mining camp.

The resolution adopting this projected route did not specifically state just how or where the engineers would build between the Salt Works and the mouth of Trout Creek. Col. Eicholtz and Major Evans, in all probability, did survey a much safer route between the two points than the one down the bed of an unpredictable mountain stream, but we can only guess as to its probable location. From knowledge of this particular region, it can be safely stated that any other route chosen between the two specified points would require much heavier construction and considerably more time than a line down Trout Creek Canon.

A route along the north side of the mountain above Trout Creek Canon, such as the Colorado Midland followed seven years later, would necessitate constructing the South Park track quite a number of miles north up the Arkansas Valley, before it could be gradually brought down to the level of the river and turn back south. Naturally, such a route would entail heavy construction and require considerable time. This would place them much closer to Leadville, but it must be remembered that this is the main line we are speaking of, which, at the time of the original survey, was considered more important than a branch line. The destination then was the San Juan country, not Leadville.

A line constructed on the south side and above the canon of Trout Creek, eventually dropping down to the Arkansas Valley, would be in the general direction of Poncha Pass, but it is assumed that preliminary surveys of this route called for too much heavy construction

work and too much mileage, and consequently was passed up. As a matter of fact, we do find mention in the Engineering News of August 16, 1879, of a proposal to build the line around by way of Cleora, a ghost mining camp near South Arkansas (Salida),[1] but the article intimated that the idea was dropped as the route was considered too long. Possibly another factor which caused the company to frown upon the Cleora route was the projected line toward Gunnison.

However, by the time the rails had been extended to the southern end of South Park, a change of major importance had come about. This was the Joint Operating Agreement which Gould had arranged between the Rio Grande and South Park after he had gained a controlling interest in both lines. The fact that it had been definitely determined that the South Park's point of destination was the Gunnison country changed the situation entirely. The South Park's construction program was somewhat behind schedule, due more or less to financial difficulties the road had encountered while building through the Platte Canon to Kenosha Summit. In the meantime, the Leadville mining boom was skyrocketing and gaining momentum daily.

Time was becoming more valuable with each passing day. The Rio Grande's line was surveyed and scheduled to build into Leadville, but a survey is not a railroad. The mining camp was yelling for supplies and cheap transportation for their ore. Any time lost by the South Park in unnecessary right of way construction between the end-of-track and the Arkansas Valley meant the loss of just that much more valuable traffic. Therefore, in view of the circumstances involved, it was evidently decided to follow the line of the original survey between the pass and the river. Trout Creek canon was the ultimate answer for a short route with a minimum of construction time.

The surveyors had laid out the safest line possible down the canon, and the fall of 1879 found the grading crews hard at work all along this section. As the line progressed down the canon, a few small stations were established. Two miles below Hill Top was a station known as Divide, while some three miles further on was located the station of McGees.

For the first few miles down the stream, the engineers could, to a certain extent, build the right of way along the so-called banks of the creek and thus partially avoid any flood hazards which would result if the grade were built directly down the bed of the stream. However, as they progressed down the canon, the banks of the creek became too high and steep to follow this procedure, and they were forced to build the right of way more or less directly in the sandy bed of the creek itself. At a point, later known as "Dead Man's Curve", just a

1. Cleora was laid out by the Santa Fe in 1878, during the time they were surveying up the Arkansas Valley. South Arkansas Station was changed to Salida in 1881.

Junction of the Rio Grande and South Park lines near the stone station at Nathrop, Colorado. The South Park tracks curve to the right past the Nachtrieb Hotel.

Engine 22, the "Crested Butte," and train on the bridge across the Arkansas River, near Buena Vista, Colorado, in the early 1880's.

short distance west of milepost 132, the line left Trout Creek, proceeded through a few cuts in some low hills and emerged out upon the floor of the great Arkansas Valley. The track crossed the Arkansas River two miles below the townsite of Buena Vista.

That part of the line between the summit and the Arkansas River was one section where the bridge crew earned their money. Between milepost 120 near Hill Top, and milepost 134, just west of the river, a distance of approximately 14 miles, there were 30 bridges varying in length from 12 to 293 feet, and in height from 2 to 48 feet. There were also numerous smaller ones of 6- to 10-foot lengths. In this section, the track crossed Trout Creek 27 times, on bridges varying from 12 to 16 feet in length. Of these 30 bridges, the larger structures had the following dimensions:

Length in feet	Height in feet		
31	5	near milepost	126.9
48	8	" "	130.6
75	18	" "	129.2
172	17	" "	129.3

The largest of the 30, of course, was the structure across the Arkansas River. This bridge was an iron truss structure built on stone piers. The main span was 152 feet long while the total length overall was 293 feet. Inasmuch as the river has cut quite a deep and narrow channel through this broad valley just below Buena Vista, this bridge was 48 feet above the water.

The maximum grades encountered (eastbound) between the river and Hill Top, ran from 2.48% to 2.76%. There were a number of 18, 20 and 22 degree curves and two 24 degree curves.

As nearly as can be determined, the South Park's rails reached the east bank of the Arkansas River, known for a time as Arkansas Station, about February 9, 1880.

Within another week the big bridge across the river was finished and a large wye connection was completed across the level valley about a mile to connect the unfinished portion of the Rio Grande's right of way at two different points. This wye was completed about February 21st. Although it was four months, as will be explained later, before the Rio Grande completed their line through from Canon City to Buena Vista, this did not prevent the South Park from continuing with their proposed construction. At that time, the north leg of the wye connecting with the Rio Grande was located south of Cottonwood Creek and the townsite of Buena Vista. For three years, this was to be the South Park's Buena Vista terminal.

Thus within a period of about eight months, approximately 59 miles of railroad had been built, making a total of 135 miles of line completed and opened to traffic between Denver and Buena Vista. The Rio Grande and South Park roads, together with the Buena Vista Townsite Company, built a joint railroad depot at Buena Vista. It was completed January 8, 1880. All expense pertaining to construction costs, rolling stock, equipment, etc., necessary to build the road and place it in operation, which had been incurred from November 24, 1877, up to this date, had been taken care of by the Denver & South Park Railroad Construction & Land Company. This included approximately 110 miles of main track and branches extending from the vicinity of South Platte station to Buena Vista. 150 miles of railroad were now completed and in operation and, as stipulated in the contract between the railroad company and the construction company, the latter now held the $1,800,000 of bonds and the $3,500,000 of stock. Details concerning the demise of this last named construction company and the organization of its successor will follow shortly.

CHAPTER VII

WHO REACHED BUENA VISTA FIRST?

In compiling this history of the South Park, one of the issues to be settled seems to be the question as to which railroad, the Denver South Park & Pacific or the Denver & Rio Grande, reached Buena Vista, Colorado, first. A few historians have made the statement that the Rio Grande reached that point first. Other authors of various Colorado historical subjects have stated that both roads reached Buena Vista at about the same time. During the early search for material by the writer, it appeared that the Rio Grande supporters were correct in their statements. However, as time progressed and more material was uncovered, the evidence seems to indicate just the opposite. It is the firm contention of the author of this book that the South Park beat the Rio Grande into Buena Vista, both with their track and trains, by a margin of some four months. This statement is based on the following newspaper items and other miscellaneous sources of material.

Railway World, March 13, 1880:

"On February 11, 1880, Denver & South Park trains started running to Arkansas Station, 133 miles from Denver and 17 miles beyond the point which the track reached on December 31, 1879. The line is nearly complete to Buena Vista, two miles further."

Author's note:

From the above, and other bits of information that have been found, Arkansas Station was a temporary name for the end-of-track on the east bank of the Arkansas River at the point of crossing. Later, this place was known as Macune.

Rocky Mountain News, February 17, 1880:

"The first ten days of this month gave the South Park road the largest passenger business in its history. At 5 p.m. last Saturday, February 14th, the South Park swung the 150-foot span of their iron bridge across the Arkansas River to the Buena Vista side. The roadbed is ready for the iron as far as Buena Vista, two miles from the river. Their cars will reach the Buena Vista depot by Saturday, the 21st."

During the writing of this book, the author directed a letter to Dr. LeRoy R. Hafen, State Historian of the State Historical Society of Colorado, inquiring as to what information he might have on the subject. Dr. Hafen replied as follows:

"In response to your letter I have obtained the information you want. It comes from Mr. Arthur Ridgway, Chief Engineer of the Denver & Rio Grande Railroad. Mr. Ridgway states that the records show that the track of the Denver & South Park reached Buena Vista, February 9, 1880,[1] and that the Rio

1. Bailey's "History of the Union Pacific" states that the Denver & South Park reached Buena Vista on February 22, 1880.

Grande track did not reach there until June of the same year. He thinks there is no question but that the South Park also established the first passenger service."

The following testimony of Governor John Evans was taken from the court records transcribed during the trial of the famous Pacific Railway Commission Case held in 1885.

"Question by the Court to John Evans: 'Did the Denver & Rio Grande reach Buena Vista first before the South Park?'

"Answer by John Evans: 'No—the South Park reached there first, but there had been a great deal of work done by the Denver & Rio Grande and the Santa Fe who were contesting the Leadville extension.'"

Due to the Rio Grande's long drawn out legal controversy with the Santa Fe over possession of the Canon City-Leadville route up the valley of the Arkansas River, construction of that section was held up by the courts. Finally, after the courts, the judges and the lawyers, together with Bat Masterson and his gunmen, were unable to get anywhere, the two roads got together and settled the issue themselves. On April 5, 1880,[1] two and one-half months after the South Park had been completed through to Buena Vista, General Palmer secured possession of the Leadville route for his railroad. The fact that the Santa Fe had completed all the original surveys and a large portion of the grading between the vicinity of the Royal Gorge and Leadville, enabled the Rio Grande to proceed with considerable speed in the completion of this line. Relative to this preliminary work on the part of the Santa Fe, we read in the Railway Age of June 10, 1880, the following:

"The Pueblo & Arkansas Valley Railway Co. (the Santa Fe's Royal Gorge line to Leadville) reports that work was continued on the Leadville extension up to July 14, 1879, at which time the grade to Leadville was nearly completed, with 22 miles of track laid. Had it not been stopped by an injunction, the line would have been completed to Leadville by September 30, 1879."

The Rio Grande completed their line through to Buena Vista on June 9, 1880,[2] four months after the South Park's arrival. By July 31st, Palmer's road was com-

1. April 4, 1880. Anderson, "Gen. Wm. J. Palmer".
   April 5, 1880. Mock, "Railroad Development in Colorado".
   April 5, 1880. Railway World, page 461 bound volume for 1880.
   April 5, 1880. Denver & Rio Grande Annual Report, 1880, page 33.

2. D. & R. G. Annual Report, 1880.

pleted through to Leadville. These statements are based on the following newspaper items and other miscellaneous sources of material.

Rocky Mountain News, February 20, 1880:

"Quoting from Wednesday, February the 18th's issue of the Leadville Democrat. . . . Mr. S. W. Eccles, General Agent of the Rio Grande, came to Leadville last night. The Democrat reporter had been asking Mr. Eccles regarding completion of the Rio Grande to Leadville and was kidding him on account of the slowness of the Rio Grande in reaching Leadville. The reporter asks 'How about iron'? Mr. Eccles' answer, 'We have a sufficient quantity of iron at Canon City to complete the railroad to Buena Vista, and enough at Denver to complete the line from Buena Vista to Leadville'. 'Which portion will be built first'? Mr. Eccles answered, 'Work on the right of way will be commenced simultaneously all along the line. Track laying will commence at Buena Vista and extend both ways. Track laying will also be started at once at the present track from Pueblo'."

Railway Age, April 29, 1880:

"The track of the Leadville extension of the Denver & Rio Grande will reach Cleora, 62 miles from Leadville by May the 14th, 1880."

Railroad Gazette, May 14, 1880:

"Track on the Leadville extension is now laid to South Arkansas (Salida) 55 miles from the old terminus at Canon City, Colorado, leaving about 60 miles to reach Leadville. Nearly all this distance is graded. Of the track now complete, 22 miles were laid by the Atchison Topeka & Santa Fe before that company's work was stopped by litigation."

Railway Age, May 27, 1880:

"The Denver & Rio Grande General Passenger Agent announced May the 10th the completion of its line to South Arkansas (Salida) where connections are made with Barlow & Sanderson's stage line to Leadville."

In Anderson's "Gen. William J. Palmer" we read:

". . . Thus after two years of expensive delay, and loss of revenue due to the fact that the Leadville line had not been in operation during the flood tide of development, the Denver & Rio Grande was at last free to proceed with the development of their line and construction of the road into Leadville. Arrangements were made early in February, 1880, for the completion of this line; however, it was not until April 4th, 1880 . . . that possession of the Canon City-Leadville line was returned to the Rio Grande road. . . . The work of construction on the Leadville line was then pushed with such vigor that the line was finished . . . into Leadville by July 31st, 1880."

Gunnison Review, June 12, 1880:

"The Denver & Rio Grande ran their first passenger train into Buena Vista from Salida last Saturday evening, June the 5th. Announcement has been made unofficially that they will reach Leadville by July the 4th." Note: The Rio Grande 1880 Annual Report gives June 9th as the date of arrival in Buena Vista.

Commercial & Financial Chronicle, August 7, 1880:

"A dispatch from Denver dated August 1st, 1880, says: 'The Denver & Rio Grande was completed into Leadville yesterday. Both the South Park and the Rio Grande will start running regular through trains today. The South Park is completed to Hortense and opened for business'."

Railway World, August 7, 1880:

"A Denver dispatch dated August 1st says: 'The joint track of the Denver & Rio Grande and the Denver South Park & Pacific was completed into Leadville yesterday, July 31st, and both companies began operating regular through trains today, August 1st'."

Engineering News, August 7, 1880:

"The joint track of the Denver & Rio Grande and the Denver South Park & Pacific was completed into Leadville July 31st, 1880, and the first trains went into the city on August 1st. At this time the South Park is open for business as far as Hortense."

As a finale to this discussion, we quote the following report written by J. A. McMurtrie, Chief Engineer of the Rio Grande, to Gen. Palmer and incorporated in the Rio Grande Annual Report of 1880.

". . . After the injunction heretofore spoken of, nothing was done on the Leadville extension until about the first of February, 1880, when the Engineering Corps, having commenced and partially completed the location of an independent line between South Arkansas and Leadville, were notified from New York that papers had been signed settling all controversies, and that we were to take possession of our original line between the Canon and Leadville and all material pertaining thereto. Contracts were made at once for completing the grading and bridging to Leadville, but owing to numerous vexatious delays, hard to forget—but too numerous to mention, the road and material were not turned over to us until about April 5th, 1880, at which time track laying was commenced where the Atchison company were stopped, and was completed as follows:

To South Arkansas .... May 20, 1880
  Nathrop .... June 1, 1880
  Buena Vista .... June 9, 1880
  Malta .... June 29, 1880
  Leadville .... July 20, 1880."

CHAPTER VIII

"OUR LITTLE ROAD IS FULL OF BUSINESS"

Some mention of the South Park's first rolling stock and the great amount of traffic handled by the road has already been made; however, this phase of the road's history had expanded so much between that time and 1880 that the subject merits further discussion. During the early days of the railroad, Spotswood & McClellan's stage lines had connected successively with advancing railhead stations by abandoning old stations and establishing new ones as the end-of-track forged ahead to such new places as Webster, Kenosha, Jefferson, and Weston. This concern was managed by Robert J. Spotswood, who at that time had achieved an outstanding reputation as a stage and freight line operator and had few equals as such in early western history. The Colorado Magazine states:

"On no other stage line in Colorado did stage coach service attain the magnitude and perfection that was reached by the Spotswood stages to Leadville in the boom days preceeding the arrival of the railroad."

A great friendship existed between John Evans and Robert Spotswood. This friendly tie between these two men resulted in close cooperation between the two transportation agencies which they represented, and was largely responsible for a great volume of traffic that was moved in and out of Leadville and surrounding areas during the early building and extension of the South Park railroad. To handle this passenger traffic between Leadville and the various rail connections, Spotswood operated four 4-horse Concord stages daily. In addition to the Spotswood & McClellan lines, there were also other stage and freight line operators, notably Barlow & Sanderson and Wall & Witter.

One of the most famous end-of-track stage connections to be established was Weston, located in the southern end of South Park, where a toll road for stage and freight wagon traffic had been built over Weston Pass in the Park Range to reach Leadville.

An article in the March, 1932, issue of the Colorado Magazine relates that inasmuch as Weston was located on an open prairie section in the southern end of the Park, there was no limit to the amount of room available for the accumulation of freight of every description. No effort was made to shelter the enormous amount of machinery and merchandise, but some semblance of order was maintained by piling articles separately and so arranging the piles that wagon teams could pass through what might have been called lanes. Exposed to the elements with no covering, this great amount of miscellaneous freight remained there until such time as it could be freighted to its destination.

For some additional material relative to the stage connection at Weston, we quote from an advertising circular issued by the Denver office of the railroad under date of October 30, 1879.

"The Denver South Park & Pacific Railroad Company is pleased to announce that their line of railroad is now completed to Weston, 107 miles west of Denver, and offers the shortest and most direct route in connection with a triple daily line of six-horse Concord Stage Coaches to Leadville, Oro City, Fairplay, Alma, Dudley, Montgomery, Mosquito, Hamilton, St. John, Montezuma, Breckenridge, Hall's Valley, Morrison, and all points in the South Park, Summit County, Gunnison Valley, and Southwestern Colorado. The railroad is being rapidly pushed through the South Park to Leadville, Fairplay, and the Gunnison Valley; mining camps that are attracting the attention of an immense number of people. It is estimated that there are now upwards of 50,000 people in their vicinity, attracted by the rich discoveries. At present there are only five miles of staging to Fairplay and 32 miles to Leadville, being 96 miles less staging than by any other route.

"New stations of the road are being opened for traffic as fast as the Denver South Park & Pacific is completed."

The completion of the Evans road to Buena Vista enabled a considerable portion of this Leadville traffic to make the transfer to the stage and freight lines at that point. With traffic funnelling into Buena Vista partly by way of Salida and the Arkansas Valley and partly via the newly arrived South Park railroad, the town suddenly found itself in the midst of this Leadville stampede, wherein the Rocky Mountain News of January 8, 1880, stated:

". . . there were over 800, six, eight and ten mule teams going through Buena Vista every day headed for the new silver camp."

By the time the rails had reached Buena Vista and regular service had been established to that point, traffic and financial returns reached an unprecedented peak. This immense amount of traffic called for all the motive power that the road's officials could muster. The locomotive builders in the east were filling the South Park's requisitions for engines as fast as their production facilities would permit. By October, 1880, the road had 36

L. C. McClure.

Looking down on Buena Vista from the Colorado Midland Railway, about 1905. The Colorado & Southern tracks and depot can be seen in the foreground, and 14,172-foot Mt. Yale towers in the background at the right.

W. H. Jackson photo,
from Francis Rizzari Collection.

The Buena Vista transfer yards in the early '80's. Here the South Park and Rio Grande interchanged freight.

locomotives in service between Denver and Buena Vista, with more on order.

The first type of engine purchased for passenger service was the Mason Bogie, while the first freight engines acquired were a group of Baldwin consolidations. These engines began to arrive in the spring of 1878, and by October, 1880, the road had 23 Mason engines and eight Baldwins in service. Including the first two engines purchased and three more Dawson & Bailey moguls acquired during 1879, the South Park now had 36 locomotives in service. For a comparatively new railroad just emerging from its embryonic stage with only 150 miles of main line trackage, this was quite an array of steam power. Still, the amount of business was such that they were totally unable to handle the immense volume of traffic that was beginning to flow through the canon of the Platte. Early in 1880, the Leadville boom was going full blast. Mining activities in the Mosquito or Park Range, Chalk Creek Canon, and the Gunnison and San Juan regions were increasing rapidly. The tremendous amount of supplies needed by these various mining camps, together with the great quantity of ore and bullion to be hauled out, literally swamped the South Park line. Their thin strand of steel, the only life line available to this teeming area up to this time, was just not able to carry the load demanded of it. In addition to this deluge of freight traffic, there was a correspondingly increased passenger traffic to take care of. Because the railroad was unable to cope with such a situation, the backlog of freight traffic began to pile up along the line like flood waters behind a dam.

Anderson, in writing of Palmer and the Rio Grande, tells an interesting story regarding some of the traffic problems of the South Park during this particular period. It seems that a final court decision relative to the control of the Royal Gorge route was scheduled to be handed down on October 21, 1879. When the day arrived, it was postponed until November 17th, and on that date, the decision was again postponed for an indefinite period. Meanwhile, the citizens of Leadville were calling for an immediate court decision, so that the line from Pueblo to Leadville could be completed by either the Santa Fe or the Rio Grande. The South Park road to Trout Creek could not bring food and merchandise rapidly enough, much less transport the coal, coke and other bulky materials required by Leadville's ore reduction mills. Only four days supplies bridged the gap between the people and complete exhaustion of food stores. It was suggested that the people would have to live on two-thirds rations or one-third of the people would have to move away. Freighting by wagon teams continued to be a thriving business between Colorado Springs and Leadville and between Trout Creek and Leadville, but railroad connections were demanded and required. Prominent men, including H. A. W. Tabor, were bitterly critical of Judge Hallett for postponing the decision.

November passed and with December came the dreaded blockade by snow of the South Park line and also of the wagon roads. These blockades lasted for days at a time and meanwhile the people of Leadville suffered for want of the necessities of life. R. F. Weitbrec, construction manager for the Rio Grande, told the people of Leadville that his road would try to be the first railroad into Leadville if Judge Hallett decided the suit in its favor; that nearly 15,000 tons of rails, 400 tons of spikes and joints, 56 locomotives, 400 freight cars, and vast quantities of supplementary material had been ordered, but delivery was being postponed pending the court's decision.

Following the settlement in April, 1880, of their long feud with the Santa Fe over the Arkansas Valley route, the Rio Grande completed their track into the silver camp in record time. The line was opened for business August 1, 1880. In accordance with terms contained in the Joint Operating Agreement, the completion of Palmer's railroad into Leadville also gave the South Park immediate access to that point. And so, at long last, the South Park's engines and cars were actually rolling into the famous carbonate camp—Leadville. Truly—it was a memorable day in the little road's history. Various announcements concerning the South Park's arrival in Leadville, along with other pertinent facts relative to business conditions, rolling stock, facilities, etc., appeared in the press.

Rocky Mountain News, July 2, 1880:
"The South Park Railroad is now operating passenger trains daily to Malta via Buena Vista".

Rocky Mountain News, July 4, 1880:
"THE SOUTH PARK
"The Pioneer Road to the Carbonate Camp.
"Elegant Coaches and Complete Arrangement.
"What the Company Has Done for the Public and Denver.

"A reporter of the News yesterday afternoon, being in that immediate vicinity in search of news, took occasion to pass through the grounds, yards and depot of the Denver South Park & Pacific Railroad, and the progress made and the improvements noted will be given here for the benefit and information of our readers. The depot is one of the most substantial and convenient buildings of the character in the country, and everything in the shops moves along with clock-like precision. As the public in general are interested more particularly in the progress and enterprise of the company as a railroad corporation, the reporter will at once proceed to set forth facts as he learned them.

"Forty-five miles of steel rails have been ordered and are now on the way. It will be used in repairing the track and keeping it as near perfection as it is at present, and always will be as long as Col. Fisher manages the road. The Colonel is rather bashful when spoken to in regard to his road, but it is a well-known fact that he is one of the best railroad men in the Union, and few other men could have built the road and carried the immense amount of freight, at the same time carrying over half a million of passengers without accident, besides carrying all the freight that Denver alone shipped out, amounting away up into the millions, besides taking the freight from the Denver & Rio Grande, Kansas Pacific and Union Pacific roads. All the departments are managed by careful, industrious, competent and sober men from top to bottom. The freight department is in the hands of Andy Hughes. Andy is the right man in the right place.

"Pringle, who will be remembered as the former master mechanic of the Kansas Pacific, has charge of the handsome two-story stone building which is used as a store house. It is forty by seventy-five feet, and is filled with nails, head lights, lamps, upholstering trimmings for cars, shovels, oils, in fact all necessary articles to keep up a first-class railroad. The company has just received from the Pullman car company at Detroit, a handsome mail and baggage car combined. It is in two compartments. The four new passenger cars are also built by the Pullman company, and they are beauties outside and inwardly, veneered head lining in light colors, hard wood finish in Japanese style. They contain twenty-six double seats, plenty of room for two on each one. They are trimmed with red velvet. The windows are broad and high, running up to the top of the car, giving the passengers a good chance to look at the wonderful scenery on this route. The floor of the cars are covered with the finest of body Brussells, bought in Denver. They are just as complete as the Pullman sleeping car in finish and style, only lacking the berths, to make them similar; in fact, an eastern railroad man says they are the handsomest in use in the world. They are also furnished with the patent Baker Heaters, hot air pipes running entirely around the car. They will make their first trip on the fifth of July. They also have the celebrated paper wheels, with steel tire which have been tested and are in use on all sleeping cars in the United States. Six large and handsome lamps light up these cars, and it will be just as easy to read THE NEWS by night, as at noon-time. The rolling stock consists of twenty-six first-class coaches, five baggage cars, two hundred and sixty flat cars, thirty coal cars, two hundred and fifty box cars, three construction trains, one to the front and one on each track district, keeping the roadbed in perfect order. They have put on two Tiffany refrigerator cars,[1] built by the company under the patent, in which they ship all perishable goods and guarantee to deliver them at their destination just as good as when shipped. In winter these cars are used to ship merchandise that is liable to freeze. The motive

1. See photo on page 236.

power consists of nineteen Mason, five Dawson & Bailey, and eight Baldwin locomotives.[1]

"The road is now completed to Malta, three miles this side of Leadville, one hundred and eighty miles of track, being about fifty miles shorter than by any other route to Leadville. The running time is about twenty miles per hour. The company sends out on an average of about fifty cars of merchandise per day and receive about the same number each day, loaded with wood and lumber, the moving of which gives employment to thousands of laborers along the line of the road, and take it all in all, makes quite a business for Denver merchants who furnish these people with their supplies.

"In going over to the depot the reporter could not help contrasting the appearance of West Denver today and the way it used to look several years ago—then everything quiet as a church yard. Now it is looking as lively as East Denver. The streets are full of teams loaded with merchandise, lumber, coal, wood, stone, brick, lime, and everything else imaginable, buggies and carriages filled, the sidewalks thronged with busy people, new stores being erected on the main street, and back of that dwelling houses going up in all directions, all of which is due to the enterprise of the South Park company."

Denver Daily Times, July 16, 1880:

"The Denver & South Park announces two freights daily to Malta, but fifteen hours being required for the journey, and made without transfers".

Rocky Mountain News, August 4, 1880:

"The track and depot arrangements in Leadville having been completed, on and after August 2nd, the Denver & South Park Railroad will run all trains to and from the depot in that city. The stage ride to Leadville is now a thing of the past".

Rocky Mountain News, August 7, 1880:

"On and after Monday, August 2nd, the South Park Railroad will run a daily fast freight leaving 6th and Larimer Streets in Denver at 9:45 PM and going clear through to Leadville in less than 15 hours. Refrigerator cars are attached for the most perfect preservation of perishable articles."

Railway World, August 7, 1880:

"The Leadville Chronicle states: 'The Denver & Rio Grande and Denver South Park & Pacific are jointly erecting a fine large depot in Leadville to be used for passenger and freight business. So rushing is the freight business of both companies that a large number of cars are on the tracks and have been there several days awaiting their turn to be unloaded. Every available team has been pressed into service to carry this freight to the warehouses in the city for temporary storage, the large platforms being found inadequate for the purpose'."

Railway Age, August 19, 1880:

"Travellers are complaining of the Denver-Leadville fare which is $16.00 for the 171 mile trip."

Close behind this news item we find the following article in the Railway World of October 2, 1880:

"The Denver South Park & Pacific has issued the following circular to all General Passenger and Freight Agents:

1. Author's note: These figures are as of February, 1880.

Denver South Park & Pacific 35, "Dillon", built by Brooks in 1882. Renumbered 162 by the Union Pacific in 1885, this engine finally became Colorado & Southern 22, during 1898.

Denver South Park & Pacific 63, a 2-8-0 built by Cooke in 1883. It was renumbered 212 by the Union Pacific, and 51 by the Colorado & Southern.

W. A. Lucas Collection.

Built by Cooke in 1884 as Denver South Park & Pacific 71, this neat little 2-6-0 became Union Pacific 113 and later Colorado & Southern 8.

'For the purpose of setting at rest all questions regarding the relations of the Denver South Park & Pacific and the Denver & Rio Grande on joint trackage between Buena Vista and Leadville, and the Western terminus of the Gunnison extension, the following contract governing the same is hereby given:

'That for the purpose of harmony and mutual profit, it is agreed that the Denver & Rio Grande shall build from the point of junction of the lines of their respective roads at Buena Vista, in the Arkansas Valley, to Leadville or Malta, on which the Denver South Park & Pacific shall have equal rights and privileges in perpetuity, for which it is to pay 8% per annum, payable monthly, one-half of the cash cost thereof, and pay one-half of the expenses of maintenance and repairs.

'In case of further extension of the main line or branches of the line between Buena Vista and Leadville, the Denver & Rio Grande shall build the same and the Denver South Park & Pacific have like rights thereon, on the like terms as above set forth.

'The Denver South Park & Pacific shall build its line by way of Chalk Creek and Alpine Pass to and through the country drained by the Gunnison and its tributaries, and the Denver & Rio Grande shall have like rights on the like terms with the Leadville line, and with any branches and extensions that may be built from the main line thereof.

'It will be seen then, that the relations between the two companies are the same, so far as relates to all traffic, as if each had its own individual track to Leadville and the end of the Gunnison extension. The Denver South Park & Pacific is 109 miles the shortest line from Denver to Buena Vista and Leadville, and 92 miles the shortest to the Gunnison. In going to Buena Vista, from which point to Leadville is on joint track, the distance via the South Park road is 135 miles; via the Denver & Rio Grande it is 244 miles. An examination of our time-card will show a difference of over 3 hours in favor of the South Park line, and our trains are run at a safe rate of speed. With these advantages, the South Park confidently looks forward to a large share of the passenger business from the Eastern lines, and with a complete outfit of coupon tickets over all lines, we are in a position to reciprocate'."

Freight statistics during 1879 and early 1880 continued to disclose Denver as the leading commercial and supply center of the region. After the completion of the Rio Grande-South Park rail connection to Leadville, this volume of Denver traffic increased to greater proportions than ever. In this connection, we read in Mock's history as follows:

"Almost without exception the South Park sent out a larger volume of freight to its single region than the Rio Grande to all its territory. In fact, the South Park shipped out more freight than any other Denver road, including the Kansas Pacific. But with respect to incoming freights, the opposite was true; here the Rio Grande was the consistent leader while the South Park line usually stood fourth or fifth in the list. Note the following brief table of representative freight statistics as published by the Denver Daily Times. The figures represent carloads received and forwarded."

		Nov. 1 1879	Nov. 10 1879	Jan. 5 1880	Jan. 12 1880	Mar. 29 1880
D.&R.G.	Rec'd	382	408	479	496	400 plus
	Fwd	183		225	248	
D.S.P.&P.	Rec'd	167	195			200 plus
	Fwd	262		289	358	
K. Pac.	Rec'd	272	292			400 plus
	Fwd	130				
C. Cen.	Rec'd	131	199			160 plus
	Fwd	90				
D. Pac.	Rec'd	40	48		88	175 plus
	Fwd					
B. Val.	Rec'd	220	225		290	200 plus
	Fwd					

At the height of the boom, transportation facilities were entirely inadequate. From November, 1879, to the following January, the Denver freight yards were badly overcrowded. A freight blockade of considerable proportions developed. The South Park simply was not equipped to handle the tremendous amount of business. New freight records were made and broken almost every week. As a result of such an enormous amount of business the South Park began to show large earnings. The following table shows the gross figures for the year 1879, as reported by the Commercial & Financial Chronicle:

Month	Earnings	Year to Date
January	$ 19,567.00	$ 19,567.00
February	30,932.00	50,499.00
March	41,366.00	91,865.00
April	44,090.00	135,955.00
May	44,354.00	180,309.00
June	58,020.00	238,329.00
July	70,354.00	308,683.00
August	91,204.00	399,887.00
September	95,532.00	495,419.00
October	132,185.00	627,604.00
November	139,077.00	766,681.00
December	136,064.00	902,745.00

A study of these figures reveals that the road's earnings, with the exception of a slight drop in December due to a snow blockade, increased every month throughout the entire year. For the last three months of the year, these earnings averaged over $4,525.00 per day. For a small narrow gauge railroad operating some 150 miles of track, this was an excellent showing. These were indeed palmy days for the South Park, making even the rosiest prophecies of its founders sound like peanuts. For those interested in a few more figures regarding the ratio between the passenger and freight earnings, the Railway World of November 22, 1879, published the following:

	Week of Oct. 1st to Oct. 8th	Week of Nov. 1st to Nov. 8th
Freight	$ 21,768.56	$ 31,072.03
Passenger	9,451.00	8,680.50
Express	706.52	1,546.29
	$ 31,926.08	$ 41,298.82

The year 1880 got off with a flying start when the road grossed over $144,000 for the month of January alone. The Commercial & Financial Chronicle reports the following gross earnings for the year 1880:

Month	Earnings	Year to Date
January	$144,300.00	$ 144,300.00
February	135,430.00	279,730.00
March	195,704.00	475,434.00
April	238,939.00	716,886.00
May	223,903.00	940,789.00
June	156,844.00	1,097,633.00
July	140,900.00	1,238,533.00
August	128,811.00	1,367,344.00

September	127,532.00	1,494,876.00
October	108,190.00	1,603,066.00
November	87,333.00	1,690,399.00
December	78,357.00	1,768,756.00

The gross figure for the year, $1,768,756.00, produced a net profit of $966,621.49, and permitted a payment of between 12 and 15 per cent interest in dividends for the year. As shown in the table, the month of April produced the maximum amount of business, $238,-939.00 or an average of over $7,960.00 per day. In the Railway Age of April 1, 1880, we read:

"An officer of the Denver & South Park writes the Editor: Our little road is full of business. We are now pushing our line towards the Gunnison country'."

History records few such instances of railroads paying for themselves during the course of construction.

The reader will recall that Palmer's Rio Grande reached Buena Vista around the first of June, 1880, and Leadville by July 31st. The competition thus introduced by the Rio Grande was the reason for the downward trend of the South Park's earnings which commenced with the month of May. Their financial skyrocket had passed its zenith; never in the history of the South Park, from this time on, was the little road to reap such a financial harvest as it had been privileged to enjoy during these two boom years of 1879 and 1880. The Evans regime ended with the passing of 1880, but it ended with a grand and magnificent flourish. Quoting from the Colorado Magazine of March, 1932, we read:

"It is doubtful if the conditions attending the construction of any other railroad equalled those met by the South Park organization. Certainly few roads, if any, paid dividends to the stockholders while the line was being built as did the South Park. Its success in handling such an enormous amount of freight, passenger, and express business under the conditions existent at the time, will long be remembered in western railroad history."

The Railroad Gazette commented:

"The world was in a hurry to get to Leadville and was glad to pay the South Park rate of something like ten cents per mile to get there. The company was coining money . . . the 1880 profits were about 40% of the actual cost of the road."

Concerning this financial record, we also read in the Railroad Gazette of October 1, 1880, the following news item:

"In connection with earnings on American railroads during the current year: The largest rate of increase is 95.2% on the Denver South Park & Pacific which has earned approximately $9,430 per mile in eight months, an amount exceeded only on the New York Central, Pennsylvania R. R., Reading, and the North Central, and more than twice as much as earnings of the Illinois Central—certainly a remarkable showing for a railroad less than ten years old."

The historian, Samuel D. Mock, writes:

"The results well justified the story that the Denver South Park & Pacific Railroad was designated as the most profitable railroad enterprise ever entered upon in the United States."

In commenting upon the South Park enterprise at this particular point in the road's history, Mock states: "The venture, which had 'started at a stone quarry and run up a tree', and of which the original incorporators had probably not 'had the slightest conception of where it was going, when, how or why', had turned out very well. In fact, the road paid fabulous returns to its backers." Mock further quotes Carlyle C. Davis in his book "Olden Times in Colorado" as claiming that those who financed the South Park road received $248.00 in return for every dollar invested. Be that as it may, whether the profits realized from the building, operating, and final sale of the road by Evans and his associates were a stroke of luck or due to Evans' keen foresight and managerial abilities, the author is inclined to give credit where credit is due. Many times when the future looked dark indeed and the critics were the loudest in their denunciation of Evans and it appeared that the stockholders were sending good money after bad, it was John Evans who said: "Gentlemen, hold on to your stock; it is the best investment you ever made, for beyond these dark clouds I can see the bright sunlight of success, which will soon burst upon us." Time proved that the Governor was correct in his advice. The old adage "to the victor belongs the spoils" seems very appropriate.

CHAPTER IX

FINAL CONSOLIDATION

By 1880, the era of the Colorado railroad pioneer was dropping into the background. He was gradually being replaced by the little men of the security markets and the Wall Street counting houses. With the 1880's, the age of big business had arrived on the Colorado railroad frontier with Jay Gould dominating the entire situation. Due to his manipulations, the Union Pacific, in fear of being destroyed, capitulated and became a part of the great Union Pacific consolidation which materialized on January 24, 1880.[1] As stated in that road's annual report of 1879, "the consolidation disposed of many questions of a vexatious and disturbing nature". Not the least of these was the tangled railroad situation in northern Colorado. Gould had temporarily cleaned the slate with a single sweep; his financial and organizing genius, whether by fair means or foul, had brought order out of chaos in the Colorado scene. Hereafter, local interests, thus far manipulated to serve their own needs, were to be subordinated to the interests of the combined Union Pacific, Kansas Pacific, Denver Pacific, and Colorado Central lines in Colorado—the powerful northern Colorado pool. Branch line acquisition and construction became one of the system's major policies.

As a result of this consolidation, all lines in Colorado with the exception of the Santa Fe, the Rio Grande, and the South Park, were now operating under one head. The relations between the first two roads had been settled amicably. The interests of the last two had been taken care of in the signing of the Joint Operating Agreement. It now remained only for the Santa Fe and the Union Pacific to come to terms.

THE TRIPARTITE AGREEMENT

This was brought about shortly afterwards by the signing of the Tripartite Agreement. This agreement, signed on March 27, 1880, included the Santa Fe, the Union Pacific, and the Rio Grande. The contract was to be binding for a ten-year period. In form, it was only the Santa Fe-Rio Grande compromise enlarged and extended to include the Union Pacific lines, and pledged the three companies to certain stipulations, for the purpose of adjusting controversies in relation to the construction of railroads in Colorado and New Mexico. Under its terms, the Santa Fe was not to construct west

1. Poor's Manual of Railroads, 1882.

of the line of the Rio Grande. The Rio Grande was not to build any railroad lines east of its north and south line. The Union Pacific agreed that it would not directly or indirectly construct or promote the construction of any parallel or competing line of railroad from any part of its line or lines to any point in Colorado south of the latitude of Denver, on the line of the Kansas Pacific. The Union Pacific and the Santa Fe agreed to divide the westbound mountain traffic equally between themselves; one-fourth of the Denver traffic was to be given to the Santa Fe, with the remainder, of course, going to the Union Pacific. All eastbound Colorado and New Mexico traffic originating west of a line drawn between Denver and El Moro was also to be divided equally between the Santa Fe and the Union Pacific. The Rio Grande, it was agreed, was to carry to Denver for the Santa Fe on the same basis as it carried to Pueblo for the Union Pacific. None of the three lines were to voluntarily connect or exchange business with any railroad which might be built into the territory of any of the participating lines. It can be easily seen that the agreement was partially designed to block any new railroad project that might be started within the above named territory. All in all, it was a very infamous agreement, one that would not dare be suggested in these days of the Interstate Commerce Commission. As a result of this agreement, when Governor John Evans launched his Denver & New Orleans project in 1881, he became involved in one of the longest, costliest, and most vindictive battles of his stormy career for, by it, he aroused the united antagonism of three great railroad systems. His ensuing struggle to free the Denver & New Orleans road from the meshes of its opponents is one of the great annals of western railroad history.

GOULD ACQUIRES CONTROL OF THE SOUTH PARK

Some of the facts concerning the story of Gould's gradual gain of absolute control of the South Park, followed by the subsequent sale of the road to the Union Pacific, are a bit obscure. The story is somewhat similar to that of the early financial structure of the road, in that some of the necessary data is missing. A few of Gould's early attempts to secure this control have already been mentioned; however, we will try to present as coherent a story as possible with what material is available.

It seems that the financial policy of the company was so organized and operated that those who controlled the construction companies building the road also controlled the road itself. As Evans stated: "When once we were satisfied that this arrangement would pay, then there was a very real object in controlling the construction company". How true this was can be seen from the interest of the several railroads in securing control of these construction companies. Although the road had experienced considerable difficulty in securing the necessary funds with which to build through Platte Canon, it had been the proud boast of its backers that the South Park company was strictly a local enterprise, and that outside aid was neither sought nor wanted. However, following the organization of the fourth construction company, the Denver & South Park Railroad Construction & Land Company, in November, 1877, the backers were frankly faced with the necessity of borrowing some $300,000 in order to push construction toward Kenosha Pass. And, according to the Denver Daily Times of November 26, 1877, they succeeded in negotiating the much needed loan. Outside capital had been invited and from that point on outside capital began to assume a dominant role. Once the South Park had successfully accomplished the difficult feat of building through the Platte Canon, and once the Leadville boom was on, the Kansas Pacific, the Santa Fe, and Gould himself, were up in the Evans office with offers to buy stock in the construction company at highly profitable figures for the owners. Commenting on this situation, Mock writes:

"The South Park road was locally controlled for some years, but that was only because it was not worth controlling. When the Leadville boom gave it some commercial value, it fell prey to outside control quickly enough. In spite of John Evans' often reiterated insistence on local control, his railroads invariably failed to remain in local hands. The lack of local capital made it both necessary and profitable to turn over to outside interests such locally-projected lines as events made valuable."

The first outside interest, other than Arapahoe County, to get their foot in the South Park's door, financially, was the Kansas Pacific. At the time the Denver & San Juan Construction Company was making an effort to build the line south of Bear Creek Junction toward the Platte Canon, ready cash was a pretty scarce item. In order to continue with construction of the road, the South Park interests entered into an agreement with the Kansas Pacific through John D. Perry, President, whereby that road agreed to transport into Denver, at a fair and low rate, according to John Evans, a considerable portion of the construction and building supplies needed by the South Park Company. In payment for these freight charges, the Kansas Pacific accepted stock in the South Park's construction company. Another angle to this deal was that Perry expected the South Park would develop into a good traffic feeder for his road. Thus it came about, that the Kansas Pacific interests gained control of $30,000 worth of Denver & San Juan Construction Company stock. Then, when the San Juan company was reorganized as the Denver & South Park Railroad Construction & Land Company in 1877, the Kansas Pacific took up its option of subscribing for stock in the new construction company on the basis of exchanging its stock in the old company for 40% of that amount in stock of the new company. Consequently, the Kansas Pacific came into possession of $12,000 worth of stock in this new and fourth construction company. In the organization of this new construction company, it was stipulated that each share of new construction company stock was worth twenty-five shares of railroad stock, thus, the Kansas Pacific also came into control of $300,000 worth of South Park railroad stock.

As a part of Gould's strategy in the promotion of his railroad program in this western region, he gained control of the Kansas Pacific in the spring of 1878 and was elected to that road's board of directors in May. During this time, he was gradually becoming more and more interested in securing control of the South Park. Among other things, this seizure of Kansas Pacific control dovetailed with his plans very conveniently, for the control of that road then gave him control of the $300,000 stake the Kansas Pacific held in the South Park, and this was Gould's first step toward gaining full control of the Evans road.

In the meantime, both Gould and the Santa Fe were making a determined effort to gain control of the Rio Grande. The Santa Fe won this round when they secured a lease of the Rio Grande on October 19, 1878, thus depriving Gould of the control of that road and its entryway into Leadville. Gould's failure at this point caused him to move upon the South Park more determinedly than ever. It is strongly suspected that Gould applied plenty of pressure behind the scenes when the Santa Fe, in December of 1878, failed in an effort to secure a partial control of the South Park road. Gould wanted the South Park and was not disposed to stand by and see his rival worm control of the road away from him.

In the meantime, as previously mentioned, Evans was attempting to negotiate a loan in order that construction might be continued through Platte Canon toward Kenosha. Gould made an offer to supply this loan, but it was rejected. His next step was an offer to buy an interest in the road. In this connection, we quote in part, from an interview published in the Denver Republican under date of January 19, 1913, by J. Sidney Brown, one of Denver's early pioneers, who was associated with Governor Evans in the organization of the various South Park construction companies.

". . . Thinking we would be easy prey, Mr. Gould sent an offer for our property through one of our stockholders, who advocated our accepting the offer. Through this party he offered to pay $450,000 cash, the approximate amount already spent on the construction of the road. For this, he wanted half of the capital stock less the $300,000 owned by Arapahoe County, and half of the bonds that pertained to that portion of the road between Denver and the vicinity of Webster. The other half of the bonds was to remain in the possession of the construction company. He also proposed that in case his offer was accepted, to continue construction of the road on to Leadville and into the San Juan country, taking bonds on that portion of the road at the rate of $16,666.67 per mile. . . . Mr. Gould's offer was submitted to the Board of Directors and rejected. Governor Evans said the substance of the offer was this: 'If we would give him all the property, he would give back half of it.' This was at the time that the stock was assigned to a trustee. Mr. Gould then sent his attorneys. One was no less a personage than the Honorable John P. Usher, former Secretary of the Interior in Lincoln's Cabinet. He submitted another offer, not much different from the first. They threatened to ask for a receiver and, in fact, did file a bill for one. We knew it was a bluff and were in shape to care for our own property."

Gould's attorneys withdrew their suit against the road, but efforts to embarrass its operation and owners continued and a certain amount of criticism began to spring up regarding the progress of the road and its management. As a result of this growing criticism, Governor Evans issued a public statement to the Arapahoe County Commissioners in defense of the South Park's affairs. This report was published in the Denver Daily Times and, as it appears elsewhere in this book, we shall not include it at this time. Sufficent to say, in the words of Mock, "The County Commissioners whitewashed the charges completely".

Again Gould had been thwarted, but he was not to be defeated so easily. Shortly after his attorney, John P. Usher, had failed in his threat to force the South Park people into submission, Gould decided on another method of approach. Quoting further from Mr. J. S. Brown's newspaper interview, we read:

"A short time later Mr. Gould came to Denver to negotiate for himself, not by bluffing, but to try and get what he wanted in a businesslike way."

Evans and his associates finally yielded to the Gould pressure. It was agreed at a meeting held on September 8, 1879, that in lieu of certain considerations on behalf of the Gould interests, he would be allowed to purchase a certain amount of construction company and South Park stock. This agreement is substantiated in the testimony of Charles Wheeler, the South Park's Auditor at that time, as given in the Pacific Railway Commission Case. We quote:

"The Kansas Pacific minutes of October, 1879, tell of an agreement made on October 8, 1879, between the Denver & South Park Railroad Construction & Land Company and Gould (acting for the Kansas Pacific and the Union Pacific), in which a stipulation was made that in consideration of the sale of certain stock to Gould, the companies he represented, the Kansas Pacific and the Union Pacific, would forbear certain discriminations against the above South Park Construction & Land Company."

As a matter of fact, Gould wanted to purchase the road outright, but John Evans refused his offer. Probably the Governor was biding his time, waiting for future developments to make the stock of the road more valuable.

As a result of these maneuvers and the agreement made with the Evans group, it was arranged that Gould be allowed to purchase a quarter interest in the Denver & South Park Railroad Construction & Land Company on the basis of paying two dollars for every dollar the backers of the road had invested in it. This financial arrangement was quite involved and the information necessary to explain the deal clearly is missing; however, it seems that this quarter interest Gould acquired in the construction company netted him $571,000 in stock of the South Park Railroad Company. At the time this deal was being negotiated, Gould received a promise from the South Park officials that they would NOT sell any of the balance of the South Park stock without first giving him due notice and selling to him at the same price offered by any other party. As events turned out, the author is very much inclined to think that the crafty Gould led with his chin in this instance and left himself wide open, an opportunity of which John Evans eventually took good advantage.

The reader will recall that it was during this same time that Gould acquired his half interest in the Rio Grande; therefore, it can now be more clearly understood how Gould, with his strong controlling influence over the two roads, was able to promote his Joint Operating Agreement as of October 1, 1879.

Gould's next move was to secure control of the $300,000 of South Park stock held by Arapahoe County. Accordingly, he approached the County Commissioners with a proposition to buy the county's stock at fifty cents on the dollar. As a result of this offer, the County Commissioners placed the proposition before the Denver citizens, and, at an election held on December 2, 1879, it was duly voted to accept his offer. Why Arapahoe County took this step is not known or understood. So far, Gould was making fairly good progress. By the end of 1879, as a result of these three transactions, he had gained control of $1,171,000 worth of the road's total stocks, which were as follows:

The Kansas Pacific interest	$ 300,000.00
The interest gained through the construction company deal	571,000.00
The Arapahoe County interest	300,000.00
	$1,171,000.00

Shortly after his acquisition of the Arapahoe County stock, Gould commenced his negotiations with Evans for the purchase of the balance of the South Park stock. In the meantime, the Rio Grande interests had been suggesting and intimating that they were also interested in the South Park road. In order to protect their

D.S.P.&P. 42 and waycar 72 at "Rolling Stone Curve" in Platte Canon, during the late 1880's.

holdings, all the parties who held paid-up South Park stock, exclusive of that which Gould controlled and $100,000 held by a New York banking house by the name of Winslow Lanier & Company, pooled their stock and placed it in the hands of Mr. J. S. Brown in Denver. Fortunately, the original document covering this agreement, dated October 6, 1879, is still preserved in the archives of the Colorado State Historical Society. This document lists forty stockholders together with the amount each owned and their individual signatures as signed to the contract. Through the courtesy of Dr. L. R. Hafen, the Society's Director, we present this list, together with other pertinent facts contained therein.

We the undersigned stockholders of the Denver & South Park Railroad Construction and Land Company, signers of a certain pooling contract dated October 6, 1879, by which our said stock was assigned to J. S. Brown, Trustee, do hereby acknowledge his fulfilment of said trust as far as its relation to the stock of the Denver South Park & Pacific R. R. Company belonging to said trust, owned by each of us.

Names of owners of stock of the Denver South Park & Pacific R. R. Co. held in trust by J. S. Brown, Trustee.

	No. of Shares	Amount
E. M. Ashley	150	$ 15,000.00
Peter G. Bradstreet	375	37,500.00
J. S. Brown and Brother	1,365.5	136,550.00
Jas. W. Bowles	150	15,000.00
William Barth and Brother	1,253	125,300.00
William B. Berger	187.5	18,750.00
Amos Bissell	93.75	9,375.00
W. S. Cheesman	1,648.75	164,875.00
S. H. H. Clark	250	25,000.00
G. W. Clayton	1,007.8125	100,781.25
J. Q. Charles	37.5	3,750.00
Birks Cornforth	37.5	3,750.00
A. B. Daniels	1,235.5	123,550.00
S. H. Elbert	487.5	48,750.00
L. H. Eicholtz	571.875	57,187.50
John Evans	5,600.25	560,025.00
John Evans, Executor	48	4,800.00
Margaret P. Evans	375	37,500.00
Cyrus W. Fisher	442.5	44,250.00
John F. Gray	28.125	2,812.50
Hallack & Brother	525	52,500.00
Bela M. Hughes	187.5	18,750.00
A. S. Hughes	187.5	18,750.00
Assyria Hall	187.5	18,750.00
A. Jacobs	93.75	9,375.00
C. B. Kountze	1,290.1875	129,018.75
G. W. Kassler	300	30,000.00
T. G. Lyster	150	15,000.00
D. H. Moffat, Jr.	725	72,500.00
John Milheim	75	7,500.00
D. C. Oakes	75	7,500.00
M. G. Palmer	150	15,000.00
J. W. Richards	75	7,500.00
John J. Riethman	525	52,500.00
Cyrus Strong	1,012.5	101,250.00
J. W. Smith	275	27,500.00
George Tritch	642.5	64,250.00
M. D. Thatcher	900	90,000.00
R. W. Woodbury	75	7,500.00
Charles Wheeler	195.5	19,550.00
Total	22,992.00	$2,299,200.00

These parties were all Denver citizens. Mr. Brown, who acted as trustee or custodian for these stockholders, held this stock under a contract made between themselves not to sell individually, but collectively. By this time, it had become fairly well known in railroad circles that the South Park was for sale. The road's profits were climbing steadily, and its future outlook was extremely promising. Perhaps John Evans figured that this was his opportunity to cash in. However, he had the reputation of being a high priced man and any offers made would have to be liberal ones.

In view of developments at this particular time, it might be well to interrupt at this point and insert the following news item published in the Railway World of January 24, 1880.

"At the recent annual meeting of the Denver & South Park, the following Directors were elected. John Evans, W. S. Cheesman, J. S. Brown, David Moffat, J. W. Smith, C. W. Fisher, C. B. Kountze, JAY GOULD and RUSSELL SAGE.

"Officers elected were: Evans, Pres.; Cheesman, 1st V. Pres.; Fisher, 2nd V. Pres.; Kountze, Treas.; and Geo. W. Kassler, Sec'y."

The two principal bidders for the South Park stock were Gould and Palmer. John Evans took advantage of this situation. He proceeded to play the two men against each other, and succeeded. The competition between Gould and Palmer for possession of the road became quite spirited. Palmer was supposed to have made some high offers for the stock; however, due to the Evans-Gould agreement wherein Gould was to have an opportunity to match any offer made by another party, Palmer failed in his attempts to close a deal with the South Park interests. Palmer soon learned of this arrangement between Evans and Gould and complained of the agreement, saying it would prevent him and the Rio Grande from getting the South Park stock, as any negotiations he might arrange would end in nothing because Gould would equal his offer; therefore, it would not be worth while for him to carry the negotiations any farther. At this point, the author might add that at the time Evans closed his deal with Gould, he had an offer of an equal amount from Palmer.

Evans and Palmer were at sword's points because of a very bitter personal quarrel. Evans felt that Palmer had broken faith with the South Park interests when he (Palmer) repudiated the Joint Operating Agreement and commenced construction of his Rio Grande branch to Gunnison. As a result of this ill-feeling between the two men, Evans preferred to give Gould the preference.

It will be remembered that one of the provisions in the Joint Operating Agreement was that the Rio Grande and South Park roads consolidate as soon as practical. Such a consolidation would be of great benefit to Gould and it is strongly suspected that he was the instigator of the many rumors which began to circulate that summer to the effect that the two roads were to consolidate. Witness the following news items:

Railway Age, June 3, 1880.

"The Denver Tribune announces that the Denver South Park & Pacific and the Denver & Rio Grande have been practically consolidated. The two lines are to be allied with the Union Pacific and controlled at Omaha."

Railway Age, June 10, 1880.

"Colonel D. C. Dodge, General Manager of the Denver & Rio Grande, denies that the Rio Grande and South Park roads are to be consolidated and says that the story is a fabrication. Gov. Evans also denies all information."

Commercial & Financial Chronicle, June 12, 1880.

"It has been confidentially reported in Denver that the South Park and Rio Grande are to be consolidated. Arrangements were supposed to have been perfected by Evans, Palmer, and Gould (who owns large interests in both roads) in New York."

Railway Age, September 17, 1880.

"It is reported that negotiations have been in progress for the consolidation of the South Park and the Rio Grande. . . The Denver Daily Times says that so far, no success has attended the efforts to consolidate the two companies and that no present prospect exists that they will be consolidated."

Railroad Gazette, November 12, 1880.

"It is reported that a substantial agreement as to terms has been reached for the consolidation of the South Park and Rio Grande roads, but that the matter is in suspense at present, because Counsel has given an opinion that authority must be obtained from the Colorado Legislature before the consolidation can be completed."

That fall Gould, accompanied by Russell Sage, who had some South Park stock through his connection with Gould and the Kansas Pacific, came to Denver to resume negotiations with Evans. While there, the group made a trip over the South Park to end-of-track near Alpine Station. As a result of this trip, Gould stated: "I was very much impressed with the South Park road and its earnings looked good." The author pauses here to say that the earnings *should* have impressed him—the South Park's net profit for the year 1880, on some 150 miles of railroad, was the enormous sum of $996,621.

Regardless of all the rumors and denials of the proposed consolidation that had been circulating during the summer and fall of 1880, it developed that Evans and Palmer turned up in Gould's New York office in October to continue negotiations. At this point, we shall quote

part of John Evans' testimony on the witness stand during the trials of the Pacific Railway Commission Case. It is an excellent account of how the final negotiations were carried out whereby Gould purchased the remaining South Park stock. Evans' testimony was as follows:

". . . But subsequently I went to New York and in conversation with Gould and Palmer in Gould's office, Gould urged that Palmer and I consolidate the Denver & Rio Grande and the South Park as a matter of great interest to both companies. After we agreed that this would be a good idea, Gould left New York and went west. Messrs. Evarts, Southmayed and Choate, Palmer's attorneys, with Palmer and myself, commenced negotiations for this consolidation. These plans were carried forward until we agreed upon every point but one. They wanted to pay the South Park Company, using stock of the Denver & Rio Grande Company, dollar for dollar, for its stock. Then they were to carry out certain extensions which had already been commenced, and they were to pay $700,000 in cash in nine months. This was all drawn up by the Palmer attorneys and the question was as to the security for the $700,000. The Rio Grande offered the company's note without any mortgage or any hypothecation, and although Messrs, Woerishoeffer & Company proposed to guarantee it, the note would NOT be bankable or subject to any discount in New York City. I turned this note down because I did not want to accept anything unless we could sell it, because the interests I represented in Denver wanted their money. Messrs. Woerishoeffer & Company thought this was very rigid and exacting on my part. Even though they thought it good paper I refused it, left the question with them and returned to Colorado, stating that perhaps Gould could help them when he returned from the west; that if Gould could make some satisfactory note or arrangements, it would be O.K. with me. (Note the strong Gould influence here.) I will say that the Denver interests owning this South Park stock, in changing from the negotiations that I had with the Denver & Rio Grande, were satisfied that they got less for the road than they would if they had closed the trade in the exchange of stock. The Rio Grande stock went up above par very soon afterwards, and they would have got all that Gould had paid them, the Denver & Rio Grande stock (dollar for dollar); remember that went up, plus this $700,000 in cash more for the road than they did get. Consequently, the Denver interests would have fared better had they carried out the proposed consolidation plan."

No information has come to light of any further negotiations between the Evans, Palmer, and Gould parties regarding the proposed Rio Grande-South Park consolidation and it is assumed that all talk on this point ended with Evans' return to Colorado. Gould returned to New York City on November 4, 1880, and upon learning that his proposed consolidation scheme had failed, decided immediately to proceed with his original plan of purchasing the Evans road outright. On that day, November 4, 1880, Gould telegraphed Evans as follows:

"Hon. John Evans:
"Have thought it wise to do nothing further in regard to proposal until I see you. Signed: Jay Gould."

On November 5th, the next day, Gould again telegraphed Evans:

"Hon. John Evans:
"The proposed contract is too complicated. Suppose, in lieu of everything, we make a cash sale at 90 up, and you remain as president. Signed: Jay Gould."

Evans wired back immediately:

"Jay Gould, Esq.:
"If we sell out for cash, why should I be president afterwards? Have we such an offer as you suggest? Signed: John Evans."

On November 6th, Gould replied:

"Hon. John Evans:
"I thought you might like to remain as president and be identified with Union Pacific. I have no direct cash offer, but I could have one if I was authorized to negotiate at the price named. Signed: Jay Gould."

Two days later, on November 8, 1880, Evans answered:

"Jay Gould, Esq.:
"Our folks think the trade for D. & R. G. stock and bonds, that is, the trade I told you we had pending at this time, is better than your offer of 90, because the South Park stock may go up. They decided not to take less than par from Palmer when he wanted a cash price. We told Palmer that his offer of par would be subject to your option, for which reason he said his parties declined to make it, for fear you would take the stock. I think I could get a cash offer at par accepted at once. I would like the Union Pacific association if in a position where I could be of service. Signed: John Evans."

Gould replied to Evans at once:

"Hon. John Evans:
"Make me a cash offer. Answer quick as Mr. Ames and other directors are in this city now. Signed: Jay Gould."

Evans replied November 9th:

"Jay Gould Esq.:
"We will take par cash for our railroad stock. Signed: John Evans."

Gould replied immediately:

"Hon. John Evans:
"Your offer is accepted. Signed: Jay Gould."

John Evans further testified as follows:

"Accordingly, in cooperation with J. S. Brown, Trustee, I assigned the stock to Mr. Gould who gave me his checks for $2,590,800. These proceeds were deposited in the First National Bank of New York City to the credit of the City National Bank of Denver, for the use of J. S. Brown, who represented the Denver pool. This accounted for all South Park stock, to wit: that which Mr. Gould had already gained control of, this last lot purchased, and the 1,000 shares that were in the custody of Winslow Lanier & Company of New York."

Evans' statement that this final transaction accounted for all the South Park stock brings up the question as to just how much actual stock Gould obtained in this final deal. Much written material has come to light regarding the distribution of the South Park's capital stock; however, the information consists only of a series of conflicting statements. It seems that the most reliable source of information available at this late date is to be found in the records of the Pacific Railway Commission Case. According to Gould's testimony during these trials, he paid Evans $2,528,300 for 25,283 shares of stock. According to Evans' testimony, he received $2,590,800 covering 25,908 shares. According to the list of stockholders participating in the trusteeship under J. S. Brown, there was available for sale 22,992 shares. Other sources give still different figures. After a careful study of all available material found, we can be reasonably certain of the following statement showing the stock distribution, exclusive of Gould's final purchase, at the time he bought the road.

	Shares	Value
Winslow Lanier & Company's holdings, account loan	1,000	$ 100,000.00
The Kansas Pacific interest	3,000	300,000.00
Gould's interest obtained through his construction stock deal	5,710	571,000.00
Arapahoe County's interest (purchased by Gould)	3,000	300,000.00
Totals	12,710	$1,271,000.00

The balance sheet of The Denver South Park & Pacific R. R. Company under date of December 31, 1880, definitely states that the authorized capital stock was $3,500,000.00. By the simple process of subtraction, this leaves only 22,290 shares available for Gould to purchase.

Therefore, after a thorough study of all material at hand, the author is unable to explain these various differences, but in view of present information known, and until proven otherwise, we are forced to accept the following statement showing the distribution of the road's stock at the time Gould made his final purchase.

	Shares	Value
Winslow Lanier & Company's holdings, account loan	1,000	$ 100,000.00
The Kansas Pacific interest	3,000	300,000.00
Gould's interest obtained through the construction stock deal	5,710	571,000.00
Arapahoe County's interest (purchased by Gould)	3,000	300,000.00
Gould's final purchase on November 9, 1880	22,290	2,229,000.00
Totals	35,000	$3,500,000.00

Two views of a mixed D.S.P.&P. train, pulled by a Mason Bogie, in Chalk Creek Cañon between Mt. Princeton station and the Cascades, enroute to Gunnison via Alpine Tunnel.

The $3,500,000 represents the total par value of the stock on the basis of $100 per share. Of these 35,000 shares, Gould controlled all but the 1,000 shares held by Winslow Lanier & Company. However, of the 34,000 remaining shares held under his control, the Kansas Pacific owned 3,000 which left Gould's personal holdings at 31,000 shares. The reader is probably wondering just what Gould's South Park holdings actually cost him in dollars and cents. By a careful study of the information available, it is believed that the following figures represent a close estimate of his actual cost.

To begin with, his personal holdings of 31,000 shares consisted of three blocks of stock; first, the 5,710 shares obtained through his construction company stock deal, second, the 3,000 shares purchased from Arapahoe County, and third, his final purchase of 22,290 shares directly from John Evans. Regarding the first block; journal entries in Gould's accounts record that during November, 1879, he paid out $159,911.99 covering construction costs, and that on April 14th, following, he received back in actual cash $68,732.25. This represents an actual cash outlay of $91,179.74. Another entry dated August 13, 1880, indicates that in return for these financial expenditures, which are supposed to represent his one-quarter interest in the construction company, he received 5,710 shares of South Park stock with a par value of $571,000.00. Regarding the second block, we have already read where he purchased Arapahoe County's 3,000 shares for fifty cents on the dollar, and as for the third block of 22,290 shares, they were purchased directly through John Evans for $2,229,000.00 cash. A recapitulation of these figures shows that Gould's actual cost of his South Park holdings were as follows:

1. The 5,710 shares obtained through his construction company stock deal....$ 91,179.74
2. The 3,000 shares purchased from Arapahoe County................................   150,000.00
3. The 22,290 shares purchased at par through John Evans.................... 2,229,000.00
                             ——————

   Gould's actual cost of his 31,000 shares $2,470,179.74

It must be added that coincidentally with his purchase of the South Park, Gould had been making the necessary arrangements to take over control of the current construction company which, by this time, had completed the line well up Chalk Creek canon. As far as is known, this fourth construction company, the Denver & South Park Railroad Construction & Land Company, had not run into any financial disaster such as befell its predecessors, but for some unknown reason, the South Park interests had found it expedient to organize a new construction company.

This was the fifth construction company to be organized by the Evans interests; however, it is strongly suspected that, for some reason, there must have been some Union Pacific influence behind the movement inasmuch as one of the Union Pacific's executives, S. H. H. Clark, was a member of the directorate. The name of this new corporation was The Denver & South Park Railroad Construction Company. It was incorporated on September 18, 1880, with the following Directors: S. H. H. Clark, G. P. Morisini, J. J. Slocum, L. H. Eicholtz, J. A. Cooper, J. F. Brown, Wm. Barth, T. G. Lyster, and A. B. Daniels. L. H. Eicholtz was President. The object, as stated in the incorporation papers, was the construction and equipment of railroads and to do all business thereunto pertaining. The principal office was listed as Denver with an added notation that the company was to carry on business in the several counties through which the extensions, branches, and lines of the Denver South Park & Pacific Railroad were to be constructed.

The contract held by the Denver & South Park Railroad Construction & Land Company was officially turned over to the new company on September 22, 1880, and was subsequently assigned to Gould upon condition that he take care of and meet the obligations incurred in pursuance thereof. Therefore, the following resolution was issued from the offices of the railroad company:

"THE DENVER SOUTH PARK & PACIFIC
RAILROAD COMPANY
"PRESIDENT'S OFFICE

Denver, Colorado. Dec. 16, 1880.

"Extracts from the record of the proceedings of a meeting of the Denver & South Park Railroad Construction Company, held at the office of the Company in Denver, Colorado, this 16th day of December, 1880. Mr. J. F. Brown offered the following preamble and resolution, which was seconded by Mr. William Barth, and unanimously adopted: Whereas the Hon. John Evans, attorney in fact for this company, did, by virtue of a resolution passed October 17, 1880, transfer to Jay Gould the contract existing between the Company and the Denver South Park & Pacific Railroad Company, for the construction of its extensions and branches: Therefore, Resolved, That his action in so doing be, and the same is hereby, ratified, confirmed, and approved.

L. H. EICHOLTZ, President."

With Gould now in control of practically all railroad stock and construction company stock, the South Park changed hands and became his property. This included everything: right of way, buildings, equipment, rolling stock, contracts, assets, liabilities, the coal mine properties at Como and Baldwin, the Morrison quarries, and other miscellaneous properties and holdings distributed along the line from the Denver Union Terminal to the end-of-track. There is no denying the fact that John Evans, in disposing of the railroad, made considerable money for both himself and his friends. Quoting from the Denver Daily Times of November 17, 1880, we read in part:

".... The Denver stockholders who so pluckily pushed ahead and now got such a handsome dividend from its sale, are to be congratulated."

To facilitate the change and to look out after Gould's newly acquired railroad interests, Evans consented to remain as president for an indefinite period; however, as will be related shortly, friction soon developed between him and the Gould-Union Pacific interests causing Evans to sever all relations with the South Park road.

As matters now stood, Gould's remaining interest in the road can be summed up in the following two statements: first, get the road under Union Pacific control; and second, make whatever profit he could off the deal.

Gould had gained a controlling interest in the Union Pacific in 1873 and served as a member of that road's board of directors from March 11, 1874, to March 25, 1885, at which date he conveniently washed his hands of Union Pacific affairs.[1] During the greater part of this period he exerted a strong influence over the road and played a leading role in setting forth the policies which the Union Pacific was destined to follow for a number of years while under the dishonest management of Gould and his associates. This policy of building up a large network of branch and feeder lines to support the Union Pacific system, especially in the Colorado region, is best exemplified in some of the testimony Gould gave on the witness stand during the Pacific Railway Commission trials. We quote in part:

"A railroad manager protects his property from invasion by other roads by throwing out feeder lines, or purchasing same. This will keep a competitive road out. This feeder system protects and holds their territory. . . The amount of business that the South Park was bringing out to give some Eastern road was very great. It also furnished a market for a very large amount of Kansas products. In the mineral country, they have to bring in everything they use."

Further evidence to show how determined the Gould-Union Pacific interests were to build up and control this powerful northern Colorado pool is confirmed, or explained, in the following story. Immediately after Gould acquired control of the South Park, General Palmer offered him a bonus of $500,000 over and above what he paid for the Evans road, but the offer was refused.[2] Gould considered the South Park road as indispensable in controlling certain Colorado traffic. This is borne out by further testimony he gave on the witness stand, which we quote in part:

"There was another purchaser for the South Park—the Den-

1. On page 54 of the Pacific Ry. Comm. Case proceedings we read: "It appears from the minutes of the books of the Union Pacific R. R. that while this litigation was pending, certain actions were taken by the directors, whereby they undertook to release themselves from any obligations or liabilities of said railroad company."

2. Pacific Railway Commission Case.

ver & Rio Grande. I was afraid that if the Union Pacific and allied interests were deprived of access to this country it would shut off a large amount of earnings on their main lines. I did not want the Union Pacific to lose access to that Leadville country and was very anxious that the Union Pacific should control it. . . ."

This refusal of Palmer's offer also brings out the point that there was more profit to be realized by Gould in peddling the South Park to the Union Pacific than in selling it to Palmer.

In building up this network of feeder and branch lines, the usual practice was to gain control of the required railroad and then unload it on the Union Pacific at a highly profitable figure. Witness the history of such roads as the Georgetown Breckenridge & Leadville, the Colorado Central, the South Park & Leadville Short Line, the Kansas Pacific, and many others. Development, sound operation, efficient management, and good equipment were of no interest to Gould, and the Denver South Park & Pacific was no exception. To build up this monopoly in Colorado, it was necessary that the Union Pacific have control of the South Park regardless of the cost; therefore, Gould saw to it that this was accomplished. Six weeks after he had gained control of the road it was turned over to the Union Pacific. The South Park's books were delivered to Omaha on December 30, 1880, and on January 1, 1881, the Union Pacific management assumed control of the road.

On January 25th, following, Gould sold 30,993 shares of his 31,000 shares of South Park stock to the Union Pacific at par, or $3,099,300. Quoting from testimony given in the Pacific Railway Commission Case, we read:

"This credit to Mr. Gould in his current account was entered in the books on January 25, 1881. No corporate action was taken on this transaction—Mr. Gould 'willed it, and it was done'."

This deal netted Gould a neat profit of $629,120.26. As a smoke screen to sanction his profits resulting from the sale, Gould contended that the new business brought to the Union Pacific by the South Park was worth it.[1] Relative to the sale the Court stated:[1]

"The general outlook is that the South Park branch hardly justifies the price paid for it by the Union Pacific."

Following this, on October 18, 1881, he transferred his control of the Denver & South Park Railroad Construction Company contract to Sidney Dillon of the Union Pacific. There never was very much importance attached to this fifth and last construction company; nevertheless, it was something else for the Union Pacific to buy, and Gould sold it to them. The extent of his profits on this construction contract deal are not known. Before closing this discussion, we might also add that it is not known what disposition Gould made of his seven remaining shares of South Park stock.

From this date on, until August 7, 1894, the South Park railroad was under the control of the Union Pacific

1. Pacific Railway Commission Case.

and was simply known as "The South Park Division of the Union Pacific". How this splendid South Park property was dissipated and eventually forced to the wall is one of the tragedies of railroad mismanagement. John Evans had been paid his price—momentarily, the road was Jay Gould's property, destined to serve him only as a vehicle in furthering his ambitious financial career. Consequently, our little road ceased to exist as an independent enterprise to expand and develop as its former owners saw fit, but instead, became only a tool in the hands of the powerful Union Pacific to be exploited for whatever the Omaha interests could squeeze out of it.

Relative to the total cost of the Denver South Park & Pacific properties to the Union Pacific company, including all construction costs up to around 1886, we again revert to the Pacific Railway Commission trials report, Vol. 1, page 65, wherein we find the following itemized statement:

30,993 shares of stock bought from Jay Gould Jan. 25, 1881	$3,099,300.00
30,358 shares issued to U. P. Ry. Co. for construction costs	1,265,412.49
$2,797,000 consolidated first mortgage bonds issued for construction costs	2,746,905.86
$1,800,000 first mortgage bonds, subject to which the purchase was made	1,800,000.00
Total	$8,911,618.35

George E. Mellen photo, from Francis Rizzari Collection.

A Grand Army of the Republic special pauses at the Palisades on Alpine Pass on August 1, 1883. The train was headed by engine 35 and another 2-6-0.

CHAPTER X

CONSTRUCTION — BUENA VISTA
WEST UP CHALK CREEK

Governor Evans and his associates, who were the original promoters of the South Park, had pushed the end-of-track into the Arkansas Valley and this was the "end of the line" for them, as far as actual control was concerned. It has already been related how these men succumbed to the strong influence of Jay Gould and relinquished control of the road's future policies and plans. From here on, the destinies of the road were in the hands of eastern capitalists who were interested in the property only to the extent of the dollar sign. It would be interesting to know just what might have developed had the road avoided the Gould tentacles and remained an independent enterprise under the wise and careful direction of John Evans. But now that the road had been dumped into the maw of the Union Pacific hopper, it was to abandon any previous plans it might have once cherished and henceforth was to exist only to serve its new masters as they saw fit, which, in this case, was merely that of an extended feeder line to fatten the coffers at Omaha. Thus, it came about that what was originally intended to be only a branch line became a continuation of the main line. The rails of the little narrow gauge railroad were pointed toward the mighty Saguache Range and the Gunnison.

GUNNISON

According to reliable sources, John Evans and his associates, when first organizing the South Park company in the early '70's, were interested in the possibilities of extending a branch of their railroad to the Gunnison country.[1] Their desire to tap this region with a railroad was based on the many reports that continued to emanate from this territory regarding the discoveries of anthracite coal beds. History also tells us that as early as 1861 a few prospectors left California Gulch to explore the region for gold and silver. They succeeded in their venture, but the country was wild and unsettled and the fear of the Indians caused the people to shy away from the district. In 1871, the Government established a cow camp for the benefit of the Ute Indians near the forks of the Gunnison and Tomichi Rivers, the future site of Gunnison.[2] Gradually, the Indian

1. McMechen, "Life of Gov. Evans."
2. "History of Gunnison," Colo. State Normal School, 1916.

menace subsided and the territory became the mecca for many new prospectors, a partial overflow from the Leadville rush. However, a temporary depression descended upon the territory. Fortune had turned a frowning face upon these gold seekers and they lost; and departing, they hurled maledictions upon the land that had defrauded them. For a time, Gunnison was a synonym for Hades among the miners.

Then all was changed during the latter part of the '70's. The lamp of Aladdin had been rubbed. Big strikes were made; marvelous veins of gold and silver were uncovered and the excitement spread like a contagious fever. From every direction came the prospectors with the frenzied lust for gold in their eyes. By 1879 and 1880, the rush was on. Thousands came weekly. A correspondent writing in the Pueblo Chieftain from Parlin's Ranch on May 17, 1880, stated:

"Yesterday I counted 250 teams bound for Gunnison, Ruby, Gothic, and the Elk Mountain country. One would think that there must be an end to this procession, but the end is not yet, for far away on the Saguache[1] Road, there is a long line of white wagon covers."

Embryo merchants, town lot speculators, bonanza saloon men, tinhorn gamblers, and the soiled doves were on hand to welcome all comers, prepared to do a flourishing business. It was a repetition of the renowned Leadville rush—only on a smaller scale. All along such streams as Quartz Creek, the Tomichi, the Gunnison, and the Ohio, and throughout the Elk Mountain and Gunnison area, camps sprang up overnight. The land beyond the Saguache Range was hailed as the new El Dorado of the west. Even Leadville would have to look to her laurels.

The boom was further augmented by discoveries of precious metals along Chalk Creek on the east slope of the range. By 1881, the entire region was in full swing. Prospecting was being conducted on a tremendous scale and hundreds of new mining camps mushroomed; Alpine, Iron City, Forest City, Hancock, Pitkin, Tin Cup, Aspen, Crested Butte, Gothic, Irwin, Ruby, Baldwin, Gunnison, Ouray, Lake City, and many others. In the dawn of the '80's, all of Colorado was smelting silver and at that time silver was worth smelting. The new camp of Gunnison was no exception. Be-

1. Pronounced, and frequently spelled, "Sawatch."

200

Engine 42 and coach 9 in Chalk Creek Canon between Nathrop and Mt. Princeton Hot Springs. The Chalk Cliffs are plainly shown in this photo, and the high peak at the right, with the snowslide run, is Mt. Princeton.

ing located in the center of the western slope area, she was thriving like a bit of scandal, supplying the miners, dispensing "mountain dew" and entertainment, promoting mining claims, building smelters, shipping silver— while at the same time, she was developing a burial ground on the banks of the Gunnison. In addition to the silver and gold, they found large deposits of good anthracite coal, some iron ore, and limestone. Soon, eastern capitalists began to visualize Gunnison as the coming Pittsburgh of the west. Money flowed in with which to erect mills and smelters and exploit the newly found resources.

But the boom soon wore itself out. Gunnison had skyrocketed quickly and she collapsed in the same manner. The mines played out, the smelters closed, the new hotel shut its front door, and the gamblers and the girls went their way. Even that public benefactor, the man with the elusive pea between two half-shells of a wallnut, silently folded his blankets and sought other fields of fortune. The multitudes had reached Gunnison all right; even the railroads put in their appearance—all in time to carry away the corpse of the dead camp. However, that is another story.

In view of what was occuring over on the west slope of the divide, it seems that our little road was approaching the banks of the Arkansas River at an opportune time. The newly discovered deposits of silver and gold, together with the abundant quantities of anthracite coal, attracted the attention of the road's management; even that of Gould who, by this time, had a goodly part of his foot in the South Park's front door. Through Gould's influence, which was becoming more and more apparent, the managing interests concluded that once they reached the Arkansas Valley, no time should be lost in pushing a railhead across the Saguache Range to tap the seemingly potential wealth that lay waiting for them. It is needless to go to any extra length explaining the great amount of business that was being created by this sudden mining boom in the Gunnison country. To all appearances, it would be a lasting source of traffic, but above all, it offered Gould an excellent opportunity to strengthen his strategic southwestern Colorado railroad position.

The details of Gould's program for the extension of his railroad properties in this territory, including both the Rio Grande and the South Park, were fully related in a previous chapter. His scheme to integrate the functions of these two railroads both as to traffic and construction was incorporated in a Joint Operating Agreement. The two roads met at Buena Vista; from this focal point, the Rio Grande was continued north to Leadville while the South Park was directed to build to the Gunnison region. Therefore, in preparation for this proposed extension, an Amendment (number 1) to the original Articles of Association was filed with the Secretary of State on August 28, 1879, which stated:

". . . to give the said company the power and right to construct, maintain, and operate an extension of this railroad starting from the most eligible point on the line of the Denver South Park & Pacific Railroad in the valley of the Arkansas River and running thence by the most feasible Route over the Saguache Range of Mountains to the confluence of the Quartz Creek and Tomichi River to the Gunnison River, thence by the most feasible Route to Ouray on the Uncompahgre River, with a Branch to Lake City and a Branch running up the Ohio Creek to the Coal and Silver Mining districts in the Elk Mountains."

Thus, while the end-of-track was moving forward across South Park, plans were perfected to extend the South Park to the Gunnison country. Major Evans, now Chief Engineer of the South Park, was directed to take immediate steps to locate a satisfactory route across the Saguache Range. In choosing the most feasible route between the Arkansas Valley and the Gunnison country, Major Evans was faced with the most difficult task of his entire career as a civil engineer. Between the Arkansas Valley and his goal lay the backbone of the Rocky Mountains—the great Continental Divide towering to heights of over 14,000 feet above sea level. Up to this date, no Colorado railroad had dared to attempt such a difficult piece of mountain construction. Even the few wagon and toll roads that laboriously wound their way through the canons, across streams, and over the mountain passes, encountered many difficulties and so it was with a great deal of faith in his engineering ability that Major Evans attempted such a feat.

For an entire season, a corps of surveyors under the direction of Major Evans and P. F. Barr, his assistant, surveyed the mountain passes and searched on both sides of the range for a suitable route for the railroad.[1] A preliminary reconnaissance disclosed two possible routes; one by way of Poncha Pass, Marshall Pass and thence down the Tomichi to Gunnison and the other by way of Chalk Creek, probably Altman Pass (later known as Alpine Pass), and thence down Quartz Creek and the Tomichi to Gunnison. Regarding the Marshall Pass route, one historical source[2] states:

"The company did not want to build around by way of Marshall Pass, over which the grade was as much as 8%."

Note: Palmer's Rio Grande later built via this route with a maximum grade of 4% and maximum curvature of 25½ degrees.

Maj. Evans chose the Chalk Creek route as the shorter and more direct line. This mountain stream, some 18 or 20 miles long and whose headwaters commence on the east slope of the divide, flows east, emerging from its mountain fastness between the towering peaks of Mt. Antero and Mt. Princeton to flow into the Arkansas River just below Nathrop. To even the most casual observer down in the valley, the massive snow-covered ramparts in the vicinity of the 14,000 foot peaks of Antero and Princeton suggest a formidable and unas-

1. New West Illustrated, July 1882.
2. Bulletin, Colorado State Normal School, June 1, 1916.

sailable barrier to any effort to gain access to the main range that lay beyond. In approaching the vicinity of the divide, Evans faced a rough and rugged terrain situated above timberline where the titanic battle of the winter elements becomes a treacherous demon, ready at any moment to engulf the puny efforts of men who would dare bring their steel rails into that forbidden domain. Terrific blizzards batter the mountain tops in the winter season and, gathering force, they howl unimpeded over the range, raging and brawling against the mountain sides as they seek to blast away every obstacle with their relentless fury. Enormous and fantastic drifts are formed by wind and snow, growing bigger and bigger until they can no longer maintain a foothold, and tumble down the jagged mountain sides in huge roaring avalanches of snow, ice and rocks, wiping out everything in their path of merciless destruction.

To assist him in running this survey, Maj. Evans had two able assistants; Messrs. P. F. Barr and Robert R. Williams. History tells us that Williams later opened up one of the first banks to be established on the western slope at Gunnison. The engineers had no great amount of difficulty in locating a line up the canon to the north and south forks of Chalk Creek. This location, some 17 miles west of Nathrop, was later known as St. Elmo. At this point, however, they were faced with the problem of approaching and crossing the lofty Saguache Range at some point which would permit a satisfactory descent down the western slope. Prominent among the better known passes along the crest of the divide, west and southwest of St. Elmo, were Tin Cup Pass, Altman Pass, Williams Pass (sometimes known as Hancock Pass), and South Pass.

Altman Pass, later known as Alpine Pass, was named after Henry Altman, sometimes referred to in early history as a colonel and sometimes as a judge. Colonel Altman, a stage line operator, discovered the pass during one of his several exploration trips in search of a more easily accessible toll road route across the range to Gunnison. Upon learning that Major Evans was attempting to locate a possible line for a railroad across the range in that vicinity, Colonel Altman informed him of his discovery and offered to lend any assistance he was capable of rendering. After careful survey and due consideration of all geographical factors on both the east and west slopes concerned, Maj. Evans chose to tunnel under Altman Pass. This route would enable him to hold the ruling grade to a maximum of four per cent, and if at all possible, hold all curvatures to 24 degrees or less on both slopes. In order to reach this pass from St. Elmo, with a minimum of steep grades and sharp curves, Maj. Evans ran his line of survey up the South Fork of Chalk Creek about five miles to a point later known as Hancock. History tells us that one Captain Hall was also of considerable assistance to Maj. Evans in helping him locate his line through this particular

section. From Hancock, the engineers turned sharply back northwest, and by clinging close to the mountain side for a distance of some three miles, they gained sufficient altitude to enable them to approach the prospective tunnel site on a grade of 4 per cent or less.

The question has been brought up as to why Maj. Evans did not follow the South Fork of Chalk Creek for a short distance beyond St. Elmo and thence bear west up the north side of Tunnel Gulch and approach Altman Pass from the north. It was contended that this would have placed the South Park's track on the south side of the mountain, where the winter sun would tend to keep the snow melted to a minimum and partially relieve a serious operating hazard. It is true that the South Park experienced tremendous difficulties with the enormous amount of snow that the blizzards blew in on this section between Hancock and the east portal; however, it is the firm belief of the writer that had Maj. Evans been able to locate a satisfactory route leading to the tunnel by way of Tunnel Gulch, he certainly would have done so. It is certain that both he and the South Park management were well aware of the advantages offered by such a location and it is highly probable that if such a route could have been located without incorporating an excessive amount of curvature and steep grades, it would have been utilized.

From Alpine Pass, the survey followed down the precipitous west slope past the Palisades to the head of Missouri Gulch, from whence it turned and followed the Middle Fork of Quartz Creek to its junction with the Tomichi. The surveying party reached this point by the first of September, 1879. From the confluence of these two streams, Maj. Evans had the advantage of a smooth water level route along the Tomichi directly into Gunnison. From this point, the line of survey was directed in a northwesterly direction up Ohio Creek toward the Elk Mountain district. According to a South Park map, as furnished to the U. S. Department of Interior and signed by Governor John Evans and Major James Evans under date of March 4, 1880, this survey followed up Ohio Creek past Mt. Carbon to the vicinity of Kebler Pass, approximately two miles south of Irwin and Ruby near the headwaters of Anthracite Creek. The survey being duly completed that fall (1879), Maj. Evans returned to Denver and made his report.

From the minutes of a meeting held by the South Park's board of directors on November 25, 1879, we read the following:

"November 25, 1879, the President laid before the Board the reports and maps of the Gunnison Valley Extension of the railroad of this company by way of Chalk Creek, Alpine Pass and Quartz Creek, Tomichi River and Ohio Creek to the Coal Fields in the Elk Mountains made under the direction of Major James A. Evans, consulting engineer of the company which were read and examined and fully explained by the Major in person, whereupon the following resolution was on motion adopted:

D.S.P.&P. 3, the "Oro City", first of the Mason Bogies, with mixed train near St. Elmo in Chalk Creek Canon, about 1883.

W. H. Jackson photo.
from Denver Public Library Western Collection.

"RESOLVED: That the route recommended by Major Evans in the reports first read, be and the same is hereby adopted as the location of that part of the line of the extension of the railroad of this company and the President is directed to file plats and profiles of the same to secure the right-of-way over the public lands according to law."

Thus, all was in readiness to commence construction of the Gunnison extension. Survey stakes were in place, the necessary legal amendment authorizing the building of the line was in order, and finally, Gould's Joint Operating Agreement, covering certain construction and traffic agreements pertaining thereto, was duly signed, sealed and tucked away in the office safe. All that was necessary now was for the end-of-track to make its appearance on the banks of the Arkansas River.

CONSTRUCTION TO GUNNISON BEGINS

The first black smoke of a little Mason engine rolled off across the fertile Arkansas Valley on February 9, 1880, and on February 21st following, the 30-pound rails and the cedar ties reached across the river to the partially completed grade of Gen. Palmer's Rio Grande. The South Park management decreed that no time was to be lost and construction got under way very shortly. As stipulated in the Joint Operating Agreement, the South Park was to be allowed trackage rights over the Rio Grande for a few miles south of Buena Vista to some mutually agreed point where it would branch off west toward Gunnison. Nathrop, of which we will hear more from time to time, and which was located near the confluence of Chalk Creek and the Arkansas River, seven and one-half miles below Buena Vista, was chosen as the point of divergence. Inasmuch as the Rio Grande had not yet completed their track to this particular point by the early spring of 1880, the South Park, in accordance with the above agreement, completed the seven and one-half miles of track. The Railway Age of March 18, 1880, stated:

"The Denver South Park & Pacific has commenced constructing its track upon the grade of the Pueblo & Arkansas Valley (A.T.&S.F.) near Buena Vista. At last accounts, three miles of iron have been laid."

This part of the valley along the Arkansas River was fairly level and as the Santa Fe had already completed most of the grading work, it was but a short time before the ringing sound of the spike maul was heard at Nathrop. At this point, the little South Park track left the Rio Grande grade and the level valley of the river and bravely headed west up Chalk Creek toward the great barriers that lay ahead, soon to disappear and be swallowed up by a vast mountain domain.

Even to this day, it is a genuine inspiration to those who really admire the South Park railroad to stand at the exit of Box Canon near the mouth of Trout Creek and view the enormous expanse of that great Saguache Range in all its glorious magnitude with snow-covered peaks towering towards the heavens and surrounded by

great blue canons that fade out and lose themselves in their own greatness, and visualize that once a little narrow gauge railroad bravely headed into the heart of that mountain domain and successfully reached its goal on the far side.

The construction crews made very good progress. By July, the end-of-track was completed to Hortense, or Mt. Princeton as it was sometimes called. By September, the railhead had reached Alpine, later known as Fisher, and by the latter part of December of that year, 1880, it had reached St. Elmo. The graders had kept well ahead of the track gang and by the middle of October had finished the grade up to the east portal of Alpine Tunnel. Construction of the tunnel had commenced in January of that year; therefore, to expedite the digging of the bore, the grade to the east portal had been pushed with all possible speed in order that the right of way might be used by the wagon teams to haul the badly needed supplies to the tunnel site.

The earliest reliable report relative to opening up the first section of the Gunnison extension to traffic is found in the Gunnison Review of August 28, 1880, which stated that passenger trains "are now operating as far as Heywood Springs". Next, we find an advertisement by the railroad in the Rocky Mountain News of October 3, 1880.

"IMPORTANT

"The completion of the Alpine & South Park Toll Road and its equipment, with a fine line of four-horse coaches, connecting with all trains on The Denver South Park & Pacific Railroad to Heywood Springs, 13 miles west of Buena Vista, makes a short route to Alpine, Gunnison City, Ouray and all points in the Gunnison Valley. This is the finest toll road in Colorado and in connection with the South Park railroad, offers to the traveling public the shortest and most desirable route to all the mining camps of the great Gunnison."

As specified in the Joint Operating Agreement, the Rio Grande was also entitled to trackage rights over this Chalk Creek line; however, the first information found by the writer concerning the movement of Rio Grande trains over this track appears in a Rio Grande advertisement in the Rocky Mountain News of October 10, 1880.

"The Denver & Rio Grande Ry., having placed regular trains on the joint trackage west of Nathrop, is now carrying passengers through to Hortense without detention and making the closest connections at the latter point with J. L. Sanderson & Company's stages for Alpine, Forest City, Pitkin, and Gunnison, and Witowiski & Dunbar's Hack Line for Virginia City and Hillerton. This route, in connection with the older and favorite one via South Arkansas and Marshall Pass, affords a choice of two excellent roads into the Gunnison, with the lowest rates and choice connections, and the quickest time always. Tickets by the Royal Gorge Route."

Next, we read in the same paper of November 9, 1880.

"Hortense: This City now has five trains each way every day, three by the South Park and two by the Rio Grande. These do not include the several freight and construction trains."

R. H. Kindig.

The roadbed at the west switch of Atlantic siding, showing the 24° curve at the east portal of Alpine Tunnel.

J. C. Thode.

The east portal of Alpine Tunnel and the ruins of the snowshed in August, 1939.

Rio Grande timetable No. 8, dated Sunday, May 8, 1881, shows the following schedule:

No. 75	No. 77	STATION	No. 78	No. 76
lv. 8:15am	lv. 8:10pm	Nathrop	ar. 7:15pm	ar. 6:45am
8:45am	8:35pm	Hortense	6:45pm	6:15am
9:20am	9:05pm	Cascade	6:15pm	5:45am
ar. 9:45am	ar. 9:35pm	Alpine	lv. 6:00pm	lv. 5:30am

Rio Grande timetable No. 14, dated Sunday, December 4, 1881, eliminates Alpine station but has the following notation:

"This timetable is valid and will be used by trainmen and trackmen between South Pueblo and Nathrop only. Conductors and engineers will provide themselves with the joint time-table of the D. & R. G. Ry. and the D. S. P. & P. R. R. before going west of Nathrop and will be governed by the rules, regulations and timetable between Nathrop and Leadville."

The same notation was also found in the following Rio Grande timetables:

No. 17. June 25, 1882.	No. 22. April 22, 1883.
No. 18. July 2, 1882.	No. 23. June 3, 1883.
No. 19. July 23, 1882.	No. 24. July 1, 1883.

It should be remembered that at the time the Tripartite Agreement was ratified (March 27, 1880), the South Park was still under the legal and independent control of the Evans group; therefore, the road's policies, plans, and projected extensions were not affected by this contract. The only agreement the South Park was obliged to adhere to at this particular time was the Joint Operating Agreement which Gould had arranged between that road and Palmer's Rio Grande. The reader will also remember that, among other things, this South Park-Rio Grande agreement stipulated that the line to Gunnison was to be constructed by the South Park, with full trackage rights allowed the Palmer road. As the season of 1880 progressed, it became more and more apparent that the South Park was gradually yielding to Gould's strong influence and that he would eventually gain complete control. During this time, Palmer was also dickering with Evans in an attempt to purchase his road outright, while at the same time, he was engaged in a series of discussions with both Evans and Gould regarding a consolidation of the Rio Grande and South Park roads, the proposal of which had been incorporated in the Joint Operating Agreement. As these negotiations continued throughout the spring of 1880, Palmer gradually began to visualize what the results might be if Gould gained control of the Evans road. He was also thinking of his own railroad's present connection, via the South Park, with the Gunnison region and anticipating what the future might hold in store. Due to his keen foresight and knowledge of Gould's reputation, methods, and policies, he felt fairly certain that Gould ownership of the South Park would soon mean Union Pacific ownership, and that Union Pacific ownership, through some subterfuge, could very easily mean a com-

peting Union Pacific line to Gunnison, regardless of any Tripartite Agreement. This could then resolve into a situation whereby the Rio Grande would lose their trackage rights over the South Park line to the Gunnison territory together with their share of the tremendous amount of business that was destined to come out of this region.

In view of this critical situation, Palmer directed his surveyors to locate a feasible route for a railroad between South Arkansas (Salida) and Gunnison. It is not known just when Palmer made this important decision, but a notice in the Railway Age of September 23, 1880, announced that the Rio Grande had let a contract for the construction of the line via Marshall Pass, to be completed within seven months. The 1880 Rio Grande Annual Report confirms this and adds that tracklaying started October 25, 1880. Relative to this rupture between the Palmer and Evans road, John Evans testified in the Pacific Railway Commission Case as follows:

"After we had been running to Leadville on the joint track for some time, and were extending our line to the Gunnison, the Denver & Rio Grande also commenced extending into the same territory. The Denver & South Park people thought this was not in good faith, because the Rio Grande had agreed to go to Gunnison in the contract for joint trackage over our line via Alpine Tunnel. But on examining the papers, Messrs. Evarts, Southmayd & Choat (D.&R.G. Lawyers) said there was nothing in the contract to prevent the Denver & Rio Grande from building an independent line, if they desired it. . ."

By building to Gunnison, Palmer distinctly broke faith with the South Park interests, or indirectly with Gould and the Union Pacific. Palmer well knew the reputation of Gould and the Omaha crowd; consequently, the writer is rather inclined to give the man credit for looking ahead with a view to protecting his Rio Grande property.

Construction of the Rio Grande's Gunnison line commenced at Salida on October 25, 1880, and the battle between the two roads was on in earnest, both making strenuous efforts to reach Gunnison first. The South Park had the advantage in time and distance, but not in ease of construction.

At the time Palmer commenced his Gunnison line, the South Park interests felt confident that they would be the first to reach the town. The entire line over the range had been completely surveyed and staked out; the end-of-track had been extended up Chalk Creek Canon some twelve miles beyond Nathrop, and track laying and right of way construction beyond that point were proceeding fairly well. Progress at the tunnel was not proceeding as had been expected; however, the road's officials were optimistic and announced that trains would be running into Gunnison by the spring or early summer of 1881.

By October, the Sanderson Stage Lines were leaving Gunnison daily, carrying passengers to the terminals of the two railroads. Both roads began a campaign of ex-

*W. H. Jackson photos,
from Francis Rizzari Collection.*

**The upper photo shows the camp at the east portal during the construction of Alpine Tunnel, and in the lower photo the camp
at the west portal is shown. These pictures were taken in 1881.**

tensive advertising, each extolling in superlative language the fact that its combination rail and toll road was the shortest, safest, most convenient route over the divide. Each passed through the "grandest, choicest scenery in nature's repertoire". Each made glowing statements that travelling over their line was a luxury. Both roads were telling the public that each day found them drawing nearer to Gunnison and that they would be the first to reach her gates. The Gunnison Daily Review carried advertisements of the South Park and the Rio Grande side by side. Never was there an article extolling one road as the "favorite short-line route", but that close by, the other would be representing itself as "The Pride of Colorado". If a reader found a statement that the South Park would be the first to enter the great Gunnison Valley, he would also be informed in some other column of the same issue that the shriek of the Rio Grande engines would be the first to be heard in the great Tomichi Valley. The timekeeper of the race was in no way partial; to him, the glory belonged to the first crew to poke their engine's pilot inside the city limits.

During the winter of 1880 and '81, both roads struggled with their many construction problems. Although the Rio Grande was not boring a tunnel through the main range, they were building a railroad up 4% grades and around 24 degree curves to cross the top of Marshall Pass, 10,856 feet above sea level, which was no easy task during the winter season. However, the engineers were relieved of many construction problems and made better progress because of the fact that the Rio Grande made good use of Otto Mears' Marshall Pass toll road which Palmer had purchased from the little man from the San Juan.[1]

Both the Rio Grande people and the Alpine Tunnel contractors were experiencing great difficulty with the labor problem. The Gunnison citizens watched with much interest for the miscellaneous news items and reports that appeared from time to time stating the progress each railroad was making. The digging of Alpine Tunnel presented many unforseen difficulties and it was soon discovered that the South Park's progress toward Gunnison was going to be seriously delayed. On June 21st following, the first shrill whistle of an engine was heard on Marshall Pass; by the middle of July, the railhead had reached Sargent, at the foot of the mountains; and on August 6th the track reached Main Street in Gunnison. On Monday, August 8, 1881, a Rio Grande train consisting of two cars of coal, a baggage car, and two passenger coaches steamed into Gunnison. The race was finished; the Rio Grande had won.

1. David Lavender, "The Big Divide".

H. H. Buckwalter photo,
from the State Historical Society of Colorado.

A special to the reopening of Alpine Tunnel arrives at Atlantic in June, 1895.

CHAPTER XI

THE CONSTRUCTION OF ALPINE TUNNEL

The toughest job to confront Major Evans had been the final selection of the location of Alpine Tunnel and its east and west approaches. In order to hold the tunnel to the minimum length and to take the best possible advantage of the mountainous terrain at the two approaches or portals, it was decided to construct the tunnel in a northeast-southwest direction. The plans called for a single track bore, 1,805 feet long with minimum dimensions of 8 feet 10 inches in width at the bottom, or rail level, 10 feet 10 inches in width at the spring of the arch, and 13 feet 9 inches in height. From the appearance of the surface, Major Evans deduced that the greater portion of the bore would have to be blasted and drilled through solid granite. The balance of the bore was to be arched and timbered where necessary with California redwood; reinforced concrete was unknown in those days. In order to negotiate the short turn at the east portal, due to a difficult approach, the first 160 feet of the bore at that end was built on a curve and constituted part of a 406-foot, 24 degree left curve. The balance of the tunnel through to the west portal, a distance of 1,645 feet, was laid out on a straight line.

The project was a stupendous undertaking and attracted much attention. The South Park interests were anxious to get underway with actual construction as soon as possible. The Rocky Mountain News under date of November 2 and 3, 1879, carried advertisements by the Denver office calling for bids on constructing the tunnel. On November 26th, this paper announced that the contract had been awarded to M. Cummins & Co. on November 25th, with the stipulation that the work was to be completed by July 1, 1880. It is almost impossible to realize anything more difficult than the inauguration of such a project as this—in midwinter, on Alpine Pass, at an altitude of 12,000 feet, where the blizzards howl in unrelenting fury, piling the snow many feet deep. However, in view of the urgent need to complete the line through to Gunnison, it was decided to commence work on the tunnel as soon as possible. Accordingly, a preliminary construction crew made its first appearance on the pass in January of 1880 and began hewing away at the backbone of the mighty Saguache. The digging of the bore was under the direction of Mr. P. F. Barr, who had charge of all tunnel work

throughout its construction.[1] Following the usual practice in tunnel construction, it was decided to commence operations at both ends. Newspapers carried advertisements calling for large numbers of laborers and soon hundreds of men were at work removing snow, ice, rock and dirt from both the east and west approaches.

With construction crews at work on both sides of the pass, one of the first major problems to face the contractors was the transportation of men and supplies to the two scenes of construction. At this date, the rail head had only progressed as far as the canon of Trout Creek; consequently, all supplies had to be hauled in by wagon teams. The wagon and toll road on the east slope followed Chalk Creek to St. Elmo, where it divided; one fork bearing to the north for the Tin Cup and Aspen districts crossing the range some 5 miles north of Alpine Pass at Tin Cup Pass. The other fork turned south by way of Hancock and across the Continental Divide at Williams Pass, sometimes called Hancock Pass, for Gunnison. The wagon teams, hauling supplies for the tunnel, followed this South Fork as far as Hancock, from which point they followed a temporary road laid out along the grade up the east slope to the tunnel site. At the beginning of the job, the contractors put in over $50,000 worth of supplies, hauled in from the end-of-track at an enormous expense. As the summer of 1880 progressed, the South Park's railhead was being gradually pushed up Chalk Creek Canon which, of course, lessened the burden to a certain extent. To handle the transportation of supplies on the west slope, the company spent over $25,300 to build a wagon road from Pitkin to the west portal. History tells us that after the railroad was completed, they sold a portion of this road, known as the St. Elmo Toll Road, to the county for $400.[2]

During the spring of 1880, when construction of the tunnel was first getting underway, it was the general opinion that the track would be completed up to the east portal long before the tunnel would be ready. Therefore, in order that construction might continue in the meantime between the tunnel and Gunnison, it was thought that perhaps a temporary switchback could

1. The New West Illustrated, July, 1882.
2. Colorado Railroad Commission Report, 1885.

be built over Alpine Pass to serve as a connecting link, until such time as the tunnel could be completed. This would enable the company to establish service into Gunnison much sooner. In this connection we copy, in part, from a newspaper item that appeared in the Denver Daily Times under date of March 18, 1880.

"While work on the tunnel is progressing satisfactorily, it is certain that the track will be completed to the tunnel before that passage through the mountain will be opened, and that tracklaying beyond that point will be delayed unless a 'switchback' over the mountain is put in—the propriety of which the company is now debating. The Times is of the decided opinion that, considering the immense rush certain to go to the Gunnison country, and the vast traffic that will follow it, a 'switchback' should be put in, not only for the benefit of the public, but for the company itself. The importance of reaching Gunnison City at as early a date as possible cannot be overestimated; and every consideration of self-interest and public policy combine to demand of the South Park company no lack of any means that will put the road into Gunnison City as soon as possible."

After due consideration, the South Park managers decided against the proposition and no attempt was ever made to build a switchback over Alpine Pass.

After the winter season of 1881 was well underway, the railroad company experienced a great deal of trouble with the labor problem. The altitude was so great at the tunnel that it was impossible for a man to do as much work in the rarified atmosphere as he could do on the plains. The winter cold was intense. The snow piled so high that merely clearing the way so that the men could get to work cost the railroad a great deal. The western approach was completely blockaded with snow. Often the laborers had to cut shafts in the snow in order to get down to their work. At times when it was impossible for them to do anything outside, the men were allowed to work inside on the heading, moving the rubble back to a position just inside the portal. This was done to keep the men occupied and to prevent them from leaving, even though it necessitated handling the material a number of times instead of once, which increased expenses. None but the experienced old timers would or could stand the battle against the winter elements. At times, the blizzards howled with such fury that the men had to form human chains extending from their boarding house to the tunnel entrance and hold to each other in order to keep from getting lost in the deep snow and freezing to death. Even on these trips, the men's clothes were often frozen to their skin due to the severe cold. Only those who have felt the effects of the midwinter winds and snow storms on the main range can realize the difficulties of trying to carry on this kind of work without the danger of loss of life or broken limb. An article written by a news reporter and published in the Pitkin Mining News under date of December 23, 1881, states: "A weather record was kept by Mr. Wm. Osborn, one of the contractors, from the time he started until the finish, which the writer had occasion to read; and it is only a wonder that one man ever worked so long in a region of such frequent blizzards." Because of these conditions, the company found it very difficult to obtain a sufficient quantity of good labor during the winter season. The payroll records show that very few men worked more than a month. Ordinary track laborers on the South Park received from $4.50 to $5.00 per week, plus their board and lodging; however, tunnel laborers, who worked inside, were paid $3.00 per day without board. Laborers who worked overtime often drew from $100 to $125 a month. Out of no less than ten thousand workmen who came to the tunnel, only a comparatively small number stayed on the job more than two or three days, in spite of this higher wage scale. The Union Pacific gave free transportation to thousands of laborers from the east, who worked, for the most part, but a very few days. In a great many cases, the class of labor that responded was a worthless and undesirable group, interested only in a free train ride to Colorado. From two hundred to two hundred and fifty new men, of all colors and nationalities, and from all parts of the world, were employed daily, and on several occasions, almost the whole force picked up and left. The story is told that during the digging of the tunnel an Italian, convicted of some crime, was hanged in Gunnison. Upon learning of the hanging, all the Italian laborers at the tunnel quit and were planning on marching into Gunnison to seek revenge, but it was a 40 mile walk from the tunnel and it seems that their craving for excitement died out before they got there. As a result of such conditions, it is easy to see why one of the biggest labor turnovers in Colorado history took place at Alpine Tunnel. The end of every shift found large groups of disgruntled workers leaving for a lower and warmer climate. Many went to the mines; others returned to their homes, and the Lord only knows where the rest scattered to. Nevertheless, the high wages paid induced some of the men to brave the wind and cold and to stay through the winter; consequently, the work was never interrupted.

In order to provide eating and sleeping facilities for the construction crews at the tunnel, the contractors built some rough log cabins. Old photographs show six of these log buildings near the west portal. Although no information ever came to light, it is naturally assumed that there were also a group of these cabins built near the east portal for use of the men working at that end. The Rocky Mountain News published a brief news item regarding one of these camps, calling it Streeter's Camp No. 2. The article went on to state that this particular camp was under the jurisdiction of one James Malone who was very popular with the men, and that the camp's cook, William Malloy, furnished the men with plenty of well-cooked food. Louisa Ward writes in her book: "Henry Weber, who owned a butcher shop

The engine house at Alpine Tunnel station, during construction in 1881. The log buildings which housed the tunnel workers are shown in the background, and the **wagon** road which crossed Alpine Pass is at the extreme right.

W. H. Jackson photo, from Denver Public Library Western Collection.

at St. Elmo, contracted to supply all the necessary meat for the construction crews at ten cents per pound."

The railroad's engineers and the contractors fully expected that in digging the tunnel they would encounter a more or less solid mass of granite. However, after actual construction got under way and the contractors had penetrated some distance from both portals, they ran ito some of the most slippery slide rock, boulder, and decomposed granite formations ever invented by Mother Nature. This condition gave them no end of trouble and caused quite a loss of time in construction work. Only about 100 feet of self-supporting solid rock was found in the entire bore. In addition to many small streams of water, three large streams from five to seven inches in diameter were intercepted. When encountered, these subterranean channels of water gushed forth, partially filled the bore, created a very dangerous condition for the laborers and caused much damage as the water ran off toward the portal. It was with the greatest of difficulty that this loose, wet, and muddy formation was held back.

This peculiar formation of loose and decomposed rock, together with the streams of water encountered, forced the contractors to arch and timber practically the entire bore. The timber used for this purpose was 12x12 California redwood, shipped from that state by the Union Pacific at an expense of from $80 to $110 per thousand feet. Four hundred sixty thousand feet of this special timber was used in the construction of Alpine Tunnel. Besides these 12x12 redwood timbers, the contractors used over 1,500,000 feet of false timbering. This timber was cut from the surrounding mountain sides and transported to the tunnel under tremendous difficulties, especially during the winter season.

Such conditions greatly interfered with the progress of construction. By April, only about 150 feet of tunnel work had been completed. Then friction began to develop between the Cummins Company and the railroad. There are references to exorbitant costs in both money and lives. Whatever the reasons were, the Cummins Company broke their contract with the railroad and gave up the job. The Engineering News, under date of May 1, 1880, carried the news item that the South Park was again soliciting bids for the completion of Alpine Tunnel. On July 12, 1880, a new contract was awarded to Fitzgerald, Cushing & Osborne, of Lincoln, Nebraska.[1] The Fitzgerald Company took charge, and day and night a thousand laborers toiled at building the tunnel. A fair rate of progress was made. On November 2, 1880, Major Evans announced in the Rocky Mountain News that 220 feet on the west end and 170 feet on the east end were completed, and that 150 feet of the east bore was completely arched and timbered. On February 19, 1881, an article in the Railway World reported that 480 feet of the west bore and 320 feet of

1. Minutes of D. S. P. & P. Board of Directors.

the east bore were completed; and on April 16, 1881, the Gunnison Review reported only 570 feet left, and that the men were going forward at a rate of about ten feet per day.

Up to this date, the end-of-track had not progressed any farther than St. Elmo; consequently, all tunnel supplies were still being hauled in by wagon. In this connection, we will quote part of an interesting news item as published in the Pitkin Mining News. "Getting supplies and materials to the scene of construction over the rough mountain trails is no small feature of the Alpine Tunnel enterprise. False timbering required in the construction of the tunnel is cut from the surrounding region and hauled over the mountains through 5 to 7 feet of snow and over snow banks 50 to 70 feet in depth. On the 23rd of May, 1881, a jack trail was cut through 16 feet of snow over the mountain to get the redwood timber to the western approach. Eighteen mules and three horses were killed and a large number of wagons smashed to pieces." As the summer of 1881 progressed, construction moved along without any unusual difficulties. On June 18, 1881, the Gunnison Review reported that all but 250 feet of the tunnel was completed. From this, we learn that the tunnel laborers were making fairly good progress. From November 2, 1880, until June 18, 1881, they had completed 1,165 feet of the bore. This was an average of about 5 feet per day, or 2½ feet for each crew, for this particular period. Then on July 26, 1881, there was great excitement and much rejoicing up on Alpine Pass. The headings of Alpine Tunnel were broken through; the South Park had pierced the backbone of the great Saguache Range in the Continental Divide. Regarding this great occasion, we find the following news item in the Denver Tribune of July 27, 1881. "The Denver South Park & Pacific Railroad has at last bored through the great Alpine Peak. The first streak of day light shot through the great tunnel yesterday morning about 8 A.M., Tuesday, July 26th." Who should be permitted to go through the opening first? The honor was given to the small child of Mr. William W. Osborn, the superintendent. Later, Mrs. Osborn and P. F. Barr, the engineer in charge, went through, after paying $10, which was suitably spent in buying a few barrels of beer for the boys.[1]

With the headings broken through, construction difficulties eased considerably, and good progress was made during the fall.

As nearly as can be determined, the railhead reached the east portal about the second week of August,[2] where

1. "Historical Sketches of Early Gunnison," Colorado State Normal School. 1916.
2. Denver Daily Times, July 27, 1881, states: "The end-of-track reached Hancock the last week in July." Denver Daily Times, July 30, 1881, states "The rails will reach the east portal in ten days." Gunnison Review, August 6, 1881, states: "The rails will reach the east portal in one week. Trains are now operating to Hancock." George A. Root states: "Both the Gunnison and Pitkin papers were silent regarding the exact date the rails reached the east portal."

Engine 157 emerging from the west portal of Alpine Tunnel.

The west portal of the tunnel, showing the remains of the snowshed, the lead to the turntable, and the harp type switch stand
as they appeared in 1940.

a siding was built and given the name Atlantic. The completion of the track to the east approach eliminated a great many difficulties that had heretofore faced both the railroad and the contractors. However, there was much unfinished work to be done before it could be announced that the tunnel was completed and ready for use. Note the following interesting newspaper item that appeared in the Gunnison Review under date of November 19, 1881.

"Operations are still progressing in the tunnel. Three shifts, consisting of 150 men, are at work at each portal. There is an immense amount of debris to be cleared away and a great amount of rock work is yet to be finished. In view of this, it is difficult to say just how soon the tunnel will be completed; however, the idea of laying track through to the west portal this season, is not altogether abandoned. The expense of keeping the men at work at this time is much greater than a few weeks ago. The construction train, including the boarding car, is stationed at Hancock and is backed up to the tunnel each morning. Because of the drifted snow that has accumulated during the night, the track has to be cleared away with shovels in order that the crew can get the train up the slope to the tunnel. Mr. Barr informs us that the cost of getting the men to their work each day is not less than $75. Only those who have frequently interviewed the job can form an idea of the immense difficulties the South Park has had to overcome since they tapped the eastern slope of Alpine Range."

By the latter part of November, all timber work inside the tunnel was completed. A snow shed 150 feet long (later reduced to 128 feet) was built at the east portal, and a shed 650 feet long (later reduced to 527 feet) was built at the west portal. William Cairns (veteran South Park engineer) writes that the end of each of these snow sheds was equipped with large doors that were kept closed during stormy weather.

The disadvantages accruing from a constant war with the snow were greatly diminished due to these sheds, which protected the track from slides. Track was laid through the bore to within 200 feet of the west entrance, thus enabling the construction train to run through practically the entire tunnel. On or about December 1, 1881,[1] it was announced that Alpine Tunnel was completed. Although the tunnel was ready for use, the winter season with its blizzards and deep snows had set in, making it impossible to continue any construction on the west slope. Consequently, all further work on the Gunnison extension was postponed until the following spring. Note the following news item from the Gunnison Review of December 31, 1881.

"It was expected that the Denver & South Park branch of the Union Pacific would reach here last fall, but owing to the many obstacles encountered in the building of Alpine Tunnel, completion of the line will be considerably delayed. That gigantic work, however, is now completed—but owing to the immense amount of snow on the summit, and the lateness at which the tunnel was finished, work has been abandoned until spring."

1. Rocky Mountain News of December 21, 1881 reports the date as December 2, 1881.

The Pitkin Mining News of December 9, 1881.

"All work on the South Park from the Tunnel to Gunnison City was shut down last Saturday the 3rd, except a little that is being completed in the tunnel on contract. All work except the bedding was stopped previous to that time and on Saturday, Mr. Scott Dickenson was ordered to shut down on that work. He has gone to take a contract in the Black Canon from the Denver & Rio Grande. We will have no South Park railroad into Pitkin before the last of next June."

Shortly after the tunnel's completion, the Denver Republican published the following item in praise of Major Evans' work.

"The whole work bears a record equal to none, in the history of railroad tunnels, and it is a wonder that the work was not discontinued and given up long ago. But today, this great trans-continental railroad tunnel is finished, with a snow shed on the Eastern approach, 150 feet in length, and one 650 feet in length at the Western approach. It is to the credit of James Evans, the Chief Engineer of this enterprise, that, as a result of careful surveying, the headings, when broken through, came together within 11/100 of a foot; the distance within 7/100 of a foot; and the level within 94/100 of a foot. This was indeed a fine piece of engineering for this day. During the construction of the tunnel, the Cummins and Fitzgerald companies had encountered and successfully overcome some of the most severe hardships ever faced by railroad contractors. Under the careful and efficient management of the Fitzgerald Company's Superintendent, Mr. Wm. Osborn, the work was carried on with a minimum of danger to the workmen."

In compiling these various tunnel figures, Mr. E. J. Haley and the author encountered a number of conflicting statements. Considering all data, and Engineer Andy Nelson's opinions along with those of some other old timers, we arrived at the following conclusions. The track entered the east portal at an elevation of 11,600 feet and bored upward on a .96% grade for 1,203 feet to the apex at 11,612 feet. From that point it descended on a 1.04% grade for 602 feet where it emerged at the west portal at an elevation of 11,605 feet.

The engineering department of the Colorado & Southern states that the correct length of the tunnel from portal to portal, exclusive of any snow sheds, was 1,805 feet. To dig this bore through the Continental Divide, the contractors excavated 1,820 cubic yards of earth, and 14,721 cubic yards of rock. Although it was anticipated, no ore veins or bodies were found during the digging of the entire bore. It required 699 days to dig the tunnel which was an average of 2.58 feet per day. The best time was made between February 19 and May 28, 1881, when the men averaged 7.19 feet per day for 98 days. Like most tunnels, Alpine was built so that it sloped both ways from the apex of the bore. This was for drainage purposes. For some reason, Alpine's apex was not in the center but was located at a point some 602 feet from the west end.

An old South Park engineer, William Wendell, told the author that a framed red glass lamp always hung overhead at the apex of the bore. This old lamp contained a big sperm candle that burned continuously and served to notify the engineer when he was over the

The west portal of Alpine Tunnel in 1885, showing a portion of the snowshed. A section of the Alpine Pass wagon road runs to the right, level with the mouth of the tunnel.

W. H. Jackson photo,
from Denver Public Library Western Collection.

hump and could shut off steam for the downgrade run out of the tunnel. Later, this candle was replaced by an oil burning lamp.

In commenting on the tunnel, Andy Nelson stated:

"The grade in the tunnel was not as steep on either side of the apex as that found just outside both portals. The short west slope was the steepest. The grade between Alpine Tunnel station and the west portal was a steep drag. This steep grade continued up to and through the west portal snow shed, but levelled out some on entering the actual tunnel bore. I was engineer on the head end, handling the air, when we took the South Park's first rotary snow plow through Alpine Tunnel. In some places there was only about three inches clearance between the plow and the walls of the tunnel. It took fifty-five minutes to take the plow through."

Although statements have been found saying that there were no lives lost during the entire job of digging the tunnel, the Gunnison Review of September 25, 1880, carried an item to the effect that one Joseph Riley, a gang foreman, was killed the previous Saturday. It seems obvious that such a dangerous job as the construction of Alpine Tunnel would claim at least a few lives. M. S. Goodale claims that 48 men lost their lives in a dynamite explosion that occurred during the digging of the tunnel.[1]

To overcome the thousand and one obstacles that confronted them, the contractors required the most dominant perserverance and skill. All of the work was carried on by hand, which proved to accomplish more in this slide rock formation than machinery, which was tried out and found to be unsuitable.[2] The underground workings of the tunnel and the tremendous difficulties under which it was built were of major interest to all the railroad and mining interests throughout the state of Colorado.

Since the building of the tunnel presented some very difficult problems and was regarded as a marvelous piece of engineering in its day, it would be well to present a few facts and figures for those interested.

Within the timbered section the minimum width at rail level is 8 feet 10 inches, with a maximum of 12 feet

1. Railroad Stories magazine, December, 1933.
2. H. L. Curtiss.

6 inches; the minimum width at the spring of the arch is 10 feet 10 inches with a maximum of 13 feet 6 inches; the minimum height above rail level is 13 feet 9 inches with a maximum of 16 feet 5 inches. Three thousand six hundred ten linear feet of 40-pound steel rail was laid on 2,444 native pine ties. One thousand pounds of track bolts and 5,500 pounds of spikes were used. The altitude at track level at the apex is 11,612 feet and is 512 feet below the crest of the Continental Divide, which, at this point, is 12,124 feet above sea level. As far as is known Alpine Tunnel, at the time of its completion, bore the very great distinction of being the highest adhesion operated railroad point above sea level ever attained. However, in later years this figure was exceeded by two other railroads in the United States[1] and some four or five roads located in the Andes Mountains (see Railroad Stories magazine, August, 1935, page 84) in South America.

The tunnel had no ventilation system, depending on the natural wind currents blowing through it to keep the bore clear of gasses, etc. As nearly as can be ascertained, the actual cost of digging the great Alpine Tunnel, including all construction labor and materials such as timber and track items, amounted to approximately $242,090.

1. List of high altitudes attained by miscellaneous U. S. railroads:

Summit (Red Mountain)—Silverton Railroad—Built 1889—Altitude 11,113 ft. Abandoned.

Climax (Fremont Pass)—Denver South Park & Pacific—Built 1884—Altitude 11,319 feet. In operation (now standard gauge).

Boreas—Denver South Park & Pacific—Built 1882—Altitude 11,493 feet. Abandoned.

Ibex Branch—Denver & Rio Grande—Built 1898—Altitude 11,522 feet. Abandoned.

Hagerman Tunnel—Colorado Midland—Built 1887—Altitude 11,528 feet. Abandoned.

Alpine Tunnel—Denver South Park & Pacific—Built 1881—Altitude 11,612 feet. Abandoned.

Rollins Pass—Denver & Salt Lake—Built 1904—Altitude 11,660 feet. Abandoned.

Mt. McClellan (end-of-track)—Argentine Central—Built 1906—Altitude 14,007 feet. Abandoned. (U.S.G.S. Bulletin No. 707.)

CHAPTER XII

CONSTRUCTION — WEST PORTAL TO BALDWIN

The first of the year 1881 still found some semblance of a race between the Rio Grande and the South Park as to who would reach Gunnison first. The Rio Grande was having less difficulty in laying their steel up the east side of Marshall Pass than the South Park was having in boring their tunnel under Alpine Pass. However, a race is not won until the winner crosses the finish line; consequently, the South Park interests had not yet given up all hope of arriving in Gunnison first. All the contracts had been let for grading the right of way and building the necessary bridges as far as Gunnison, with the stipulation that work was to get underway as soon as local weather conditions permitted.

The building of a right of way, even for a narrow gauge railroad, down the west slope of Alpine Pass was destined to be a difficult job at best. For a distance of about one-half mile west of the tunnel the right of way is fairly level, but at this point it curves sharply to the left and it is here that the actual descent of the west slope begins. Ernest Ingersoll, an early day journalist, describing a trip over Alpine Pass in his book "Crest of the Continent" stated: "I let my mule down into Quartz Creek valley by hitching his wiry tail around the base of successive saplings which acted as snubbing posts." Steam engines could not follow the trail of Ingersoll and his mule, so Maj. Evans had to find a more gradual descent. Standing at this location and viewing the valley far below, one wonders what Maj. Evans must have thought when he was confronted with the problem of building a railroad over that seemingly impassable section. It was on the western slope of the Saguache Range that the South Park's engineers were confronted with more of the same difficult construction problems encountered throughout the entire line of the railroad. Only those adventurous souls, who have sufficient interest to climb Alpine Pass and observe with their own eyes the nature of this mountainous terrain, can appreciate the difficulties which faced these engineers. The problems which Eicholtz had encountered in his climb up the east side of Kenosha were not to be compared with this stretch of track.

Maj. Evans had only one choice in laying out a route between the pass and the floor of Quartz Creek Valley; to pick his way with caution along a precarious and winding route, hugging the west face of the mountain

until he could reach the far end of Missouri Gulch whence flowed the Middle Fork of Quartz Creek. Upon reaching this point he would then be able to curve sharply back to the right and gradually descend along the east side of this gulch to the head of the valley. He was further handicapped in that he must stay within the maximum of a 4% grade and if at all possible, 24 degree curves.

Soon spring brought a partial letup of the heavy snows and with the right of way staked and marked out, the contractors went to work. To provide a suitable support for the track, they literally blasted and carved out benches for the roadbed along the steep sloping mountain sides and through many projecting arms of solid granite as they advanced. They constructed numerous and substantial rock cribs or walls to support the roadbed across the many defiles that offered little in the way of a foundation, even for a narrow gauge mountain railroad. In one place, after negotiating a reverse curve of 28 and 22 degrees, closely followed by a 14 degree curve, all within a track distance of less than 1,400 feet, the right of way then approached that formidable and almost impassable granite barrier, the Palisades. This famous rock formation, located between mileposts 163 and 164, slightly over a mile and a quarter by rail from Alpine Tunnel station, is a smooth, almost perpendicular wall of solid granite, which rises upward for hundreds of feet. The face, or wall, of this great cliff is over 400 feet wide and is directly parallel with the path of the projected right of way. To blast out a bench across the face of this huge rock wall would have been an exceedingly long and costly proposition.

Some thirty feet below the projected track level, the face of the cliff leveled out a bit to form a shelf-like formation which extended along the face of the mountain. In fact, the old South Park & Alpine Toll Road between Pitkin and Hancock followed up the side of the mountain along this ledge-like formation as it wound its way up and over the crest of the Continental Divide at Williams Pass. It was decided to construct a large rock wall or crib and fill the intervening space with rock using the ledge-like formation as a foundation. This would then serve as an embankment to support the track across the face of the Palisades. A suitable foundation was blasted out at the base to support

Looking past the Palisades toward Paywell Mountain. Note the man seated on one of the large blocks of masonry which formed the wall that supported the right of way. Directly below are the remains of the Williams Pass stage road, descending into Brittle Silver Basin, sometimes called Missouri Gulch.

the rock work or crib. Hundreds of men worked many months building up this great rock wall with stone, hewn by hand from the surrounding mountain side. When completed, the wall was two and one-half feet thick, 33 feet high, and 452 feet long. It was so well constructed that it is in a remarkable state of preservation, even to this day. Just beyond the Palisades lay another rock formation which necessitated the construction of a similar crib, 6 feet high and 550 feet long.

After passing these two long rock cribs and continuing along the side of the mountain for about a mile, curving both right and left as it dropped down a three and four per cent grade, the track approached Sherrod Curve. This huge curve lay at the south end of Missouri Gulch which in turn led down into the valley of Quartz Creek. Sherrod Curve had a curvature of 24 degrees, with a radius of 238¾ feet, and lacked only 132 degrees of making a complete circle. When the railroad was first built, the curve was known as the Woodstock loop or curve. Later, in October, 1903, a station, which was nothing more than a flag stop, was established here and given the name Sherrod.

Due to the immense amount of rock work, this section of the railroad between Alpine Tunnel station and Sherrod Curve was the scene of much activity throughout the entire year of 1881. The right of way here consisted of almost one continuous length of bench and crib work, as it followed along the precipitous slope of the mountain side. All summer, large numbers of men drilled and blasted away at the hard granite rock and the reports of giant powder explosions, followed by the usual smoke and dust, were continually echoing against the surrounding mountain sides. It is estimated that it cost the company approximately $100,000 per mile to build this section of the railroad.

Meanwhile, the contractors, in an effort to accelerate the speed of construction between the tunnel and Gunnison, established additional grading camps farther west along the projected line of the right of way. However, the same difficulties were encountered here which faced them on the eastern slope and at the tunnel, including the shortage of labor. Despite the high wages paid, from $4.50 to $5.00 per week with board and lodging, the contractors experienced considerable difficulty in keeping a sufficient quantity of good labor in the grading camps. It seemed to be the popular belief among the men that the adjacent hills were fabulously rich in gold and silver. They had the habit of borrowing picks and shovels from the railroad and then leaving singly or in groups to try their luck at prospecting. Some returned and others were never seen again.

West of Sherrod Curve, the construction problems encountered by the engineers eased considerably and the grading crews were able to advance at a more rapid pace. Following down Missouri Gulch, they soon reached the head of Quartz Creek Valley. Here the right of way made a sweeping 24 degree left curve to the west, and keeping high on the north side of the valley, followed a long rambling chain of mountains, winding in and out of numerous gulches that reached up into the hills from Quartz Creek Valley.

Continuing in a southwesterly direction, the grade, after passing through Pitkin, crossed Quartz Creek twice and arrived at Parlin, 28 miles from the tunnel. At Parlin, located near the forks of Quartz and Tomichi Creeks, the South Park entered the great Tomichi Valley. Here the road came face to face with its competitor, the Rio Grande. It probably grieved the South Park interests to observe, at close hand, the first concrete evidence that they were the losers in the great railroad race to Gunnison. For here in the Tomichi Valley, lay not only the Rio Grande grade, complete with ties and rails, but diamond stacked engines were shuttling back and forth on it. However, all was not lost; the Gunnison region was still digging and shipping silver, and from all indications there would be plenty of traffic for both roads.

After reaching Parlin, the region leveled out considerably and the water level route along Tomichi Creek afforded a comparatively easy grade into Gunnison. Following Maj. Evans' line of survey stakes, the contractors built the South Park's grade along the north bank of the stream. The Rio Grande lay on the south side, and although Tomichi Creek wound around a bit, crossing and recrossing both railroads a number of times, the two tracks remained more or less parallel as they continued west. With no further difficult construction problems to hinder their progress, aside from two wooden trestles of 125 and 119-foot lengths, located at mileposts 193 and 194.4, respectively, the contractors made fairly good time in their progress down the valley.

The bridge and trestle gang finished most of their job by September. By November of that year, 1881, the entire right of way between the west portal and Gunnison, including the heavy rock work in the vicinity of the Palisades, was completely graded and a large portion of the ties cut and distributed along the grade ready for the rails. Some of the rail was purchased and ready to lay, but it was getting late in the season and the coming winter months, with their accompanying blizzards and snow storms, would hinder any construction work attempted. Furthermore, the tunnel was not yet completed, which would have facilitated transportation of rails and supplies; consequently, all further construction was postponed until the following spring. Commenting on this suspension of work, the Gunnison Review of November 19, 1881, stated:

"All work on the D. S. P. & P. has been suspended until next spring; however, the company expects to keep a force of men at work in the tunnel."

220

Dr. C. H. Scott photo,
from Francis Rizzari Collection.

A passenger train, with the 26-foot business car B-3 on the rear, pauses at Sherrod on its way to Alpine Tunnel.

S. L. Logue.

The roadbed on Sherrod Curve as it appears today. The upper level of the railroad, climbing toward Alpine Tunnel, shows in the distance.

LAYING THE RAILS AND COMPLETING THE LINE FROM THE TUNNEL THROUGH GUNNISON TO THE BALDWIN MINES

Before leaving for that land where the lights are always green, Lewis Lathrop wrote a short sketch on the old South Park. The article, later published in Railroad Magazine, stated in part:

"Beneath the rubble which perpetually slips down from the slopes of Alpine Pass on the Continental Divide, there used to be a keystone bearing the legend 1882 upon its weathered face. This was the west portal of the great Alpine Tunnel. Westward from that point, for some five or six hundred feet, lay the ruins of what was once a curved snow shed. Huge timbers mark its skeleton course, for tons of winter dross have caused the roof to cave in and the side wall sheathing to collapse. A stream of crystal clear water trickles along between the thirty-five pound rails that rest on hand-hewn red spruce and cedar ties. Thus have desolation and wilderness come near to reclaiming the last vestiges of the Denver South Park & Pacific, a narrow gauge railroad, which, when built over fifty years ago, crossed the highest railroad pass in North America. In its heyday, the little road had a daily passenger train each way, and innumerable freights, laden with coal, timber, livestock, ore, and mountain timothy hay. A small turntable pit, walled with stout boards, mutely testifies that panting little engines were once turned here. The rails of the spur track leading to it are still solid enough to bear the weight of a locomotive, and the switch on the main line operated by an old time harp type switch stand with the date 1883 moulded in its cast frame, is not yet locked with rust.

"As for the telegraph office, or Alpine station itself, it still stands today, a tiny frame depot with a fixed signal hanging above the door and a weather-beaten sign with the name 'Alpine Tunnel' perched across the pinnacle of the roof. A two-story frame lodging house, the ruins of a hand-hewn stone engine house, with a wooden water tank in one corner, and the crumbling remains of what was to have been an ambitious granite hotel are also there."

Since Mr. Lathrop penned the above words, the elements, with the assistance of mankind, have heaped further depredation and ruin on this famous old South Park station. Mining interests in the vicinity have pulled up many of the rails, while other persons have carried away the Alpine Tunnel sign and the old fixed signal. Today, Alpine Tunnel station is a picture of loneliness and desolation, but not so in the spring of 1882.

While the Rio Grande had been basking in the sunlight of success as a result of their winning the race across the range, the South Park's contractors had been patiently at work boring their tunnel under Alpine Pass. As previously mentioned, all grading and bridge work

between the west portal and Gunnison had been completed before work was suspended the previous fall. Meanwhile, the tunnel had been completed during the winter and the end-of-track extended to within 200 feet of the west portal. Consequently, as soon as the spring of 1882 rolled around, with its more favorable weather, activity was again resumed upon the pass. The Union Pacific was very anxious to get rail laid, station facilities established, and other miscellaneous construction work started without further delay in order that the line to Gunnison might be completed as quickly as possible. Concerning news of their efforts to resume work, we read in the Pitkin Mining News of April 14, 1882, the following:

"Mr. Fred Mack, who was local engineer of the Denver & South Park Railroad at Pitkin last season, but who has been at Fairplay in the interest of that road for the last two months, returned to Pitkin Tuesday evening and on Wednesday, a reporter for the News cornered him with the intention of pumping some reliable news out of him relative to the building of the South Park to Pitkin. What a railroad man knows, and what he will tell you, are two different things. Generally, a fellow after pumping one of these dignitaries for two or three hours, and blowing in two or three dollars for 'tea', knows little more than when he commenced the interview. But we got enough from Mr. Mack to lend encouragement to our citizens in their wishes for a railroad. He told the reporter that he knew positively that work upon the road between the tunnel and Pitkin would commence between now and the first of May, and probably by the last of next week. It was his opinion that after work was resumed it would not take longer than three or four weeks to lay the track to Pitkin, as enough iron is on the Hancock side of the range to lay the track a few miles below this camp, and that it was the intention of the management to build on to Gunnison as soon as the iron could be obtained. The drawback to the prosecution of the work at this time is the heavy snow upon the east side of the range. The rail and ties are buried very deep, and the company, he said, desired to be sure no more snow would fall before they commenced shoveling out the track. The tunnel is more than 1,800 feet in length and the track is now laid to within 200 feet of this end, making the distance of laying track to Pitkin only about 13 miles. We can rest assured that the road will reach Pitkin by the 25th of May at the outside and then business will be very lively."

One of the first stations to be established on the pass was just beyond the west portal. This was the only location along the line in the vicinity of the tunnel suitable for constructing any station facilities. In fact, it was the only site between Hancock and Quartz Creek Valley where the right of way was wide enough to set anything but a telegraph pole. In view of this, a station was located slightly over a quarter of a mile beyond the west portal. At the time the railroad was building up Chalk Creek, a small station some five miles below St. Elmo had been given the name "Alpine", and in order to eliminate confusion between that station and the tunnel, the name was changed to "Fisher" and the west portal station was given the name "Alpine Tunnel".

Due to the severe winters on the pass, the buildings were constructed of stone. Old Union Pacific records disclose that the engine house was 54 feet wide and 153 feet long. Inside this structure a large coal bin and a 9,516 gallon wooden water tank were built. The coal bin was 14x40 feet, large enough to hold a good supply of coal. The water tank, located in the west end of the engine house, was supplied by a spring located up on the side of the mountain. This spring water, which the Union Pacific records state was of excellent quality, was fed by gravity through 640 feet of four-inch pipe. How such a long pipe was kept from freezing solid throughout the long winter months is not known. In addition to the engine house, the construction crew built a bunk house 14x16½ feet, a store house 10x18 feet, and a section house 29½x56 feet with a 16x25½ foot addition. These last two structures, containing ten rooms, consisted of a dining room, sleeping quarters, and station facilities for the agent, the tunnel watchman, and other employees. The telegraph office at Alpine Tunnel station was not opened until February 20, 1883.

Many a train crew found protection at this station from the howling blizzards as they spread their fury over the range. William Wendell, an old time South Park engineman, told the author that in the early days shortly after the road was built, the management had a colored cook at Alpine Tunnel station. She was around forty years old, weighed well over 200 pounds, and was an A-1 cook. Wendell added that he had enjoyed many a nice hot meal at Alpine Tunnel station.

Later on, shortly after the turn of the century, the Colorado & Southern built a two-story frame boarding house beside the telegraph office across the tracks. Today, this old frame building leans like the Tower of Pisa; some invisible hand of the past must be holding it up, for, at last reports, it was still standing, having defied the blizzards, the wind, and the rain for some forty years. In the early days there was approximately 660 feet of side track at the station. Later on, this was increased to approximately 1,350 feet of track.

It is not known on exactly what date track laying was begun at the tunnel. The Gunnison Review of April 15, 1882, stated that track laying began that day. On the other hand, the Pitkin Mining News published the following lengthy news item under date of May 5, 1882.

"A force of 30 men and three locomotives and a snow plow were set to work on the Denver South Park & Pacific Railroad last Monday the 1st, at Alpine Tunnel above Hancock, clearing the track of snow and uncovering the ties and rails. Mr. Scott Dickinson, who was a contractor in building the road last season, was present at the commencement of the work. He told our reporter that the greatest difficulty encountered was in reaching the tunnel from Hancock, a distance of between three and four miles. The snow on that side of the range is still deep, and has melted sufficiently to form a layer of ice on the rails, making it almost impossible to move the engines over the track. Consequently, the progress of work will be very much retarded until the tunnel is reached. No difficulty of any consequence will be encountered on this side of the tunnel, as the snow has almost disappeared.

"The company has put as many men to work as can be ac-commodated, until the boarding train, which is partially under snow, can be reached, then the force will be increased. T. J. Reed received a telegram Wednesday, to send over 15 men for work on the tunnel. Mr. Dickinson says it is the intention of the Superintendent to put an extra large number of men at work next Tuesday and it is thought the force will then number about 100 men.

"It is known that the railroad will be completed to Pitkin early in June. On Tuesday evening the 2nd, Mr. D. Morgan, the watertank contractor, came into Pitkin with three teams and eleven men and struck camp at the junction of State and Third Streets, where the tank is to be erected. Work will commence at once."

Each passing day brought an improvement in the weather. After opening the line between Hancock and the tunnel, the company was able to bring in additional men and supplies. While the stone masons were making preparations to erect the various station buildings just beyond the west approach, the track laying gang was busily engaged in getting ties, spikes, and rail in place. Soon construction was well under way. On May 12th, the Pitkin Mining News again published a small article of interest which stated:

"Hand bills were scattered in and around Pitkin today, advertising for 300 more men to lay track from Alpine Tunnel to Elk Mountain. About 100 men are now employed at this job."

Steady progress was made and soon the ringing sound of the spike maul was echoing against the face of that mighty wall of granite, the Palisades. Gradually, the railhead advanced toward Sherrod Curve. Just beyond this great curve the original station of Woodstock was established. Woodstock will be long remembered in the minds of the old timers as the scene of a terrible snow slide, the full details of which will be related later in our story. Relative to the completion of the track to this station, we find the following news item in the Pitkin Independent of Saturday, June 3, 1882.

DENVER & SOUTH PARK RAILWAY RAPIDLY PUSHING WESTWARD

"Word was received yesterday from Engineer Barr that the construction train would be in Woodstock tonight. Considerable of the work done this week, has been on sidetracking at the tunnel, for convenience of construction. We learn that the bridge work this side of Woodstock can all be completed in five days, and as the grade is all complete and part of the ties laid, the nine miles to Pitkin can be laid in a couple of weeks."

And in the Gunnison Daily Review of June 12th, we read:

"The Gunnison extension of the Denver & South Park Railway is making good progress, considering the great amount of snow with which the track layers have had to contend on either side of the Alpine Tunnel, which is located near timberline. The rails are now laid below Woodstock about four miles west of the tunnel and about nine miles east of Pitkin, which point will be reached about the 25th instant. Better headway may be expected after leaving Pitkin, and Gunnison City will doubtless enjoy the advantages to be derived from railway competition by the first of August next.

"We learn from a gentleman recently arrived from Tin Cup, that the South Park road is expected to reach Pitkin on the 15th—which we do not believe."

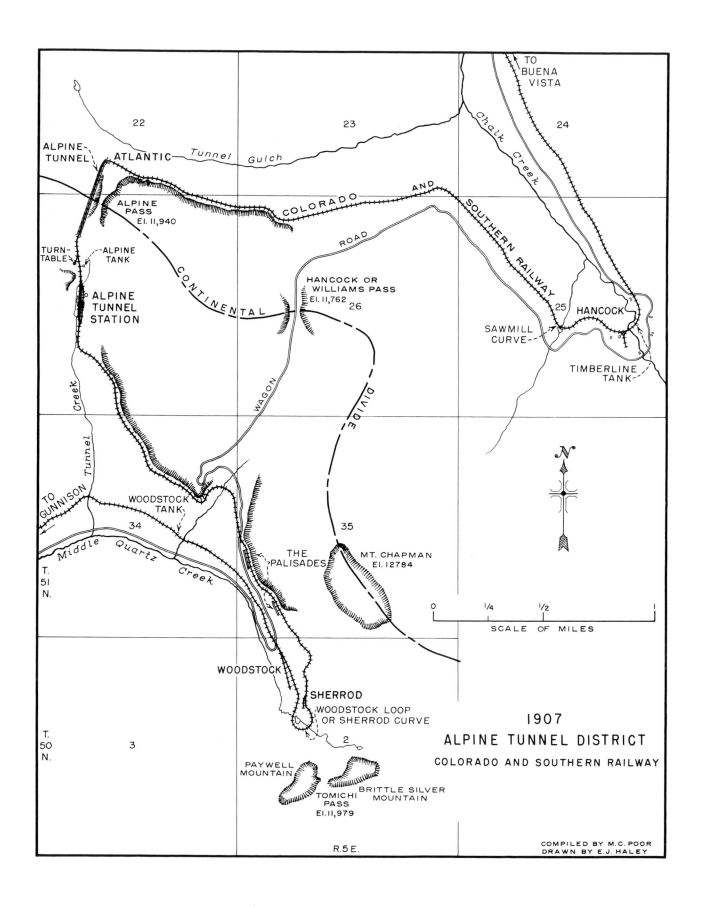

22

23

24

TO
BUENA
VISTA

ALPINE
TUNNEL
ATLANTIC

Tunnel Gulch

Chalk Creek

ALPINE
PASS
El. 11,940

COLORADO AND

SOUTHERN RAILWAY

TURN-
TABLE
ALPINE
TANK

CONTINENTAL

ALPINE
TUNNEL
STATION

HANCOCK OR
WILLIAMS PASS
El. 11,762 26

25 HANCOCK

ROAD

SAWMILL
CURVE

TIMBERLINE
TANK

WAGON

DIVIDE

Creek

N

TO
GUNNISON

Tunnel

WOODSTOCK
TANK

34

35

T.
51
N.

Middle Quartz Creek

THE
PALISADES

MT. CHAPMAN
El. 12784

0   1/4   1/2   1

SCALE OF MILES

WOODSTOCK

SHERROD
WOODSTOCK LOOP
OR SHERROD CURVE

2

1907
ALPINE TUNNEL DISTRICT

COLORADO AND SOUTHERN RAILWAY

T.
50
N.

3

PAYWELL
MOUNTAIN

TOMICHI
PASS
El. 11,979

BRITTLE SILVER
MOUNTAIN

R. 5 E.

COMPILED BY M.C. POOR
DRAWN BY E.J. HALEY

NIGHT TRAIN TO GUNNISON

Up the canyon of Chalk Creek, so lonely and white
The little train to Gunnison climbs through the night
The Mason Bogie barks as the grade grows steeper
For she's trailing a combo, a coach, and a sleeper

As I ride, cozy and snug, in a lower berth
My mind's filled with thoughts of home and of "Peace on Earth"
'Tis the night before Christmas and I'm on my way
Back home to Gunnison to spend that happy day

Pullman windows present an ever-changing view
And an occasional glimpse of the Bogie too
When the firebox is opened, there's a bright red glow
And squares of yellow coach light flicker 'cross the snow

The Bogie noisily struggles to hoist her train
Along Tunnel Gulch's bleak and rocky terrain
Her Congdon stack gushing a bituminous plume
Boiling upward to blot out the pale winter moon

A warning shriek from the whistle, a muffled roar
Our little train plunges into Alpine's black bore
Coach lights illuminate tunnel sides slipping by
'Cross the Divide, then out under the starlit sky

One long blast announces Alpine Station's ahead
Though I can't see it I know the order board's red
For the Bogie's stack is mute and the brake shoes growl
While round the snow laden depot the cold winds howl

Down Tunnel Creek, along the Palisades great wall
Around Sherrod's sharp curve, on through Woodstock we crawl
Down Quartz Canyon we drift, with the night almost gone
Along Tomichi's broad valley we race the dawn

To Gunnison at last, and so my journey ends
As I step to the platform 'midst fam'ly and friends
Down the years to you, old friend, I send at long last
This hearty Christmas greeting from out of the past

E. J. Haley
1959

A cold winter wind blows out of the west, and the full moon illuminates Alpine Pass in this mid-1880's scene. The night Pullman train for Gunnison, with oil head lamp and red markers aglow (at this time red markers on the front of the engine indicated a following section), pulls away from Alpine Tunnel station with the yellow squares from its coach windows flickering across the uneven surface of the snow. With quickening exhausts a Mason bogie, Denver South Park & Pacific 58, formerly the 14, named "Twin Lakes," passes the engine house as D.S.P.&P. 194, a Baldwin Consolidation, and the 53, another Mason bogie, enter after helping an eastbound freight from Pitkin to Alpine Tunnel.

Painting by Philip Ronfor
"Night Train to Gunnison"

Following this, we then read in the Pitkin Mining News of June 23rd:

"TRAINS TO WOODSTOCK

"Trains on the Denver & South Park were to have commenced running to Woodstock, nine miles above Pitkin on this side of the range, on Tuesday the 20th, but owing to a heavy land slide that occurred at the other end of the tunnel, the first regular train did not get through until Wednesday. However, regular trains are now running to Woodstock, arriving there at 10:45 am, and returning at 2:00 o'clock pm. Darrell & Watson are running a regular conveyance to and from the train. The track layers are less than seven miles from Pitkin. Trains will be running here in two weeks at the outside."

Thus, the end-of-track gradually advanced down grade from Woodstock and it was not many days before the shrill whistle of engine 57, a Baldwin consolidation which was being used as construction engine at this time, was heard in Quartz Creek Valley.

Valley Spur, Midway Tank, Quartz, and finally Pitkin, celebrated the arrival of the South Park railroad. On Wednesday, July 12, 1882, the first train, a special carrying a large number of company officials and their guests, arrived in Pitkin, drawn by engine 10. The special train had a wreck near Midway Tank, in which several members of the party were slightly injured. We are greatly indebted to Mr. H. L. Curtiss of Paonia, Colorado, for the story of this eventful occasion. Mr. Curtiss' story is as follows:

"The first train to arrive in Pitkin was a special pulled by engine 10, the 'Granite', with Ed Granger, engineer, and George Bernard, fireman. The train consisted of one sleeping coach carrying about twenty South Park officials and their wives on a tour of inspection. The special had left Alpine Tunnel station with engine 11, the 'Ouray'. It seems the train got out of control near Midway Tank. The engineer applied the brakes (they were vacuum brakes) but something went wrong. In some manner the sleeping car broke loose from the engine. A number of the passengers, in attempting to jump off the car while it was traveling at a fairly good rate of speed, were injured. Among those hurt was the South Park's Chief Engineer, Mr. L. H. Eicholtz, who had an arm and leg broken, which necessitated in his being under the care of a Pitkin doctor for several days. Other officials who were on the trip included C. W. Fisher, Sidney Dillon, a Mr. Armstrong and Mr. Canfield. Due to some trouble with her vacuum pump, No. 11 was set out at Quartz and No. 10 which was working with the construction gang was brought up to take the special on into Pitkin."

Mr. Curtiss' story is confirmed by a similar report of the wreck which was published in the Gunnison Review of July 21, 1882. Details and comments on the arrival of the first regular passenger train in Pitkin are found in the same paper under date of July 14th, as follows:

"PITKIN JUBILANT
"ARRIVAL OF THE DENVER SOUTH PARK & PACIFIC RAILWAY
"GREAT ENTHUSIASM THROUGHOUT THE CAMP

"Special correspondence of the Review.

"Pitkin, July 13th. Yesterday was a day long to be remembered by the citizens of Pitkin, on account of the arrival of the railroad. After waiting patiently, two years for the event, outsiders cannot blame us much for manifesting our enthusiasm in a pretty demonstrative way. Night before last the track was laid within half a mile of the city limits, and one mile of the depot grounds. About 3 o'clock, p.m., some 150 workmen, together with the construction train, arrived at the grounds between 6th and 7th streets on State Street, where they were met and welcomed by the citizens of Pitkin. They fired giant powder, and a neat and appropriate welcoming speech was made by Honorable J. F. Drexilius, which was well received by all, after which the boys gave three rousing cheers for the Denver South Park & Pacific Railroad. But the surprise of the railroad men can better be imagined than discussed, when they were invited to partake of three or four barrels of beer and several boxes of cigars. All seemed to appreciate the hearty welcome they received.

"Today at 12:30 o'clock, the first passenger train of three or four coaches arrived, bringing the U. S. Mail, a party of excursionists, and William's Theatrical Troupe, who propose giving several entertainments here this week, including a Saturday afternoon matinee.

"It was amusing to witness the surprise of parties arriving, who, a year ago had never heard of Pitkin, to see what a neat and thriving little city we have here, and we cannot help feeling proud of ourselves to know and feel that we are a self-made camp, against the opposition of all our neighbors. We are steadily advancing on to success and making, for ourselves, a name which is being 'noised' abroad throughout the whole Union. With the permission of our neighboring cities we feel that we must rejoice a little.

"The railroad men are now putting in side-tracks, erecting a temporary office, and cleaning up. They will make their way toward the setting sun and Gunnison City."

Regular train service was established as far as Pitkin on July 13th, and in connection with this, we find the following interesting item as published in the Pitkin Mining News of July 14th.

"Mr. E. Wilbur, Road Master; W. G. Self, Auditor of the Union Pacific; Addison Jones, General Agent; W. Griffiths, Sup't. of the Pacific Express Company; and F. W. Juneman, Agent; all arrived in Pitkin on the first regular train on July 13, 1882. The railroad reached the townsite of Pitkin about noon on July 12th, and reached the depot at 3:30 P.M. Most of the population turned out to greet the iron horse, several hundred people being on the ground. Kegs of beer and boxes of cigars were set out, these being furnished by Mayor Williams, and other prominent citizens. Regular trains will hereafter reach Pitkin at 12:05 P.M. and depart at 2:00 P.M."

Leaving Pitkin, the railhead advanced quite rapidly. Soon the citizens of Ohio City were watching the black smoke curl from the big balloon stack of No. 57 and roll back into the Tomichi hills. On August 19th, the

Three views of trains in the vicinity of the Palisades on Alpine Pass are shown on this page. The upper photo shows D.S.P.&P. 51 on an eastbound freight. At the lower left another balloon-stacked engine heads a westbound freight. The lower right picture shows South Park 39 with an eastbound passenger train.

rumble of a South Park train was heard in Parlin, milepost 189.8. Only the home stretch now remained—twelve miles to Gunnison, and track was being laid at the rate of one mile per day. One can almost hear the clear ring of their spike mauls as those experienced tracklayers build up a mighty crescendo, driving spikes into the cedar ties. On August 29th, the Gunnison Review-Press reported that the rails were laid to within four miles of the city. Soon the shining steel would glisten along San Juan Avenue. On Friday, September 1st, as the rails approached the city limits, this paper sent a news reporter out to the scene of construction to get a story. His findings, published that day, read as follows:

"A Review-Press representative visited the Denver & South Park railway this morning about 10 o'clock, and for half an hour, watched the lively work of track laying. A force of fully 150 men is employed in stringing the ties, laying the track, and such other work as is necessary for rapid track laying. The rails put down are 30 feet long, and the time of spiking down a rail was just a minute and a half, or 1,200 feet of rails per hour. . ."

Although the track had only reached the city limits, the officials evidently felt that there was little time to waste and made preparations at once for the inauguration of passenger service. Note the following interesting announcement as carried in the same issue of this paper:

"A special morning excursion train for Denver, will leave Gunnison over the Denver & South Park road on Sunday morning at 6 o'clock. This excursion train will consist of six passenger coaches, three of them elegant Pullman day coaches. The crew will consist of Conductor F. W. Graham, Engineer George Ardell, Fireman Ben Biggery, and Brakemen A. Barney and C. L. Hanna. The representatives of the South Park say it will be the most elegantly equipped train of cars that ever crossed the Continental Divide. This special will give excursionists a complete day-light run from Gunnison to Denver, and will enable everyone who has not seen the magnificent scenery along the South Park line, to behold it all in day-light, from Quartz Creek to the end of Platte Canon.

"Between these points are Alpine Tunnel, the South Park, and Kenosha Summit, with the towns of Ohio City, Pitkin, Hancock, St. Elmo, Alpine, Buena Vista, and Como. Breakfast in Gunnison, dinner at Como, and supper in Denver, over the best line of railroad in Colorado. Another train will leave Gunnison on this line at 2:00 o'clock Sunday afternoon, Sept. 3rd, and will arrive in Denver on the following day at 7:00 o'clock. Excursionists can also ride, at the same rate of fare, on this train. Pullman day coaches on the morning train without extra charge, and excellent accommodations on all other trains. Fare $11.50 for the round trip, with one admission to the Exposition, and good for 7 days. Tickets will be on sale in Gunnison, by Mr. Henry Ames, Agent."

A later article stated that the "day-light special" left Gunnison at 6:15 a.m. and arrived in Denver at 8:00 p.m. with 206 passengers.

In the meantime, the contractors continued with their tracklaying west, along San Juan Avenue. Through the kindness of Mr. George A. Root, of the Kansas State Historical Society, the author is able to present a series of newspaper items covering the arrival of the South Park in Gunnison, and the celebration that followed on September 5th. Mr. Root writes: "I well recollect the celebration, for as a kid a little over 15, I was 'thar' and saw the whole affair." Mr. Root possesses a large file of the Gunnison Review-Press, which he inherited from his father, who published the paper. These news items, which are considerably more interesting than mere statements covering the South Park's arrival, are as follows:

September 1, 1882.

"During all the weary months the people of Gunnison were waiting for the coming of the South Park road, the Review-Press cheered their drooping spirits by repeatedly assuring them that the road would be built to Gunnison. It therefore, affords us all the more pleasure to be the first to announce that the road is completed, today, to Gunnison, and a second iron band unites this city with Denver and the East."

September 2, 1882.

"The Denver & South Park reached the Denver & Rio Grande's track between Spruce and 14th Street at noon today."

September 4, 1882.

"Mr. Henry Ames, the South Park Agent, informs us that their road will have a switch put in tomorrow, so that regular trains and the construction cars can pass. The water tank will also be in condition to take water from it by tomorrow morning. The ticket office is now in the basement of the Tabor House, but Mr. Ames thinks he will be in his new quarters at the depot by Sunday. Regular trains will also probably be running by that time. The frogs at the crossing of the Crested Butte branch of the Denver & Rio Grande road were put in by the South Park construction gang today. It is expected that regular passenger trains will be run to the South Park depot by Wednesday."

September 5, 1882.

"Henry Ames, Agent for the South Park road, will move into his new quarters in the passenger depot on Ninth Street this evening. Tomorrow, trains will leave from the depot instead of from Main Street. The work of putting up the Water Tank will be completed today. Work is also progressing on the Turntable."

September 6, 1882.

"The South Park ticket office was removed from the Tabor House Basement to the depot on Ninth Street last evening. The office will soon be fitted up in excellent style, and will be presided over by Henry Ames, Ticket Agent, assisted by D. D. McLaughlin, Telegraph Operator."

This September 6th issue also included a long and most interesting editorial in honor of the celebration which was held on the evening of the 5th. It is as follows:

Looking downgrade at Pitkin during the winter of 1903.

Colorado & Southern 71, ex-U.P.D.& G. 9, at Pitkin in 1903. Note the C.& S. monogram on the cab.

"THE JOLLIFICATION

"A Rousing Reception Tendered the South Park Railroad Men

"Quite extensive preparations had been made yesterday for the reception tendered the South Park railroad men. The scheme was inaugurated by residents of the West end though participated in by citizens of the entire city, to property owners west of the Boulevard belong the credit of making the affair a success.

"During the day Ed Hoel and Richard Morrison took up a collection to defray expenses, meeting with a liberal response from the people. With the money they purchased a generous supply of cigars, beer, and powder. The buildings in the neighborhood were draped in flags. A rope was stretched across New York Avenue on which floated the stars and stripes. Early in the evening a bonfire was built in the middle of the street, and in a short time had attracted a large crowd to the vicinity. Hoel and Morrison erected a temporary bar on the north side at which they dispensed free beer and cigars to all hands, and did a rushing business all evening. A platform was built in front of Parson and Pancake's for the speakers, while their office was used as a waiting room. A couple of anvils were brought down and an attempt made to 'wake the echoes', but it was sometime before the echoes would wake. There appeared to be something wrong either with the powder or those who attempted to fire it, for the first forty or fifty trials resulted in total failures. Giant powder was next secured, and with this, reports loud enough for the purpose, announced to the city that the celebration had opened in earnest.

"Captain C. T. Russell, with the members of Hose Company number 2, appeared in full uniform, and had their hose cart handsomely decorated.

"A little before nine o'clock, Hon. Alexander Gullett ascended the speaker's stand, and after securing the attention of the crowd, introduced Col. J. H. Phillips. Mr. Phillips spoke for some time, complimenting the people upon having at last secured a second railroad. 'I am a grasshopper', said he, 'and I am proud of it. Colorado owes much to Kansas; but I'm prouder tonight of this city among the hills; proud of our new railroad'. The speaker then went on to state how only a few years since it was deemed impossible to build railroads through these mountains, but tonight we are here to celebrate the second iron band that unites Gunnison with the eastern world. 'One railroad is a good thing; but two railroads are better. The one holds the other in check . . .' (Part of the next three or four lines of the newspaper mutilated.) 'Thus the people who have grumbled at the high freights they have had to pay over the Denver & Rio Grande, will now find that a second railroad is completed and that there will be competition between the two, and freights will come down. In this manner a railroad corporation benefits everyone'. Mr. Phillips

closed by proposing three cheers for the South Park road, which were responded to with enthusiasm.

"Aaron Heims was announced as the next speaker. Mr. Heims congratulated the people upon having secured a second railroad. It would not become him, he said, to speak in terms of laudation of the Denver South Park & Pacific Railroad Company, for the reason that he was connected in a legal way with the company.

"Judge Morgan was called for and made a few remarks. His health was such as would not permit him to make an open air speech. He joined with every other citizen who had the welfare of Gunnison at heart in welcoming the new road.

"Col. Ford was loudly called for, and came upon the stand. He had been to Leadville, where everybody had a bad cold and a sore throat; he was in the same condition, and hoped the audience would excuse him from attempting to address them.

"Mr. O. P. Abercrombie was the next speaker introduced. He particularly complimented the people upon having secured such good men to represent the South Park Company in this city. He was sure that as long as Henry Ames remained as the Gunnison Agent, our citizens would receive good treatment at his hands.

"Mr. Henry Ames was called for, and made a short speech, thanking the people for their hearty reception of the road, and promising them that he would do everything in his power to retain the affections of the citizens of Gunnison for the new enterprise.

"None of the other speakers being present, Hon. Alex. Gullett took the stand. His address was principally noted for the number of anecdotes he told. Said he, 'Do you know how it came to be discovered that railroads could be built across these mountains? No? Well, I will tell you. A party of eminent engineers had met in council, and they were discussing the problems of crossing the mountains. One man said the curves could not be made so that engines could safely climb around and over the hills. Another said it could; and one said this thing and another said that; but no one seemed to know just how the feat was to be accomplished. There was, however, a man sitting in one of the front seats who was slightly, what they call in the east, tipsy— ('full' suggested a voice in the audience)—yes, 'full'; and while these eminent engineers were earnestly discussing the subject in hand, this fellow who was 'full', suddenly spoke up: 'Sot 'em up! Sot 'em up!' This was the whole secret, and a sharp engineer caught onto the idea, and hence by setting one rail higher than the other, a railroad can be made absolutely safe on the sharpest curves.'

"Mr. Gullett's remarks were greeted with prolonged cheers, and then he announced that there would be a recess of ten minutes while the boys across the street would proceed to set 'em up.

"After recess Mayor Moses, who had put in an ap-

*W. H. Jackson photo,
from E. J. Haley Collection.*

The west side of the Denver Union Station about 1881. Note the large amount of narrow gauge trackage.

Richard B. Jackson.

The South Park's stone depot at Gunnison in 1939. The white stone pillars at the right once framed the doorways of the roundhouse.

pearance, was called to the stand. Mr. Moses' speech was the shortest of the evening, but directly to the point. Said he, 'Boys, I'm not much of a speech maker but if you'll follow me I'll set 'em up'!

"Three cheers were given for the Mayor, and the entire crowd followed Mr. Moses into the nearest refreshment stand where the lady behind the bar was kept busy for nearly an hour handing out cigars and drawing beer for the thirsty multitude.

"While in the saloon, Judge Karr was discovered in the crowd and immediately a speech was called for. The Judge mounted one of the card tables and made a short but very witty speech, which was enthusiastically cheered.

"The bonfires were then put out and all hands retired to their homes well pleased with the evening's celebration".

Another old timer from the early west who witnessed Gunnison's South Park celebration was Mr. William B. Thom. Mr. Thom's version of what happened on that memoriable occasion, and which was published in Railroad Magazine, is as follows:

"The town was wide open that night. Hundreds of boxes were piled up in the middle of New York Avenue, near the railroad, and set afire. On either side of the roaring flames were long rows of beer kegs, all inviting the thirsty—and believe me, there were plenty who acted as though their throats were in need of the freely flowing beer. The Mayor was one of the most noted celebrators. I can still see him mounted on a poker table in the midst of the throng, haranguing the multitude. It was a great day for Gunnison, when the first South Park train entered the town."

With both the South Park and the Rio Grande making Gunnison a sort of Division headquarters, the place very soon developed into quite a railroad town. In entering Gunnison, the South Park's right of way ran along San Juan Avenue west to Ninth Street where it divided and formed a large wye. This wye with its three legs formed the heart of the South Park's Gunnison yards. In the center of this wye they built a 50-foot, hand operated turntable, and a six stall roundhouse. The roundhouse faced south and a little west. It was built of stone and was 127½ feet wide and 65 feet long. At last report the large keystone, or marker, with the date 1882 carved in it, was still laying on the ground near the site of the roundhouse. In all probability it is too heavy to carry off, or some enterprising collector would have had it long ago. The little depot and telegraph office, located on the north leg of the wye on the line to Baldwin, was built about 500 feet northwest of the roundhouse, at the corner of Ninth and New York Streets. It was of stone construction, 38 feet long and 20 feet wide, and contained a ticket and telegraph office, waiting room and baggage room. Construction of both the roundhouse and the depot was started during 1881, and they were completed by the time the rails reached the city. According to the Gunnison Review

of May 29, 1880, the contract for the construction of the depot was let at this early date. The South Park's telegraph line, which followed the right of way the entire distance between Denver and Gunnison, was completed to the latter point on October 22, 1880.[1]

Other buildings and facilities consisted of the usual miscellaneous assortment such as pump house, well, 47,500 gallon wood water tank, stock pens, coal bins, sand house, tool shed, freight house, scales, rip track, etc. The interchange, or connecting track with the Rio Grande was near 14th and San Juan, a block south and east of the La Veta Hotel. The stone roundhouse and the turntable have long since disappeared; nothing remains except the foundation wall and the pit. To an old timer or a good South Park fan, the scene west of Ninth Street today is a sorrowful and forlorn picture indeed. About the only thing left is the little stone depot at the north end of the yards; in fact, a family was living in it at last report.

Although Gunnison was the major objective point for the moment, it was not proposed to allow the city to remain as the end-of-track. The first amendment tacked on to the South Park's original Articles of Association back in August, 1879, which directed the road to build toward Gunnison, was not the end. Gould had some ambitious plans laid out for our little railroad. These plans not only included proposed lines to be extended in a southwesterly and also a northerly direction from the new silver camp, but incorporated other projected railroad lines in the Colorado region, the discussion of which will come later. These proposals were all contained in two additional amendments. The second amendment was filed with the Secretary of State on February 10, 1880, and is as follows:

"Right to construct, maintain and operate the following described branches and extensions, to be designated as the Utah and Arizona Extensions.

"Extending the said Railroad from the most eligible and feasible point on the Ouray Extension of said Railroad in the Uncompahgre Valley and thence by the most eligible and feasible route by the way of the waters of the San Miguel River and the Dolores River, thence to a point on the Western Boundary Line or the Southern Boundary Line of the State of Colorado, and within a distance of twenty miles from the southwestern corner of said State, this extension to be designated as the Arizona Extension of said Railroad.

"Also to extend the said Railroad from the terminus of the Branch of said Railroad which runs up Ohio Creek to the Elk Mountain Coal Fields, thence by the most feasible route down the North Fork of the Gunnison River to the Grand River, and thence by the most eligible and feasible route to the Western Boundary Line of the State of Colorado, with a branch on the most feasible point on the line of said Railroad and down the

1. Rocky Mountain News, October 23, 1880.

231

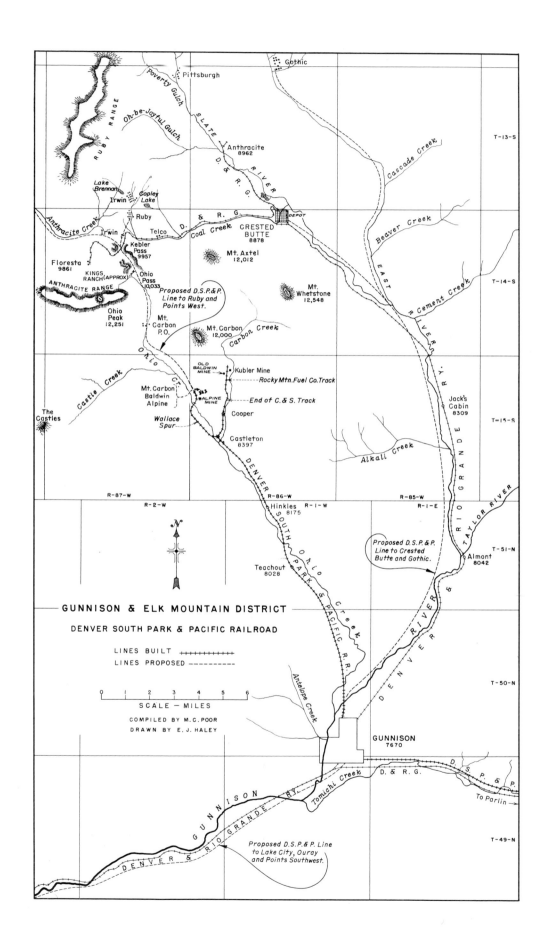

Gothic
Pittsburgh
Poverty Gulch
Oh-be-Joyful Gulch
RUBY RANGE
SLATE
D. & R. G.
RIVER
Cascade Creek
T-13-S
Anthracite 8962
Lake Brennan
Copley Lake
Irwin
Ruby
Telco
Irwin
Anthracite Creek
D. & R. G.
Coal Creek
CRESTED BUTTE 8878
DEPOT
Beaver Creek
EAST
RIVER
Cement Creek
T-14-S
Kebler Pass 9957
Floresta 9861
KINGS RANCH (APPROX)
Ohio Pass 10,033
ANTHRACITE RANGE
Ohio Peak 12,251
Mt. Carbon P.O.
Mt. Axtel 12,012
Mt. Whetstone 12,548
Proposed D.S.P.&P. Line to Ruby and Points West.
Mt. Carbon 12,000
Carbon Creek
Ohio
Ct.
Castle Creek
OLD BALDWIN MINE
Kubler Mine
Rocky Mtn. Fuel Co. Track
Mt. Carbon Baldwin Alpine
ALPINE MINE
End of C. & S. Track
Cooper
Wallace Spur
Castleton 8397
The Castles
Jack's Cabin 8309
T-15-S
Alkali Creek
DENVER
RIO GRANDE
RY.
R-87-W
R-2-W
R-86-W
R-1-W
R-85-W
R-1-E
Hinkles 8175
SOUTH PARK & PACIFIC R.R.
Ohio Creek
Proposed D.S.P.&P. Line to Crested Butte and Gothic.
TAYLOR RIVER
Almont 8042
T-51-N
N
Teachout 8028
GUNNISON & ELK MOUNTAIN DISTRICT
DENVER SOUTH PARK & PACIFIC RAILROAD
LINES BUILT ++++++++++++
LINES PROPOSED - - - - - - -
0 1 2 3 4 5 6
SCALE — MILES
COMPILED BY M.C. POOR
DRAWN BY E.J. HALEY
Antelope Creek
DENVER RIVER &
T-50-N
GUNNISON 7670
D. & R. G.
D.S.P.& P.
To Parlin
T-49-N
GUNNISON
DENVER & RIO GRANDE RY.
Tomichi Creek
Proposed D.S.P.&P. Line to Lake City, Ouray and Points Southwest.

Roaring Fork of the Grand River, this Extension and Branch or Branches of said Railroad to be designated as the Utah Extension of said Railroad.

"Also to construct, etc., Branches to coal and other mines.

"Capitalization increased to $5,000,000."

The third amendment was filed with the Secretary of State on September 20, 1880, and is as follows:

"To construct . . . Broad or narrow gauge lines of Road from any eligible point or points on the line or lines or branches of said Railroad, or from Denver to Colorado Springs, Pueblo, Canon City, Silver Cliff, and Rosita in the several Counties of Arapahoe, Jefferson, Douglas, Park, El Paso, Pueblo, Fremont, and Custer, to connect the lines of said Railroad and branches with the main line or other branches of said Railroad of the said Company;

"Also a branch of said Road from a point on the Tomichi River up, along and near to Cochetopa Creek by the most eligible route in the Counties of Gunnison and Saguache to the Town of Saguache, also a branch from the line of the said Road on Ohio Creek by the most eligible route to Crested Butte in Gunnison County; also to extend the Dudley branch of said Railroad (provided for in said original Articles of Association) by way of the 'Hoosier Pass' to the Town of Breckenridge, through the Counties of Park and Summit, all in the State of Colorado.

"Capitalization to be increased from $5,000,000 to $20,000,000."

Relative to the various projected lines as included in the second amendment, the Denver Daily Times of March 18, 1880, carried an interesting news item from which we quote in part:

"SOUTH PARK PLANS

". . . At Gunnison City the line branches. The Utah extension will follow up Ohio Creek, thence to Anthracite Creek, thence down Anthracite Creek to the North Fork of the Gunnison, down the North Fork to the main Gunnison River, and thence by way of the Grand River to the State line.

"The other branch from Gunnison City will run down the Gunnison to the Grand Canon of the Gunnison, where it crosses the river and passes in a southwesterly direction via the Uncompahgre River to the State line. The Lake City branch leaves this line just before reaching the Lake Fork of the Gunnison and runs up this Fork to Lake City. The Ouray branch runs up the Uncompahgre to Ouray.

"Exact data as to grades, distances, dates of completion, and times of letting grading contracts, cannot yet be given by the company, but the completion of these extensions will be pushed as fast as money and muscle will permit. The company is fully alive to the advantages to be gained by the early completion and opening to traffic of their various lines, and fully realize the vast

resources, the immense trade, and the quickening influence of railways upon industrial development—all of which will be assured by the speedy completion of their lines. To Denver, as well as to the great valley of the Gunnison and its tributaries, these lines, running as they do, like a spider's web across the western slope, are of special importance. Their completion will give to our merchants a wholesale trade limited only by the possibilities of the Gunnison valley for growth and improvement. The prediction of Governor Evans will be fulfilled. The South Park road will open to Denver a new empire, whose resources, industries, and commercial importance will add untold wealth to Colorado, and new glories to its chief city—Denver."

However, the most important project to be considered at this time was the "Utah", or the Ohio Creek extension which was to include the newly discovered Elk Mountain coal fields. Among others who were attracted by the discovery of these rich bituminous coal deposits, especially in the vicinity of Mt. Carbon and Crested Butte, and who foresaw that a lucrative revenue was to be had in the transportation of this coal, was one Captain Luden (sometimes spelled Louden) Mullin of Gunnison. Accordingly, on November 17, 1877, Captain Mullin and two other Gunnison citizens organized the Mt. Carbon Gunnison & Lake City Railroad & Coal Company.[1] Their plans called for the construction of a railroad from the vicinity of Mt. Carbon, south through Gunnison to Lake City in Hinsdale County. Captain Mullin's company owned certain properties and rights but had not entered into any actual construction.

It seems that some of the rights and properties possessed by Captain Mullin's company in and near Gunnison were desired by the South Park, especially the location wanted for the Gunnison depot and for the right of way up Ohio Creek. Negotiations were entered into between the two interests, with the result that the South Park purchased outright all the stock, rights, privileges, and the franchise of the Mt. Carbon company for $1,000.[2] The deed conveying the property to the South Park was dated March 9, 1881, and recorded in Gunnison County the following July 18th. The South Park was now in a position to construct their Ohio Creek line to the Mt. Carbon coal fields without infringing upon the rights of any competitor.

The Rio Grande was also attracted by the discovery

1. Historical sources disagree both as to the name and date of organization of this company.

The U. S. I. C. C. Val. Docket No. 716 gives the date as Dec. 10, 1877, and the name as the Mt. C. G. & L. C. R. R. & Coal Transportation Co.

The C. & S. Corporate History states that the date was Nov. 21, 1877, and the name as the Mt. C. G. & L. C. R. R. & Telegraph Co.

The Colo. Ry. Comm. Report, 1885, gives the date as Nov. 17, 1877, and the name as the Mt. C. G. & L. C. R. R. & Coal Co.

2. Minutes of the South Park Board of Directors.

of these valuable coal deposits and upon the completion of their line into Gunnison in 1881, they built a branch line north into this region. The Rio Grande's line followed north along the Gunnison and Slate Rivers to Crested Butte, reaching that place in October, 1881. In 1882, they extended their line northwest to Anthracite, and in 1883, built west to Irwin and Floresta.

Although Major Evans had completed his survey and staked out the right of way for the Ohio Creek extension, completion of the line was slow. The first reference to any actual work on the line is found in the Gunnison Review of November 19, 1881, where it was stated that the work of grading the Ohio Creek line through to Ruby Camp was in progress. Later, in the January 14, 1882, issue of the same paper we read:

"Two hundred men are at work finishing the grading between Gunnison and Ruby. All grading is expected to be finished by spring."

Following this, we read in the Pitkin Mining News of January 27th:

"Mr. P. F. Barr, resident engineer of the South Park Railroad, arrived at the Tabor House in Gunnison last night. He will leave tomorrow to inspect the work between Gunnison and Ruby. A large force of men are employed on the grade above Kings.[1] Most of the grading between Gunnison and Irwin is all finished except three miles just this side of Ohio Creek Pass."

And then we read in the Gunnison Review of September 5th:

"Iron is being laid on the South Park railroad north of the depot."

The distance between Gunnison and the nearest coal fields in the vicinity of Mt. Carbon was only some 17 miles, yet for some reason, the Union Pacific chose to delay completion of the line. This was at the time when the Omaha management, being unfamiliar with the South Park's local economic problems, were instituting some of the measures that eventually proved so disastrous to the South Park, the details of which we shall discuss more fully later on. There are references that competition from rival roads threatened to force the Union Pacific to seek a new route to Salt Lake City. Just how much truth is contained in these statements, or what influence they had on the extension of the Ohio Creek line, is not known. Then, there is the statement in the Railway Age of September 14, 1882, to the effect that the Union Pacific might be forced to extend the South Park into the Elk Mountain district in search of coal. This can be easily understood; no doubt their need for coal was steadily growing due to the greatly increased growth of the Union Pacific system. This statement can be partially confirmed by the fact that in the years to follow, the Union Pacific hauled many a ton of coal out of the Mt. Carbon and Baldwin mines.

1. Colorado Magazine, January 1947, states that King's Ranch was located approximately three miles below Irwin. This would place it in the vicinity of Ohio Creek Pass.

Possibly another factor to be considered was that the Union Pacific, in view of the decline of the Gunnison boom, did not deem it necessary to spend any extra effort toward completing the line. Regardless of what the reason might have been, the Union Pacific evidently was not in any great rush to complete the 17 mile branch. We find a notice in the Railway Age of November 22, 1883, that the Ohio Creek line was finally extended as far as the Mt. Carbon mining district. The notice also carried an added statement that the Union Pacific would probably extend the line to the Irwin and Anthracite coal fields beyond. The word "probably" was very appropriate; the end-of-track was never advanced beyond the Baldwin Mine.

In an attempt to ascertain the correct location of the original South Park trackage, as well as early station sites and settlements in this particular district, the writer ran into many conflicting maps and statements. We do know that when the line was first built, a station was established at a point 14.7 miles north of Gunnison near the confluence of Ohio and Carbon Creeks which, according to old Union Pacific records, was known as Baldwin. Shortly afterward this station was given the name of Castleton. Early history tells us that one of the first coal mines worked in the Mt. Carbon field was the old Baldwin Mine, located near Carbon Creek, northeast of Castleton. Sometime later it seems that this property was abandoned and a new mine, known as the New Baldwin Mine, was opened up over on Ohio Creek. According to an early U. S. Geological Survey map, the railroad company originally built a track up Carbon Creek to a point about two miles northeast of Castleton to the old Baldwin Mine. This map also shows another line of track extending up Ohio Creek in the direction of a settlement called Mt. Carbon Post Office. As nearly as can be determined, the line up Carbon Creek did not last long and was abandoned, leaving only the Ohio Creek extension, which was built up that stream in 1883 for a distance of about 2.80 miles northwest of Castleton to serve the New Baldwin Mine. Over a period of years, the end-of-track seesawed back and forth for small distances as mining operations probably required. It seems that the line attained its maximum length in 1914, when the track was extended to a point 3.11 miles above Castleton. And as nearly as can be accurately determined, this was as far as the South Park railroad ever penetrated up Ohio Creek toward the Elk Mountain district.

Around 1895 the Rocky Mountain Fuel Company, headed by Frank Trumbull, opened up the Kubler Mine, on Carbon Creek about three miles north of Castleton. In order to serve the Kubler Mine properties, the South Park, in 1896, built 1.56 miles of new track up Carbon Creek. For some unknown reason, the intervening trackage between the South Park's end-of-track and the mine, a distance of approximately 1.79 miles, was constructed by the Rocky Mountain Fuel Company. Thereafter the Ohio Creek line was known as the Baldwin branch and the Carbon Creek track was known as the Kubler branch. The South Park continued the operation of both branches until 1911. At this time, they were taken over by the Rio Grande, the details of which will appear later on.

Before closing this chapter, mention should be made of the proposed Arizona and Utah extensions, as previously outlined in Amendment No. 2, neither of which ever advanced any farther than the paper they were written on. Relative to the Utah extension, the reader will recall that this projected line, which came to be known as the Ohio Creek line, was surveyed to a point known as Kebler Pass. This line was to extend on to the headwaters of Anthracite Creek in the Elk Mountain district and thence west by way of the Gunnison and Grand Rivers to the Colorado-Utah State line. For some unknown reason, probably because of the rough and mountainous terrain encountered north of Mt. Carbon, it was decided to abandon further plans of extending the Ohio Creek line beyond the terminus at Baldwin and search out a more favorable route to, and through, the Elk Mountain area and regions to the west, as provided for in Amendment No. 3.

Apparently a feasible route was supposed to have been located, for, in the minutes of a Board of Directors meeting, held on June 26, 1883, we find it was unanimously resolved that the new line to the Elk Mountains, as surveyed and mapped by Major Evans, be adopted as the location of the company's proposed extension to Crested Butte and Gothic. The new route, according to the survey, branched off the Ohio Creek line three miles north of Gunnison, and followed the Gunnison and Slate Rivers to Crested Butte, a distance of 26½ miles, paralleling the Rio Grande's Crested Butte line the entire distance. Just below the confluence of the East and Slate Rivers, a secondary projected route branched off north to Gothic, a distance of 13½ miles. In this connection, we read in the Railway Age, under date of May 24, 1883, the following announcement:

"The Crested Butte extension of the Union Pacific has been surveyed to that point and construction is to begin at once."

Both the Lake City section of the southwestern extension and the new Elk Mountain projects were surveyed by Major Evans, and the usual resolutions were adopted to build them; however, this is as far as either proposal ever advanced. They were never built.

GRADES AND CURVATURES ON THE ALPINE PASS ROUTE

Unfortunately, no large scale track chart and profile map covering the section of the South Park west of Buena Vista is known to exist. However, reference to the profile chart will give one a fairly accurate conception of the various curves and grades encountered. In travelling from Buena Vista south to Nathrop, a distance of some eight miles, the track dropped from an elevation of 7,952 feet to 7,710 feet, but after turning west up Chalk Creek Canon the track maintained a steady rate of climb all the way to the tunnel. West of Mt. Princeton this grade averaged 3.26% with a maximum of 4%.

On the eastbound line between Gunnison and Parlin, the maximum grade encountered was only 1.29%, and while the average grade between Parlin and Pitkin reached 1.63%, the grade from the latter point to the tunnel was a different story. Between these two stations the grade averaged over 3.46%, with a maximum of 4%. When one stops to consider that a grade of 3.46%, for example, indicates a rise of 3.46 feet for every hundred feet of track distance, it will be understood why three locomotives were required to drag a 12 or 15 car freight train over Alpine Pass.

That section of the line between Hancock and Quartz, with its great assortment of sharp curves and steep grades, plus the added attractions of Alpine Tunnel and the Palisades, constituted the most spectacular stretch of track on the entire South Park railroad. Beginning at Hancock, the track climbed from an altitude of 11,027 feet to the apex of the Alpine Tunnel at an elevation of 11,612 feet and then dropped down to Quartz, where the elevation was 9,649 feet. The air line distance between the two stations is six and one-half miles, but it required some 13.8 miles of track to connect the two points. This 13.8 miles of track, with its three and four per cent grades, included an assortment of eleven 20 degree curves, two 22 degree curves, nineteen 24 degree curves, and one 28 degree curve. The longest tangent in this entire section was an 1,800-foot stretch on the eastern slope about one mile below the east portal. The only other tangent of any appreciable length was an 800-foot section at Woodstock. The 28 degree curve just east of the Palisades and the great curve at Sherrod have already been mentioned. The most crooked section in this entire stretch was located just above Quartz. Here, in a distance of not more than a mile, was an assortment of reverse curves that resembled a serpent's tail.

It is interesting to note that a compilation of all grades and curves between Nathrop and Gunnison discloses the following:

Total mileage	65
Total miles of curvature	20.25
Per cent of curvature	31.15
Number of curves	373
Maximum curvature	28.00 degrees
Total degrees of curvature	10,294 degrees and .05 minutes
Number of complete circles	28.60
Maximum grade eastbound	4.00%
Maximum grade westbound	4.00%

A South Park freight headed downgrade below Woodstock, at the mouth of Tunnel Gulch. Note the white refrigerator cars; these were lettered "Tiffany Summer & Winter Car". A double headed freight train is shown on the upper level of track.

The Ohio Creek branch between Gunnison and Baldwin did not present any great construction problems. The maximum curvature encountered on this branch was 24½ degrees and the maximum grade was 2.50%, both of which were located beyond Castleton. Three miles north of Gunnison, this line crossed the Gunnison River on a 261-foot iron truss bridge.

The reader will remember that mention was made of the immense amount of rock cribbing which was required to support the right of way along the face of the mountain on the western slope of Alpine Pass. It is interesting to note that between Hancock and Quartz there was constructed a combined total of 4,127 feet of these rock wall cribs. The average length of the rock cribs, excluding the 452-foot Palisades wall and a 550-foot rock wall just beyond, was over 69 feet. These cribs varied in height, up to a maximum of 30 feet. Many South Park fans who have journeyed up to the east portal will probably be interested to learn that the long rock crib at this point was 189 feet in length. The right of way here was built to support a 489-foot passing track, known as Atlantic.

Quite often, the question as to the existence of snowsheds on the eastern and western slopes of Alpine Pass has been brought up. With the exception of the two previously mentioned sheds built at the east and west approaches of the tunnel, the writer has located conflicting evidence concerning snowsheds along this particular section of the road.

H. L. Curtiss, who lived in Pitkin at the time the road was built through there, states:

"There were one or two snowsheds located in the vicinity of the tunnel, but it was my understanding that when the railroad purchased their first rotary snow plow the snowshed was removed and the material transferred to the Leadville branch. A considerable quantity of timber and snowshed lumber that had been distributed along the right of way between the Palisades and Sherrod curve on the upper track level above Woodstock, preparatory to the construction of some sheds in that section, was swept away in the Woodstock snow slide that occurred in 1884."

Joe Plunkett, of Grand Junction, writes:

"There were some snowsheds on the pass but they were smashed by the slides."

William Cairns writes:

"There were some sheds located about one mile east of the tunnel. I went to work for the South Park in 1898, and they were all down then. I understood that the snow slides were more than the sheds could stand up under and that the company did not rebuild them."

Confirmation of what these gentlemen say is found in the following sources:

The Gunnison Review of January 6, 1883, carried this news item:

"The South Park Railroad is now pushing their snowsheds rapidly on the east side of the Range between Hancock and the tunnel. They are to build in all about a mile of new sheds."

The 1886 Official List of all Building and Structures, including snowsheds, does *not* list a single snowshed between Como and Gunnison. From some early engineering records found in the Denver office, we find the following notation:

"The snowshed at Alpine Hill was removed to Boreas in September, 1885."

In the Railway Review of August 20, 1887, we read:

"The South Park management is debating the installation of snowsheds on the Gunnison line in order to keep it open all winter."

In the Colorado & Southern's Annual Report for 1901, we read that $868.57 was spent on snowsheds on the Gunnison division. No explanation for this particular reference has ever been found.

Relative to the cost of the Denver-Gunnison line, the following engineering report and itemized statement, dated October 15, 1887, was found in the Pacific Railway Commission Case Report:

Right of way	$ 50,000
Grading, bridging and culverts	2,241,400
Ties	267,800
Main track, rails, etc.	788,000
Side track, rails, etc.	151,400
Tracklaying and surfacing	133,900
Fencing	10,000
Snow fences	25,000
Telegraph line	27,900
Buildings	111,600
Locomotives	223,100
Passenger and freight equipment	133,900
Tools, stationary power, etc.	44,700
Engineering and contingencies, 10%	420,870
The impact and adaption[1]	223,100
	$4,852,670

1. The writer is unable to explain the meaning of this item.

CHAPTER XIII

THE HIGH LINE TO LEADVILLE

The full and complete story of the details underlying the construction of the high line over Boreas Pass to Leadville is, by far, the most difficult part to write in the entire history of the South Park, but we shall do the best we can with the material available.

This particular chapter covering the antics of the Rio Grande and the Union Pacific over a five year period from 1880 to 1885 reminds one of the famous feud between the Hatfields and the McCoys. It has been stated that by 1880, Gould's financial and organizing genius, whether by fair means or foul, had seemingly reduced the Colorado railroad situation to something approaching orderliness, as far as he was concerned. This he had achieved by successfully consolidating the Union Pacific and Kansas Pacific lines, and by exercising a co-ordinating control over Colorado's two major railroad systems, the Denver & Rio Grande and the Denver South Park & Pacific; however, his Rio Grande control was short-lived. His Rio Grande-South Park control culminated in the Joint Operating Agreement and was concluded with the Tripartite Agreement between the Union Pacific, the Rio Grande, and the Santa Fe. All was now supposed to be peaceful and everyone concerned on friendly terms; but nothing could be further from the truth. Actually, this orderliness was more apparent than real. Even before the end of 1880, there were signs that Gould's carefully arranged structure was beginning to crack. The leader of the revolt was the Rio Grande. Palmer's disregard of the Joint Operating Agreement, and the subsequent construction of the Rio Grande's Marshall Pass line to Gunnison, as brought out in a previous chapter, was the signal that precipitated a bitter five year struggle between the latter road and the Union Pacific for control of the coal and mineral traffic in the Gunnison and Leadville districts, and the surrounding regions. It was a period of unrestrained railroad promotion and expansion which ended rather disastrously for both railroad systems.

One of the principal reasons Palmer kicked over the traces was his refusal to trust his cosigners, especially the Gould-Union Pacific interests in the Joint Operating and Tripartite Agreements. Palmer apparently concluded that if perchance something happened to these contracts and the parties concerned (the Omaha group) refused to abide by their agreements, the Union Pacific

would come into possession of a railroad to the Gunnison, and his valuable trackage rights to that region would be subjected to the dire peril of being cancelled. And if such a situation came to pass, his Rio Grande system would then be left out on a limb with no railroad connection to the area in question. Therefore, to insure himself a Gunnison connection, Palmer renounced the Joint Operating Agreement and started pushing his Marshall Pass line to that territory.

The next break to occur in Gould's Colorado empire was another dispute between the two roads relative to the Rio Grande's Buena Vista-Leadville section of track, over which the Union Pacific had an entryway into the silver camp. Prior to the Union Pacific's acquisition of the South Park, the Evans and Palmer roads were working together more or less harmoniously in the joint use of this track under arrangements incorporated in the Joint Operating Agreement. However, after the Union Pacific came into control of the South Park road, friction arose between the former and the Rio Grande over certain agreements contained in this contract. The first issue dealt with the division of profits derived from traffic hauled by the two roads over this piece of track. The second concerned a clause in the contract wherein the Union Pacific was to pay an additional fee of eight per cent for certain rights and privileges, plus additional fees covering track maintenance, etc. It was this dissention between the two roads, revolving around Palmer's construction of his Marshall Pass line to Gunnison, and their wrangling over the Buena Vista-Leadville segment, that forms the nucleus of the story behind the construction of the high line to Leadville.

The quarrel over the division of traffic receipts between the two points in question hinged on that section of the Joint Operating Agreement which stated: "all receipts to be pooled—and the gross amount to be divided equally". During March, 1880, a short time prior to the completion of the Buena Vista-Leadville section of track by the Rio Grande, the South Park's gross earnings, while still under the Evans control, stood at $195,704, and for the first five months of the year, they amounted to $940,789. Mock states: "For the same period, the Rio Grande grossed $191,693 and $785,500, respectively. But by 1881, when the Gould and Union Pacific influence began to manifest itself, all this had changed sharply. In spite of the adverse showing for the first half of the year, the Rio Grande wound up the year 1880 having done 75% of the Leadville business. From that point on, the advantage became even more pronounced." Further discussion of this particular phase of friction between the two roads over the unequal division of the Leadville traffic is brought out in a series of four Denver newspaper items. These items are as follows:

From the Denver Daily Times of June 3, 1881.

"Railroaders, like newspaper men, are close-mouthed, and to pump them for information is a matter of considerable difficulty. The following, however, is a brief and fair statement of the existing causes of dispute between two powerful corporations, the D. & R. G. and the U. P.

"In entering into the pooling arrangement last year, the two parties to the agreement did so with very different ideas. The Union Pacific having access to Leadville over the joint track, and having by the South Park, a line 110 miles shorter than its rival, felt reasonably sure that it would be able to handle at least half the traffic. On the other hand, the Rio Grande, being a home corporation, felt assured that state pride and local patriotism to home industries would give it the majority of the business, and events have proven the correctness of this anticipation. Why this is so, is a debatable question between the two roads. The Grande claims that their liberality is the cause, while the Union Pacific contends that it is due to the control of the Moro coke traffic by the D. & R. G. But whatever the cause, one thing is certain; the April accounts show that while passenger business is about even between the two, the Grande is carrying about 75% of the freight. This state of affairs gave rise to the appointment of Mr. Sickles for the Union Pacific and Colonel Danforth for the D. & R. G., as a committee on arbitration.

"Now comes the rock upon which these arbitrators split. Col. Danforth claims that the pooled traffic should be divided on the basis of the past year, which shows that the Grande carried three-fourths of the freight, and the Union Pacific one-fourth, and having fairly won this by their liberality and fairness, they hold that the division of profit should be in precisely the same proportion. On the other hand the Union Pacific points to the equality of the passenger traffic, which they claim shows that the public generally prefers neither road over the other, and that the preponderance of freight traffic over the Rio Grande is due to unfair influence, and will not be a permanent situation, and they therefore, insist upon the present division of profits. As each side argues from a different basis, a settlement seems as far away as ever."

The Denver Daily Times of June 4, 1881.

"During November and December of last year the Rio Grande carried 96% of the Leadville freight traffic, and during January, February, March and April of the present year, 85%."

The Denver Republican of July 28, 1882.

"RAILROAD RACKET

"The speck of war between the Denver & Rio Grande and the South Park roads over Leadville business is increasing in size hourly and is liable to burst with disastrous effect soon. The trouble arose from a demand of the South Park which the Rio Grande refused to accede to. The latter road secures about 85% of the Leadville traffic, and the South Park, determining to have more than 15%, threatened to cut rates. This unsettled affairs, and it is an open secret that heavy reductions have already been made. One of the Officers said yesterday, that he did not believe there would be a war on passenger rates, but that it was possible."

The Denver Republican of August 1, 1882:

"The Denver & Rio Grande put one over on the South Park in railroad business, and the latter are very angry. When the Leadville militia concluded to come to Denver, both roads began to cultivate the soldiers, who number over 500. The Rio Grande had about completed arrangements when the South Park began to cut the throat of its rival by cutting rates to almost nothing. The committee on Transportation signed an agreement with the South Park, but the Denver & Rio Grande soon broke this up by a magnificent offer of free transportation, and free Pullman cars. It is said the Rio Grande will have to pay the Pullman Company $2.00 each way for each man, and the trip would therefore cost them about $1,600 but the Giant of the Rockies, when it wants anything right bad, generally gets it."

At the time the Joint Operating Agreement was drawn up, such an unequal division of the traffic was not considered. After this situation developed, the Palmer interests felt that since they were obtaining and transporting a major portion of the traffic in question, a 50-50 division of the receipts was entirely out of line. Thus, the question of dividing the business and the profits on a different basis than that stipulated in the agreement became a paramount issue.

The second cause for a dispute between the two roads is to be found in that section of the agreement which stated: ". . . the party of the first part, the Denver South Park & Pacific, shall have equal rights and privileges in perpetuity, for which it is to pay eight per cent per annum, payable monthly on one-half of the cash cost thereof, and pay one-half of the expense of maintenance and repairs."

The Union Pacific contended that in view of the fact that they were not receiving their share of the Leadville business, the eight per cent as stipulated in the contract was too much to pay for these rights and privileges, and that six per cent was sufficient. The Omaha road refused to comply with the agreement. As a result of this edict from Omaha, we read in the Denver Republican of September 30, 1882:

"The D. & R. G. will seek an injunction to prevent the Union Pacific from using their joint track between Buena Vista and Leadville. If this is granted, as is supposed will happen, the U. P. will have to stop at Buena Vista and reship via the D. & R. G. into Leadville. This will be ruinous to the U. P. It would force the Union Pacific (D. S. P. & P.) to build its own line to Leadville—a big job."

In September, 1882, the Rio Grande entered suit for $350,000 against the Union Pacific, claiming this amount to cover accumulated track rental and maintenance expense incurred on the Buena Vista-Leadville track. Regarding this suit, we read in the Railway Age of October 5th the following item:

"The Denver & Rio Grande have brought suit against the Union Pacific to recover $350,000 for the use of the Grande's track between Nathrop and Leadville by the Union Pacific Company. The D. & R. G. claim that the U. P. has had use of this track and telegraph since 1880, under an agreement made, which provided that it was to pay a certain amount of money for such privilege. It appears that the Union Pacific has never paid anything and the suit is brought to recover the accumulated debt. The Union Pacific, under its purchase of the South Park, has used this portion of the Rio Grande without ever having paid anything for it."

According to the Leadville Democrat of September 30, 1884, the Union Pacific was supposed to be paying the Rio Grande an annual fee of $10,000[1] to cover trackage rights between Buena Vista and Leadville and all office expense at the latter point. Arguments over the amount and payment of the claim continued between the two roads until the spring of 1883, at which time a settlement was reached.

However, we must get on with our Leadville story. By this time the mining industry in the Leadville area had spread over into Summit County and was developing quite rapidly. Many rich strikes were being made in the Tenmile, Blue River, Montezuma, and Breckenridge districts. With the growth of this new mining development, traffic in ore and mining supplies between these areas and the outside world grew proportionately and, as a natural consequence, drew the attention of the Rio Grande and Union Pacific interests. In addition, control of transportation in the Grand River area to the north of this territory was also claiming their attention. (Note: The Grand River is now known as the Colorado River.)

Many objectives were common to both roads and both strongly realized the strategic value of gaining control of the choice routes leading into and across the areas involved in order that their lines might advance more easily and rapidly. This resulted in some keen competition as to whose railroad might reach the area first—not that there might not be enough business for both, but because of the advantage to be gained in favorable entrenchment with respect to the mines and occupation of the more easily negotiated passes, canons, and defiles. This additional rivalry only served to add more fuel to their bickering and dissension.

Both roads, but especially the Union Pacific, began to fortify themselves with an array of projected railroad lines that were to descend on the region involved from various directions. Some were old abandoned projects, dusted off and brought out into the open once more, while others were newly created plans to support their sponsor's program and strengthen his chances of success. It was a case of trying to outbluff the other fellow, and yet have an ace up the sleeve should the right opportunity present itself at an unforeseen moment. A partial list of the various proposed lines being nourished by the Union Pacific management is shown:

Incorporated

1. Grays Peak Snake River &
   Leadville R.R. ....Feb. 12, 1878

2. Georgetown Leadville & San Juan
   R.R. ....Dec. 5, 1878
3. Denver South Park & Tenmile
   R.R. ....Dec. 13, 1878
4. Denver South Park & Leadville
   R.R. ....Dec. 13, 1878

Acquired

5. Denver South Park & Pacific
   R.R. ....Jan. 1, 1881

Incorporated

6. Greeley Salt Lake & Pacific R. R. ....Feb. 1, 1881
   (This was the Boulder Creek line
   to Sunset and Ward, Colorado.)
7. Georgetown Breckenridge &
   Leadville Ry. ....Feb. 23, 1881
8. Loveland Pass Mining & R.R.
   Tunnel Co. ....July 15, 1881

Those fostered by the Rio Grande were as follows:

Incorporated

1. South Park Railway 1870
2. Western Colorado Railway 1870
3. Upper Arkansas San Juan &
   Pacific Railway 1878
4. Leadville Tenmile & Breckenridge
   Railway ....May, 1880
5. Monarch Pass Gunnison &
   Dolores Railway............................Mar. 1880

Incidentally, the reader might be interested to know that there were innumerable small independent lines projected by various individuals and groups who had hoped to get their finger in the pie, providing dame fortune and their ability to sell railroad stock stayed with them. The complete list would fill a book, but a partial list of these projects follows:

1. Atlantic-Pacific Tunnel & Grays Peak Ry.
2. Atlantic-Pacific Railway Tunnel Co.
3. South Park & Leadville Short-Line R.R.
4. South Park & Horseshoe Ry.
5. Leadville Breckenridge & Denver Ry.
6. Clear Creek & Summit County R.R.
7. Como Breckenridge & Pacific R.R.
8. Fairplay Alma & Dudley R.R.
9. Fairplay Mt. Sheridan & Leadville Ry.
10. London South Park & Leadville R.R.
11. Red Hill Fairplay & Leadville R.R.

This endless array of projected railroads, all headed for the "pot of gold", reminds one of flies buzzing around the sugar barrel.

The Union Pacific management faced two problems: first, they must build to the Summit County area, often spoken of as the Blue River area; and second, they must solve a major problem—that of a Leadville connection or entry. We shall take up the Blue River proposition first.

_____

1. This figure of $10,000 is evidently an error. According to the treasurer's office of the D. & R. G., this annual payment was approximately $96,000, or $8,000 per month.

The Union Pacific's desire for an independent line of their own into this territory had been a favorite topic of discussion across the directors' table for a long time. To enumerate and go into the full details concerning the numerous projected and partially surveyed lines into this particular region would make a story within itself. As a double threat against the Rio Grande in the Blue River area, they planned to advance into the region from two different directions. Of a number of proposed northern entries, it gradually developed that the strongest appeared to be the Georgetown Breckenridge & Leadville Railway, the history of which has already been told. Briefly, this road, a short cut between Denver and the Leadville territory, was to be an extension of the Clear Creek line of the Colorado Central beyond Georgetown. The road was organized by the Union Pacific in February, 1881, one month after their acquisition of the South Park line, with the intention of extending it over Loveland Pass and thence by way of the Snake and Blue Rivers to the confluence of the latter and Tenmile Creek. Branches were projected from this vicinity in three directions—Breckenridge, Leadville and the Grand River area. Construction of the road commenced at Georgetown in January of 1882. During this time considerable publicity was given to the proposed extensions of this railroad. Obviously, a large portion of this propaganda was disseminated for the benefit of the Rio Grande interests. The question of whether the Union Pacific seriously intended to complete this railroad west of Graymont is open to debate. In view of the great height and rugged character of that section of the Continental Divide between the headwaters of Clear Creek and Summit County, it is doubtful if they would have attempted to carry out the actual construction of a railroad between the two points. Charles Francis Adams stated that the construction of this fifteen miles of railroad would be a stupendous undertaking and would cost a million dollars.

Be that as it may, contruction of the Georgetown line progressed very slowly. On April 1, 1884, the line was completed west to Bakerville (Graymont) at the foot of Loveland Pass. In the meantime, the South Park line had been completed to Buena Vista, with access to Leadville via the Rio Grande, and for reasons best known to the Union Pacific management alone, the much publicized Georgetown Breckenridge & Leadville never advanced beyond Graymont.

The Union Pacific's southern entry to the Blue River territory was to be an extension of the South Park railroad by means of a branch line which the Evans management had included in their second Articles of Incorporation on June 14, 1873, and which was also mentioned in amendment number 2 which Jay Gould had a hand in writing. Obviously, the Union Pacific's strongest weapon, and their major support in this conflict with the Palmer road, was their control of the South Park. Consequently, they began an early campaign to push the construction of this road's proposed Breckenridge, or Blue River extension. The early activities of the Summit County mining industry had commanded the attention of the South Park interests to such an extent that a proposal to build a branch line into the Breckenridge district had been fostered by the Evans management for almost a year before the Union Pacific had gained control of the road. Evidence of this interest is best described in an article published in the Denver Daily Times of March 27, 1880.

"A BRECKENRIDGE BRANCH
"A Proposed Extension of the South Park Road
to the Carbonate Fields of Summit County

" 'What are the latest newspaper reports from Breckenridge?' asked a prominent South Park official of a Times reporter yesterday afternoon. 'Nothing especially new', replied the reporter, 'only an undiminished interest in the new mines discovered, and the firm belief that a vast field of carbonates will be developed in that vicinity the coming summer—greater in extent, if not equal in richness, to that about Leadville.'

" 'So I had concluded', observed the railway man, 'and in this connection perhaps I can give you an item of interest. The South Park Company have been considering the propriety of building a branch over the range to Breckenridge. The matter will be brought up formally before the Board of Directors at their next meeting, and no doubt considered favorably.'

" 'What is the proposed route?' queried the TIMES reporter.

" 'That cannot now be stated, and will be determined by surveys yet to be made. There are two routes and two passes over which this branch can be built. Which is the better one, the engineers will have to determine . . . Exact surveys may change these ideas entirely, but in any event, it can hardly be doubted that this Breckenridge extension will be constructed the coming summer, or before next winter's snow flies in the South Park. There is now an immense travel to this Summit County district, as well as a constantly increasing freight traffic, both of which would be largely augmented by the extension of the iron rails to this new and promising field of carbonates. Self-interest will compel its speedy construction.'

"The interview here ended, but the TIMES presents the facts as an assurance that Denver will soon have railway communication with the rich mines of Summit County."

Following this, we read in the Denver Tribune of April 7, 1880, this item:

"The Directors of the Denver South Park & Pacific held a meeting April the 6th, at which a resolution was adopted determining the immediate extension of the road into Summit County by way of Breckenridge. The engineers will leave immediately and as soon as their surveys have been approved, construction will be started and pushed rapidly."

However, for some reason action was delayed and it was not until July that Major Evans and his surveying parties went into the field.[1] They faced a difficult task. Ahead of them lay the great ramparts of the Park Range and the Continental Divide, where the only available passes were eleven to twelve thousand feet high. To one standing along the east rim of South Park and viewing this great chain of mountains, the task of projecting and constructing a railroad through their lofty rugged masses would seem to be an impossibility. No wonder Eicholtz had chosen the Trout Creek Pass route to reach the Arkansas Valley and Leadville.

Preliminary surveys had disclosed three possible routes. One left the main line at the north end of South Park just below Kenosha Pass, skirted along the north rim of the Park, thence by way of Jefferson Creek and across the main Range at Georgia Pass at an elevation of 11,598 feet.[2] From this pass, the line followed down French Gulch into Breckenridge. The second route commenced at Como, followed up Tarryall Creek through Hamilton and thence across the Continental Divide at Breckenridge Pass, later known as Boreas Pass, at an elevation of 11,493 feet. From this pass, the survey followed Indiana Creek and Illinois Gulch down into Breckenridge and the Valley of the Blue. The third route commenced at Survey Station number 1280 and thence up the South Platte River by way of Fairplay, Alma, and Dudley; thence across Hoosier Pass at an altitude of 11,541 feet.[2] From this pass, the survey followed down the Blue River directly into Breckenridge. The writer is unable to give the definite location of this Survey Station 1280. We can only assume that it was near Garos where the Fairplay and Alma Branch, built in 1881, connected with the main line.

After due consideration of all factors involved, the Boreas Pass route was chosen. On September 20, 1880, President John Evans laid before the board of directors the plats of the proposed extension of the South Park railroad from Como to Snake River, whereupon the following resolution was adopted:

"RESOLVED: That that part of the Summit County line of road of this company extending from Como to Snake River in Summit County be located as surveyed by the Chief Engineer of this company and the President and Chief Engineer be directed to file the necessary plats and profiles with the Secretary of the Interior as required by law to secure the right of way over the public lands."

According to the Rocky Mountain News of November 2, 1880, ground was broken on the previous October 30th, at a point just outside of Como on the spur that led to the Upper Como Coal Mine, and this marked the commencement of the high line over Boreas. The same paper, under date of November 9th, stated:

"Contractor F. O. Brown has completed two miles of the Breckenridge extension. He has 300 men at work and if they

1. Railway Age, July 8, 1880.
2. U. S. Geological Survey Map.

can be found, he will increase his force to 500 by next week. The railway companies are experiencing great difficulty in finding labor. The South Park company pays $1.50 a day. This extension will reach Breckenridge, if possible, ahead of the Rio Grande. The rivalry between these two railroads is doing the State good."

The responsibility of locating and staking out a feasible route between Como and Boreas had been placed in the hands of Colonel Eicholtz and Major James Evans. The job presented almost as many difficulties as did the right of way through the tortuous canon of the Platte River or the hazardous descent down the west slope of Alpine Pass. They were faced with the problem of ascending from an altitude of 9,796 feet at Como, to the summit of Boreas Pass, whose elevation was 11,493 feet. This called for a rise of approximately 1,700 feet within a distance of 10.5 miles. Throughout that winter and the following summer, the contractor kept the graders and their teams at work, but they made little headway. Relative to their progress we read in the Rocky Mountain News of October 3, 1881:

"The grading on the Breckenridge branch will be completed to the summit by October the 15th."

For reasons best known to themselves, the Union Pacific did not elect to lay any rail on this extension during 1881, and with the exception of some minor attempts to carry on the work, further construction was halted until the following spring.

In the meantime, while the Union Pacific was pushing the construction of their two projects, the Rio Grande was also engaged in the further promotion of their schemes. Among the more important projects fostered by the Rio Grande were two roads known as the Leadville Tenmile & Breckenridge Railway and the South Park Railway. The former was a reorganization of the Leadville & Tenmile Narrow Gauge Railway by a group of Leadville citizens headed by E. B. Litchfield and George M. Pullman, the latter of sleeping car fame. The new road was incorporated on May 14, 1880. Its object was to build a narrow gauge railway from Leadville, by way of Tenmile Creek, Kokomo, Frisco, and up Blue River to the new mining camp of Breckenridge. The Rio Grande, realizing the strategic value of the route controlled by this newly organized road, purchased the company and all its rights and privileges on August 6, 1880, and thereafter, the line was known as the Blue River branch of the Denver & Rio Grande.

The new mining camps of Robinson, Kokomo, Wheeler, Frisco, etc., scattered along Tenmile Creek were growing rapidly and the Rio Grande moved fast. A grading contract was let the following September, and by December the line had been extended to Robinson. By September, 1881, the end-of-track had been pushed down Tenmile Creek to Wheeler and by the latter part of November, 1882, the rails reached Dillon, 36 miles from Leadville. From Dillon, a proposed branch of this line turned south and followed up the Blue River to

Breckenridge. It was the Rio Grande's intention to push their line through to the new mining camp as soon as possible.

The second railroad project which the Rio Grande had hoped to use as a countermeasure against the Union Pacific during their current fight for the Leadville traffic was the South Park Railway. Incidentally, the following paragraphs will perhaps answer some of the questions of many South Park fans who have been curious to learn the details about all the grading work they used to be able to see when riding the South Park trains through certain sections of Platte Canon.

The author is indebted to Mr. H. O. Brayer for much data relative to the South Park Railway. The South Park Railway was one of the original six branch lines organized and incorporated along with the Rio Grande by General Palmer in 1870. It was the line that Palmer had proposed to build at the time he and Governor Evans were at odds over the South Park bond issue in 1873. The project had been more or less abandoned for a number of years but was pulled out of the archives in the early part of 1879, with the hope that some use might possibly be made of it during their conflict with the Santa Fe over the Royal Gorge route.

The project branched off at a point on the Rio Grande 13½ miles below Denver, slightly north of the confluence of Plum Creek and the South Platte River, near the present station of Wolhurst. This junction point, 3.2 miles north of Acequia, was known as Platte Junction in the early days. From this point, the line followed up the canon of the South Platte River, parallel to the South Park railroad, to the confluence of the North and South Forks of the South Platte River at the station of South Platte. Here it turned south and followed the South Fork of the South Platte across South Park to Fairplay; thence across the Continental Divide by Hoosier, Hamilton, or other suitable pass to the valley of the Blue River, and thence by the most eligible route to western Colorado and Salt Lake City, Utah, with a branch or branches to Salida and the Salt Works. The route was actually surveyed to Fairplay and Salida, and 29.7 miles of the line between the main line junction and a point near Deckers was located and staked ready for the graders. According to a report by J. A. McMurtrie, Chief Engineer of the Rio Grande, in the annual report of 1880, page 38, the grading on this project commenced on May 1, 1879. The majority of information that has come to light seems to indicate that only grading work was done; however, we find in the Railway Age of July 14, 1881, a report to the effect that construction was being vigorously pushed on the Rio Grande's South Platte line and that the road had inaugurated an aggressive campaign against the Union Pacific by commencing the laying of track on this extension.

Thus, it appears that what was originally intended to be a threat to the Santa Fe regarding Leadville traffic, was now being used in a similar manner toward the Union Pacific. In the meantime, however, certain factors materialized which, evidently, caused the Rio Grande interests to change their tactics. The Royal Gorge war had been brought to a successful conclusion, giving them an entryway into Leadville. In addition to this, the Blue River branch was being gradually extended into the region northwest of Leadville. Mr. Brayer adds the statement: "The conflict with the Santa Fe over the Royal Gorge, together with the extreme cost of the Rio Grande extensions built in the south, caused Palmer to continually delay construction of the South Platte line." In view of this situation, the Rio Grande management evidently felt that further work on the South Platte line was unnecessary and called a halt to its construction on January 30, 1882. At this time, 25 miles of grading had been completed. According to a report by the Chief Engineer on November 8, 1883, the Rio Grande spent $190,539.06 on the grading and survey work of this project.

CHOOSING THE LEADVILLE ENTRY

The Union Pacific's second and most important problem concerned their entryway into Leadville. At present, they were enjoying the privilege of trackage rights between Buena Vista and the camp, afforded them through the Joint Operating Agreement. Regardless of whether collusion was being practiced during the early stages of their relations with Palmer or the competition was on the square, the Union Pacific's only hold on their share of the Leadville traffic was through the ability of the two roads to cooperate and time was not improving relations between the two managements. The Omaha interests realized that something infinitely stronger than a trackage connection on another fellow's railroad would eventually be required if they expected to promote and protect the growth and business of their Colorado interests. There is little doubt but that the final answer lay in an independent line of their own. Proof of an early decision in this matter is shown when Sidney Dillon, President of the Union Pacific, refused to yield to Palmer in March, 1881, regarding certain interpretations of the Tripartite Agreement. Therefore, as a protection to their future security, a satisfactory route had to be decided on and a sufficient amount of construction had to be expended thereon. The progress of this work would be governed by the success of their Rio Grande relations—the extent of local Rio Grande railroad construction—mining activities—and a host of additional existent factors to be considered as future developments materialized.

It is this writer's opinion that, in the light of existing conditions, the Union Pacific managers decided to rely on the Joint Operating Agreement and use the Rio Grande's trackage as an economical means of maintaining their Leadville connection as long as they possibly could, or until such time as their negotiations with Palmer reached the breaking point and then—and not until then—would they seriously attempt the completion of their own Leadville connection. Some evidence of this attitude is found in a Denver News item published in the Railway Age of August 30, 1883, from which we quote in part:

"Heretofore the Union Pacific has been content to use the track from Buena Vista to Leadville jointly with the Denver and Rio Grande, but last month the Union Pacific manifested a desire to have their own line."

It was only a matter of some twenty miles, air-line distance, between the South Park's track along the east slope of the Park Range and Leadville on the other side. But the great Park Range, which extended along the entire western side of South Park, presented a formidable barrier some three-quarters of a mile high that defied man's efforts to discover some feasible pathway where he might build a steel trail for his iron horse. A few sanguine souls conceived the idea that such a feat was possible, e.g., a group of Denver citizens organized a company known as the Red Hill Fairplay & Leadville R.R., with a capital stock of over twelve million dollars. This company proposed to dig a two and one-half mile tunnel under Mosquito Mountain at an estimated cost of $400,000 and thereby effect a short cut through the mountains to Leadville. Like many other starry-eyed Colorado railroad projects, this proposition never advanced any further than the paper it was written on.

This left the Union Pacific with only two possible routes by which they might gain access to Leadville. The first, and the one which in all probability they would have greatly preferred, was to build up the Arkansas Valley from Buena Vista. The second was to enter from the north. Meanwhile, an estimated cost of building the high line by way of Boreas Pass, the Tenmile, and Fremont Pass was prepared and appeared to be an economical figure—the grave error was admitted later. After the usual consideration of this, and other pertinent matters, the Boreas Pass route was chosen. In the light of what later transpired it seems very evident that, although the growth and development of the mining industry in the Breckenridge and Blue River districts justified the extension of a railroad into that area, the Union Pacific interests never lost sight of the fact that Leadville was their goal.

This brings up the old and difficult question: WHY did the Union Pacific choose to build over the expensive Boreas Pass route to Leadville instead of constructing some 35 miles of inexpensive track up the Arkansas Valley?

Charles Francis Adams, President of the Union Pacific in 1885, stated: "The Union Pacific chose the Boreas Pass route because it would be 21 miles shorter than the Denver-Leadville route via Buena Vista." True—

the Boreas line was 21 miles shorter, but this extra 21 miles included the more or less flat South Park region and the low, water level route up the Arkansas Valley, which fact more than compensated for the huge expense of building a railroad over the Continental Divide twice[1] at heights above 11,000 feet, plus the added expense of keeping it open during the severe winter seasons. In the writer's opinion, Mr. Adams' statement was pure propaganda and nothing else.

From another source of information relative to this question, we read:

"The Denver & Rio Grande obtained its claim to the route between Buena Vista and Leadville; first, on prior survey and planning, in accordance with the provisions of the Act of Congress granting the Rio Grande certain rights of way; secondly, the Atchison Topeka & Santa Fe controversy definitely left the Rio Grande in possession of a prior right to this route. (Remember that the Santa Fe had already built part way along this same route at the time their line was turned over to the Rio Grande.) Furthermore, the Union Pacific, Santa Fe and Rio Grande signed a Tripartite Agreement on March 27, 1880, agreeing not to infringe upon each other's territory. Since the Union Pacific controlled the Denver South Park & Pacific, the principle naturally applied to that line.

"The reason that the Colorado Midland built into and through this area without opposition—in so far as that placed in the way of the South Park line—was that the Midland was not bound by the Tripartite Agreement mentioned above.

"There was no controversy with the Midland over the right of way here, because the Courts had later decided that no exclusive right existed to any single route. It all depended upon the competing railroad finding a second suitable right of way on which to build."

It cannot be denied that General Palmer had prior claim to this Arkansas Valley route. Confirmation of this fact is to be readily found in the study of early Rio Grande history. Relative to the Colorado Midland not being bound by the Tripartite Agreement, that road was nevertheless a serious competitor to the Rio Grande; consequently, it is difficult to reconcile the fact that the Palmer road, regardless of any court rulings, failed to raise any objections when the Colorado Midland intruded upon their Arkansas Valley route. Undoubtedly, there must be more to the story.

On the other hand, during the Pacific Railway Commission Case trials, John Evans testified from the witness stand as follows:

1. Although Leadville was situated on the east slope, this crossing of the Continental Divide twice was necessary because of the rough mountainous terrain peculiar to this area of Colorado. The Continental Divide forms the east boundary line of Summit County, then swings west by way of Hoosier, Fremont, and Tennessee Passes, turning south again to form the west boundary line of Lake County. The ruggedness of the formidable Park Range, which extended south, like a huge thumb, from the Continental Divide near Fremont and Hoosier Passes, formed an almost unsurmountable barrier between Como and Leadville. This forced the engineers to bear north, cross the main range at Boreas, drop down the west slope, turn south and again recross the Continental Divide at Fremont Pass (Climax) in order to reach their goal —Leadville. Reference to a Colorado map of the area will further assist in understanding this explanation.

"The Union Pacific built a track over to Breckenridge instead of continuing the present South Park line up the Arkansas River from Buena Vista into Leadville as the road's owners had originally surveyed[1] and planned to do before they entered into a trackage agreement with the Denver & Rio Grande. *There was nothing to stop the Union Pacific from extending this Buena Vista line up to Leadville.* The Colorado Midland took advantage of this route and built a standard gauge line parallel with the Rio Grande directly into Leadville."

In making this statement, Gov. Evans, for some unaccountable reason, did not mention the Tripartite Agreement whereby the two companies had agreed not to build a competing railroad into each other's territory. It is thought that perhaps the following explanation might be the answer.

As a result of Palmer's previous actions, the reader may be prompted to accuse him of breaking his word when he commenced construction of his Marshall Pass line to Gunnison—therefore, why could not the Union Pacific do likewise and build a line up the Arkansas Valley? It must be remembered that the Tripartite Agreement did not interfere with Palmer in respect to his Gunnison extension; and also that there is not one word in the Joint Operating Agreement stipulating that Palmer was *not* to build a railroad to Gunnison. On the other hand, the tripartite contract drawn up between the Santa Fe, the Rio Grande, and the Union Pacific, bound the three companies to certain agreements regarding controversies, and construction of new lines in certain territories. As far as the South Park was concerned, at the time this Tripartite Agreement was ratified (March 27, 1880) the road was under the independent ownership and was not included in the agreement; therefore, it did not affect any of the proposed South Park extensions. When the Union Pacific came into control of the South Park, nine months later on January 1, 1881, the Omaha interests maintained that the status of the South Park extensions was as before—unaffected by the agreement—and claimed the right to push these extensions in any direction. Palmer contended that the South Park, on becoming a part of the Union Pacific system, was subject to the rules of the agreement and that the privileges of their independent extension, which would be a violation of the agreement if carried out, were therefore lost. The Union Pacific refused to accede. In March, 1881, Sidney Dillon, the road's President, directed a letter to General Palmer stating that the South Park would be extended to Gunnison.[2] Wrangling over the issue continued between the two parties; finally, Palmer announced that the South Park must be restrained by the stipulations contained in the Tripartite Agreement, or else the Union

Pacific must accept the alternative of a free fight.[1] Thus, by the middle of 1881, it appeared that the great Tripartite Agreement had been thrown in the ash can, with the result that each road went its own way.

In this case, the Union Pacific had respected the agreement up to this time and had refrained from trespassing on the Rio Grande's Arkansas Valley route. Therefore, with the Tripartite Agreement being more or less discarded, it seems hardly possible that it could be counted on as a factor in preventing the Union Pacific from attempting to build up the Arkansas Valley after that date. In view of this situation, it appears that John Evans was correct when he stated:

"There was nothing to stop the Union Pacific from extending this Buena Vista line up to Leadville."

As partial answer to this question, the writer very strongly suspects that the Union Pacific was well aware of the fact that any attempt they might have made to build up the Arkansas Valley at that time would have precipitated an endless and expensive legal battle of major proportions between themselves and the Rio Grande company.

In conclusion, the question, "Why did the Union Pacific choose the Boreas Pass route instead of the Arkansas Valley route?" is still unanswered. The writer is unable to offer a satisfactory and fully acceptable explanation at this time. Perhaps some day some one will uncover additional facts. The Colorado historian, McMechen, in his book, "The Moffat Tunnel of Colorado", comments on this vexatious question by briefly stating: "The Union Pacific, for reasons of its own, relinquished the valuable joint trackage rights with the Rio Grande and built over Boreas Pass to Leadville."

Thus, by the first of 1882, the strategy of both roads was fairly well defined. The Rio Grande had gained control of the Royal Gorge route into Leadville and was pushing their Blue River extension down the Tenmile toward Dillon with the expectation of completing it to Breckenridge as soon as possible.[2] For reasons already explained, their South Platte project had been dropped. In the interim, the Union Pacific, to all intents and purposes, was pushing both their major projects, namely, the high line over Boreas Pass and the Georgetown line over Loveland Pass. In respect to the Leadville entry, it had been definitely decided to enter the great silver camp from the north. In anticipation of extending either or both the South Park and Georgetown lines into the vicinity of the confluence of Tenmile Creek, Snake River, and Blue River, further plans

1. See resolution adopted by the South Park Board of Directors, May 24, 1879.
2. Railway Review, July 9, 1881.

1. Railway Review, July 9, 1881. Palmer's official note to the Union Pacific informing them of their violation of the Tripartite Agreement was dated May 13, 1881. (Courtesy H. O. Brayer.)

2. The company completed their grade to Breckenridge (D. & R. G. Annual Report, 1881) but due to the lack of finances and the disapproval of some of the Eastern stockholders, the Rio Grande track was never extended beyond Dillon.

were made relative to the actual construction of the line. It was tentatively decided that the Leadville entry, which would be built between the Dillon area and Leadville by way of Tenmile Creek and Fremont Pass, would connect with the track of either of the other two lines, depending upon which reached the Dillon vicinity first.

It was a bold scheme. In view of the fact that both routes would be forced to cross the extremely high and mountainous terrain of the Continental Divide, it was assumed that the Union Pacific interests concluded that if one project failed, they would have the other to fall back on. The completion of either route would give them an independent line, not only into the Lake and Summit County area, but into Leadville as well. It was a stupendous undertaking, regardless of which route succeeded. Notwithstanding the fact that Leadville is on the eastern slope of the Continental Divide, the final completion of the line into Leadville would entail the building of a railroad over two great mountain ranges, both in excess of 11,000 feet in altitude.

The Dillon-Leadville segment was to be built under the name of the Denver South Park & Pacific. At the same time, plans were also made covering the extension of the South Park line up the Snake River toward Keystone and another extension down the Blue River to the Grand River. In connection with these projects, we read from the minutes of a meeting held by the South Park's Board of Directors on January 10, 1882, as follows:

". . . . show the approval of the company's line of location from station 895 on the Blue River to the crossing of the Grand River, a distance of 42.26 miles; also, from Leadville to Dillon, a distance of 33.93 miles; also location in the valley of the Snake River for a distance of 9.18 miles . . . the surveys being adopted, maps were ordered filed with the Secretary of the Interior."

At this point, it might be well to add that although John Evans and his South Park associates had been interested in extending a branch of their railroad into the Breckenridge area, they had definitely decided against building into Leadville via this route. The Boreas-Tenmile-Fremont route was strictly a Union Pacific idea, and as it so happened, the Breckenridge project fitted in very advantageously with their scheme. But to return to our story. The Snake River project had a twofold purpose. First, the construction of a railroad up this stream would enable them to gain control of the ore traffic which was developing at that time in the Montezuma and Chihuahua mining districts. Second, it would serve as a means of connecting the South Park system with the proposed extension of the Georgetown line over Loveland Pass. The Blue River project was a further attempt by the Union Pacific to gain control of the traffic in this region and incorporated plans whereby this proposed extension of the South Park could be tied in with various other projected lines of the Union Pacific system northwest of Denver. According to the Railway

World of September 10, 1881, it was proposed to extend the South Park down the Blue River to the Grand River and thence up that stream to Hot Sulphur Springs in Middle Park. This scheme then included the proposed extension of the narrow gauge division of the Greeley Salt Lake & Pacific from Boulder to Ward (see author's history of the Denver Boulder & Western in R. & L.H.S. Bulletin number 65) and thence across the Continental Divide to the headwaters of the Grand River to a connection with the South Park at Hot Sulphur Springs.

In line with these plans it appears that during 1881, previous to their official announcement in January of 1882, the Union Pacific had done some preliminary construction work along the Blue River north of Dillon. Concurrently, in addition to their extension down the Tenmile to Dillon, the Rio Grande had also proposed the construction of a line north from that point down the Blue River toward the Grand River. This Dillon-Blue River-Grand River line, incidentally, was a part of one of General Palmer's original six branch lines organized along with the Rio Grande in 1870, and was known as The Western Colorado Railway. The proposed route of this line commenced at the mouth of the South Arkansas River, at the site of Salida, and thence by way of the present site of Leadville, Tenmile Creek, Blue River to the Grand River, then west into Utah. As a result of these various schemes on the part of both roads, another dispute arose between them over certain right of way claims along the Valley of the Blue and they took their troubles to the courts. The Rio Grande maintained that they had the first location here and claimed priority through the valley by reason of a special Act of the Congress passed in 1872. The Palmer road further alleged that the construction of a railroad down the Blue River by the Union Pacific was in violation of the terms as outlined in the Tripartite Agreement. Further details of this conflict were published in the Railway Age of September 1, 1881, of which we quote in part:

"The Union Pacific, which has begun to extend its Denver South Park & Pacific line along the Blue and Grand Rivers, has commenced a suit in Leadville to restrain the Denver & Rio Grande from proceeding with the construction of a railroad along the same line. The Union Pacific claims a prior location. The Denver & Rio Grande admit the prior location for a few miles along the line but claim that they have the right of way by a continuous location. The portion of the right of way that is conceded to the Union Pacific by the Rio Grande is about thirteen miles below the mouth of the Tenmile, and this is where the difficulty occurs. The South Park claims that the D. & R. G. is interfering with them in the construction of their line at the above mentioned point, and upon this ground their application is based. The Denver & Rio Grande hold that the Union Pacific, in order to procure a basis for an application to enjoin them, made a jump over the grade of their line as defined, for four miles, and commenced work on the ground which was being approached by Denver & Rio Grande graders."

As the situation developed, the whole affair turned into the usual side show of suits, countersuits, injunc-

The Pacific Hotel at Como as it appeared in 1886. Behind South Park engine 209 is the railroad station.

The ruins of the Pacific Hotel at Como after the disastrous fire on November 9, 1896. The photographer, Dr. Scott, lost most of his possessions in this fire. The station, which can be seen at the right, was not seriously damaged.

tions, etc., such as was often conducted by early day railroad entrepreneurs. The threats of the Union Pacific to extend the narrow gauge division of the Greeley Salt Lake & Pacific over the Continental Divide to Hot Sulphur Springs never advanced beyond the projection stage. As a partial gesture toward carrying out their projects and plans, both roads did a considerable amount of grading work between Dillon and the Grand River, but that constituted the extent of their activities along this section of the valley of the Blue River. During the next few years, a few news reports appeared from time to time in various railroad publications stating that the Union Pacific interests expected to complete this Blue River extension to the Grand River and Glenwood Springs. In fact, the minutes from a meeting of the Board of Directors, dated September 30, 1886, included a resolution to the effect that the company still proposed to build the line. Finally, the Railway Review of August 20, 1887, stated that the Union Pacific had postponed this Blue River extension because of differences with the U. S. Government. It is not known what these differences were. This was the last the writer ever heard of the project. Before concluding this particular section of our story, the author desires to add a few comments made by Mr. W. E. Mahony, a student of Colorado railroad history.

"About 25 years ago, while traveling down the Blue River highway, I noticed an old railroad grade, well located and constructed, with many deep cuts and high fills. I found that this grade extended almost the entire distance of 38 miles between Dillon and the Grand River. Being interested, I made local inquiry as to when the old grade was built and who built it. I was informed that it was constructed many years ago, supposedly by the Denver & Rio Grande as an extension of their three-foot gauge line then ending at Dillon. The strange part is that this old grade, with all its expense of construction, never had a tie or a rail laid on it."

As previously related, the Union Pacific had completed the grading between Como and the summit of Boreas Pass by October, 1881. Some attempts were made that winter to continue with the work but the winters on Boreas Pass, with their terrible snow storms and blizzards, are something to be reckoned with, for they defy any puny efforts that man might make toward building a railroad in that high and mountainous region. Consequently, little progress was made. In March, 1882, Colonel Fisher, Superintendent of the South Park, announced that laying of the rail would commence as soon as the weather permitted. In line with this statement, the contractor started laying rail at Como in April. Meanwhile, the graders were following the survey stakes down the north side of Boreas Pass toward Breckenridge. Considering the many difficulties encountered, the contractors made good progress throughout the summer of 1882, and by September 1st the end-of-track reached Breckenridge. That section of the line between Breckenridge and Dillon, a distance of approximately nine miles, followed straight north down the Valley of

the Blue with a minimum of curvature, and offered little in the way of constructional difficulties. The railhead advanced rapidly and the Union Pacific reported in the Railway Age of December 7, 1882, that the South Park's line was completed through to Dillon, a distance of 30.7 miles from the main line connection at Como.

Upon reaching Dillon, the Union Pacific continued with construction eastward up the Snake River, and by January, 1883, the end-of-track reached Keystone, a distance of 6.8 miles. Commenting on this, the Gunnison Review of January 27th stated:

"The present terminus of the Breckenridge extension is now Keystone. From this point stages will run daily to Montezuma, six miles, and Chihuahua, 7 miles."

It was their intention to extend the South Park some 12 or 15 miles farther up the Snake River to serve the Montezuma and Chihuahua mining districts. This extension was also supposed to make a connection with the much publicized Georgetown Breckenridge & Leadville, whose line had been surveyed over Loveland Pass to the vicinity of the confluence of Peru Creek and Snake River. The closure of this gap would have afforded them a shorter and more direct route between Denver and Leadville than that of the Rio Grande or the proposed Colorado Midland, but it would have been far less favorable from an operating point of view. However, as previously related, construction of this line beyond Georgetown proceeded slowly and the track did not reach Bakerville until the spring of 1884. Meanwhile, a number of major changes had come about. For various reasons explained in the chapter covering the Georgetown road, the Union Pacific discontinued further construction of that line. In the meantime, the small amount of traffic coming out of the Montezuma district was insufficient in itself to justify the extension of the South Park to that vicinity. As a result of these factors, this branch of the South Park was never extended beyond Keystone.

With the Breckenridge extension now completed to Dillon, the Union Pacific's long cherished desire to have their own independent line into Leadville began to assume a tangible form. Its completion would place them in a position whereby they could offer the Rio Grande some stiff competition in their proposed attempt to gain control of the great ore traffic that was flowing out of Leadville. They went to work quietly and industriously in their attempt to outwit the Rio Grande. The first of their strategic moves revolved around the ore smelting industry in Colorado.

It seems that two prominent Union Pacific officials, Sidney Dillon and Frederick L. Ames, were large stockholders in an ore smelting concern in Omaha known as The Omaha Smelting & Refining Company. At this time, there was also a large smelting works in operation in Denver known as The Grant Smelting Company. In Dillon's and Ames's opinions, an amalgamation of these two large smelting concerns to work in harmony with the Union Pacific railroad would give them a gigantic monopoly of the smelting industry in the west. The completion of a branch of their railroad into Leadville would then make the competition of the home smelters worthless and unavailing against the combined strength of the Union Pacific Railroad Company and the Omaha & Grant Smelting Company. In commenting on this move, the Denver Republican stated:

"The stockholders of the Omaha & Grant Smelting Company, the incorporation of which was announced recently, have elected the following gentlemen as directors: Guy C. Barton, Edward W. Nash, James B. Grant, Edward Eddy, Wm. H. James, Charles Babcock, and J. H. Millard. The company was constituted by the combining of the Grant Smelting Company, of Denver, and the Omaha Smelting & Refining Company, of Omaha. The combination probably makes the greatest ore smelting company in the United States. The consolidation was consummated on July 5, 1882. The capital stock is fixed at $2,-500,000. There will be no changes in the location of the works or the administration of affairs. The ore smelted by the Grant smelter has been refined at the Omaha Company's works for the past three years, and the two concerns have been co-operating that length of time. They are now placed under one management, with Sidney Dillon, President of the Union Pacific, as a conspicuous figure connected with the deal."

This move on the part of the Union Pacific meant only one thing; a bitter conflict with the Rio Grande over the Leadville traffic. In this connection, the Leadville Herald stated:

".... it is estimated that the Union Pacific freight rate can be reduced to a point lower than the Rio Grande can compete with. The through line will be from Leadville through Robinson and Kokomo, but instead of going to Dillon, it will probably be turned from Frisco to the Breckenridge branch, making a saving of about ten miles. Thence it will go over the range again to the Como junction. It is said that the ore rate will be reduced to one dollar a ton to Denver. Those of the local smelting men who have spent any time in figuring, claim that even at a dollar rate to Denver, the Rio Grande, through its coke supply at Trinidad, and a liberal reduction on the bullion rate, can hold the Union Pacific and the Grant-Omaha syndicate to an equal division of the business. The inevitable result will be a bitter war, and at this date it is impossible to even conjecture as to the influence upon the industry and prosperity of the country. . . . It yet remains to be seen whether the wiping out of the local smelters by the Union Pacific can be accomplished, as the Rio Grande will unquestionably contest for the immense freight to the end."

During this time there was also another matter that required the attention of the Union Pacific officials. This was the aforesaid suit which the Rio Grande had brought against them the previous September in an effort to collect a sum of $350,000 which the Palmer road alleged the South Park owed for maintenance and rental fees in connection with their use of the Rio Grande's track between Buena Vista and Leadville. The South Park's rails were still 34 miles from Leadville and until this gap could be closed, their only connection depended solely on the not too trustworthy Joint Operating Agreement. To have Palmer cancel the agreement at this time would be disastrous. Therefore, as a part of

their strategy, and as a probable appeasement to the Rio Grande in an attempt to insure their not being deprived of their Buena Vista-Leadville trackage until the Dillon-Leadville gap could be closed, they deemed it advisable to liquidate this debt. The Union Pacific agreed to pay the Rio Grande $280,000 in settlement of all claims relative to operating infringments, contract violations, etc. Through the courtesy of two Rio Grande men, Mr. Walter Leaf and Mr. R. J. Herring, we learn the terms of this settlement. Mr. Leaf writes:

"The agreement was signed May 26, 1883, by the D. & R. G. Ry. Co. on one side and the Union Pacific and the Denver & South Park Ry. on the other. The settlement was for $280,000 covering rental of the Buena Vista-Leadville line from July 1, 1880, to June 1, 1883, being at the rate of $8,000 per month for 35 months. The agreement specified a payment by the Union Pacific of $10,000 per month starting June 1, 1883."

The third move was to get underway with actual construction of the Dillon-Leadville line. In preparation for the job, 50,000 spruce ties and a large quantity of rails were contracted for. On July 21, 1883, the Union Pacific, through the South Park company, signed a contract with C. W. Collins & Company of Omaha, Nebraska, for the construction and equipment of the Tenmile Creek line. One source states that the contract called for a payment of $32,000 per mile, while another source gives the figure as $20,000 per mile; the latter figure appears to be more accurate. The Collins company then let out various portions of the construction work to subcontractors. Incidentally, Chester W. Collins was Sidney Dillon's brother-in-law; that should add up to something. In discussing this contract, the Denver Republican of August 5, 1883, stated:

"The contracts require that the work shall be completed within sixty days. Some figures on this basis will be of interest. When the Rio Grande branch was built to Kokomo, 3,000 men were given employment for four months. That point being about midway between Dillon and Leadville, and the work being just as heavy on the Tenmile River as it is on this side of the range, it will require 12,000 laborers to build the road within the time stipulated. It is thought however, that the contracts are provisional and flexible, and that the limitation will be stretched to 90 days. Even then, nine or ten thousand men will be needed. One of the principal contractors is a brother-in-law of Sidney Dillon. Messrs. Corrigan & Carlyle, of Pueblo, are also prominent in the letting of the contracts. . .

"There are three corps of surveyors out, under the general supervision of Major Evans, the full force being about fifty men. Their primary work will be finished next week. The road will parallel the Rio Grande on the line or outside the fifty foot limit prescribed by Court decision. The latter road, of course, has selected the most practicable route and easiest grade, which will, naturally, increase the hardship and cost of the new branch."

On Friday, August 3, 1883, actual construction of the line between Leadville and Dillon commenced. The Leadville Herald came out with the following article:

This view of Como, made about 1900, shows various railroad facilities.

The new Como eating house, which was built to replace the Pacific Hotel. This photo, taken about 1902, shows the day train arriving from Leadville.

"RAILWAY WAR INEVITABLE
"The South Park People Commence Work
on Their Short Line

"The first shovelful of dirt was thrown on the extension of the South Park Railway between Kokomo and Dillon. There is not a remnant of doubt that Leadville is soon to become the objective point of the most bitter rail-war ever witnessed in this state. . . . Messrs. Carlyle & Corrigan, of Pueblo, are now driving 300 mules up the Arkansas Valley, and these will all be employed on the South Park grades within a few days. Yesterday a special freight train arrived in Leadville loaded with their utensils, including carts, shovels, and numerous excavating implements."

In the meantime, the Rio Grande people apparently woke up to all this activity on the part of the Union Pacific. As an initial move, General Palmer arranged to cancel the all important Joint Operating Agreement, which covered the South Park's trackage rights into Leadville over the Rio Grande's Buena Vista-Leadville track. The agreement was cancelled in lieu of a new contract which contained a clause stating that the agreement was terminable on six months notice.[1] This new contract went into effect on August 6, 1883, and was no sooner signed than General Palmer gave notice to the Union Pacific of its cancellation. In the words of John Evans:

". . . with this cancellation went the last hopes of the South Park road of ever enjoying the principal source of its revenue—the Leadville ore traffic."

The next move on the part of the Rio Grande to counteract the ambitious scheme of the Union Pacific to corner the market on the Leadville ore traffic is best described in an article published in the Denver Republican of August 28th. The article is as follows:

"The past week has been an unusually animated one in railroad circles. There promises to be some lively competition between the Denver & Rio Grande and Union Pacific. For a long time the association of the competitive lines into Leadville has been harmonious, but the inauguration of a new scheme by the Union Pacific to extend the South Park line to the Blue River has given things a rather exciting turn.

"When the Rio Grande folks felt assured that the Union Pacific Company meant business, they went vigorously at work to off-set the Short Line scheme. While the Union Pacific people have been so quietly and industriously arranging for the construction of the South Park Short Line, as it is called, and purchasing rights of way into Leadville, it is now evident that the Rio Grande people have been on the alert, and it appears that they had caught their competitors dozing. The first intimation of the Rio Grande's shrewd move was had at a meeting of the Lake County Board of Commissioners. On this occasion a right of way was granted to a man named S. L. De Lan to construct a street railway for passenger and traffic purposes over and across the county road up California Gulch. At the time the Commissioners adopted the resolution which ceded this privilege, nobody who paid any attention to it divined the intent. The next move was on Friday afternoon, when a special train consisting of fourteen cars, loaded with workmen, implements, and mules, was pulled into the terminus of the California Gulch branch of the Rio Grande. It then became whispered around that the privilege granted to S. L. De Lan to lay a track up California Gulch was a Rio Grande scheme.

1. Carl Hewett, of the Denver & Rio Grande Western R. R.

"This road will run its cars, as it can, on street car tracks, and will tap all the principal mines and smelters in that district. De Lan was simply acting as an agent, and the moment he obtained the favor of the Commissioners, Orman & Crook, the well-known railroad contractors were instructed by telegraph to come with their outfit, which is now encamped.

"The project is to give the Rio Grande access to the California Gulch region. The street railway, so termed, while it may be constructed on the bob-tail plan, will be narrow gauge. It will also be owned and operated by the Denver & Rio Grande Company. The object is plain. The California Gulch section yields one-half the output of the camp—about 1,500 tons a month. The teaming contracts, some of which are for a year, were entered into upon the condition that they shall be abrogated when a railroad is built to facilitate the transportation of ores. The completion of the railroad through the gulch will make the competition of mules and wagons useless.

"The Rio Grande in making this movement a success, secures a little monopoly of its own. It enters into the railroad fight as a rival in behalf of the Leadville smelting industry, to all appearances. The South Park Short Line is shut out from one of its objective points, and, if it desires to handle this ore it will never be able to lay it down in Denver for $1.00 a ton as it has threatened to do. The Rio Grande will be in a position to discriminate in favor of the several large smelters which are located lower in the Gulch, to a very large extent. The movement was a brilliant one, and if all reports attached to it are true, several interesting revelations may be expected in time."

From such evidence, it might appear that the battle of the century was on, but a pause for an analysis of the situation tends to prove otherwise. Railroad companies sometimes operate under a peculiar code of ethics, with the result that the historian is often forced to wonder just what the true facts of the case are. During all this feverish activity on the part of both roads in question, a reporter for the Denver Republican interviewed Mr. Horace Newman, a Union Pacific official, regarding the latest news from the Leadville sector. In answer to some questions concerning matters of cooperation in Leadville, Mr. Newman informed the newspaper man:

". . . . the D. & R. G. had consented to our use of their yards at Leadville and thus-far everything was progressing smoothly."

The reporter then inquired as to prospective railway war and its effects on freights. Mr. Newman replied,

". . . . that, no one can tell, but its tendency may be towards reduction, and then again there may be a pool for the protection of existing rates. It is one of those matters that can only be solved by the future." . . . "Good-day."

Furthermore, this Rio Grande cancellation, followed by two subsequent renewals, serves to support this writer's contention that Rio Grande-Union Pacific competition during the years 1881 to 1884 was not strictly on the level. No railroad management could possibly be so blind to a competitor's moves as not to be able to observe that the Union Pacific's ultimate goal was Leadville. Thus, there is ample reason to believe that a certain amount of collusion, or cooperation (call it what you will) was going on behind the curtain; otherwise Palmer would have taken this step when dissension first developed between the two managements in 1881.

As previously mentioned, actual construction on the Leadville-Dillon line commenced on August 3rd. Inasmuch as the Union Pacific was entremely anxious to complete the line before the winter season with its deep snows and zero weather set in, construction was commenced at numerous points throughout the entire length of the line. With this view in mind, they exerted a strong effort to get as many laborers on the job as possible. In this connection, the Denver Republican of August 14th carried an interesting item which stated:

". . . . The work on the extension of the South Park is being rapidly pushed forward. The Union Depot last evening presented a lively appearance. About 200 Italians were there with their gripsacks. They were put on board the South Park train, and will arrive in Leadville this morning and will be put to work at once. The men seemed very much elated over the pleasing prospect of having a job all winter, and jabbered in their native language at a lively rate. . .

"It is reported that within a day or two about 1,500 laborers will have been enlisted and deposited on the ground. Messrs. Carlyle & Corrigan, who will construct the road, have brought from the Oregon Short Line, 365 teams. Besides these, a number of contracts have been made with local team owners at this point. They think that the branch will be completed and ready for the running of trains in three months."

The Railway Age of August 30th quoted an item from the Omaha Herald which stated:

"The Union Pacific has been hiring and forwarding to Colorado, all the able bodied laborers to be had in this country to work on its new short cut to Leadville. The wages offered are: trackmen,$ 2.25; rock men, $2.50 per day, with board at $5.00 per week. Transportation to Colorado free."

The original surveys specified that the connection to the Breckenridge line was to be made at Dillon; however, the plans were changed in favor of making the connection at Placer Junction, later known as Dickey, 2.7 miles south of Dillon. The new route, which effected a saving of some 4 miles of track, turned west at Placer Junction and followed a fairly easy grade around the north end of Tenmile Range, joining the original survey on Tenmile Creek just above Frisco. From this point, the line followed along the banks of Tenmile Creek through the mining camps of Wheeler, Kokomo, and Robinson to the summit of Fremont Pass whose altitude at the point of crossing was 11,320 feet. The entire distance to this point was a continuous climb up grades that reached a maximum of 4.30%, with numerous curves running between fifteen and twenty degrees. From Fremont Pass, the line descended the west slope of the mountain range following the headwaters of the Arkansas River for a number of miles and then entered Leadville from the north side of town. The total mileage between Placer Junction and Leadville was 34.6 miles.

The Rio Grande, having had first choice of a right of way between Leadville and Dillon, naturally controlled the more favorable route. In view of this Major Evans faced a very difficult task in his effort to stake out a feasible right of way between the two points. Between Fremont Pass and Dillon, the Rio Grande's right

of way lay on the west side of Tenmile Creek, practically the entire distance. It was through this section that Maj. Evans encountered his greatest difficulty; that of avoiding coming closer than fifty feet from the center line of the Rio Grande's grade, as was specified by law. His greatest trouble in locating a grade line was encountered at Kokomo. At this point, the Rio Grande's grade approached from the north on the west side of Tenmile Creek. Near the center of the Kokomo townsite, this grade swung east about one-half mile and crossed the Tenmile where it then proceeded south along the east side of that stream. The South Park's grade approached Kokomo from the north on the east side of Tenmile Creek. In attempting to survey a line through the south end of the Kokomo townsite, Evans found it to be practically impossible, due to the limited amount of space between the creek and the mountain side, to abide by the one-hundred foot ruling without incurring a tremendous expense, plus the added inconvenience of locating depot and yard facilities. Therefore, in order to keep construction expense at a minimum, and to gain the benefit of necessary station and yard facilities within Kokomo, Evans found it necessary to run his survey within the two-hundred foot right of way strip controlled by the Rio Grande.

The Rio Grande immediately filed suit on August 27, 1883, and secured a temporary injunction which prevented the South Park from entering upon their right of way. This injunction applied to their entire line in Summit County and their depot grounds at Robinson and Summit Station (Climax). This injunction also specified that the South Park company was not to interfere with any of the Rio Grande's snowsheds, snow-fences, telegraph lines, etc., and prohibited the defendent from diverting any of the waters of Tenmile Creek or its tributaries. The South Park then filed a countersuit in answer, basing their rights upon the Act of 1875, by which the Congress granted railways the right of way through government land. They also contended that the nature of the region was such that they could not avoid coming within the prescribed one hundred foot limit of the Rio Grande's right of way at certain points. The South Park's lawyers also argued that the railroad's contract with the Rio Grande, by which it had access to Leadville over Rio Grande tracks from Buena Vista, would terminate on February 6, 1884; that the season for railway construction in that high altitude was very short, and that unless relief was granted by the Court, irreparable injury would result. They then entered a motion to dissolve the injunction heretofore issued, but the Court failed to render any decision in their favor at this time, with the result that the injunction stuck.

Sheriff Hanley of Leadville spent three days serving the injunction notices to various South Park employees and representatives. No one paid any attention to the Court's decision, so the good Sheriff left Leadville on

The siding at Frisco, at the mouth of Tenmile Canon, in the 1890's.

A South Park work train in Tenmile Canon. The Rio Grande's Blue River Branch crosses the creek on a Howe Truss bridge.

August 30th, armed with warrants to arrest all who failed to obey the notices, stating that the first man to be arrested would be Major James Evans. In the meantime, a large force of track laborers, working within the city limits of Leadville, were arrested and jailed. The next day Major Evans and one of his assistant engineers, a Mr. Bowen, were arrested. Both gave bail of $1,000, and were released. By this time, it was apparent that the injunction was to be enforced, with the result that construction in the Kokomo sector and at other minor points along the line was halted.

As things now stood, it began to look rather doubtful as to whether the South Park would be able to complete their line through to Leadville before the winter season set in. However, their hopes were brightened when on September 5th, the City of Leadville, which had been rather antagonistic toward the Union Pacific company, granted the South Park a right of way within the city limits. The ordinance passed by a vote of eight to seven. The hasty action of the Council gave rise to some unfavorable comment. In all probability, it would be interesting to know just how much connivance took place between some of the Council members and Union Pacific interests.

Here is an interesting episode that has come to light which concerns the attempts of the Rio Grande to prevent the South Park from entering the City of Leadville. The story, published in the Railroad Gazette of September 14, 1883, is as follows:

"A dispatch from Denver dated September the 1st says: 'The Union Pacific is having all sorts of trouble getting into Leadville, as its enemy, the Denver & Rio Grande, seems to be exhaustless in its filibustering resources. Injunctions, and every device known to railroad men are adopted to retard the construction of the South Park's line across the Cummings & Finn switch in East Leadville. At a point where the South Park expects to cross the Grande, a locomotive has been stationed for a week past, rendering it impossible for the construction force to complete the connection. At regular intervals the stationary locomotive is supplied with coal and water and there it stands day and night.' "

Inasmuch as the injunction which the Rio Grande had obtained against the South Park only specified that the latter's grade was not to be built within one hundred feet of the Rio Grande's right of way, there was nothing to prevent the contractors from continuing with construction on the balance of the line. Therefore, with the exception of the Kokomo section, they proceeded with the work at hand. The winter season was approaching and much remained to be accomplished if the line was to be completed while good weather was present. By September, according to the Leadville papers, there were nearly two thousand men at work on the line between Leadville and Placer Junction. It seems, however, that a great majority of these men came from the East, and not being used to such heavy labor, together with exposure, in the high altitude of the Colorado Rockies, many of them contracted a sort of mountain fever which had a tendency to develop into pneumonia. These sick men sought relief in Leadville, at the expense of the city. Soon their number increased to alarming proportions. Newspaper references state that the Union Pacific did not live up to promises made when hiring the men; failed to provide proper living conditions on the job; and that they paid the men in scrip good only at company stores.

The following story,[1] told to a Leadville newspaper man, seems to be a typical case.

"James Connors, one of the patients at the City's poorhouse, was questioned as to the method of his employment and experience. 'You see,' he said, 'we were hired to come here for $2.25 and $2.50 a day. "Mancatchers," that's what I calls 'em. They were the fellows who hired us. We had to pay 'em $2.00 for the hiring. I came from Kansas City. We were to pay $6.00 a week for board. Nothing was said about how we were to be paid. I came and you see I am not a very strong man. I don't know what it is, but the first day I went to work up here in the mountains, I was taken down. I couldn't work, and that night I went to my boss and told him so. My day's wages was $2.25. He couldn't give me the money, he said, and all he offered me was an order on the store for that amount. I took it. What do you think I got? Here it is.' And the laborer took from his pocket a fifteen cent package of Bull Durham tobacco, a ten cent plug, and a five cent box of matches.
'Is that the way everybody is treated?' he was asked.
'That's just the way. You can't get blankets until you have worked for them at this discount, and then you have lots of trouble.'
'Did you have any blankets?'
'No, but I was told that I would have plenty of them, and clothes and a nice place to sleep.'
'Are many of the men suffering in the same way?'
'Yes, half of them. They are all from the East, you know, and can't stand it here. I wish I was back.'
'Where have most of them come from?'
'Kansas City, Chicago, St. Joe, and Omaha. We were all told that it was a beautiful climate and all that, and you know that $2.25 and $2.50 a day and board and lodging at $6.00 a week is a big inducement to a poor fellow who is struggling along back there for $1.25 and $1.50 a day and at about the same expense for board. I wish I could get back at the same old wages.' "

Dr. Law, the Lake County Physician, stated: "From all accounts the Union Pacific is not keeping the contracts which its agents in the East are making. The grade hands are coming to Leadville under misapprehension, caused by misrepresentations on the part of the Union Pacific. Lake County cannot stand the evil."

Although the contractors were faced with many difficulties including labor, engineering problems, and the continual enmity and harassment on the part of the Rio Grande, they made fairly good progress. Speaking of the Rio Grande's hostility toward the South Park road, the Commercial & Financial Chronicle, in writing about the strong opposition by the Rio Grande, stated ". . . at times it was necessary to keep armed men on guard and occupy the completed track with loaded trains as fast as the rails were laid in order to prevent Denver & Rio Grande men from tearing it up."

1. Denver Republican, Sept. 11, 1883.

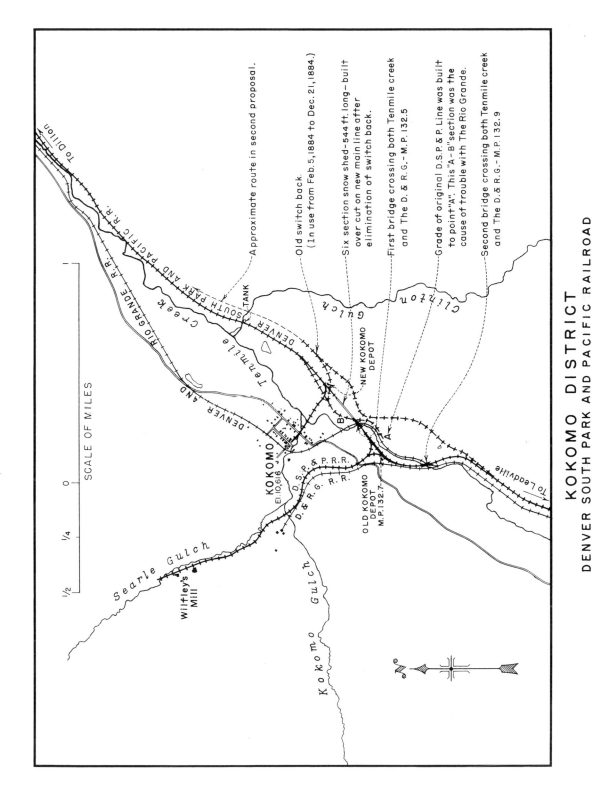

Approximate route in second proposal.

Old switch back.
(In use from Feb. 5, 1884 to Dec. 21, 1884.)

Six section snow shed—544 ft. long—built over cut on new main line after elimination of switch back.

First bridge crossing both Tenmile creek and The D. & R.G.—M.P. 132.5

Grade of original D.S.P. & P. Line was built to point "A". This "A-B" section was the cause of trouble with The Rio Grande.

Second bridge crossing both Tenmile creek and the D.& R.G.—M.P. 132.9

To Dillon

RIO GRANDE R.R. R.R.

DENVER SOUTH PARK AND PACIFIC

Tenmile Creek

DENVER AND RIO GRANDE R.R.

TANK

NEW KOKOMO DEPOT

Gulch

Clinton

B

A

To Leadville

KOKOMO
El. 10,616

D.S.P. & P.R.R.

D.& R.G. R.R.

OLD KOKOMO DEPOT
M.P. 132.7

Searle Gulch

Wilfley's Mill

Kokomo Gulch

SCALE OF MILES

1/2   1/4   0   1/4   1/2

KOKOMO DISTRICT
DENVER SOUTH PARK AND PACIFIC RAILROAD

COMPILED BY M.C. POOR
DRAWN BY E. J. HALEY

During November, Judge Hallett, of Royal Gorge fame, appointed a railway commission of three men, which included Colonel L. H. Eicholtz of Denver, F. E. Calvert of Lincoln, Nebraska, and Andrew N. Rogers of Central City, to visit the scene of dispute at Kokomo with instructions to get all facts and details with the view of settling the case one way or the other. The results of this committee's findings are best described in the Denver Republican of December 6, 1883, which we quote in part. Reference to the Kokomo map will assist the reader in following the story.

"THE KOKOMO COMMISSION RENDERS ITS REPORT TO JUDGE HALLETT

"It Reviews the Cost of Projected Lines
"South Park Must Seek a New Route

"Yesterday afternoon, Wednesday, December the 5th, the Commissioners appointed to view the routes of the Denver & Rio Grande and the Denver South Park & Pacific in Tenmile Canon made their report to the United States Circuit Court. The question involved is whether there was any necessity that the South Park should locate its road on the right of way of the Denver Rio Grande, as it attempted to do, claiming that this was the only available route by which it could get through the canon. The Rio Grande denied this, and claimed that the other road could be built just as well without encroaching on its right of way, and that the only thing which the South Park gained by so encroaching was a reduction in the cost of building. The commissioners found that the South Park had located its line at certain points only thirty-two feet from the Rio Grande track although at an elevation of fifteen feet above it and on the same side of the creek. They found that it could be moved directly back off the right of way of the Denver & Rio Grande at an increased cost of less than $50,000 and that it could cross to the other side of the creek without in any way interfering with the Denver & Rio Grande, at an increased cost of about $13,000. The interference is on the townsite of Kokomo and work on the proposed South Park line at that point has heretofore been prevented by an injunction. As the report of the commission sustains the allegations of the Denver & Rio Grande, it is probable that the injunction will be made permanent.

"THE COMMISSION'S REPORT

"The Commission, being bound by oath to impartially and faithfully discharge their duties, do hereby submit the following report:

"First: The Road of the Denver South Park & Pacific Railroad Company as projected, surveyed, and partially constructed is upon the same side of Tenmile Creek as that of the Denver & Rio Grande Railway Company within the townsite of Kokomo. The point of conflict where the two lines approach within the one-hundred

foot limit, and where the Denver South Park & Pacific thus encroaches upon the right of way of the Denver & Rio Grande, occupies a distance of 1,775 feet. Within this 1,775 feet the South Park has located its line at distances varying from 32 to 72 feet from the Rio Grande's right of way, and from 13 to 15 feet above it.

"Second: In the operation of the two roads, if so constructed, there might be no necessary obstacle to occasion interference between them, unless it be the possible inconvenience which may arise in clearing the tracks of snow in case of heavy storms and much drifting. This may be obviated by the construction of snow sheds at the requisite points.

"Third: In locating and constructing the South Park grade at the prescribed distance of one hundred feet from the grade at the Denver & Rio Grande, the obstacles encountered will depend materially upon the gradient employed. To remove the line into the hill so as to clear the Denver & Rio Grande track sufficiently and yet conform to the present fixed gradient, would present serious obstacles. It would necessitate a great amount of rock work and excavating. The cost of the present located Denver South Park & Pacific line is stated to be $7,536. The estimated cost of constructing a new line through the side of the hill is $54,642. To eliminate this excess cost of construction is would be necessary to abandon the present depot site and select a different line.

"Fourth: The Commission proposes two different routes through Kokomo which the Denver & South Park might use in lieu of the present route:

"The first proposal is a plan whereby the Denver South Park & Pacific, by means of an overhead crossing, could pass to the westerly side of both the Denver & Rio Grande and Tenmile Creek, and then by recrossing the Denver & Rio Grande and Tenmile Creek reunite with the present grade of the Denver South Park & Pacific. Both of these crossings could be located within the townsite of Kokomo. This plan would accommodate the business of Kokomo, avoid interference with the Rio Grande right of way, and should prove mutually satisfactory to both parties. The cost of this proposed line is estimated to be $20,380, exclusive of right of way.

"The second proposal is a plan whereby the Denver & South Park would leave its present location near the upper end of the townsite and pass to the east of the Denver & Rio Grande right of way and the town of Kokomo at a greater elevation upon the mountain side, reuniting with their present grade at a point near the lower edge of the townsite. This is a practicable line possessing the same general characteristics of alignments and gradients as their present located line. It is estimated that this line would cost $18,810. However, such a location, being more remote from the town and at a higher elevation, might be objected to on account of the sacrifice of depot facilities, and its inconvenience of access in respect to the accommodation of business. Also the railroad would have less available ground for sidings and yard room with which to secure business and serve the community."

Judge Hallett reviewed the Commission's report and three days later ruled that the South Park road adopt the first proposal whereby they would enter and leave the town of Kokomo by means of the two overhead crossings over the Rio Grande. The Union Pacific's attorney, Mr. Teller, reported that they were well satisfied with the decision, adding the statement: "On the located route the use of snowsheds would be required, and it was estimated that they would cost about $7,000. This expense would be avoided on the route adopted, and in consequence, the increased cost would be only about $6,000."

The Rio Grande management, having gained their point that the South Park should keep off their right of way, was also satisfied with the decision.

Then, for reasons which we have been unable to determine, the engineers decided against the plan of building the two overhead crossings as outlined by the Commission, and chose a third route. This newly proposed line followed the suggestion as outlined in the second proposal to a certain extent. They followed along the mountain side east of the Rio Grande track and the Tenmile, keeping their required distance from the former, but instead of extending the line a sufficient distance to hold the required gradient, they chose to shorten this particular section of track and built a switchback. In view of the fact that the lower leg of this switchback was located along the base of the mountain side in close proximity to Tenmile Creek, sufficient ground room was available for such station and yard facilities as were required.

Construction of this switchback had hardly commenced when they encountered further difficulties. In the Denver Republican of December 19, 1883, we read:

"SOUTH PARK IN A NEW DILEMMA

"Major Evans, Chief Engineer of the South Park railroad, says another difficulty is arising in connection with the Leadville extension. No sooner has the road been ordered off the Rio Grande's right of way, than it is hindered from advancing in any other direction. As soon as the South Park left the Tenmile Canon, it graded a line over a switchback. There would be no interference there, supposed the engineers, but it was a mistake. Now that it was beginning to lay track over the switchback, the owner of the land is stepping up and asks an immense price for the strip of land, not over 2,000 or 3,000 feet in length. The sum is so exorbitant that the South Park will have to go to the Courts. It looks as though the completion of the road was a question of the distant future."

Relative to this lawsuit, we read in the Denver Republican of January 20, 1884:

"SOUTH PARK ENJOINED

"Restrained from entering any part of the Crown Mining Claim, between Big English and Dutch Gulches, for purpose of building a railroad or cutting any timber. $5,000 damages asked for grade already built."

Offhand it appeared that the South Park was again blocked. However, an agreement was reached with the owner of the land in question and the railroad completed their switchback. The completion of this switchback closed the last gap in the line between Dickey and Leadville.

Before leaving the story of the Kokomo switchback, the reader will be interested to learn that this arrangement did not last very long, being in actual use only about ten months. The switchback served until the latter part of 1884, at which time the South Park reverted to the first plan suggested by Judge Hallett's Commission, and built the two overhead crossings over the Rio Grande's track. This new line was completed and opened to traffic on December 21, 1884, thus obviating further use of the switchback. Parts of the old switchback grade can still be seen.

On February 5, 1884, the first South Park locomotive passed over the route between Como and Leadville. Concerning this important event, the Leadville Daily Herald of Wednesday, February 6, 1884, stated:

"The completion of the South Park railroad to this city, which was shown by the running of the first locomotive over the new line into Leadville yesterday, is an event of no small importance. It means competition in freight and passenger rates to Denver and through Denver to all the east. It opens up a new territory to the trade and enterprise of this city, and sets the business of Leadville free from the chains which have heretofore bound it to one railroad. Both Leadville and Denver have reason to rejoice over the completion of this great work which ended yesterday." Author's note: This particular news item probably gave the Union Pacific and Rio Grande "Big-Wigs" a hearty laugh.

Officially, the Como-Leadville line was completed, but owing to the accumulation of an excessive amount of snow and ice along the line, especially between Leadville and Dickey, it was impossible to open the high line to regular traffic. This placed the South Park in a rather difficult situation for the time being, for it must be remembered that General Palmer's six months notice to the Union Pacific of the termination of their Buena Vista-Leadville agreement expired February 6, 1884.[1] In commenting on this situation, the Railway Age stated:

"The contract between the Denver South Park & Pacific and the Denver & Rio Grande for trackage rights between Buena Vista and Leadville is about to end. An extension of time will be asked for in the hopes that the South Park will not have to drop Leadville from its list of stations."

In view of this predicament which faced the Union Pacific, the Rio Grande extended the agreement to May 1st, with the expectation that the line could be cleared of all snow and any necessary repairs made by that date. Throughout March and April the snow and cold weather continued to such an extent that it was impossible to get any work done. As a result, the Rio Grande again extended their agreement. It was not until July that a sufficient amount of snow had disappeared to allow work to commence. The job of clearing the track of snow and making the extensive repairs necessary to get the line in operating condition was then pushed vigorously in order that the high line could be opened to traffic as soon as possible.

1. Denver Republican, January 30, 1884.

Engine 115 (later C.& S. 10) with an eastbound passenger train on the trestle over Tenmile Creek and the Rio Grande's tracks at Kokomo.

*Graves photo,
from T. G. Thomas Collection.*

THE NATHROP CUTOFF

During 1883, while preparations were being made to open the Boreas Pass line, steps were also being taken to change the various track connections between the South Park and the Rio Grande in the vicinity of Buena Vista and Nathrop.

From the time the South Park first built into the Arkansas Valley in February, 1880, until the completion of the high line between Como and Leadville, they used the track of the Rio Grande between Buena Vista and Nathrop as a connecting link with the Gunnison extension. This was in accordance with terms incorporated in the Joint Operating Agreement drawn up between the two roads. The completion of the high line terminated this agreement and necessitated some changes in the South Park's trackage facilities between Buena Vista and Nathrop. These changes required the construction of an independent line to connect their Trout Creek line with the Chalk Creek line which branched off the Rio Grande at Nathrop, some five miles south.

As previously related, the South Park's original track had been built down Trout Creek to a point near milepost 132 where it then left the canon and turned northwest toward Arkansas Station and Buena Vista. The shortest route between the Trout Creek exit and Nathrop led down the canon through an extremely narrow and crooked cleft in the mountains known as Box Canon, a brief description of which seems necessary.

On its approach to the Arkansas Valley, the banks of the creek bed gradually become higher and steeper until a good sized canon is formed. At this point the gorge, or Box Canon, makes two sharp left and right turns similar to the letter "S". The canon proper is not more than 75 to 100 feet wide at the bottom, while the perpendicular walls of solid granite tower straight up for 200 feet or more on either side, forming a narrow chasm which was to spell disaster for that section of the railroad in the years to follow. Upon emerging from this gap in the rocks, Trout Creek sprawls out over the flat sandy bottom of the valley until it empties into the Arkansas River.

For some unknown reason, the Union Pacific engineers chose to build the connecting link down Trout Creek through Box Canon where the track then turned south toward Nathrop. It seems to the author that had this connecting link been commenced at Macune, the railroad would have been able to avoid some of the disastrous washouts that occurred along this section of the stream in later years. However, as we have explained, Trout Creek in the early eighties did not appear to be such a dangerous stream as it later turned out to be. In fact, William J. Coogan, an early South Park runner, wrote the writer:

"When the Union Pacific built their line down through Box Canon in 1883, there was just a small stream and it kept in its banks and there was plenty of room for both the stream and the track."

The work of contructing this Nathrop cutoff, as the Union Pacific called it, was begun in 1883 and completed and put in service in January, 1884. This included the construction of approximately five miles of new main line track between the Trout Creek connection and Nathrop. The building of this segment of track necessitated the construction of quite a large bridge over the Arkansas River just above Nathrop. This bridge was an iron truss structure built on stone piers. There were two main spans, each 125 feet long, while the total length, including the two approaches, was 304 feet. The bridge was 48 feet above the river. Some three miles of track was also built to connect Buena Vista, by way of Macune, with the new main line at a point known as Schwanders. The south leg of the large wye below Buena Vista, originally built to form a connecting link with the Rio Grande, was taken up. See the Buena Vista and Nathrop District map, in pocket on back cover of this book.

The north leg of this wye remained to form part of a new line built into Buena Vista proper. Another section of track, 1.48 miles in length, which formed a part of the original main line between Trout Creek and Macune, was also taken up. In the following year, 1885, all physical connections between the two roads at Nathrop were removed. The Union Pacific reported that the Nathrop cutoff, including all track changes mentioned, and the bridge across the Arkansas River, entailed a total expenditure of $97,342.60.

The job of putting the finishing touches on the Leadville extension continued unabated throughout the summer of 1884. By September all was in readiness and on September 30, 1884, the high line was opened to traffic.[1] Thus, the much publicized "Short Line to Leadville" was finally completed. The air-line distance between Denver and the silver camp was only 77 miles but it required 151 miles of railroad track that wound around the equivalent of 97 complete circles and climbed over three mountain passes to get there. Relative to the opening of the line, we read in the Leadville Democrat of September 30, 1884, the following news item:

"The South Park will commence regular operation of trains via the High Line Wednesday, saving 1 hour and 5 minutes running time between Leadville and Denver.

"It has been using the Grande's Buena Vista-Leadville line for the past four years, paying $10,000[2] per year for trackage rights. This charge also includes all office expense at Leadville. The South Park will now have their own depot and offices. A freight depot has been erected at 9th and Hemlock Streets and the company has remodeled a two-story building at 327 East 8th

1. Union Pacific Annual Report, Dec. 31, 1884.
   Railway World, Oct. 11, 1884.
2. This figure is in error, as previously explained. The annual fee was approximately $96,000.

George E. Mellen photo,
from Morris W. Abbott Collection.

One of the narrowest spots on the South Park's track in Box Canon, beside Trout Creek, just below Dead Man's Curve.

Street for temporary use as a passenger depot. The first passenger train for Denver will leave Leadville at 8:45 Wednesday morning and arrive in Denver at 6:15 PM. The full fare is $12.50 each way. There will also be two freight trains per day. The South Park office force, heretofore directly in the employ of the Rio Grande, will be paid off this evening and leave the old Union depot for the temporary station on 8th Street. The South Park contemplates building a new and elegant passenger depot at an early date. (Author's note—the new depot was not constructed until 1893.)

"From Denver to Leadville by the old route was 171 miles; by the new line it will be 151 miles, while by way of Colorado Springs, Pueblo and Salida on the Rio Grande, it is 277 miles.

"The South Park's new roundhouse is practically completed. It will accommodate eight locomotives. The new turntable and water tank have been completed. The South Park force consists of Colonel George W. Cook, General Agent for both railroads; J. Hughes, Cashier; John Salter, Ticket Agent, and four other gentlemen. The rifle in Colonel Cook's office is loaded for 'Pass hunters'."

The writer regrets that no newspaper items could be located giving the details regarding the first official train, engine number, crew, etc. The only information was that Mr. Philip Kaub was engineer on the first regular passenger train to run from Denver to Leadville.[1] Perhaps some day this interesting story will come to light. Before concluding this section we might add that on this date, the Rio Grande ceased using the Chalk Creek line to Alpine (later known as Fisher), and the South Park ceased using the tracks of the Rio Grande between Buena Vista and Leadville.

It is rather difficult for the ordinary layman to give a satisfactory written description and explain the difficulties Major Evans encountered in locating a feasible route for a railroad between Como and Leadville. Like many other difficult but interesting exhibitions of railroad construction, a complete technical description of this route would be highly desirable. However, most amateur railroad historians have to be content with descriptions based, too often, on the ill-directed admiration of some dreamy-eyed advertising agent, or a news reporter who is entirely devoid of the capacity for properly describing the subject in question.

Standing in Como, Maj. Evans was faced with a great mountain barrier—a solid pile of granite that reached heights of thirteen and fourteen thousand feet, and whose peaks and canons seem to elbow one another as if to array themselves in a closer formation to exclude an encroaching civilization. His goal was on the far side and his job was to find a path for the steel rails, mark the ledges where the tracks could hang, and stake out a right of way with curves and gradients over which

1. Fritz G. Nagel, great-grandson of Mr. Kaub.

trains could run. His was a hard task, but he succeeded and laid a steel trail over two great mountain passes, both in excess of 11,300 feet. To reach this goal, Maj. Evans started out at Como at an altitude of 9,796 feet, climbed to the summit of Boreas Pass, 11,493 feet, dropped down to the valley of Blue River near Breckenridge and thence to the station of Dickey at an elevation of 9004 feet, and once again climbed to a height of 11,320 feet, before he was able to drop down into Leadville. There were no great chasms or deep gorges of rushing rivers to span, no tunnels to bore, or long rock retaining walls to build, but it did require the blasting of many benches and cuts in the granite mountain sides, and the construction of numerous bridges and fills to accommodate the steep and curving track. It was one continuous procession of curves, cuts, fills, and trestles, requiring 62.9 miles of track to travel an air-line distance of 23 miles.

The following figures will give the reader some idea of the great amount of curvature and steep grades encountered in the ten miles between Como and Boreas. With the exception of some 525 feet of track located about three-quarters of a mile north of Como, this entire section was one continuous climb. From milepost 91.8, just beyond Peabodys, to the summit, a distance of 7 miles, it was a continuous climb of 4% or more. Included in this 7-mile stretch was a 1.1 mile section near milepost 93.0 that was a continuous climb of 4.49%, and it included twelve curves, of which five were 20 degrees each.

The descent from Boreas to Breckenridge was indeed a notable achievement in this man's career. Unfortunately, it is very difficult to give by printed description or illustration any correct idea of the many problems encountered by Maj. Evans in locating and surveying this line down the rugged north slope of Boreas Pass. Similar to the line up the opposite side, this descent into Breckenridge was one continuous line of curves, cuts, fills, and bridges. The air-line distance between the summit and Breckenridge is approximately six and one-half miles, and the difference in elevation is 1,925 feet; to negotiate this intervening distance and maintain a gradient somewhere within the limits of 4%, required 11.2 miles of track and involved 108 curves of from one to 25 degrees. Another interesting item is that over 82% of this 11.2 miles was on a 4% grade. Between Rocky Point, at milepost 104.9, and Mayo Spur, milepost 106.5, a distance of 1.6 miles, there were four 20 degree curves, and six 24 degree curves on a steady 4% grade. The greatest concentration of curvature on the entire high line was between Baker Tank and Mayo Spur. Within this section, a distance of 4.3 miles, the track negotiated fourteen 20 degree, eighteen 24 degree, and one 25 degree curves, all on 4% grade. One of the most interesting views throughout this entire section is to be seen at a place called Rocky Point. Standing at this point of the right of way, where the elevation is some

Otto Westerman photos,
from Elmore Wehrly Collection.

The upper two photos show Denver Leadville & Gunnison 113 (note initials on sand dome) just below Rocky Point on the west slope of Boreas Pass, headed upgrade. The lower picture shows D.S.P.& P. 213 in the valley of the Blue River between Dickey and Breckenridge.

10,450 feet above sea level, one can clearly observe how the railroad curved around Nigger Hill and back to a point almost directly below the observer on a constantly descending grade to reach the bottom of Illinois Gulch. The track then disappears around the far side of Little Mountain, following Illinois Gulch to Breckenridge.

In the face of such tremendous odds, one sometimes wonders how the early Colorado railroads were able to lay their steel rails over such mountainous regions. It is a safe prediction that in the hands of engineers, not driven to economy by necessity, or railroad construction by unorthodox methods, such railroad projects as that through Platte Canon, or over Boreas or Alpine Passes, would have cost many times what they actually did, or would have been wholly impossible. One of the secrets of this economy was the comparatively free use of sharp curves. Eliminate all curves sharper than 15 degrees from this section between the summit and Breckenridge and we would multiply the cost four or five times. It would also render impossible such railroad construction as was to be found along this section of the South Park since the turn could not have been made around Illinois Gulch, Nigger Hill or Illinois Park. A far steeper grade on an entirely different route would therefore have had to be chosen, thus increasing construction expense considerably. In commenting on this particular section of the South Park, a reporter for the Railroad Gazette stated:

"It is interesting to note that one rides over these curves on Boreas Pass without the slightest sense of insecurity or danger, nor have they proved to be especially dangerous in operation. The motion around them is as smooth as around the six degree curves which so many engineers were formerly disposed to look upon as the ultimate limit for first class work, and which have been held to at such large expense on many lines. . . . The Westinghouse pressure retaining valve used on all South Park freight and passenger trains in descending these grades works like a charm. The train is always under control, and there is no difficulty in handling it down the grade at nearly uniform speed. The rail and wheel wear likewise, we are told is by no means excessive, although of course, far larger than it would be on a flat prairie road. The track was in fine condition last summer when this reporter rode over it."

After leaving Breckenridge the line followed the Blue River toward Dickey with a minimum amount of curvature. Within this section was a 1.6-mile tangent, the longest piece of straight track in the entire line between Como and Leadville. Leaving Dickey, the track skirted the north end of Tenmile Range, where it entered Tenmile Creek Canon and began the climb toward Climax at the summit of Fremont Pass, whose altitude is 11,320 feet. In negotiating this intervening distance, many sections of the track contained grades of 3.80%, with a maximum of 4.30% located between Curtin and Solitude. The descent from Climax down the west slope of Fremont Pass into Leadville was a 2% drop practically the entire distance. This last mentioned section also contained the greatest amount of curving track found

west of Dickey. However, with the exception of one 20 degree curve at Birdseye, the maximum was 15 degrees; but there were plenty of curves, especially between Climax and Birdseye. On the branch from Dickey through Dillon to Keystone, the maximum curvature reached was 11 degrees, while the maximum gradient was 3%.

For those interested in statistics, the following table of facts and figures concerning the line between Como and Leadville should prove interesting.

Total miles..63.83
Total miles of curvature 59.53
Per cent of curvature:
    Como to Breckenridge 47.75
    Breckenridge to Leadville................29.36
Number of curves 435
Maximum curvature............25 degrees, 20 minutes
Total degrees of curvature .... 13,266 degrees, 44 minutes
Number of complete circles 36.85
Maximum grade east, per cent 4.03
Maximum grade west, per cent.............4.49

A study of the profile map will give the reader additional information regarding the mountainous terrain encountered in this section.

Another interesting phase of the high line is the snowsheds, most of which were constructed during 1884-85 shortly after the completion of the line. As far as is known, all the sheds on this Leadville branch, with the exception of two, were located on the east slope between Como and Boreas. Regarding the two exceptions, one was located east of Breckenridge and the other was located over a long cut just west of the Kokomo depot. The following data, taken from the January, 1886, list of D.S.P.&P. buildings and bridges, gives the details and locations of the road's snowsheds on this division.

Shed Number	Clearance from base of rail	Width	Length in feet	Location
1	18 feet	15'8"	450	Located on east slope of Boreas
2	"	"	1500	Pass between
3	"	"	208	Half Way, Mile-
4	"	"	344	post 93.9, and
5	"	"	272	Selkirk, Mile-
6	"	"	336	post 96.1.
7	"	"	384	
8	"	"	384	
9	"	"	420	
10	"	"	600	Boreas, Milepost 98.8
—	"	"	150	On a side track at Boreas
—	16'4"	13'4"	527	Milepost 108.6 near Little Mountain Spur
—	—	—	544	Located over a rock cut just west of the Kokomo depot

The 1,500 foot snowshed, No. 2, was known as the Selkirk shed.

South Park engineering records disclose that there

A view from Rocky Point, looking toward Little Mountain and Breckenridge. Hookeye Curve in the foreground.

The mixed train, locally dubbed "The Tomcat", struggling up Nigger Hill (also shown in center of top photo).

Looking down Illinois Gulch toward Breckenridge from Puzzle Spur. Little Mountain at left and Nigger Hill at right.

were 58 trestles, bridges, and open culverts, totaling 3,040 feet, between Como and Leadville. These trestles and bridges varied in length up to 200 feet and in height up to 29 feet. Data relating to the larger structures is as follows:

Location Milepost	Spans	Length in Feet	Height in Feet	Construction	Remarks
90.8	12	191.5	6	Wood Frame	Over Tarryall Creek
95.8	10	157.0	15	" "	
96.0	12	191.5	16	" "	Selkirk Trestle
108.0	10	158.0	19	" "	Gold Pan Trestle
109.5	9	135.0	13	" "	Over Blue River
111.9	12	192.0	11	" "	Over Blue River
113.7	5	80.0	5	" "	Over Blue River
132.3	5	79.0	8	" "	Part of switchback at Kokomo
132.5	8	132.0	26	" "	Over D.&R.G. track at Kokomo
132.9	12	200.0	29	Iron Girder (later wood)	Over D.&R.G. track at Kokomo
138.4	5	79.5	18	Wood Frame	Over East Fork Arkansas River
143.2	11	175.3	24	" "	Over Birdseye Gulch
144.4	8	125.0	9	" "	
145.0	10	160.0	10	" "	

Fortunately, a few details regarding the construction and costs of this Leadville line have been found. Many early photographs disclose that construction of the grade followed the usual practice prevalent in the Colorado region during that early day. No solid rock or cinder ballast was used. As a rule, the grade consisted of dirt, and whatever rock was on hand, scraped up from along the edge of the right of way. Over this earthen grade the pine ties were distributed with some additional dirt tamped between them. However, after being in use year after year, a fairly good cinder ballast was built up on the steeper sections of the grade as a result of laboring engines shooting great quantities of cinders out of the stacks. In the more mountainous sections where it was all rock, necessary earth required had to be hauled to the scene of construction. An engineering report published during the Pacific Railway Commission Trials stated that the Boreas line used 3,000 pine ties per mile. Of the 62.9 miles of track between Como and Leadville, 55.0 miles were laid with 40-pound rail, 2.5 miles with 52-pound rail, 4.1 miles with 56-pound rail, while the remaining 1.3 miles were laid with 35-pound rail. The 6.8 miles on the Keystone branch were laid with 56-pound rail. The rail used cost the Union Pacific $68.80 per ton.

This report also stated that Fisher rail-joints were used in connecting the rail ends. The rails were spiked directly to the ties; no tie plates were used. All switches were of the stub-end type, using the old harp type switch stands.

During the Pacific Railway Commission Trials, Charles Francis Adams stated that the estimated cost of the high line was placed at $300,000, but that it cost "fully a million", adding the remark "it was an error of judgment". As nearly as can be accurately determined, the Como-Leadville line cost $1,134,399.59. This is an average of approximately $18,000 per mile. The Keystone branch cost $69,000, or an average of $10,147 per mile. An interesting item found in connection with the letting of the contract was the statement that all ties, rails, switches, water tanks, buildings, depots, etc., were to be furnished by the Union Pacific Company.

G. M. Best Collection.

D.S.P.&P. 70 stands atop Boreas Pass, elevation 11,493 feet, beside the newly constructed stone engine house in 1884.

CHAPTER XIV

EARLY BRANCH LINE CONSTRUCTION

During the decade following the Denver South Park & Pacific's acquisition by the Union Pacific, the little railroad had a rough and rugged road to travel. It is a tragic story of how the property was dissipated, mismanaged, and forced into a receivership which eventually caused the Union Pacific to lose control of the road entirely. However, before taking up the discussion of the details which led to receivership, the author will endeavor to cover the branch line construction that occurred during the period of Union Pacific control. The underlying purpose of the construction of these branches and extensions was to gain some strategic advantage over a rival road, to effect a shorter route between various points, or to connect the main line with some profitable source of traffic. Some of these projects were proposed prior to the sale of the road to Gould and the Union Pacific; others were projected afterward. Some of them were sound; others were not.

These plans entailed a wholesale group of projected extensions which spread out over southwest Colorado like an octopus. The Denver News of September 22, 1880, carried the story of a proposed change in the original Denver South Park & Pacific's Articles of Association whereby it was proposed to increase the capital stock of the company from $5,000,000 to $20,000,000. Their plans also called for the organization of a new construction company for the purpose of building certain extensions, branches, and telegraph lines. Among the new incorporators were S. H. H. Clark, G. P. Morosini, J. J. Slocombe, Jay Gould, and Russell Sage, most of whom will be readily recognized as Union Pacific men; indicative of the strong influence which that company was exerting over the South Park management. It seems that Gould and Sage were to furnish most of the money.

The amended articles proposed the construction of a line to branch off the South Park near South Platte station, following up the South Fork of the Platte River and thence down Oil Creek to Canon City and Grape Creek to Silver Cliff and Rosita. Another projected line was to branch off the Gunnison extension just beyond Parlin and follow Cochetopa Creek south along that stream to the town of Cochetopa. From this point the line was to follow the most practical route southeast to

the Saguache River, and thence along or near that stream to the town of Saguache. Another projected line on the Gunnison extension followed the Gunnison River northwest to Crested Butte. Their plans also called for the extension of the Gunnison line southwest to Lake City, and another to the Uncompahgre River region. This last line was to be extended to Ouray and the rich and undeveloped territory near Rico in Dolores County. The reader will remember that mention of a few of these projects radiating directly out of Gunnison was made in a previous chapter. They also planned to extend the so-called Dudley branch of the South Park (provided for in the original Articles of Association) by way of Hoosier Pass to the town of Breckenridge. This projected branch line was to leave the main line at or near the crossing of the South Platte River near the vicinity of Garos; thence, up that stream by way of Fairplay, Alma, Dudley, Hoosier Pass, and down the Blue River to Breckenridge. Their plans even included a standard gauge line from Denver to Pueblo via Colorado Springs. In commenting on this last plan, the Denver News stated: "This revives the fact that in its agreement with the Rio Grande, the Santa Fe was guaranteed against broad gauge competition into Pueblo. But the Santa Fe, it seems, was not proscribed from aiding any other line that might want to enter into competition with the Rio Grande. There is no agreement between the South Park and the Santa Fe in this new South Park enterprise, but there can be no doubt that when and if the new road is completed, it will be of mutual advantage to both."

Of the many projected branches or extensions all except two came to naught. The Cochetopa and Saguache projects, the Rico and Lake City extensions, and the Denver-Pueblo standard gauge line were never attempted. Neither was there any attempt made at the time to build the South Platte extension toward Canon City; however, agitation to construct this line was resumed again in 1888, with the same results. Finally, in 1896, a portion of this route was included in a proposed line to Cripple Creek, the story of which will follow later. As the reader already knows, the Ohio Creek line was eventually extended as far as the Baldwin and Kubler coal mines, where it stopped. This leaves only

266

David S. Digerness Collection.

C.B.& Q. 537, an outside frame 2-8-0 from the Burlington's narrow gauge Black Hills line (leased to the C.& S.), on an eastbound freight at Breckenridge in 1936.

Otto Westerman photo,
from Francis Rizzari Collection.

Breckenridge from Shock Hill, with 14,000-foot Mt. Baldy jutting up in the background. Rounding the hill at the far right, the grade passes Rocky Point, and near the center of the photo it can be seen descending Nigger Hill.

the Dudley branch to be taken care of. This project became known as the Alma branch and its history follows.

THE ALMA BRANCH

First and foremost of these smaller branches was the line built from Garos up the North Fork of the South Platte River to connect with the Alma mining district. This district came into existence around 1860, hence it dates back to the State's pioneer days. It was then that prospectors were roaming this wild and rough section of the Rockies searching for gold in the alluvial soils. The gulches along the western rim of South Park soon disclosed their valuable contents and the rush was on.

The first settlement in this particular region was established in 1859 by a group of prospectors who had worked their way over the range from Gilpin County.[1] History tells us that this party of weary men, in pausing to rest beside a small stream before proceeding farther west, discovered gold deposits in the bed of the stream. As a result of their success, they established a camp and named it Tarryall. The news of their success spread fast and the population of the gulch was quickly augmented by many new arrivals. The newcomers were promptly disappointed at finding all of the desirable alluvial ground taken up by the first contingent of prospectors, who refused to share with them.

The unwelcome men left and soon found their luck in the gravels of the South Platte River near the point where it issues from the mountains into the western edge of South Park. They named their newly established camp Fairplay and shared their discoveries with all comers.[2] The news of their success spread rapidly and prospectors rushed to the vicinity. These pioneer prospectors began to work their way gradually upstream. Rich placers were discovered on the site of Alma; however, it does not appear that any settlement was made there until a few years later in 1873.[2] Gold was found, not only in the gravel of this river's bed, but also in the many small gulches near the Platte. As the prospectors gradually extended their search up the many gulches and the mountain sides, numerous rich deposits of gold and silver were discovered. As a result, many famous mines such as the Phillips, London, Orphan Boy, Moose, Excelsior, Dolly Varden, Sacramental, etc., were opened up. The operation of these mines resulted in the establishment of many new mining camps, and such places as Fairplay, Buckskin Joe, Dudley, Montgomery, Alma, Park City, Quartzville, and others soon mushroomed into existence.

In 1873, the Boston & Colorado Company erected a smelter near Alma. By the latter part of the '70's, the region was humming with activity. The United States Government report on mining in Colorado gives the

1. Colorado State Geological Survey Bulletin No. 31.
2. Colorado State Geological Survey Bulletin No. 3.

following yearly production figures of all minerals such as gold, silver, lead, copper, and zinc, for Park County.

1858 to 1867	$2,490,000.
1868	50,000.
1869	40,000.
1870	80,000.
1871	60,300.
1872	241,200.
1873	533,142.
1874	587,800.
1875	633,000.
1876	525,900.
1877	471,800.
1878	450,200.
1879	473,300.
1880	445,800.

Governor Evans and his associates were fully aware of all the mining activity present in the Alma district, even before the railroad was built across South Park. Although they were well aware of the potential value of this immense amount of traffic and its importance as a source of revenue to the railroad, plans for the actual construction of a branch line into the district were held in abeyance until 1880. During the fall of that year, it was decided to construct a branch line to Alma, the center of business for that region. Accordingly, on October 4, 1880, the following resolution was passed by the board of directors.

"On motion of Mr. Moffat it was Resolved, That the line of road of this company extending from Garos to Fairplay and Alma in Park County be located as surveyed by the Chief Engineer of this Company and the President and Chief Engineer be directed to file the necessary plats and profiles with the Secretary of the Interior as required by law to secure the right of way over the public lands."

Due to the rather rough nature of the terrain between Fairplay and the main line, and also because of scattered mining activities along the South Platte, Eicholtz chose Garos, a station located near the crossing of the Middle Fork of the South Platte, as the connection point. From Garos the line more or less followed the South Platte River past Fairplay to the foot of Mosquito Gulch, a short distance below the site of Alma.

A construction gang was put to work immediately but progress was slow. One year later, we read in the Railway Age of November 17, 1881, that the end-of-track was completed to Fairplay, ten miles above Garos, and opened for business. During the early part of 1882, the line was extended to a point known as London Junction—sometimes called Alma Junction, 1.1 miles below the town of Alma. This branch line was 15.4 miles in length and cost $169,400 to build.[1] The track crossed the South Platte River four times on wooden trestles of 96, 96, 111, and 80-foot lengths, respectively. The maximum grade west was 3.58%, while the maximum curvature encountered was 24 degrees. Included in

1. Pacific Railway Commission Trials.

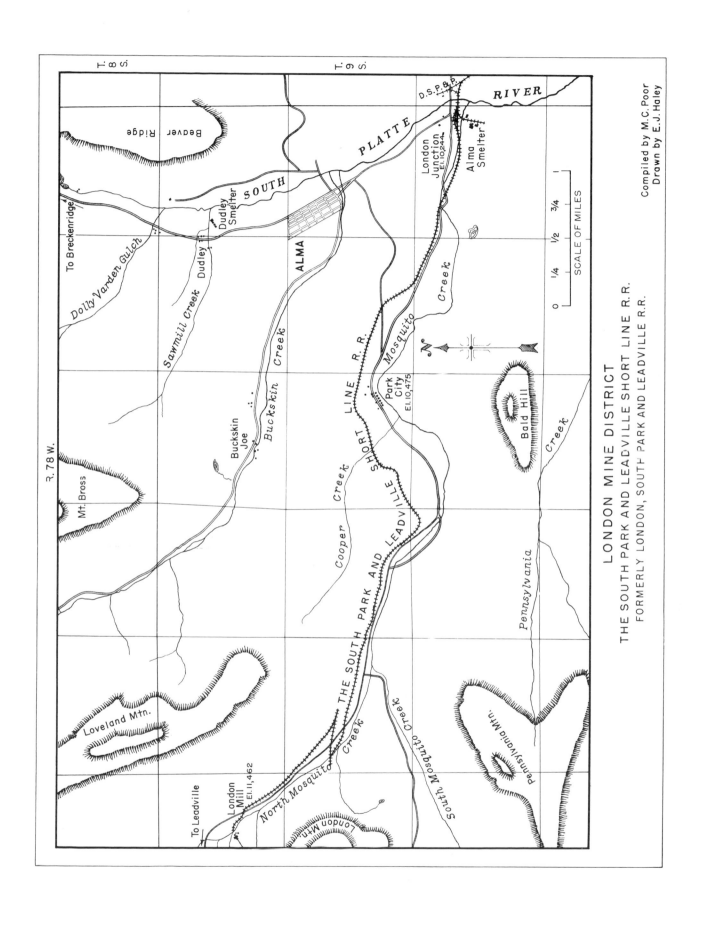

LONDON MINE DISTRICT

THE SOUTH PARK AND LEADVILLE SHORT LINE R.R.

FORMERLY LONDON, SOUTH PARK AND LEADVILLE R.R.

Compiled by M.C. Poor
Drawn by E.J. Haley

SCALE OF MILES
0   1/4   1/2   3/4   1

the Alma branch was a straight section of track 7.84 miles in length, the longest tangent found on the entire South Park railroad. The Alma branch was operated more or less continuously until the time of the abandonment of the last of the Colorado & Southern's narrow gauge lines.

THE LONDON SOUTH PARK & LEADVILLE RAILROAD

Contrary to the belief of many South Park fans, the London South Park & Leadville Railroad was never, at any time, an official part of the Denver South Park & Pacific Railroad Company, or its successor companies. Because of the fact that it was built to operate in connection with the South Park railroad and because it eventually passed into control of the Union Pacific, it is necessary that the history of this railroad be included.

Among the many mines opened up in the Alma district was the famous London Mine. This mine, discovered in the early seventies, was located on the north side of London Mountain at the head of Mosquito Gulch about six miles west of Alma. The main opening or portal was located on the south side of the old Mosquito Pass wagon road, which was built in 1879, between Fairplay and Leadville, by way of Mosquito Pass. Incidentally, the old wagon road is still in fair shape even today. The writer, accompanied by Ed Haley, travelled by auto up the road which utilizes the old railroad grade part of the way, to the end-of-track at the abandoned London Mine, in 1945, and from appearances one could still make his way over the pass to Leadville. London Mine was opened in 1875, and was worked more or less continuously from that date until 1932, producing, during that period, over $8,000,000 worth of gold, silver, copper and lead.[1] The principal owners of the mine during this early period were a group of eastern capitalists headed by H. J. Jewett and George R. Blanchard, who were at that time connected with the Erie Railroad.[2]

In view of the fact that the Union Pacific had completed the extension of the South Park's track to Alma, Blanchard and his associates concluded that it would pay them to build a railroad up Mosquito Gulch to serve as a connection between their London Mine Mill and the South Park's track at Alma. Accordingly, on February 16, 1882, they organized the London South Park & Leadville Railroad Company. According to the incorporation papers, the directors of this road were Hugh J. Jewett, George R. Blanchard, Herbert R. Smith, Charles G. Barber, John F. Moulton, and John T. Herrick. These papers further stated:

"The places from and to which said railroad shall extend are as follows: Commencing at a point in the County of Park and State of Colorado, between the towns of Fairplay and Alma; at or near the point where Mosquito Creek empties into the Platte River, thence following up the course of said Mosquito Creek to London Mountain, thence by the most available course across the Park Range of Mountains and into the City of Leadville, Lake County, Colorado, with such branches from said main line and within said Counties of Lake and Park as may from time to time be advisable."

The company was capitalized for $100,000 on the basis of 1,000 shares at $100.00 each. The principal office was listed as Fairplay.

Construction was commenced immediately, and must have been pushed quite rapidly, for we read in the Railway Review of October 14, 1882, that the line was completed. Very little of the engineering details are known regarding this railroad. It was of narrow gauge construction and was 7.37 miles in length. According to elevations shown on an early U. S. Geological Survey map for the region, the road climbed from a height of 10,244 feet at London Junction to an elevation of 11,462 feet at the London Mill, a difference of 1,218 feet. These figures show the average grade to be approximately 3.12%. An examination of old maps and a greater portion of the old grade does not seem to indicate an excessive amount of curvature. In order to gain sufficient altitude at the upper end of the gulch a double switchback, approximately 2,375 feet long, was built. As nearly as can be determined, the grade on the middle leg of this switchback was between 5% and 6%. There were four wooden trestles on the line; two were 48 feet long, one was 79 feet long, and the fourth 80 feet long. They varied in height from 6 to 10 feet. Thomas St. John, well-known conductor on the Colorado & Southern, tells the writer that the old London Mine branch was an "awful hunk of railroad", and about four empties was all one locomotive could drag up the wobbly iron rails to the mine.

Very little information has come to light regarding the rolling stock. During the Pacific Railway Commission Trials, Chas. F. Adams stated that the road owned one engine and some cars.[1] The author has been unable to locate any mechanical details concerning this engine. In attempting to run down a story about this engine being stolen by some South Park men, Ed Haley was successful in securing this unconfirmed information:

"Both Tom St. John and Andy Nelson had heard about this incident, but Ed Haight, of Morrison, seemed to know more of the details, although he had no actual data such as names, dates, etc. It seems that the London Mine owned a light engine of which the South Park men were envious. So what did they do but slip up one dark night and steal this engine. They ran her down the Fairplay branch to Garos and up to the Como shops. They then painted the engine, gave her a new number, made a few other changes to further disguise her, and put her to work on the South Park road. Ed Haight related that he ran this engine more than once in later years but cannot recall the number."

1. U. S. Geological Survey, Vol. 911.

2. Railroad Gazette, March 10, 1882.
   Poor's Manual of Railroads, 1882.

1. Jim Delaney of Denver informs the writer that Davey Bones, early South Park runner, delivered this engine and seven cars to the London Mine road.

According to information printed in the Fairplay Flume, one of the very early newspapers published in Fairplay, the portal of the London Mine was located near the top and on the north side of London Mountain at an elevation of 12,280 feet, while the mill and loading bins were located on the mountain side below the mine opening. The mill and bins were about 800 feet lower in elevation than the portal of the mine and an aerial wire rope tramway, the first in Colorado,[1] was built to transport the ore down the mountain side to the mill, a distance of some 3,300 feet. The railroad was extended up to this point and the track so built that the cars were loaded by gravity from the ore bins. The steel cables used on this old tramway are still hanging there, swinging in the wind between the squat wooden towers.

In 1883, the London Mine interests built a second stamping and concentrating mill at London Junction. During the first seven months after its completion this mill, known as the Alma Smelter, treated an average of 850 tons of ore per month, which was a remarkable production figure for those pioneer times. The mill, in this seven month period, produced $124,000 in gold and shipped 240 tons of concentrate to Denver and Black Hawk smelters.[1] With such an output from this and other highly productive mines in the Alma district, the South Park expected to receive a great amount of ore traffic.

For some unexplainable reason, the London Mine railroad ran into financial difficulties and reorganized as the South Park & Leadville Short-Line Railroad Company. The incorporation papers, which were dated April 10, 1885, listed the directors as David H. Moffat, Henry R. Wolcott, Samuel N. Wood, John T. Herrick, and Edward O. Wolcott. The object of this railroad was as follows:

"The railroad of this company shall be constructed from a point in or near the town of London Junction, Park County, Colorado, beginning at the switch where the track of the present line of The London South Park & Leadville Railroad leaves the line of The Denver South Park & Pacific Railroad Company and running thence up the course of Mosquito Creek to a point known as the upper terminus of the track of the present line of The London South Park & Leadville Railroad near the head of Mosquito Gulch in said Park County, and thence through the north ridge of said Mosquito Gulch to the nearest available point (governed by grades not to exceed 240 feet to the mile) to the present Highline track of the said Denver South Park & Pacific Railroad Company in Bird's Eye Gulch in Lake County, Colorado, and thence down the valley of the Arkansas to the City of Leadville in said Lake County, Colorado."

The company was capitalized for $100,000 on the basis of 1,000 shares at $100.00 each. Denver was listed as the principal office.

Apparently, the reorganization failed to improve the financial situation of the railroad and the company soon fell into the maw of the powerful Union Pacific. It seems that the latter road had advanced a considerable amount of second hand track material to the London South Park & Leadville Company at the time of the original construction, during 1882. In the meantime, Union Pacific interests had bought an $8,000 note (for $4,490.01) that was held against the London Mine road, and took a mortgage on the property. The London Mine interests, who controlled the road, failed to meet their debts and the Union Pacific foreclosed on them. According to the 1885 annual report of the Union Pacific, they took possession of all assets of the South Park & Leadville Short-Line Railroad Company, including the 1,000 shares of stock, certain equipment and appurtenances and their one engine and some cars.

Due to the inability of the road to meet its operating expenses, the Union Pacific made little or no attempt to operate it for the next few years. In the 1897 report of the Statistics of Railways, we find the following statement:

"The South Park & Leadville Short-Line Railroad, controlled through ownership of the entire capital stock by the Union Pacific, is operated by the Denver Leadville & Gunnison who keep the track in repair, furnish motive power and rolling stock. The South Park & Leadville Short-Line Company is charged with maintenance and is allowed 50 per cent of the freight earnings."

Around the turn of the century, the London Mine, due to the exhaustion of ore bodies in the old workings, opened a new portal on the south side of London Mountain at an elevation of some 11,970 feet. This rendered the little Mosquito Creek railroad practically useless, with the result that it was abandoned altogether.[1]

THE ASPEN PROJECT

Another Union Pacific project which involved South Park trackage was their proposed extension into Aspen. As a result of important mining developments in the vicinity of Aspen around 1885, a conflict arose between the Union Pacific, the Rio Grande, the Colorado Midland, and to some extent, the Burlington, for control of traffic in that area. By this time, the Rio Grande had pushed their railhead about 25 miles north of Leadville to Rock Creek, and they proposed to continue west along the Eagle and Grand Rivers to Glenwood Springs and thence up the Roaring Fork to Aspen. The Colorado Midland's projected line ran west from Colorado Springs via Buena Vista, Leadville, Basalt and thence up the Roaring Fork to Aspen.

The Union Pacific considered two routes into Aspen. The first involved the construction of a line from Fort Steele, a station located on their main line 180 miles west of Cheyenne, south by way of Kremmling, Dillon, Leadville, and Glenwood Springs.[2] This line, incorporated on September 28, 1886, was known as the Un-

1. Colorado State Geological Survey Bulletin No. 3.
2. Colorado Magazine, January, 1946.

W. H. Jackson photo,
from the Denver Public Library Western Collection.

D.S.P.&P. 48, formerly D.S.P.&P. 13, the "Ruby", with a mixed train at London Junction about 1886. Snow-covered Mt. Bross rises in the distance.

John Marks photo,
from Francis Rizzari Collection.

C.&S. 30, used for many years between Como and Alma, standing at the Alma depot in 1902. Alma is a mile north of this station, which was formerly known as London Junction.

ion Pacific & Western Colorado Railroad.[1] Regarding their second projected entry into Aspen, which involved certain South Park trackage, we read in the Railway Age of September 28, 1888:

"Engineers have completed the survey for an extension of the Denver South Park & Pacific from Leadville via Twin Lakes and Independence Pass (sometimes designated as Hunters Pass) to Aspen, Colorado, a distance of 50 miles. It is stated that construction will begin at once. An Aspen dispatch says: 'It is understood that the line will be constructed jointly with the Denver & Rio Grande and that a joint track will also be built from Aspen to Ashcroft, the South Park obtaining in exchange, the right to use the Rio Grande track from Aspen to the Rock Creek coal fields.' "

Further information concerning this second entry, but which involved certain proposed changes in the South Park's main line, is also found in the Railway Age of November 16, 1888.

"The Denver Republican says: 'The Union Pacific has recently made some important surveys, which, with reports, show that the Union Pacific intends to modify the South Park route to Leadville. The main line for a distance of about 30 miles in the section along Kenosha Hill is to be changed. It is their intention to go by the way of the South Platte to Como, thence by Mosquito Gulch or some pass to the south of Leadville, thence by Mosquito Pass to Aspen and thence southwest.[2] A corps of surveyors recently broke camp at Canon City and it is reported that a branch from this new line will run to that city which will make a line of 101 miles from the point 35 miles up the Platte River to Canon City.' "

Although the gauge of these projected lines is not known to the author, it is assumed that they were to be narrow gauge inasmuch as they were to be built and operated in conjunction with the Denver South Park & Pacific.

Considerable money was spent by the Union Pacific on survey and location work[3] and some actual grading was completed on the line south of Ft. Steele; however, no track was laid and work was suspended in 1886.[1] In

1. Union Pacific Annual Report, December 31, 1886.
2. Writer's note: Some newspaper reporter evidently slipped here. In all probability he meant: ". . . by way of the South Platte, Garos, Fairplay, Mosquito Gulch, Mosquito Pass, Leadville, Twin Lakes, Independence Pass, Aspen and southwest."
3. Colorado Magazine, January, 1946.

commenting on the fact that the Union Pacific suspended all further action on their projected Aspen extensions, the Colorado Magazine of January, 1946, states:

"A possible explanation lies in the fact that soon after the three-cornered contest between the Union Pacific (through the Denver South Park & Pacific), the Midland and the Rio Grande had taken place, Jay Gould, being already in the driver's seat on the Rio Grande and being president of the Missouri Pacific, acquired control of the Union Pacific. From his standpoint, there was no need of one road which he controlled invading the territory of another which he also dominated."

For a thorough review of the details relating to this struggle between the Union Pacific, the Rio Grande, the Burlington, and the Colorado Midland for the Aspen traffic, the reader is referred to the Colorado Magazine of January, 1946, and the July, 1945, issue of the Brand Book, official organ of the Westerners. Both papers were written by Judge William S. Jackson, Justice of the Supreme Court of Colorado. These papers cover an important epic in early Colorado railroad history.

Another piece of branch line construction proposed by the Union Pacific for the South Park, before the road went into receivership, was the Horseshoe or Leavick branch. During 1888, the company's engineers completed a survey for a line between Fairplay, on the Alma branch, and the Horseshoe mining district, and announced that construction would commence immediately,[1] but this was as far as their plans proceeded. For reasons best known to themselves, they shelved the idea and it was not until 1896 that Frank Trumbull, in connection with the Denver Leadville & Gunnison management, constructed the line.

During the period of Union Pacific control, a few news reports appeared from time to time regarding the completion of the Blue River line to the Grand River and Hot Sulphur Springs, and the Georgetown Breckenridge & Leadville extension from Graymont by way of a tunnel under Loveland Pass to connect with the South Park's Keystone branch. With the failure of these proposals, development and expansion of the South Park under Union Pacific control came to an end.

1. Railway Age, Sept. 7, 1888.

CHAPTER XV

MISMANAGEMENT AND RECEIVERSHIP

We shall now attempt to discuss some of the details or factors which eventually led to the South Park's receivership and the Union Pacific's loss of the road entirely. For a few years during the heyday of the Leadville boom, the little railroad did a land office business, but its subsequent history is a story of disaster and failure. Two factors were responsible for this situation. The first was mismanagement of the road by the Union Pacific; the second was the decline of Colorado's mining industry, more especially of the Leadville boom. The South Park, like numerous other early Colorado railroads, was built and maintained by gold and silver—the decline of this industry also sounded the death knell of the very roads it had nurtured and nourished. We shall take up the Union Pacific's managerial policies first.

Previous to, and during this period, the Colorado region was ripe for exploitation and the Union Pacific was exerting every effort in the promotion of their interests therein. During the scramble between the various railroad interests for control of transportation in the commonwealth, Gould had purchased the South Park railroad and immediately passed it along to the Union Pacific at a neat profit to himself. Without any consideration of their interest in the proposition, Gould ordered the transaction made and his orders were obeyed. The South Park was theirs and it was up to the Omaha management to make the best of the deal. Being a transcontinental railroad, their maximum efforts were directed toward the promotion of the more profitable long haul traffic. The Union Pacific management concluded that if the South Park was to fit into their program, it would be necessary that the road serve as a feeder line to their great railroad system. With this in mind, and with the rich Leadville haul waiting like the proverbial pot of gold at the foot of the rainbow, it appeared that perhaps the Evans road might become a valuable possession. They therefore bent every effort to see that the South Park be utilized as a feeder line over which some of Colorado's great ore traffic might flow to Denver, Omaha, and the East. In their attempt to gain this long haul Leadville traffic, it developed that the Union Pacific, much to the detriment of the welfare and future success of the South Park, began sacrificing local business in favor of their long haul traffic policy. A good example of the attitude of the Omaha office toward the

South Park is reflected in a comment made by Joseph K. Choate, Superintendent of the Union Pacific's Colorado Division during the latter eighties. Mr. Choate stated in the Union Pacific's annual report for the year 1888:

"The South Park Road has never paid a dividend to us, and yet it is claimed by railroad men in the West to be one of the most valuable franchises that the Union Pacific owns. On this line are the finest coal mines in the West. It is a controlling line in the ore shipments from Leadville. . . . As a feeder to the Union Pacific it is very valuable in that it controls $1,500,-000 worth of business per year from the smelters, and a large percent of the business from the Missouri River to the west; that if the road cost the Union Pacific a million dollars annually instead of the fifty to sixty thousand that it does cost, it would still be valuable."

It appears that immediately after the South Park properties were turned over to the Union Pacific, the Omaha management instituted their new policy and manner of conducting the road's business. Upon orders from New York, the management of the road was transferred from Denver to Omaha, whereas the previous board of directors and management were substantial Denver business men interested in the general good and welfare of the South Park railroad and the territory in which it operated. In the application of their new policies, the absentee Omaha management, knowing little about the road's peculiarities and the difficulties which the owners had encountered in obtaining and holding business, did not meet with any degree of success.

Fulfilling his promise to the Union Pacific, and to facilitate the change and look after the South Park's interests, Governor Evans agreed to remain as president of the road; however, the Union Pacific sent their representative, Mr. E. P. Vining, to Denver to act as general manager, and to carry out the Union Pacific's policies. Governor Evans soon became greatly dissatisfied with Vining's inefficiency and his Union Pacific policies and as a result wrote to T. L. Kimball, General Passenger and Ticket Agent at Omaha. An excerpt from this letter, dated January 6, 1881, is as follows:

"The rules about carload rates and turning all through business over to the Denver & Rio Grande, and the new local rates, have literally suspended business along the line. Many of our best customers will be bankrupt by it, and the road left without traffic, unless these conditions are changed at once. Orders to agents not to ship without prepayment of freight, issued from

Omaha today, do not touch the case. Unless a change is made soon, the business will be ruined and the road will not pay operating expenses.

Signed, John Evans"

The next day Governor Evans wrote to Jay Gould, who was principal proprietor of the Union Pacific and dictator of its policy and management. The letter follows in part:

"Denver, Colorado
January 7th, 1881.

"Jay Gould, Esq.,
Dear Sir:

". . . The Legislature is now in session and many members propose to regulate our tariffs and prohibit all pooling between railroads in the state, etc. This would be a serious blow to us, account of our agreements with the Denver & Rio Grande between Buena Vista and Leadville.

"Just at such an unfortunate time, Mr. Vining, without any consultation, either with me, Colonel Fisher, or Colonel Hughes, our late general freight agent who had arranged our tariffs and made our rules by which he began to get business and make the most out of it, issues a new tariff raising the prices on our local business to a prohibitory point, and adopting rules which will throw most of our through freight over to the Rio Grande, and increase our operating expenses greatly. For instance, we had at great pains got up cars to carry 12 tons and thus save dead weight. He charges double rates for all over eight tons in our carload rates. The quarries at Morrison produce a great amount of freight, and mainly belong to the South Park company. His rates for stone and lime are double the highest we had ever been able to get. This suspends work at your own quarries and throws the business into the Denver & Rio Grande.

"We had, with great care, worked up a lumber, wood, and tie business from the forests along our road, and by liberal rates for timber from our own lands, had built up a very large and profitable traffic at high rates from this source. Vining's tariff of the products of the forests are so great, that the business is suspended. His charge for wood from Buffalo is double what we had, and is nearly as much as the wood is worth. It has not only stopped shipments, but will bankrupt the men we have induced to come on our road to do business. Coal, too, is put at prohibitory rates. Some, ordered before knowing of the rise, is refused at the depot because the freights are more than the price of coal in the market. This unfortunate blunder is followed up today with orders, not to ship any more to parties refusing to take their goods and pay more freights than the goods are worth, unless freights are prepaid. Of course this makes the matter, serious as it is, ridiculous in the extreme. The road will not pay operating expenses long, under such management. The master of transportation, Mr. McCormick, says his empty cars are filling the side tracks for want of business, already. If continued much longer, this management will ruin the property. It will now require a long time to re-establish the business interrupted. Perhaps the most unfortunate aspect of the case is that it comes just as our Legislature is convened. The men, whose business is interrupted, builders, shippers, quarrymen, lumbermen, wood choppers, etc., raise a great hue and cry against the operations of the Union Pacific monopoly as they call it, and demand legislative protection. The papers have been pointing out the shortcomings of the Union Pacific and praising the Denver & Rio Grande, to our detriment, for a week or two, and now urge legislation. Our board of trade took up the question last night and appointed a committee to prepare a bill. We had a pretty solid sentiment against any legislation at this time, least it interfere with building roads, when this blunder was made. Now I fear it will be difficult to prevent hostile legislation. I doubt the practicability

of operating the South Park Road from so great a distance as Omaha, where local questions cannot be well understood. The difficulty of hurrying the completion of our extensions without the aid of the Union Pacific in getting forward men to work on contract is serious; but of this I will have time to speak hereafter.

"As I now hold a place of nominal responsibility, without any definition of my authority, I ask to know your wishes and that of the Union Pacific Company, before the matter gets any more unpleasant. Of course I cannot stand in place to be censured for acts I ought to correct, without any control over them. I shall be glad to hear from you by return mail.

Very truly yours, etc.,
Signed: John Evans"

Gould referred the letter to the Omaha officials. The warnings were ignored; John Evans received no reply from either Gould or the Omaha office and the Union Pacific policy continued to remain in force.[1] Further complaints and protests from Evans were to no avail. On December 20, 1882, the Union Pacific held their annual meeting and, for reasons best known to themselves, dropped John Evans and his two able assistants, Col. C. W. Fisher and John S. Brown, from the South Park's directorate.[1] This ended, for all time, Governor John Evans' connections with his beloved South Park railroad. From here on his further energies were to be directed toward the organization and construction of other railroad enterprises, the story of which forms an interesting chapter in his active career as a railroad builder of the early west.

In the past, one was led to believe that the Rio Grande's success in securing the major portion of the Leadville traffic was the result of fair competition, but after considerable research, the historian becomes suspicious and doubts the veracity of statements supporting the idea. There are numerous references regarding the existence of certain pooling arrangements whereby the Union Pacific, for a price, sat back and allowed the Rio Grande to carry the larger share of this traffic. Note the following testimony as given by John Evans during the Pacific Railway Commission Trials, (page 1856). We quote in part:

"The Leadville business was a great part of the South Park value. The road was hauling feed, grain, hay, coke, and miscellaneous supplies into Leadville, and bullion and ore out of the camp, in connection with a large lumber and coal business along the balance of the line. . . . The pooling of freight business between the D. & R. G. and South Park caused the South Park to lose much of their Leadville business and this, together with the high freight rates imposed by the new Union Pacific management, has just about ruined the South Park's Leadville business during the years 1881 and 1882. The Denver & Rio Grande was getting most all the business here through an agreement to pay the Union Pacific a flat sum of $800,000 a year to let them handle the Leadville business because they could do it at less expense."

Note the statement in Evans' letter to T. L. Kimball under date of January 6th, wherein he states: "The rules about carload rates and turning all through busi-

1. Pacific Railway Commission Trials.

275

W. H. Jackson photo,
from Denver Public Library Western Collection.

D.S.P.& P. 21, the "Pitkin City" beside the little frame station at Dome Rock, in Platte Canon.

ness over to the Rio Grande . . . have literally suspended business along the line". Note also Evans' statement in his letter of January 7th, to Gould, wherein he tells of Mr. Vining issuing new tariff rates and adopting rules that tended to throw much of the South Park's through freight over to the Rio Grande. Note Evans' statement made on the witness stand during the Pacific Railway Commission Trials wherein he stated: "Shortly after the transfer of South Park stock to Gould, steps were taken to increase rates on the South Park, which threw the business over to the Grande". This statement was subsequently denied by Charles Francis Adams, the Union Pacific President, but the denial carries little weight. Note a newspaper article in the Denver Republican under date of January 30, 1884, wherein are mentioned rumors of large royalties in connection with D. & R. G.-U. P. contracts.

In an effort to analyze this situation, one is faced with the question: Why did the Union Pacific propose to reduce local traffic on the South Park road in favor of long haul traffic, if this latter business was being turned over to the Rio Grande? Such a practice would only result in a more or less idle railroad and it is difficult to reconcile such a situation here. The fact that they discouraged local traffic in favor of the long haul business tends to refute arguments that the Union Pacific management entered into a pooling agreement to let the Palmer road have the greater share of the business. However, numerous statements to the contrary and the two letters of Governor John Evans, which have been quoted, are public records and cannot be overlooked. In view of such conflicting evidence, the author is faced with the debatable question as to whether this apparently unfavorable or unbalanced condition was the result of honest competition, or secret agreements made behind closed doors. Little progress has been made in the search for an acceptable explanation or definite answer. Truly, the policies and workings of the Union Pacific, not forgetting the Rio Grande, during this period, are hard to understand.

Other policies which tended to bring ruin upon the little road concern the Gunnison and Leadville extensions. The Union Pacific suspended construction of the proposed extension to the Gunnison and Elk Mountain coal fields and beyond, although much of the expense including surveying, grading and tie purchase had been incurred.[1] The act that proved most disastrous was the loss of the Buena Vista-Leadville trackage agreement which was responsible for the construction of the high line over Boreas Pass. Not only did this section of the railroad cost a terrific amount of money, but the company incurred a tremendous expense in operating it. Coping with the winter snows and two mountain ranges, with their accompanying steep grades and snow blockades in the high passes, wreaked havoc with the

road's operation. From testimony given during the Pacific Railway Commission Trials we learn that Boreas Pass was so blocked by snow during the winter of 1885 that for three months the line was impassable. Because of this tie-up the South Park was forced to move their traffic in and out of Leadville by way of Buena Vista. The Rio Grande's charges for this service during March were $10,823.69. In April the charges amounted to $11,889.46, and in May they were $13,577.37. It would be interesting to know how much the South Park paid out for similar services for this reason, in other years. The Boreas Pass line cost the South Park thousands of dollars, both in interest on their indebtedness and in operating expenses. The valuable Buena Vista-Leadville trackage agreement was the South Park's key to their Leadville business—never again could they operate as a successful rival to the Rio Grande. In the words of Governor Evans, ". . . with the loss of this contract went all chances the Denver South Park & Pacific had of ever enjoying its principal source of revenue, the Leadville traffic".

During one particular period, after the high line was completed into Leadville, the Rio Grande and the Union Pacific drew up a new pooling agreement wherein, for certain considerations, the Rio Grande practically controlled the Leadville business. Although very few actual figures have come to light, it seems that the South Park was allowed to have approximately one-third of Leadville's outbound traffic in lieu of certain traffic advantages which the Union Pacific was to have at other points in Colorado along Rio Grande lines. William S. Jackson (Colorado Magazine, January, 1946) states:

"Colonel D. C. Dodge, of the Rio Grande, had reported to his company in the year 1883 . . . that the division was roughly 60 per cent to the Denver & Rio Grande and 40 per cent to the Denver South Park & Pacific in spite of the fact that the haul to Denver was 100 miles longer via the Denver & Rio Grande."

Under the percentages which prevailed in 1886, the Rio Grande was entitled to about $1,700,000 of the gross earnings of the Leadville business and the South Park to about $800,000.[1] However, the South Park had not carried its full allowance and the remainder was made up to it by the Rio Grande. From what can be learned through the great amount of testimony brought out during the Pacific Railway Commission Trials, the Rio Grande was, from all appearances at this time, working hand-in-hand with the Union Pacific in the promotion of a goodly number of these schemes. By running all of Leadville's traffic through one common wringer and charging all that the traffic could possibly bear,[1] the Rio Grande and the Union Pacific were squeezing the maximum amount of revenue out of the community. This satisfied the Union Pacific interests, for their share went indirectly to the benefit of the Omaha management at the expense of the South Park.

1. McMechen, "Life of Governor Evans".

1. Pacific Railway Commission Trials.

Leadville not only received no advantage from having two railroads into Denver, but was seriously injured by the combination. The citizens of Leadville declared that on certain articles, it was cheaper to haul them by wagon team than to ship by rail. Railroad managements often make strange bedfellows; one minute they are fighting tooth and nail and the next they are working together harmoniously for the mutual benefit of each other. At times it is very difficult for the average layman to understand their policies.

The South Park was also a victim of other schemes at various times whereby it was deprived of freight revenue, e.g., in order to choke off a certain fuel company, the Union Pacific hauled coke from the Missouri River to Denver for $1.00 per ton, and from Denver to Leadville for nothing. Another example of this sort of treatment revolved around the Omaha & Grant Smelting Works in Denver. Two prominent Union Pacific directors, Sidney Dillon and Frederick Ames, were large stockholders in the Omaha & Grant company. These gentlemen decided that their Denver smelter needed some more business, and saw no reason why their Union Pacific connections could not be used to further their nefarious scheme. Accordingly, the Union Pacific issued a new tariff covering the shipment of ore and bullion from Leadville to Denver over the South Park. The new rate was $5.00 per ton on ore and $12.00 per ton on bullion. The ore rate was extremely low while the bullion rate was very high, the effect being to force the smelting business into the Denver branch of the Omaha & Grant company. The big mining and smelter operators of Leadville long suffered under this arrogant freight rate policy imposed on them by the Union Pacific and Rio Grande interests. They complained of these unbalanced rates, declaring that either the rate on ore was too low or the rate on bullion was too high. The $12.00 rate on bullion began to force the smelters out of business. As a result, less than half of the 23 furnace stacks in Leadville were in operation by 1887 and 1888. Thus, the Leadville smelter industry was crushed along with the South Park's freight revenue in favor of the Omaha & Grant Smelting works in Denver. The president of the Union Pacific, Charles Francis Adams, admitted that this was a great evil, but confessed his utter inability to remedy the situation.

By these and other means, one of the most spectacular successes in western railroad history, which had been paying all fixed charges, operating expenses, and eight per cent on the capital stock, was brought from wealth to ruin within a period of ten years—the same railroad of which Jay Gould wrote to Governor Evans on December 21, 1879, "all that you have ever said about it has more than proved true already".[1]

The second factor to be considered in the downfall of the South Park was the decline of the Leadville min-

1. McMechen, "Life of Governor Evans".

ing industry. This is clearly illustrated in the following table showing the annual production in dollars, for the period in question, of all minerals mined in Lake County such as gold, silver, lead, etc. The figures are from the United States Government report on mining in Colorado.

1879	$11,285,200	1885	$ 9,640,900
1880	14,910,900	1886	10,750,500
1881	12,108,300	1887	10,304,200
1882	15,256,400	1888	8,737,400
1883	15,242,350	1889	9,282,300
1884	12,042,300	1890	8,121,500

The Union Pacific had assumed control of the South Park January 1, 1881. During 1881-82, the Lake, Summit, and Gunnison County mines were at their zenith in production and the South Park's profits held up fairly well despite Union Pacific control. Following this period, the mining activity in these counties began a gradual decline, and this factor, together with the Union Pacific's mismanagement, turned the little road's profits into deficits. From 1884 to 1889, the operation of the road was very disastrous. In 1884, the expense of the road was $1.25 for every dollar taken in, and this railroad, which in 1880, returned $996,621 in net earnings, or $6,644 per mile on approximately 150 miles, netted a loss of $4,649 per mile on 321 miles. The following table shows the financial results from 1880 through 1889.

Year	Operating Revenue	Profit or Deficit
1880	$1,768,756.00	$996,621.49
1881	1,464,228.04	309,757.28
1882	1,558,723.48	377,449.60
1883	1,557,021.00	48,748.29
1884	1,194,069.17	549,193.22*
1885	1,145,494.40	320,869.32*
1886	1,246,539.77	368,081.16*
1887	1,282,681.78	289,430.33*
1888	1,065,386.86	315,897.48*
1889	1,008,234.80	248,497.53*

* Denotes deficit.

The statement of operations for the year 1887,[1] is a typical example of how the earnings and expenses were running during this particular period. It is as follows:

Earnings

Passenger	$ 242,380.76
Freight	962,319.09
Mail	20,351.45
Express	40,311.45
Miscellaneous	17,319.03
Total ($3,942.83 per mile)	$1,282,681.78

1. Poor's Manual of Railroads, 1888.

```
                 Expenses
Transportation ..................$  281,252.05
Motive Power ...................    517,619.86
Maintenance of Cars..............   117,188.16
Maintenance of Right of Way...     264,114.59
General Expenses .................    30,035.70
                                   _____
Total ($3,664.73 per mile)......$1,192,210.36
```

Interest on bonds, taxes, and other miscellaneous items amounted to $379,901.75, leaving a deficit of $289,-430.33. The accumulated deficit for the year ending December 31, 1889, was $2,091,969.04.[1] This was certainly a very unhealthy condition for a railroad only 325 miles long.

Shortly after the Union Pacific acquired the road, the South Park's bond issue rose from the original $1,800,-000 to $4,725,000, of which the Union Pacific held $2,797,000. The balance, $1,928,000, was in the hands of the public. It is interesting to note here that of the amount held by the public, $128,000 of these bonds had been issued to the Westinghouse Company in payment for air brake equipment that had been installed on South Park rolling stock. Even though the road was going into debt every year the Union Pacific continued to pay interest on these outstanding bonds until 1887. The interest payments amounted to approximately $130,-000 annually. Finally, on May 1, 1888, according to Poor's Manual of Railroads, they defaulted. Ames, of the Union Pacific board of directors, was asked why such a policy had been followed. He replied:

"The amount of business that the Union Pacific was able to control in Colorado by the South Park line gave them the benefit of the long haul east out of Denver, which more than offset the $126,000 interest they paid out. Also that it was not that people and business along the South Park would cease to ship via the South Park if this bond interest stopped, but that if the Union Pacific gave up control of the road, the whole of the Leadville business would be grabbed by the Denver & Rio Grande which would result in them losing much profitable long haul eastern traffic."

It is plain to see that the pursuance of such a program as the Union Pacific had followed over a period of years would eventually bring the South Park to the end of its rope. Even as early as 1885, the management began to observe the handwriting on the wall. In this connection we quote from an interview between Charles Francis Adams and a Denver newspaper man, wherein Adams attempts to blame economic conditions, and the actions of Colorado citizens themselves, as the causes of the railroad's plight. For some reason he forgot to

1. Compiled from financial statements contained in Poor's Manual of Railroads.

mention that perhaps Union Pacific policies and methods of doing business in Colorado might be partly responsible for any of the aforesaid troubles, or that Dillon and Ames's Omaha & Grant smelter deal could have any bearing on the subject. This interview, published in the Railway Review of July 18, 1885, is as follows:

"President Charles F. Adams of the Union Pacific tells the Denver Republican that his road would be better off if all the Colorado railroads owned by the Union Pacific would be swallowed up by an earthquake or otherwise lost. President Adams stated that the whole Colorado system was not paying operating expenses. The low market price of lead and other metals compel us to haul ores at a losing figure in order to allow the mine operators to operate their mines. He believed the principal reason for this depression in Colorado was due to its too rapid growth. During the 1879-82 boom, everything was prosperous but there was no foundation for it to rest upon. He stated that if the people of Colorado would forget their insane search for gold and silver and spend more time developing other natural resources, such as coal, iron, paving stone, etc., that the state would be better off."

Author's note: Later on, in July, Mr. Adams addressed the Colorado Chamber of Commerce in Denver and attempted to apologize and salve over some of his previous remarks. However, we are reminded of a line from Omar Khayyam, which goes something like this: "The moving finger writes, and having writ moves on. Nor all thy piety nor wit shall lure it back to cancel half a line, nor all thy tears wash out a word of it".

True, the decline of the Leadville mining industry did have its effects on the South Park's operating revenue, but knowing the policy and methods under which the Union Pacific operated the road, it is hard to reconcile all of Adams' remarks. During the Pacific Railway Commission Trials in 1887, Adams lamented, ". . . if the Union Pacific could only construct some 16 miles of railroad between Graymont and Keystone, the old South Park line would be worthless. But it would be a very difficult and expensive piece of railroad construction. It would require a tunnel under Loveland Pass that would cost fully a million dollars, but it would give us a 120-mile line between Denver and Leadville that could be made standard gauge and would solve our problem". However, it was too late for lamentations now. The damage which they had wrought upon the South Park could not be repaired. In May, 1887, the Farmers Loan & Trust Company of New York City went before Judge Moses Hallett, U. S. District Judge, in Denver and requested to have a receiver appointed for the South Park property.[1] One might begin to think that the good Judge played a large part in shaping the destinies of the Colorado railroads.

1. Railway Age, May 27, 1887.

CHAPTER XVI

THE DENVER LEADVILLE & GUNNISON RAILWAY CO.

The burden of the extremely heavy construction account, the great expense of operation, together with a diminishing income, finally brought the Denver South Park & Pacific Railroad Company to bankruptcy. The road was sold under a foreclosure decree on July 17, 1889, and was bought in by a purchasing committee selected by the bondholders, consisting of Messrs. Frederick D. Tappen, William H. Hollister, and Francis L. Leland for the sum of $3,000,000.[1] At the time of this sale, the South Park road, including all rolling stock, equipment, terminals, real estate, properties, right of way, etc., was valued at $9,727,553.78. Following the sale the purchasing committee then transferred the property of the South Park Company to the Denver Leadville & Gunnison Railway Company on August 29, 1889. This latter company had been incorporated under the general laws of Colorado on July 6, 1889, by the Union Pacific officials and interests owning the Union Pacific Railway Company. Through the usual system of railroad financing, the Union Pacific became owner of all the stock and securities of the new company. At the time of the sale the property consisted of an aggregate mileage of 325.21, together with valuable terminal property in Denver. This 325.21 miles of railroad property, which represented a total construction cost of $5,331,851,[2] consisted of the following trackage:

	Miles
Denver to Como	88.27
Como to Gunnison	113.49
Gunnison to Castleton	14.71
Castleton to Baldwin	2.80
Schwanders to Buena Vista	3.75
Garos to Alma (London Jct.)	15.41
Bear Creek Jct. to Morrison	9.97
Garfield Quarry branch	2.75
Soda Lake branch	.25
Como Jct. to King Mines	2.97
Como to Leadville	63.83
Dickey to Keystone	7.01
Total	325.21

By virtue of these proceedings all of the property formerly owned by the Denver South Park & Pacific

Railroad Company, including railroad trackage, property, station terminals, franchises, etc., became the property of the Denver Leadville & Gunnison Railway Company, and its further history will appear under that name until it is absorbed by the Colorado & Southern Railway Company in 1898.

THE UNION PACIFIC DENVER & GULF RAILWAY COMPANY

Shortly after the organization of the Denver Leadville & Gunnison, it went under control of a new corporation known as the Union Pacific Denver & Gulf Railway Company. In view of the South Park's connection (the author will continue to use the name "South Park") with the new corporation, we shall include a brief resume of the new organization. By 1890, the Union Pacific was pretty well in command of all local railroad transportation in Colorado north of Denver, east of the Continental Divide, and the two mountain roads—the Colorado Central and the Denver Leadville & Gunnison. Their policy of building and annexing feeder lines had caused the system to expand to the point where it became too cumbersome to manage. As a result of this situation, the railroad financiers who were directing the destinies of the Union Pacific and its allied lines determined upon absorbing, consolidating, reorganizing, and making more surely tributary to their ulterior purposes, all the local lines in Colorado within their reach. Some of these lines were, and had been for several years, more or less under Union Pacific control, either by ownership of their securities or by arrangements with the proprietary companies.

The Union Pacific and Kansas Pacific companies had previously been consolidated into one corporation; control of the Colorado Central lines (including the narrow gauge Clear Creek division) had long been held, and the Denver South Park & Pacific, now reorganized as the Denver Leadville & Gunnison, was still under their jurisdiction. To carry out the plans in view, control of various other roads, either by agreement, purchase, or sale, had been acquired until, by the close of 1889, domination over half a dozen or more additional roads of varying importance had been secured. In fact, the Union Pacific system had just about reached the acme of top-heaviness.

1. Corporate History, Colorado & Southern Railway.
2. Smiley, "History of Denver".

D.L.& G. 109, later C.& S. 4, on an Order of Railway Trainmen excursion in Clear Creek Canon at Roscoe in 1898.

U.P.D.& G. 9, later C.& S. 71, at Black Hawk in 1898.

The merger included twelve separate railroads, all of whom adopted certain "Articles of Consolidation and Agreement" to form a new corporation known as the Union Pacific Denver & Gulf Railway Company. The date of the incorporation was April 1, 1890. The new road's officers consisted of President Charles F. Adams, Vice President William H. Holcomb, Second Vice President Gardiner M. Lane, Secretary Alexander Millar, Treasurer James G. Harris, Comptroller Oliver W. Mink, Assistant Secretary Charles Wheeler, and Assistant Secretary and Treasurer Luther S. Anderson. The general offices were listed as Boston, Massachusetts, and Denver, Colorado.

The aggregation thus marshalled together to form the new corporation consisted of the following railroads:

		Miles
1.	Colorado Central Railroad Company of Colorado.	
	Narrow gauge	71.46
	Standard gauge	203.10
2.	Georgetown Breckenridge & Leadville Railway Co.	
	Narrow gauge	8.47
3.	Denver & Middle Park Railroad Co.	
	Narrow gauge	4.56
4.	Denver Marshall & Boulder Railway Co.	
	Narrow gauge	30.09
5.	Greeley Salt Lake & Pacific Railroad Co.	
	Narrow gauge	14.43
	Standard gauge	48.10
6.	Denver Texas & Gulf Railroad Co.	
	Standard gauge	138.06
7.	Denver Texas & Ft. Worth Railroad Co.	
	Standard gauge	170.03
8.	Road Canon Railroad Company.	
	Standard gauge	3.00
9.	Chicosa Canon Railway Company.	
	Standard gauge	4.05
10.	Canon de Agua Railroad Company.	
	Standard gauge	3.29
11.	Cheyenne & Northern Railway Co.	
	Standard gauge	125.14
12.	Colorado Central Railroad Co. of Wyoming—See note.	
	Total	823.78

NOTE: The Colorado Central Railroad Company of Wyoming was organized in 1877 to build 8.62 miles of standard gauge connecting line between Hazard (Colorado Junction) on the Union Pacific's main line in Wyoming, and the northern end of the Colorado Central Railroad of Colorado, at the Colorado-Wyoming state line. In 1888-89, this line was abandoned and was not in operation at the time of consolidation on April 1, 1890. Further details of this road may be found in the

section covering the history of the early Colorado Central Railroad.

The Union Pacific Denver & Gulf Railway Company, with an authorized capital of $36,000,000, was organized to absorb all these lines and operate them as one dependent system tributary to the Union Pacific. Under the arrangements, the Denver Leadville & Gunnison was a part of the new setup, but continued to operate as an independent and separate corporation. In reality it was a tail to the Union Pacific Denver & Gulf kite. The new corporation took possession of the consolidated roads and began business on April 1, 1890.

A period of general prosperity existed throughout the country through the years 1888 to 1892. Curiously enough, it was generally known as the period of Railroad Prosperity, but the Union Pacific lines and affiliated roads in Colorado failed to reap any of the benefits. To make matters worse, this so-called era of prosperity came to a sudden end in the latter part of 1892. The depression that followed was known as the Silver Panic of 1893.

It seems that bankers and world economists had become alarmed over the fact that a ten mile square area like Leadville could produce such huge annual amounts of silver. The price of the precious metal went into a serious decline. Money changers on the Atlantic seaboard refused further issuance of capital for the needs of the west. On June 26, 1893, the mints of India, the world's most important silver market, closed to the coinage of silver.

Mines ceased operations; the fires in the smelters went out; jobless miners and others with their families crowded into Denver creating an unemployment problem so serious that relief camps were established on the outskirts of the city.[1] The panic reached its crisis in the summer of 1893. On July 17th, three Denver banks closed their doors; and within three more days, nine other suspended business.[2] Real estate values crashed overnight. Advertisements of land and real estate for sale filled 73 pages of one issue of the Rocky Mountain News. Thousands lost their homes and affluent men were pauperized in a day.[1]

In November, the Congress of the United States repealed the silver purchasing clause of the Sherman Act, whereby the Government was required to purchase silver at a fixed price. Thus, with silver robbed of its ability as a debt-paying function, together with its depreciation in the markets of the world from $1.29 an ounce, its coinage value, to $0.50 an ounce, its value as a base metal, the mining industry of the west, including the great silver state of Colorado, received a vital blow from which, even to this day, it has not fully recovered.

The situation was critical indeed. The population of Colorado had increased from less than 40,000 in 1870,

1. McMechen, "The Moffat Tunnel of Colorado".
2. Gene Fowler, "Timberline."

U.P.D.& G. 7 with a Silver Plume-Denver train at Empire station on August 7, 1894. This engine later became C.& S. 12.

to nearly half a million in 1890. Reduction works, mills, smelters, etc., had been established as a direct result of the phenomenal growth of the mining industry. Foundries, machine shops, and manufactories for supplying the needs of both mining and smelting activities had been established and built up. All those, as well as the mountain railroads, depended upon the production of the mines for their continued sustenance. Consequently,

porate existence, the aggregate deficit far exceeding the solitary surplus. According to a report made on October 12, 1893, the day before the receivers took charge, the total construction account was $45,152,866, and the floating indebtednes amounted to over $73,000,000.

According to the annual reports, the South Park, like its sister enterprise, the Union Pacific Denver & Gulf, never earned its way even through the so-called pros-

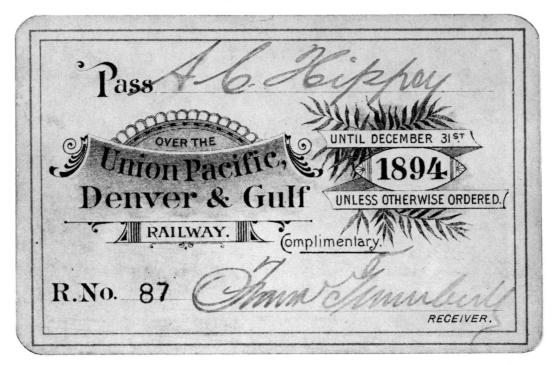

the financially fateful year of 1893, with its far-reaching tale of disaster, was a year long remembered in the annals of Union Pacific history.

By this time the far-reaching Union Pacific system was a sick and sorely beset leviathan. Its debt was over four hundred million dollars and rapidly increasing.[1] It had been reaching for business throughout the entire west, operating under the theory that traffic should bear the highest possible rates. From the deserts and from the mountains, the Union Pacific attempted to wring prosperity for itself, while, at the same time, it sowed the seeds of discontent among its patrons and connections. The prosperity of 1879-80 gave it a great stimulus, but now rival railroads were springing up and taking their share of the profits. High rates were a thing of the past.

The Union Pacific Denver & Gulf Railway failed from the start to make both ends meet. With the exception of 1894, after it had passed to the receivers, and in which year there was a surplus of $111,524, its operations resulted in a loss year after year during its cor-

1. Smiley, "History of Denver".

perous years of 1889 to 1892. The following table shows the results of the road's operations for this period.

Year	Operating Revenue	Profit or Deficit
1889	$1,008,234.80	$248,497.53*
1890	991,958.51	165,276.86*
1891	967,447.86	208,062.51*
1892	1,032,495.25	145,887.19*
1893	685,677.81	245,678.43*

* Denotes deficit.

The statement of operations for the year 1890 is a typical example of how the earnings and expenses were running during this particular period. It is as follows:

Earnings

Passenger	$ 158,358.56
Freight	790,669.33
Mail	21,630.21
Express	15,912.40
Miscellaneous	5,388.01
Total ($3,061.31 per mile)	$ 991,958.51

Expenses

Transportation	$ 262,073.39
Motive Power	391,144.44
Maintenance of Cars	107,080.65
Maintenance of Way	229,322.00
General Expenses	16,754.89
Total ($3,105.81 per mile)	$1,006,375.37

Interest on bonds, taxes, and other miscellaneous items, together with the deficit from operations, amounted to a total deficit of $165,276.86.

Thus, by 1893, it had become evident that a receivership for the Union Pacific could no longer be avoided. The controlling interests deemed such a procedure necessary in order to prevent the giant enterprise from being dismantled, dissipated, and dismembered. Accordingly, the Omaha road went down in a heap, carrying all its allies and dependents with it, the entire aggregation having obligations on stocks, bonds, and a floating debt that exceeded the enormous total of $470,000,000.[1] On October 13, 1893, the entire Union Pacific system, including the Kansas Pacific, the Denver Pacific, the Union Pacific Denver & Gulf, and the Denver Leadville & Gunnison, was placed in the hands of three receivers: Messrs. S. H. H. Clark, Oliver W. Mink, and E. Ellery Anderson. Clark was president while the other two were officers under him. On November 1st, John W. Doan and Frederick R. Coudert were appointed additional receivers on petition of the Attorney General of the United States, Doan then being one of the Government Directors of the road. On November 13th, Doan and Coudert were made additional receivers for the two dependent bankrupt corporations, the Union Pacific Denver & Gulf and the Denver Leadville & Gunnison.

Notwithstanding the fact that the receivership was an avowed attempt to prevent the Union Pacific system from disintegrating, a number of important auxiliary lines were soon placed in the hands of separate receivers. As early as August, 1893, Governor Evans, who was a prominent stockholder in the Union Pacific Denver & Gulf, petitioned for an accounting, alleging that this branch of the Union Pacific system was being "bled" for the benefit of the parent Union Pacific Company. He filed suit on September 15th. As a result of Governor Evans' petition, the five receivers who controlled the Union Pacific Denver & Gulf, all of them nonresidents of Colorado, were removed, and Mr. Frank Trumbull of Denver, a most capable man, was appointed successor receiver on December 18, 1893. This appointment was made in the face of much opposition from the Omaha road.

At the beginning of August, 1894, judicial proceedings were instituted, by parties interested in the securities of the South Park road, to take it out of the hands

1. Smiley, "History of Denver".

of the Union Pacific receivers and place it in those of an independent receiver. On August 7, 1894, Mr. Frank Trumbull was appointed as a separate receiver for the Denver Leadville & Gunnison, and upon orders from the court, the Union Pacific receivers were directed to turn all property of the South Park road over to Mr. Trumbull. A committee, consisting of Messrs. Henry Budge, Charles A. Peabody, and Henry de Coppet, were appointed to protect the interests of the bondholders. The appointment of Frank Trumbull as receiver for the South Park ended the Union Pacific's control of the road. Thirteen years previously they had taken the road over from John Evans; now they relinquished this control. These thirteen years had seen a prosperous and efficiently operated railroad property exploited and brought to ruin.

MR. FRANK TRUMBULL

In view of the fact that Frank Trumbull was to be the guiding spirit of the South Park for a number of years and play an important role in its history, we deem it advisable to devote a few lines to his life.[1] Mr. Trumbull was born in Arcadia, Missouri, on November 11, 1858. He began his railroad career in the autumn of 1874, when he went to work for the Missouri, Kansas & Texas, as a clerk in the comptroller's office at Sedalia, Missouri. He remained with the Katy until December 1, 1880, at which time he became associated with the Missouri Pacific. While with this road he served in various capacities. In January, 1886, he was appointed head of the auditing department of the Texas & Pacific, which was in receivership at the time. In 1888, he moved to Denver and engaged in the wholesale coal trade. It was in Denver that he began his second railroad career when he was appointed receiver for the Denver Leadville & Gunnison Railway Company. As we advance with the history of the South Park, we shall be hearing more of Mr. Trumbull.

Effective August 7, 1894, the Denver Leadville & Gunnison was placed under the leadership of Frank Trumbull, who was more or less free to operate the South Park system as he and his associates saw fit. The officers consisted of the following: Receiver and General Manager, Frank Trumbull; President, S. H. H. Clark; Vice President, Edwin F. Atkins; Treasurer, Charles Wheeler; Secretary, Alexander Millar; and Auditor, Alexis D. Parker. The principal office was located in Denver. With the benefit of skill and economy behind the counter in the person of Frank Trumbull, and an increasing business in front of it as the country recovered from the disastrous effects of the 1893 panic, the officials had hopes that the railroad could be developed into a valuable piece of property.

Among the first important steps taken by Trumbull

1. Smiley, "History of Denver".

to put the road back on its feet was to remove a rockfall in Alpine Tunnel and reopen the Gunnison line to traffic once more. The cave in, which occurred east of the apex of the tunnel about 1888,[1] had been neglected by the previous management for 7 years. In the interim, with Hancock as the end-of-track, all Gunnison and Baldwin through traffic on the South Park had been rerouted and shipped by way of the Rio Grande's Marshall Pass line.

count is furnished by J. M. Cuenin, Chaffee County Surveyor and long a resident of Gunnison and Salida. Mr. Cuenin writes:

"During the summer of 1895, engineer Dad Martinis,[1] Conductor Mike Flavin, and two other trainmen, (I forgot their names), were on a work train engaged in cleaning out Alpine Tunnel. On one of their trips into the tunnel the engine created so much gas and smoke that the crew had to back out to get some fresh air. Mike Flavin forgot and left his coat inside the

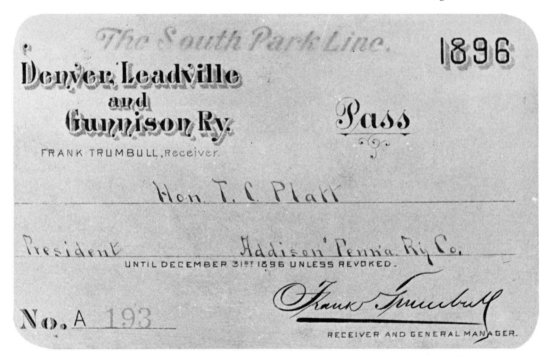

Charles Ryland Collection.

shall Pass line. A run was made from Gunnison up to Pitkin and Quartz two or three times a week to take care of local traffic. The failure to remove this obstruction in the tunnel at the time of the accident and keep the line open is another concrete example of the destructive policy of the Union Pacific management toward the South Park road during the time it was under their control. Another factor instrumental in the opening of the Gunnison line was Trumbull's financial interest in the development of the Kubler coal mine properties northeast of Castleton. The Kubler Mines were operated as a private business enterprise by Trumbull and some associates. Reopening the line from Gunnison to Denver would enable the South Park to obtain the long haul revenue on traffic which they originated at Gunnison and Baldwin.

Concerning the opening of the Alpine Tunnel we have two stories relating to various incidents which occurred in connection with the work. The first story, of which there are a number of versions, involves the tragic death of four South Park trainmen. The first ac-

tunnel. Martinis, under protests from others of the crew, said they would run back in and get the coat. The engineer, the conductor, and two other men—I believe they were the fireman and a track laborer—never came out of that place alive."

The second account of this story is told by William Cairns, veteran South Park engineman. Mr. Cairns writes:

"In 1888, a cave in occurred some distance east of the apex of Alpine Tunnel. The rock that piled up made a dam that backed up a considerable amount of drainage water. In 1895, the railroad company decided to open up the tunnel. They worked from both sides. A crew consisting of conductor Mike Flavin, engineer Nathan Martinis, a fireman by the name of Byrnes, and Elmer England, a brakeman, had come up from Gunnison to work from the west end. This crew went into the tunnel with their engine in an attempt to siphon the water out. After passing over the hump they went too far and the water got into the ashpan and the live fire. This created a gas that killed Mike Flavin, Dad Martinis, and the fireman, Byrnes. The brakeman, Elmer England, realized what had happened and got down on the ground where he was able to crawl back out to safety."

Other accounts of this tragedy are to be found in the

1. William Cairns, veteran South Park engineer.

1. Many early references to this man spelled his name Martinez.

286

Gunnison News-Champion. In the April 17, 1947 issue, Oscar Hurlock of Lincoln, Kansas, writes:

"Fifty-three years ago I was firing the 197 over the South Park road. I was sent from Denver in 1893 to Gunnison to act as night watch. The tunnel had been closed for some time, but the Union Pacific maintained a stub run from Baldwin to Pitkin.

"In 1895 they decided to open the tunnel which had caved in. We were sent to clean off rocks and repair tracks, and were stationed at a siding some three miles west of the tunnel. The crew consisted of N. Martinis, engineer; Mike Byrnes, fireman; Michael W. Flavin, conductor; and Elmer England, brakeman.

"Byrnes asked me if I would fire for him when they were working in the tunnel as he was troubled with asthma. He said they would get through the tunnel the next day. They got there sooner than expected and went in to try out a siphon. The cave in was near the east end and left only a two-foot hole.

"While they were busy, the gas from the engine was filling the tunnel behind them about one-fourth mile. Dad Martinis, Flavin, Byrnes, and a laborer named Oscar Cammann died in the tunnel. England got out, with the help of the second crew getting there a few hours ahead of time."

In the May 22, 1947 issue of the same paper we read:

"In connection with Oscar Hurlock's story, Ernest Miller has mentioned the fact that he participated in the Alpine Tunnel tragedy when four men took an engine into the blocked tunnel to furnish power to siphon the water impounded by a cave in about 300 feet from the east portal.

"The engine was taken in from the west portal, Dad Martinis on the engine, Mike Flavin conductor, Elmer England brakeman, and Mike Byrnes fireman. The gas of the engine in the 1,800-foot tunnel was too much for the men: Nathan Martinis was found dead with his hand still on the throttle of the engine, which had got out of control and pushed into the soil of the cave in; Byrnes had fallen from the cab and lay in two feet of water several feet back of the engine; and Mike Flavin was dead at his post of duty. England escaped on his own power.

"Ernest Miller, then a lad of 19, was timbering near the east portal, under the direction of Andy Lejune of Pitkin, who was superintending the attempted opening of the tunnel. With him was another workman, Oscar Cammann.

"Twice the two entered, hoping to get over to the west side through a connecting hole which had been excavated at the apex of the cave in.

"'Let's hold each other's hands and try it,' urged Cammann a second time. Miller demurred, but finally agreed. The smoke forced them out. His companion was determined to make a third attempt. He retrieved a coat he had left where he had been working and climbed the scaffolding used in the retimbering work, expecting to crawl through the hole to the other side, since he was living near the west portal. Overcome by the fumes, he fell from the scaffolding and was found dead on the floor of the tunnel.

"'They are all dead in there!' was the next information conveyed to Miller from the west side. Cammann was lifted the 16 feet to the hole connecting the two parts of the tunnel and taken with the bodies of the other three to the west portal. The rescuers made their way by pushcar to Pitkin and relayed the dread news to Gunnison.

"A commandeered train met them as they were carrying the bodies, and took them back to Gunnison."

An Editor's note in the April 17th issue of the same paper stated:

"The exact date of the tragedy was Saturday, June 8, 1895. Mike Flavin, 41, left home May 1st, never to return. Nathan Martinis, with 36 years (sic) on the railroad, was found with his hand still on the throttle of his engine which had been taken into the tunnel. Byrnes, 44, who had fallen from the cab, was found, stiff and cold under two feet of water, several feet from the engine. Oscar Cammann went back into the death tunnel to get his coat, and was overcome by the gas.

"They went into the 1,800-foot tunnel at four in the afternoon. No relatives in Gunnison knew of the awful events. It was not until Sunday morning that Elmer England, rescued by Andy Lejune of Pitkin, went on a pushcar to the nearest telegraph office and let the people in Gunnison know.

"The Masonic Lodge secured an engine and coach and started for the scene of the disaster. Three miles from the west portal of the tunnel they met the men carrying the dead bodies on improvised stretchers. They got here at seven. The funerals were at three different hours on Tuesday, and to use the words of Tennyson in Enoch Arden, the 'little town had seldom seen a costlier (not in the sense of money) funeral'."

The second narrative is by Cy Warman, a railroad engineer who wrote a vivid story relating other details of the occasion. Mr. Warman was evidently aware of the tragic death of the four trainmen, but he does not include the incident in his story. It seems that he has seasoned it with a little fiction based on the tragedy, but just how much, the writer is unable to say. However, it is interesting and no South Park history would be complete without the story. The article is found in Mr. Warman's book, "Short Rails".

"THE OPENING OF ALPINE TUNNEL.

"'The highest point reached by any railroad (not a cog road) in the Rocky Mountains is at Alpine Tunnel on the Denver Leadville & Gunnison. Marshall Pass on the D. & R. G. is 10,856 feet high and Tennessee Pass is 10,239, but Governor Evans, who built the road over Alpine Pass, climbed up and up, until he reached the timber line, and then diving under the eternal snow, he tunneled through the top of the towering range of the Continental Divide and came out on the Pacific slope.

"It cost a mountain of money to make the grade and bore the big hole in the hill, but the Gunnison country at that time was attracting the attention of the mining world and the cost of the railway was not taken seriously into consideration, so long as it tapped the Gunnison.

"The timbering in this great tunnel came from the redwood forests of California and had to be hauled up the mountain on the backs of burros. Finally the railroad was completed, but the Gunnison boom was dying; the winter came on, and the railway was closed up, for no amount of bucking with pilot plows could keep the heavy drifts from the deep cuts. In five years the road was almost entirely abandoned. A few years later when the breaking up of the Union Pacific system came, the narrow gauge reverted back to its original owners, and the ambitious manager undertook to reopen the railway over Alpine Pass. It was a big undertaking. The snow near the tunnel had been there for many months, some of it for years, and when June came you might still walk over the top of six feet of hard snow where the right

A special passenger train, headed by Denver Leadville & Gunnison 197, pauses in its eastbound journey to allow the passengers to admire the magnificent view of Quartz Creek far below.

Little Art Studio, Gunnison, from Colin Moore Collection.

of way lay. It was a novel sight to see three or four powerful locomotives pushing a rotary snow plow through the white waste, for the furrow in the forest showed where the railroad wound its way up among the high hills. Where the mountainside was steep, the solid stream of snow about two and one-half feet in diameter shot up from the rotary and clear over the tops of the telegraph poles and went crashing down through the tall spruce and pine, stripping them of their branches, until the whole mountainside was covered with green boughs that had been torn from the trees. After many days of constant and persistent pounding they reached the east portal of the Alpine Tunnel, only to find it filled up solid with snow and ice.

"It was like boring a new tunnel, almost, but they worked away until they were about halfway through, and then they began to have trouble. There were no ventilating shafts for the bad air to escape through, and when they began to use locomotives to haul the snow and ice out of the tunnel, the coal gas from the engines made it almost unsafe for a man to work inside the tunnel.

"In the meantime the publicity department of the railroad was trying (but failed, for no man can do it) to paint pictures of the wonderful scenery on Alpine Pass. And it is wonderful; there is nothing like it, but all the grandeur of the world is not enough to hold men where they can feel upon their throats the cold fingers of the grim reaper, and every day the force decreased. Dozens of lives had been lost in the building of Alpine Tunnel. The bore, when full of black smoke, seemed to the workmen to be alive with the ghosts of the men whose lives had been lost in the building of the tunnel. Every night now the men rehearsed the old stories of the building of this great tunnel, at the boarding train at the foot of the hill. Every day new men went up to the pass, and old men with time checks tramped off toward the Arkansas. The ice near the west portal of the tunnel became so hard that it had to be blasted out and a number of lives were lost on this particular job. Expert miners were brought up from Leadville, but they smelled death in the damp of the place and in the coal gas belched out by the locomotives. The noise and smoke of the blasting added to the other dangers of the work, and now the men worked with one eye on the exit or toward the open end of the tunnel. If an engine slipped or snorted the men would start, ready to stampede like a herd of Texas steers. It was an awful strain upon the nerves of men to work in that way from day to day, and then add to the anxiety by rehearsing their experiences in the boarding cars at night. One day an engineer became scared at some incident, blew his whistle, and backed away hurriedly, killing and crippling six men.

"Things were beginning to be so bad that the Gen-

eral Manager took his private car and camped on a spur near the mouth of the tunnel to help to encourage the workmen.

"Great preparations had been made for a grand excursion over the pass on July 4th. It was now the last week of June and the tunnel was not open yet. Down at the Denver shops they were constructing observation cars to carry the people over the divide through the Alpine Tunnel. An especially elaborate car had been built to accommodate the Governor and his staff.

"But there came a day around July 1st when the clouds lay heavy upon Alpine Pass and there was not a breath of air stirring. By this time a hole had been broken through the ice near the west portal, and encouraged by the fresh air and another exit, the men worked with a will to clear the place. The engine kept going in and out with three flat cars in front of her, while the miners kept blasting and the men kept shoveling the loose ice, rock, etc. upon the flat cars. It was about noon, the tunnel, in spite of the new opening at the west portal, gradually filled with powder smoke from the blasting and coal gas from the engine. The men working on the ground near the entrance had felt no inconvenience. The fireman of the engine had gone up to the front of the locomotive to make some sort of a repair on a marker light, when suddenly he was overcome by the gasses and fell among the workmen, who quickly carried him through the doorway and out into the open air. Other miners and shovelers seeing this became excited and ran for the mouth of the tunnel, thus saving their lives. Meanwhile the heavy cloud hung like a wet blanket over the mouth of the tunnel, holding the poisonous gasses in the tunnel and keeping the fresh air out. Noticing the confusion, the engineer leaned far out of his cab window trying to make out in the smoke and darkness what had happened.

"He was a new engineer in the tunnel. Suddenly, he felt a strange sensation. In another second, he realized he was alone in the tunnel with the ghosts of the dead. He had strength and presence of mind enough to open the throttle. Becoming unconscious, he fell across the arm rest of the cab window. A moment later the General Manager, looking from his car window, saw the locomotive coming out of the tunnel mouth at a tremendous speed, with the limp form of the engineer hanging out the window of the cab. The throttle being wide open, the locomotive rushed down the steep grade. At a curve in the road the engine jumped the track, went tearing down the mountain side, overturning great rocks and crushing large trees as though they were weeds. This sudden lurch of the locomotive threw the engineer from the cab, leaving him unhurt in a snow drift. The cool air soon revived him, and he came to without a scratch, but pale and perspiring, for he had been pretty close to death."

THE LEAVICK BRANCH

The only additional construction of any importance that occurred on the South Park system while it was known as the Denver Leadville & Gunnison was the Leavick branch to connect with the Horseshoe mining district, and the Kubler branch to connect with the Kubler coal mines.

Another gold and silver mining district of considerable importance that developed in this region during this period was the Horseshoe Mining District. This district was located in the Park Range some six miles south of London Mountain and about nine miles due west of Fairplay. Among the more important mining properties located here were the Hill Top, Last Chance, Badger Boy, Mudsill, etc. The town of Horseshoe, the first locality of any importance in this district, was established in 1877. A small smelter was built here in 1879 and operated for a short time; however, during some labor trouble, it was burned and never rebuilt.

Chief among the mining properties in this district were the Hill Top and Last Chance Mines owned by some mining operators in Denver and headed by Frank T. Trumbull. As was the case at the London Mine, some means of transportation other than by wagon was required to serve the Horseshoe district and particularly the Trumbull properties. The mine owners proposed to build a narrow gauge line to connect the Hill Top mines with the Denver Leadville & Gunnison line at Fairplay.

The Trumbull group were not the first to contemplate the building of a railroad into this district. In the Railway Age of September 7, 1888, we read:

"Union Pacific engineers are surveying a line of railroad from Fairplay to the Horseshoe mining district, a distance of eleven miles. Contracts will be awarded at once."

Following this, another article appeared in the same publication under date of September 21, 1888, stating:

"The survey from Fairplay to the Horseshoe mining district is completed and construction is to begin at once."

However, this was as far as the Union Pacific proposal ever advanced. Nothing more was done.

In line with the Trumbull plans, the Denver, South Park & Hill Top Railway Company was incorporated under the general laws of Colorado on August 31, 1896. The Articles of Incorporation were filed in the office of the Secretary of State on September 1, 1896. The Directors were: Thomas F. Dunaway, Frank T. Trumbull, Bradford H. DuBois, Silas L. Rainey, and Felix Leavick. The object was as follows:

"To build a line of railroad, with appurtenant property . . . which shall extend from the town of Fairplay, in the County of Park, in the State of Colorado, in a general westerly direction through the town of Horseshoe to a point in section one (1), township ten (10) south, of range seventy-nine (79) west of the principal meridian, where the Hill Top Mine is located by the particular route deemed most advisable, direct and practicable, after a detailed survey thereof; said line of railroad may be extended beyond such point in such direction, and into

such other counties, as may be hereafter determined and deemed expedient."

The road was capitalized for $100,000, on the basis of 1,000 shares at $100.00 each. Denver was listed as the principal office.

By virtue of an agreement made with the Denver Leadville & Gunnison Railway Company, the road was built jointly by the railway company and the private individuals interested in the Hill Top Mines.[1] It is interesting to note that Frank Trumbull was Receiver and General Manager of the Denver Leadville & Gunnison at this time. On completion of the building of the road, the stock was issued to the two respective interests in proportion to the expenditures contributed by each; approximately 51 per cent to the Denver Leadville & Gunnison Company and 49 per cent to the Hill Top mine interests.

Construction of the Horseshoe branch commenced in October, 1896, and the road was completed in December of that year. The road branched off the Garos-Alma line at Hill Top Junction, some three-quarters of a mile below Fairplay. It continued in a southwesterly direction to Four Mile Creek, from which point it followed up the north side of this stream through Horseshoe and Mudsill to Leavick, the end-of-track. The elevation at Leavick is 11,249 feet, which is 1,449 feet higher than Hill Top Junction. The charter had stipulated that the line was to be extended as far as the Hill Top Mine, but this mine is located midway between Mount Sherman and Mount Sheridan, at an altitude of some 13,000 feet. Such a location was practcially inaccessible as far as reaching it with an adhesion type railroad was concerned. An old map showing the proposed route of the railroad between Leavick and the mine discloses some interesting data. Just beyond Leavick, this map shows a 4.7% grade; the next section shows a 7.0% grade; while the third and last shows a proposed grade of 11.8%. The map shows a continuous line of track, i.e., no switchbacks were proposed. Such figures may be more easily comprehended when it is known that the difference in elevation between Leavick and the Hill Top Mine is approximately 1,750 feet, and the air line distance is only two and one-half miles. The length of the narrow gauge line between Hill Top Junction and Leavick was 11.33 miles. The maximum curvature was 20 degrees. The maximum grade west, located between Horseshoe and the end-of-track, was 5.85% and was the steepest grade encountered on the entire South Park system. The maximum grade east was 1.68%.

Relative to the Leavick branch, Ed Haley reports the following story as told by Ed Haight to himself, Andy Nelson and Tom St. John. Concerning these three grand old men, Haley writes:

"Haight, Nelson and St. John are South Park veterans. In

1. Corporate History, Colorado & Southern Railway.

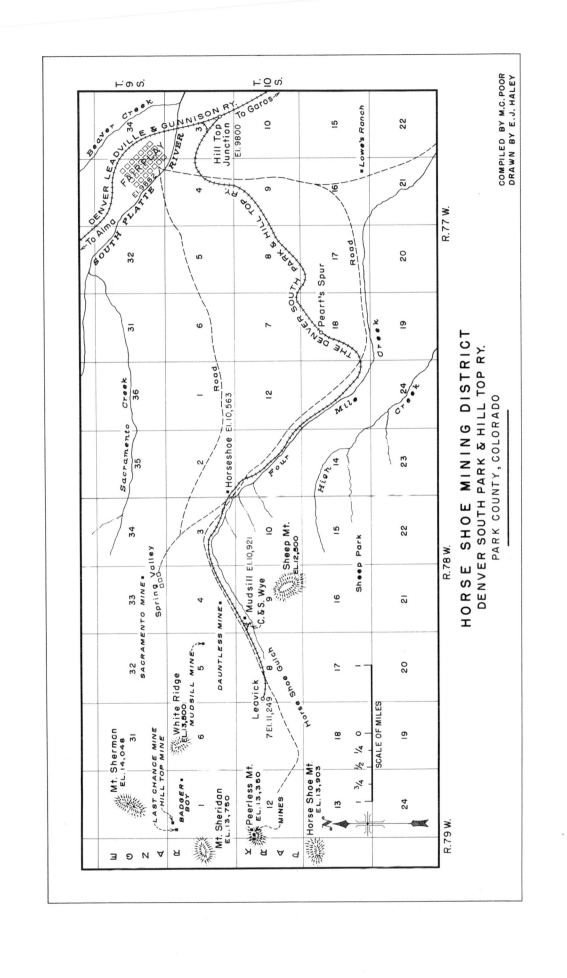

HORSE SHOE MINING DISTRICT
DENVER SOUTH PARK & HILL TOP RY.
PARK COUNTY, COLORADO

COMPILED BY M.C. POOR
DRAWN BY E.J. HALEY

the early days when this group first went to work on the South Park, St. John was braking and Nelson was firing. Ed Haight is 82 years old; Andy Nelson is almost 85 and hard as nails. Sometimes these two tease Tom St. John about being just a kid because he is only 77.

"Mr. Haight relates that the Leavick branch was the toughest stretch of railroad track he ever ran an engine on. The last three miles had grades of around 6 per cent. He told how he and his fireman once ran a trainload of ore across a high rickety trestle on that branch. Just before reaching the trestle they stopped the train and Ed got off and walked across to the other side. The fireman then opened the throttle sufficiently to move the train and jumped off. When the engine reached the far side where Ed was, he hopped on, stopped the train, and waited for his fireman to walk across. Then they proceeded on their way."

Shortly after the road's completion on October 1, 1897, Frank Trumbull exercised his rights to an option and purchased the entire 49 per cent of the Hill Top's stock at a cost of $49,030.36,[1] thereby becoming sole owner of the Denver, South Park & Hill Top road. Following this, the Hill Top interests, through an agreement with Trumbull dated October 18, 1897, operated the road until December 28, 1898, at which time it was acquired by the Colorado & Southern company at the time of that road's organization, through a purchasing committee.

THE KUBLER BRANCH

As previously mentioned, a group of Denver interests headed by Frank Trumbull had organized the Rocky Mountain Fuel Company. Among the various mining enterprises taken over and developed by this concern was the Kubler coal mine which had been opened about 1895 by the Kubler Mining Company. This mine was located on Carbon Creek about three miles above Castleton, a station on the Baldwin branch, which ran north out of Gunnison. In order to provide railroad connections between the mining property and the South Park track at Castleton, a narrow gauge extension, 1.56 miles long, was built north up Carbon Creek from that point. A United States Government Bulletin on coal mining in Colorado states that the Kubler branch was built in 1896. Details regarding curvature and grades are

1. U. S. Interstate Commerce Commission Valuation Docket No. 716.

not known by the writer. The balance of the track required to reach the mines, a section 1.79 miles long, was built by the owners of the mining property. Why the railroad company did not extend their track the entire distance to the mine is not known. In all probability the South Park built to a certain property line and the mine owners then constructed the balance of the necessary track on their own property.

Relative to Trumbull's connection with the Kubler Mines, Thomas St. John, veteran South Park passenger conductor, related the following incident to the writer.

"Prior to Trumbull's acquisition of the Kubler Mines, Alpine Tunnel had been closed down for a number of years due to a cave in. In view of the greatly increased production of Baldwin coal brought about by the opening of the Kubler, and other mines in the vicinity, Trumbull took the necessary steps to get the tunnel repaired and opened up again by 1896, to facilitate the transportation of this coal into Denver, which was then averaging from 60 to 70 cars per day."

William Cairns writes:

"Many a coal train screeched down that 4% Alpine grade with Kubler and Baldwin coal destined for use by the railroad and some of the settlements between there and Denver."

The Kubler branch was operated intermittently along with the Baldwin branch by the South Park until it was taken over by the Rio Grande in 1911.

THE WILFLEY'S MILL SPUR.

Mention should also be made of a short spur that was built west from Kokomo to Wilfley's Mill. It seems this mill was built in 1895 by one A. R. Wilfley who invented some sort of an ore separation apparatus known as the "Wilfley Table". Construction of this spur commenced September 21, 1895, and was completed the same year. It was of narrow gauge construction and was 1.14 miles in length from the main line connection (milepost 132.80) to the end-of-track at the mill. The Kimberly Mine, located on the line, was also served by this spur. The entire line was an uphill climb to the mill, with a maximum grade of 5%. The maximum curvature was 24 degrees. The Wilfley Mill spur was operated by the Denver Leadville & Gunnison until such time as it was taken over by the Colorado & Southern in 1898.

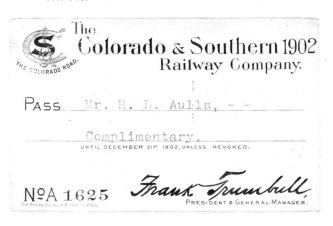

CHAPTER XVII

THE COLORADO & SOUTHERN RAILWAY COMPANY

At this point we come upon a new name in Colorado railroad history—The Colorado & Southern Railway Company. Although the name is new, the constituent roads that were combined to form this new company are old ones whose past history has been unfolded in the preceding pages of this book. To present an understandable account of the circumstances which led to the organization of this new company, we shall briefly review the constituent roads and some of the principal causes that finally led to this latest consolidation. For a more complete treatise on this particular subject, the reader is referred to Smiley's "History of Denver", a reliable source of information from which this writer acknowledges much assistance.

Prior to 1890, the parties in control of the Union Pacific and its allied roads determined upon absorbing, consolidating and reorganizing all the local lines in Colorado which were under their control, either through ownership or by arrangement with their owners. The Union Pacific and Kansas Pacific companies had previously been made one corporation; control of the Colorado Central lines had long been held; and the Denver South Park & Pacific had been theirs since 1881. To carry out their plans, control of these various roads had been gradually acquired until by 1890 domination over twelve lines had been secured. The aggregation thus marshalled together, consisting of some narrow gauge and some standard gauge lines, and which have been previously listed in this history, were consolidated on April 1, 1890, into the Union Pacific Denver & Gulf Railway Co.

Following this wholesale consolidation, some minor construction was carried out in the southern part of the state, while in the northern part 42 miles of the Colorado Central's line between Ft. Collins and Colorado Junction were abandoned. Other small abandonments included a portion of Loveland's old line between Golden and Longmont, and between Ralston and Louisville. A number of other changes were also made in the new system. However, they are irrelevant to this book.

The Union Pacific Denver & Gulf, together with its most important subsidiary, the Denver Leadville & Gunnison, failed from the start to make both ends meet. With one exception, its annual operations resulted in a loss every year during its corporate existence. Then came the great panic of 1893, with its far-reaching entailment of disaster. The Union Pacific and all its dependents went bankrupt, leaving obligations in excess of $470,000,000. Our own Denver Leadville & Gunnison was saddled with an indebtedness of approximately $1,-000,000.[1] Receivers for the entire group were appointed, but due to charges of mismanagement the South Park system was removed in 1894 and placed in control of Frank Trumbull, an independent receiver. Under the efficient direction of Trumbull, the Denver Leadville & Gunnison property was considerably improved.

Meanwhile, arrangements were in progress among holders of the securities of the two former dependents of the Union Pacific, for their reorganization into one new company on a general scaling down of valuations that would bring the paper and the real values somewhere near a common level. On November 18, 1898, the Denver Leadville & Gunnison Railway Company was sold in Denver under a foreclosure decree; the purchasers being Messrs. Henry Budge, Charles A. Peabody, and Henry de Coppet, committeemen representing the road's bondholders, who bid it in at $1,500,000,[2] and were the only bidders; that sum having been the minimum as specified in the decree. At the time of the sale the Denver Leadville & Gunnison Railway Company was valued at $5,289,983.57. This included all rolling stock, terminal grounds, right of way, equipment and land. This also included an investment of $25,000 in the Alpine Coal Company at Baldwin, $50,000 in the Park Coal Company in Park County, $15,377 in the Leadville Mineral Belt Railway Company, and $49,030 in the Denver, South Park & Hill Top Railway Company and Hill Top Mining Company.[3]

On November 19, 1898, the Union Pacific Denver & Gulf Railway Company, under a decree for foreclosure, was sold at Old Line Junction, two miles north of Pueblo, for $6,250,000,[4] the minimum price, to three committeemen, Messrs. Henry Budge, John Kennedy Todd, and Edward C. Henderson, representing the

1. The I.C.C. gives the figure as $869,030.44.
2. Corporate History, Colorado & Southern Railway Co.
3. U. S. I.C.C. Valuation Docket No. 716.
4. Smiley, "History of Denver", Railroad Gazette, Dec. 2, 1898.

CORPORATE STRUCTURE CHART

Narrow gauge Colorado & Southern trackage indicated by solid lines.

1. COLORADO CENTRAL R.R.
   Feb. 9, 1865 - Apr. 1, 1890.
2. GEORGETOWN BRECKENRIDGE & LEADVILLE RY.
   Feb. 23, 1881 - Apr. 1, 1890.
3. DENVER & MIDDLE PARK R.R.
   Apr. 17, 1883 - Apr. 1, 1890.
4. DENVER MARSHAL & BOULDER RY.
   May 14, 1885 - Apr. 1, 1890.
5. GREELEY SALT LAKE & PACIFIC RY.
   Jan. 17, 1881 - Apr. 1, 1890.
6. DENVER TEXAS & GULF R.R.
   Jan. 25, 1881 - Apr. 1, 1890.
7. UNION PACIFIC DENVER & GULF RY.
   Apr. 1, 1890 - Dec. 28, 1898.
8. ROAD CANON R.R.
   Aug. 3, 1889 - Apr. 1, 1890.
9. CHICOSA CANON RY.
   Jan. 16, 1889 - Apr. 1, 1890.
10. CANON de AGUA R.R.
    Jan. 16, 1889 - Apr. 1, 1890.
11. COLORADO CENTRAL R.R. of WYOMING.
    Sept. 19, 1877 - Apr. 1, 1890.
12. CHEYENNE & NORTHERN RY.
    Mar. 1, 1886 - Apr. 1, 1890.
13. DENVER TEXAS & FT. WORTH R.R.
    Apr. 12, 1887 - Apr. 1, 1890.
14. COLORADO & SOUTHERN RAILWAY.
    Dec. 28, 1898 - Aug. 25, 1943.
15. DENVER LEADVILLE & GUNNISON RY.
    Aug. 29, 1889 - Dec. 28, 1898.
16. DENVER SOUTH PARK & PACIFIC R.R.
    Oct. 1, 1872 - Aug. 29, 1889.
17. MT. CARBON GUNNISON & LAKE CITY R.R. & TEL. CO.
    Nov. 17, 1877 - Mar. 9, 1881.
18. DENVER SOUTH PARK & HILL TOP RY.
    Sept. 1, 1896 - Dec. 28, 1898.
19. DENVER CRIPPLE CREEK & SOUTHWESTERN R.R.
    Jan. 10, 1896 - Sept. 13, 1899.
20. LONDON SOUTH PARK & LEADVILLE R.R.
    Feb. 16, 1882 -
21. LEADVILLE MINERAL BELT RY.
    Oct. 29, 1898 - Jun. 26, 1900.
22. GILPIN R.R.
    Jul. 29, 1886 - Jun. 2, 1917.
23. COLORADO RAILROAD
    Jul. 6, 1906 - Mar. 28, 1930.

1870 1880 1890 1900 1910 1920 1930 1940

C.C.R.R.

G.B.&L.

D.S.P.&P.

D.L.&G.

U.P.D.&G.

COLORADO & SOUTHERN RY.

C.R.R.

AUG. 25, 1943

POOR & HALEY-1949

bondholders, and in this instance also they were the only bidders.

On December 19, 1898,[1] the Colorado & Southern Railway Company, with a capital of $48,000,000,[2] was organized and chartered by the holders of the Union Pacific Denver & Gulf and the Denver Leadville & Gunnison securities, under the general laws of the state of Colorado, for the purpose of acquiring all the railroad properties, rights, franchises, etc., of those two corporations.[1] The Denver Leadville & Gunnison property was conveyed by its purchasing committee to the Colorado & Southern on December 28, 1898, while the Union Pacific Denver & Gulf property was conveyed by its committee to the new company on December 29, 1898. The Colorado & Southern Railway Company took official charge of their two constituent railroads at midnight, January 11, 1899.[3] The new company's Board of Directors was constituted almost wholly of eastern men, and included Grenville M. Dodge, Henry Budge, John Kennedy Todd, Luther Kountze, and Frederick P. Olcott of New York; Harry Walters, of Baltimore, Maryland; Oliver Ames, of Boston, Massachusetts; Frank Trumbull, of Denver, Colorado; and Norman B. Ream of Chicago, Illinois. The direction and management of the new system was placed in the hands of the following men:

Grenville M. Dodge, Chairman Board of
Directors _____New York, N. Y.
Frank Trumbull, President and General
Manager _____Denver, Colo.
B. L. Winchell, Vice Pres. and General
Traffic Manager_____Denver, Colo.
Charles Wheeler, Secretary and Treasurer_Denver, Colo.
A. D. Parker, General Auditor_____Denver, Colo.
T. F. Dunaway, General Supt.
and Purchasing Agent _____Denver, Colo.
T. E. Fisher, General Passenger Agent____Denver, Colo.
H. A. Johnson, General Freight Agent ___Denver, Colo.
H. F. Parke, Supt. Trans. and Telegraph_Denver, Colo.
J. Forsher, Supt. of Motive Power_____Denver, Colo.
W. E. Fowler, Master Car Builder_____Denver, Colo.
H. W. Cowan, Chief Engineer_____Denver, Colo.
A. Zimmerman, Supt. Bridges and
Buildings _____Denver, Colo.

Principal office, Cooper Building, Denver, Colorado.
Eastern office, 1 Broadway, New York, New York.

The total mileage of all railroad lines, both standard and narrow gauge, acquired by the Colorado & Southern at the time of its organization was 1,085.61.[1] The new company's standard gauge lines formed an important link in Colorado's railroad transportation, but inasmuch as this book is a history of the narrow gauge lines of

1. Corporate History, Colorado & Southern Railway.
2. Poor's Manual of Railroads, 1899.
3. 1899 Annual Report, Colorado & Southern Railway.

the Colorado & Southern, we shall forego any discussion of the company's standard gauge divisions. With reference to the narrow gauge lines, we now arrive at that important milestone in our history where we find the entire narrow gauge mileage of all roads concerned consolidated under one management.

In order that the reader might have a more comprehensive and concise picture of how these miscellaneous narrow gauge lines eventually gravitated toward one control under the name of the Colorado & Southern Railway Company, the author has drawn up a corporate structure chart, and a control and ownership chart. These two diagrams should give the reader a better understanding, or continuity, of the corporate history of these railroads.

The following table gives a breakdown of all narrow gauge mileage acquired by the Colorado & Southern on January 11, 1899, when they assumed control. In an effort to arrive at an acceptable and fairly reliable figure, the author was confronted with a maze of conflicting statements and encountered considerable difficulty. Construction of new branches and spurs, abandonment and extension of others, resurveying of established lines, together with vague information regarding miscellaneous minor changes, all lent themselves to the complexity of the problem. After much consultation and diligent study of many Colorado & Southern mileage reports, corporate and otherwise, employees' timetables, maps, Interstate Commerce Commission Reports, Poor's Manual of Railroads, etc., the writer believes the following table represents a fairly reliable set of figures.

South Park Lines	Miles
Denver to Como	88.27
Como to Gunnison	113.49
Gunnison to Castleton	14.71
Castleton to Baldwin	2.80
Castleton to Kubler	1.56
Schwanders to Buena Vista	3.98
Garos to Alma	15.41
Sheridan Junction to Morrison	9.97
Soda Lake Spur	.25
Garfield Quarry Spur	2.75
Como to King	2.97
Como to Leadville	63.83
Dickey to Keystone	7.01
Kokomo to Wilfley's Mill	1.14

Total mileage of Denver Leadville &
Gunnison Lines _____328.14
Hill Top Jct. to Leavick (Denver, South Park
& Hill Top Railway) _____ 11.33

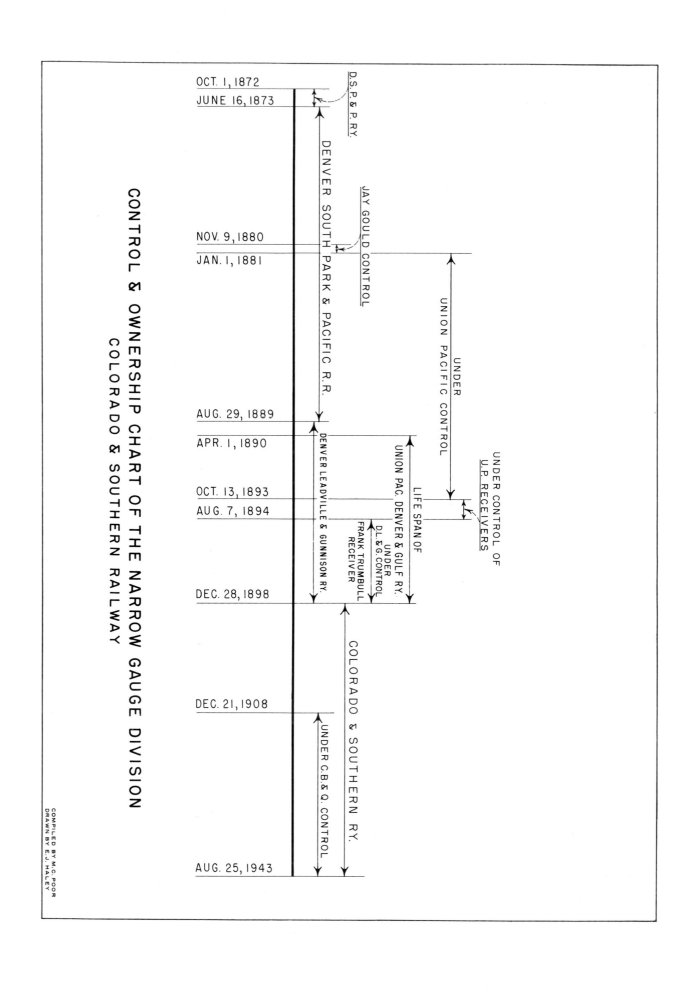

CONTROL & OWNERSHIP CHART OF THE NARROW GAUGE DIVISION
COLORADO & SOUTHERN RAILWAY

OCT. 1, 1872
JUNE 16, 1873
NOV. 9, 1880
JAN. 1, 1881
AUG. 29, 1889
APR. 1, 1890
OCT. 13, 1893
AUG. 7, 1894
DEC. 28, 1898
DEC. 21, 1908
AUG. 25, 1943

D.S.P. & P. RY.

DENVER SOUTH PARK & PACIFIC R.R.

JAY GOULD CONTROL

UNDER UNION PACIFIC CONTROL

DENVER LEADVILLE & GUNNISON RY.

UNION PAC. DENVER & GULF RY.
LIFE SPAN OF

UNDER DL.& G. CONTROL
FRANK TRUMBULL RECEIVER

UNDER CONTROL OF U.P. RECEIVERS

COLORADO & SOUTHERN RY.

UNDER C.B.& Q. CONTROL

COMPILED BY M.C. POOR
DRAWN BY E.J. HALEY

Clear Creek Lines

Denver to Silver Plume (3.01 miles beyond Silver Plume abandoned 1898)	55.09
(Denver to milepost 15.81 just beyond Golden was 3-rail)	
Church's Brick Yard Spur out of Golden	1.70
Forks Creek to Central City	11.66
Total	407.92

The turn of the century found our newly hatched **Colorado & Southern** with a clean slate and an opportunity for those in charge to display their ability as efficient railroad managers. Through ownership and trackage agreements, the company controlled a transportation system reaching from the mountains to the gulf. From an economic standpoint, the next dozen years in Colorado was not altogether an unfavorable period. Strikes by embryo miners' unions cropped up now and then in mining areas, silver lagged between 52 and 68 cents an ounce, and a small panic occurred around 1907. However, such conditions were partially offset by a fairly steady production in the state's mining industry. In 1898, gold again took the leading role at Leadville and for a decade or so the camp poured out her golden treasure from deep quartz veins previously overlooked. The little "Kingdom of Gilpin" up Clear Creek, Chaffee County and the St. Elmo diggings, the Breckenridge district, Park County, and even the almost forgotten Gunnison area, came through with some fair production records. The following figures were taken from the U. S. Government report on mining in Colorado, especially in areas affecting Colorado & Southern narrow gauge lines.

	1900	1905	1910	1915
Clear Creek	$ 1,580,900	1,181,580	1,029,200	1,124,200
Gilpin	1,967,150	1,764,275	852,700	739,100
Park	157,800	378,300	465,500	233,700
Lake	10,691,900	10,889,600	7,360,700	13,839,400
Summit	865,500	590,500	973,700	1,870,400
Chaffee	416,500	322,800	270,600	1,242,600
Gunnison	256,000	80,147	298,300	300,000
Entire State	$50,614,424	44,699,000	33,671,000	43,426,000

For the first few years the narrow gauge freight drags kept fairly busy plying across the mountain passes with their ore shipments, but the days of annual earnings of a million dollars such as the South Park enjoyed in the boom years of 1879-80 were past history. Unfortunately, we do not know what the annual operating revenue of the South Park lines was for the years 1899 to 1909 inclusive, as the records were destroyed by a flood; but the following figures, furnished by the road's engineering department, will indicate to some extent the volume of traffic carried during the latter part of the period in question as compared to a previous period.

Period	Average Operating Revenue per Year
1891-1898	$738,304
1910-1920	465,331

It was not a very healthy record and did not inspire much confidence in the future. We shall take up this discussion later.

Shortly after the Colorado & Southern acquired control of its constituent roads, the management took steps toward improving its properties, some of which we are able to list. The Denver Daily Times of January 25, 1900, announced that a 40-acre tract had been acquired in West Denver and that new shops, including $100,000 in new machinery, a 35 stall roundhouse, a 70 foot turntable, car shops, paint shops, and approximately six miles of three-rail track would be built. The place was known as the Seventh Street Yards, and was located not far from the spot where the first cabin on the site of the city was erected in 1858.[1] The new shops were completed and the company moved on December 1st. The improvements, which cost $350,000,[2] constituted a very important addition to Denver's industrial establishments. Since its organization the company had been a tenant in the old Union Pacific shops in the northern part of the city, and which had long been utilized by the Union Pacific Denver & Gulf, the Union Pacific having transferred their principal shop facilities to Cheyenne.

Other improvements made throughout the next few years were as follows:

1900. New depot at Central City costing $3,394. This depot, located across the street from the place where engine 71 now stands on exhibition, is completely buried under a mine dump.

40 box cars, one new rotary snow plow costing $16,959, and three new passenger coaches, all equipped with automatic couplers and air brakes.

1901. $2,828 spent on new snowsheds in Leadville district. $868 spent on new sheds on Gunnison division.

1902. New coal chute at Dickey costing $4,397.

1903. New engine house at Dickey costing $3,073.

1905. New track ballast and third narrow gauge rail laid between Denver and Boulder to promote

1. Smiley, "History of Denver".
2. Colorado & Southern annual report, 1900.

additional passenger and freight traffic between the Colorado & Southern and the Colorado & North Western Ry., later known as the Denver Boulder & Western. Cost $83,924.

1907. New two story frame boarding house at Alpine Tunnel station costing $1,701. Turntable installed at Alpine Tunnel station.

1908. New water tank at Alpine Tunnel station costing $1,184.

1910. 125 new box cars, 50 stock cars, and 50 coal cars built at the Denver shops.

Other improvements included plans for both extensions to the main lines and construction of some branch lines. Some were carried out, others were never attempted. The stories of these proposed lines follow.

In the Denver Daily Times of April 26, 1899, we read:

"The report is out that Frank Trumbull is to raise $20,-000,000 to extend the Clear Creek line to Middle Park and thence south to connect with the Dillon line."

In the Denver Daily Times of October 20, 1909, we read:

"Due to the increasing popularity of Morrison and the Garden of the Red Rocks as a summer tourist resort, the Colorado & Southern is proposing to build a funicular railroad to the top of Mt. Morrison. The company proposes to standard gauge the entire line to Morrison."

In the Denver Daily Times of October 23, 1909, we read:

"There are rumors that the C. & S. are proposing to extend the Baldwin branch to Paonia and Delta by way of Ohio Creek Pass and the North Fork of the Gunnison River. About 75 miles of new line would be required. Such a line, if built, would cut off about 100 miles between Denver and Paonia. C. & S. officials reply that such a line would require standard gauging the entire Gunnison division, including Alpine Pass, which is usually blocked with snow three months out of the year, and would be too expensive, adding that local interests must have pepped up the idea."

Commenting on this news item, W. E. Mahony of Denver states:

"It seems that some citizens of Delta and surrounding vicinity met with Colorado & Southern officials to request them to consider the extension of their Baldwin branch to the Delta fruit district. The Delta group contended that considerable fruit was spoiled each year due to the inability of the Rio Grande to supply the sufficient box cars and reefers to haul it to market. The railroad officials replied that the transportation of large quantities of fruit out of this area would require standard gauging the whole Gunnison division and that the cost would be prohibitive."

None of the above projected lines were ever attempted, with the exception of the Mt. Morrison Funicular, which was later built by other interests.

THE LEADVILLE MINERAL BELT RAILWAY COMPANY

During the progress of the reorganization negotiations of the Denver Leadville & Gunnison Railway Company,

a separate corporation was organized to build certain lines of railroad in and near the City of Leadville to connect the main line of this road with various mines located in and near Leadville. Accordingly, the Leadville Mineral Belt Railway Company was organized under the general laws of the State of Colorado on October 28, 1898. The directors behind this road were Frank Trumbull, A. DuPont Parker, H. W. Cowan, Elmer E. Whitted (all Colorado & Southern officials) and James R. de Remer. (de Remer was a very famous early day Rio Grande civil engineer.) The Articles of Incorporation were filed the following day, October 29th.

The Leadville Mineral Belt branched off the main line at milepost 149.9 just north of the Leadville city limits at a point about three-quarters of a mile north of the Leadville roundhouse. Construction was commenced during that month and the line was placed in operation in April, 1900. By building numerous spurs and side tracks, this line served quite a number of prominent mines, such as the Robert E. Lee, Denver City, Robert Emmet, The Mab, and the Blind Tom, all located in the immediate area to the east of Leadville. The total length of this line was 2.99 miles. This included a .65 mile extension to the Penrose Mine, which was built on to the end of the main line of the Denver Leadville & Gunnison on the south side of Leadville under the charter of the Leadville Mineral Belt.

The line was built 3-rail, and connected with both the Rio Grande and the Colorado Midland at a number of points in and around Leadville. Inasmuch as the Colorado & Southern and the Rio Grande Western (controlled by the Denver & Rio Grande) had come into the control of the Colorado Midland on July 2, 1900, this facilitated the shipment of ore regardless of what gauge car was loaded. The narrow gauge cars went out via the South Park line, while the standard gauge cars went via the Colorado Midland.[1]

On June 26, 1900, all the properties, rights, and privileges of this company, valued at $15,377.23[2] were sold to the Colorado & Southern Railway Company. Immediately after this purchase, an extension of .10 miles was added by the Colorado & Southern, which gave this particular branch a total length of 3.09 miles. The purchaser continued the operation of the line until the time of its abandonment in 1938.

THE NIGHTHAWK BRANCH

Once again we take up the subject of construction of a railroad up the South Fork of the South Platte River. During Colorado's early railroad history, numerous railway projects designated that their line should follow this well known stream, but 98 per cent of them failed to advance any further than the talking stage. It was a popular route for would-be Colorado railroad

1. A. T. Million, Colorado & Southern valuation engineer.
2. U. S. I.C.C. Valuation Docket No. 716.

builders. Surveyors and engineers probably had a well-worn path marked out, up and down this branch of the Platte River, stumbling over each other's survey stakes as they proceeded along its banks. It reminds the writer of all the tunnels and railroads that were proposed to be built under and over Loveland Pass. General Palmer chose to use the canons of this stream as a route for one of his early projects and, as previously related, did go as far as to complete some 25 miles of grading up the stream and then quit. The reader will also remember that the South Park company, under Union Pacific influence, passed certain resolutions in September, 1880, which included among other things a projected line from the South Platte station up the South Fork and thence down Oil Creek to Canon City, Silver Cliff, and Rosita.[1] This project was brought up again in 1888, but like the majority of other roads that proposed to build along this route, nothing further developed.

The cry of gold, heard in the Cripple Creek district in the early '90's, once again revived the old idea of building a railroad up the canon of this stream. As a result of numerous rich ore discoveries, the new camp possessed vast potentialities in the matter of ore traffic. Accordingly, a group of Denver capitalists organized the Denver, Cripple Creek & South Western Railroad Company for the purpose of constructing a narrow gauge railroad between Denver and that district. The directorate was composed of the following men: F. W. Crocker, Cyrus W. Fisher, Alexander Berger, William W. Borst, John W. Nesmith, William G. Evans, Joseph T. Cornforth, Earl B. Coe, Michael Spangler, James A. Fleming, Harvey C. Lowrie, John P. Heisler, and James H. Blood. The incorporation papers, dated January 10, 1896, stated the object as follows:

"The line of this railroad shall extend from the City of Denver, in the County of Arapahoe, in the State of Colorado, in a Southwesterly direction through the counties of Arapahoe, Douglas, Park, and El Paso, to the City of Cripple Creek and the City of Victor, in the County of El Paso, in the State of Colorado, by the particular route that may be found most feasible and available after a careful survey therefor; thence, Southwesterly by the most feasible route through the counties of Fremont and Custer to Silver Cliff in the County of Custer; thence Southwesterly by the most feasible route through the Southern Counties of the State of Colorado, as may be determined, by survey, to the Southern boundary line of the State of Colorado; thence, Southwesterly through the territories of New Mexico and Arizona to Tidewater."

The road was capitalized for $2,500,000 on the basis of 25,000 shares at $100.00 each. Denver was listed as the principal office. During 1895 and 1896, the company made certain surveys, located two different routes, obtained some rights of way from private individuals as well as through the public lands of the U. S. Government, and filed their location maps with the Department of the Interior, Washington. According to an old map furnished by Robert Hicks, the line branched off the

Denver Leadville & Gunnison at South Platte station and followed south along the South Fork of the Platte River to a station known as Deckers, located at the confluence of Horse Creek and the South Fork of the Platte. At Deckers the surveyed line split; one line continued up the Platte River past Lake George, thence across the Colorado Midland at Florissant and down Oil Creek to Cripple Creek and Victor. The second proposed route turned southeast at Deckers and followed a stream known as Trout Creek, through Dellwood Springs and thence across the Colorado Midland track at Divide and thence south to Cripple Creek and Victor. The company did a small amount of construction above South Platte station and by May 12, 1900, had extended the grade to a point about two miles below Nighthawk.

The old records disclose that the company's expenditures covering these efforts amounted to the meager sum of $2,253. A short time later, on September 13, 1899, the Denver, Cripple Creek & South Western Railroad Company sold all their property, rights, and privileges for the sum of $2,253[1] to the newly organized Colorado & Southern Railway Company which had just recently absorbed the Denver Leadville & Gunnison. It was at this time that the Colorado & Southern interests were entertaining some lofty ambitions. Together with the Rio Grande Western, they were dickering for a controlling interest in the Colorado Midland road and it appeared for a time that this Cripple Creek short cut might serve a twofold purpose; that of having a direct short line between Denver and Cripple Creek, and, secondly, becoming part of a transcontinental route in connection with the Colorado Midland, the Rio Grande Western, and the Santa Fe. At this point we shall revert to the Denver Republican of October 5, 1899, wherein was published a long and interesting article regarding this new Cripple Creek short line route. We quote in part:

"CRIPPLE CREEK SHORT LINE
"Midland Wants a Short Line to Leadville and the Colorado & Southern One to Cripple Creek

"Recent developments in railroad matters, and especially the building by the Colorado & Southern Railway, of a line through Platte Canon, which probably will be the much-looked-for Denver & Cripple Creek road, have brought to light the close connection formed within the last year between the Colorado & Southern and the Colorado Midland road. So close has this connection become that among the railroad men the rumor is abroad that the Colorado Midland is to have a share in the benefits to be reaped by the Colorado & Southern from its proposed new line to Cripple Creek.

"The arrangement includes for the Colorado & Southern a short line to Cripple Creek, using the tracks of the Colorado Midland and Midland Terminal, and for the Colorado Midland a short line from Leadville to Denver which will enable it to compete on more than an equal footing with the Rio Grande.

"The Atchison, Topeka & Santa Fe, recognized to be hand

1. Railroad Gazette, October 8, 1880.

1. Corporate History, Colorado & Southern Railway.

*Dr. C. H. Scott photo,
from Francis Rizzari Collection.*

Six engines push the rotary snowplow across Selkirk Trestle, on the east slope of Boreas Pass, in the spring of 1899. The plow, hidden in the cut, is followed by C.& S. 63, 57, 70, 37, 39, and D.L.& G. 202.

Elmore Wehrly Collection.

A South Park rotary snowplow, minus its wooden housing, after being caught in the Uneva Lake slide in Ten Mile Canon.

in glove with the Midland, also will come in for a share of the benefits, in that it will have a short and valuable middle country route which will give it a Pacific connection that will compete with the Union Pacific on the North, and the Rio Grande on the South.

"The statement is made upon good authority and has been all but admitted at the offices of the two railroads that the bonds of the Colorado & Southern, at the time of the reorganization of the road, were bought by capitalists who already owned the controlling interest in the Midland. Further, the close traffic arrangement which is now in operation between the Santa Fe and the Colorado & Southern and the Midland between Colorado Springs and Denver is another evidence of the way in which the roads are working together.

"In addition to this, the Pacific Express Company, which so long operated on the old Gulf section of the present Colorado & Southern, has been supplanted by the Wells-Fargo Express Company, a distinctly Santa Fe and Midland company. These straws, say men wise in railroad matters, are blowing in the direction of a consolidation of interests between the Colorado & Southern and the Midland as far as the road up the South Platte canyon is concerned. The plan is to build up the South Platte River via Lake George to a connection with the Colorado Midland at Florissant; from Florissant the Colorado & Southern would have trackage rights over the Midland east to Divide, and from Divide, further trackage rights over the Midland Terminal would give them access to Cripple Creek.

"People who are in touch with the situation at the place at which construction of the Colorado & Southern's Cripple Creek line is going on say that there is every indication that the track to be laid out will not be narrow gauge, as is the South Park branch from which it will extend, but broad gauge as is the Midland, with which it will connect. Contractors who are furnishing ties for the road have been instructed to deliver the 8-foot and not the 7-foot length, showing that when the controversy has blown over, the track which has been hastily laid to hold the site will be replaced by a broad gauge track. The work which is being done on the cuts and in blasting out curves which were in the original narrow gauge survey made by the Rio Grande is also on a scale to indicate the wider track will be built. This scheme will, of course, mean that the track from South Platte to Denver will have to be laid with a third standard gauge rail.

"The short line to Leadville, for the Midland, if the plan is carried out as conditions seem to indicate it will be, is up South Platte canyon to Florissant, where connection will be made with the Midland route, thence over a smooth upgrade to Leadville. This will replace the roundabout course now taken which goes first from Denver to Colorado Springs and from Colorado Springs to Florissant. In addition to the extra length there are two heavy hills on this second route, one between Palmer Lake and Denver and the other between Colorado Springs and Divide. The new route will be almost water grade from Denver to Leadville, which will make it possible to bring down from that point almost an unlimited amount of freight, thus putting Denver, as a smelting center, in the closest connection with the two greatest mining camps in the state. Out of the agreement the Colorado & Southern will get its close connection with Cripple Creek over the Midland tracks.

"Should this agreement go into effect it would put the Midland as a transcontinental line on a footing to enter into competition with the Rio Grande in a manner which it has never yet been able to do. It would also make Denver the natural terminus of the line, where it is now a terminus only by courtesy of other lines.

"In the great scheme of transcontinental traffic, the Santa Fe, as the copartner of the Midland, would reap its benefits in being able to cover the territory in the middle of Colorado,

in a way it has never been able to before. Denver would then become a terminus of the Santa Fe, rather than a way-station on the big system, which is the position it now occupies.

"The Denver Power & Irrigation Company, organized by the Rhodes Brothers on January 25, 1896, secured an injunction against the Colorado & Southern, keeping them out of the canyon. The fight between the irrigation company and the railroad began early last month when James E. Rhodes telegraphed to his Denver attorneys to obtain an injunction against the railroad which was hurriedly constructing tracks over the land in dispute. Before the restraining order could be secured, the railroad company heard of the action and rushed the work of laying their track across the reservoir site. Since the injunction was served, no work has been done, both sides awaiting action by the Courts.

"Yesterday the railroad filed an application to dissolve the injunction. Judge Moses Hallett being out of the city, the case was transferred to the United States Court at St. Louis, Missouri. The Colorado & Southern charged that the Denver Power & Irrigation Co. was organized to generate and sell power only, and that it has no intention of promoting irrigation enterprises; and further, that all of the water in the South Fork of the South Platte is appropriated, leaving none for the new enterprise. The chief engineer of the railroad company, the resident hydrographer, and the State Superintendent of Irrigation, have made affidavits in favor of the railroad company, which were filed with the notice yesterday, and which will be presented to the Court at St. Louis on October 7th.

"H. W. Cowan, Chief Engineer for the Colorado & Southern, has issued the statement that the railroad company is the sole owner of a certain right of way up the South Fork of the Platte River, heretofore granted to the Denver, Cripple Creek & South Western Railroad Company, and to the Denver, Leadville & Gunnison Railway Company in accordance with the Act of Congress approved March 3, 1875; that the company is now engaged in the construction surveyed by the Denver, Cripple Creek & South Western Railroad Company. He asserts that the Denver Power & Irrigation Co. is attempting to construct a dam 160 feet in height across the South Fork at Eagle Rock, just above the junction with the South Park's track at South Platte Station. This part of the canyon is narrow and precipitous and that if this company is successful in building their dam, the railroad tracks will be flooded and under water for two miles. It is alleged that a large force of workmen are on hand ready, at the behest of the Rhodes representatives, to tear up the tracks which are already laid across the land in dispute.

"The records of the land office show that the water is being sought for power purposes and not for irrigation, as claimed by the Denver Power & Irrigation Company, this being confirmed by a representative of the power company who stated to Mr. Cowan that it was the intention of his company to furnish power for the Tramway Company, the paper mills, the smelters and other industries in Denver. Any change in the line of the railroad as located will necessitate an expenditure of at least $250,000 by the railroad company.

"Charles H. Allen, Chief Engineer of the South Platte Canal & Reservoir Company (another organization who proposed to build a dam farther up the Platte above Deckers to provide water for irrigation purposes) also makes a statement, in effect, that all of the available water in the canyon at the point is appropriated by his company, which has spent more than $100,000 since 1893, in improvements and that the power company has no right whatever to any of the water.

"The wording of the application gives ample evidence of the intention of the Colorado & Southern to carry through its short line to Cripple Creek. President Trumbull said that there were now no employees working beyond the contested strip, that they had been taken off because of the scarcity of labor and the use the road had for them elsewhere. Between South Platte Station and the dam site, however, a gang of laborers is still working completing the track. Asked what would be done in case the suit in the United States Court were decided in favor of the road, President Trumbull answered: 'I should say that we should certainly go on building up the canyon until we have absolutely protected our right of way.'

"After leaving the canyon the Colorado & Southern has rights of way in two directions, one via Trout Creek and Divide, on the Midland Terminal, and another via the South Fork of the Platte, Florissant, and Oil Creek. On neither of these is there any contest, and once through the canyon of the South Platte the matter of building to Cripple Creek will be easy. Which route would be chosen President Trumbull would not tell. The wording of the application filed yesterday, which says that the road is engaged in the construction of a railroad 'over and across the right of way from South Platte Station to the junction of Horse Creek (also known as Trout Creek) and thence in a southerly and westerly direction toward Lake George' seems to indicate that the Florissant route had been settled upon."

Meanwhile, negotiations on the part of the Colorado & Southern and the Rio Grande Western (a Denver & Rio Grande controlled railroad) for control of the Colorado Midland were completed and the two roads assumed control of the Midland on July 2, 1900. Concerning this move, Graves's The Colorado Midland Ry., (R. & L. H. S. Bulletin No. 36) states:

"The Colorado Midland continued to operate as a separate railroad since the laws of Colorado prohibited the consolidation of parallel or competing roads. With the transfer, Frank Trumbull, President of the Colorado & Southern, was elected President of the Midland and Colonel D. C. Dodge became Vice President. . . . Colonel Dodge, who was also Vice President and General Manager of the Rio Grande Western, made the following statement for the Denver Republican in explanation of the purchase:

" 'The move was made by the Rio Grande Western and the Colorado & Southern Railways to keep conditions stationary. It was not to gain any advantage over a rival, but to keep a rival from gaining an advantage over us, and especially over the Rio Grande Western. The combining of the interests of the three roads will not materially affect the railroad situation in Colorado.

" 'The Colorado Midland will operate as a separate organization, and in all respects, for its own interests. The property will have the advantage of closer connections with the Colorado & Southern on one hand, and the Rio Grande Western on the other. The Colorado Midland management will do nothing for the benefit of the two connecting systems that might be harmful to the Midland.

" 'The Colorado & Southern, even now, will be able to reap some benefit from the connections into the mountains, which the Colorado Midland will afford it, while the Rio Grande Western will be able to maintain its original divisions on traffic with its connection, which, under other circumstances, it would not have been able to do'."

Immediately after this joint control of the Midland was obtained, plans were laid for the construction of the new Cripple Creek cutoff. The newly projected route was to diverge from the main line of the South Park at

South Platte station, located at the confluence of the North and South Forks of the Platte River, some 30 miles above Denver. From this point the line was to extend up the South Fork of the Platte by Lake George to a connection with the Colorado Midland at Florissant, and thence by way of the Midland's tracks east to Divide. From Divide, the Colorado & Southern was to have access to the famous Cripple Creek district by means of a trackage agreement with the Midland Terminal Railway Company. It was estimated that about 45 miles of new road, costing approximately $2,000,000, would be required to construct this cutoff. In view of the fact that both the Colorado Midland and the Midland Terminal were standard gauge, the plans stipulated that the line was to be of standard gauge construction and included the laying of a third rail on the Colorado & Southern's line between Denver and the point of divergence, South Platte station. Actual construction of the cutoff was held up pending the Court's decision as to who was entitled to control of the canon. Meanwhile it was reported that both sides had armed forces in the vicinity to protect their claims. It seems that "guns and Judge Moses Hallett" were an important adjunct to the building of early Colorado railroads. Their well-laid plans were short-lived. In the court fight for control of the canon, both the railroad and the Denver Power & Irrigation Company lost out and a dark horse, the City of Denver itself, emerged as the victor. In August, 1900, the City of Denver signed a contract with the South Platte Canal & Reservoir Company and the Denver Union Water Company for the construction of a dam across the South Fork at a point some five miles above Deckers. The project, known as the Cheesman Dam, was completed by January 1, 1905. This dam formed a huge reservoir known as Cheesman Lake and is today a part of Denver's water supply system.

Although the Colorado & Southern had lost their Cripple Creek cutoff, they were not to be deprived of an entry into the new gold camp. Access to the area was obtained a short time later when they secured complete control of the Colorado Springs & Cripple Creek District Railway in January, 1905.[1] This standard gauge road, built at the turn of the century between Cripple Creek and Colorado Springs, connected with the main line of the Colorado & Southern at the latter point, thus giving them control of a through route between Denver and the Cripple Creek gold fields. Meanwhile, during 1902 and 1904, the C. & S. built 4.28 miles of narrow gauge track south from South Platte station to Nighthawk. Curiously enough, this branch was used primarily to haul construction materials used in the building of the Cheesman Dam, the very object that caused them the loss of their proposed Cripple Creek extension. The Nighthawk branch was abandoned in 1916.

1. Poor's Manual of Railroads, 1936.

Looking through the mouth of Box Canon into the Arkansas Valley about 1900.

A view taken in 1946 at approximately the same location as the upper photo, showing the depth of the sand deposited on the grade by numerous Trout Creek floods.

THE GILPIN RAILROAD

In writing the history of the Colorado & Southern's narrow gauge lines, mention should be made of the Gilpin Railroad. Briefly, the Gilpin was a two-foot gauge railroad built in 1888, under the name of the Gilpin County Tramway Company. The little road was built to serve the numerous mines in the vicinity of Central City and Black Hawk. The road which attained a total length of some 26 miles, connected with the narrow gauge Colorado Central just north of Black Hawk. On February 24, 1904, the Colorado & Southern acquired control of the road and operated it from that date until 1917, at which time operations were discontinued and the road abandoned on account of the decline of mining activity in that region. For further details the author suggests that the reader see Mr. H. T. Crittenden's complete history of the Gilpin Railroad, which was published in the Railway & Locomotive Historical Society's Bulletin No. 57.

TROUT CREEK FLOOD IN AUGUST, 1908

As previously explained, the South Park's track between Trout Creek Pass and the Arkansas Valley was built along the bottom of the canon and crossed and recrossed the small creek many times as it twisted its way downstream. As the years rolled by, the Trout Creek region, like any other Colorado mountainous region, received its share of rains; and the railroad, located along the bottom of the canon, practically in the very bed of the stream itself, became an open invitation to disaster.

When first constructed, the right of way was practically immune from damaging floods, but as time passed some of the excessive rains commenced to play havoc with our little railroad. During the latter part of July, 1908, ominous clouds began to gather in this vicinity and soon the rains came. Peaceful little Trout Creek became a raging torrent, and Box Canon, which served as both the railroad's and the stream's outlet to the broad Arkansas Valley, formed a veritable funnel through which drained the entire water shed between Trout Creek Pass and the Arkansas River. The high perpendicular granite walls of Box Canon held its victim securely within its grasp. The flood reached its greatest intensity on August 1, 1908, and completely washed out over a mile of the main line between milepost 131.5, about where the old charcoal ovens were located, and Schwanders, milepost 132.6.

The reader will recall that the author attempted to defend the South Park's engineers' decision on their final location of the Trout Creek line, on the basis that conditions existing at the time of construction justified their act. Regarding possible flood conditions along the canon, Mr. Hugh C. McLean, resident of Buena Vista, offers a good explanation of one of the major factors that eventually brought about a change in the creek's

behavior. Before civilization had advanced into this region, the slopes of the mountain sides along Trout Creek Canon were plentifully supplied with an abundance of timber and, as nature intended it, these densely timbered areas retained much of the water, thus preventing floods to a great extent. Construction of railroads through these regions created a heavy demand for ties and the South Park was no exception.

In addition to furnishing railroad ties, the timbered area in this vicinity was also exploited by some local interests who built some charcoal ovens near the mouth of the canon. To supply their demands, the tie contractors and charcoal interests cut away much timber, and to move this timber down into the canon, they had cut numerous trails up and down the mountain sides. Every tree the tie cutters and the charcoal operators removed lessened the forest's ability to retain the rains, and every trail they cut became a potential gully to carry these rains down to the canon floor below.

Mr. McLean's explanation seems plausible indeed. Regardless of the reasons Trout Creek developed into a trouble maker, time had proved that Eicholtz and Evans made a serious error when they chose the bed of Trout Creek canon as a right of way for the South Park railroad. However, the damage was done now and it was up to the present day owners to make the best of their bargain.

The Colorado & Southern engineers realized the folly of rebuilding this section of washed-out track through Box Canon and, to eliminate further trouble here, decided to abandon the route and rebuild the track over the old original grade built by Maj. James Evans in 1879. This route, which the Union Pacific had abandoned in 1884, diverged from the canon near milepost 132 at a point later known as Dead Man's Curve. The story behind this odd name will be related later. From this point the grade followed through a few cuts in some low hills and thence across the floor of the valley to the South Park's first Arkansas River crossing, originally called Arkansas Station. At this point the relocated line connected with the Schwanders-Buena Vista track. A wye was built at the point of connection and the place was given the name Macune.

In addition to rebuilding the new line over the old grade between the canon and Macune, it was also necessary to rebuild a small section of track that had been washed out in the canon immediately above Dead Man's Curve. William Cairns states that the new line via Macune was completed on October 10, 1908. The rebuilding of this segment thus completed the main line connection between Como and Gunnison. Reference to the Buena Vista and Nathrop map, included in the pocket inside the rear cover of book, will show the reader the various changes in trackage that occurred in this vicinity from time to time.

THE SILICA BRANCH

Following in chronological order, we next come to the construction of the Silica branch. This branch left the main line at the station of Platte Canon, later known as Waterton, 20 miles from Denver. It was built by the Colorado Railroad Company, a subsidiary of the Colorado & Southern Railway.[1] Title to the Colorado Railroad Company's equity in the line was conveyed to the Colorado & Southern on March 28, 1930.[2] The branch was built to serve the feldspar deposits located in that vicinity, owned by the Western Feldspar Milling Company. Feldspar is a mineral product used in the manufacture of glass, pottery, porcelain and other ceramic products. There were also some rock quarries located along the line, and a brick plant at Silica.

Construction was commenced in September, 1908, and the line was completed and placed in operation in August, 1909. It was narrow gauge and was 3.89 miles in length from the main line connection to the end-of-track, which was known as Silica. A close study of maps indicates that a portion of this branch, after crossing to the south side of the Platte River and turning east, followed the old grade of the Rio Grande between Acequia and the South Platte River for about a quarter of a mile before turning south toward Silica. The entire line was an uphill climb with a maximum grade of 3.04%. The maximum curvature encountered was 24 degrees. The Silica branch was used intermittently until it was dismantled in 1941.

COLORADO & SOUTHERN CONTROL ACQUIRED BY THE CHICAGO, BURLINGTON & QUINCY R. R.

Control of the Colorado & Southern did not remain in the hands of its original incorporators very long. Some four years after its organization, control of the Colorado enterprise was acquired by purchase in the open market in 1902,[3] by the Edwin Hawley interests who, at that time, also controlled the Minneapolis & St. Louis and the Iowa Central roads. The next important step in the corporate history of the South Park road was the acquisition of Hawley's Colorado & Southern control by the Chicago, Burlington & Quincy in 1908.[4] The Commercial and Financial Chronicle of December 26, 1908, spoke of this deal as the most important event of its kind in railroad finance during that year.

How long the Burlington had been interested in acquiring control of the Colorado & Southern property is a debatable question. There are those that contend that although the Burlington had appeared on the Colorado scene in 1882,[5] they were unable for some reason

to gain a suitable foothold whereby they might expand their transportation system in that region; and that because of this situation it was Burlington manipulation of finances which assisted materially in the 1898 consolidation of the old Union Pacific Denver & Gulf, and the Denver Leadville & Gunnison, which emerged as the Colorado & Southern system. Although the writer has no concrete evidence to confirm this theory, we do know that when the Colorado & Southern embryo made its appearance, one Norman B. Ream of Chicago was sitting on the new company's Board of Directors,[1] and that on November 5, 1902, this same gentleman was duly elected to the Chicago, Burlington & Quincy's Board of Directors.[2] Mr. Ream remained as a member of the two boards for some years.

As previously related, in 1902 Edwin T. Hawley had secured Colorado & Southern control and if the Burlington was biding its time waiting for the Hawley decision to sell, it had not long to wait. The opportunity to acquire the Colorado & Southern came in 1908. In the Railway Age-Gazette of December 25, 1908, we read:

"The Chicago, Burlington & Quincy's Board of Directors have ratified the purchase of a controlling interest in the common stock of the Colorado & Southern Railway Company. Enough of the 31,000,000 shares of outstanding common stock have been purchased from Edwin T. Hawley and associates to give them the desired control."

The transaction involved the transfer of $23,657,500[3] in common stock at a cost of $16,416,337.50.[4] The Burlington assumed control of its new property on December 21, 1908.[5]

Through this transaction the Chicago, Burlington & Quincy acquired approximately 2,000 miles of railroad operated by the Colorado & Southern and its various subsidiaries, including the Denver & Interurban, Ft. Worth & Denver City, Colorado Springs & Cripple Creek District, and the Wichita Valley. Thus, the C. B. & Q., through its alliance with the Great Northern and the Northern Pacific,[6] acquired a new short route extending from Puget Sound in the Pacific Northwest to tidewater at Galveston, Texas.

In addition to this, the Burlington also came into control of a very valuable interest in the Denver Union Station.[7] In commenting on the transaction the Railway World of December 25, 1908, stated:

"Colorado & Southern stock, held by the Edwin Hawley

1. Corporate History, Colorado & Southern Railway.
2. Poor's Manual of Railroads, 1930.
3. Graves, "Colorado Midland Ry.", R. & L. H. S. Bulletin No. 36, and Railway Age, December 25, 1908.
4. Chicago, Burlington & Quincy Annual Report, June 30, 1909.
5. Burlington & Colorado R. R. reached Denver May 29, 1882.

1. Poor's Manual of Railroads, 1899.
2. Poor's Manual of Railroads, 1903.
3. Graves, "Colorado Midland Ry."
4. C. B. & Q. Annual Report, June 30, 1909.
5. Overton, "Burlington West".
6. These two railroad systems, controlled by the James H. Hill interests, had held joint control of the C. B. & Q. since April 17, 1901. (Overton, "Burlington West".)
7. A report published by the Union Pacific at Omaha under date of Feb. 17, 1890, stated: "The Denver Leadville & Gunnison terminal grounds, property, etc., was worth well over $3,000,000."

Three Colorado & Southern locomotives; the 4 and 61 were photographed at Denver in 1926, and the 74 was taken at Leadville in 1941.

interests for the last seven years, was recently sold to the Chicago, Burlington & Quincy for cash. President Frank Trumbull stated: 'The transaction is good for both parties. It will give the Burlington access to Pueblo, the Leadville, Clear Creek and other mining districts of Colorado, and Galveston and other tidewater terminals. Colorado & Southern credit is greatly improved and is therefore advantageous to all present security holders.' Mr. Hawley stated: 'Colorado & Southern is in a snug shape in every respect. The net earnings are ten times what they were during Frank Trumbull's first year of receivership'."

Mileage of the South Park lines at the time the Burlington assumed control, December 21, 1908.

	Miles
Denver to Como	88.27
Como to Gunnison	115.75
Gunnison to Castleton	14.71
Castleton to Baldwin	2.62
Castleton to Kubler	1.56
Macune to Buena Vista	2.25
Garos to Alma	15.41
Hill Top Junction to Leavick	11.33
Sheridan Junction to Morrison	9.97
Soda Lake Spur	.25
Garfield Quarry Spur	2.75
Como to King	.26
Como to Leadville	63.83
Dickey to Keystone	7.01
Kokomo to Wilfley's Mill	1.10
Leadville Mineral Belt	3.09
Nighthawk Branch	4.28
Denver to Silver Plume	54.64
Golden to Church's Brick Yard	1.70
Forks Creek to Central City	11.66
Total	412.44

As a sort of eulogy relative to the passing of the Colorado & Southern system into outside hands, the Denver Republican of December 23, 1908, published a very timely article which we shall include:

"PASSING OF A COLORADO RAILROAD

"Fully forty years ago a band of patriotic pioneers of Colorado, headed by the late Governor Evans, undertook to place Denver in communication with the outside world—a herculean undertaking at such a time. A railroad system radiating through the territory was outlined by Governor Evans. The Government-aided trunk line, the Union Pacific road, was leaving Denver a village in the wilderness. This could not be permitted; the leaders of the day were men who could not be rebuffed. From this determined stand to put Denver on the map grew the system which later became the Colorado & Southern road. It had many an up and down—the Colorado Central, the Denver South Park & Pacific, the Union Pacific Denver & Gulf divisions. But Governor Evans lived to see his vision a practical fulfillment, a connecting link between Denver and the Gulf states. Now comes official announcement that the Colorado road is to become a part of the great Hill system of something like twenty-four thousand miles of railroad.

"It is significant of the evolution that has taken place in railroading and business generally that the absorption of this local road is accepted as a matter of fact. The doctrinaire state rights' man is philosophical about it and materialistic in his philosophy. As a small part of a giant system, it may benefit Denver and parts of Colorado. Perhaps this is true, perhaps it is not true. Time will tell. One thing is certain—the Colorado & Southern railroad will be conducted as part of one great organization. Denver has no significance to the new owners apart from its trade sheets. If this city is the natural center of the cities on the 'trade currents' it will be taken into account. If not, the Colorado & Southern management will pass it up in favor of some other city. In these days of gigantic Wall Street combinations, state pride and local associations cut no figure. Once upon a time the local directors and officers of Colorado railroads—the Colorado & Southern, the Denver & Rio Grande, the Rio Grande Western, Colorado Midland, and others—looked closely to Colorado and to Colorado sentiment. Each of the roads were of Colorado. Railroad commissions and railroad laws were not encouraged in those days—a personal 'kick' was sufficient. The tariff schedule was made to be broken. A shipper was dealt with as an individual factor. With changed conditions, with new ownership, with dictation from Wall Street, new conditions have arisen at home and at the seat of centralized government. The Interstate Commerce Commission has had the breath of life breathed into it, and Colorado has been trying, somewhat ineffectually up to the present, to have a state commission supplement the work of the federal body.

"Colorado is no different from other states. Indeed, it is a bit better off for there is the Moffat road, still independent and local to Colorado, for how long we do not know, but it is to be hoped for a long time to come."

Around 1917 rumors were afoot whereby a section of the South Park line was once again considered as a possible connecting link in a cross-country hookup in connection with the Colorado Midland.

During the years 1910 to 1912, general economic conditions were at a low ebb and the incomes of many Colorado railroads suffered, including the Colorado Midland which was under joint control of the Rio Grande Western and the Colorado & Southern. As a result of this state of affairs, the Colorado & Southern saw that its investment in the Midland road was in danger of becoming valueless and received permission during the year 1912 to sell their half interest. After a great deal of legal controversy revolving around the Colorado Midland, the road was sold at auction in 1917 to Albert E. Carlton, a Colorado Springs banker, and some associates who had become wealthy through their recent Cripple Creek mining investments. It seems that this group of men were vitally interested in the old Midland and were opposed to seeing the road pass into the hands of opposing bidders who merely intended to junk the entire line. Concerning Carlton's acquisition of the Midland property, we quote from Graves's "Colorado Midland Railroad":

"Of this latest transaction of the Colorado Midland Railway, the Denver News, under date of April 22, 1917, had the following to say:

" 'The joining of Denver and Salt Lake City with the rich copper fields of the Watson and Vernal regions in Utah is contemplated by Mr. Carlton and his associates. Plans so far indicated provide for the building of two links in the system that will connect the Colorado and Utah capitals, while two other links necessary to the chain already are owned or controlled by the Colorado Springs group headed by Mr. Carlton.

" 'The new owners propose, it is understood, to use the South Platte branch of the Colorado & Southern Railway from Denver to Bath, 120 miles, thence to Grand Junction via the Midland. From Grand Junction to Fruita, Colorado, the company will acquire for the Midland the interurban system operating 21 miles of track, now plying between those towns, and, incidentally, controlled by Mr. Carlton and his associates. A stretch of nine miles from Fruita to Mack, Colo., must be built up to connect with the Uintah Railway at Utah City. The Uintah road (extending from Mack, Colorado, on the D. & R. G. to Watson, etc., 68½ miles) is said to be controlled or owned outright by the Carlton group. The new owners have an option on the road from Watson, north to Vernal, Utah, the heart of the copper district, and from Vernal to Salt Lake City it will be necessary to construct a new road'."

The Carlton group immediately took steps to rehabilitate the Midland road and extend it westward. To carry out their plans, it would have been necessary to change the South Park's track between Denver and Bath, and the Uintah line, to standard gauge, an exceptionally expensive proposition in both cases. The first world war resulted in the total abandonment of the Colorado Midland in 1918 and put an end to all their plans.

The remaining corporate history of the South Park, including the old Colorado Central Clear Creek line, more or less revolves around the abandonment of the two divisions, related in full later in this book.

Otto Westerman photo,
from Elmore Wehrly Collection.

D.S.P.& P. 157, formerly D.S.P.& P. 30, the "Morrison", on the Keystone branch in the late 1880's.

CHAPTER XVIII

POTPOURRI.

Few states have ever cradled and nursed such a galaxy of railroads as has the state of Colorado. A partial list would include such well-known roads as the Denver & Salt Lake, Crystal River & San Juan, Argentine Central, Manitou & Pikes Peak, Colorado Central, Uintah, Denver & Rio Grande, Gilpin Tramway, Denver South Park & Pacific, Rio Grande Southern, Silverton, and other San Juan roads, the Colorado Midland, Denver Boulder & Western, and many others. They strung their ribbons of iron and steel from the depths of the dark canons to the top pinnacles of the Continental Divide. A few are still with us but most of them are gone. But the greatest of them all was the Denver South Park & Pacific.

What was the South Park like? To the old time railroad man or boomer, it was a symbol of link and pin days, of runaway cars, rock and snow slides, hazardous work, and late trains. To the tourist, no more beautiful pictures of glorious mountain scenery were ever framed by a passenger coach window. To the mine owner and rancher, it was a life line between himself and civilization. But where trains, and people, and traffic once rambled up and down its busy rails, nothing remains today but abandoned sections of trackless right of way, with a few rotted ties to be found here and there, balanced across a washed and eroded grade. It is like the passing of an old friend. And inasmuch as we like to hear and know about old friends, the writer will attempt to tell something about this particular one—the old South Park.

* * * *

CONSTRUCTION AND MAINTENANCE.

In attempting to describe the physical characteristics of the Denver South Park & Pacific we must take cognizance of factors not ordinarily associated with the standard gauge type of railroad. The narrow gauge type of railroad was adopted for mountain construction mainly because of the very nature of the rugged terrain through which it was to be built and because of the economy of construction. A roadbed and track capable of supporting heavy standard gauge equipment and high speed trains was a factor which did not demand consideration by the original builders. Their major problem was the location of a satisfactory route whereupon they might lay their pine ties and light rail;

while their second problem was the overcoming of the many difficulties encountered in the building of their right of way along the boulder-strewn banks of some rushing mountain stream, between the high walls of a precipitous canon, or along the steep face of some mountain side.

Throughout the entire South Park system, including the Clear Creek line, the roadbed was primitive and unfinished, with no surface or ballast.

Very little grading was done, and a minimum amount of earth was scooped up along the right of way for use as ballast between the ties. In the more mountainous sections, where blasting was necessary to carve out the roadbed, fragments of small rock were conveniently utilized, along with some earth, to tamp between the ties. As the years rolled by, deep layers of cinders were gradually built up along the steep grades—mute evidence of the laborious exertions of the little engines as they blasted their way to the top with a heavy drag. The only exceptions to this earthen ballast occurred near Denver and a few of the larger division points where small sections of the grade were ballasted with slag or cinders.

Relative to the drainage of the right of way by means of bridges and culverts, we find the following interesting data in an old bridge report dated January 1, 1885.

	Number of Open Bridges and Culverts	Combined Length In Feet
Golden to Central City	67	2,265
Forks Creek to Graymont	44	1,990
Denver to Baldwin	124	4,463
Como to Leadville	58	3,040
Bear Creek Junction to Morrison	27	936
Garos to London Junction	19	1,102

During the construction of the South Park, red spruce and yellow pine, as a rule, were conceded by the engineers to be the best tie material. However, due to the great abundance of cedar in the mountain regions of Colorado, ties of this material were also used in the construction of the road. The ties were laid at the rate of 3,000 per mile on the main line and 2,800 on the branch lines and spurs. They were untreated, being used just as the tie cutters prepared them in the forest.

The first rails used on the road were of iron and weighed thirty pounds to the yard. During the early '80's, the road began the replacement of these rails with steel rail of a heavier design. The Railroad Gazette reported that much of this steel was used rail shipped to the South Park from the Union Pacific. Relative to some of the first steel rail, the writer received the following interesting note from Mr. B. J. Blecker, a former Union Pacific engineer. Mr. Blecker stated:

"I once found some steel rail just west of Idaho Springs with the name DOWLAIS STEEL cast in the web. It took me a number of years to find out that this steel was made in Cardiff, Wales, in England, and that it was some of the finest steel laid on the Union Pacific in the 1860's. When it became worn badly, the Union Pacific took it up, cut the ends off, bored new holes for fish plates and used it on the Colorado Central. It was in various lengths of ten, fifteen, and twenty feet. They first used 'iron chairs' for the rail ends to set in. They also used two flat pieces of iron bolted to both ends of the rail and called them fish plates."

The 1885 Colorado Railway Commission's report carried the following figures relative to the type and weight of rail used on all main lines and branches:

	Miles
30, 35, 40, and 56-pound iron rail	95.05
40 and 45-pound steel rail	227.10
Total	322.15

The Commission's report also added that the average life of iron rail on the main line was six years, while that of steel rail was eight years. The average useful life of ties was given as four years. Although the weight of rail used increased to some extent, both iron and steel were to be found on the South Park up to the time of abandonment, being distributed as follows:

Denver to Como

40 to 85-pound mixed, with 52-pound steel predominating, with a very small amount of 85-pound.

Como to Gunnison

40 to 56-pound mixed, with 40-pound steel predominating. With the exception of the tunnel, the section over Alpine Pass between Hancock and Quartz was all 40-pound iron. The tunnel itself was laid with new 40-pound steel at the time it was built and relaid with new 50-pound steel in 1908. It is also of interest to note here that the writer once found some 40-pound iron rail laid between the west portal of the tunnel and Alpine Tunnel station with the wording "JOLIET 1881" cast in the web, indicating that this rail had been rolled in Joliet, Illinois. The Baldwin branch was laid with 35-pound iron rail.

Denver to Central City and Graymont

The Clear Creek line was laid with 50 to 56-pound steel rail with 52-pound predominating.

All branch and spur lines of the entire system were laid with a mixture of 35 to 60-pound rail with the lower weights predominating.

During the early years the South Park used the Fisher rail joint, held together by a "U" bolt, but later used the regulation type angle bar to connect the rails.

However, the author found a considerable number of the old type Fisher rail joints scattered here and there. A photograph elsewhere in this book shows one of the Fisher joints which still remained on the Gunnison division between Alpine Tunnel and the Palisades at the time this section was finally abandoned in 1923. The tie plate was a modern railway appliance that seldom found its way to the narrow gauge division of the Colorado & Southern system. The rails were usually spiked directly to the ties. Stub switches, usually operated by the old harp type switch stand, were standard equipment. Stub switches had a distinct advantage in Colorado's mountain regions in that it was practically impossible for snow and ice to collect between the point and the main rail, as very easily happens to the modern split type switch.

We find many references, in the construction of some of the narrow gauge railroads through the mountainous regions of Colorado, to the fact that the engineers chose to lay their track around a large tree, boulder, or projecting mountain arm, in preference to removing the obstruction. Cy Warman writes: "The little locomotives could curve on the brim of a sombrero, and it was not an uncommon thing for the locating engineers to run around a big boulder or a large tree, rather than blast it away". This is easily explained. In the absence of modern mechanical equipment, a few extra ties and sections of rail were cheaper than the powder and labor, especially the latter, necessary to remove these obstructions. The winding characteristics of the South Park, together with the apparent policy of the builders to "just lay track" without paying too much attention to cuts and fills, were often a favorite topic of discussion. In a spirit of fun, one writer even went so far as to state that a jackass would have to have hinges in order to negotiate some of the sharp curves found along certain sections of the right of way. Many used to speak of it as "the toboggan road" because of the numerous up and down grades. And the kids often called it "The Dam Slow Poke & Pretty Rough Riding". However, not all the line was made up of curving track. Several long sections of tangent, or straight track, were to be found along the line as it made its way across South Park or in the Blue River section north of Breckenridge. Also, there was a tangent approximately three miles in length between Schwanders and Nathrop. The longest section of straight track was a 7.84-mile tangent on the Fairplay branch between Garos and Hill Top Junction. For a more detailed discussion of curvature, tangents, grades, bridges, and other similar track data, see the individual chapters covering the construction of various sections of the road. Through the courtesy of Mr. Donald Ashton, Publicity Director of the Burlington, the writer is able to present a chart giving all grade and curvature data on the main line of the South Park system.

STATEMENT OF GRADES AND CURVES

Narrow Gauge Division
COLORADO AND SOUTHERN RY.
Main Lines Only

	Miles Total	Miles of Tangent Track	Miles of Curving Track	Per Cent of Curving Track	Number of Curves	Maximum Curvature	Total Degrees of Curvature	Number of Complete Circles	Maximum Grade (%) West	Maximum Grade (%) East
Denver County Line to Waterton	14.32	10.60	3.72	26	34	12°00'	593°08'	1.65	1.86	1.50
Waterton to Kenosha	55.76	25.29	30.47	55	560	32°00'	19911°38'	55.31	4.00	2.03
Kenosha to Como	12.08	9.47	2.61	22	35	28°30'	1268°59'	3.53	2.38	4.20
Como to Breckenridge	21.73	11.37	10.36	48	201	25°20'	7379°14'	20.50	4.49	4.00
Breckenridge to Leadville	41.19	29.10	12.09	29	234	20°00'	5887°30'	16.35	4.30	2.73
Como to Nathrop	48.48	36.68	11.80	24	147	24°00'	5394°01'	14.98	2.82	2.76
Nathrop to Gunnison	65.01	44.68	20.33	31	373	28°00'	10294°05'	28.60	4.00	4.00
Totals	258.57	167.19	91.38	35	1584	32°00'	50728°35'	140.92	4.49	4.20

Additional information covering station mileages, station facilities, grades, curves, elevations, etc., will be found in the complete profile charts which cover the South Park and Clear Creek lines, and in Chapter XXII. At this point the author desires to include a few words regarding maximum, or ruling grades, and curvature. The best nontechnical definition of ruling grades found by the author is furnished by Mr. E. W. Mureen in his "Fulton County Narrow Gauge History," R. & L.H.S. bulletin 61-A. Mr. Mureen states:

"The ruling grade on any railroad is that grade which fixes the maximum train tonnage that can be hauled over the road. The grades of a narrow gauge road may permit the haul of a 300-ton train over the entire line with the exception of a short distance where an unusual grade or curvature might limit the haul of the train to 200 tons. Unless 'doubling' or additional motive power is resorted to, this particular grade limits all trains to a maximum of 200 tons and thereby becomes the ruling grade of the road."

It is a difficult task to give a good definition of the term "20-degree curve." Briefly, the curvature of a track, figured in degrees, is equal to the angle subtended at the center of a simple curve by a 100-foot chord on the circle. A one-degree curve has a radius of 5,730 feet; a two-degree curve, 2,865 feet; three-degree, 1,910 feet; 10-degree, 574 feet, and a 20-degree curve has a 288-foot radius.[1] For an excellent description on this subject, supplemented by diagrams, the reader is referred to page 42, August, 1945, issue of Trains Magazine.

referred to page 42, August, 1945, issue of Trains Magazine.

The South Park was burdened with the usual amount of right of way maintenance that is encountered on any railroad. However, due to its geographical location, maintenance on this narrow gauge mountain railroad was an expensive proposition, no matter how you looked at it. According to testimony given during a court hearing relative to the abandonment of one of the narrow gauge sections, the maintenance-of-way cost on the narrow gauge division was 51.3 per cent of the operating revenue as against 28.8 per cent on the entire Colorado & Southern system. The greater portion of this huge expense resulted from floods, rock slides, and snow. Snow was one of the South Park's greatest enemies; on flat sections it would pile up to depths of from two to ten feet; it filled up cuts to tremendous depths; and snow slides in the canons caused no end of trouble for both train and maintenance crews.

Flood waters in Clear Creek and South Platte Canons would wash out sections of the track and tie up the road for days and weeks at a time. One of the many examples of flood damage occurred on May 3, 1900, when a temporary diversion dam, on Goose Creek near the site of Cheesman Dam, then under construction, broke because of heavy spring rains, and washed out over six miles of the railroad between South Platte Station and Platte Canon station (later known as Water-

1. Railroad Stories magazine, May, 1932.

ton). This caused the suspension of all traffic on both the Leadville and Gunnison Divisions until May 28th, when the damage was repaired. Incidentally, the Colorado & Southern entered a suit for $100,000 against the Cheesman Dam owners for this damage. However, the results of the suit are not known. In all probability the railroad company never collected. Trout Creek Canon was another location where the railroad suffered considerable damage from floods. The story of the great 1908 Trout Creek flood, which resulted in the relocation of part of the line in this vicinity, has already been told. The 1908 flood was not the last to damage the South Park tracks through this canon. They continued to occur with more or less intensity from time to time, washing out track and causing great damage to railroad property throughout the canon. By 1910, the company finally gave up the fight against Trout Creek flood waters and abandoned the entire line from Garos south to Buena Vista.

Speaking of floods in Trout Creek, one night in Denver while the author and a few devotees of the South Park were spending a convivial evening in genial Ed Haley's home, that venerable old South Park engineer and champion snow-bucker de luxe, Andy Nelson, related the following incident:

"A common expression heard around the Como Yards when it looked cloudy off to the south was 'Oh! Oh! Washout in Trout Creek!' One afternoon I was called to help get a drag of empties, scheduled for the Baldwin Mines, over the hill. It looked rather threatening south and east of Como but I never paid any unusual attention to it. Late that afternoon we double headed out of Como with our drag. I was running the lead engine. At Trout Creek Pass I cut off, and as it was dark I hung a red lantern on the rear right side of my tender and proceeded to run light down the canon toward Schwanders.

"While drifting down the track, about half way between McGees and Box Canon, I suddenly observed what appeared to be some one swinging a red light across the track in front or me, waving me to a stop. I slammed on the brakes, stopped and got out to investigate. Sure enough, just about twenty feet ahead of my engine a section of track had been washed out. However, strange as it seems, I could not locate the person who had warned me of the damaged track. My fireman and I looked all around and could find no one. We finally solved the mystery.

"Believe it or not, the red lantern I had hung on the hind end of my tender had got to swinging on its hook and its reflection in the front cab window of my engine led me to think that I was being flagged down. To this day, I still think that it was an Act of God that saved me from wrecking my engine and possible injury to the fireman and myself on that dark rainy night in Trout Creek Canon."

The Clear Creek line was another section often menaced by flood waters. An example of this is found in the 1933 annual report, which stated that it cost $19,-759 to repair flood damage to the railroad between Golden and Black Hawk. The Morrison Branch, along Bear Creek, also came in for its share of flood damage.

Another factor which caused considerable damage to both roadbed and rolling stock was rock slides. Certain sections of Clear Creek, especially between Chim-

W. H. Jackson photo,
from David S. Digerness Collection.

A washout in Clear Creek Canon, near Chimney Gulch, which occured July 24, 1896.

W. H. Jackson photo,
from David S. Digerness Collection.

The same flood washed out Huntsman Bridge, just west of Chimney Gulch in Clear Creek Canon.

ney Gulch and Forks Creek; Platte Canon; and Tenmile Canon, together with the mountainous sections over Boreas and Alpine Passes, were all subjected to rock slides at various times. Roy Morton, ex-South Park brakeman, tells of an incident near Grant where a big rock from a slide came down the mountain side, during a rain, just as a passenger train was passing. This huge boulder hit the rear end of the baggage car, caving in the whole side. Mr. Morton reports that, fortunately, no one was hurt. Numerous statements, concerning other incidents, due to rock slides, have been made to the author by old time employees, telling of engineers rounding a curve and encountering rock, snow, and even earth slides, that had come down some adjacent mountain side and spread over the track.

Head and shoulders above all maintenance expense encountered on the South Park was the eternal problem of snow during the long winter seasons. The Colorado Railroad Commission report of June 30, 1885, stated that the South Park's expense for removing snow and ice during the winter of 1884-85 amounted to $55,525.17. A typical example of some of the difficulties which the little railroad experienced with snow blockades is found in the Gunnison Daily Review of February 2, 1883, in which we read:

"SOUTH PARK SNOWBOUND

"No train from east of the range has arrived on the South Park road since last Sunday, five days ago, and it is beyond the power of any human being to tell when there will be another. The railroad is clear of snow from Gunnison to Ohio City, but from there to Pitkin the trouble begins. All of the cuts are full of snow and at Pitkin the snow is reported to be three feet deep on the level, which fell last Tuesday and Wednesday.

"The only mode of conveyance between Tincup and Pitkin is over the range on snowshoes. The road between Quartz and the Silent Friend Mine is closed up by the snow but hopes are that it will be opened soon. The snow on the railroad track between Pitkin and Quartz is reported to be from three to four feet deep.

"Construction trains are still working east of the range but when the track is cleared it requires only a few minutes for the drifting snow to fill up the cuts. The snow in the cuts near the tunnel on this side of the range is reported to be twenty feet deep. A large force is employed near the tunnel trying to open the road. The snowslide at Woodstock is a serious drawback and may delay trains for some time. A telegraph office was established at the tunnel on January 20th, which proved to be an important office and a convenience to the railroad."

Author's note: The same paper of February 17th stated that the railroad was finally opened to traffic.

Through the courtesy of Carl Hewett and Dick Kindig, we find some interesting sidelights, relative to the road's troubles with ice and snow, in the following messages and train orders:

Apr. 10, 1901. For Dickey, to C & E of all west.
Keep sharp look out for snow slides from Curtin to 2 miles & half west, especially 300 ft. east of Grippe siding.

JAR   7:32 am

314

Mch. 16th, 1902. For Dickey, to C & E of No. 72.
No. 72 will run nine 9 hours & fifteen 15 mins late Dickey to Como.

JAR   8:31 pm

Denver, 3/2/1909. To C & E, all east. At Dickey.
Look out for ice on track at Baker's Tank account tank leaking.

WMB   2:33 pm

Denver, 3/11/1909. To Engs 10—64 & 72. At Dickey, Colo.
Order No. 34 is annulled. Engs 10—64 & 72 will run as one extra Dickey to Leadville, protecting against extra 6 east Kokomo to Sand Spur, and look out for engs and cars in snow between Kokomo and Climax. These engs and cars may not be protected.

WMB   7:57 pm

E F Lott   3/22/32
CCW
No. 71 left good rail all the way from Leadville—stormy at Climax and the 10 mile. If wind will not start to blow will not be necessary to run car flanger tomorrow—we ran flanger thru Climax and Solitude sidings.

Tony Palucci
DDK   3:06 pm

CCW   EFL   3/30/32
I cut eng 8 off train Selkirk tank—went to mile post 97¼ Windy Point—snowing so hard I could not pull train after I plowed it out—if I had stayed bucking it out would get eng 8 stuck and would be out of coal—going to Boreas light eng.

St. John
D 4:15 pm

CCW   Como   April 3 33
Snow from 10 to 18 inches deep on Alma branch and still snowing.

Sanches
3:18 pm

Como, Jan. 26, 1934. To C & E engs 73—71—74 & 75.
Eng 73 run extra Como to Leadville.
Engs 71—74 & 75 help extra 73 west Como to Climax then run extra Climax to Como.
Eng 71 run extra Dickey to Dillon then run extra Dillon to Dickey.

EBM   3:56 pm

In order to eliminate as much grief as possible, snowsheds were built along certain sections of the line, where conditions were generally the worst. About a dozen

Otto Westerman photo,
T. St. John Collection.

Colorado & Southern 69 with a passenger train snowbound just north of Como station in 1904.

T. St. John Collection.

C.&S. 10 at Halfway on Boreas Pass in the winter of 1901. Conductor Tom St. John and brakeman beside the engine.

sheds of various lengths were constructed on the east slope of Boreas Pass. Other sheds were located near Breckenridge, Kokomo, and at the west portal of Alpine Tunnel.

Snow fighting equipment consisted of the rotary snow plow and the wedge plow. The wedge plow crews did their share to help keep the lines clear, but it was up to the rotary, or the big vacuum cleaner, as some called it, to keep the badly blocked sections open. As nearly as can be determined, the railroad possessed only one rotary snowplow up to 1900.[1] The Colorado & Southern annual report for that year states that a new plow was purchased for the sum of $16,959.86. A note added that the machine was equipped with the new automatic couplers and air brakes. Speaking of the rotary, the author ran across an interesting anecdote that happened while the rotary crew was opening up a section of the line. It seems that the rotary snowplow was working through a cut into which a herd of cattle had drifted to protect themselves from the cold and had frozen to death beneath about fifteen feet of snow. The big rotary went right through the cut, throwing refrigerated beef steaks all over the adjacent mountain-side.

The wedge plow, sometimes referred to as the butter-fly plow, was bolted to the front end of an engine, and was highly successful as a means of clearing the track of snow, providing it was not too deep or packed too hard. Through continued use of these wedge plows, many old-time South Park engineers developed into some of the most competent "snow buckers" ever found in the Rocky Mountain area. A snow bucking outfit usually consisted of three engines. The head engine, which received the brunt of the punishment, carried one of the wedge plows bolted securely to her front end. This plow, an ungainly steel butterfly, almost completely obscured the view of her crew. The operation of the wedge plow is probably best described by quoting a few stories from some of the enginemen who ran them. One of the most interesting is told by the late Lewis Lathrop. We quote in part from his article, "The Alpine Tunnel Route," as published in Railroad Magazine, June, 1941.

"On numerous occasions, Denver South Park & Pacific heads displayed their own particular brand of ingenuity. I remember one snow-sparkling December's morning back in 1898. Colin Moore had been called that day, to fire an engine for Walt Parlins from Gunnison east. They picked up a couple of helper engines at Pitkin, and a coach loaded with snow shovelers.

"Colin's engine was equipped with a hinged flanger, so she was left in the lead. Hammering steadily along she didn't have a great deal of trouble in clearing the light drifts up to Alpine Tunnel station. But beyond, the snow lay deep and the track leading to the tunnel was completely choked.

"It was while the outfit was battering away at this approach that the track behind them blew full again. After innumerable

1. William Wendell, South Park engineer, reports only one rotary in the early days.

316

hours of enthusiastic but futile toil, it suddenly dawned upon the gang that they were stuck tighter than a drumhead. There was no chance of opening the line through the tunnel and down the east side, and less of backing down to Pitkin. Coaches never were designed for bucking snow.

"They held a parley. During the course of the argument, they decided they could still get back to Pitkin—if they only had an engine with a plow on her, headed west. The trouble was that all of theirs were headed east. Furthermore there was at that time no turntable at the mouth of the snowshed leading to the west portal of Alpine Tunnel. Could they swing the plow engine around in any other manner?

"They decided they could. On the train were half a dozen hydraulic jacks, capable of lifting thirty tons. There was plenty of valve oil which would make rails laid at right angles to the wheels slick enough so ponderous weight would slip on them. No sooner thought of than they went to work. They discon-nected the engine from her tender. To get actual practice, they decided to turn the tender first. Five or six hours later the loco-motive and tender were back on the rails and headed west!

"Colin Moore, who is still alive and going strong, claims that, 'There wasn't nothin' to it. A fellow had to use his head, is all. Even the engine didn't give much trouble, once we got her flanges above the rails so she'd slide. And after we'd dragged her back as far as the side tracks at Alpine Tunnel station, where we could rearrange our train, we went sailing down that four per cent grade into Quartz, like a bucket drop-ping into a deep well.'

"With the kind of country through which they worked, the D. S. P. & P. boys were about as colorful a gang of don't-give-a-damn railroaders as ever assembled under one banner. Among them were 'Silver Tip' Adams, Dad Martinis, Mike O'Hara, Tom Flavin, Joe Plunkett, Patrick 'Curley' Colligan, William Cairns, Tommy St. John, Andy Nelson, Billy Wendell, Pat Gibbony, Billy Kerns, Charlie Squires, Jerry Regan, Billy Westall, and maybe a few others. Daredevils and loyal heads, every one of them. Today most of them have crossed the Great Divide, 'from whose bourn no traveller returns'.

"One January evening back in the '90's, I was loafing in the cigar store when Silver Tip Adams came in. It had been a beautiful day in Gunnison, cold but not a breath of wind blow-ing. Silver Tip was a little fellow who wore a beard every winter. Although he was in his thirties, this chest-protector was white as snow on the end, hence his moniker.

"'You ought to see my engine, Lew,' he opened the con-versation. 'What happened? Turn her over?' I asked.

"He pulled up a chair and sat down. 'No,' he said, 'I just moved the cab back eighteen inches on the boiler.'

"'How?'

"Then he told me the story:

"'Well, we got out of here early this morning. You know how pretty the day was? Just like Spring, all the way up the west side of Alpine. I'd begun patting myself on the back thinking what a good run we were going to make when we stopped at Alpine Tunnel station to register.

"'I was ahead. Mike O'Hara was behind me and Andy Nelson and Johnny Olson were on the other two engines at the hind end of the train. After our brakeman looked them over, we whistled off. We passed the red light in the center of the tunnel going slow and I held 'em down until we nosed around the curve to where we could look out of the east portal.

"'I've never seen such a blizzard as was blowing there. The track was buried deep with drifted snow. I could hardly see my hand in front of my face. I kicked off my brakes, whistled a couple so the boys behind me could work steam, pulled my windows and doors closed, and got to my feet.

"'We hit it harder than I ever hit snow before. I felt my cab move. My front door smashed open and a white avalanche

Dr. C. H. Scott photo,
from Francis Rizzari Collection.

D.L.&G. 206 helping the Gunnison-Como mixed train past the engine house at Alpine Tunnel about 1897.

Dr. C. H. Scott photo,
from Francis Rizzari Collection.

C.&S. 64 bucking snow near Woodstock in 1900, showing the butterfly plow in raised position, for backing out of snowdrifts.

came through and shoved me out of the cab. I wound up half-buried in the coal pit. We were stuck plenty. The hind end managed to drag the loads back to Alpine, and after steaming and shoveling out, they pulled my engine free.'

"Silver Tip hadn't exaggerated. Those South Park heads would waltz up the west side of Alpine Pass with a full train. The weather would be perfect, with an afternoon sun melting the snow between the rails. But east of the tunnel they'd run into a glorified hell of howling wind, flying snow, and filled cuts. The springs that dripped through the roof of the tunnel made ice which would have quickly choked the bore, had it not been chopped out every day. The company tried to operate through several winters, but after losing plenty of money maintaining from fifty to a hundred shovelers at the pass, and bucking drifts with as many as a dozen coupled engines, they began closing down the line about mid-December each year, resuming operations along about the following April. What freight originated on their line from the Baldwin coal fields was routed over the Denver & Rio Grande during the interim. A stub run operated between Gunnison, Baldwin, and Alpine Tunnel station. It carried mostly freight.

"As I've already stated, those South Park hoggers were snow-bucking fools. In a way they had a better break than we Rio Grande fellows. It wasn't long after the rails were laid over Alpine Pass that the D. S. P. & P. officials realized that something must be done to battle the blizzards and the slides. So one day they came out with a new departure. This was called a 'Priest' flanger and was hung beneath the pilot, directly ahead of the pony truck wheels. It could be raised or lowered by an air valve in the engine cab. That device was all right. I know, because years later the little 169, which I ran in passenger service west of Gunnison, was equipped with one of those snow battlers. When lowered, it left a clean, ice-free rail.

"But the South Park officials were not entirely satisfied with the Priest flanger. Their next innovation was a butterfly plow which was hinged on the pilot. This plow was also raised and lowered by air. When bucking snow, an engineer would ram his mill into a drift as hard and fast as steam and speed allowed. When he plugged, he simply raised the plow and his Priest flanger and backed out. With the fixed plows which we had on the Rio Grande, backing always filled the track behind us with ice and snow which the rig dragged in."

Another interesting story centering around Mr. Clarence Adams was published in the Gunnison News-Champion of May 12, 1938. This is the same "Silver Tip" Adams spoken of by Lewis Lathrop. The article, from which we quote in part, is as follows:

"One of Gunnison's pioneer residents, Clarence Adams, has a fund of stories about the early days in Colorado, and among them are his experiences on the old Denver & South Park railroad. For fourteen and one-half years Mr. Adams fired and ran an engine over that scenic route. Mr. Adams was born in Kentucky in 1859, but moved to Gunnison with his parents in 1881. Some time later he started to work for the railroad. Mr. Adams retired in 1902, to go into business for himself.

" 'There really isn't much of anything of interest to tell about my experiences on the South Park,' began Mr. Adams, when interviewed. 'That is, nothing that was not everyday work.

" 'One day after twenty-four hours of work and a few hours of rest in Gunnison, I was called to take a train out of Gunnison at noon. We started east up the slope for Alpine Tunnel with eleven cars of coal and one passenger coach. Three locomotives were on the hind end pushing. Upon reaching the tunnel station we stopped for orders. Two of the pushers were returned to Gunnison and the other engineer and myself re-ceived orders to continue on east. While weather conditions on the west slope were all right, it had been reported to the west portal operator that a storm was blowing on the other side of the range. My conductor was not in favor of spending the night in the snow, but I concluded that 'orders were orders' and that we should go ahead until we were stopped.

" 'The two pushers that were to return to Gunnison gave me a push to get my train into the tunnel, then the coupling pin was pulled and they went on back down the hill to Gunnison. When I rounded the curve at the east portal and passed Atlantic siding I was going down that four per cent grade at a fairly good speed. I hooked my cab door back so that in case of an accident, I would not be thrown back under the coal tender.

" 'On the east slope the snow was piling up and drifting down the mountain which was on my side of the locomotive. Shortly after leaving the tunnel the engine hit a big snow drift with full force. The cab door broke and I was thrown back into the tender and completely buried with snow which had been swept in all over the cab. My fireman helped extricate me. An examination of the engine showed that the cab had been pushed back three inches on the boiler. By that time the conductor had fought his way through the snow to the engine to see what the trouble was. We decided that the only thing to do was to go back to the other side. Bracing ourselves against the strong wind, we started walking back and finally got into the tunnel.

" 'We reported our predicament to the operator at the tunnel station and then returned to our train. The conductor bedded down in the coach (fortunately, there were no passengers) and my fireman and myself sat up in our engine all night. The rotary snow plow finally dug us out about four o'clock the next day. We then proceeded to Como on our own engine. Our eleven cars of coal were being taken to Leadville. This Baldwin coal had to be pushed over the Continental Divide three times to get it there.

" 'The biggest snows I have ever seen in my life were on the east side of the range. Invariably, there was always more snow and rain on the east slope of the three passes than there was on the western side. There were never any rains heavy enough to cause floods on the west side like they did on the east.

" 'We had no trouble to speak of where the railroad passed through heavy timber, but the open sections that were laid bare by either man or fire permitted heavy drifting of the snow and gave the railroad much trouble.

" 'I never was in a wreck, but once, when firing, I looked back in time to see a car leave the rails and turn over. For a while I had the regular run on the Pitkin-Baldwin section. Dad Martinis was engineer and I was fireman. Once during this time the locomotive on the regular Denver passenger run broke down in Gunnison. Dad Martinis' engine was new and we were called to take the passengers to Denver and return. On the return trip we left Denver about seven o'clock in the morning and reached Gunnison around six o'clock in the evening. It was an all-daylight run over a magnificent scenic route. On clear days the passenger train would stop at the Palisades to let the passengers gaze across the Gunnison Valley, the Uncompahgre, past the hills west of Montrose and on into the mountains of Utah. It was a very spectacular and beautiful view.' "

William Cairns, another old timer whom we have spoken of before, relates:

"One time two snow-buckers, Ed Gross and Fred Williams, were attempting to clear the track between the east portal of the tunnel and Hancock. Ed was running engine 69 and Fred was running the 67. George Gray, a traveling engineer, was riding with Williams on the 67. They had brought their two engines up from Gunnison. As they came out of the east portal, they were picking up speed rapidly so that they would have a good run at the drifted snow. There is a very sharp curve at the mouth of the tunnel and as the two engines came out, they both left the rails, turned over on their sides, and slid down the mountain side three or four hundred feet below Atlantic siding. Fortunately, no one was seriously hurt."

In searching for material relative to snow conditions encountered on the Clear Creek line, the writer inquired of Mr. Robert Hicks as to what information might be had. Mr. Hicks, who was connected with the Vice President's office in Denver, replied as follows:

"I put this question up to General Manager J. D. Walker, who has been in the operating department of the Colorado & Southern since around 1900. Mr. Walker's knowledge of this matter plus additional data which he obtained from talking to the retired Chief Dispatcher, Mr. C. C. Whitman, is as follows: As far as the old timers, including Mr. Ed Osborne, who ran engines up and down the Clear Creek line for many years, and others now pensioned, can recollect, it was necessary to take the rotary up Clear Creek Canon but once. That was during a terrible snow storm that occurred in the Denver region in 1913. This storm commenced on December 4th, and when it let up the snow was 47 inches deep on level ground in Denver. This one trip of the rotary up the canon was further verified by records in the General Superintendent's office.

"A few of the engines used on the Clear Creek line were equipped with the Priest flanger. This device, which was successfully used to clear the rails of snow and ice, was placed immediately ahead of the pony truck wheels. Some of the engines were also equipped with a butterfly plow.

"No one recollects any bad snow slides in Clear Creek Canon, and they were never particularly bothered with snow on this line. There may have been a few occasions when butterfly plows and Priest flangers were helpful, but snow was not a hindrance or a very great expense on this line as compared to the South Park's line. The Clear Creek line was located in the Front Range and did not cross the Continental Divide. There was no great amount of wind to speak of except between Idaho Springs and Georgetown and this wind blew the snow off the track instead of on it.

"And here is some additional information. The Colorado & Southern had two special cars on the South Park line called 'rail flangers'. They were built somewhat on the order of a flat car, and were equipped with four flangers or plows, one at each corner of the car. These flangers, located just above the rail center, were set at an angle, and could be raised or lowered as conditions required to scrape snow off the rail and throw it to one side.

"The short plows were not only used to clean the ice and snow from the rail, but would plow out just far enough to clear the right of way so that the journal boxes would not drag in the snow. As a rule these cars were always operated between Como and Leadville. Their use was never required on the Clear Creek line.'

* * * *

ROLLING STOCK

During the discourse on rolling stock, we shall attempt to hold discussion pertaining to the road's locomotive power to a minimum, as this particular subject merits a section to itself. The author spent considerable time in searching for material regarding the South Park's rolling stock; unfortunately, the resulting information leaves much to be desired.

Relative to the road's original passenger cars, Albert Sandford (Colorado Magazine, October, 1928) states:

"For the first three years or more, the system's rolling stock consisted of a pair of small locomotives and four passenger coaches, two of which were designated as smokers and the other two as ladies' cars. . . . Their Sunday excursion business grew to such proportions that the management ordered six flat cars which were reconstructed as 'excursion cars'. On these rebuilt cars, the passengers were protected from the weather by a light roof supported by strong uprights. The seats were of common lumber, smoothed off and painted."

From the information which has come to light, these so-called excursion cars were built by Halleck (or Hallack) Brothers, located in Denver. Note the following statement found in the road's annual report for the year 1874, page 27.

". . . it has been the policy of the company in every practicable way to encourage home industry. With this in view they have had all their cars manufactured in Denver. And it is safe to say that no better freight cars or more elegant passenger cars are to be found than those made for your road, by Messrs. Halleck Bros. of Denver."

Additional passenger car information occurs in Poor's Manual of Railroads for the year 1879, wherein we read that the road owned six passenger coaches and two baggage, mail and express cars. Evidently a Denver news reporter was not favorably impressed with these "elegant coaches." After making a trip through Platte Canon in the spring of 1879, he wrote:

"Travelers who have been accustomed to Pullman Palace cars for night travel find an all night ride in a narrow gauge passenger car with low-backed cushionless seats not a little fatiguing and hardly a good preparation for the next day's duties, etc."

Following this, we find an item in the Denver Daily Times of September 10, 1879, concerning passenger car No. 7, which states:

"The Denver & South Park shops in this city have just turned out a new and elegant passenger coach designated as the 'Como', No. 7. The car is similar to those now in use upon the road. It has two rows of double seats and a newly perfected and easily operated window latch which allows opening and closing the windows with little trouble. The cost was approximately $2,600."

Evidently our friend George Pullman was not the first to have trouble opening car windows. Then in the April 8, 1880, issue of the same paper we read where the road purchased sixteen secondhand passenger cars from the New York City Elevated Railroad.

By the latter part of 1879, the South Park had mastered the difficulties of Platte Canon, surmounted Kenosha Summit, and stretched out across South Park to the Arkansas Valley; business was booming. The railroad had reached that stage in its growth where the passenger lists began to include others beside railroad construction crews, roughshod miners plying to and fro, and the tougher element usually found riding a new railroad in a new country. Therefore, in order to cater to the higher class of clientele that was beginning to patronize the line, the South Park management

W. A. Gibson.   *M. C. Poor.*

W. A. Gibson.   *W. A. Gibson.*

Richard B. Jackson.   *Richard B. Jackson.*

Some examples of Colorado & Southern narrow gauge rolling stock.

added a piece of fashionable passenger equipment—a Pullman Palace Car. It is hard to determine just what type of car this first Pullman Palace Car was. In view of miscellaneous statements found, it must have been some sort of a combination sleeper, diner, and parlor car. Commenting on this ornate new car with the red plush cushions, the fancy chandeliers, and other elegant appurtenances, the Rocky Mountain News of October 19, 1880[1] stated:

"The South Park Company furnishes to ladies and to such of their gentleman passengers as wear a clean shirt and do not swear, a Pullman car without extra charge.'

Following one of Jay Gould's inspection trips over the South Park, the same paper added these comments:

"During an inspection of the line, Mr. Gould said he liked the road's nickel, red plush cushions and mirrors. He said, 'They gave us plenty of shine and color as good measure in berth length.' The easy spending, well-to-do mine operators enjoyed the comfortable diners with their inviting alcoves, up to date poker tables and buffet bars."

By the latter part of 1882, the South Park had gained entrance to both Leadville and Gunnison. The fact that both of these places were twelve to fifteen hours away from Denver created a demand for overnight schedules. The management foresaw possibilities of additional passenger revenue and decided to establish a sleeper service between Denver and the two prominent mining camps. Accordingly, arrangements were made for the use of four Pullman Palace Cars. In those days the Pullman Company built two types of narrow gauge sleeping cars. One type contained double berths running down one side of the car only, with the corridor on the opposite side as was standard practice in European cars of similar construction. The other type was much like the standard gauge sleepers, except that the berths, which were built on both sides of the aisle, were single ones. Upon receipt of the four cars the Rocky Mountain News of October 7, 1882, says:

"The Union Pacific has just received a superb shipment of new Pullman sleepers for its Gunnison trains, the first of which went out last night, well filled. The South Park trains leave Denver at 8:00 p.m. daily and will hereafter run a Pullman sleeper through to Gunnison via the famous Alpine Tunnel route.

"This much needed car service has been the only feature lacking to render the great Alpine Tunnel route the most popular in the State. With the advantage of nearly one hundred miles in distance, its great saving time, its unrivalled scenery and superior equipment and construction, it must always take the business between Denver and Gunnison."

Concerning this de luxe equipment, we are indebted to the Railway Age for a description of these cars.

"The Pullman Company has just supplied the Denver South Park & Pacific with four very elegant and comfortable narrow gauge Pullman Palace Cars. They are now running. The Pullman Company owns the cars, which were built at the Detroit works, and furnishes and maintains them on a contract similar to that made with other railroads through the country. The

cars, which are appropriately named, 'South Park', 'Leadville,' 'San Juan', and 'Bonanza', each contain ten sections—upper and lower berths—and can thus accommodate twenty passengers. They are 42 feet long, 8 feet 4 inches wide, and 8 feet high inside, and weigh 15 tons. They run on 30-inch paper wheels with the Pullman standard truck reduced. Externally, they are painted in the rich dark color adopted as the Pullman standard, ornamented in gold after the Eastlake style. The interiors are beautifully finished. The ceilings (which are of wood) and sides are finished in Marquetrie, with mahogany, burl, prima verra (white wood), amaranth, ebony, and rosewood. The seats, seat covers, curtains, mattresses, and other appurtenances are up to the degree of excellence for which this company is famed. The windows are large—nearly equal to those in the standard car. Eames' vacuum brake attachments, Baker heaters, and Hicks & Smith's improved lamps, and various minor conveniences are included. In short, these cars, both in appearance and in actual comfort for the traveler, are very similar to the full sized Pullman sleepers, and their workings are perfectly satisfactory."

Reference to one of the sleeping cars is found in a newspaper story of a wreck. In the Gunnison Review of March 19, 1881, we read:

"At 3:30 this morning a South Park train of sleeper,[1] coach and baggage cars met with a serious accident near Thompson, 46 miles from Denver. The rear trucks of the sleeper jumped the tracks dragging the other two cars off the track, but leaving the locomotive on the rails. The sleeper turned a somersault down the bank, some 30 feet into the Platte River, where water soon filled the car to a depth of 12 to 18 inches. The passengers escaped by crawling through windows. Of the 26 that were on the train, two were seriously injured. The railroad soon secured a box car and continued on their way into Denver."

Further reference to the Leadville and Gunnison sleeper service was found in an old Denver newspaper clipping (name unknown) of October 22, 1882.[2]

"AN UNLUCKY ACCIDENT

"At six o'clock yesterday morning the regular night express from Gunnison and Leadville arrived at the station at the entrance of Platte Canon, just 20 miles from Denver. The train, drawn by the engine 'Pitkin City', consisted of a baggage car, the ordinary passenger cars, a Gunnison sleeper and a Leadville sleeper.

"At this station there is a siding where this passenger train often passes the westbound freight, it being the duty of the latter, however, to keep out of the way. No freight was there, and the passenger pulled out toward the city. It had an upward grade with which to contend, and when it had run about one-quarter of a mile had acquired a speed of about four miles per hour. At the point it had then reached, there is a sharp curve where the track rounds the base of a hill. As the engine rounded this curve, Engineer Latham saw the outward bound freight, a double-header, almost upon him, not over one hundred feet away, and moving at a good rate in order to make the siding where it should have been. There is another passing track on this side where it seems as if the freight train ought to have waited, considering the orders under which it was running. All hands on the freight engines jumped, after the steam had been shut off. Engineer Latham remained at his post. When the crash came he was struck severely in the back, but not seriously injured, as was thought at first. The pas-

---

1. Evidently this must have been the "Pullman Palace Car" referred to in the Rocky Mountain News of October 19, 1880.

2. Courtesy D. W. Yungmeyer.

1. Courtesy Jack Thode.

senger engine climbed the front of its first opponent, but the speed at which the trains were running prevented any serious damage. The passenger tender was partially jammed into the baggage car, and the baggage car broke the end of the car behind it. Of the freight tenders, the first was overturned and the second sent partly into the car next to it, which was loaded with iron machinery. This was not injured. Latham was the only man hurt. The engines were not badly damaged at all, though they lost some paint, and a cow catcher or two was turned awry. A wrecking train was sent for and reached the spot at nine o'clock with fifty men. The delayed passenger train arrived at the Denver depot at one o'clock. The passengers were scared at the time of the mishap and some of them were shaken up, though not one was the least bit hurt.

"This is the whole source of the terrible rumors that floated about yesterday in regard to dire loss of life and property, the worst affair of the kind, it was said, that ever occurred in Colorado. The foundation of all these stories, as the account shows, was slight. Only one man was hurt and he in a trifling degree. The track was only blocked for a few hours and after that, travel and traffic went on as if nothing had happened. A story of railroad disaster, run down, in nine cases out of ten comes like this, almost to naught."

A news note, elsewhere in this same paper, stated:

"Mr. N. P. Babcock, of Gunnison, was among the passengers on the sleeper which was stopped suddenly on the South Park yesterday. He was the only man who did not wake up. 'Bab' was in the midst of a beautiful nightmare and refused to be disturbed."

Shortly after this, according to the annual report of December 31, 1885, the Union Pacific Company entered into a contract with the Pullman Company whereby the Union Pacific purchased a three-quarter interest in the 28 Pullman Palace Cars to be used on the entire Union Pacific system, including the South Park Division. Three-quarters of the earnings went to the railroad company and the balance reverted to the Pullman Company. The annual report stated that the investment proved profitable.

Regarding the Pullman service between Denver, Leadville and Gunnison, an 1886 public timetable discloses that the Night Express, carrying sleepers for Leadville and Gunnison, left Denver at 8:30 p.m. Upon reaching Como, the train divided. The Leadville section left Como at 2:25 a.m. and arrived in Leadville at 7:15 a.m. The Gunnison section pulled out of Como at 2:30 a.m. and arrived in Gunnison at 11:15 a.m., having stopped en route at 7:30 a.m. for breakfast at Alpine Tunnel station. On the return trip, the Leadville train pulled out at 8:45 p.m. The Gunnison section left at 4:30 p.m. (dinner at Alpine Tunnel station). Connections were made at Como at 1:20 a.m., with arrival in Denver at 7:00 a.m. Concerning the meal stops at Alpine Tunnel station, an 1883 employee's timecard states the meal stop was at Alpine (Fisher). This is confirmed by H. L. Curtiss.

The writer pauses to wonder just how many South Park fans would like to make one of these round trips, especially the one to Gunnison. The line forms at the right—"have your money ready." However, sad to

relate, the demand for Pullman service on the South Park did not continue any great length of time. By 1887, business on the Gunnison division declined to a point where it did not justify continuance of sleeping car operation. According to H. L. Curtiss, former Pitkin resident, Pullman sleeper service to Gunnison was dropped in July, 1887. For some time after that the sleeper was cut off at St. Elmo to accommodate traffic to and from the Tincup, Aspen and Glenwood Springs districts. However, a short time afterward in October, 1887, both the Colorado Midland and the Rio Grande reached Aspen. This eliminated any further need for the St. Elmo sleeper and as a result all further Pullman service on the Gunnison Division was discontinued in November, 1887. Concerning sleeper service between Denver and Leadville, Thomas St. John states that this class of service was discontinued in 1896. This was the last of the narrow gauge Pullmans on the South Park.

Meanwhile, the passenger car roster had been further augmented by purchase of additional chair cars, tourist cars, and baggage, mail and express cars. The writer has been unable to locate any record of the South Park's rolling stock for the years 1881-82. However, in 1883 the record discloses that the road possessed 28 passenger coaches, 5 Pullman cars,[1] and 6 mail, baggage and express cars. The sudden increase also shows up in the freight car rolling stock and was undoubtedly caused by a combination of two important factors which occurred at this time, the acquisition of the road by the Union Pacific, and the increased traffic due to the newly acquired Gunnison and Leadville connections which caused a demand for additional cars.

Albert Sandford,[2] in commenting on the road's first rolling stock in 1874, stated that the company had a few flat cars and box cars. The Rocky Mountain News of March 19, 1874, published an item to the effect that Hallack Brothers would build 52 freight cars for the South Park. Evidently this and additional orders were filled, for the list of rolling stock as given in Poor's Manual of Railroads for 1879 lists 45 box cars and 109 flat cars. Following this, we read in the Railway Age of July 20, 1882, that the Union Pacific shops in Omaha were building 80 box cars and 100 flat cars for the South Park. According to H. L. Curtiss, the South Park, during the early '80's, acquired considerable rolling stock from the old Utah Northern, another Union Pacific subsidiary. Cy Warman writes: "The first coal or ore cars had four wheels, a dump in the bottom, and held about as much as an ordinary farm wagon."

The passenger car equipment that carried people up and down Clear Creek, the Platte, and over the moun-

1. H. L. Curtiss states that the name of this fifth Pullman car was the "Hortense."
2. Colorado Magazine, October, 1928.

An excursion train, headed by C.&S. 10, wrecked in Platte Canon near Foxton, after a runaway in September, 1901.

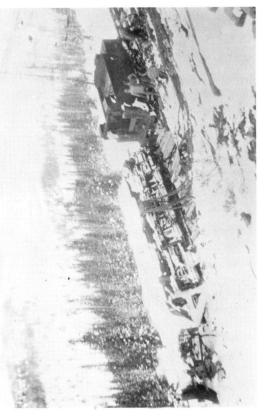

A wreck on Boreas Pass above Peabody's Spur, in April, 1926, caused by an over-loaded baggage car.

D.L.&G. 115 and train, overturned on the Mudsill Branch in 1895.

C.&S. 73, wrecked east of the summit of Boreas Pass, in 1935.

tains, was typical of almost any early day coach found in this country in the '80's and '90's. The open end coaches were illuminated by gaudy coal oil lamps that swung in a constant arc as the car bounced along over the rough and uneven track. Coal burning stoves, bolted to the floor of the car, furnished what little heat was to be had. Link and pin couplers were standard equipment.[1] An 1883 South Park rule book states that signals were transmitted by the conductor to the engineer by an overhead bell cord running the entire length of the train and attached to a brass gong on the ceiling of the engine cab.

The Eames vacuum brake was also standard equipment on all South Park rolling stock up to the early '90's, at which time it was gradually replaced with the more reliable and efficient Westinghouse air brake. Thomas St. John says that to the best of his recollection, the first air brakes appeared in Denver in February, 1893. Evidently, link and pin couplers did not last long on South Park passenger equipment, for the 1885 Colorado Railway Commission Report states that the Miller automatic coupler was standard equipment on all passenger cars of the road as of that date. With the exception of the automatic coupler and air brake, little or no improvement was made in the narrow gauge passenger coaches throughout the entire history of the road. The few coaches which were left at the time of abandonment in 1937, still remained the old high backed plush or leather seats, coal oil lamp illumination, and coal burning stoves for heat.

Similar to the early passenger equipment, all Colorado Central and South Park freight cars were equipped with Eames vacuum brakes and link and pin couplers. Like the passenger cars, it was not until the early '90's that the Westinghouse air brake replaced the vacuum brake. However, before the vacuum brakes were replaced, many a good trainman took his last ride on some of the South Park's steep grades. An example of what happened, due chiefly to this inefficient type of braking, is found in the September 9, 1883, issue of the Denver Republican.[2] The article tells of two bad wrecks; one on Kenosha Hill, and the other near Webster:

"TWO FEARFUL WRECKS
"TWO ACCIDENTS HAPPEN ON SOUTH PARK RAIL-
WAY YESTERDAY
"SEVEN MEN INJURED—THREE OF THEM THOUGHT
TO BE FATALLY HURT
"ONE SECTION OF FREIGHT TRAIN JUMPS THE
TRACK, THE OTHER COLLIDES
"WOUNDED BROUGHT TO DENVER AT MIDNIGHT—
SCENES AND INCIDENTS

1. One of these old couplers, complete with link and pin, can be seen on display at the State Museum in Denver.
2. The Denver Republican apparently had little use for the Union Pacific Company and availed themselves of every opportunity to play up and publicize wrecks and other mishaps that occurred along the Union Pacific controlled South Park railroad.

324

"Two frightful accidents occurred yesterday on the South Park Railway, and within a very short time and distance of each other. Seven men were injured,, three of them, it is thought, fatally. The first accident occurred just above Webster, and the second on Kenosha Hill. Conductor Livingstone's freight train had been made up into two sections to come down the hill. The first section made the grade successfully, but at its base, ran into a construction train, injuring four men. The second section was even less fortunate. Just at the top of the immense grade, while running at more than the usual rate of speed, the engine jumped the track and the eight cars back of it were telescoped down the embankment. E. S. Fister, the engineer, Edward Lake, the head brakeman, and Conductor Livingstone were badly injured. The wreck was a terrible one. The wounded men were extricated from the ruins and taken to Webster, where the wounded from the first wreck had also been taken. At a late hour in the afternoon the seven injured men were placed aboard a train and brought to Denver, arriving here about midnight."

Further comments regarding the Eames vacuum brake are to be found in Railroad Magazine in an article by M. S. Goodale. We quote in part:

"I can well remember the stiff grades on the Leadville line. Some of them were more than four per cent; it required three engines to take 14 cars up the east slope of Boreas Pass, for example. But the old time railway officials were generous. They ordered us down old Boreas with fifty or more cars. The helper engines were coupled in the middle of the train, for the grade was so steep they weren't able to run back down hill without a train for braking power.

"In those days we used the old 'wind jam' or Eames vacuum brakes. If you broke in two, it was goodby and farewell. And in case you started to run away, it was useless to set the hand brakes, for as soon as you started to tie one down the train would enter a low snow shed and you'd have to lie flat on the running board to keep from knocking your head off. As almost any one knows, you can't set brakes in that position.

"One dark night we had a doubleheader and 60 cars. It was blowing snow terribly. Then our air failed. Our hand lanterns went out, so we frantically held on to the running board and prayed. In this way we went about five miles until the top of the head engine struck the overhanging and snow-laden limbs of a large tree which took the big diamond stacks off both locomotives. A reverse curve, together with the deep snow drifts, finally stopped us altogether. We were within a mile of Como. Believe it or not, even in that cold and snow there were 43 hot boxes blazing when we stopped!"

Mr. A. M. Hains also wrote in Railroad Magazine:

"Early South Park rolling stock was all equipped with Eames vacuum brakes. Going down hills, all hands were on top with their brake clubs, the steam siphon on the engines were wide open trying to keep air out of the train pipe, while the engines were in back motion with their water brakes in operation.

"A supply of loaded ore cars was always kept on the siding at the summit of Kenosha Hill for helper engines to pick up to help in braking down the stiff grade. In 1882, a 17-car train, with Conductor Sherman and rear brakeman Bill Toler, started down Kenosha Hill. The engineer lost control of his train and the whole outfit jumped the track and went several hundred feet down the mountainside. As Sherman had had several wrecks before, Trainmaster Huntington discharged him, saying that if the road kept him it would soon have no cars to run."

It seems that as early as 1885 the company was carrying on some experiments with the Janney freight

O. C. Perry.

A. W. Whiteford Collection.

Robert LeMassena Collection.

The top photo shows engine 21 in Denver in 1916. Note the cone-shaped cinder device in use at this time. In the center is the 49 just west of the coal chute at Pitkin about 1903. The curtain over the headlight was pulled down at night when the engine was in a siding for a meet, to avoid extinguishing the oil flame. A view of C.&S. 63 with combination car 22, about 1905, appears at the bottom of the page.

coupler, but just what success they had with them is not known. On March 4, 1893, Congress passed the Safety Appliance Act, requiring railroads engaged in interstate commerce to equip all cars with automatic couplers. The South Park's rails did not extend beyond the Colorado state line and any interstate traffic they had must have been of small consequence. Therefore, it is not known for certain whether they came under the new ruling or not. If they did, the company was rather slow about complying with the requirements, for it was not until 1900 or later that the old link and pin system on the South Park's freight cars was replaced with the automatic coupler. William Cairns says that the job of installing the new couplers on all the freight equipment required about six months. He also added that although a number of couplers from various manufacturers were used, the greater portion were Climax couplers.

Regarding the adoption of the modern coupler, it is interesting to note in the Colorado & Southern's annual report of 1901 that 160 new coal cars, 50 new stock cars, 40 box cars, 3 passenger coaches and one rotary snow plow were purchased, all equipped with automatic couplers and air brakes as specified by the Interstate Commerce Commission. Relative to this changeover in couplers, it is also interesting to note how the South Park's link and pin inventory gradually disappeared, These figures are from the road's annual reports.

Link and Pin Inventory

June 30, 1900	$1,586.31
June 30, 1902	838.41
June 30, 1905	238.56

* * * * *

"The pay car will pass over the South Park on the 10th." This not unusual notice appeared in the Rocky Mountain News on November 2, 1880. Like most early railroads, the South Park ran their pay car up and down the line, carrying the cash with which to pay the employees their wages. A bit of color relating to this long since discarded piece of rolling stock, and which aptly applies to the subject at hand, is found in the August, 1943 Railroad Magazine, written by Stuart Covington. We quote in part:

"Side by side with the diamond stack, the link and pin, the open platform coach and the oil headlight, the pay car has a place all its own in the recollections of old timers. Little known to the novice, the traveling bank was a byword to all true rails. Dilapilated, unpainted, sometimes attached to the local passenger, sometimes not, the creaking chariot rolled up and down the system, visiting the bustling terminal as well as the sleepy branch lines, bringing excitement and drama to each place as it distributed the 'mazuma'.

"Sometimes part of a three-car train, the paymaster's buggy was glassed in, with a wicket cut in the partition where the official stood to distribute the payroll. The bunk car was the general center of living for the train, the place where the crew ate, slept and worked until the round was completed. Coupled on behind sometimes, the oil car supplied some of the

smaller section houses and depots on the division with coal, signal oil, and other necessities.

"The paymaster, the grand lama of these rolling banks, was frequently pompous and awesome. He presided over the cash with dignity and no employee who filed past his window dared to question his authority.

"But time and hazards of the road soon overtook these traveling exchequers. Long relegated to the junk pile or put to duty on some work train, they roll today only in the memories of old trainmen gathered at the sandhouse to recall the 'good old days'."

William Wendell once wrote the author:

"Locomotive No. 2, an old Dawson & Bailey 4-4-0, with Jim Burke as engineer and Mike Keefe as fireman, often pulled the South Park's pay car up and down the road."

Other miscellaneous rolling stock, such as is found on any railroad, included such equipment as oil and gas cars, private cars for the brass hats' use, construction and work cars. Even a narrow gauge pile driver was in use on the South Park at various periods during its lifetime. William Cairns writes:

"Around the turn of the century Patrick Gibbony was wrecking boss. It was surprising how Pat and his crew, with the aid of a 'dead man', jacks, and block and tackle, could re-rail engines and cars. Most of the early cars only had four wheels and when one was derailed, the crew just got out and jacked her back on the rail and that was all there was to it".

Regarding the rotary snow plows, Roy Morton writes:

"As I heard the story from some of the old timers, the rotary plow purchased by the Union Pacific sometime prior to the famous snow plow trials held in the spring of 1890, was small but served its purpose very well. Shortly after the purchase of a new plow around the turn of the century, the older plow was scrapped. This new plow was built to standard gauge specifications but was mounted on narrow gauge trucks".

Charlie Squires writes further regarding the big plows:

"The statement has been made that the South Park never had a rotary snow plow that would not go through Alpine Tunnel. Well I want to tell you of an incident that I saw at Atlantic, the east portal. One time during the first week of March, 1897, three engines pushed the D. L. & G. rotary up the east slope to Atlantic. Before proceeding further, all of us in the crew together with Sam Churchill and Superintendent Rainey stood around the big plow while a photograph was taken. Immediately after that picture was taken they moved the rotary up to the tunnel very slowly. Supt. Rainey had ordered the machine to be taken over on the west slope to clear out some slides, providing they could get the plow through the tunnel. They measured both the plow and the tunnel and decided to try it. Well, there is a very sharp left curve at the mouth of the tunnel and as the rotary would not bend she began to take pieces of timber off the right side from one to three inches thick, so they had to give it up. That was one rotary snow plow the South Park had that would not go through Alpine Tunnel. As I recall, this plow was a standard gauge machine mounted on narrow gauge trucks".

Author's note: At the time the Leadville-Climax section was changed to standard gauge, the narrow gauge trucks under this plow were replaced with standard gauge trucks.

Andy Nelson adds to the snowplow discussion:

"Shortly after the 1890 snow plow trials were completed the Superintendent ordered the rotary taken over on the west slope to clear out some of the line between the tunnel and Gunnison. Four locomotives pushed the big vacuum cleaner through the hole. I had the honor of being at the throttle of the lead engine on this occasion, the first trip of a rotary through Alpine Tunnel. Upon entering the east portal we traveled very slowly, checking to make sure that there was sufficient clearance in the tunnel to allow the plow to pass through. This trip through the tunnel required a full 45 minutes".

H. L. Curtiss adds:

"I well remember the last time I went through the tunnel. We had a train made up of three engines, the rotary snow plow, the private car of Mr. W. M. Bacon, the Superintendent of the South Park Division, some coal cars and one combination coach. Mr. Bacon's car was on the hind end. He had a Jap cook on his car and we had supper at the Alpine Tunnel station about 2:00 a.m."

As the hind end of a freight drag always carries a caboose, we should not fail to mention the little four-wheel South Park caboose at the end of this discourse on freight equipment. H. L. Curtiss tells us that the caboose first made its appearance on the South Park about 1882. Although cupolas were standard equipment on all South Park cabooses in later years, the first one did not possess this added convenience for the trainmen. As far as is known, all cabooses on the South Park and Clear Creek lines were of the four-wheel variety. They reminded one of an overgrown packing box. Roy Morton states that these little four-wheel dinkies that weaved and bounced along at the hind end, were often dubbed "bouncing betties" by the train crews. At the time of abandonment of the Clear Creek line, one of these little crummies, number 1006, was set up as a permanent exhibit at Silver Plume. While passing through Silver Plume on a trip up Clear Creek in search of data in 1945, Ed Haley pointed out number 1006 to the author. There it sits on four crossties, forlorn and neglected, as if waiting for the inevitable end, which somehow seems close at hand.

Before concluding this discussion on rolling stock, we should include a letter written to the author in 1938 by Mr. T. B. Aldridge. Mr. Aldridge worked in and around the Colorado & Southern shops and yards in Denver for a number of years prior to the first World War. This letter, in part, follows:

"The old Denver, South Park & Pacific roundhouse in Denver was at what is now a junk yard at 5th and Lawrence Streets. On some of the present C. & S. narrow gauge box cars from which the paint has weathered off, may be seen the letters D. S. P. & P., and U. P. D. & G. Some of the old lettering and numbers can be seen through the C. & S. identification, clear enough to photograph. My first recollection of these cars is when they had 'continuous stem' draft gears, having just been changed from link and pin. The C. & S. narrow gauge cars used some link and pin couplers, along with split or open knuckle 'Jennies' as late as 1912. Up until just a few years ago they still had some of these cars stored in the old Argo Yard. Some of the link and pin castings are still to be found, or were a few years ago, in scrap piles around the Denver shops. These cars were first built prior to 1890, but of course rebuilt probably several times since. Some were modernized with safety appliances and all of them now have automatic couplers. I equipped some of the cars with what is known as 'Small Miner' tandem draft gears, removing the stem-connected link and pin drawbars.

"Some of the old C. & S. standard gauge switch engines that worked in the Denver yards had three-way couplers on them so that the engine coupled onto either narrow or standard gauge cars. This combination coupler slot was in the shape of an inverted 'T'. When coupled to a broad gauge car, the coupler was placed in the top position; when coupled to a narrow gauge car, the coupler would be placed in either one of the lower positions, depending on which side the third rail was located in the track. Some of the old standard gauge cars in the Denver yards were also equipped with this three-way coupler. Last January, in the narrow gauge portion of the Prospect (38th Avenue) yard in Denver, I saw one of these old three-way cars passing through on a Rio Grande train.

"After the Civil War, my maternal grandfather came west and worked on the Union Pacific before the transcontinental line was completed. Eventually he located in Denver and lived there the rest of his life until 1924. He was the first general yard master of the D. S. P. & P. in Denver. This was in the days when it was often required that the men be on duty for as much as 24 hours at a stretch. He recalled many instances, especially wrecks, of the 'chippie gauge' trains along the banks of the South Platte in the Denver yards.

"My first train ride was on the old South Park narrow gauge line from Denver to Morrison. In later years I worked for the Colorado & Southern as car repairman and inspector for about nine years. Within that length of time I traveled over most of the narrow gauge lines, or all that were being operated. One winter I lived for a month at Singleton's Lake in Platte Canon, where I took care of the ice cars. Two engines would bring up about 30 empty cars. They returned to Denver with about 12 to 15 cars each."

Relative to the disposition of all remaining Colorado & Southern narrow gauge rolling stock on hand at the time of abandonment, Mr. George E. Lundberg, Master Mechanic at the Denver Shops, writes:

"With the abandonment of all narrow gauge lines operated by the Colorado & Southern, there was no further use for the narrow gauge freight and passenger rolling stock. Quite a number of cars had already been retired in former years as they wore out, and the remaining freight cars, except for a few on exhibit, were either sold or scrapped by 1943. 125 freight cars were sold to the Rio Grande Southern Railroad in 1938 and 1939. About 125 cars were sold to the Chicago Freight Car Parts Company, of which the company's records indicate that 31 cars went to the Navy and some to Alaska. Practically all of the narrow gauge passenger equipment had been sold or scrapped by September, 1943, except those on exhibit or being held for exhibit."

The only known narrow gauge South Park rolling stock, excluding locomotives, that was saved, consists of one combination baggage and passenger coach, number 20, and one gondola or ore car, number 4319, set up as a permanent exhibit at Central City; one passenger coach, number 70, set up as another permanent exhibit at Idaho Springs; caboose number 1006 on exhibit at Silver Plume; two cars, including baggage and mail car number 13 and passenger coach number 76 that went with engine number 9 to the New York Fair in 1939; and a business car, number 911; engine 9 and these cars were used at the 1948-49 Railroad Fair at Chicago.

COLORADO & SOUTHERN RAILWAY

ROSTER OF NARROW GAUGE PASSENGER EQUIPMENT

This information compiled and revised by J. W. Maxwell, using records from Master Mechanic's Office, Colorado & Southern Shops.

NEW NUMBER 1911	OLD NUMBER	TYPE CAR	LENGTH OVER END SILLS	SEATING CAPACITY	WEIGHT IN TONS[1]	BUILDER	DATE	REMARKS AND DISPOSITION
1	102	Baggage	34' 0"	—	13	Union Pacific	1874	Rebuilt by C. & S. in 1915[2]. Dismantled May, 1939.
2	104	Baggage	34' 0"	—	16	Union Pacific	1874	Rebuilt by C. & S. in 1915. Retired January, 1939. Body on farm near Longmont, 1959.
3	101	Baggage	35' 0"	—	13	Union Pacific	1873	Rebuilt by C. & S. in 1915. Retired January, 1939.
4	105	Baggage	40' 0"	—	16	Union Pacific	1874	Rebuilt by C. & S. in 1915. Retired January, 1939.
10	110	Baggage-Mail	40' 0"	—	16	Union Pacific	1880	Rebuilt by C. & S. in 1915. Dismantled Jan., 1929.
11	111	Baggage-Mail	40' 0"	—	16	Union Pacific	1880	Rebuilt by C. & S. in 1915. Dismantled May, 1939.
12	112	Baggage-Mail	40' 0"	—	16	Union Pacific	1880	Rebuilt by C. & S. in 1915. Dismantled May, 1939.
13	114	Baggage-Mail	42' 0"	—	13	Pullman	1880	Rebuilt by C. & S. in 1905 and 1915. Stored in Aurora, Illinois, shops of C. B. & Q. Exhibited at New York Fair in 1939 and Chicago Railroad Fair in 1948 and 1949.
20	121	Baggage-Coach	32' 0"	14	16			Rebuilt by C. & S. in 1915. Became No. 025 in February, 1925. Renumbered No. 20 and set up on permanent exhibit at Central City, Colo.
21	120	Baggage-Coach	32' 6"	19	13	Union Pacific	1876	Rebuilt by C. & S. in 1915. Became D. & I. M. 903.
22	122	Baggage-Coach	34' 9"	22	13	South Park	1880	Rebuilt by C. & S. in 1915. Sold to A. T. Herr Supply Co., June, 1926.
23	123	Baggage-Coach	34' 0"	24	17	South Park	1880	Rebuilt by C. & S. in 1915. Sold to Herr Rubican Supply Co., February, 1923.
24	126	Baggage-Coach	35' 0"	28	20	Bowers & Dure	1875	Retired—date not known.
25	125	Baggage-Coach	40' 0"	20	16			Rebuilt by C. & S. in 1905 and 1915. Sold to Herr Rubican Supply Co., February, 1924.
26	127	Baggage-Coach	40' 0"	26	17	Ohio Falls		Rebuilt by U. P. in 1893, by C. & S. in 1915. Rebuilt into tool car. Stationed at Leadville until 1943.
27	124	Baggage-Coach	40' 4"	28	17	Union Pacific	1880	Rebuilt by C. & S. in 1915. Sold to Herr Rubican Supply Co., February, 1923.
28	129	Baggage-Coach	40' 4"	28	17	Union Pacific	1882	Rebuilt by C. & S. in 1915. Converted to outfit car No. 99362, October, 1922.
29	128	Baggage-Coach	41' 10"	28	17	Barney-Smith Brill	1875	Rebuilt by C. & S. in 1915. Destroyed after 1940.
30	130	Baggage-Coach	42' 7"	28	13		1873	Rebuilt by C. & S. in 1915. Rebuilt into tool car. Stationed at Leadville until 1943. Car body at Leadville, 1959.
40	115	Mail-Coach	42' 5"	28	20	Pullman	1906	Dismantled after 1940.
41	116	Mail-Coach	42' 5"	28	20	Pullman		Rebuilt by Pullman, 1906. Dismantled Mar. 1929.
42	117	Mail-Coach	42' 5"	28	20	Pullman		Rebuilt by Pullman, 1906. Dismantled May, 1939. Car body at end of Silica branch.
43	118	Mail-Coach	42' 5"	28	20	Pullman		Rebuilt by Pullman, 1906. Dismantled April, 1939.
50	155	Coach	35' 0"	44	17	Bowers & Dure	1874	Rebuilt by C. & S. in 1915. Dismantled about 1939.
51	156	Coach	35' 0"	44	17	Bowers & Dure	1874	Rebuilt by C. & S. in 1915. Dismantled about 1939.
52	157	Coach	35' 0"	36	17	Bowers & Dure	1874	Rebuilt by C. & S. in 1915. Dismantled about 1939.

NEW NUMBER 1911	OLD NUMBER	TYPE CAR	LENGTH OVER END SILLS	SEATING CAPACITY	WEIGHT IN TONS[1]	BUILDER	DATE	REMARKS AND DISPOSITION
53	141	Coach	40'0"	44	17	Union Pacific	1880	Rebuilt by C. & S. in 1915[2]. Dismantled about 1939.
54	142	Coach	40'0"	44	17	Union Pacific	1880	Rebuilt by C. & S. in 1915. Dismantled about 1939.
55	143	Coach	39'10"	42	18	Union Pacific	1880	Rebuilt by C. & S. in 1915 and 1917. Dismantled about 1939.
56	160	Coach	40'5"	43	17	Barney-Smith	1885	Rebuilt by C. & S. in 1915. Dismantled May, 1939.
57	159	Coach	40'6"	48	15	Brill	1875	Rebuilt by C. & S. in 1915. Sold to Herr Rubican Supply Co., February, 1923.
58	151	Coach	41'11"	48	20	Union Pacific	1883	Rebuilt by C. & S. in 1915. Dismantled May, 1939.
59	161	Coach	42'0"	50	20	Pullman	1886	Rebuilt by C. & S. in 1915. Dismantled Oct, 1929.
60	152	Coach	42'0"	48	17	Pullman	1873	Rebuilt by C. & S. in 1915. Dismantled Oct, 1929.
61	149	Coach	42'8"	50	18	Ohio Falls	1879	Rebuilt by C. & S. in 1915. Dismantled Jan, 1939.
62	153	Coach	42'5"	46	15	Pullman	1873	Rebuilt by C. & S. in 1915. Dismantled May, 1939.
70	168	Coach	40'0"	44	17	St. Charles	1896	Rebuilt by C. & S. in 1915. On permanent exhibition at Idaho Springs, Colo.
71	169	Coach	40'0"	44	17	St. Charles	1896	Rebuilt by C. & S. in 1915. Dismantled Apr., 1939.
72	170	Coach	40'0"	44	17	St. Charles	1896	Rebuilt by C. & S. in 1915. Dismantled Apr., 1939.
73	171	Coach	40'0"	44	17	St. Charles	1896	Rebuilt by C. & S. in 1915. Dismantled May, 1939.
74	172	Coach	40'0"	44	18	Amer. Car & Fndry.	1902	Rebuilt by C. & S. in 1915. Dismantled Apr., 1939.
75	173	Coach	40'0"	44	68	Amer. Car & Fndry.	1902	Rebuilt by C. & S. in 1915. Dismantled May, 1939.
76	174	Coach	40'0"	44	18	Amer. Car & Fndry.	1902	Stored in Aurora, Illinois, shops of C. B. & Q. Exhibited at New York Fair in 1939 and Chicago Railroad Fair in 1948 and 1949.
77	158	Coach	40'0"	44	20	Barney-Smith	1873	Rebuilt by C. & S. in 1915. Body sold. Balance dismantled April, 1939.
78	162	Coach	42'0"	46	20	Pullman	1886	Rebuilt by C. & S. in 1915. Dismantled Mar., 1929.
79	163	Coach	42'0"	46	20	Pullman	1886	Rebuilt by C. & S. in 1915. Dismantled Mar., 1929.
80	164	Coach	42'0"	46	22	Pullman	1886	Rebuilt by C. & S. in 1915. Dismantled Oct., 1929.
81	165	Coach	42'0"	46	22	Pullman	1886	Rebuilt by C. & S. in 1923. Sold to Herr Rubican Supply Co., February, 1923.
82	166	Coach	42'0"	46	22	Pullman	1886	Rebuilt by C. & S. in 1923. Dismantled Oct., 1929.
83	167	Coach	42'0"	46	22	Pullman	1886	Rebuilt by C. & S. in 1923. Dismantled Oct., 1929.
120-131	181-192	Observation	40'0"	58	13	Colorado & Southern	1900	Rebuilt by C. & S. in 1915. Sold to Herr Rubican Supply Co., February, 1923.
132-136	193-197	Observation	37'3"	54	11	Union Pacific	1883	Rebuilt by C. & S. in 1915. Sold to Herr Rubican Supply Co., February, 1923.
137	198	Observation	37'3"	54	11	Union Pacific	1883	Destroyed August, 1912.
138	199	Observation	40'0"	58	13	Colorado & Southern	1903	Rebuilt by C. & S. in 1915. Sold to Herr Rubican Supply Co., February, 1923.
139-148	200-209	Observation	40'0"	58	13	Colorado & Southern	1903	Rebuilt by C. & S. in 1915. Dismantled Jan., 1929.
910	B-1	Business	42'6"	10	27	Pullman	1875	Rebuilt by C. & S. in 1915. Dismantled Mar., 1929.
911	B-2	Business	36'2"	6	27	Union Pacific	1872	Stored in Aurora, Illinois, shops of C. B. & Q. Exhibited at Chicago Railroad Fair in 1948-49.
912	B-3	Business	26'0"	4	15	Union Pacific	1872	Rebuilt 1915. Rebuilt and converted to No. 089 in April, 1926. Disposition not known.

1. Weights are as listed in 1912 Employees Timetable.
2. During the 1904 to 1915 rebuilding program, platforms were removed from both ends of baggage and baggage-mail cars. Front platforms were removed from baggage coaches and mail coaches.

COLORADO & SOUTHERN RAILWAY

ROSTER OF NARROW GAUGE FREIGHT AND NON-REVENUE EQUIPMENT

This information compiled and revised by J. W. Maxwell, using records from Master Mechanic's Office, Colorado & Southern Shops.

NEW NUMBER 1911	OLD NUMBER	TYPE CAR	LENGTH	UNDER-FRAME	TRUCKS	CAPACITY TONS	BUILDER	DATE	REMARKS
1000-1011	300-314	Caboose	12' 4"	Wood				1883	
1005-1008		Caboose	13' 0"					1882	
1003	304	Caboose	14' 10"					1882	No. 1006 on exhibition at Silver Plume.
1006	308	Caboose	12' 11"					1884	Out by 1923.
1050	1104	Flat	26' 0"	Wood	Arch Bar	20	Union Pacific	1880	Out by 1912.
	1000-1054	Flat	30' 0"	Wood	Arch Bar	12	Union Pacific	1884	Out by 1923.
	1055-1075	Flat	30' 0"	Wood	Arch Bar	20	Union Pacific	1902	Out by 1923.
	1078-1098	Flat	30' 0"	Steel	Bettendorf	25	C. & S.	1909	1098 in Leadville August, 1943.
1100-1119	500-519	Refrigerator	30' 0"	Wood	Arch Bar	25	St. Charles	1898	1113, 1116 and 1108 became RGS 2101, 2102 and 2103 in 1938.
1120-1125	550-555	Refrigerator	30' 3"	Wood	Arch Bar	12		1880	
1126-1127	575, 580	Refrigerator	26' 5"	Wood	Arch Bar	14		1883	Out by 1923.
1128-1130	590, 596, 598	Refrigerator	27' 0"	Wood	Arch Bar	25	St. Charles	1898	Out by 1923.
	4003-4245	Coal	30' 0"	Wood	Arch Bar	25	C. & S.	1902	No. 4319 on permanent exhibition at Central City.
	4246-4407	Coal	30' 0"	Wood	Bettendorf	25	C. & S.	1907	Retired.
	4408-4497	Coal	30' 0"	Wood	Bettendorf	25	C. & S.	1910	Retired.
	4498-4547	Coal	30' 0"	Steel	Arch Bar	20		1884	Out by 1923.
	4809-4997	Coal	28' 0"	Wood	Arch Bar	25	Am. Car & Fdry.	1900	6 cars to RGS 1938, 7200's.
	7015-7064	Stock	30' 3"	Wood	Bettendorf	25	C. & S.	1907	7016 to RGS 1938, 7304.
	7016, 7046, 7058	Stock	30' 0"	Wood	Bettendorf	25	C. & S.	1907	38 cars to RGS 1938, 7300's and 7400's.
	7065-7083	Stock	30' 0"	Steel	Bettendorf	25	C. & S.	1910	
	7085-7134	Stock	30' 0"	Wood	Arch Bar	12		1880	Out by 1912.
	7200-7226	Box	24' 4"	Wood	Arch Bar	12	Union Pacific	1884	Out by 1912. Body of 7298 now at St. Elmo.
	7273-7348	Box	26' 4"	Wood	Arch Bar	14		1900	Out by 1923.
	7353-7615	Box	27' 3"	Wood	Arch Bar	20	C. & S.	1898	7727, 7728 and 7743 became RGS 8505, 8511, 8509.
	7642	Box	27' 0"	Wood	Arch Bar	25	C. & S.	1900	8030, 33, 35 and 47 became RGS 8506, 13, 16, 03.
	7722-7746	Box	27' 0"	Wood	Arch Bar	25	St. Charles	1898	9 cars to RGS 1938, 8500's.
	8025-8064	Box	30' 3"	Wood	Arch Bar	25	C. & S.	1907	
	8065-8102	Box	30' 0"	Wood	Arch Bar	25	C. & S.	1906	
	8066	Box	30' 0"	Wood	Arch Bar	25	C. & S.	1907	
	8103-8142	Box	30' 0"	Wood	Bettendorf	25	C. & S.	1908	15 cars to RGS 1938, 8601-15.
	8143-8192	Box	30' 0"	Wood	Bettendorf	25	C. & S.	1909	
	8193-8292	Box	30' 0"	Steel	Bettendorf	25	C. & S.	1910	29 cars to RGS 1938, 8701-29.
	8293-8417	Box	30' 0"	Steel	Bettendorf	25	C. & S.		
013-016		Flanger	18' 2"	Wood	Arch Bar				Dismantled July, 1943.
068		Outfit	27' 0"	Wood	U. P.				Retired April, 1934.
071	4826	Outfit	27' 0"	Wood	U. P.				Converted from 4826. Dismantled June, 1932.
084	1070	Track Car	30' 0"	Wood	U. P.				Converted from 1070. Dismantled February, 1931.
088	B-3	Tool Car	30' 0"	Wood	Arch Bar		Union Pacific	1872	Rebuilt from Business Car 912, April, 1926.
089		Wrecker	26' 0"	Wood	Arch Bar				Dismantled November, 1934.
099			30' 0"	Wood	Arch Bar				
0100-0107	4000-4085	Cinder Car	30' 0"	Wood	Arch Bar	25	St. Charles	1898	Rebuilt by C. & S.
0108	4796	Cinder Car	30' 0"	Wood	Arch Bar				
0200-0208	2000-2008	Side Dump	30' 0"	Wood	Bettendorf	25	C. & S.	1908	Renumbered April, 1920. Retired.
0209	2009	Side Dump	30' 0"	Wood	Bettendorf	25	C. & S.	1908	Destroyed April, 1920.

Due to the almost total absence of information on passenger and freight car equipment on either the South Park or Colorado Central roads, it has been practically impossible to compile any sort of a roster of early-day rolling stock, prior to the turn of the century. Efforts to collect such information from early photographs or other vague sources, only led to a maze of conflicting numbers or series of numbers that were impossible to reconcile. The only usable information found, concerning this early rolling stock, consists of miscellaneous inventory figures on South Park equipment as shown in the following table:

SOUTH PARK ROLLING STOCK FOR VARIOUS YEARS.[1]

EQUIPMENT	1880	1885	1889	1894	1900	1911
Passenger	26	28	28	20	46	56
Combination Mail, Baggage & Express	5	6	6	6	19	23
Pullman-Parlor	1	5	5	—	—	—
Box	250	550	550	517	*	431
Stock	—	6	9	8	*	79
Coal-Ore	30	329	329	390	*	644
Flat	260	322	322	131	*	42
Refrigerator	2	27	27	27	*	31
Caboose	—	21	21	11	15	12
Pay	—	1	1	1	—	—
Official	—	1	1	1	3	3
Flanger	—	—	—	—	4	4
Snow Plow	?	?	?	1	2	1
Pile Driver	—	—	—	—	1	—
Work—Construction and Wreck	16	3	3	8	10	23

*In 1900, a total of 1280 box, stock, coal-ore, flat, and refrigerator cars was listed, but no breakdown was given.

Relative to similar information for a later period, the author is greatly indebted to Mr. John W. Maxwell for compiling a fairly complete roster of both passenger and freight car rolling stock. This data is based upon a complete renumbering change which occurred in 1911. The compilation of these two rosters was made possible through valuable assistance given by Mr. George E. Lundberg, Master Mechanic of the Colorado & Southern's shops in Denver.

* * * *

SCHEDULES—TRAFFIC—OPERATION

One of the most interesting phases of the great old South Park's history revolves around the various schedules governing the movements of the little trains, the traffic they carried, and the operation of the road. It

1. Above data compiled from:
   Poor's Manual of Railroads.
   The Rocky Mountain News of July 4, 1880.
   Various annual reports of the road.
   Official Railway Equipment Registers.

is the author's honest opinion that someone more gifted at the art of writing, should compile this particular section; it is the nucleus of a glorious and colorful chapter on Colorado mountain railroading.

One of the first public announcements concerning the departure of a scheduled South Park passenger train is found in the Rocky Mountain News of June 26, 1874. This news item, relative to an excursion celebrating the opening of the Morrison branch, stated:

"The first grand excursion over the South Park Railroad leaves this morning at 8 o'clock from Larimer and Sixth Streets. Lose no time in getting aboard."

The earliest public schedule covering regular train movements, to be found by the writer, appears in an 1875 Official Railway Guide. This small announcement stated:

DENVER SOUTH PARK & PACIFIC RAILROAD

John Evans, President. B. M. Gilman, Superintendent
General Offices Denver

Trains leave Denver 8:00 a.m. and 3:00 p.m. arriving at Morrison (16 miles) 9:15 a.m. and 4:30 p.m.

Returning—Leave Morrison 9:45 a.m. and 5:00 p.m., arriving at Denver at 11:15 a.m. and 6:15 p.m.

Connections with all diverging roads out of Denver.

A similar notice published in the guide the following year under the date of June 23, 1876, carried little change in the schedule except for an added note that "Sunday trains leave Denver for Morrison, 10:30 a.m. Returning leave Morrison 4:30 p.m."

The first information regarding schedules beyond Morrison to come to light is found in the Gunnison Review of May 22, 1880, shortly after the line was completed through to Buena Vista.

"A new time card took effect on the Denver South Park & Pacific last Sunday, May 14th. The Day Express leaves Denver 7:30 a.m., arrives Buena Vista 5:25 p.m. Leaves Buena Vista 9:20 a.m., arrives Denver 6:05 p.m. Night Express leaves Denver 7:00 p.m., arrives Buena Vista 6:50 a.m. Leaves Buena Vista 7:15 p.m., arrives Denver 7:00 a.m."

A little study here discloses the interesting fact that the westbound "Day Express" averaged 13.6 miles per hour in making the 136-mile run from Denver to Buena Vista, while the eastbound "Express" averaged 13.2 miles per hour. The schedule was somewhat slower for the two night trains, the average being slightly over 11 miles per hour. After the track was built up Chalk Creek and regular service was extended to Alpine, the Gunnison Review of May 14, 1881, stated:

"After Sunday, May 8, 1881, a scheduled passenger train on the D. S. P. & P. leaves Denver at 7:45 a.m., arriving at Alpine at 9:00 a.m., laying over at Buena Vista from 5:15 p.m. to 6:55 a.m. en route."

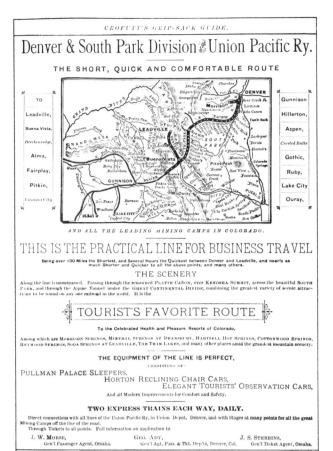

An advertisement from the 1881 edition of Crofutt's Grip-sack Guide.

Among the guides to western tourist travel published during this period was Crofutt's Grip-Sack Guide. An 1881 issue of this guide carried a very interesting advertisement. Note the many projected extensions which the railroad proposed to build.

It appears that one of the best ways to tell a part of the story of the many and varied passenger schedules that existed on the South Park system throughout its lifetime is to treat the various sections separately. The following notes relating to passenger schedules have been compiled from old newspaper advertisements, Rand-McNally Guides, Rocky Mountain Railway Guides, the Official Guide, and public and employees' timetables published by the railroad. The various guides and timetables consulted cover the operation of the railroad from the time the first train pulled out of the Denver depot on June 26, 1874, bound for Morrison, to April 10, 1937, when the last scheduled passenger train pulled into Denver after completing its final run over the mountains from Leadville.

THE DENVER-GUNNISON LINE
Service inaugurated in September, 1882

The earliest employees' timetable available to the writer is dated November 11, 1883. At this time the Leadville trains were running by way of Buena Vista. No. 263, the *Leadville Express,* carrying both Leadville and Gunnison sleepers, left Denver at 8:00 p.m., arriving in Buena Vista at 5 o'clock the next morning. The Gunnison section, known as No. 287, left Buena Vista 45 minutes later, made a 20-minute stop at 7:20 a.m. for breakfast at Alpine (Fisher), and arrived in Gunnison at 11:50 a.m. On the return trip, the Denver train, No. 288, left Gunnison at 3:05 p.m., made a 20-minute stop at 7:25 p.m. for supper at Alpine, made connections with No. 264, the Leadville-Denver section, at Buena Vista at 9:10 p.m., and arrived in Denver at 7:00 a.m. the next morning. As previously related, this sleeper service between Denver and Gunnison was inaugurated in October, 1882 and lasted until July, 1887. With few exceptions, there was never enough traffic to justify the running of more than one daily passenger train between the two points. Examination of a number of timetables throughout the above period discloses that at times this train operated on a day schedule, while other tables show it as a night train. From this we conclude that Pullman service was not a regular feature on the Gunnison division, and that the Pullman car probably served as a parlor car, when and if used, on the day train.

Mr. J. M. Cuenin, Chaffee County Surveyor, writes that some of the early Gunnison passenger trains consisted of only two cars—one baggage and one passenger coach. However, Mr. H. L. Curtiss writes that the four-car passenger train, when used, consisted of one baggage car, one mail car, one smoker, and one Pullman car. A study of the various timetables, together with what these and other old timers report, seems to indicate that the makeup of the train varied according to the seasonal demand for passenger accommodations on the Gunnison division. Mr. Cuenin adds an interesting note to this passenger service:

"From Parlin to Gunnison, the South Park and the Rio Grande ran nearly parallel for a distance of about 12 miles, and there were many races between the two railroad crews. It used to be a popular practice among the Gunnison citizens to leave town in the morning and arrive in Denver in time for a nice supper and then a good show at the old Tabor Grand Theatre".

In addition to the regularly scheduled daily passenger train, some of the early timetables show a mixed train operating between Como and Gunnison, or between Pitkin and Gunnison. Just how long the daily passenger service between Denver and Gunnison was maintained is not known. An employees' timetable, No. 10, dated November 7, 1897, shows only a mixed passenger and freight operating daily except Sunday. Official Guides dated 1901 to 1905 show a daily train but do not state whether it is a passenger or mixed train. A May, 1907, Colorado & Southern public timetable lists a mixed train operating daily except Sunday.

Roy Morton tells us that during 1903 and 1904, the years of the St. Louis World's Fair, the South Park put on a daily passenger train each way between Como and Gunnison to compete with the Rio Grande. The eastbound train left Gunnison about 7:30 a.m. while the westbound train arrived in Gunnison about 5:00 p.m., being scheduled to connect at Como with the Denver-Leadville passenger run. Engines 8 and 9 were usually used on this Como-Gunnison schedule. Andy Nelson and John Olson were the engineers while George Burris and Pete Newberry were the conductors on the run. Morton adds: "I have a photograph taken during that period showing Andy Nelson coming into Pitkin with engine 9 and three coaches."

When the Baldwin branch was first completed, traffic must have been fairly heavy. The November, 1883, employees' timetable shows two daily mixed trains, including Sunday, operating between Gunnison and the Baldwin Mines. Number 293 left Gunnison at 7:00 a.m., arriving in Baldwin at 8:10 a.m. The southbound run then left Baldwin as number 294 at 10:45 a.m. and arrived in Gunnison at 11:55 a.m. Number 295 left Gunnison at 1:00 p.m., and arrived in Baldwin at 2:10 p.m. The southbound train then left Baldwin as number 296 at 5:30 p.m., and arrived in Gunnison at 6:40 p.m. During the following year, service on this branch line was reduced to one round trip per day by the usual mixed train. In the latter part of the '90's, the schedule was reduced to a tri weekly service and seems to have remained as such until 1907 or 1908, when passenger accommodations were eliminated altogether. A 1910 Official Guide lists this branch but does not schedule any train service. The Baldwin Mines branch was taken over by the Rio Grande in February, 1911.

The Colorado & Southern continued mixed service on the Gunnison division until 1910, when a second bad flood washed out the roadbed in Trout Creek Canon, and a cave in occurred inside Alpine Tunnel. The last through schedule published in the Official Guide of July, 1910, just prior to these two disasters, showed a mixed train operating each way daily except Monday, between Como and Gunnison. These two serious ruptures in the main line ended for all time the through service between Denver and Gunnison. In commenting on the cave in that occurred in the tunnel in October, the Gunnison News-Champion of October 14, 1910, stated:

"We have positive information that the Colorado & Southern has decided to close the road to Denver for the winter, perhaps permanently. A mixed train will run each day between Gunnison and Pitkin, also between Buena Vista and St. Elmo."

This news item states that a mixed train was to operate daily between Pitkin and Gunnison. However, if it did, the service was short-lived, for the engineering

department in Denver reports that all train service beyond Alpine Tunnel ceased in October, 1910. Lewis Lathrop wrote in Railroad Magazine (June, 1941) as follows:

"In the autumn of 1910 the last South Park train pulled out of Gunnison and headed east. It seemed the whistles of the chuffing little locomotives were mournful and the steam which squirrel-tailed from the safety valves seemed almost to sob. One of the most colorful of all Colorado's narrow gauges was abandoning its line that day, and this was a clean-up train."

Clarence "Silver Tip" Adams wrote in the Gunnison News-Champion of May 12, 1938:

"The excursion from Gunnison to Denver on July 4, 1910, was probably the last considerable movement of people over the entire division."[1]

F. C. Buell, South Park veteran now living in Cheyenne, Wyoming, writes that the last train to go through Alpine Tunnel was a freight with one combination passenger coach on the rear. The exact date is not known.

Because of the Trout Creek flood, all service between Garos and Buena Vista was eliminated. However, a mixed train operated between Buena Vista and Hancock. The company maintained a triweekly mixed service between these two points until about August, 1915. Service to Hancock was then discontinued and Romley became the end-of-track. Thereafter, a mixed train made a round trip from Buena Vista to Romley three times a week until September 11, 1924,[2] when this service was discontinued, thus ending all train service on the South Park beyond Garos. As a passing note, we might add that the number of passengers between Buena Vista and Hancock had decreased from 3,711 in 1916 to a mere 725 in 1922.[3]

ALMA BRANCH
Service inaugurated about December, 1881.

When this branch line was first opened to business in the latter part of 1881, there was considerable traffic between the main line connection at Garos, through Fairplay and up to London Junction. The November, 1883, employees' timetable lists two trains per day, each way, between Garos and London Junction, or Alma Junction as it was sometimes called; one passenger and one mixed train. However, this service was soon reduced and for many years afterward one mixed train per day made the trip each way between Garos and Alma. After the line south of Garos was abandoned in 1910, Como was made the end of the run and the usual daily round trip was made between that point and Alma. The Como-Alma service was reduced to two runs per week about 1928, and this schedule was more

1. The Gunnison News-Champion of March 6, 1947, also indicates that this was the last passenger run between Gunnison and Denver.
2. 94-ICC-657.
3. 86-ICC-395.

or less maintained until the entire South Park system was abandoned in 1937.

The author is sorry to report that no information has ever come to light regarding either passenger or mixed service on the London Mine Branch up Mosquito Gulch. What passengers were hauled on this line probably rode in the caboose with the train crew. The writer, accompanied by Ed Haley, followed the old grade clear to the end-of-track at the abandoned London Mill and can say it must have been one grand train ride, with rough and curving track, a steep switchback, deep canons, and towering mountains all around.

LEAVICK BRANCH
Opened early in 1897.

Inasmuch as this branch was built for the express purpose of transporting ore and mining supplies to and from the Horseshoe mining district, no regular passenger trains were ever scheduled to operate on this line, as far as is known. At the time of the opening of this branch in 1897, and for a few years afterward, some Official Guides show a daily mixed train service between Hill Top Junction and the end-of-track. About 1905, service became rather irregular, ranging from one train per day, each way, down to one per week. Many issues of the Official Guide failed to show the line at all, while two employees' timetables show the line but do not list any scheduled service. According to the Interstate Commerce Commission reports, all traffic on the Leavick Branch ceased in 1923.

At the extreme end of the Leavick branch, for less than a mile (from the wye at Mudsill to the mine at Leavick) the grade was over 7%. Ed Haight, who ran an engine on this branch for a number of years, recalls that passengers for Leavick had to ride on the coal in the gondola which was usually hauled up to the mine, as the engine would not pull both the loaded gondola and the combination car up this grade.

KING MINES BRANCH
Opened in 1879.

In view of the great amount of mining activity that was carried on at the King Mines, it is to be supposed that some sort of passenger service was furnished to the patrons using this branch. However, only one of the many timetables consulted by the writer, an employees' timetable dated August 1, 1889, listed a schedule on this short line. This table listed two mixed passenger and freight trains operating daily except Sunday between King Mines and Coal Branch Junction. No. 461 left King at 9:35 a.m. and arrived at the junction at 10:05 a.m. No. 463 left King at 3:35 p.m. and arrived at the junction at 4:05 p.m. Eastbound, No. 462, left the junction at 8:00 a.m. and arrived at King at 8:30 a.m. No. 464 left the junction at 2:00 p.m. and arrived at King at 2:30 p.m.

THE MORRISON BRANCH
Opened in 1874.

Exclusive of newspaper items announcing the initial run, the first regular schedule covering passenger service on this line is found in an 1875 Official Guide, the contents of which were noted near the opening of this chapter. For many years thereafter, passenger service to Morrison varied with the seasons. At times the service required only a mixed train, while at other times regular passenger service was scheduled. For many years Morrison and vicinity was a great place for Sunday picnic parties. During the summer season as many as four passenger trains were sometimes operated out of Denver into Morrison for the benefit of the Sunday excursionists.

Traffic to this point began to diminish about 1912, and service was gradually reduced. The Interstate Commerce Commission reports that 1918 saw the end of the Morrison passenger business. However, Official Guides as late as 1920 list two or three daily trains. There may have been some reason for the I. C. C. statement. Triweekly mixed service was maintained as late as 1924, after which date all passenger service to Morrison was discontinued.

DENVER TO LEADVILLE
Service inaugurated August 2, 1880.

Immediately upon completion of the Rio Grande's track into Leadville in August, 1880, the South Park, on the basis of terms incorporated in the Joint Operating Agreement, established through passenger service between Denver and the famous carbonate camp, via Buena Vista. The earliest schedule covering the operation of passenger trains between the two points, so far as the writer knows, is shown in the 1883 employees' timetable. This Denver South Park & Pacific employees' timecard, No. 4, dated November 11, 1883, was presented to the writer by Mr. Robert Hicks of Denver. The timecard shows two passenger trains per day, each way, between Denver and Leadville. No. 263, the *Leadville Express*, pulled out of Denver at 8:00 p.m. carrying both the Gunnison and Leadville sleepers. This train arrived in Buena Vista at 5:00 a.m., dropped the Gunnison sleeper and proceeded to Leadville, arriving there at 7:00 a.m. The 171-mile run was made in eleven hours even. The return train, No. 264, left Leadville at 7:30 p.m., arrived at Buena Vista at 9:32, picked up the returning sleeper from Gunnison, and arrived at the Union Station in Denver at 7:00 a.m. the following morning. The second passenger train, known as the *Day Express*, was No. 261. This train left Denver at 8:35 a.m., arriving in Leadville at 6:55 p.m., or ten hours and twenty minutes later. The return *Day Express*, No. 262, left Leadville at 7:30 a.m. and arrived in Denver at 6:00 p.m. that evening. The night run averaged slightly over 15

Westbound passenger train No. 70, hauled by engine 5, about to enter the snowshed at the summit of Boreas Pass, elevation 11,493 feet, on August 8, 1929.

The 73 rounds a sharp horseshoe curve in Hall's Valley above Webster, as it begins the climb up Kenosha Pass on July 14, 1938.

miles per hour while the day run averaged about 17 miles per hour.

Construction of the high line began in 1882, and passenger service on the new line was established as the end-of-track advanced to such points as Boreas, Breckenridge, Dillon, and Keystone. The 1883 timecard shows No. 279, a mixed train, leaving Como at 2:30 p.m. and arriving in Keystone at 6:40 p.m. The returning train left Keystone at 7:00 a.m., and arrived in Como at 11:30 a.m., making the 35-mile run in 4½ hours.

An attempt to dig out the complete story on the passenger service between Denver and Leadville has proved rather futile. As we have stated, when through service was first established into Leadville via Buena Vista, the company operated two daily passenger trains each way. By 1884 the night train carrying the Pullman car must have been dropped temporarily because the January 1885 Official Guide mentions only one daily train, operated on a daylight schedule. 1886-87 schedules again list two trains per day, one night run and one day run. However, an employees' timecard dated August 1, 1889, again schedules only one daylight run. Evidently the Leadville Pullman service was similar to that on the Gunnison division—the sleeping car being operated only due to seasonal demand, and it was not long-lived. Thomas St. John tells the writer that Pullman service between Denver and Leadville was discontinued altogether about 1896.

From 1896 to about 1910, the passenger facilities again included two daily trains. However, at certain times, especially after the turn of the century, schedules show one mixed and one passenger train. The January 1911 Official Guide, together with a January 1912 employees' timetable, states that mixed service only was available between Denver and Como and between Breckenridge and Leadville. However, this was due to an attempt by the Colorado & Southern to abandon all freight and passenger service between Como and Breckenridge. But, as related elsewhere, the courts forced the railroad to resume this service in January, 1913.

The regular daily service to Leadville, which at times was only a mixed train, was continued until March 31, 1931. On this date it was reduced to a triweekly affair and was continued as such until April 10, 1937, at which time all service was discontinued. During the period of triweekly service, the westbound train left Denver on Monday, Wednesday, and Friday, while the eastbound train left Leadville on Tuesday, Thursday, and Saturday.

THE KEYSTONE BRANCH

From construction days until the '90's, a mixed train (daily except Sunday) provided service from Breckenridge to Dillon and Keystone. Prior to 1900, the mixed train was discontinued, and the two regular passenger trains provided service to Dillon by means of a stub run, backing in one direction between Dickey and Dillon. In 1931, with the reduction of passenger service to a triweekly basis, service to Dillon was reduced to one train a day—in the afternoon on days when the westbound train ran, and in the morning when the eastbound train was operated.

Freight service was operated to Dillon or Keystone whenever necessary, either by running a train from Breckenridge or by using the engines and crews of through freights. Service on the Keystone branch was discontinued in 1937, when the Leadville-Denver line was abandoned.

THE CLEAR CREEK LINE

Authentic schedules showing passenger train service between Denver, Silver Plume, and Central City in the early days are rather scarce. The reader will recall that by 1873 the Colorado Central's tracks had been extended only as far as Floyd Hill and Black Hawk, hence the inclusion of the stage line information between these points and Georgetown and Central City, as shown in this schedule:

COLORADO CENTRAL RAILROAD[1]

H. M. Teller, President. Central City, Colorado

T. E. Sickles, Chief Engineer and Superintendent, Golden, Colorado.

D. F. Carmichael, General Passenger and Ticket Agent, Golden, Colorado.

Acn. p.m.	Exp. p.m.	Mail a.m.	Miles	Ticket Fare	Stations	Exp. a.m.	Acn. p.m.	Mail p.m.
6:30	4:05	8:35	0	00	Denver	*10:30	3:45	6:00
6:40	4:15	8:45	2		Denver Jct.	10:20	3:35	5:50
7:00	4:25	8:55	7		Vasquez	*10:08	3:20	5:38
7:08	4:35	9:05	9		Arvada	*10:03	3:15	5:33
7:32	4:50	9:20	15		Golden Jct.	* 9:50	2:55	5:20
7:40	5:00	9:30	17	$1.00	Golden	* 9:45	2:45	5:10
Mxd. a.m.	p.m.	a.m.				a.m.	p.m.	p.m.
9:55	5:20	9:45	0	$1.00	Golden	* 9:30	2:40	5:00
10:15	5:42	10:06	3		Chimney Gulch	9:07	2:17	4:37
10:36	6:02	10:26	6		Guy Gulch Beaver	* 8:47	1:57	4:17
10:47	6:15	10:37	8	$2.20	Brook	* 8:36	1:45	4:06
10:55	6:23	10:45	9		Elk Creek	* 8:30	1:37	4:00
11:20	6:45	11:10	13		Big Hill Forks	* 8:07	1:12	3:37
11:27	6:52	11:17	14		Creek	* 8:00	1:05	3:30
11:55			18	$3.60	Floyd Hill		12:40	
					Via Stage			
			33	$6.60	Georgetown			
	7:10	11:35	16		Cottonwood	* 7:40		3:10
	7:30	11:55	18		Smith Hill	* 7:20		2:50
	7:50	12:15	21	$4.00	Black Hawk	* 7:00		2:30
					Via Stage			
			23	$4.50	Central City			

*Indicates shipping points

Mixed Trains

Leave Denver 11:00 a.m.   Arrive Golden 12:15 p.m.
Leave Golden 2:45 p.m.   Arrive Denver 3:45 p.m.

1. Rand-McNally Railway Guide, October, 1873, from D. W. Yungmeyer collection.

Miscellaneous Information

Black Hawk is present terminal of branch to Caribou, 20 miles from Central City. Stages connect with all trains. Floyd Hill is present terminal of branch to Georgetown. Stages connect with all trains for Idaho Springs and Georgetown. Population of towns along the Colorado Central Railroad

Denver	4,759
Golden	800
Georgetown	1,200
Black Hawk	400
Central City	2,000

The Georgetown line was extended to Graymont in 1884, but very little information has come to light regarding definite passenger schedules in effect beyond Silver Plume. The writer has found only two time-tables showing service as far west as Graymont. An 1892 issue of the Official Guide carries a schedule dated April 10, 1892, showing two daily trains operating to Graymont. A Rocky Mountain Railway Guide, published in October, 1893, shows only one train operating to the station in question.

As a rule, passenger service on the Clear Creek line consisted of two daily trains operating throughout the year in each direction between Denver, Silver Plume, and Central City. During the summer tourist season a third train and frequent extras were operated to take care of the additional business. The famous Georgetown Loop and the Argentine Central, a narrow gauge scenic line which ran between Silver Plume and the top of Mt. McClellan (See Author's history of this railroad in R.&L.H.S. Bulletin No. 64) were a source of considerable revenue to the Clear Creek line in the heyday of Colorado tourists and sightseers. The Argentine Central line connected with the Colorado & Southern's track near the old pavilion beside the wye in Silver Plume.

After 1912, winter season service was frequently reduced to one train per day. Passenger travel on the Georgetown line gradually decreased and in 1927 all passenger trains, except such extras as might be required now and then to take care of a little seasonal business, were discontinued. After that year the few passengers that desired rail transportation up Clear Creek were accommodated in the caboose of a freight train which operated on a triweekly schedule between Denver and Silver Plume. Later, in July, 1932, the triweekly schedule was reduced to two round trips per week as far as Idaho Springs, with an occasional run to Silver Plume. After March, 1940, only one trip per week was made. Early 1941 Official Guides carried cheerful announcements by the Colorado & Southern to the effect that "Bus Service" was available between Idaho Springs and Silver Plume. They might have gone one step further and announced: "See the wondrous beauties of Clear Creek Canon, a region of panoramic magnificence, while joyfully bouncing along in a swaying bus—breathe the delightful fresh mountain air, delicately blended with odorous fumes as dispensed by a leaky exhaust pipe." The line from Silver Plume to Idaho Springs was taken up in 1939, and the remainder of the Clear Creek line was abandoned in May, 1941.

Service on the Black Hawk branch was eventually reduced to a mixed train which, at first, made two round trips daily between Forks Creek and Central City, but was later cut to one trip per day. In February, 1925, all train operation beyond Black Hawk ceased. After 1927, service to Black Hawk consisted of side trips made by the Silver Plume freight train on its regular triweekly run up the canon. As this weekly schedule was reduced, so was service to Black Hawk reduced. It ceased altogether in May, 1941, when all operation up Clear Creek Canon was discontinued.

Regarding passenger fares on the Clear Creek line, the following figures were found in the Pacific Railway Commission reports:

	Rate in Cents Per Mile					
	1881	1882	1883	1884	1885	1886
Colorado Central	.047	.044	.043	.042	.039	.035
Georgetown, Breckenridge & Leadville	—	—	—	.045	.039	.045

This report stated:

"The Union Pacific Company operated on the policy of charging all that the traffic could possibly bear."

* * * *

MISCELLANEOUS FARES AND RAILROAD MILEAGES ON THE COLORADO CENTRAL RAILROAD AND THE DENVER SOUTH PARK & PACIFIC RAILROAD AS REPORTED IN CROFUTT'S GRIP-SACK GUIDE TO COLORADO, January 1, 1881

All fares and mileages quoted are from Denver, Colorado

Alpine	$12.85	149 miles
(Alpine was later known as Fisher)		
Alma	10.80	117 miles
Arthurs	8.60	102 miles
Baileys	4.35	54 miles
Black Hawk	2.85	35 miles
(Stage coach fare, Black Hawk to Central City [1½ miles] 50c)		
Buffalo	2.95	40 miles
Buena Vista	11.65	135 miles
Como	7.35	88 miles
Crossons	3.75	48 miles
Divide	10.35	122 miles
Dome Rock	2.25	31 miles
Estabrook	4.05	51 miles
Fairplay	9.80	112 miles
Free Gold	11.40	133 miles
(Free Gold was 1½ miles south of Buena Vista on the D. & R. G.)		
Forks Creek	2.15	28 miles
Georgetown	4.30	52 miles
Garos	8.80	104 miles
Grant	5.35	66 miles
Hancock	13.75	158 miles
Heywood	12.20	142 miles
Hortense	12.20	143 miles
Idaho Springs	3.00	36 miles
Jefferson	6.70	80 miles

Kenosha	6.25	76 miles
Leadville	15.00	171 miles
(Via Buena Vista)		
McGees	10.80	126 miles
Morrison	1.00	16 miles
Nathrop	11.65	137 miles
Pine Grove	3.20	42 miles
Pitkin	16.90	175 miles
Platte River	9.55	113 miles
Red Hill	7.85	93 miles
Slaghts	4.70	58 miles
St. Elmo	13.25	153 miles
Summit	10.20	120 miles
(Also known as Trout Creek Pass or Bath)		
Webster	7.00	70 miles

An effort to obtain sufficient data to show a comparison in miscellaneous traffic figures between certain periods on the South Park was made, but met with little success, due to the old records being destroyed at Denver. The following table represents a typical year in the early history of the road:

PASSENGER

Average miles traveled by each passenger	50.02
Average number of cars per train	2.90
Average number of passengers per train	41.2
Average passenger fare per mile	.063
Total passengers carried for the year	59,566
Average speed in miles per hour	15

FREIGHT

Average number of cars per train	8.90
Average rate per ton mile charged	.0542
Total tons of freight carried for the year	191,807
Average speed in miles per hour	8

* * * *

TOURISTS' ATTRACTIONS

Throughout the history of the South Park railroad, from its beginning to about 1910, when the little road began to sink into the quagmire of despair, certain sections along the route were a regular haven to vacationists, tourists, health seekers, fishermen, hunters, and others, seeking peace, recreation, and rest. There was considerable revenue to be had from this class of travel and the passenger traffic department did a good job of advertising and promotion work.

The Railway Review of September 30, 1882, carried a report by the Union Pacific concerning the completion of the Gunnison extension, including therein some publicity on the scenic value of the line. We quote in part:

"In the Tunnel Range, far above timberline at the altitude of eternal ice and snow, the railroad enters the great Alpine Tunnel piercing the most rugged of the Rockies. The tunnel approaches on either side of the range are marvels of engineering skill, being laid through scenes unrivaled for grandeur and magnificence. Emerging from the tunnel on the Pacific slope, over 11,000 feet above sea level, the enchanting valley of Quartz Creek and its numerous tributaries, and 150 miles of mountains stretch before the eye—a view of stupendous peaks and rugged canons unexcelled for grandeur on this continent."

Another spot that was well advertised, especially in the early days, was a health resort known as Hortense Hot Springs. This place was located up Chalk Creek a few miles west of Nathrop in the shadow of Mt. Princeton. A rambling four-story hotel of frame construction was erected here to serve the guests. The place experienced a rather checkered career, the details of which we shall read about later on.

Various guides were published now and then telling the tourist of the magnificent mountain scenery, vacation and health resorts, and the excellent fishing that was to be enjoyed along the line. Here are a few excerpts picked at random from the 1881 edition of Crofutt's Grip-Sack Guide to Colorado:

"After reaching the mouth of the canon, the road turns west, crosses and recrosses the Platte River many times while ascending the narrow gorge between towering mountains. Some are 2,000 feet in height, and almost overhanging the road. In places these mountains are sloping and covered with pine, spruce and cedar trees; in the summer the shrubs, moss, ferns, and countless flowers clinging to and growing from every nook and crevice presents a scene of gorgeous beauty, a scene where Mother Nature has displayed her handiwork far beyond the comprehension of mortal beings . . . Dome Rock, a station three miles above the station of South Platte, is named for a mammoth dome-shaped rock on the south side of the road, far up the mountain side. A short distance above is a foot bridge across the river to a little park, which, in the summer time, is a great resort for picnic parties from Denver and the valley towns. . . . Passing Dome Rock, we are whirled over a solid roadbed through and around many projecting mountain spurs, with rapid and ever-changing scenery on either side, and soon the train stops at Vermillion. . . . A few more revolutions of the wheels . . . . the mountain sides slope away and we are at beautiful Estabrook Park. This place represents some attractions as a summer resort, particularly to those fond of hunting and fishing. In the adjacent country, deer, bear, and other game are quite plentiful, and in Deer Creek and other small creeks that flow into the Platte near this vicinity, trout of the finest quality are abundant. . . . Jefferson, the first station after descending Kenosha Summit, is located at the north rim of the 'Great South Park'. The settlers in this region are mostly engaged in mining for gold and silver, coal and other minerals. Others are raising cattle and sheep. None are idle. . . . Game such as deer, elk, bear, mountain lion, grouse, and occasionally mountain sheep, are plentiful in the park and vicinity, while the streams are stocked with an abundance of the finest mountain trout."

In addition to Crofutt's Guide, there were two other pamphlets that we should not fail to mention. These two booklets, issued by the passenger traffic department in 1896, were titled: "Boreas, Breckenridge and the Blue" and "South Park and Alpine Pass." The two publications, each containing about 32 pages and well illustrated, go to considerable length to give a short history of the railroad from the romantic angle, describe the "unsurpassed scenery", the fine fishing and hunting, the numerous vacation and health resorts, etc., that were to be found along the "Great South Park Line". Fortunate is the man who owns either or both of these little booklets.

First and foremost, however, above all the miscellaneous attractions to be found along the little road,

C.&S. 46 leads a parade of picnic trains which halt to disgorge a swarm of passengers, bound for the little park across Platte River. The spherical formation known as Dome Rock looms in the left background.

was the fishing and summer resort area that grew up along a 50-mile section of the South Platte River between Platte Canon station and the vicinity of Webster. A description of this area, written to attract the eye of the tourist, was included in a publication called "Empire of the West" by Brent. His description of the canon as an ideal resort area is as follows:

"Twenty miles from Denver is Platte Canon, and through this sinuous rift in the mountains rushes the Platte River, dancing out of its shadowy channel into the full light of the valley. The South Park line enters the canon where the river leaves it. The general aspect is much like that of Clear Creek Canon, of which it is a friendly rival. It is the same, in being a rocky chasm, its bed a rushing stream, but different in its wild contour.

"To reach Platte Canon, the trains pass through the western suburbs of Denver, skirting the wooded banks of the Platte, and, twenty miles out, enter the somber canon between lofty and forbidding walls which continue for 50 miles, receding at times to make room for picturesque little hamlets like Buffalo, Pine Grove, Slaghts, Grant, etc. At all these places tourists can be accommodated, and trout and game abound.

"At times the train seems to dash against the face of the cliff, but, following the rails, it turns suddenly and passes by in safety. The way through the canon is a series of graceful curves, close to the overhanging rocks, crossing the turbulent Platte River seven times between Denver and Baileys. In places, the tops of the canon almost seem to touch each other and exclude the sun. The canon is a geological study; the different formations and the terrific forces which have combined them will tell their own stories.

"Dome Rock is like the top of a buried mosque and is as regular in shape as if fashioned by the hand of man, except that one side is partly broken away. Cathedral Spires are in sight for miles, despite the winding canon, and keep reappearing long after they are passed.

"The canon affords fine opportunities for camping out. There is shade in plenty, trout, game, and bathing, and good board to be had in neighboring houses. But the best way is to live in a tent and hire a servant to do the cooking, etc. This is especially recommended for the invalid tourist. There are 50 miles of this varying panorama, and, after the train climbs Kenosha Hill, the great South Park is seen stretching away for over 40 miles—one vast level picture as different from the canon as night is from day."

With plenty of fish in the Platte River, and since it was close to Denver, the stream became a regular mecca for the disciples of Izaak Walton. Inasmuch as the canon was accessible by train only, the railroad soon inaugurated a regular schedule to accommodate the fishermen. An old timer once told the author that "at times, the week-end and Sunday trains between Denver and the canon were jammed to the roof." Copying from Trains Magazine, we read:

"Probably the best known trains to run over this road were the fish trains, which were inaugurated in the '90's. Fish train No. 75 ran out of Denver daily except Sunday, at 5:00 p.m., going as far as Grant; and on Saturdays there was still another, No. 73, at 2:05 p.m. Through the Platte Canon, trout fishing was good, and available right off the ends of the railroad ties. Outbound, the fisherman would pick his spot and ask the conductor (probably Tommy St. John) to stop the train. By early next morning, his creel full of choice Rocky Mountain trout, the fisherman had but to get up from the end of the tie at the sound of the approaching train, and wave his handkerchief for the inbound fish train to stop. These trains often ran in two and three sections."

An anecdote of the days when fishing was good along the Platte is told by Grant Jordon in Railroad Magazine. Mr. Jordon relates:

"One Saturday night I rode my bicycle to the mouth of the Platte Canon, hiked up the track during the night to South Fork above South Platte station, and began fishing. Ever see a Colorado cloudburst? About noon a stage driver rattled along down the old wagon road shouting to every fisherman: 'Better come down to South Platte; there's a flood coming! You'll get marooned if the water washes out the track below!' Nine of us piled into his wagon and rode down to South Platte; and sure enough, the Fisherman Special chugged along an hour early. Was that string of varnish loaded! They had picked up eight or nine coaches and every one was packed; three people to a seat, and swarms in the aisles, and on the tender. I was happy to find a place on the bottom step of the rear car.

"That downhill ride was like a roller coaster. We could see the river swelling and hear its roar as the water came up higher and higher. Soon it was lapping the ties. When that heavy train rolled over the weak spots I could feel the track settle. Two miles from the mouth of the canon there was a fill, and as we rolled along I saw the dirt drop from beneath the ties, leaving the rails strung out like a ladder!"

Finally, the building of roads and the coming of the automobile enabled larger numbers of persons to get into the canon at South Platte station, Buffalo, Baileys, and other good fishing spots. Eventually, the hordes of fishermen, together with irrigation projects, both large and small, robbed the stream of a great portion of both fish and water, with the result that the former fisherman's paradise was all but ruined.

Today one can observe many small summer cottages and resorts scattered up and down the canon, but the shrill whistle of the little South Park engine is gone, and the bobble of a fisherman's cork or the whine of his reel has nearly disappeared. In its place you may perchance see a few of the cottages occupied by persons seeking a bit of rest and quiet along the shallow stream while trying to escape the carbon monoxide, and sounding horns of the endless stream of trucks and automobiles plying to and fro. Man's eternal greed for more and more brought about the end of most of his pleasures along the Platte River.

Tourist travel on the Clear Creek line consisted principally of excursion trips up the Georgetown section to view and ride over the world-renowned Georgetown Loop, with a side trip to the summit of Mt. McClellan via the Argentine Central Railway. Inasmuch as the details revolving around this famous bridge and its value as a center of attraction for tourists have already been discussed in this book, further comments are unnecessary.

The second drawing card on the line, and one which greatly benefited the Colorado & Southern company indirectly, was the narrow gauge Argentine Central Railway, which ran from Silver Plume to the summit

B. B. Buckwalter photo,
from C. C. Rogers Collection.

D.L.&G. 109 (later C.&S. 4) on the high bridge of the Georgetown Loop in July, 1895. Part of Georgetown may be seen at the lower right.

R. H. Kindig.

C.&S. 70 crossing the high bridge with a 3-car train on May 14, 1938, about a year before the bridge was dismantled. Note the additional girders which were applied when the structure was strengthened.

of Mt. McClellan. Quoting from the writer's history of this particular railroad,[1] we read:

"The construction of this railroad to the summit of Mt. McClellan in 1906 furnished an unsurpassed scenic attraction. The line was called 'The Gray's Peak Route,' and was well advertised as America's most scenic one-day trip, or a lifetime in a day. This slogan was a very appropriate one, for the trip, which started in Denver, included the spectacular and beautiful mountain scenery along Clear Creek, the famous Georgetown Loop and bridge, climaxed by the climb through the large and interesting snow bank formations and ice palaces, to the summit of Mt. McClellan, 14,007 feet[2] above sea level.

"The Colorado & Southern Railway took these tourists' trains directly from Denver via the famous Clear Creek route of the old Colorado Central to Silver Plume. Here the Argentine Central would couple on one of their Shay engines and drag the little train to the summit. . . Due to the decline of this tourist business, and other factors, the Argentine Central was abandoned and dismantled in 1919."

Further information relative to passenger traffic is found in a story, compiled by Mr. Robert A. LeMassena, of a special group excursion made over certain sections of the South Park and Clear Creek lines. It follows:

THE T. P. A. SILVER PASS

There are few students of Colorado railroad history who do not know of the unique, gold, silver, fob, and buckskin passes which Otto Mears issued to shippers and his friends, ostensibly to provide the bearer with free transportation over the Silverton Railroad, which Mears owned. While these passes were, no doubt, actually tendered in lieu of valid tickets, on this rugged, 18-mile long mining railroad, it is doubtful if they were more than expensive, though beautiful, souvenirs. And it is somewhat strange that, at the same time, the three largest railroads in Colorado jointly issued a solid silver pass in large numbers, only to have it become virtually unknown.

Although it was issued in 1890, the T.P.A. pass can be traced back to Lincoln's Birthday of 1882. Lima, Ohio, was snowbound that day, and about twenty five travelling men were confined to the interior of the Lima House. Lively stories were unearthed at the bar, while "bull-sessions" were to be found in every corner. The subjects of discussion ran the gamut of human knowledge, but one of them, protection for the travelling man, produced tangible results, and on that day, the Traveller's Protective Association was formed, with the stranded drummers as the nucleus of the organization. The Association spread, and by 1890 had 25,000, or 60,000 members, depending upon which Denver paper you read in 1890. National gatherings were a natural "necessity," the eighth of which was bestowed upon Denver. The Executive Committee of the Denver Division planned an elaborate, week-long celebration for the boys, which it divulged in its report at a meeting of the local members on May 28, 1890. It was this report that suggested the idea of a silver pass to be used for the special railroad excursions which were to follow the convention activities in Denver. The idea of a special pass must have created great interest, as it was the first item on the report, and required a major portion of the available time for its discussion. When it was realized that this token would be retained by the recipient, and carried back to his home town, its value as advertising for Colorado was most evident. Consequently, it was decided to increase the quantity to be issued, from 500 to 1500. Contemporary reporters differed as to the cost of the passes. One advised his editor that it was only $700, while another submitted a figure of $2000. There is nothing to indicate that any design, other than the final one, for the pass was submitted, since the newspapers spoke of the *silver* design being accepted. This would imply that proofs, one at least, in silver, were struck from engraved dies. It would have been foolish and expensive to have had dies made for each proposed design, hence this implication seems reasonable. It is further supported by the fact that the State Museum in Denver has a T.P.A. pass, which is apparently half copper and half brass, and it is quite likely that this is one of the proofs submitted by the Committee. The name of the designer of the pass is not mentioned anywhere. It could have been the engraver of the die, Beddo, whose name is cut into the design in tiny letters. Nor is the name of the man who suggested the idea of a silver pass to be found in the literature. Perhaps a member of the Transportation Committee (Philip Troustine, J. H. Clute or Herbert George) was responsible. But it seems more logical that both the idea and the design were conceived in the fertile brain of one Shadrack Kemp Hooper, the General Passenger Agent of the Denver & Rio Grande R. R. During his regime, Colonel Hooper quintupled the passenger business of his railroad, by means of every advertising strategem in the books, and it is inconceivable that the resourceful Shadrack would have let this golden opportunity pass unexploited to its limit. Thus, it can be thought with reasonable certainty that S. K. Hooper fostered this project.

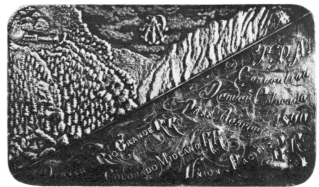

Robert LeMassena Collection.

1. R. & L. H. S. Bulletin No. 64
2. U. S. Geological Survey Bulletin number 707.

The pass was 2"x3¼" in size, of horizontal format. It weighed almost an ounce, and was made of 900 fine, Colorado silver. Fortunately, its maker is known, as he had the foresight to engrave "The Colorado Gold and Silver Mfg. Co., Denver" along the bottom in microscopically fine characters. The face is divided diagonally into two parts, the upper showing a scene on the Rio Grande in Toltec Gorge, which is on the line between Alamosa and Durango, but which, ironically, is in New Mexico. The lower half bears the names of the participating railroads, Union Pacific, Colorado Midland, and Denver & Rio Grande. (To be perfectly precise, the pass was valid on the Union Pacific, Denver & Gulf Railway, which was controlled by the Union Pacific, the Colorado Midland, and the Rio Grande.)

With the arrival of the first delegates via a Union Pacific special train from Kansas City, the Convention got under way on June 23, 1890. Certain members, who had entrained at Chicago on the Santa Fe, missed the first day. They had "succumbed to the seductive wiles" of Kansas City, thereby delaying the special just long enough for a freight train to mess up its track with a tangle of shattered rolling stock. From the first moment there was continuous activity of all sorts, receptions, processions, marches, addresses, business sessions, elections, carriage-rides ("for the ladies and escorts"), entertainment ("rich, and strictly travelling salesmen's"), plus some uninhibited hell-raising which did not appear on the printed program. The last two days, Friday and Saturday, were devoted to the special railroad trips, which were designed to show off the incomparable scenic wonders of the Centennial State.

It was originally intended that the pass be valid for two trips. One was via the U.P.D.&G. from Denver to Silver Plume, (the narrow gauge Colorado Central R.R.) over the Georgetown Loop, and consuming but one day. The other was a four-day affair via the Rio Grande and Colorado Midland to Manitou Springs, Leadville, Glenwood Springs, Buena Vista and Pueblo. (A special ticket was issued for this latter trip, but none of them are known to exist today.) With understandable acumen the Union Pacific, seeing that almost everyone would take the longer trip, announced that it would honor the silver pass on any of its regular trains to Silver Plume, either before or after the longer excursion on the other roads. Although the Santa Fe was not a party to any of the special convention trip arrangements, it felt that it would be ill considered if it did not offer some sort of a free trip also. Consequently, it honored the pass on a special train to Pueblo and back on June 29th and 30th, to coincide with the Pueblo activities of those who had taken the long trip. It would seem that one of these many trips would have been suitable to any delegate, but this was apparently not the case, as Mr. Hutton wrote to the Rio Grande for rates on another trip, which would include scenery on all three lines, and operate through Leadville, Glenwood Springs and Manitou Springs, over somewhat different routes from the scheduled, long trip. This latter trip carried the visitor between Denver and Leadville over South Park trackage by way of Como; Leadville to Glenwood Springs and return via the Colorado Midland; and from Leadville back to Denver over the D.&R.G. by way of Pueblo. It would take three days, but would cost $10.00 for the fare, as the silver pass would not be honored for it.

Some 550 delegates filled the two special trains for the long trip, which officially began at 7:30 a.m. on Friday, June 27. Behind immaculate engines were a well-filled commissary car, six day coaches, and a Pullman Palace Sleeping Car. Colonel Hooper was in charge of one train, while Charles S. Lee, General Passenger Agent for the Colorado Midland, had command of the other. (It is interesting to observe that the Denver Brewing Co. furnished an endless supply of beer for "Club Room" use, that Zang's supplied the "compressed hops" for the special trains, and that Herren Schlitz and Anheuser participated in the dispensing of brew for "medicinal purposes".) The alternate, long trip netted 130 customers who had $10.00 to spare for the purpose, while the Santa Fe's special to Pueblo on Sunday hauled about 400 members. Since the U.P.D.&G. honored the silver pass on so many different days, it is not known just how many delegates took advantage of their silver pass for the ride to Silver Plume. All trips were completed on schedule, without mishap, and Denver was pretty much back to normal on July 1st, after the last delegate, saturated with beer and scenery, had headed homeward. While those who went on the excursions were probably a little tired from the four-day rolling frolic, Shadrack K. Hooper was exhausted. He promptly took a week off, to rest up at Glenwood Springs.

From present records, the T.P.A. pass is the rarest pass of any railroad which operated in Colorado. This seems odd, when 1500 were distributed. But it must be remembered that almost all of them were taken out of the state, then to be forgotten or lost. There was no personal interest in them, as was the case with the Mears passes which had the names of the recipients engraved upon them. Hence, they were not cherished as family memorabilia, to be handed down from father to son, as so many of the Mears passes have come down. At this date, only six of them are known to exist. Two, plus the proof, are in the State Museum in Denver. Robert A. LeMassena and George H. King, both of Denver, each have one. The fifth, a long way from home, but in the hands of a Colorado native son, is owned by Morris W. Abbott of Milford, Conn., and the sixth is owned by Douglas Huntington of Bellevue, Washington.

343

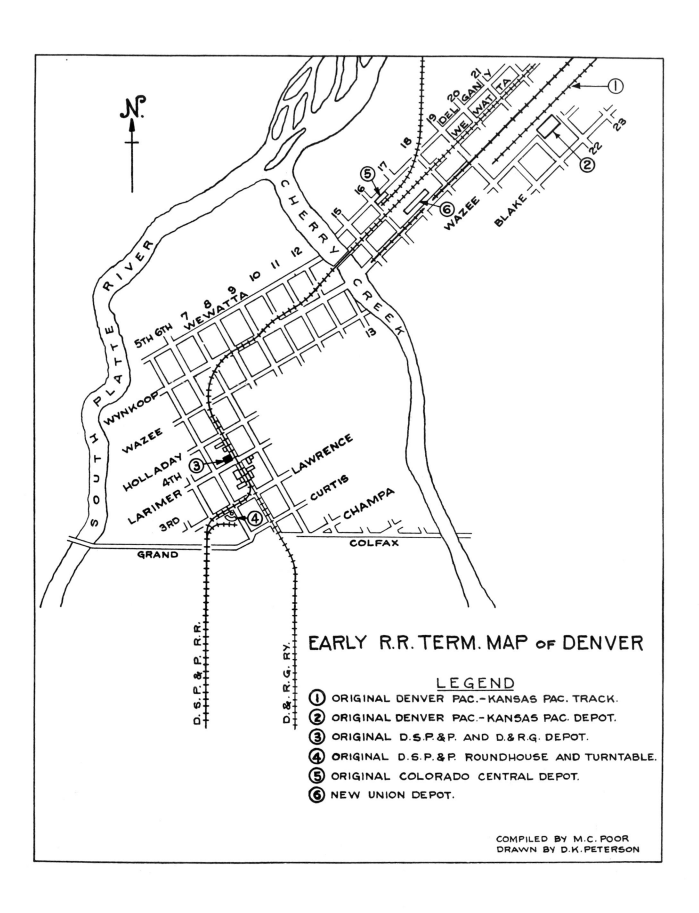

EARLY R.R. TERM. MAP of DENVER

LEGEND

① ORIGINAL DENVER PAC.-KANSAS PAC. TRACK.

② ORIGINAL DENVER PAC.-KANSAS PAC. DEPOT.

③ ORIGINAL D.S.P.&P. AND D.&R.G. DEPOT.

④ ORIGINAL D.S.P.&P. ROUNDHOUSE AND TURNTABLE.

⑤ ORIGINAL COLORADO CENTRAL DEPOT.

⑥ NEW UNION DEPOT.

COMPILED BY M.C. POOR
DRAWN BY D.K. PETERSON

REFERENCES—Denver Times, May 29, June 23, 26, 27, 28, 1890.

Denver Daily Republican, May 29, June 23, 24, 25, 26, 27, 29, 30, 1890.

Rocky Mountain News, May 29, June 23, 24, 25, 26, 27, 1890.

* * * *

THE DENVER DEPOT

In the early period of railroading in Denver there were several passenger stations in the railroad district of the city. Late in 1870, when the pioneer roads, the Denver Pacific and the Kansas Pacific, had been completed to Denver, they united in the construction of a very creditable building where their tracks intersected 21st and 22nd streets between Blake and Wazee Streets. It was a rather large two-story brick structure, and for that time was regarded as a very liberal provision for the accommodation of passengers, even though it was then on the outskirts of the city in that direction.

Depots remind most of us of telegraph offices. Therefore, it will interest the reader to learn that the telegraph line beat the railroad to Denver by some seven years. On October 1, 1863, the first telegraph line reached Denver; it was opened for business on October 10th.[1] The line connected with the outside world by means of a branch line to Julesburg, where it connected with the main telegraph line running east and west. Ten words to New York cost $9.00, while the rate to St. Louis was $7.50. In November, 1863, the line was extended west to Central City. However, we are told that this early service was sometimes intermittent since roaming buffaloes, irritated by fever ticks and other parasites, found the telegraph poles so good to rub against that they snapped one off every now and then. Other interruptions were caused at times by Indians who would cut a section down to obtain a supply of wire.

As previously stated, the South Park's first depot, which they shared with the Rio Grande, was located on the northwest corner of 6th and Larimer Streets, west of Cherry Creek in West Denver. The Colorado Central, after it had withdrawn from its brief association with the Kansas Pacific, built a frame passenger station on the east side of 16th Street on part of the present site of Denver's Union Station.

These arrangements continued until the autumn of 1879 when, on October 24, D. C. Dodge, of the Rio Grande, Governor John Evans of the South Park, and W. A. H. Loveland, then at the head of the Colorado Central, made an agreement under which the three narrow gauge roads were to use the Colorado Central's passenger station at the foot of 16th Street. The Rio Grande and the South Park then bridged Cherry Creek,

1. Smiley, "History of Denver."

and ran their trains to the not very inviting nor commodious station of the Colorado Central.[1]

This movement was the beginning of a plan to bring all the passenger business of Denver under one roof, for, within a few weeks afterward, the organization of the Union Depot & Railroad Company was undertaken. On November 24, 1879, there was a meeting of the representatives of all the roads, at which the Union Depot organization was effected. The incorporators of the company were Walter S. Cheesman, D. C. Dodge, A. A. Egbert, Bela M. Hughes, and J. F. Welborn. The arrangement provided for five trustees, and W. S. Cheesman, S. H. H. Clark, D. C. Dodge, A. A. Egbert, and Sylvester T. Smith were chosen for the first year. These trustees elected W. S. Cheesman President of the company; S. T. Smith, Vice President; George W. Kassler, Treasurer; and D. C. Dodge, Secretary. The organization's capital stock was $400,000.

Concerning this organization, the Denver Republican of January 1, 1913, carried the following story as told by Mr. J. S. Brown, one of the stockholders of the new company:

"After completing our negotiations with the different companies, seemingly to the satisfaction of all parties, we had a meeting to ratify and close the deal. There were present at this meeting all of the officials of the different roads and Mr. C. F. Woerishoffer of Woerishoffer & Co., New York, who were the bankers of the Denver & Rio Grande Railroad. Someone suggested that we should now have a Union Depot. The Rio Grande and the South Park passenger depot was located on the west side, and the Union out at Twenty-second and Blake.

"The South Park owned the block between Sixteenth and Seventeenth Streets and Wynkoop and Wewatta, and the Colorado Central owned the block in rear of the one owned by the South Park. Mr. Woerishoffer suggested that a Union Depot Company be organized and incorporated, and if they could acquire the blocks north of the two owned by the South Park and the Colorado Central, he would promise to sell $300,000 in bonds of the company, which he did as soon as the Depot company had use for them, and thus we built the Union Depot."

W. S. Cheesman negotiated for twelve acres of land lying between Sixteenth and Eighteenth Streets, with Wynkoop Street as its southern boundary and Delgany Street the northern boundary. On December 10, the company issued $300,000 in seven per cent, twenty year bonds and prepared to erect a suitable passenger station. On February 2, 1880, at a meeting of representatives of all the roads, agreements were made under which all their passenger trains were to begin and end their trips at the new station upon its completion.

The plans having been perfected, construction work was let by contract and begun about the first of June. The building was to be 503 feet long, 65 feet wide, two and one-half stories high, built of sandstone and lava, with a central tower 180 feet high, and quite a large area of park in front of it.[1] The main, or central part of the building only, was undertaken at that time, and within a year construction was far

1. Smiley, "History of Denver."

345

enough along to permit use. The original cost of construction was $458,461.58[1]. On June 1, 1881, it was opened to the public, and the next day all Denver trains began using the new station.

Later, the Union Pacific, the South Park, and the Rio Grande came into control of all the Union Depot & Railroad Company's stock, their interest being divided as follows: the Union Pacific controlled three-fifths, the South Park one-fifth, and the Rio Grande one-fifth.[2] The Gunnison News-Champion of August 6, 1942, states that the original South Park holdings were one-fourth. All other railroads using the station and the facilities it afforded them, paid a fixed rental per month, which, together with express company and office rentals, constituted the terminal company's revenue.

Several years later a wing was built on each end of the main building, which completed the structure according to the original designs. In the pamphlet "South Park and Alpine Pass," owned by H. L. Curtiss, we read:

"A great painting by Charles Partridge Adams hung at one time in the Denver ticket office of the Denver, South Park & Pacific. It was titled: 'A Glimpse of South Park'."

On the morning of Sunday, March 18, 1894, a fire started under the roof of the main building and before the flames could be brought under control, the larger part of the structure's interior was burned out—an unusual experience for a building of its quality and character. The loss was covered by $125,000 insurance. It was decided to rebuild on an improved plan at a cost of about $200,000. At that time some of the other railroad companies using the depot acquired proprietary interests. In the reconstruction and repairing that followed immediately, changes were made in the interior arrangement and exterior appearance.

On August 17, 1912, the Union Depot & Railroad Company was reorganized as The Denver Union Terminal Company, taking over the property on April 1, 1914. The corporation owned 5.90 miles of trackage and was used by six railroad companies: the Union Pacific, the Denver & Rio Grande, the Colorado & Southern, the Chicago, Burlington & Quincy, the Atchison, Topeka & Santa Fe, and the Chicago, Rock Island & Pacific. Each of the above railroads owns a one-sixth interest in the property of The Denver Union Terminal Company.[3]

* * * *

FREIGHT TRAFFIC

Earlier in this book the writer stated: "A new field of operations, the great South Park country, located southwest of the Denver region, began to draw the interest and attention of Governor John Evans . . .

1. Poor's Manual of Railroads, 1886.
2. Poor's Manual of Railroads, 1911.
3. Poor's Manual of Railroads, 1921.

he sincerely believed that a railroad built into this part of Colorado could be developed into a successful and profitable venture, and that a systematic development of large belts of timber, stone quarries, limestone ledges, gypsum beds, mineral and agricultural resources, would furnish ample traffic for his railroad."

In the Denver South Park & Pacific's first annual report, 1874, the Governor stated:

"It is believed that no route for a railroad . . . has ever offered such abundant sources of local business throughout its entire line."

John Evans built his railroad directly into an undeveloped and sparsely settled region whose inhabitants had to depend solely on the rough and slow wagon road method of travel and transportation. There was much potential wealth in the quarries, the forests of timber, the mines, and the agricultural areas. The arrival of the railroad promoted the growth and development of the Morrison quarries and opened up the South Platte timber belt. It enabled ranchers and farmers to move into the fertile South Park area and furnished them transportation for the shipment of large numbers of cattle and agricultural products to profitable markets. But the young giant who was just raising his head above the Colorado horizon at that time, the mining industry, exceeded all others in potential wealth. The Leadville discoveries quickened the pulse of industry all over the state; not only did it revive confidence and bring in thousands of immigrants, but it brought unlimited capital to the aid of the railroad. The South Park threw an extension over Alpine Pass and helped develop the Gunnison region.

Wherever the end-of-track reached, its arrival was a blessing to the mine owners and operators, and, being a direct route, the road was jammed with business. The tremendous wealth given up by the mines in the early days not only brought riches to their owners, but furnished an extremely lucrative traffic, to all the railroads which were fortunate enough to be on hand. The transportation of ore was the lifeblood of the railroad, for the Evans road was principally a mineral road rather than an agricultural road.

The Colorado Railroad Commissioner's Report for the year 1885 states that the line transported 191,807 tons of freight during the year ending June 30, 1885. The tonnage was divided as follows:

	Tons	Per Cent
Grain	4,686	2.44
Flour	3,543	1.85
Provisions (beef, pork, lard, etc.)	655	0.34
Animals	1,129	0.59
Miscellaneous agricultural products	5,459	2.85
Iron, lead and mineral products	56,917	29.67
Lumber and forest products	48,580	25.33
Coal	29,623	15.45
Plaster, lime and cement	1,000	0.52
Salt	102	0.05
Petroleum and oil	528	0.28

Steel and castings..................................	1,292	0.67
Stone and brick..	29,970	15.63
Manufactures—articles shipped from point of production............................	107	0.05
Merchandise and other articles not enumerated above	8,216	4.28
Total Tons Carried............................	191,807	100.

A general list of the major classes of traffic handled in and out of the various territories served by the South Park railroad was as follows:

1. Morrison branch: Quarry and timber products
2. Platte canon: Quarry and timber products, ice and feldspar
3. South Park:
   a. King branch. Coal, inbound mining supplies
   b. Alma branch. Ore, inbound mining supplies
   c. Garos district. Hay, cattle and sheep
4. Chalk Creek Canon: Ore and timber products
5. Quartz Creek and Gunnison district: Ore, timber products, cattle, sheep and agricultural products shipped out; general merchandise and mining supplies shipped in
6. Baldwin branch: Coal and some ore shipped out; general merchandise and mining supplies shipped in
7. Leadville district:
   a. Breckenridge district. Ore and timber products
   b. Keystone branch. Ore and timber products
   c. Tenmile-Leadville district: Mineral products shipped out; coal, coke, mining supplies, feed, grain, hay, and general merchandise shipped in

The freight traffic far exceeded the passenger traffic on the South Park. Note the gross revenue for a few typical years, as shown in Poor's Manuals:

		Passenger	Freight
1881	Gross earnings..................	$402,006	$ 990,145
1882	Gross earnings..................	383,802	1,092,050
1890	Gross earnings..................	158,358	790,669
1896	Gross earnings..................	140,219	567,833

Consultation of Official Guides and other timetables will disclose passenger train schedules, but only employee's timecards, plus other vague data will tell us how many freight trains were scheduled. From four employees' timetables—1883, 1889, 1897, and 1912, which the writer possesses, we find the following data. The figures represent daily freight trains each way (except Sunday, unless noted).

	Denver to Como	Como to Gunnison	Como to Leadville
Nov. 1883	3	1	2 via Buena Vista,
Aug. 1889	3	Como-Pitkin 1 Pitkin-Gunnison, 1 mixed	7 days per week 2
Nov. 1897	1 way freight 1 mixed	1 mixed	1 mixed
Jan. 1912	1 mixed	Como-Garos, 1 mixed Buena Vista-Hancock, 1 mixed, tri-weekly	Como-Breckenridge, no service. Breckenridge-Leadville, 1 mixed

Mention of freight traffic transported in the Clear Creek district has already been made earlier in this book. The type of commodities hauled up and down Clear Creek canon changed very little from the time the line was first completed until the day the last train whistled out of Forks Creek for Golden. One of the major reasons for constructing the Colorado Central was the transportation of ore and throughout its lifetime ore and concentrates continued to top the list of all tonnaged hauled out of the mountains. Inbound freight consisted largely of such items as coal, coke, mining supplies and general merchandise. Like the outbound ore traffic, this inbound freight constantly diminished until the time of abandonment.

An idea of the proportionate amounts of freight transported by the Clear Creek lines in later years is contained in a table published in an I. C. C. pamphlet. This table covers the years 1929 to 1935.

Commodities	Average
Ore	10,840 tons
Coal	7,892 tons
Sand and gravel...................................	710 tons
Gasoline	677 tons
Forest products....................................	572 tons
Sheep	422 tons
Cement	377 tons
Miscellaneous	1,580 tons

In the Railroad Gazette of February 26, 1886, we read:

"The Denver, South Park & Pacific R. R. has the smallest freight trains in the United States. In 1883, the average freight train was 9⅜ cars, or 31⅜ tons. In 1884, the average was 7⅞ cars or 24 tons per train, while the average for the whole of the U. S. during these periods was 129 tons per train."

H. L. Curtiss writes:

"In the early days it required three engines to take nine cars and a combination passenger coach up the west slope to Alpine Tunnel. The engines left Pitkin with full tanks of water, refilling at Midway tank and Tunnel Gulch tank, at the same time consuming about all the coal that could be piled on the tender."

William Cairns writes:

"Eight empties, or three loads, or four small loads, was tonnage for one engine. During normal times or operating conditions, the average freight train consisted of four engines, two ahead and two at the rear, ahead of the caboose or coach, with perhaps 30 to 35 empties, or 12 to 15 loaded cars. When there was not much business they ran trains of two and three engines and a smaller number of cars. During the winter months these averages dropped while in the summer season they were sometimes increased."

Mr. J. M. Cuenin adds:

"Oftentimes the freight trains coming from the Gunnison country would go to Macune via Schwanders and tie up. The crew would then proceed up to Buena Vista by the short stub, stay over night there, return to Macune the next morning and proceed up Trout Creek to Como."

South Park freights never moved very fast. A typical

schedule found in an 1897 employees' timecard shows that it required about 10 hours to move a freight train over the 88 miles between Denver and Como. Thirteen hours elapsed in making the 114-mile run from Como to Gunnison, and it required 6 hours to travel the 63 miles between Como and Leadville. Such schedules average approximately 9 miles per hour.

* * * *

SNOW

Boreas and Alpine Passes, two of the highest railroad passes in North America, were the "Achilles Heel" of the operating department. At times, these two passes, together with Fremont Pass, defied all attempts to keep the two lines open throughout the entire year. With the approach of each winter season the rotary crew, with the help of the flanger-equipped engines, exerted a superhuman effort to keep the rails clear of snow. However, quite frequently they were defeated by Old Man Winter and his two dependable allies—heavy snowfall and slides.

J. C. Ashford writes:

"I have an early Union Pacific timetable stating that on account of snow conditions in the high altitude of Alpine Tunnel, service is very uncertain between Buena Vista and Gunnison from October 15th to about May 30th."

Because of these unusually heavy snowfalls on the Continental Divide, we find numerous references to the closing of a part of the Gunnison Division because of severe winter conditions on Alpine Pass:

Railway Age, September 3, 1885:

"Alpine Tunnel was closed throughout the winter of 1884-85 because of snow blockades."

Rocky Mountain News, April 3, 1887:

"Work on the Gunnison branch of the D. S. P. & P. will be commenced Monday to open Alpine Tunnel. The road will be open to Gunnison by the 10th of April. In previous years the road has never been open to this point before July 1st."

Denver Post, February 15, 1901:

"The Gunnison branch from Romley on has been closed for several weeks. Alpine Tunnel is blockaded. President Trumbull stated this morning that the road has been closed temporarily, as is often done at this season of the year, because of heavy snows. The line will be reopened in the early spring."

Denver Republican, December 15, 1901:
"ALPINE TUNNEL TO CLOSE
"Cold and snow make the operation of the
line unprofitable.

"Tuesday will see the closing of Alpine Tunnel for the winter. This tunnel is located on the Gunnison branch of the Colorado & Southern Railway. The last train will leave Gunnison Monday afternoon and there will be no through rail connections until springtime, according to the Superintendent's office.

"Four feet of snow was reported at the Tunnel yesterday with zero weather forming a crusty combination that delayed the passenger train for an hour and a half. The big rotary snow plow has been hard at work on the Division since last Friday afternoon, barely keeping the line clear.

"The closing of the tunnel does not mean that the Gunnison Division is entirely abandoned. Trains will be run on Tuesdays and Fridays from Gunnison to Pitkin west of the Tunnel, and from Como to Romley on the eastern slope, leaving a distance of 22 miles which must be covered by wagon or 'Balloon' as one official facetiously remarked yesterday."

Another notation, found in the Colorado & Southern engineering department records, stated that Alpine Tunnel was opened for business on Sunday, June 2, 1907. H. L. Curtiss states that now and then they were able to keep the tunnel open to traffic all winter.

From the meager information available, it does not appear that the high line over Boreas and Fremont Passes was closed down as often as the Alpine Tunnel route. Testimony given during the Pacific Railway Commission Trials discloses that Boreas Pass was blocked by snow for three months during the winter of 1885. Thomas St. John tells that during the winter of 1911-12, the Leadville line was blockaded with snow for something like six months. As in all cases when the high line was snowbound, the Leadville traffic was re-routed via Buena Vista and the Rio Grande during the blockade period.

THE WOODSTOCK SNOWSLIDE

As nearly as can be determined, the station of Woodstock was established by the railroad at the time they were building the line to Gunnison in 1881 and 1882. The place consisted primarily of a boarding house, living quarters, telegraph office, water tank, a few miscellaneous buildings, and a double track spur over 500 feet long. The station served a two-fold purpose. It afforded simple living quarters for the contractors and their forces at the time of construction; and the double track spur was put in to facilitate the forwarding of freight during the time that Woodstock served temporarily as the end-of-track. Mr. H. L. Curtiss says that a great amount of merchandise and supplies was freighted west from this station by wagon team until the road reached Pitkin. Some mining was also carried on in the vicinity.

The boarding house was in charge of an Irish widow, Mrs. Marcella Doyle, whose husband had died and left her with six children. The telegraph operator was J. S. Brown. Wm. Cairns relates that the settlement, which also boasted a few miner's cabins, a saloon, and some other small buildings, was located just a short distance down the mountain below the right of way. Located in such a remote region and at such a high altitude, where the winter blizzards and snow storms raged unabated, the place afforded shelter and sustenance to many a cold and hungry train crew, as well as other individuals who happened along.

Woodstock was the scene of one of the worst disasters along the South Park railroad. This was the great Woodstock snowslide, which occurred on March 10, 1884. The huge avalanche of snow completely buried the settlement, killing thirteen people including the telegraph operator and all of the Doyle family except Mrs. Doyle. The snowslide started high up on the mountain side above the South Park's upper track level. The railroad company had piled a large amount of heavy timbers and planking beside the right of way along the upper track level, preparatory to building a snowshed. The avalanche crashed across the South Park's track at the point where all these heavy timbers had been placed, carrying them along with the great mass of snow and rocks, directly down the mountain side across the lower level track straight toward Woodstock and Missouri Gulch below.[1] Great damage was done due to the extreme steepness of this particular section of the mountain side.

Strange as it may seem, an eastbound South Park passenger train had just pulled out of Woodstock, rounded the big curve, and was working its way up the grade toward the Palisades when the disaster occurred. Whether vibrations caused by the train or the heavy exhausts from the two laboring engines had anything to do with the initial starting of the slide, is a matter of conjecture. One of the passengers was a Mr. Eugene Teets, who afterward included the story of what he witnessed in his book, "Foundation Stones." It seems that Teets and two companions had succeeded in making their way from Whitepine, a settlement some six miles south, to Woodstock in order to catch this afternoon passenger train for Denver. In view of some minor discrepancies found here and there in his writings, the author of this book cannot vouch for Teets' veracity, however, we will quote part of his story of the snowslide:

"We finally reached Woodstock after many hardships. All three of us were within the little eating shack refreshing ourselves with hot coffee. About an hour after our arrival the belated train came in with two engines, one baggage car, one combination passenger car, and one Pullman car. Never have I seen anyone more pleased than we three, as we hurried into that Pullman—far from home and safety, but the comforts of the Pullman were our only thoughts. We did not know Altman Pass (Alpine Tunnel) had yet to be overcome before darkness set in.

"After a brief stop the 'All-aboard' call of the conductor was welcome indeed, and off we started up the grade, toward where we had come from—only on the opposite side of the gulch. Here we could look across the awful peril of snow we so recently left. We had to go quite a way up Missouri Gulch to gain the necessary grade to take us over Altman Pass. We had not been long on the return track and well out of the gulch up on the mountain side, before we were stalled in a deep cut filled with snow packed so hard that our double-header could not buck its way through. It was then that we beheld one of the most alarming sights that I ever experienced. The air became surcharged with snow, so fine, so dense, simply a snow fog without the fog horn, and the crashing and roaring like the tearing away of the mountain side.

"Looking from the windows and doors we could see a moving mass. The whole mountain side seemed to be sliding into, and filling up the gulch, and it was then that we realized

1. Some of the old timbers can still be seen, scattered haphazardly among the boulders on the mountain side between the two track levels.

how lately we had left the very spot, or side of the mountain from which this great avalanche of snow had come. My friends and I harked back to just how narrow an escape we had had when we were pulling and coaxing our human burden down to safety. The great body of snow moved with the speed of birds. Finally it reached the lower railroad level and had seemingly selected the very spot where we had so recently boarded the train at Woodstock station. This station, comprising miner's shanties, eating house, living and sleeping houses, work shop, car shed, tool house, chicken house—everything—was completely buried, and with it went thirteen lives. The overpowering avalanche of snow had done its death dealing work, and had swept everything before it, taking rocks, bushes—everything from the top of the mountain to the bottom, leaving in its path a bare swath. How thankful we were that we had escaped its awful rush. We on the train did not dream of the fate of those who had lately administered to our wants. . . . We did not reach safety until the next morning after a hard battle with the snow. Food was low and even though we were within a few miles of relief, yet to reach safety, we had to go through a tunnel over three miles long. (Teets errs here—Alpine Tunnel is 1,805 feet in length). My but that section house did look good, and the hot coffee, pancakes, ham, and eggs, was the most satisfactory meal we ever had. . . . . . .".

Mr. Teets' article speaks of the many difficulties the crew had in getting the train to the tunnel and through it. He makes no mention of the stone hotel and engine facilities located at Alpine Tunnel station. It is presumed that the ham and eggs were obtained at Hancock.

Through the courtesy of Mr. H. L. Curtiss of Paonia, Colorado, we quote the following newspaper item regarding the Woodstock catastrophe:

"A terrible snowslide disaster occurred at Woodstock about 6:00 P.M. on March 10, 1884. The avalanche completely destroyed the section house, telegraph office, water tank and some other buildings. A rescue party from Pitkin returned with the bodies of ten who were killed. They were as follows: Martin Doyle, 23; Andrew Doyle, 19; Katy Doyle, 18; Marcella Doyle, 14; Maggie Doyle, 12; Christopher Doyle, 10 years of age; Jasper M. Caswell of Tomichi, James Tracy, George Alexander, and Michael Shea. The bodies of J. S. Brown, the operator; Joseph Gerazo, and the saloon keeper, Joseph Royegno, are still in the slide. Miss Celia Dillon, engaged to Martin Doyle, was rescued alive after being buried in the snow for fifteen hours. Old Mrs. Doyle, who had been buried in the snow for almost twelve hours, was also rescued alive".

As a result of this tragedy to her family, Mrs. Doyle, some time later, entered suit against the South Park company for $50,000 damages. Regarding this suit we quote from the Railway Age of January 21, 1886:

"Mrs. Marcella Doyle who lost her entire family of three sons and three daughters, brought suit in the United States Court against the Denver South Park & Pacific to recover $50,000. She says her husband died in 1880 and left her penniless. Her three boys were 23, 19, and 10 years old respectively, while her three daughters were 18, 14, and 12 years old. Mrs. Doyle contends that she was induced by the railroad company to take charge of the boarding house at Woodstock near which place the company had a large force of men at work. Mrs. Doyle says that she and the girls cooked and that her three boys worked for the railroad. She contends that the Woodstock station was built directly in the path of where numerous snow slides had occurred, but of this fact,

C. W. Erdlen photo,
from Francis Rizzari Collection.

A gang of snow shovelers clearing the lower level of track of snow and debris brought down by the Woodstock slide of March 10, 1884.

C. W. Edrlen photo,
from H. L. Curtiss Collection.

South Park engine and refrigerator car used to carry the workmen from Pitkin to the Woodstock snowslide.

she alleges, she was kept in ignorance. The slide, which occurred March 10, 1884, swept all the Woodstock buildings away, killing all her family and others. Mrs. Doyle was carried down with the avalanche of snow, but was rescued sometime later, more dead than alive. She states that she depended on her children for support, and by their loss she is left without means. The aged Mother claims $5,000 for each child and $20,000 for injuries and damages to herself and personal property.

"Eighteen persons were buried in the snow, thirteen of whom were found dead. It was one of the worst disasters from snow avalanches known in the history of the state. The only person to escape made his way to Pitkin, ten miles away, to report the disaster. Those rescued alive were Mrs. Doyle, Hugh Alexander, Peter Wallpole, Walter Hoyt, and Mrs. Doyle's niece, Miss Celia Dillon. Miss Dillon was found standing among some timbers beneath the snow where she had been held for over fifteen hours. Mrs. Doyle was rescued a few hours before. The rescuing party worked for forty-eight hours, but only ten bodies were recovered, it being impossible to rescue the other three bodies until later in the spring. One of the bodies, a saloon keeper by the name of Joe Royegno, was not found until the following June. Others killed were George Alexander, Michael Shea, Jasper Caswell, and James Tracy.

"The corpses were tied on hand sleds and pulled over the snow to Pitkin. It was claimed that the side of the mountain had been covered with a heavy growth of timber which would have prevented the slide, but that the railroad company had cut away practically all of this timber for tie and building purposes thus making the deadly avalanche possible".

The result of this lawsuit is not known to the author. As far as is known the settlement of Woodstock was never rebuilt. Old employees' timetables indicate that the spur was later extended to a length of 947 feet and that the place retained the name of Woodstock. Union Pacific records show that a new two-room bunk house and a hand car shed were built there. In August, 1889, a new water tank, constructed in a square shape, was built a half mile west. Although this new tank was located on Williams Pass Creek, it was generally referred to as Tunnel Gulch Tank. Mr. Curtiss relates that in walking along the grade near Woodstock switch, a close observer will see six stone blocks and an old water pipe with water still running from it; that is where the old Woodstock tank was located before the slide.

* * * *

Relative to relations between employees and management in the early days, the following item was found in the Railway Review of August 14, 1880.

"The Denver South Park & Pacific has adopted a novel method of adjusting questions which have grown out of accidents to railway employees. The Directors have passed resolutions which provide that if employees agree that they will not join or act in concert with any Brotherhood of Engineers, Firemen, Conductors, or other trade unions, and if they also relieve the company from pecuniary liability for injuries inflicted by accidents, the company will agree in case any Conductor, Brakeman, Engineer, Fireman, Yard Master, or Switchman becomes sick or disabled by accidents while in discharge of his duties, to furnish medical and surgical aid, to give one-half pay during sickness, and to pay $1,000 to the legal representative of the injured, in case of death".

* * * *

All dispatching of trains through-out the entire South Park system was handled by telegraph. Messages were also handled for the public. Concerning this service, we find the following advertisement in the Rocky Mountain News of October 6, 1880:

THE DENVER, SOUTH PARK
&
PACIFIC
TELEGRAPH
OFFICES.

358 Fifteenth Street., Evans Block.
Union Depot, foot of 16th Street.
and corner Fourth and Lawrence.

Messages for all points on the line of the Denver South Park & Pacific Railroad promptly transmitted and delivered. Offices in:

Leadville, Buena Vista,
Heywood Springs,
Breckenridge,
Alpine and Pitkin.

A few days later, on October 23rd, the same paper stated that the telegraph line had been completed to Gunnison on October 22nd. Notice of completion of the telegraph lines was published in the Railway Age of November 11, 1880, as follows:

"The South Park now has two telegraph wires from Denver to Buena Vista, one to Leadville, one to Morrison, and a line to Gunnison".

* * * *

While type was being set for this book, the following item about the South Park's Pullman cars (described on page 321) was located by J. W. Maxwell in the National Carbuilder of January, 1880:

"The interior decoration and finish are original in design . . . There is an entire absence of gilding, which enhances the effect of the exquisite inlay work in leaves and flowers, outlined after the Queen Anne style. The ceiling is in figured white oak, beautifully paneled and decorated with vines and flower pieces, this being one of the noted improvements in headlinings introduced by the Pullman Company. Glass of windows, 22"x24" and 9"x24"; dome lights, 5"x24".

"At one end of the car are the ladies toilet, a large linen closet, and Baker heater; and at the other end, the gentlemen's lavatroy and saloon. The toilet conveniences are great improvements upon former plans, and the heater has an automatic attachment which prevents any liability to explode. Narrow mirrors occupy the spaces between the windows, the sections are richly upholstered in Buceau plush, and the carpets and curtains harmonize with their surroundings. The upper berths have steel safety cords, and a newly-invented clothes rack. Each car is lighted with five Hicks and Smith's two-light hurricane lamps, suspended from the ceiling.

"The outside is painted in the usual chocolate color, relieved with gilt designs of the Queen Anne style. The windows are polished French plate glass. Everything pertaining to the cars, even the silvering of the mirrors and the etching of the ornamental glass, is the product of the Pullman shops."

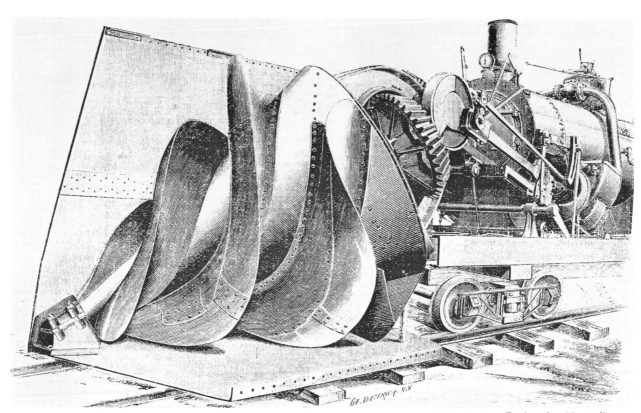

Engineering News diagram,
from M. C. Poor Collection.

A general view of the mechanism of the Jull Centrifigal Snow Excavator, with two sides of the plow-shell removed.

W. H. Jackson photo,
from H. O. Brayer Collection.

The Jull plow, after stalling in a cut above Hancock.

CHAPTER XIX

THE COMPETITIVE SNOWPLOW TRIALS AT HANCOCK

One of the great high lights in early South Park history was the battle between the machines of two rival snowplow builders, on the east slope of Alpine Pass in the spring of 1890. The railroad had experienced some very severe snowstorms that winter on both Boreas and Alpine Passes. Numerous heavy snowslides had occurred, often exceeding 20 feet in depth along the tracks. These slides brought down snow, rocks, timber, and earth, and since the snow was extremely compact, it was very difficult to handle. Also, due to many springs located on the sides of the mountains along the track, solid blue ice would form over the rails. Their one rotary snowplow, which the Union Pacific had purchased in 1888,[1] finally succeeeded in getting through some sections of the line with no great delay except where rocks and trees were brought down along with the slides, and were buried in the mass of snow. On several occasions the rotary blades were badly damaged on coming into contact with these obstacles. It had been a very difficult matter to keep the lines open that winter with only one plow. Finally, in view of all the difficulties, a new type plow with a rotary screw, or worm type excavator, which had recently been perfected by Mr. Orange Jull, of The Jull Manufacturing Company, was ordered *on trial*, to be tried out against the rotary on the Gunnison Division.

In contrast to the usual blades of a rotary snowplow, the Jull plow or Centrifugal Snow Excavator, as it was sometimes called, consisted of an immense, oblique, or cone-shaped auger. Power for this gimlet-pointed screw, or auger, was furnished by an 800-horsepower horizontal boiler mounted on a heavy frame and trucks similar to those on the rotary plow. In operation, this auger revolved at a speed of from 300 to 500 or more revolutions per minute; the power being transmitted through an ingenious set of bevel gears. The purpose of this auger, which always rotated in the same direction, was to bore into the snowdrift and draw the snow up into the machine as chips are drawn from a hole by a revolving auger bit. The discharging apparatus, which was able to throw the snow either to the right or left,

was similar to the rotary plow. The auger itself, excluding any of the surrounding housing and other mechanism, weighed about six tons. The total weight of all the mechanism on the front trucks was approximately twenty tons. This enormous weight projected fifteen feet and four inches in front of the boiler frame at the front trucks. The over-all length of the plow was fifty feet, and the whole machine weighed some 65 tons. An ordinary locomotive tender, carrying coal and water, was attached behind the plow. The complete unit was then supposed to be pushed at a speed of about eight miles per hour through the snowdrifts by a group of from two to four locomotives in the usual manner. This Jull Plow was built by The Rogers Locomotive Works at Paterson, N. J., for the Jull Co.[1]

According to reports the Jull excavator had successfully removed some bad snow blockades in the east; however, the Union Pacific management wanted to try it out on one of their mountain divisions to see for themselves just what it could do. The Alpine Pass line between St. Elmo and the east portal had been blockaded by snow for over three months. In view of the particularly steep grades, sharp curves, and deep snows here, it was decided that this particular section of the South Park line would be an excellent place to hold the trials.

The rotary needed no such test in order to demonstrate its merits. This type of machine had been in use by various railroads for some time and had successfully demonstrated its capacity to remove snow under many severe conditions. Nevertheless, many peculiar difficulties would be encountered in this forthcoming trial, the details of which were considered to be of much interest. Advertisements were sent out by the Jull Company, requesting all railroad officials who were interested in these competitive trials to be on hand to witness the results. Accordingly, representatives of various railroads were sent for that purpose. Over fifty photographs of these two machines in action were taken by the famous William Henry Jackson, official Union Pacific photographer at that time. Among the more important Union Pacific officials present were Mr. J. B.

1. Railway Review, May 24, 1890. (See Roster for further details.)

1. Railway Review, May 24, 1890.

The South Park rotary below Hancock on April 17, 1890.

W. H. Jackson photo,
from Morris W. Abbott Collection.

Gilchrist, Assistant Superintendent, and Mr. M. F. Egan, Master Mechanic of the Colorado Division.

The Jull excavator arrived in Denver during the latter part of March, 1890. Upon its arrival, the Union Pacific, under the supervision of Mr. Jull, took every precaution to put the excavator in good operating order. After being assembled and put in first class mechanical condition, the front-end mechanism was run for several days in order to limber it up and also to detect any flaws that might be present.

Meanwhile, the South Park's rotary was very busy on the high line. According to the Railroad Gazette of May 23, 1890, 22 snowslides had occurred between Como and Leadville, bringing snow, rocks, timber and earth down on the line. In attempting to clear this blockade, the rotary's blades suffered a great deal of damage due to rocks being embedded in the snow. At one time, above Breckenridge, the rotary hit a large blockade of rock buried in a mass of snow, causing four blades to be torn off, besides doing considerable damage to the plow's machinery in general. In view of this damage to the unit, it was returned to the Denver shops with orders to overhaul it as quickly as possible. The plow was partially repaired and on its way back to the mountains within 31 hours. In view of the urgent need for the rotary to keep the high line open, the broken blades were not replaced, and the rotary was returned to service on Boreas Pass and in Tenmile Canon without them. According to Leslie Brothers, the rotary's builders, the plow was still in this condition when ordered to St. Elmo to enter the competitive trials against the Jull plow.

Because of the minimum amount of traffic along the line on Sunday, it was decided to take the Jull plow to the scene of the forthcoming trials on Sunday, April 13, 1890. Accordingly, at 5:00 a.m. on this date, the contingent left Denver for St. Elmo.[1] Mr. Nasmith, a Union Pacific machinist, was in charge of the Jull excavator. Considerable difficulty was experienced in getting the Jull machine to the scene of action. The enormous weight of the auger mechanism caused the bearings of the front wheel trucks to heat up, forcing them to proceed at a very slow pace. The great amount of weight bent and spread the rails at several places, causing derailments; also, it broke the stringers on two bridges while en route. On one occasion, on Monday, the machine jumped the track and spread the rails, causing so much damage that it required seven hours to rerail the behemoth and repair the track. This caused a tie-up of regular traffic which necessitated the transferring of passengers from one train to another in order that they might continue their journey. The projecting weight of this overhanging auger unit also developed a swaying and swinging motion at times, and extreme care had to be taken while negotiating some of the

1. Railway Review, May 24, 1890.

South Park's 20 and 24 degree curves, to prevent the plow from derailing itself.

The Jull crew finally reached St. Elmo on Tuesday night. The rotary had arrived the previous day. On Wednesday morning three special trains arrived bringing Union Pacific officials, representatives of other railroads, interested members of the press, and William H. Jackson. With plenty of snowplowing to be done, two plows to do the work, and a clear day ahead, all was in readiness to get under way with the trials. An account of the three-day battle that followed between the two competitive plows is found in the Railway Review of May 24, 1890, which we quote, in part:

"At 8:00 a.m. on Wednesday, April 16, 1890, four South Park consolidation engines pushed the Jull excavator out of St. Elmo. When the Mary Murphy Mine was reached a halt was made for the purpose of enabling Mr. Jull to have the ice-cutters on his machine readjusted as a result of Monday's wreck. After this, a start was made for the snow a short distance above the mine. The first snow encountered was about three feet deep on one rail and about thirteen inches on the other. Considerable ice was found over the rails under the snow, and in order to give the excavator every chance, the Division Road Master had a gang of shovellers remove the snow off one rail and pick the ice out of the flange to prevent the Jull from being derailed. The excavator was then moved into the snow with its auger turning about 400 revolutions per minute. It had only advanced a few feet when pilot Nasmith whistled for brakes and the excavator was found to be off the track. A gang of men jacked it back on the rails after which it was backed out and the rails shovelled off clean, up to the edge of the snow, and another start was made with similar results. The Jull plow was again rerailed and a third start was made with no better results. The officials in charge then ordered the Jull machine to be retired and the rotary brought up from St. Elmo.

"On its arrival the ice cutter and flanger were dropped into working position and it proceeded about 100 yards to a point where the officials were standing. The rotary was then stopped and backed out in order that the gentlemen present might observe the condition of the track at that point. It was found that the rotary had cut its way through one to three inches of solid ice over the top of the rails under the snow. The party then boarded the engine and the rotary, and another start was made through snow and ice from two to five feet deep. A run of two and one-half miles was then made in thirteen minutes. When light snow was reached again, the officials in charge ordered a halt and the rotary was retired in order to give the Jull plow another trial in this light snow.

"After lunch the excavator was brought out. Its flanger was chained down as an extra precaution and a start was made. Although the snow was but fifteen inches deep, with very little ice on the rails at this point, the auger had to be run at a high rate of speed to keep it from choking up. Before fifty feet of track had been cleared the excavator left the rails again, and then followed a repetition of the Jull's performance that morning. The excavator had to be rerailed nine times, during which time it had succeeded in clearing about 300 feet of track. This occupied from 1:30 p.m. until 8:40 p.m. The officials decided during the evening to order the rotary out the next morning to open the line up the side of the mountain to a point beyond Hancock where continuous deep snow was to be found in order that the Jull machine might be tried out in deep snow without a continuation of the tedious delays experienced on the first day.

"Thursday morning the rotary left St. Elmo about 9:00 a.m.,

355

The South Park's rotary gets under way from Hancock, during the snowplow trials, on April 18, 1890.

W. H. Jackson photo,
from M. C. Poor Collection.

with a special train following with the officials on board. When the rotary arrived at the point where the excavator had quit the night previous, a start was made with two engines pushing. On this run snow was encountered at an average depth of from three to four feet through which the rotary proceeded at a speed of about eight miles per hour. A halt was then called for the purpose of affording the gentlemen present an opportunity of examining the track. Leaving Hancock, the line is very steep and crooked. Just beyond the Hancock water tank, snow seven feet deep was encountered on a 24 degree curve on which the rotary left the rails. On examination it was found that a blanket had been dropped on the track in a cut, saturated with water from nearby springs, and frozen solid to the rail and ground. The safety bolts of the ice cutter were sheared off. This was not discovered until the plow had left the rails a second time. After replacing the ice cutter, another start was made. The plow then went through the cut and around the curve to a point where the snow had decreased from five feet to about eighteen inches within a distance of 200 feet. The rotary was then retired in order that the Jull might be put in again the next morning.

"Meantime, the rotary opened the side tracks in the Hancock yard, which had been under snow for three or four months. Here the snow was thrown across the main track in order to show that it could be thrown to a sufficient distance to clear one or more tracks. The snow was from three to five feet deep and the rails covered with ice. The rotary ran through this at about six miles per hour. When one-half the track had been cleared the mechanism was reversed to throw the snow to the left. Although the performance of the rotary on this occasion was very fine, Mr. Egan stated that he did not think it comparable with the work they had experienced with the same machine in Tenmile Canon between Dickey and Leadville the previous month.

"Mr. A. L. Humphrey, Master Mechanic of the Colorado Midland, stated that the performance of the rotary at Hancock was no more than that which their rotary had been doing all winter on his line. In fact the Midland's plow had been operating three winters without ever having been disabled and had only been derailed once, and that was when it ran over a replacing frog which had not been taken off the rail after a derailed freight car had been put back on the track. Mr. Leeman of the Denver & Rio Grande stated that his road's plow had not been derailed or disabled during the entire winter's work.

"Friday morning, April 18th, the Jull plow was ordered out again to work in the deep snow between Hancock and Alpine Tunnel. The track was examined at the point where the rotary had retired the previous day, and found to be in good condition. With four locomotives pushing and pilot Nasmith aboard, the excavator was put to work with the auger revolving about 500 revolutions per minute and throwing the snow to the left. The snow rolled up in front of the screw and over the sides until the machine stalled and left the rails. Mr. Jull came forward and said that there was no use in trying any more to make the excavator throw the snow to the left and requested that the machine be reversed. This necessitated the loosening of the gate from its support on the front of the machine and it was removed down onto the snow and then elevated back into position. This heavy gate required twelve men to handle it and occupied an hour and twenty minutes to complete the job. The Jull was then put back into operation, but after about two and one-half hours of futile efforts to make it work and to keep it on the track at the same time, Mr. Jull said that there was no use trying any more to make it work, and requested that the machine be returned to Denver.

"The rotary was then put in at this point and ordered to continue on up to the tunnel if possible. The machine went through from four to eight feet of snow at a speed of about four miles per hour. At various points in its progress the plow was stopped and backed out in order that those interested might examine the results. This is a very bad piece of road, as there are many springs in the mountain sides which caused ice to form on the track. It was found that there was from two to five inches of solid blue ice over the top of the rails. This particular section of the South Park had been blockaded for more than eleven weeks, and a succession of thaws and storms had settled and packed the snow very solidly. The stream of ice and snow thrown out by the rotary along this section of the line was so solid that it broke off small limbs and tops of trees. The rotary completed the job by removing the snow blockade clear through to the east portal of Alpine Tunnel. This concluded the snowplow trials.

"The party then returned to St. Elmo and the officials and their special train left immediately for Denver. The Jull excavator followed soon afterward in charge of Trainmaster Saunders and Roadmaster Merriam with orders to proceed very cautiously to guard against derailment or other troubles. Notwithstanding all the precautions taken, the Jull machine left the rails near the vicinity of Nathrop and turned over on its side in a small ditch. When the official party arrived at Como a message was awaiting Assistant Superintendent Gilchrist, informing him of the derailment of the excavator. This news necessitated the return of Messrs. Gilchrist and Egan to the scene of the accident to facilitate the getting of the Jull machine out of the ditch and back on the rails again."

After reading the Railway Review's article describing the three-day trials between the two plows, one can observe that the author of the article was somewhat prejudiced against the Jull machine, and that undoubtedly he was slightly influenced by Mr. Leslie, the builder of the rotary plow. The following week, the Railroad Gazette printed a letter from the Jull Company refuting a great many of the statements made in the Review's article. They attempted to defend some of the auger plow's inabilities to successfully break the snow blockades encountered on Alpine Pass; while at the same time, they admitted that part of the cause for so many derailments was due to too rigid a design of certain parts of the excavator for negotiating this particular type of mountain railroad. They also criticized the poor construction and inequalities of the South Park's track. Further comments were also carried by the Gazette which stated in part:

"In the tryout, the Jull, or auger machine, went to work between Hancock and the tunnel with the auger turning 500 revolutions per minute in snow four to eight feet deep. This part of the line up to Alpine Tunnel had been blocked for eleven weeks, and there was from two to five inches of solid ice, from the springs, on the rails and ties. A succession of thaws and storms had settled and packed the snow very solidly. Here the Jull machine cut out a stream of snow, ice, rocks, etc., with such force as to break the limbs and tops off near by trees.

"The South Park's rotary had to be stopped frequently to allow firemen to get up enough steam to keep the blades turning. The rotary's boiler was too small. Sometimes the boiler of the locomotive just behind the plow was connected to the boiler of the rotary in an effort to keep up enough steam to keep the blades rotating. Another one of the troubles they had with the rotary was derailment, due to ice, etc., on the rails. On one trip the plow was derailed four times in one afternoon and the tender of the plow jumped the track twice.

W. H. Jackson photo,
from M. C. Poor Collection.

A view west of Hancock, showing where Mr. Jull acknowledged failure of his plow, April 18, 1890.

W. H. Jackson photo,
from H. O. Brayer Collection.

A head-on view of the Jull plow on Alpine Pass above Hancock.

The average speed of the rotary was from four to ten miles per hour. On another trip they hit two hand shovels that had been left on the track. The shovels were cut to pieces and thrown 150 feet off the side of the right of way".

The Gazette also reproduced one of Mr. Jackson's photographs showing the Jull excavator boring through seven feet of hard snow and throwing it over 200 feet in the clear to the right of the machine. Nevertheless, the Jull plow was rejected by the Union Pacific officials for mechanical reasons and returned to its manufacturers.

Through the courtesy of Mr. Mel Langhans, we have another version of this event as seen through the eyes of Cy Warman, who tells the story in his book, "Tales of an Engineer," published in 1896. Warman's story was published in McClure's Magazine for June, 1896. Warman's tale of what took place during these trials differs slightly in some places from the previous story, but it has an added human element about it that makes his story extremely interesting. We quote:

"Once at Alpine Pass, on a branch of the Union Pacific, I saw one of their snow plows working in six feet of snow that had been there for six months, and was so hard that men walked over it without snowshoes. It was about the middle of April in 1890; the weather was almost warm at mid-day, but freezing at night. A number of railroad and newspaper men had gone up there, 11,000 ft. above sea-level to witness a battle between two rival snowplows or excavators. The trial was an exciting one, and lasted three days. Master Mechanic Egan, whose guest I was, was director general, and a very impartial director, I thought. The two machines were very similar in appearance; but instead of a wheel with knives on it called a rotary, one had a great 'auger' in front, the purpose of which was to bore into the snow drift and draw the snow into the machine, as the chips are drawn from an auger hole by the revolving of the screw. The discharging apparatus was similar in the two plows, i.e., the snow was thrown out in a stream from one side.

"There was a formidable array of rolling stock on the two sidings at the foot of the mountain at Hancock, where we had our railway car and where we stayed nights. On one side-track, stands one of the plows, with three engines behind her; on another, the other plow with three engines behind her. You could tell the men of one from those of the other, for, the two armies dwelt apart.

"It was perfectly natural for the men on the different machines to be loyal to their respective employers, and a little bit jealous of the rival crew; but I was surprised to see how quickly that feeling extended to the crews of the half-dozen locomotives, all working for the same railroad company, and in no way interested in the outcome.

"On the morning of the first day of the trial, when the six engines came down the track from the coal yards, a switchman stood at the three-throw switch, and gave a locomotive to each of the two machines alternately. They all knew where they belonged, and they kept the same place, each of them, until the battle was over.

"There was no betting, but there was a distinct 'favorite' from the start; and when the engines were all hooked up, the men on the favorite, began good naturedly enough, to josh the other crew.

"Mr. Egan decided that one of the plows should go forward; and when it stuck, stalled, or stopped, for any reason, it should at once back down, take the siding and give the other plow a chance.

"It was nearly noon when the railway officers and pencil-pushers climbed to the storm deck of the first plow, and the commander gave the signal to start. The whistle 'off-brakes' was answered by the six locomotives and the little engine that brought up the rear with the special train. The hungry machine gathered up the light drifts which we encountered in the first few miles, and breathed them out over the tops of the telegraph poles. At a very sharp curve where there was a deep drift, the snowplow left the track, and we were forced to stop and back out. The engineers looked sullen as they were forced to back down to let the other crew pass, and the fresh crew laughed at them. The snow was lighter now so that instead of boring into it, the second plow only pushed it and piled up the snow in front of her until the whole house was buried, when she choked up and lay down. Now the frowns were transferred to the faces of the second crew and the smiles to the other.

"For two days we see-sawed in this way, and every hour the men grew more sullen. The mad locomotives seemed to enter into the spirit of the fight; at least, it was easy to imagine that they did, as they snorted, puffed, and panted in the great drifts. It was a beautiful sight to see them, each sending an endless stream of black smoke to the heavens and to hear them scream to one another when about to stall, and to note with what reluctance they returned to the side track.

"In the little town of Hancock at the foot of the hill, the rival crews camped at separate boarding houses. This was fortunate, for it would have not been safe for them to live together. Even the enginemen, by the end of the second day, were hardly on speaking terms. Bob Stoute said that somebody had remarked that old number 265, a Rhode Island consolidation, wouldn't make steam enough to ring the bell. He did not know who had said it, but he did know that he could lick him. After supper that evening when the 'scrappy' engineer came out of the Red Wood Saloon, he broadened the statement so as to include any 'rotary man' on the job, see?

"When we went into the field on the morning of the third day, not more than two miles of snow remained between Hancock and Atlantic, the east portal of the tunnel, where the race would end. All the forenoon the engines steamed and snorted, and banged away at the great mass of snow, that grew deeper and harder as we climbed toward Alpine. The track was so crooked that the plows were off the rails half the time, so that when we stopped for noon lunch, we had made less than one mile.

"The least promising of the two machines, the auger plow, was the first out after lunch, and as the snow was harder up here, she did fair to win great credit. She rounded the last of the sharp curves that had given so much trouble, successfully. But as the snow grew deeper she smothered, choked up and stalled. Then even her friends had to admit that, 'she was not quite right', and the engine men looked blacker than ever, as they backed down and took the siding.

"Up came the rival rotary, every engine blowing off steam, the three fireman at the furnace doors, the engineers smiling and eager for the fray. As they turned into the tangent where the other had stalled, the leading locomotive screamed 'off-brakes', and every throttle was pulled wide open. Down went the reverse levers, until every locomotive was working at her full capacity. While waiting in the siding, the engineers had screwed down their pops, or relief valves, so that each of the engines carried about twenty pounds more steam than usual. There were no drifts now, but the hard snow lay level and six feet deep. The track was as good as straight, just one long curve; and the plow would hit the timber line at the mouth of the tunnel. The right of way here lay along the side of the mountain through a heavy growth of pine. The snow was granulated, and consequently was very heavy. By the time they had gone 100 yards, a great stream of snow was flowing

The rotary churning its way through a cut below Atlantic, with three inches of ice on the rails.

W. H. Jackson photo,
from M. C. Poor Collection.

from the spout of the rotary plow out over the telegraph wires, over the tops of the tall spruce and pines, crashing down through their branches until the white beneath them was covered with the green carpet of tree-twigs. On and up the laboring locomotives pushed the plow. Higher and higher rose the black smoke; and when the smoke and snow came between the spectators and the sun, which was just then sinking behind the great mountain, the effect was marvelously beautiful. Still,

on they went through the stainless waste not stopped nor stalled until the rotary had touched the edge of the tunnel snow shed.

"The foreman gave the signal to back up; and with faces wreathed in smiles, and with their machines covered with cinders, snow, and glory, the little army drifted back down the mountain side to Hancock. The three days fight was at an end, and the rotary was the victor."

At this point Mr. Jull acknowledged failure of his machine to throw snow to the left, after the rotary had opened the line to this point.

W. H. Jackson photo,
from E. J. Haley Collection.

Four engines shoving the rotary up the east slope of **Alpine Pass**, above **Chalk Creek Canon**. The three rear engines are
D.L.&G. 263, 207, and 261.

W. H. Jackson photo,
from E. J. Haley Collection.

The South Park's rotary arrives at Atlantic siding, near the east portal of Alpine Tunnel, after clearing the line from Hancock.

CHAPTER XX

PERSONAL REMINISCENCES

In commenting on the operation of the South Park and the men who ran it, it seems appropriate to open this section of our story by quoting a paragraph from H. W. Stevens' "Adventure on the High Iron," as published in the October, 1946, Esquire Magazine. Mr. Stevens writes:

"When old timers gather in the round house, the caboose, or even in the front office, the air grows thick with yarns which might hint at Paul Bunyan to an outsider. But these are no tall tales—railroading's past has high adventure and glamour in plenty without need of embroidery. And bright in the legends of the rails are the men who took 'er round the mountains and lived to tell about it. In the Rockies and the Appalachians, and in many an unnamed sawtooth range in the West and South, they fought gravity and worse with only the half-support of their primitive locomotives and brakes. But they were a tough breed, and kept a hand on the throttle always, lest Death reach out for it. For the mountain railroaders, danger lurked at every turn and frowning canon slope. It could be death on the downgrade with runaway cars pushing violently from behind, or death from the boulders hurtling down from above. It could come on some flaming trestle, or in the white rumble of an avalanche. It could come when a dog-tired dispatcher slipped up on orders, and a train plunging downhill met head-on with one panting up the grade."

As to the men who ran the South Park, Roy Morton, ex-brakeman who worked on the western end between Buena Vista and Gunnison, very aptly covers the subject by stating:

"It was a wooden railroad operated by iron men."

And from the many tales that have been recorded and told by such men as Charlie Squires, Thomas St. John, Andy Nelson, Billy Cairns, Ed Haight, Roy Morton, William Wendell, Horace L. Curtiss, William Coogen, Clarence "Silver Tip" Adams, and others, it must be fairly conclusive that there were no "pansies" on the payroll; a fellow had to be able to take it standing up. Charlie Squires worked for the road during the 90's when it was known as the Denver Leadville & Gunnison. He was the company's lineman whose responsibility it was to keep the telegraph lines and the stations "in the clear."

In response to some inquiries, Charlie Squires replied:

"I was a division lineman on the Denver Leadville & Gunnison from February, 1896, until November, 1898. When I went with the road, Si Rainey was Superintendent with headquarters at Como. I became fairly well acquainted with Mr. Rainey and slept in his private car, No. 025, many times,

both over at Gunnison and up at Alpine Tunnel. I remember working with him one night at Tenmile Canon just above the section house at Curtin, as we both handled a No. 2 shovel fighting a snow slide sixty feet deep. Just beyond, on about 500 feet of clear track was a helper engine and back of that engine was another slide, 40 feet deep. These two slides were full of trees and rocks and after coming down they froze to such an extent that the rotary was unable to handle them. Everybody manned a pick and shovel almost continuously for three days and nights.

"Among others whom I recall were Patrick 'Curley' Colligan, 'Buddy' Schwartz, John Olson, Thomas St. John, and Bert Lintz. Bert Lintz worked for my good friend Al Litchenheld, who was agent at Como. Bert Lintz's brother, who now lives in Oakland, California, ran an engine there during the late '90's and after the turn of the century. Tommy St. John lives in Denver today and must be well along in years himself; I am over 75 and I think Tommy was older than I.

"I certainly loved that old South Park railroad, but it took a real man to hold down a job there, whatever department he was in, if he filled it faithfully. I have never heard it described as well as when you wrote, 'It was a wooden railroad run by iron men'. I know that I went through some very strenuous experiences, many of them aside from what would ordinarily be considered my duty. I have said many times that in my fifty odd years of railroading, I never saw a bunch of men on a railroad that were more like a big family; they never thought such things as 'I'm the engineer', or 'I'm the conductor', or 'Who are you to argue with the Superintentent or Dispatcher?'. There was no aristocracy on the old South Park—where I made the least money, but enjoyed my fellow employees more than any other place I ever worked".

The men previously mentioned include only a few of the old timers who made names for themselves running the railroad, driving engines, dispatching trains, handling train orders, and fulfilling many other miscellaneous duties required to keep traffic moving over the mountains to Leadville and Gunnison. There were many others such as Pat Gibbony, wrecking boss during the '90's; Bert Whitney; Walt Parlins; William A. Brown, local griever for the Brotherhood of Locomotive Engineers on the South Park for many years and who put in plenty of time running engine 7 up and down Clear Creek; Colin Moore; Joe Plunkett; S. L. "Si" Rainey, General Superintendent during the '90's; Davey Bones; A. A. "Brownie" Anderson; Al Latham; Pete Newberry; Ed Conahan; Chauncey Burnsides; Ted Williams; Dale Tomkins; Jim Burns; Billy Thomas; Jerry Regan; Bill Galligher; Andy Anderson; Billy Kerns; George Mason; Fred Williams; Ed Brady; Joe Fortney; Lou Fowler; Billy Westall; Dad Martinis; Mike Flavin;

Tom Flavin; M. S. Goodale; Ed "Rastus" Haight; Mike Burke; Henry F. Kirchner; Joe Delaney; Ed Haskins, who was later Master Mechanic for the Rio Grande at Salida; James L. Morton, (Roy Morton's father) who worked as agent, operator, and dispatcher at various times at Como, Gunnison, Leadville, Forks Creek, Black Hawk and Central City; George H. Colson, early telegraph operator at Alpine Tunnel station; Tony Schmitz; John Rapelje and J. P. Schimerhorn, who were roadmasters during the '80's. Later A. "Gus" Melin, a very colorful and efficient roadmaster, took up where these roadmasters left off. There was M. V. Egan, shop foreman at Como around 1886 and later Division Master Mechanic at Denver; C. J. Shaughnessy, Road Foreman of Engines; John F. Farthing and Robert Terrill, the engineer and fireman who made the last passenger run to Leadville; Roy Hight; Billy Maas, veteran conductor on the Clear Creek Division; Fred Maas; Bob Taylor; C. C. Rogers; and Squire Thorne, another Clear Creek veteran. There was Al Litchenheld; Blain Markel; Wes Soper; Frank Soper; George Haines; Larry Colligan; Jimmy Dooner; and Stanley Andrews. Old timers tell that Andrews, who was assigned engine 65, one with deer horns mounted on the headlight, always kept a black tailored broadcloth suit of clothes in his seat box to wear when off duty. Andrews was strong on diamonds and had a great way with the ladies.

There were many more of these men—men who fired, ran engines, twisted down brake wheels on the icy tops of box cars as the flanges squealed around the curves rolling down Boreas and Alpine Passes, punched tickets, kept the track in repair, and kept rolling stock moving; in other words men who kept the old pike going in the picturesque days before efficiency caught up with the railroads.

In order to give the reader some conception of how the South Park was operated and how these men performed their duties at times when the going really got tough, the writer is pleased to include the following "true tales" in this book. They are stories of men who worked on the South Park railroad during the days of diamond stacks, straight air, oil headlights, link and pin couplers, open platform coaches, and "armstrong" stokers. As one old timer put it, it was railroading in the raw with no holds barred, flying switches, reckless hoggers, and no brakes. The track ran two ways—either up hill or down—trains were either stalled or running away. A portion of these articles are written by men yet living; others have gone on to the land where the "lights are always green". All their stories have been reported just as they were written.

⁕   ⁕   ⁕   ⁕

Several of the following stories and poems were written especially for this book by Charlie Squires.

CONCEALED WIRING ALONG THE OLD SOUTH PARK

By Charlie Squires

"During the summer of 1897, while I was employed as a division lineman on the old South Park line in Colorado, I received a trouble report one day from the wire chief, stating that all the wires between Grant and Jefferson were grounded and to get after the trouble quick. I left on train No. 1 for Grant. At that place I got up in the engine and stood in the gangway in order to watch the wires as we went up Kenosha Pass. Engineer Latham kidded me about thinking that I could see anything wrong with the line while engine 112 was literally jumping around those sharp curves, but there are tricks in all trades, and, in a large percentage of cases of ordinary trouble, I could locate the cause from the engine. But this was not that kind of trouble. I could not see a thing wrong with the line. I thought perhaps that I had been given the wrong location, so I stayed on the engine to Como. On entering the Dispatcher's office, I was informed right away that they still had no clear wire. Well, I covered that territory back and forth on freight trains all afternoon without any success.

"As the location included both sides of the pass I was unable to use my velocipede to any advantage, and I fully expected to find the cause of the trouble any minute. Things were getting pretty warm around the Dispatcher's office, but I want to say that they acted very nice about it. They ran a crew out from Denver the next morning at three o'clock, with orders to wait at Jefferson until I told them it was light enough for me to see the line, and to stop and let me examine it whenever I wished to. Where the line would cut across a hill, I would get off and walk under it until the line reached the track again, where the train would be waiting for me. In spite of our combined efforts, we arrived at Grant with the line still tied up.

"I was getting pretty much bothered by this time, so I released the train crew and started the fifteen mile climb, walking right under or beside that pole line all the way up over Kenosha Pass and down into South Park. If there was a pole that looked suspicious, I climbed to the top and inspected it, and there were several that had to be climbed. I finally reached a point just about ten poles east of the Jefferson depot, where it seemed as though I could not go another step, when the top of a pole came in line with the sun and I saw something that glistened. In spite of my exhausted condition, I put on my climbers and went up that pole in record time, where I found the trouble. Some one had taken a fine piece of new copper wire and made a few turns on the far wire, then down the pin and along on top of the cross-arm, wrapping it around all the wires, including the ground or lightning wire. This shorted and grounded all the wires.

"I was pretty mad and reported that some one had purposely done this job. A short time later I was called into the Denver office by the Superintendent of Telegraph, who sent me in to interview the Chief Special Agent. On getting my report, he went to the general store in Jefferson and inquired for some of the same kind of copper wire that I had given him. He found out that a young boy, who lived there in Jefferson, had bought some of this same wire a few days before. The Special Agent then called at the boy's home, where he found the young lad down with typhoid fever. He questioned him and finally the boy broke down and confessed that he had connected the wires to see if he would get a 'shock of electricity'.

"I was asked if I could swear from the way I found it, that it was put on with malicious intent. I replied that I couldn't do that, and this ended the case. I am glad that I wasn't asked that question on the day that I found the trouble. That boy certainly was good at concealing a wire."

A TIMBER FIRE ON BOREAS
By Charlie Squires

"One day during the summer of 1896, I was at Como when I was informed by the Chief Dispatcher that both the message wire and the dispatcher's wire were open west of Boreas Pass and that there was a fire on the west side of the mountain. So I got my velocipede out and took it apart ready for loading at about where the baggage car would stop on the next westbound train. I also took along about 500 feet of line wire and my tool grip.

"I unloaded at Boreas station, and after assembling my car and tools, had a talk with Wes Soper, the agent, who told me that there was a pretty big fire a couple of miles below, and which he hoped wouldn't get any closer to the snow shed at Boreas. I got astride my three-wheeled 'buggy,' got hold of the brake and started off down the hill. About two and one-half miles down, the air became so filled with smoke and fine ashes that I could hardly see or breathe. The timber was a little thin along the track at this point, but the fire had crossed over the track and had set some stumps to burning on both sides.

"There was one thing that struck me as odd, and that was the fact that a lot of squirrels and rabbits, along with many other small animals I did not recognize, were running around in the open. There was also a porcupine about eighteen inches long with his quills standing out just like a pin cushion, which, by the way, was the only porcupine I ever saw. The animals did not seem to pay very much attention to each other, and very little to me. I suppose they were pretty badly frightened after having been driven out of the woods by the fire.

"I certainly had a time making temporary repairs. I went back up the hill a ways and cut some short poles that I could handle alone. Some of these I lashed to old stumps and others I propped up between some big rocks, and then piled more rocks around them. At last I got them standing strong enough to hold my weight. I finally got the wires back on the poles and in working order again. By this time it was getting late in the afternoon, and as I was too tired to push that 'buggy' up to the top of the hill so that I could coast down to Como, I just drifted down the west side of the mountain and spent the night at Dickey with my good friend John Mars, the agent. John was always glad when I showed up, as it gave him a chance for a change in cooking. I used to like to 'hash up a Mulligan stew', and that's what we had that night."

THE RUNAWAY GRAVITY CAR
By Charlie Squires

"One summer day in 1896, after I completed some repairs on the telegraph line up on Kenosha Pass, I got astride my little three-wheeled Sheffield and dropped down the east side of the hill. This section of track contained some 24 degree curves and 3% to 3¾% grades. On arriving at Hoosier siding, I found the section gang just removing their gravity car from the track in order to eat their lunch. When their car was removed from the track, the fellow who was carrying the brake stick dropped it down on the ground beside the car. The King Snipe noticed what the fellow had done and ordered him to pick it up and put it on the car where it belonged. I was thinking that it was a small matter to get so fussy about, but while were were sitting there eating our lunches he related the following story which explained why he always kept an eye on the brake stick.

"'The family living in the section house at Kenosha Pass and our family are close friends, and we visit back and forth very often. One Sunday morning last summer I loaded my wife and two children on train No. 1, tied my gravity car to the rear end, and we went up to Kenosha to spend the day. Our pleasant day passed by quickly and it was soon time to start

for home. After putting the car on the track, I placed my wife and two kids on the car, then placed the brake stick through the hole made for it, in the deck of the car just above the front wheel. I then took my position on the side of the car with the brake stick extending in front of me under my arm, so that just a little pressure would control the speed of the car. We came sailing down that steep grade from Kenosha in a hurry. You will notice that the track along here by Hoosier is nearly level for about three-quarters of a mile, which slowed us down to almost a walk. I removed the brake stick so that it would not rub the wheel and laid it on the car, behind me.

"'I was just wondering if I would have to get off and push, or if she would make it without my help, when the car began to pick up speed again. I reached back for the brake stick but *it was gone!* One of the children had dropped it off the car. I did not say anything but looked over the car for something I might be able to use for a brake stick, but there was absolutely nothing to be had. About this time my wife looked across at me and said, "John, isn't the car going pretty fast?" I was too busy thinking to try and answer her. The scenery was going by like a cyclone. Just then I had the best

Charlie Squires
1942

idea that I ever had in my whole life. I took off both my shoes and, turning them top to top, toes down, I shoved them, like a wedge, into the hole in the car deck where the brake stick belonged, pushing them down between the top of the wheel and the sill of the car. By this time the speed of the car was tremendous, and the shoes didn't seem to be doing much good. But pretty soon they began to take hold and I could feel the car begin to slow down a trifle. The car soon lost its speed and gradually slowed to a stop, much to the relief of a very frightened man.

"'My shoes were nearly gone, but they had paid for themselves many times over. I then found a piece of sapling to use as a brake stick and we resumed our trip down the hill toward home, at the slowest speed that I ever went down that grade. That is the reason why I keep an eye on the brake stick.'"

A DREAM OF THE OLD SOUTH PARK

By Charlie Squires

"I'm dreaming tonight in my memory
Of my railroading days long ago,
High in the Colorado Rockies
With their crooked track, steep grades and snow.

"Coming through the Canon from Denver,
Winding on and up Kenosha's steep grade
Where the air is so light and balmy,
'Like a new man' at once you are made.

"Leaving there, look out the left window
The South Park, far below, comes in view;
That is what I always called scenery,
One of the best, (between me and you.)

"'Cross the Park. the small town of Como,
In its background was old 'Silverheels',
This the railroad chose for headquarters
And the trains all stopped here for meals.

"Now Como was no 'City wonder',
Its people were just honest and plain,
Of course there were no automobiles
Everything had to move on the train.

"That was sure some little headquarters,
Nearly ten thousand feet in the air,
Grand, were the few days they called summer,
But the winter was 'Winter for fair'.

"Winter up on Boreas and Alpine
Were the busiest times for us all,
For the trains had to be kept moving,
The rotary always 'hitting the ball'.

"It took gritty men on those engines,
And the trainmen had their share of nerve,
For they had not the least assurance
What they'd find just around the next curve.

"There were times when their 'rights' were contested
By the great rocks that no hammer could crack;
Sometimes they'd resort to 'black powder',
Before they could clear up the track.

"I've been on the train in Platte Canon
Where the track, 'round the curve just ahead,
Was found to be buried with gravel,
With no warning or flag colored red.

"But the baggage car held lots of shovels
That were kept there for just such a time,
All took number 2's by the handle
And I spent all that night there with mine.

"I know that all hands on the South Park,
Like others, had their problems to meet
And each in his own way would face it,
Very seldom would they admit defeat.

"Just a bunch of dandy good fellows
That made you happy, just to be with.
Sometimes with your pocketbook empty,
They'd go deep in their pocket to give.

"Never a thought — 'I'm a Conductor',
Or again that 'I'm an Eagle Eye',
They knew it took all kinds of labor
To make sure that the trains rolled by.

"Now deep in that abandoned Canon,
There's a silent monument holds sway
Beside the rippling old South Platte,
But the railroad's not there today.

"It marks a spot of great sacrifice,
A passenger engine hit a slide,
'Twas there Engineer Billy Westall,
On his engine, bravely stayed and died.

"All the passengers were well shook up
As the cars in that train lost their speed,
'Twould have been a very different thing,
But for Billy Westall's deed.

"We may see, perchance, in his brave deed,
His thought of trusting lives, in his hands,
As he always lived, just so he died
A Brother true to his fellow man.

"He might have jumped from his engine there,
Leaving the train to its fate, alone,
But by staying on, he cut the speed,
Saved passengers' lives but lost his own.

"I'll never forget the South Park nor the men,
For of their deeds I have always sung,
But I guess I will have to stop here, by saying
They were a fine bunch of men to have mingled among."

MEMORIES OF THE OLD SOUTH PARK

By Charlie Squires

"I recall the two Soper brothers,
'High minded' on their jobs pounding brass.
Frank lived a high life at Alpine,
Wes with family, atop old Boreas Pass.

"A train over Alpine was put on,
I remember, in summer, each year;
Buddy Schwartz on the engine to fire,
Jimmy Dooner, the fine engineer.

"Combination baggage and smoker
Plus a coach and one engine was sent,
Brakeman Wolf and Conductor Hoffman,
Then away o'er the tunnel they went.

"They never rolled up high speed records
Like their broad gauge brothers could make,
If with Dooner, you rode the engine,
It would be about all you could take.

"One eve I was up at the tunnel,
I was to sleep at Romley below,
Twelve minutes on that three-wheeled speeder,
The exact time it took me to go.

"Steep hill 'till I got in the tunnel,
Very little straight track to be met,
If I'd left the track on a short curve,
I believe I would be going yet.

"Once a rock fell down in the Canon,
Cut a telegraph pole right in two,
Stopped all the Morse circulation,
Giving the linemen plenty to do.

"They caught me, the lineman, at South Platte,
Where at the supper table I sat,
Message said 'twas time to get going,
So I grabbed for my tools and hat.

"Then astride my car down the Canon,
In the dark on a curve I was hit,
By an engine, without a headlight,
Mussed up myself and car, quite a bit.

"On my line-up of trains, they forgot
A helper engine, in its lone flight.
'Ours was the road' each one of us thought,
Slipping down through the Canon that night.

"They smashed up my car and tore my clothes,
Left me lay on the end of the ties,
But soon I found that I was quite sound,
And persuaded myself to arise.

" 'Twas a stumbling hike through that Canon,
Made repairs with a pole, from a pine,
I have put in nights I liked better,
But the dispatcher needed that line.

"Without tools or car or light to see,
I got the wires working that night,
And I thought myself pretty lucky,
With no damage to me but the fright.

"Left Leadville one Sunday morning
On No. 2, with hopes of getting home,
But at Dickey I got a message
That the wires were dead as a stone.

"I unloaded my 'buggy' at Boreas
And followed No. 2 out of there,
Six stops in snow sheds to check the line,
But between them I rambled for fair.

"Near the loop by 'Tarryall Placer',
There I pulled some hay wire off my line,
So up that pole and back on the car
And into Como in record time.

"I was in time to reload my car,
Get a sandwich to smooth wrinkles out,
Then back on No. 2 to Denver,
And the home I was thinking about.

"While I was employed on the South Park
In Colorado's wonderful air,
We were blessed—a family addition,
They were twins, and a wonderful pair.

"My thoughts always favored the South Park,
And everything pertaining thereto,
Its scenery, fine men and officials,
Were of the best, between me and you.

"I'll close these tales of the old South Park,
Of the times that I kept up their wires,
Dear is the memory of those old days,
To their ex-lineman, Charles C. Squires."

Another retired veteran who worked for the South Park and who has given considerable assistance in the preparation of this book is William Cairns of Salt Lake City. As an introduction to Mr. Cairns, we will quote from the Buena Vista News of February 24, 1908.

"Engineer Billy Cairns, and his fireman J. S. Burnham, had a narrow escape from instant death today. As three engines on the Gunnison branch of the C. & S. were going down hill just beyond Alpine Tunnel on the Pacific slope, the head engine, No. 63, struck a snow bank, left the track and rolled down the mountain side about 150 feet. Engineer Cairns stuck to his engine and escaped without injury. The fireman jumped as the engine left the track and was not hurt. The accident occurred where the track winds around the cliff close to what is known as the Palisades. The three engines had been bucking snow all day on the eastern slope of the mountain and had opened the right of way to the tunnel. After going through the tunnel, they had started down the mountain toward Gunnison to clear the track for the regular train which was following close behind. The head engine, when it struck the snowdrift, jumped the track, broke loose from the other two engines and did not damage the track. Those who saw the accident say the engine raised in the air and turned partly over before it struck the earth again, and went rolling down the mountain. When rescuers reached the ill-fated engine, they found Engineer Cairns standing at the side of his engine taking things in a matter-of-fact way."

A SECOND WOODSTOCK SNOWSLIDE

By William Cairns

"This is a story about a second Woodstock snowslide that occurred on February 8, 1909. We left Como with the rotary snowplow and three engines pushing us. I was running engine 58, and was coupled to the rotary. Everything went fine until we hit the snowslide that occurred almost at the same place as the avalanche that destroyed Woodstock back in 1884. We hit the slide just below the Palisades where it crossed the track. We got through that o.k. and went on down the hill around Sherrod Curve and down past Woodstock spur. There, in a cut, was the largest slide that I had ever seen. It was about 500 feet long and in the center it was about 40 feet deep. No. 93, the regular freight train, followed us down the hill, and as Lady Luck would have it they had three cars of merchandise which contained foodstuff of all kinds. We did pretty well that afternoon and the next day, but when we got near the center of the slide it was just like solid ice and the rotary wheel would not touch it. In the meantime the short frame on engine 58 broke, so I had to be switched out and another engine put in my place. We had no supervisor.

"There were seven engine crews and two train crews. Well, I saw that some one had to make a suggestion, so I proposed that we get up on top and knock the snow down in front of the plow and let it throw it out, which it did very easily. We got about six or eight feet out this way and then tried the rotary again and it worked very well. We were there seven days and nights. We all had to work and shovel snow in the tanks to melt it for water for the engines and cut wood for fuel. We kept all the engines alive and got into Pitkin about 6:00 p.m. the seventh day. When we got to the water tank, we had to let all the water out of the tenders and get inside each tank with a broom and sweep the cinders and dirt out. Those little engines scattered lots of cinders with that Baldwin coal.

"The snow also used to get awfully deep between Hancock and the tunnel. In stormy weather it would drift and slide in on the track and fill up the deep cut that the rotary would make. Sometimes the snow would get so deep that you could not see out to the right or left; it was just one big long cut in the snow from above Hancock to Atlantic."

THE TROUT CREEK FLOODS
By William Cairns

"In 1900, I was firing for Andy Nelson on engine 62. On August 1st of that year we were at Schwanders ready to start up Trout Creek. As it was storming up the canon, I suggested that we walk up the track and around the curve to Box canon and see just how the water was in there. Andy Nelson thought it was a good idea. Accompanied by Conductor Pete Newberry, we walked up to Box Canon and made an inspection and returned to our train. There was a little more water than usual but we thought it looked safe. Engineer Nelson whistled off and as we started I was watching very closely and saw the water coming. I yelled to stop and back up, which Nelson did. The flood came down through Box Canon and spread out over the flats and around the section house and office to a depth of three feet over the tracks. We were there thirty days. The company went to work making repairs and were doing fine for about fifteen days, when down came another flood and took it all out again. This flood washed out about eleven miles of track between Newett and Schwanders. Box Canon was very narrow—just wide enough for a train to go through and make the turn. The narrow part was about 700 feet long. We measured the high water mark in the canon and it was 18 feet above the track level. There were about 32 bridges between Newett and Schwanders and nearly all of them were washed out".

A SOUTH PARK ENGINE RUNNING ON FROZEN GROUND
By William Cairns

"One time in February, 1895, engineer Joe Plunkett and fireman Dale Tomkins left Como on train No. 93 at 2:15 a.m., with a drag of empties for the Baldwin Mines north of Gunnison. The weather was very cold and the wind was blowing hard. If there is ever a place that can get cold and the winter winds can make you feel it, it is along the flats in South Park. About 3:00 a.m. they were wheeling their little drag of empties along some of the track just north of Arthur's spur, where farmers loaded cattle and hay. Nearby was a crossing where the farmers could drive their stock at a point which was low and level with the rails. Some cattle had been driven across here the day before and left the crossing full of packed snow.

"The storm was still raging when Plunkett and Tomkins rounded the curve just before Arthur's and hit this cattle crossing. At this point Plunkett looked out through the storm and lo and behold, the next thing he saw was a large haystack looming up in front of him. He stopped his engine as soon as possible. The crew came up to find out what the trouble was and decided that some farmer had built his hay stack on the right of way, but further investigation disclosed that the engine had left the track and had rolled out across the frozen and snowcovered ground into a meadow. They sent in a call to Como for an engine and crew to come out and pull them back on the rails, but Plunkett's engine was so far away from the track that they had to send clear to Denver for a cable long enough to reach his engine."

AN INCIDENT ON THE HIGH LINE
By William Cairns

"The date of this story is February 15, 1900. I was firing for Jim Burns on engine 65. Billy Thomas was firing for Ed 'Rastus' Haight on engine 68. Harry Surles was firing engine 69 for engineer William Galligher. This trip started at Dickey where there was a section house, coal chute, sand house, water tank, depot, and a wye. We left Dickey for Climax, which was at the top of the hill, but we got stuck in the snow before we got to Kokomo. Passenger train No. 71 came up behind us. We decided that we would all back up to Dickey. We started backing down the 4% grade toward the Wheeler water tank, where we all took a full tank of water, which was a good thing as we needed it badly before this was over. We set our train out at Wheeler. The passenger train backed down the hill ahead of us. It was getting dark by this time. Engineer Miller who was running the passenger train's engine, the 21, stopped about half a mile above Curtin and sent his fireman back to flag us. We approached the passenger train and found that the coaches had hit a snow slide and went up on the slide about 40 feet. The coaches stood right-side up, but the rear one was ten feet above the rails. There we were; we could neither go ahead nor back. There was a section house at Curtin, so the next morning we broke a trail down to this place, and got something to eat. While there we learned that the rotary plow was bucking snow over on the Gunnison line. That left us with little chance to get out of this area. We were there ten days before we got out of that snow slide. The section house began to run out of food; they started giving us only two meals per day for a few days, then this was cut down to one meal per day. We were just about to run out of food, when the rotary showed up. They had brought along a good supply of food. We had straightened the coaches up so we could sleep in them and had cut wood to keep the engines alive. Water was obtained by shoveling snow into the tanks where it would melt into water for the boilers.

"When the rotary crew got the slide cleared out the engines were all in shape ready to go. It was a great relief to get home and get cleaned up. We had not had our clothes off for ten days."

MORE TROUBLES ON THE HIGH LINE
By William Cairns

"One day in February, 1903, I was running engine 52 and left Como on train No. 81, the fast freight between there and Leadville. We got to Climax about 7:00 a.m. I was on the helper engine so the brakeman cut me off and gave me a high-ball and I lit out for Leadville. I got down the hill about seven miles below Climax and broke a tank journal. I had a student fireman, John Snee, so I told him to go back and flag No. 81. There was a pile of ties close by so I got a tie all ready and when the train came we got a jack out of the coach, jacked up the tank, shoved the tie under the broken journal and over the truck frame and skidded the tank into the Bird's Eye spur about one-half mile down the track. No. 81 went on into Leadville. In a short time the car repairmen came out with a switch engine and a flat car with a pair of wheels for my tank. It did not take long to change the wheels and I went on into Leadville.

"When we left Leadville the next morning for the return trip it was snowing hard. There were three engines on the train; Engineer Andy Anderson had the 55, Walter Parlin had the 57, and I had the 52. We had plenty of trouble with the snow before we got to Climax. I was on the rear end of the train. Parlin and his engine, the 57, was at the head of the train with Anderson and the 55 coupled in behind him. We had to double into Climax. We finally got our train coupled together with a few more cars that had been set out at Climax, making 19 cars altogether, pulled up and spotted the coach opposite the office. The red board was out. Soon the conductor came up with the orders. Walter Parlin was ahead because his engine had a flanger and snow plow on

Colorado & Southern 9 at Sheridan Junction in October, 1938.

Colorado & Southern 76 at Climax in June, 1937.

the front end, I was next with 52, and Anderson with 55 was coupled behind me. The conductor told Parlin to go to Dickey. I was told to stop at Kokomo as he had some switching to do there.

"The brakeman pulled the pin on Walter Parlin and his 57 (we still had link and pin couplers at this date) and gave him a highball for Dickey. He then came back and pulled· the pin on me and gave me a highball for Kokomo. Anderson, with engine 55, was to bring the train down the hill to Kokomo. Parlin was about a quarter of a mile down the track ahead of me. I read my orders, released the air on my tank, as we had no driver brakes at that time on the engine, and as we were standing on a 4% grade I got off in a hurry. In a few minutes I looked back and here came the 55 at me like a mad bull after a red flag. Wham! I got it. Not having automatic couplers of course, the two engines did not couple together. I tore out and soon caught up with Walter Parlin. I whistled him ahead as he did not seem to know what was happening. He tore out and did not stop until he got to Dickey, 21 miles away. Wham! Engine 55 hit me again harder than before. I set the air and reversed the engine in an effort to stay against him, but he had hit me too hard. I lost my whole tank this time as the draw bar and safety chains broke. My tank went into a side cut, took everything off the left side of Anderson's 55, including blowoff cock, cab and running boards, and ditched the 55 and all her train. Bullion and ore were scattered all over the mountain side. Those cars tried to climb all over one another until they were four high. There I was on that steep grade, no brakes and a student fireman. I backed my engine up to the 55 and had just room enough to get on Buffer spur. I told my fireman to throw the switch and then go back and see if anyone was hurt, and if he might help. I got my engine in the clear on this spur and then blocked the wheels to hold her in place. Then I went back to see if I could be of any help.

"By this time engine 55 was dead. Andy Anderson had been thrown about twenty feet from the track and was in snow up to his neck, unable to move. We had to shovel a trail to him in order to get him out. The fireman, Frank Peabody, was in the tank of 55 when my tank had cleaned the left side of their engine. No one was seriously hurt. The company fired the train crew, and Andy Anderson, who afterward went blind, was sent back to Sweden by his friends. It took Pat Gibboney and his wrecking crew several days to clean up that mess."

Author's note: Mr. Cairns neglected to state what had caused Anderson to lose control of his 19 car train.

A WRECK NEAR ST. ELMO
By William Cairns

"This bad wreck which killed two men happened on November 17, 1906. I was running engine 63, Walter Parlin was running the 67, Frank Parlin was running the 69, and Ed Conahan was running engine 73. We were on an extra working loads up the hills. We had Hancock siding filled up with loads, so the dispatcher sent us to Bath. When we reached Newett, the dispatcher gave us orders to run extra from Bath to Pitkin and that train No. 94 would wait at St. Elmo until 9:05 for extras 63, 67, 69 and 73. We had to hurry to make St. Elmo before 9:05, but we made it there on time. We were standing on the long spur near the depot. No. 94 did not come along for about an hour. We were all tired and I guess some of us went to sleep. I heard the train coming down the hill from Hancock and I called to my fireman to wake up and get the engine hot.

"No. 94 whistled for the 'red board' but did not stop. That train went through St. Elmo about 30 miles per hour, which was mighty fast for a narrow gauge engine to travel on that 4% grade. When the train went by we all ran for the telegraph office. Everybody was more or less excited. Our conductor came in (his name was Hamilton) and said, 'Well, let's go.' No one said anything, so I said, 'Where are you going?' He replied, 'I have orders to go to Pitkin.' I told him I was not going until we found out whether No. 94 got stopped or not. Just then the dispatcher called and wanted to know if we knew anything about 94. The St. Elmo operator was all excited and wanted to know what to tell him. I said, 'Tell him No. 94 went by unable to stop and ask him if we can follow down the hill and see what has happened.' The dispatched replied 'O.K.'. Conahan with engine 73 and a caboose was out first, so we all decorated the rear end of the caboose, lit fusees and started down the hill. About a half mile below St. Elmo we found the fireman where he had jumped off in the snow and rocks. He was skinned up a little but was not hurt bad. The engineer, C. K. Robbins, had joined the birds before the fireman did, on the curve just below St. Elmo, and ran down the track after the train. The train had stopped about one and a half miles below St. Elmo. When we came in sight of the coach, which was a combination baggage car and passenger coach, the tail lights were burning bright and it looked good. But the coach and one car was all that was on the track. The train, which had consisted of 14 cars of coal and two cars of ore, was piled up in a cut in a space not more than six car lengths long. The engine, No. 39, had rolled up out of the cut and was stripped clean of all the pipes, pumps, etc., and the cab was torn off. Then we started hunting for the train crew.

"We found one of the brakemen, Frank Smith. He had just regained consciousness from a bad bump on his head, which he never got over. Then we found the other brakeman, Chauncey Burnsides, who was a good friend of mine. He was buried in a car of slack coal with just his head sticking out. I had known Chauncey since childhood. I asked him how he was and he said all right except that one of his feet was caught and that if we could get that foot loose he would be O.K. So we got a shovel and started digging the coal away from him, and found what was holding him. The brake wheel had broken off the staff and the staff had rammed through his thigh. One end of the brake staff was on the car which was standing on its end and the other end was in some tangled truss rods. We got a saw out of the passenger coach and proceeded to saw the brake staff in two. This took us an hour or more before we could get him freed from the staff. In the meantime we sent for a doctor at St. Elmo and he came down. Not one of us had presence of mind enough to tie a cord above the wound so as to stop the flow of blood. They rushed Chauncey to the Salida Hospital as soon as possible but he only lived three days. He died from the loss of blood.

"All this time some of the crew were hunting for the conductor, Frank Land. We did not find him that night. When it got light enough in the morning we found two cars about a half mile above the place where the train had piled up. They were about one hundred and fifty feet from the track. Frank Land went down with them and was killed. We never did find out what part of the train those two cars jumped out of. At the spot where they left the rails they barely marked the ties. That was a sad night for me as I lost two very close friends in Chauncey Burnside and Frank Land."

"A somewhat similar accident occurred in February, 1905. Ted Williams was running engine 72 and Pete Newberry was his conductor. As they were coming down the grade from the east portal of Alpine Tunnel, Williams' train got away from him and piled up on what we called 'Saw Mill Curve' about a half mile above Hancock. No one was hurt, but the engine and 14 loads of coal piled up in a large pile of sawdust from the old mill there."

※ ※ ※ ※

The following interesting story was told by Andy

Nelson, veteran South Park engineman, to Ed Haley of Denver. We are most fortunate to have such an interesting and true story as told by the man who is the hero of the article. In speaking of Mr. Nelson, Roy Morton writes:

"Andy Nelson was the grand old man of the South Park. For over 50 years he was engineer and travelling engineer. His favorite engine was No. 71, a Baldwin consolidation."

BUCKING SNOW ON MARSHALL PASS
By Ed Haley

"The narrow gauge railroads of Colorado had many expert 'snow buckers', but those who ran on the South Park were the best of the lot. With light power they could clear a pass that would stop the heavier engines of other lines dead in their tracks. A great deal of their success was due to the fact that their engines were equipped with the Priest flanger, and it might also be mentioned that they had plenty of practice. The Priest flanger was an ingenious device—almost like an ordinary flanger except that it was equipped with ice knives that actually scraped the inside edge and top of the rail. Because of this, it had to be raised and lowered (by air) at all crossings and switches.

"One winter shortly after the turn of the century, the weather along the Continental Divide was especially nasty. A howling blizzard had so solidly blocked Alpine Pass that it would be impossible to open it before spring. Marshall Pass, where the Rio Grande crossed the Continental Divide, was farther south and much lower but it too was blocked with snow. The sudden storm had caught Andy Nelson and his engine 71, and Billy Kerns and his 65, far from their regular hangout, at Como, in South Park. It looked very much as if they were stuck in Gunnison until spring. They hung around for a few days and then Andy had an idea. He knew it was out of the question to get back to Como via Alpine Tunnel, but what about Marshall Pass? It was lower and probably had less snow. He went to the Rio Grande operator at Gunnison and had that gentleman contact the dispatcher at Salida and ask for permission for the two South Park hoggers to make an attempt to clear Marshall Pass for the Rio Grande. Andy knew that the South Park would be only too glad to get their two much needed engines and crews back to Como, no matter how they got there. Permission was granted and so that same afternoon—it was a Sunday and the thermometer stood at forty degrees below zero—at 2:00 p.m., two South Park engines, Nos. 71 and 65, steamed boldly eastward toward Marshall Pass. The 71 with Andy at the throttle and Verden Murdock firing was in the lead. Then came 65 and Billy Kerns with two cars of coal and a combination coach. A Rio Grande traveling engineer rode the 71 as a pilot.

"It was easy going up the wide level valley of Tomichi Creek to Sargent at the foot of the pass. Just west of Sargent, the 71's left rear driving box began to run hot. At Sargent, Andy found that there was no pit, so he crawled underneath the engine and repacked the driving box. The temperature was then 56 degrees below zero. The crews went over to the eating house and had a good hot dinner plus a little liquid stimulant to keep them from freezing up. The operator at Sargent gave them their orders to Marshall Pass and told them where to look for ten dead engines on the pass. Then began the long uphill fight against the deep snow and steep grade.

They found three of the ten engines on the west side of Marshall Pass still alive, so they coupled them into their train behind the two South Park engines, but the air was not cut through. About three-quarters of a mile from the top of the pass, the 71 became uncoupled and broke away from the rest of the train; however, as she was going good, Andy didn't stop but plowed on through to the top of the pass alone. Imagine the Marshall Pass operator's surprise when the first sign of activity he had seen in days turned out to be a lone South Park engine.

"The Marshall Pass operator had orders to hold the 71 and the 65, as two Rio Grande engines were working up the east side of the pass with a large wedge plow. So Andy and Billy waited 21 hours in the snow shed atop Marshall Pass. Finally orders came for them to run down light and see what had happened to the Rio Grande crew and their plow. They found them hopelessly stuck four and one half miles east of the pass. They plowed to within a few feet of the Rio Grande plow, dug out the remaining snow by hand and got it on its way again. Between Marshall Pass and Salida they passed six dead engines, all on sidings.

"Tuesday morning engines 71 and 65 chuffed proudly into the Rio Grande's Salida yards, having opened blockaded Marshall Pass for them. Shortly afterward they were routed over the Rio Grande's main line to Buena Vista, where they switched over the interchange track to the South Park's line and headed up Trout Creek for Como and home. However, the trip was not over yet, for about a half mile out of Garos, the 71 jumped the track and plunged pilot first into a ditch alongside the roadbed. That was the first time Andy ever had to call the wrecking crew to put his engine back on the rails. The damage was slight and the two small engines finally steamed into the Como yards, having come home by the long way.

"Engine 71, a Baldwin consolidation, stands today on a short section of track at Central City, Colorado, a monument to a glorious era of railroading that has gone forever. And Andy Nelson, with a twinkle in his eye, as he tells this story, hale and hearty despite his 83 years, lives on among the memories gathered in 53 years of mountain railroading."

* * * *

Another old timer is William Wendell, who writes:

"I went to work on the old South Park when it was under construction and I knew the road from one end to the other. I turned over with locomotives three times while working for the old pike.

"The pitchover in Alpine Tunnel is about 1,200 feet from the east portal. A big spume candle was kept burning there in a glass frame to notify engineers when they were over the top of the grade. There was always a bad slippery rail inside the tunnel and a hoghead wanted to be sure sand was running good and heavy before he entered or he would not get very far, and if he should hang up inside Alpine Tunnel he would smother in a few minutes. I had some close calls myself. At Hancock, three miles east of the tunnel, where we took water, I always examined my sand pipes with a hammer to be sure sand was running good and free. I would also get myself a bucket of cold water and set it beside me in the cab. I always had a big hunk of cotton waste which I soaked in the water. On entering the tunnel I would hold the wet waste over my mouth and nose so I could breathe, for the gas in that tunnel was a fright.

"In 1883, No. 287, the Gunnison passenger train, was going west through the tunnel when a big rock fell on top of the sleeping car and caved in the roof.

"Another time engine 213, a Cooke consolidation, with Billy Hemes, a young engineer just promoted, climbed the rail and landed in the tree tops 500 feet below the track at Romley. Billy went with his engine but the fireman jumped off safe. When the train crew got down to the engine Billy was sitting on a tree stump looking at the engine. He never got a scratch."

The following episode was published in the Locomotive Engineers Journal some years ago, and was sent by Mr. Wendell for inclusion in this book.

HOGGER GETS HIS ENGINES
By William Wendell

"It happened on November 7, 1905 on the old Denver, South Park & Pacific, now the Colorado & Southern. I was called to go out on a Climax, Colorado, turnaround. I had my regular engine, the 71, and my regular fireman, Frank Goring. It was a three engine train, an extra. I was the head engineer, engine 63 was next with Engineer Hogue and Fireman Bill Thomas, and engine 68 followed with engineer John Morganfield and Swede Hansen, his fireman.

"When we got to Climax we set out our empty train of ore cars at the Climax Mines. The 63 and 68 returned to Dickey light. I coupled on to the ore train of 12 loads and took it to Dickey, 27 miles from Como. At Dickey we picked up seven more loaded ore cars, which was quite a train for three engines to take over Boreas Pass, and got orders to run extra from Dickey to Boreas, the top (inclosed in a long snowshed), and to meet passenger train No. 71. The 68 was on my hind end. We met as per orders.

"The conductor, Tyler, came to me and said, 'Billy, I want you to follow passenger train 71 down the mountain.' He added that he was afraid to let Morganfield with 68 follow the train. Morganfield was a new man just off the Missouri Pacific and was no mountain engineer. Ordinarily Morganfield should have followed the passenger train, then Haig with his 63, then I would follow with the 71. I told my conductor, Tyler, that he was running the train and whatever he thought best was O.K. with me, for he was a good railroad man.

"I coupled the dinky caboose on the front end of 71 and was the first to follow the passenger train. The 63 followed me and the 68 was last. As I was rounding the curve at Baker's Tank I looked back in the direction of the tank and saw the 63 coming like hell. It was 3:10 p.m. I whistled him down and then the sun shone through the cab of the 63. It was empty! No engineer or fireman were to be seen. I was getting dangerously close to the passenger train and it was up to me to do something very soon.

"I knew what to do to save that passenger train. I yelled over to my fireman: 'Frank, there comes the 63 hell bent for election, and there's nobody on her! She's running away and you'd better jump off for I am going to catch the 63 on the hind end with this dinkey caboose!' The train crew had jumped off and I decided there was no use in both of us getting killed. But Frank was a Welshman and retorted, 'I can ride the bloody engine as fast as you can, don't you know.' I told him to put in a good fire, to keep her hot and to watch the water, as I was going to use the water brake. He was to use the injector on his side.

"We were backing down from Boreas to Dickey and I had to either catch the 63 or go to glory before we got to the Pittsburg spur, for it is on a sharp curve and the 71 would not stay on the rail, not at the speed she was going. If I got too close to that passenger train before I got to Pittsburg spur, I would throw the 71 into the 63 and trust to luck.

"As far as Frank and I were concerned, hell was staring us straight in the face. That passenger train must be saved, for there were 167 persons on it, not counting the train crew and two coaches loaded with school children going to Leadville on a picnic. I kept track of the 63 as best I could around the curves and let her gradually gain on the 71. I caught the 63 on the hind end of the dinkey caboose and the whole top of that caboose above the frame went up in the air and over the mountainside. What was left of the caboose, the 63 pushed up on the front end of the 71 and the headlight was broken beyond repair. The angle cock on the front end of the air pipe was broken off and three slats in the pilot were damaged.

"I was using a straight air brake and I had to struggle with the Johnson bar. After I got everything under control I saw the 68 coming. I caught her on the front end of the 63 and got everything stopped as I got to Pittsburg, just as I had planned. I climbed down and examined everything. I took the white flag, which was on a flag stick, and drove it into the end of the air line pipe where the angle cock had broken off and had brakes once again. Frank, my fireman, was looking over what was left of the caboose and I secured a red flag and three torpedoes from engine 71 and told him to get back and flag an extra freight that was to follow us from Boreas to Dickey. I did not know what had become of my train crew and I would not take any chances of having that express piling into what I had saved.

"Then I began to size things up. I got up on the 63; no one there—reverse lever in the back notch of the quadrant. Then I went over and climbed up on the 68 and there was the engineer, John Morganfield, laying back in the coal pit. It was almost empty, as the engine had used most of the coal getting the train up to Boreas. His right leg below the knee was crushed. He told me he tried to get off but he slipped and his leg was caught between the engine frame and the tender under the apron, but he managed to get back into the coal tender. I asked him what the matter was and why he could not keep a light engine from running away. I told him he had good straight air brakes and a water brake, and then he told me he did not know anything about a water brake or straight air. He had set his brakes, but the engine kept gaining speed and then he hit the 63 and tried to get off.

"I looked at the engineer's brake valve. It was in the nine hole for automatic which was in full release in straight air. Straight air and automatic work the reverse of each other as a brake. I told Morganfield so and he said he did not know anything about straight air, which proved that my conductor had good reasons for not letting Morganfield go down first after the passenger train.

"My fireman got back after flagging the extra freight. We got engineer Morganfield, who weighed about 220 pounds, over in the coal tender of the 71, and I had the brakies get some new ties that were piled up beside the tank. I put the ties up back of the 63 and blocked both engines so that they could not get away. The conductor told both of his brakies to stay there, and then we took engine 71 and went to Breckenridge where we put Morganfield in the station agent's bed. A company doctor who was there, examined Morganfield's leg and said it was in very bad shape. The leg below the knee was removed 24 days later. I made out a statement and it was wired into Como to the master mechanic. I had asked him to send two engine crews for the deserted engines 63 and 68.

"When I caught the two runaway locomotives, the passenger train had just rounded the curve at the Pittsburg spur. When it arrived in Breckenridge, the conductor, Tommy St. John, sent a message to the trainmaster saying that it looked as though all the engines on the mountain were running away, but Wendell was catching them with his 71. When we got back, I went to the two engines and they were both about dead. There was an extra run from Como which brought two new crews.

"Engineer Hoag and Fireman Thomas unloaded in the rocks when the 68 hit the 63. Both were badly injured, but recovered fully. The 68 was the cause of all the runaways. Swede Hansen, the fireman of the 68, unloaded the first thing and walked back and found the 63's crew. When I got to Breckenridge with Morganfield it looked as though the whole town was at the depot. The town at that time had a population of about 1200 and it seemed that they were all talking at the same time. When I got back to Como there was another excited gathering. I didn't stop at the depot, but kept on going until I got to the roundhouse. I reported the work to be done on the 71 and I skipped out the back of the roundhouse and

372

went to my room. My fireman and I had had enough for one trip.

"The company thanked me by awarding me a month's credit, 200 merit marks and a fine letter from Frank Trumbull, who was President of the South Park at that time. However, the fine letter which I received is just a memory now; I left it in a suitcase in Cechal in Old Mexico, both of which I never saw again."

Author's note: "Uncle Billy" Wendell, as he was known to all his friends, passed away on May 6, 1944, in Ventura, California. He was 91 years old.

* * * *

A SCHOOL TEACHER'S EXCURSION TO ALPINE TUNNEL
By Roy Morton

"In August, 1905, a school teachers' convention was being held in Gunnison. During the convention a group of the teachers decided that they would like to take a train trip up to Alpine Tunnel. The Baldwin crew was delegated to take the special excursion, after their return trip from the mines that day. This crew consisted of conductor, George Mason; engineer, Pat Colligan; fireman, Fred Williams; brakemen, Ed Brady, Joe Fortney, and myself. Our train was made up of engine 58, two South Park coaches, one coach borrowed from the Rio Grande, and one observation car which was nothing more than a coal car with waiting room seats placed crosswise. The 'observation car' was placed on the hind end.

"We left Gunnison about 2:00 p.m., meeting No. 93 at Ohio City. When the special arrived at Alpine Tunnel station, conductor Mason had the operator ask the dispatcher at Como if there were any westbound extras in sight, and for permission to turn 58 on the wye at Hancock. Everything was in the clear.

"The school teachers were informed that those who wished to walk up over the Continental Divide could do so as the section foreman, who happened to be at the tunnel that day, would act as their guide. They were also informed that the brakemen and some of the section crew with lanterns would accompany all who would like to walk through the tunnel and back. Ice cold water continually ran out along the edges of the tunnel and a good lantern was needed to keep from stepping in it. However, they would not be permitted to enter the tunnel until the 58 returned from Hancock. For the convenience of the teachers, we had moved the four cars up to the west portal and shoved them back in the clear on the short spur at that point.

"The head brakeman and myself then went along with the 58, through the tunnel and down the east slope to Hancock to turn the engine on the wye. Upon the return of the engine, some of the teachers made the walk through the tunnel to the east portal. There they were joined by the party who had walked over the Continental Divide, and all returned through the tunnel. On this occasion I walked through the tunnel both ways, myself.

"After the passengers were all accounted for, they boarded the train at the west portal. We had switched the fancy observation car to the hind end. We then shoved the four cars up to the telegraph office, uncoupled, ran around them on the passing track, coupled on the front end, and departed. After a short stop at Pitkin, we continued on to Gunnison. All teachers reported a pleasant trip."

DYNAMITING A SOUTH PARK BRIDGE
By Roy Morton

"The place known today as Baldwin was formerly called Mt. Carbon. Alpine Mine, the largest in the district, was located there. The South Park men, who worked on the Ohio Creek branch, would allude to this place as Alpine as often as they called it Mt. Carbon. The line out of Castleton up Ohio Creek was called the Baldwin branch. The old Union and Kubler Mines were located northeast of Castleton on Carbon Creek. The coal vein in the Union Mine was a fine grade of soft coal and was reached by means of a tunnel instead of a slope, as at the Alpine Mine. The old Kubler Mine was located some distance beyond the Union.

"About June of 1902 or 1903, there was a strike at the Mt. Carbon Mines, closing them down for about a week. A settlement could not be reached, so the mine owners imported a bunch of non-union men and a large bunch of negroes in an attempt to break the strike.

"The mine started up on a small scale and had been in operation for a few days, when about 6 o'clock one morning, the residents of Gunnison heard two or three loud explosions. An investigation disclosed that the South Park's steel bridge and part of the pile bridge approach across Ohio Creek, two and a half miles north of Gunnison, had been dynamited.

"The job was charged to mine strikers as an attempt to prevent the railroad company from furnishing empty cars for loading at the mines. A poor job of placing one charge of powder on one of the stone abutments gave the South Park company a break; had it been placed right, it would have knocked out the abutment and would have put one end of the bridge down in the creek bottom. As it was, practically all the damage was done to the pile and stringer portion of the bridge.

"The railroad rushed Harry James and his bridge gang, along with their narrow gauge pile driver and plenty of material from Como, to repair the job as quickly as possible. In about three days the bridge was in as good or better shape than it was before.

"In the meantime, the owners and the miners had reached an agreement and settled the strike. The South Park's Special Agent and the County Sheriff investigated the bridge dynamiting, but were never able to locate any of the guilty parties."

SNOW—THE SOUTH PARK'S WINTER ENEMY
By Roy Morton

"During the many years I lived in Gunnison, the winter season with its heavy snowfall usually signified the closing of the Alpine Pass section. The closing date depended upon the progress of the cold weather; one year it would be the latter part of December, while the next it might occur in January, or perhaps even run into February. Similarly, the opening dates also varied, but as a rule the road would be opened by the latter part of March or early in April.

"At the beginning of the winter season the engine pilots were removed, and a butterfly snowplow or flanger would be installed. In addition to flanger-equipped engines, good use was made of the rotary snowplow, which was usually pushed by two to four engines. With the combined aid of the flangers and the rotary, the South Park's snow buckers, who were among the best in the country, did a marvelous job of utilizing the road's power to its best advantage in an effort to keep the line open as long as they could in the winter, and to get it opened up as early as possible in the spring.

"When springtime came they would put a batch of engines behind the rotary, take a crew of snow shovellers, plenty of explosives, and give the snowdrifts hell. After the Alpine Pass route was opened up, all the excess explosives were taken to Gunnison and turned over to my father. He then had the section men destroy the stuff in the nearby Gunnison River. I have cut the paper off many a stick of powder when I was a kid."

PATRICK "CURLEY" COLLIGAN
By Roy Morton

"One of the most colorful of the old time South Park en-

Andy Nelson and Tom St. John at the C.&S. roundhouse in October, 1944.

Left to right: Engineer Curly Colligan, Conductor Tom St. John, and Brakeman Roy Hight (fourth person unknown) beside engine 9 ready to leave Leadville on the last run.

gineers was Patrick Colligan, better known as Curley Colligan. He was born in Oberlin, Ohio, and raised in Ellis, Kansas, the son of a cattleman. Curley grew up with the expectation of following in his father's footsteps, but the call of the iron horse overcame his affection for his cow horse, and he went to work firing an engine on the Union Pacific. It was while working for the Union Pacific that Curley met my father. Through my father's influence, Curley came to Colorado in 1887, and hired out on the South Park at Como. It was not long before he was promoted to the right side. In 1898, he met a Chicago girl whom he later married. After living in Alma and then Gunnison for a few years, he and Nellie Colligan moved to Como in 1913, and established their home.

"Curley's favorite engine was a Rhode Island consolidation which first carried the number 261. This was a Denver, Leadville & Gunnison number. Later this engine became Colorado & Southern 58. Curley bought a big steamboat whistle and mounted it on 261's steam dome where it could be heard far and wide. He also bought an expensive nickel plated clock which he mounted alongside the steam gauge. Next he acquired some green enamel paint and painted the inside of 261's cab. These fancy appurtenances were topped off by a big spring seat which he bought and placed in the cab.

"The genial Irishman made a lot of friends up and down the line and was the idol of any crew he worked with. He considered it his duty to contribute freely to the poor and could out-cuss any sailor that ever sailed the seven seas.

"Curley's first bad wreck occurred on December 14, 1897, about a mile west of Bird's Eye on the Leadville line. Tommy St. John was his conductor. No one was able to explain how the mishap occurred, as Curley was an expert at handling the air. Anyway, his engine left the rails and rolled down the hill where it finally came to a rest on a ledge some 200 feet below the track. Jerry Regan and his crew were sent to the scene to get Curley's engine back on the track and clean up the wreck. At this time our old friend Charlie Squires cut in a temporary wire to Jerry's caboose to facilitate clearing the wreck and to assist in keeping the high line traffic moving.

"Curley was badly injured and was in the hospital several months. It began to look as if he might never pull another throttle. But the intestinal fortitude of this western born Irishman gained the upper hand, and he reported for duty once again.

"Another time in the spring of 1904, Curley was going east out of Gunnison with train No. 94. He had a second engine coupled in the middle of the train with Colin Moore as engineer. Just west of Ohio City, Curley's engine, the 58, hit a herd of burros near a cattle guard. The engine was derailed and turned over. The Irishman's leg was injured this time, but he soon recovered.

"He then took the Gunnison-Baldwin run where he stayed until 1910, when Alpine Tunnel caved in. After that he took over the Garos-Fairplay-Alma run. Later, he moved to the Leadville-Como run where he remained until retirement.

"I am indeed glad that I knew Curley Colligan as a friend. He was a great engineman and was one of the best the South Park ever had. I have ridden many a mile with him on his seat box; he used to let me run old 58 quite often."

Author's note: Patrick Colligan died September 11, 1941, at the age of 74 years. He was mourned by a host of friends in the South Park region. In September, 1945, Ed Haley and the writer enjoyed a most pleasant visit with Nellie Colligan at her home in Como. No finer little Irish lady ever lived. Curley's big nickel plated clock was hanging on the kitchen wall—still ticking away.

A FAST RIDE DOWN THE WEST SLOPE OF ALPINE PASS
By Roy Morton

"This is the story of an incident that happened to an uncle of mine, R. B. Morton. He started his railroad career as a telegraph operator for the Union Pacific in Kansas. Pounding a telegraph key became too monotonous for him, so he started braking on the Union Pacific out of Ellis, Kansas. From there he drifted to the Rock Island and was soon promoted to conductor. He grew tired of Kansas and at the suggestion of my father, who was agent for the South Park at Gunnison, came to Colorado. He hired out to the South Park in the fall of 1900, and was sent to Como.

"He had only been there one day when, due to a shortage of empties for the Baldwin branch coal mines, he was called for his first trip on an extra west to Gunnison. The drag was scheduled to leave Como at 11:00 p.m. The conductor on that run was Jerry Regan. Jerry was an old boomer who could always work for the South Park, for he was a combination desert and mountain railroader. He had also served as dispatcher and conductor for the Santa Fe and the Southern Pacific in the Sierra Nevada Mountains. Jerry was a typical Irishman and wore a long red handlebar mustache.

"The engineer on that trip was Clarence 'Silver Tip' Adams. My uncle did not recall the name of the fireman, nor the other brakeman. However, they were all experienced South Park men. As it was my uncle's first trip over the big hill, Jerry said to the other brakeman, 'Pard, we got a plainsman with us tonight; you take the head end and I'll work with the new man on the hind end this trip—I want to see what he knows and break him in on mountain railroading.'

"They finally arrived at the tunnel where their helper was cut off. Adams made an air test and the brakeman set the retainer cocks up to half position on each empty and to full position on each loaded car. Just west of the tunnel Silver Tip made an application with the air to pinch her before they hit the steeper section below the station. The air took hold on this application. By the time they rounded the sharp curve just before swinging around the Palisades shelf, the train had gathered considerable speed. Silver Tip gave the train a sharp application of air but it failed to take hold as it should. The whole crew, including Jerry Regan, were out on top with their brake clubs. Adams then whistled for brakes and they went to work tying them down.

"My uncle said, 'When we began to approach that curve I was not much afraid—just figured it was the usual procedure; but when I saw the fireman coming out over the tank of the engine with a brake club in his hand, I was really scared. We went to work twisting those brake wheels wholesale.' When they hit the big curve at Sherrod, Silver Tip slacked her and let her go. As they squealed around the curve, the engineer again charged the train line the best he could and managed to check their speed; but they made darn good running time into Pitkin.

"Jerry Regan said, 'Morton, I believe you will make a good South Park trainman.' My uncle was then given a drink out of Jerry's bottle. It's a queer thing, but the South Park train crews mixed a little whiskey with their railroading to good advantage, and got into very little trouble. The road's officials knew of it, and a few of them openly stated that a railroad man had to mix a little booze with mountain railroading."

* * * *

SNOWBOUND AT ALPINE TUNNEL

Mr. F. P. Roesch, who was connected with the mechanical department of the South Park line in the early days, related an interesting story to the author.

Mr. Roesch is now Vice President of the Standard Stoker Company of Chicago.

Mr. Roesch said that one winter day he and some other fellows were waiting at the tunnel for an eastbound freight train from Gunnison to pick them up. A very heavy snowstorm came up and conditions became very disagreeable. The freight train finally showed up but got stuck in the snow near the west portal. It seems that the rotary snowplow, which had been stationed at Hancock at the time, was in Como for some repairs. There was nothing the snowbound men could do except wait until the plow could return and open up the line. Mr. Roesch stated:

"In the meantime the eating situation became quite serious. After eating up all the section foreman's pork and beans, we killed and ate a burro. When that ran out one of the fellows found a fox den near the tunnel and we killed and ate three red foxes. By that time we had used up all the coal in the tender in an effort to keep the locomotive alive. Fortunately, the plow arrived shortly afterward and opened up the line. It was quite an experience and one I will never forget."

* * * *

BILLY WESTALL
By Ed Haley

"Another famous South Park character was William G. 'Billy' Westall. In memory of an heroic deed by this man,

M. C. Poor.

The Westall Monument.

there stands today, as a lasting tribute to his courage, a large granite monument near Dome Rock in Platte Canon.

"On the afternoon of August 28, 1898,[1] engineer Billy Westall was pulling a seven car passenger train loaded with some 450 excursionists on a return trip from the mountains into Denver. Just as the engine rounded a blind left curve near Dome Rock, engineer Westall caught sight of a large pile of sand and gravel on the track directly ahead, which had been washed down the mountain side by a recent heavy rain. He could have easily 'joined the birds' and jumped in the clear, but chose, instead, to stick to his engine and try his best to stop the train with its human cargo. His fireman, Joseph Nichols, also stayed with the engine but was thrown into the clear as the engine turned over and escaped injury. Westall was successful in saving the lives of all his passengers at the expense of his own. His body was pinned to the ground by the handhold on the right side of the tender. He lived 12 hours, dying in the arms of his fireman. Westall's last words were: 'Tell my wife I died thinking of her'.

"The monument erected to his memory is located a short distance west of the station of Dome Rock in Platte Canon. It is hewn from Platte Canon granite, weighs 34,000 pounds, and stands ten feet high. In the polished stone oval is inscribed the letters, 'A.O.U.W.' (American Order of United Workmen), and their emblem. Beneath the A. O. U. W. is a small line which says, 'Tell my wife I died thinking of her'. Below all this is the name WESTALL in large letters. The monument was unveiled on Labor Day, Monday, September 4, 1899. Three train loads of persons attended the exercises."

Author's note: Billy Westall must have been well known and greatly admired by his fellow employees on the South Park. Many old timers have mentioned his name in their letters.

* * * *

A story is told about elephants riding on the South Park. It seems that a circus train got stuck on a steep grade and was unable to reach the top until the elephants were unloaded and put to work pushing at the rear end. In attempting to learn the details of this little episode, three different versions of the story were uncovered. Not knowing which story is authentic, the writer will include all three—the reader can take his pick. J. M. Cuenin, veteran Chaffee County Surveyor at Salida, writes:

"In the early '80's a circus train was en route to Leadville. It was probably the John Robinson Circus that played in Gunnison that year, 1882. In coming up Kenosha Pass the circus train became stalled and could not make the grade. Two elephants were unloaded and helped push the train to the top of the pass."

Another version of this story appears in Lewis R. Lathrop's article "The Alpine Tunnel Route," published in Railroad Magazine, June, 1941. This article carries an interesting pen sketch showing the elephants at work pushing the circus train up the grade past the Palisades. Mr. Lathrop writes:

"Old timers still talk about the Barnum & Bailey circus train that stalled on the line, back in its heyday. Naturally, regular circus cars couldn't be used on the narrow gauge track, but, disguised beneath bunting and banners, three South Park box cars and a coach took on a mildly impressive carnival air. All went well until the chuffing little Mason engine at the head end lost her footing on wet rail, as she approached the Palisades.

"The South Park train crew had never heard of another Alpine grade-buster by the name of Hannibal. In their own

1. Denver Daily Times, August 27 and September 5, 1899.

376

way, however, they lit on the same method of getting over the hump. In one of the box cars were a couple of elephants, with three tons of weight, apiece, upon their 'driving wheels'. Brought around to the rear of the special, they boosted it steadily on to the summit."

Last, we read in the Rocky Mountain News of November 8, 1936, an article by Edith Townsend, who writes:

"W. D. Penny, South Park engineer, was hauling a three-car circus train up Boreas Pass (no date given) when the engine stalled on a curve. No amount of steam could budge the cargo of wild beasts. Time was pressing. The lions were hungry. The one-track line was being held up and night was coming on. Finally, the fellow in charge of the elephants offered to take them from the car and use their pushing power at the rear of the train. The brakeman gave the signal—the caretaker swore in 'Arabic', and Mr. Penny whistled off for the start up a 3½ per cent grade. Mr. Penny said, 'The big boys jammed their heads against the rear car, grunted a powerful snort, and up we went. I could feel the force of their shove while they were putting us over the three miles of grade. It was a mighty queer hook-up but damn lucky for us'."

* * * *

M. S. Goodale writes in Railroad Magazine, December, 1933:

"We had all kinds of men working on the old South Park. Some good, some bad. But most of them knew how to railroad. There were a few exceptions. There was a young man by the name of Heard, who had married the General Roadmaster's daughter. Mr. Heard craved promotion, and in this craving, he was sustained by General Superintendent C. W. Fisher.

"First of all Heard wanted to be a train dispatcher. However, Fisher advised him to get a job as a brakeman, and learn something about the railroad. So old John McCormack, the trainmaster, lined him up for a run with conductor 'Dad' Hinkle. Dad was crabby and all business. They made a round trip to Leadville, and when they got back Hinkle was fit to be tied. He asked Mac where in the hell he had picked up that 'hayburner', and told him that if he went out again on his run he would make a whistling post out of Mr. Heard.

"McCormack tried Heard out with several other conductors, and they all reported him as no good. These recommendations had no effect. He was turned over to Fisher who set him up as third trick train dispatcher at Buena Vista. This job was the heaviest of them all. It called for first class talent, as the South Park used the Rio Grande's track between Buena Vista and Leadville. This was before the South Park built their high line over Boreas Pass from Como.

"Well, Mr. Heard thought he had talent, and he started out with all the confidence in the world. To begin with, he had three trains meet on a 30-car spur at Malta where there was already a work train waiting for orders. This was just a starter. By the time morning came he had everything tied up so tight that it took the day dispatcher three days to untangle them.

"Heard knew when he had enough. He raved and fumed and threw away his office key. Notwithstanding his influence, he never came back."

* * * *

Excerpts from "South Park Memories" by Gibson H. Johnston, Railroad Magazine, June, 1934.

"The D. S. P. & P. was the most thrilling, hell-roaring little one-horse railroad on the American continent. On my first trip I fired No. 190, a Baldwin consolidation—a rough riding, knockneed old gal that could make all of 20 miles per hour. We ran from Denver to Como, and Lou Fowler (rest his soul) was my hoghead. I guess he was a bit skeptical of my ability to stoke the old mill, for all the way to Como he kept saying: 'You are doing fine; keep it up'.

"On the return trip, after we were over Kenosha Hill, he told me the 190 was a good steamer and a hard puller, but he added other things that weren't so complimentary.

" 'You know,' he told me, 'we all hate and fear this old rocking horse. So far she has killed sixteen men, and she ain't done yet'. To drive his point home he showed me the various places along the right of way where the 190 had turned over. Well, it seemed that the old coffee grinder had flopped so many places between Denver and Como that Fowler was kept busy the whole trip pointing them out to me.

"My next trip was with Bill Klett. He was a funny dude; when the engine's pops (safety valves) would blow he would invariably reverse the old gal and slip her drivers until the pops were quiet again. The second time he pulled this trick I got down and baled coal into the firebox, for my fire was almost gone. " 'Hey there son,' he yelled to me, 'quit that. I'm trying to stop the noise of that steam blowing off. We can't use too much steam on this gunboat.' That pleased me, and I saw to it that he had as little steam as possible from then on.

"Another time the train ahead of mine was wrecked. Her hind brakeman had stuck with her and had been injured. When the investigation came (there were at least two a day on the old South Park), the superintendent asked the boomer brakeman why he hadn't jumped.

" 'Jump?' asked the brakeman. 'Where in hell could I have jumped to? On one side was a canon a mile deep, and on the other side a granite wall so close to the cars that there wasn't even room for a skinny superintendent to stand'. The super took that one and liked it. He had to.

"All the interesting boys on the South Park weren't boomers. Buddy Schwartz was a home guard, but he got into and out of more scrapes than any two boomers. About once a week he was in a wreck, but he seemed to lead a charmed life, for he was never hurt. In the end though, his 'charmed life' was blotted out like many others.

"Crown sheets on many of the old South Park engines were in bad shape from topping the hill with water shy; yet I never heard of one of them blowing up. Moreover, they carried no water glasses, and we often let the water get too low without realizing it.

"Which reminds me: one day several engineers from another road came in and hired out. They had never been on locomotives without water glasses, so they went to Master Mechanic Sprigg and asked about it.

" 'Why, hell boys,' said Sprigg, 'you don't want water glasses on them bullgines. You would probably be scared to death if you was able to see where the water was all the time!'

"With the coming of the Westinghouse brakes things tamed down a bit. I remember that they were given a grand tryout on Kenosha Hill. They had made several trips down the hill with the engine; then the demonstrator ran the locomotive around the cars, pumped up the air, closed the angle cock and gave the cars a good kick. After that he pulled the pin and signaled the crew to stop. By this time they were rolling at a fast clip. But the brakes set and stopped the cars, and thus the air brake was a proven success on the South Park."

* * * *

From Railroad Magazine, August, 1937:

"Fireman R. A. Townsend of Denver recalls the time on the South Park when C. & S. 75 jumped the track and landed flat on her back in the Platte River at Deer Creek, dragging Engineer Mott and Fireman J. F. Farthing along with her. Her throttle was opened up a little. And there she lay in the middle of the river, her stack buried in the river bottom, her wheels up in the air and turning. The wheels continued to chug merrily along as if nothing unusual had happened until she ran out of steam.

"When they found Mott he was sitting on a rock in the middle of the stream all wet and shivering—mountain water is icc cold—the most forlorn human you ever saw. The hoghead never knew how he had got onto that rock. But he wasn't hurt except for a few minor bruises. Farthing wasn't hurt much either. Later John Farthing pulled the throttle on the 'last run' to Leadville.

"One time a double header consisting of engine No. 75 with Engineer Williamson and Fireman Eshe, and No. 73 with Engineer Thomas and Fireman Starbush jumped the track on Boreas Pass. Williamson was killed and the other three men suffered minor injuries. No. 75 was re-railed, but on account of the heavy snow and hazardous location, the other old gal was left where she had fallen until the following summer, when they built about a quarter mile of new track and finally got her back on the iron again.

"Referring to the thrills of railroading on this pike, Mr. Townsend cited snow slides, rock slides, washouts, and cloudbursts that often washed huge piles of loose dirt and gravel down the mountain side onto the track. Sometimes a crew would get stuck in the snow for days at a time. They then would have to shovel snow into the tender in order to get water for the engine, then crack the injectors and let them blow back into the tank and melt the snow."

Speaking of getting water into an engine tender, Andy Nelson related to the writer that he was once marooned in Alpine Tunnel because of snow. By using the injector, he managed to fill the tender with water from the drainage ditch alongside the tunnel track.

* * * *

J. C. Daugherty, who made a round trip between Denver and Leadville a few weeks previous to the last run in April, 1937, writes:

"When I asked for a round trip for a friend and myself to Leadville over the C. & S., the agent looked somewhat surprised and remarked that these were the first complete round trip tickets between Denver and Leadville he had written up in eight months. . . Leaving Como, in South Park, little old No. 9 buckled down in earnest at the job of climbing the 4% grade up to Boreas Pass, the roof of the world. It was snowing steadily before we reached the summit and the heavy fall continued all the way to Leadville. This added greatly to the beauties of the scenery. . . . While climbing up the north slope of Fremont Pass at Climax, we were stopped behind a freight stalled in the snow about halfway up. Our engineer added our little train to their sixteen cars and four locomotives, and all five engines fought their way up the steep grade, at one time barely moving two or three miles per hour. The show those five old gals put on was well worth the price of the train trip. The brakeman had started a fire in the stove at the opposite end of our car by this time, and we finished the journey by the light of the old coal oil lamps—a sight I had never expected to see again."

Mr. Fritz G. Nagel, who was also a passenger on this trip, has furnished the writer with some additional material concerning this run to Leadville. Mr. Nagel writes:

"Our train consisted of engine 9, baggage car 13, a regular passenger coach and the private car of Mr. Robert Rice, Colorado & Southern official. . . . Everything went very well until we ran into a freight stalled on the grade just above

Kokomo. Four locomotives were trying to get this freight up the hill. Our engine and cars coupled on behind and all five of them went to work. . . . After those five engines had snorted and fought their way through some ten foot snow drifts, we finally reached Climax, only to find a huge Diesel tractor, nearly as large as a South Park engine, stalled on the track. It took over two hours to get this tractor off the track. We finally reached Leadville two hours later.

"On the return trip the next day all went well until we reached Boreas Pass. Here we struck a terrific blizzard, and had to stop and 'blow up' steam no less than five times. Coming down Platte Canon, the air brakes suddenly went on with a jolt. I looked out the window and saw a woman running down the track with a letter in her hand. The engineer slowed up enough for one of the crew to pick up her letter on the fly. On the flats between Waterton and Denver I thought we would be blown off the track by a bad dust storm. That is something-- a blizzard and a dust storm all in one day."

* * * *

Frank Buell writes in Railroad Magazine, September, 1935:

"One winter about 1905, I lived at a mine above Hancock on the Gunnison branch of the old South Park. My brother and I saw a rotary pushed by three engines coming down the grade from Alpine Tunnel. We put on our skis and went over to the track. The plow had stopped and we went inside to warm up. The fireman was brewing some tea over a scoop shovel of live coals. He got out a few crackers and asked if we wanted something to eat. We declined and asked if that was all he had to eat. He answered, 'Boys, that's all I've had for two days!'

"Others of the crew of fifteen were no better off, so taking two men, we hiked to Hancock for provisions. My mother cooked until 9 o'clock, and how those railroaders ate! The roadmaster was sick, so mother sent him some lunch and some medicine. After that, no one of our family ever paid fare to ride on the South Park."

* * * *

E. C. Huffsmith writes in Railroad Magazine, August, 1935:

"Years ago I worked on the Leadville branch of the Colorado & Southern, better known as the South Park. I was with Conductor Larry Colligan and Brakeman F. Sawdey. The company sent us over to Breckenridge; we had a Shay geared engine which had come from a small road between Boulder and Ward,[1] and another helper. We would pick up a train at Breckenridge, go to Boreas and sometimes take the train on down into Como.

"On one of these trips I had a little old hoghead who had never before worked on the road, nor on any mountain railroad. We pulled out, but I did not tell my partners about him until we reached Boreas, where we stopped for air inspection and orders. We decided to run no chances with the new engineer, so we turned up all retainers and had six good brakes clubbed down. I went back to the middle of the train and visited with Brakeman Sawdey. It wasn't long before we were rolling too fast, so we both cinched up some more brakes. Up till now, our hero in the cab had made one application of air. Finally, when we got to Mayo we struck another letup and he had to work steam again.

"A few miles out of Breckenridge there's a long curve called the Race Course, on a gentle grade. There we decided to have some fun with our hogger. Figuring he could easily make the Breckenridge stop, we kicked off all our binders. Boy, how those box cars did go! It seemed as if they would jump from

1. Denver, Boulder & Western

under us. Our hero was calling for brakes, which were impossible to apply, as those old narrow gauge cars were plenty hard to stay on, let alone get over.

"Well, we were getting close to Breckenridge, but we could not tell if there was anything on the main line. I was trying to pick a good place to light. At length we began to slow up a little. I got a few binders cinched, and we finally stopped the train. Luckily our helper was in the clear and No. 81 was late, or we sure would have hit them. Later we found out that the air had been frozen between the engine tank and the first car, and we had no air down that whole hill! If Mr. Hoghead had made a reduction, the whistle of the retainers or the release of the brakes would have warned us. But the only application he made was when we came from the sheds. As I was on the first car, I heard the engine tank release and it fooled me. It was about 30 below zero that night and clear as crystal. The snow was almost all melted and there would have been very few spots for a fellow to light. After that I never played any more smart tricks."

* * * *

Fred R. Whitsett writes in Railroad Magazine, March, 1935:

"As a small boy in 1901 I remember the Colorado & Southern. At that time they still used the link and pin,[1] and would run four engines on a train of five or six cars and a caboose. My father, Frank Whitsett, had just been hired by Roadmaster G. Miller, and we were sent to live at a place called Halfway. One cold wintry day in January, 1902, engine 10 on a passenger train threw a spark under our front porch, setting the house afire and burning everything we owned. We waited in a bunk car until Dad came home, then we took a train to Argentine, Colorado. It had four engines, four cars, and a caboose. Dad and I rode in the caboose. Our train had a tough job bucking snow and about ten miles from Como, near Boreas, we got stuck in a drift. A flagman went back a short distance and laid two torpedoes. Dad and I were left alone in the caboose. Some time later Dad said: 'Here comes No. 71 up behind. I didn't hear her hit those guns or answer the flagman.'

"He was right. No. 71's engine had snow flangers which pushed the torpedoes off the rail! The engineer hadn't seen our flagman, who was out in the swirling blizzard with a lantern. Dad waited until the train was within 20 feet of us, then threw me off the caboose and jumped across me. Those trains sure hit! Our caboose was in a snow shed. The locomotive (the same one which had set our house afire) split the caboose in half and shoved it and a box car into a coal car. Our four engines finally came back after clearing the track, and we rode one of them into Argentine."

* * * *

George F. Lewis of St. George, South Carolina, writes:

"I went to work for the South Park in 1886 as agent and operator. The South Park was a good road to work for. At Como we had a roundhouse full of engines, a switcher and a yard crew. The coal mine at King nearby was running full time shipping coal to Denver.

"We had two passenger trains each way between Denver and Leadville, and two between Como and Gunnison every day. A local freight also operated between Denver and Leadville and between Como and Gunnison, and there were two or three through freights every day. I have seen three engines shoving a rotary snowplow, followed by a flanger with two engines, clearing the way through the deep snow for a double

1. Although officially ruled out in 1893, a few link and pin couplers were still to be found on the South Park around this date.

header, and sometimes a triple header passenger train which followed them. Sometimes it would take all day and night to make the trip from Como over Boreas to Leadville.

"At Pine Grove the railroad had three to five helper engines, a coal chute, three coal shovellers, and an engine hostler. During part of my time, engineers on these helper engines at Pine Grove were Ed Grainger, Si Jefferies, Davey Bones, John Owerea, and Lew Fowler. The South Park's chief dispatcher in Denver was A. F. Vickroy; his assistants were Henry Flavin and Charles Douglass. I left the South Park in 1893, to come south. I used to return now and then but the last time I made a visit to Colorado, all my old South Park friends were gone."

* * * *

Another old timer, F. M. Page, writes from San Diego, California:

"Don't forget to mention the time Walt Parlins and myself turned engine 9 over in the snow up on Boreas Pass during the winter of 1906. We had lots of trouble with snow that winter. While on the South Park I worked with 'Jumbo' Miller, old 'Daddy' Hall, 'Bad-Eye' Nichols, Tom Colligan, Walt Parlins, Ed Gross, and old man Hayes. They were all good mountain railroad men."

* * * *

Another very interesting story that gives additional light on the subject of South Park transportation facilities and some of the men who were connected with the road in its early days, is told by Mr. Albert Sandford in the Colorado Magazine of October, 1928. Mr. Sandford's story follows:

"It was the writer's good fortune, in his boyhood days, to enjoy a rather wide and happy acquaintance with the trainmen of the South Park railroad, almost from its very start. This association enabled him to deadhead on work trains, freight trains, and even the de luxe limited, The Leadville Express.

"Perhaps it was a particularly impressionable age, when a boyish enthusiasm in seeing a railroad operating through the mountains, where formerly a covered wagon or rolling stagecoach were the only means of travel, that left me with certain pictures of the old South Park and those who were intimately associated with its construction and operation. Of them all, none stand out clearer than that on a spring morning at the depot in West Denver, when the end-of-track was near the foot of Kenosha Hill.

"The morning passenger train had been backed in, headed by two engines that took turns popping off. Already there were many passengers boarding the coaches to find the best seats and a place for bundles that varied in size from an ordinary bedroll to a fairly complete prospecting outfit, which, before leaving time, were frequently gathered up by a pair of brawny brakemen and thrown carelessly into a box car ahead. At least half of the train consisted of cars formerly used on the New York Elevated. These cars had been purchased and reconditioned to meet the rapidly increasing rush to Leadville. To original equipment that was used on the Morrison branch, a few new coaches had been added, and on this occasion a special car was attached to the rear.

"Now, among my railroad friends was 'Long Bill' Draper, a brakeman who was stationed at the entrance to the special car with a list of those having reservations. Something happened up ahead. Draper was called from his post, and hurriedly passing the list to me with orders to admit no others, disappeared, and a thrill came to me that has never been duplicated to this day.

"I had completed an examination of this roll of honor, and discovered that with few exceptions, I knew every man by sight, when my first test came with the arrival of a carriage and I checked in David Moffat, Walter Cheesman, and Eben Smith.

"In the meantime Draper returned and another carriage rolled up in a cloud of dust and its occupant jumped to the ground before the vehicle stopped. A large, broad shouldered man with a heavy, drooping mustache, who seemed to know everybody and everybody knew him, came up. He was a man whose millions had just begun to be poured out of the carbonate beds of Leadville, with a good part, even then, being so invested in Denver that makers of new maps began to give the city more prominence—Horace A. W. Tabor—and he had time to grasp the hand of this passenger brakeman and say, 'Howdy, Bill'.

"The next arrival came in an express wagon, seated with the driver, with an overcoat and a large carpet bag, the only baggage. Perhaps a rather close acquaintance in later years has helped preserve this picture more clearly. He did not jump from his perch, but rather made the descent backwards with a firm grip on the seat, as any old person would do. The smile of that expressman, as a fee and a tip, too, no doubt, was handed him, broadened as his passenger said, 'Tom, you made it in good time, but I don't think you missed that darn sprinkling cart by six inches. Goodbye, good luck'. This man, short and rather stout of build, was dressed in 'digging clothes' that showed stains from mine drippings and candle grease, with trousers tucked in the tops of heavy boots. He also wore a heavy dark mustache, and sideburns reaching halfway down his cheeks and kindly eyes, shaded by heavy brows. Some one asked as he was being cordially greeted by all 'How is the 'Morning Star'?' This was John L. Routt, owner of one of the latest bonanza strikes and Governor of Colorado.

"Both engine bells were ringing and two men, apart from the crowd, were so engrossed in conversation over freight and passenger problems to Leadville that, apparently, the time card was forgotten. 'Stuttering Bill' Jackson, the conductor, hurried to them and, partly overcoming his impediment to speech, said, 'Don't want to rush you and the Colonel, Governor, but we're ready to pull out,' and as 'Billy' waved a signal to engineers Frank Kaub[1] and 'Little Joe' Horgan; the President of the South Park, John Evans, and 'Bob' Spotswood, the veteran stage man, got aboard as the long slack of the train started the rear car with a jerk."

* * * *

In the March 6, 1947 issue of the Gunnison News-Champion we read:

"The unusually open winter of 1946-47 recalls to Colin Moore, by contrast, the March, 42 years ago, when 50 trainmen, sleepless and cold, pulled into Gunnison at 1:00 A.M. on the old C. & S. tracks, with seven engines and a broken rotary, after 16 days blocked in the snow at Alpine Pass, then the highest usable pass in the United States, 11,612 feet above sea level.

"Moore says, 'In the year 1905, I was working for the Colorado & Southern as a fireman for Walt Parlin, engineer on engine 57. The last of March marked the worst series of snowslides in the entire history of the Colorado & Southern. On March 14th, the rotary with three engines and a small train left Como to cut through the drifts on both sides of the pass, which were at that time impeding traffic. One by one the cars of the train were backed down the pass and abandoned at St. Elmo. Among them was Superintendent Bacon's private car, although Mr. Bacon kept on with the rotary.

"'One-fourth of a mile east of Alpine Tunnel the rotary

1. A great grandson of Mr. Kaub, Fritz Nagel, gives the name as Philip Kaub.

broke down in 18 feet of snow, and a train was ordered up from Gunnison to help them out. Four engines with five cars of coal went up and were stuck on the side track just west of the tunnel. On March 16th, the Baldwin crew went up and succeeded in getting down the hill from the train. This last train plied back and forth between Pitkin and the nearest they could come to the train.

"'The snow was level with the cab windows. We kept our engines alive by carrying coal about 100 feet through the deep snow from the Gunnison coal cars, and shoveling snow into the engine tank and keeping our heaters on to melt it.

"'The rotary ran into a snow avalanche which had come from the high mountains above, bringing rocks and trees with it, which broke the blades. The slide was 300 feet long and 18 feet deep. It was one-half mile from the east end of the tunnel and two and one-half miles west of Hancock.

"'The rotary blades were carried by the fireman and section men to the Midway water tank. At the tank they were picked up by engine 38, Conductor George Mason and Engineer Pat Colligan. They took the blades to the Salida machine shop (Denver & Rio Grande) for repairs, brought them back as far as Tunnel Gulch from where they were carried up the mountain and over the pass to the rotary and installed.

"'When the rotary was sufficiently repaired it opened the way down the east slope permitting the train to be backed down. Then it undertook the task of opening the line between Como and the tunnel.

"'And there we turned engine 57 and went to Pitkin for the night. We bucked out the road for the train crew to go to Como the next morning.

"'Our boarding house for the 16 days at the tunnel, consisted of two box cars—one a dining room, the other a kitchen. There were two tables down through the center of the car, with benches for seats.

"'For a week the cook fed us three meals a day, of bread, meat, potatoes, and coffee. The second week he reduced the schedule to two meals with menu of beans, carrots, and coffee. The last few days it was just carrots and coffee, and he boiled the coffee grounds until they had no taste.

"'Superintendent Bacon, in Gunnison, said in all the history of the road there was never such a siege as this. The 50 men were sunburned to the color of a boiled lobster, and had a luxuriant growth of whiskers. They were a sorry looking outfit, as most of them had not even had a blanket on which to sleep. The engine men spent most of the 16 days on their seats in the cabs of their engines.

"'Conductor D. E. Gutchell was in charge of the rotary train. Conductor P. C. Newberry of the train snowbound on the west side, and Conductor George Mason made the trip to Salida for the repairs'."

* * * *

In the Gunnison News-Champion of April 17, 1947, Oscar Hurlock writes:

"I fired engine 197 for some two years for John Stapleton and was promoted about the same time as Walt and Frank Parlin, 'Curley' Colligan, Stanley Andrews and Bert Cunningham.

"Snowslides were the dread of winter railroading. We were always glad when the Woodstock slide was down. It was about three miles west of the tunnel, where there still remained what was left of a section house. They say the slide struck in the '80's, killing 13 people.

"Another slide near Breckenridge was said to have killed two engine crews and a rotary crew.

"The winter of 1898 was the worst during my time. I was one of four engineers, a rotary crew, and train crew stuck for four days west of Como. We had beefsteak three times a day—nothing else. Once we were trying to free a train stuck in the snow at Wheeler but failed. We were the last train out of Breckenridge for two or three months as they gave it up and went back to Como—10 engines, a rotary and two coaches.

"The crew at Wheeler lived for two or three weeks from the merchandise car, then made skis out of a snow fence and got to Breckenridge. Waiting for better weather, a passenger who was with them decided to try to make Como—they found his body when the snow melted in May.

"In those days the hours were long and the pay was short. Engineers received $4.40 per day; firemen $3.10. I remember one trip of 61 hours. A day was 10 hours or 88 miles. . . .

"There was an old saying that the conductor tossed cash fares up and all that stuck to the bell cord went to the company. I was with George Mason one day when he took in a cash fare. I told him to throw it, but he refused to take a chance."

* * * *

Mr. H. N. Barr of Grand Rapids, Michigan, writes:

"My father, P. F. Barr, was Division Location and Construction Engineer working with Major James Evans at the time the South Park was constructing their line over Alpine Pass to Gunnison. With our father and mother, my sister and myself went by stagecoach from Buena Vista to Chalk Creek Desert Ranch, which was owned by Mr. Charles Nachtrieb, before the actual construction started from near this place to Gunnison. We later moved to Heywood Springs, about five miles up Chalk Creek, where my father built a house. It had two rooms down stairs and two rooms upstairs and was built of green lumber. The house was located near the bank of Chalk Creek where a mess of mountain trout could be had with very little effort at any time. Being near the Hot Springs, we had hot water day and night.

"I was at Hancock before the tunnel was finished and afterward my mother sent me to stay a couple of weeks with my father in his office car before the road was finished to Gunnison. My mother, my sister and I were on the first through passenger train from Buena Vista to Gunnison. In order to get our meals, while we were at Hancock with father in his office car, we had to go through a big tent where the gambling tables and bar were located to get to the so-called dining room, also in a tent. I can see my mother yet, her nose in the air, her skirts held *almost* to her shoe tops and looking straight ahead with two trailing kids taking in the sight of roulette wheels, faro, poker, painted ladies, drunks, gamblers and bad men. It is something to remember.

"One of the contractors on the Gunnison side of the tunnel was a bad man, who wore two guns, and was a general nuisance and crooked to boot. Father had to cancel his contract and the bad man then let it be known that the old man was his meat the first time they met. So Dad bought a .41 short barrel gun, thinking he might have a chance to use it, and scared to death at the idea. He had never gone armed and knew as much about handling a six-shooter as a hog knows about a holiday. But carry the gun he did and no bad man showed up. Father and Major Evans had been scouting the country on horseback and when night arrived, they stopped at a ranch. After supper they were taking a well earned rest in the main room of the ranch house when who should walk in but our bad man all togged out in his war paint, six-shooter and everything. Father reached for his gun but found he had left it in his office car, so he stuck his hand in his coat pocket and sat still. Mr. Bad Man passed a pleasant evening to everyone, backed out of the room and father never saw him again.

"In connection with Gov. Evans, I must tell you a story told to me by my father. Gov. Evans was, of course, well along in years, probably over seventy-five at the time this incident occurred. The governor, while talking to my father one day, said: 'Barr, you know where that corner lot opposite the Windsor Hotel is? I have leased the lot for ninety-nine years and here are the plans for a four story building to be erected there, and at the end of the lease the building will be mine'. Now I would say that the governor was somewhat of an optimist, considering the fact that the lease still had some thirty odd years to go, before it was terminated."

* * * *

The following incident concerning an heroic act on the part of Governor Evans was taken from McMechen's "Life of Governor John Evans".

"Colonel C. W. Fisher, General Superintendent of the South Park, related in after years, an interesting ancedote about the Governor that occurred while the two were riding the cowcatcher of a locomotive on an inspection trip above Baileys. As the train rounded a curve they saw a little girl seated on one of the rails. The engineer was on the opposite side of the cab from the child, and could not hear the shouts of warning. So suddenly did the situation occur that Col. Fisher thought a disaster inevitable, but Governor Evans was ready for the emergency. Although his motions were always slow, they were sure, and his calm, deliberate presence of mind that controlled his every thought and action did not desert him. Without an instant's hesitation he slid down the high, old fashioned cowcatcher, grasped a rod and, leaning forward, pushed the little girl away from the track with his free hand. It all happened within a cycle of seconds, yet the Governor was as unperturbed when he climbed up the cowcatcher to his seat as he had been a moment before, while surveying the scenery."

* * * *

Here is a rare tale found in an early issue of the Railroad Gazette. It is farfetched, but was undoubtedly believed by many persons in the elite east who lived in the belief that civilization ceased to exist beyond the western bank of the Hudson River.

"Out Leadville way, when a passenger on the Denver South Park & Pacific will not pay his fare and refuses to get off when invited, the Conductor does not call for the brakeman to put him off—he just takes out his Colt six-shooter and shoots him—i.e., unless the passenger gets the drop on the Conductor and shoots him first. In either case the 'stiff' is dumped along side the track and the train continues on its way".

Another shooting episode, this one concerning James Evans, was reported in the Railway Age via a dispatch from Buena Vista on November 10, 1881, which stated:

"James Evans, Chief Engineer of the Denver South Park & Pacific, was shot and seriously wounded this afternoon, November the 4th, by a discharged employee. The assailant was arrested and locked up".

Evidently Mr. Evans' injury was not as serious as reported, for he lived to continue his duties of pushing track over many more miles of South Park right of way.

* * * *

A PASSENGER TRAIN RIDE FROM DENVER TO LEADVILLE.
By Ed Haley.

Let's pretend that we can turn time back to the year 1934 and we'll take a trip in memory together over the old Colorado & Southern narrow gauge line to Leadville.

First we'll see the man behind the ticket window at the **Denver Union Station.** Boy—that fellow got a surprised look on his face when we asked for two round trip tickets to Leadville via the Colorado & Southern. Guess he doesn't have many requests like that. It cost us $9.44 apiece. Just think: $9.44 for 300 thrilling miles of the best scenery in the United States.

Grab your suitcase and let's beat it down the ramp and through the underpass, way out to track number nine. It's only a few minutes until train time and we'll want to look her over before we start. Up these stairs now and there she is. Compared to the rest of the trains in the station, ours is amazingly small. As is usually the case we have engine 9, baggage car 13, and passenger car 70. It's not much of a train to look at, but if all goes well, it will take us to Leadville, crossing the Continental Divide twice before nightfall.

Doesn't this old open platform coach look odd? Let's climb aboard and stow these bags. We'd better grab this end seat by the stove—it's liable to get mighty chilly up at 11,000 feet today. Old No. 70 was quite a car in her day, and these black leather seats are still plenty comfortable. This half is the smoker and beyond those sliding doors in the middle is the regular section with its red plush seats. Notice the oil lamps hanging from the green ceiling. The beautiful wood paneling, the mirrors, the gold paint. All this, like the big old potbellied stoves in each end of the car, is typical of South Park coaches back before the turn of the century.

Well, we have five minutes, so let's hop off and take a look at engine 9. She's an old-timer all right, as you can tell by her square wooden cab. Put a balloon stack and oil lamp back on her and she would look just as she did back in the '90's when she was making her way up and down the narrow canons as the 114.

There's Tom St. John, our conductor, talking to engineer John Farthing. St. John is kind of sober faced isn't he? Well, don't let that fool you. He is a very congenial fellow and he can tell you many an amazing tale of railroading on the old South Park. He has been on the line for fifty years and he knows almost everyone between here and Leadville by their first name.

I guess we'd better climb on again as it looks like we're about ready to pull out. Yes, there's St. John calling "Booo-ard". St. John's highball is answered by the hiss of escaping air as the brakes release. A jerk, a few protesting squeals, the sound of No. 9's quickening exhausts, a rumble as we cross Cherry Creek bridge, and we're off to Leadville.

Our little train carefully threads its way through the maze of yard tracks south of the station, with many a stop to set switches. We cross to the west bank of the Platte River and leave the third rail—from here on it's narrow gauge only.

Look toward the west. The early morning sun sure gives those snow-covered peaks a rosy look. The train is slowing for a stop—must be Sheridan Junction. Yes, it is—there goes the Morrison Branch out to the west along the banks of Bear Creek. But we will follow the windings of the Platte River as it wanders through grove after grove of cottonwood trees on its way from the mountains.

We're coming into Waterton now. This is where Denver gets part of its water supply from the Platte River. There are the filtering beds. And there's the Silica branch of the railroad leading off to the south along the base of the mountains. We turn to the west at this point and leave the last vestige of the level plains behind us. Following closely along the boulder-strewn banks of the river, our little train pushes boldly into the shadowy depths of the narrow and twisting confines of the canon where the cliffs rise like great frowning fortresses and soon we are buried in the solitude of Platte Canon. As you can see, there's only room for the roadbed

and the river and at times it surely seems as if the car will scrape the sheer rock walls of the canon on some of these sharp curves.

Let's go ride the rear platform for a while. It's plenty chilly down here in the bottom of the canon, and the smoke from the engine hangs low over the train. The roar of the river can at times be heard over the noise that No. 9 is making on the grade. There's Strontia Springs, first sign of civilization in the canon. It is a summer resort so the train won't stop there. Did you ever see such a twisting, turning roadbed? It follows every bend of the river and even adds a few it-self. We're slowing down, must be South Platte station coming up. Yes, there's the old gray frame South Platte Hotel and there's the South Fork of the river. If you look closely you can see the roadbed of the long-abandoned Night-hawk Branch following the South Fork of the river. Also there is a section of the old Rio Grande grade, where they had planned to build up the South Fork.

As we proceed west from South Platte station to Webster, you'll find the canon a lot less forbidding. There are many summer resorts and cabins along this section. We're coming to Dome Rock now—great place for picnics a few years ago. See that huge dome-like rock formation across the river? That's what gave this place its name. Got to watch now for Billy Westall's monument. There it is, on the river side. That big gray stone monument was erected by the A.O.U.W. in memory of Engineer William Westall who was killed on this spot when an afternoon passenger train hit a rock slide back in August, 1898.

Here we come into Buffalo. There goes the baggage man taking some mail over to old man Green's store and post office. It's that stone building just south of the tracks. It is only a short run to Pine, another important stop on the line. It's quite a summer resort. We'll take on water here. It's a pleasant ride through this section. The grade is not very steep; the curves are more sweeping and our path crosses one meadow after another, interspersed by groves of trees.

There is Crystal Lake; all frozen over at this time of the year. There are lots of small lakes along this section of the canon.

We are slowing up again—must be coming into Baileys. There is always mail for Baileys as there are many people in this section who live here the year around. See the highway coming down out of the mountains from the north? It joins the railroad here in following the course of the river. If you'll look over here to the left while we pass Maddox, you will see them harvesting and storing ice. The railroad will haul it to Denver later on.

I'll tell you a little story about the next station, Alturia. Tom St. John tells me it was always called Slaghts until some French woman bought up all the surrounding land and renamed the place Alturia. But it's still called Slaghts by all the train crews and I can't say that I blame them.

Lots of meadows and pasture land along here now. There's Shawnee up the hill to the left; great spot for Sunday picnickers not so many years ago. The canon now begins to narrow and we swing around this bend into Cassells. There's camp Santa Maria for underprivileged children. Look across the canon on the top of that high hill to the right. That huge statue is the largest statue of Christ in North America. Mt. Logan forms a majestic background.

We stop for a moment at Grant and then on to Webster and famous Kenosha Pass. See that low spot in the peaks ahead—that's Kenosha Pass. In 1875, civil engineers said a railroad could not be built over it, but the South Park built one anyway. The east slope of Kenosha Hill has been the scene of some of the nastiest smashups and runaways in the South Park's history. Now we are slowing down for Webster, the last town in Platte Canon. Webster has quite a history. At one time, when it was end-of-track, it was a rip-roaring town. See that little knoll off to the south across the creek? Within that picket fence on its crest, lay forty men who "died with their boots on". It was here that the Leadville stage line used to meet the train.

We swing north now into Hall's Valley. Here is the big curve where we reverse directions. There have been some very bad wrecks at this spot. By the sound of No. 9's exhausts and the rain of cinders that come cascading down, you can tell we're on a mighty steep grade. There is Webster far down below us in the valley. Look at the deer grazing along the right of way; they look up but don't run. Here we are at the summit of Kenosha Pass, 9,991 feet above sea level. There's the Kenosha section house. They tell me it used to be a station on the old stage line.

Now watch for one of the most beautiful scenes in the Rockies. There it is—the great South Park! Stretching for forty miles to the south and twenty miles across—a beautiful, fertile, rolling plain in the heart of the Rockies. It is a fast run down off the pass to the floor of the park.

Let's see—it's almost noon so let's eat this lunch we had packed. Just prop your feet up on the opposite seat and use your lap for a table. What could be nicer? Eating lunch while rockin' and rollin' across South Park with its fields of timothy hay waving in the crisp mountain breeze. Not a speck of cloud in the bright blue sky that really contrasts with those snowy mountain tops surrounding the park. There go the brakes again. We will be stopping here in Jefferson for a minute. Then we're off again on our run across the park—that was Michigan we just breezed through. Here's Coal Branch Junction. I want you to be sure now and notice the peculiar method they use to get the train into Como, over there to the west. First we head south along the wye and out to what was the branch to the King coal field southeast of Como. The switches are set and then back north we go along the other leg of the wye to the main line and continue north for about half a mile. This sharp curve swings us completely around so that we back into Como, past the old eating house, and come to a stop in front of the depot with our engine headed north, pointing at austere Boreas Pass on the west shoulder of 14,000-foot Mt. Baldy.

As Como is a lunch stop, our few fellow passengers wander over to the little store and lunch counter near the depot, but we're free to snoop around the roundhouse and other railroad facilities. It's hard to realize, looking at Como today, with its boarded up store fronts and tumble-down buildings, that this place was once a busy division point with 26 trains a day. There goes engine 9 down to the water tank south of town. She'll fill up with coal too and be ready for the long drag up Boreas Pass which lies ahead of us. See the rails leading off south through the park? That was once the main line to Gunnison through the famous Alpine Tunnel. Now it is merely the Fairplay-Alma branch with tri-weekly service.

Well, let's get back to the train. I see Engineer "Curley" Colligan, a genial Irishman with fifty years on the South Park, oiling around No. 9. Looks like we have a new passenger. Seems to be a miner or a prospector with that long white beard and that sack he's carrying. There's Curley whistling so I guess we'd better climb aboard. A few protesting squeals and we slip past the Como eating house, clatter across the switch that leads off east toward Denver and, plunging into thick aspen groves, we begin the second half of our journey.

This grade we're starting up now is the beginning of the long drag to Boreas. Look—St. John is signalling to Curley Colligan to slow down; our passenger with the long white beard hops off. That trail he is trudging down leads to the old Tarryall diggings that were famous before there was a Leadville. Listen—it sounds like Curley has the Johnson Bar

down among the oil cans—No. 9 is really working—those cinders are falling like rain. Come on, let's get out on the rear platform and enjoy this scenery. Look at South Park spread out below us like a map. It will soon be lost to view. We're slowing down again—must be coming to Halfway Tank. We'll have to fill up. Notice how the trees are beginning to thin out—we are approaching timberline. We're mighty lucky this trip. The pass is usually pretty stormy this time of year, but the good weather seems to be holding out. Right in this section was the famous Selkirk snowshed—the longest on the line. It burned down many years ago. It won't be long now 'til we're on top of the pass.

Here we are, at Boreas—the highest railroad pass in North America, 11,493 feet elevation. Notice the peculiar arrangement here. The main line and the long passing track are all covered with a snowshed while the depot is built right into the shed. It is pitch dark in there where the train stops.

And now begins the ride down to Breckenridge (and I do mean down), a drop of 1,925 feet in 11 miles. We'd better get inside as Tom St. John has to ride the rear and work the air. The brakeman rides the front platform and tightens the brakes on the baggage car by means of that large hand wheel.

Over to the west there, across the valley of the Blue River is the majestic Park Range, sometimes called Mosquito Range. Those highest peaks are Bross, Lincoln and Quandary, all over 14,000 feet in elevation. Leadville lies on the other side of that range, but it's a long hard trip yet before we'll be there. The reverse curve through that rock cut is called Rocky Point. It is a sheer drop here to the Blue River, many hundreds of feet below. Look to the north on this next curve and you'll see three levels of track where our line swings around the crown of Nigger Hill, down to the loop at Puzzle Switch and through Illinois Gulch to Breckenridge. From the top of Nigger Hill, Breckenridge looks like a little toy town. The grade is plenty steep here as we drift along the side of the hill and 'round the loop. This mountain we're passing is called Little Mountain. We are slowing for Breckenridge. Have mail to leave and orders to pick up. There goes Tom St. John over to the little white station. The gold dome over there is the Summit County Court House. Here we go again— this time following the Blue River. This was a great mining country a good many years ago. Notice the numerous mine workings dotting the mountain sides.

We're stopping for Dickey now. There goes the brakeman out to set the switch for the Dillon branch. It's only a little over three miles to Dillon and the track is straight almost all the way. You can see the town ahead now. We will only stop long enough to leave the mail. See the track beyond the station, curving east toward Loveland Pass? That is the Keystone branch; Keystone is a lumber camp. The branch is hardly ever used nowadays. They tell me that it was the plan of the railroad in the early days to build a line between Dillon and Graymont, under Loveland Pass, to connect this point of the South Park line with the Colorado Central that ran up Clear Creek past Georgetown and Silver Plume. I guess this Keystone branch was as far as they ever got with their plans.

There is No. 9's shrill whistle and we're off again. Tom St. John rides the rear platform as we back up toward the main line at Dickey. It's not a very pleasant ride out there when the days are really cold. We clatter across the switches of the wye at Dickey and start forward again. This time we are headed west toward the long drag up rugged Tenmile Canon. Between Dickey and Kokomo in Tenmile Canon is the most treacherous snowslide area on the entire South Park line. All through the winter the snow comes cascading down from jagged Tenmile Range, which towers so forebodingly on our left. If you'll look closely you will see, running parallel

W. H. Jackson photo,
from the State Historical Society of Colorado.

A South Park passenger train and a Rio Grande mixed train on parallel tracks near Alicante, just west of Fremont Pass. Note the three trestles across the headwaters of the Arkansas River, near the snowshed on the Rio Grande's Blue River branch. The Continental Divide stretches across the background, with 14,142-foot Mount Democrat at the left.

to us and between us and Tenmile Creek, the Rio Grande's Blue River branch, which was built between Leadville and Dillon. The rails have been gone for many a year, but in many places the old pine ties are still to be seen.

Now we are coming to Solitude, where we take on water. The place is aptly named for there isn't a human habitation in sight. The stop on the Rio Grande just across the creek was called Wheeler and many of the South Park men call the place Wheeler. Sections of this Tenmile Canon are very beautiful. See those beaver dams along the creek? The water tank we just passed is Kokomo tank—that means it's only half a mile to Kokomo. There's the town over across the creek, nestled at the foot of Jacque Mountain. Kokomo is a fairly busy little place compared to some of the stations along the line and we sometimes pick up a passenger or two for Leadville. Notice the spur track running from the main line across Tenmile Creek and into Kokomo? It is seldom used since the railroad moved the depot from the town over beside the main line. This rocky cut we're passing through used to have a snowshed covering it, but it burned down a few years ago. We cross the auto road and the creek twice within a few hundred feet. The auto road is the old Rio Grande roadbed. To your right is the spur running up Kokomo Gulch to Wilfleys Mill. The rails have been removed. If you will observe closely, you can see over there to the left where the original South Park grade was built along the side of the hill. It was a part of the Kokomo switchback, which was abandoned many years ago.

Watch now for Robinson on the right. That's it—the tall brick stack, the mill and those houses. It used to have a big population but it's a ghost town now. The grade here is steep but it isn't far to Climax, on the Continental Divide at an elevation of 11,320 feet. A peculiar situation exists here. Since leaving Como we have crossed the Continental Divide twice, ending up on the same side from which we started. All those buildings, the big hotel, hospital, and houses belong to the Climax Molybdenum Company, as one of the world's largest molybdenum mines is located here.

Look at that beautiful Colorado sunset; those few scattered clouds bright gold against a blue sky. And the long rays of the setting sun slanting down across the purple hills light up the green valley of the Arkansas River for one last lingering moment. It is a picture hard to forget. We follow along the top of the ridge almost all the way to Leadville, while the Rio Grande's old roadbed drops swiftly away as we leave Climax and is soon lost in the blue shadows of the valley below.

Here comes the brakeman, from the rear platform, with the marker lamps. Has to get his signal oil and fill them, light them up and get them hung for it gets dark quickly, once the sun is gone. These car lamps are next. You have to be an acrobat for that job. See how he places one foot on the arm of this seat and his other on the arm of the seat across the aisle and, holding the fragile glass lamp shade in his hand and fumbling in his vest pocket for a match, he strives to keep his balance as Curley Colligan really "rolls 'em" down the Arkansas Valley to Leadville. It's getting chilly—guess I'd better throw a little more coal in the stove and poke up the fire a bit. We might as well be comfortable the rest of the way in.

That water tank that just flashed by is called Birds Eye. Only about six more miles to Leadville; down hill all the way. The way Curley's rolling them, it won't be long now. There—I see the lights of Leadville twinkling in the distance. We turn around out here on the wye and back into town past the roundhouse and freight depot. Here we are at the Leadville station; grab your bag and let's beat it down to the Saddlerock Cafe for a good steak and a beer, and a chat with St. John and Colligan. And then for a good night's sleep, because when the sun turns snow-clad Mt. Massive and Mt. Elbert red again in the morning, we'll be on our way back to Denver.

W. H. Jackson photo,
from E. J. Haley Collection.

The Jull plow derailed above Hancock during the snowplow trials on April 16, 1890.

CHAPTER XXI

ABANDONMENT.

There is no pleasure in writing or reading an obituary column in a daily newspaper; the same applies to the last chapter of South Park history—its abandonment. Concerning the policies of the Colorado & Southern company relative to the operation, management, and gradual abandonment of the narrow gauge division, there are two schools of thought; one faction criticizes the management, while the other upholds them. Distance, lack of time, and difficulty of access to all the records (if they exist) prevents the writer from entering into a long discourse as to why the South Park road went the way it did. Research has produced some material supporting both sides; we shall report the findings and let the reader form his or her own opinion.

The elimination of the South Park railroad from the Colorado scene is difficult to reconcile by many individuals. They feel that the management, contrary to assertions made, was not truly and vitally interested in the future welfare of the narrow gauge division of the Colorado & Southern system. There are those who contend that the Burlington, after extending their line into Denver in 1882,[1] was nursing some ambitious plans to expand its transportation system throughout Colorado and adjacent areas. An opportunity presented itself in the dissolution of the Union Pacific Denver & Gulf combination during the '90's. It is contended that Burlington interests, operating behind the scenes, helped promote the organization of the Colorado & Southern company for the purpose of eventually gaining control of a north and south standard gauge transportation system extending from Wyoming to Texas. This trackage included the old Denver Texas & Gulf, Denver Texas & Ft. Worth, and the Ft. Worth & Denver City. At the same time they conveniently acquired the narrow gauge Denver Leadville & Gunnison, mainly for the extremely valuable one-fifth (some records say one-fourth)[2] interest which the road controlled in the Denver Union Depot terminal. What became of the Colorado Central Railroad's interest in this terminal property is not known by the writer.[3] The South Park

1. This was the Burlington & Colorado Railroad which reached Denver May 29, 1882.
2. The Gunnison News-Champion, August 6, 1942.
3. The 1885 Report of the Colorado Railroad Commission states the Colorado Central R. R. Co. owned 150 shares of Denver Union Depot stock valued at $15,000.

road had apparently served its purpose, and although the new owners could not discard it like so much chaff, they had no further use for the narrow gauge line and seemingly looked upon it as an unwanted child. If the road made any money for them, either as an artery of commerce or as a feeder line, well and good; if it developed into a liability—time would take care of that. Accordingly, they refused to nourish it and left the road to shift for itself with the probable idea that sooner or later it would die on the vine.

A representative of the South Park Railroad Company, one of a number of organized groups interested in taking over the Denver-Como Leadville line during the 1937 abandonment proceedings, stated: "Plain stupidity of the railroad has not only failed to develop new business, but for some years past has done everything to discourage and drive away existing business".[1] Other individuals added to this indictment by claiming that the management was not desirous of purchasing any new locomotives or rolling stock, or properly maintaining the right of way, and purposely destroyed business in order that the records, which would eventually be submitted to the Interstate Commerce Commission, would look bad.

Other individuals cite the 1910 cave in of Alpine Tunnel as an example of the company's destructive policy. These persons criticize the management for letting it appear that the tunnel was damaged beyond repair, forcing them to abandon the line; when in reality the cave in was of small consequence and could have been readily repaired, thus keeping the Gunnison division open. Photographs taken thirty years later bear out this contention that the cave in, or rock fall, was of a minor nature.

On the other hand, those who uphold the management in their actions and policies also have some strong points. First, and of no little importance, was the gradual decline of Colorado's mining industry over a period of years. This fact cannot be denied. The South Park was definitely a mineral road. True, the road transported various other commodities, but its very life blood, from the beginning, was ore traffic. For years, the mine owners and operators skimmed off the cream of the gold and silver ores. Eventually they reached the more com-

1. Railroad Magazine, August, 1937.

plex and less accessible ores, which made mining less and less profitable. Capital, acquired as profits from previous operations, had been squandered with the result that there were few funds left for the necessary improvements to continue operations.[1] Many mines closed down due either to the exhaustion of ore or decline in prices. The myriad of abandoned mines and mills, ghost camps and deserted communities, bear out this fact.

However, lest the reader gain a wrong impression, it should be pointed out that the state of Colorado as a whole is still very much a mining state, its output exceeding $30,000,000 annually.[2] Cripple Creek, Alma, the San Juan region, and Boulder, Gilpin and Clear Creek Counties still have some good gold and silver mines; the Climax Molybdenum Mine produces about two-thirds of the world's molybdenum; while lead, zinc, copper, tungsten and various other minerals are being obtained in respectable quantities. Many of Colorado's early mining camps were either founded on poor judgment or on indications of extensive mineral resources that failed to materialize. In some cases they were abandoned, not because the ore gave out entirely, but because there was no process available for profitably treating the complex ores. It is possible that, with the present advanced metallurgical technique, many of these abandoned mines could be made to pay and that some of them will one day be revived. Colorado is also discovering that its greatest source of wealth is not altogether found in the mining of gold and silver, but in a rapidly developing agricultural industry.

Another economic factor to be considered was the introduction of cheap electrical power transmitted into the Leadville area around 1907. The gradual rise in the use of electricity in and around the mines eliminated the need for coal brought in by the railroad. This resulted in the loss of considerable inbound traffic which the railroad had enjoyed heretofore. And still another point which should probably be mentioned, is that the South Park road, being a narrow gauge system, was unable (without undue cost) to ever become a part of any standard gauge transcontinental system. Had the road been of standard gauge construction there is the very remote possibility that at some time a section of it might have been included in such a scheme. Although remote, the idea is not without foundation; around the turn of the century such a scheme was being considered in connection with the Colorado Midland and the Santa Fe.

Following on the heels of the decline in the mining industry came the improved highway with its attending growth of the private automobile and the bus and truck business. The growth of the bus and truck industry had a very telling effect on the railroad's busi-

1. Colorado Geological Survey Bulletin, 1912.
2. Compressed Air Magazine, July, 1941.

ness, depriving it of more and more traffic each succeeding year. During the course of the hearings before the I. C. C. relative to abandonment of the road, this important fact was brought up time after time. Each time the protestants promised to favor the railroad in preference to the truckers, but soon forgot their promises. They were sternly warned by the I. C. C., more than once, that the inevitable result of failure to support the railroad would hasten its abandonment. But for some reason the public chose to patronize trucks and busses, using public highways instead of supporting a railroad which built and maintained its own right of way. Thus, they not only had to dig down in their pockets for tax money to build and maintain a first-class highway, but also killed a lucrative source of revenue—for an abandoned railroad pays no taxes to any community. The cost of maintaining hundreds of miles of mountain highways, which have to be kept free of snow in the winter season, has proved to be an enormous burden to Colorado taxpayers.[1]

In summarizing the case, both sides have their strong points. Possibly many readers, because of a great affection for the old line from an historical point of view, close their eyes to the cold facts, but it must be remembered that a railroad becomes a commercial factor only to the extent that it vitalizes trade. It cannot exist upon so unsubstantial a sentiment as personal pride. It must be useful to be important. It must have traffic to exist. In forming an opinion as to whether management destroyed this traffic or attempted to hold it, the writer desires to let the reader make his own decision.

However, on the strength of a declining Colorado mining industry, a growing truck and bus system, augmented by the private automobile, a disinterested clientele along its lines, and a management who apparently exerted little or no effort to prevent the road's downfall, all climaxed by a period of depressed business activity in the early '30's, the Colorado & Southern company secured that which it desired—abandonment of the narrow gauge lines. Statistical data is included which shows the reduction in business handled by Colorado & Southern narrow gauge lines in later years. Abandonment of the varous sections of the system will be discussed in detail.

VOLUME OF BUSINESS

Year	Passengers Carried	Tons of Freight Hauled	Operating Revenue	Operating Expenses	Deficit (Including Taxes)
Ending 6-30-85	59,566	191,807	$1,145,494	....	$320,869
1910-27 average	....	....	330,000	$490,000	240,000
1920	....	....	444,813	800,713	....
1923	34,366	109,165	....	....	....

1. "Colorado". American Guide Series, 1941. Sponsored by The Colorado State Planning Commission.

Year					
1924	....	95,244	....	....	(1920-27
					Average:
1925	....	100,971	....	....	$339,170)
1926	....	108,738	....	....	....
1927	24,114	102,430	266,859	463,650	....
1928	....	94,786	321,051	438,114	236,354
1929	....	93,834	....	....	193,045
1930	....	87,525	....	....	224,309
1931	....	69,756	223,202	....	176,031
1932	....	87,288	263,956	....	91,623
1933	....	60,595	185,141	....	138,140
1934	5,658	70,915	222,971	295,171	160,605

This data was compiled from the 1885 report of the Colorado Railroad Commissioner, various Colorado & Southern reports, and 217-I.C.C.-370.

* * * *

CHRONOLOGICAL RISE AND FALL OF COLORADO & SOUTHERN NARROW GAUGE MILEAGE.

Denver South Park & Pacific trackage.

Year	Section	Acquired	Removed	Balance
1874	Denver (6th & Larimer) to Bear Creek Junction	6.67		6.67
1874	Bear Creek Jct. to Morrison	9.71		16.38
1878	Soda Lake Spur	.25		16.63
1878	Garfield Quarry Branch	2.75		19.38
1878	Bear Creek Jct. to Grant	58.60		77.98
1879	Grant to Trout Creek Pass	53.69		131.67
1879	Coal Branch Jct. to King Mines	3.32		134.99
1879	Extension from original D.S. P.& P. Depot north to new Denver Terminal	.88		135.87
1880	Trout Creek Pass, via Arkansas Station to D. & R. G. Switch No. 1	14.46		150.33
1880	Nathrop to St. Elmo	16.89		167.22
1880	Arkansas Station to Buena Vista, D.& R.G. Switch No. 2	2.11		169.33
1881	St. Elmo to Alpine Tunnel	7.99		177.32
1881	Garos to Fairplay	9.98		187.30
1882	Fairplay to Alma	5.43		192.73
1882	Alpine Tunnel to Gunnison	40.46		233.19
1882	Como to Dillon	30.90		264.09
1883	Gunnison to Castleton	14.71		278.80
1883	Castleton to Baldwin	2.80		281.60
1883	Dillon to Keystone	4.20		285.80
1883	Dickey to Kokomo	16.20		302.00
1884	Kokomo to Leadville	19.43		321.43
1884	Connection from old line to new Buena Vista station	1.56		322.99
1884	Connection from old line to D.& R.G. Switch No. 2, put into side track		1.48	321.51
1884	Macune to D.& R.G. main line taken up		1.00	320.51

Year	Section	Acquired	Removed	Balance
1884	Trout Creek connection on main line to Macune taken up		1.48	319.03
1884	Macune to Nathrop, via Schwanders	5.42		324.45
1884	Trout Creek connection on main line to Schwanders	1.09		325.54
1884	Portion of King Coal Mines branch taken up		.35	325.19
1885	New main line connection at Nathrop	.48		325.67
1885	Main line connection with D. & R.G. at Nathrop taken up		.83	324.84
1888	Extension of Keystone branch	.11		324.95
1888	Extension of Morrison branch	.26		325.21

Became Denver Leadville & Gunnison Ry. August 29, 1889.

Year	Section	Acquired	Removed	Balance
1892	Extension of Buena Vista station track	.23		325.44
1895	Kokomo to Wilfley's Mill	1.14		326.58
1896	Castleton to Kubler	1.56		328.14
1898	Hill Top Junction to Leavick	11.33		339.47

(The Denver South Park & Hill Top Ry.)

1870 to 1898 Colorado Central R.R. (Clear Creek line.)

Denver to Graymont 58.10
Mile Post 55.09 (beyond Silver Plume) to Graymont abandoned in 1898 3.01
_____
55.09
Golden to Church's Brick yard 1.70
Forks Creek to Central City 11.66
_____
68.45 68.45 407.92

Control acquired by the Colorado & Southern, December 28, 1898.

Year	Section	Acquired	Removed	Balance
1899	Coal Branch Jct. to King Mines abandoned		2.71	405.21
1900	Leadville Mineral Belt built	2.34		407.55
1900	Leadville Mineral Belt extension	.10		407.65
1900	Extension of Main Line at Leadville	.65		408.30
1902	South Platte to Nighthawk	4.11		412.41
1903	Abandonment of portion of the Clear Creek line near Silver Plume		.45	411.96
1904	South Platte-Nighthawk extension	.17		412.13
1905	Castleton to Baldwin reduction. (Approximate date)		.18	411.95

Year	Section	Acquired	Removed	Balance
1905	Kokomo to Wilfley's Mill reduction		.04	411.91
1908	Trout Creek line above Schwanders washed out		.85	411.06
1908	Trout Creek connection to Macune	1.55		412.61
1908	Buena Vista station track reduced. (Approximate date)		.17	412.44

Control Acquired by the C.B.& Q. Dec. 21, 1908.

Year	Section	Acquired	Removed	Balance
1909	Waterton to Silica	3.76		416.20
1909	Silica branch extension	.13		416.33
1911	Morrison Line extension	.20		416.53
1912	Dickey to Keystone reduction		.17	416.36
1912	Buena Vista station track extension. (Approximate date)	.22		416.58
1912	Coal Branch Jct.-King Mines; remaining line put into side track		.26	416.32
1914	Castleton to Baldwin extension	.49		416.81
1916	South Platte to Nighthawk taken up		4.28	412.53
1919	Morrison line reduced		.41	412.12
1919	Garfield Quarry Branch taken up		2.75	409.37
1919	Soda Lake Spur taken up		.25	409.12
1922	Garos to Macune taken up		28.73	380.39
1923	Hancock to Quartz taken up		13.80	366.59
1923	Parlin to Gunnison taken up		11.98	354.61
1926	Buena Vista to Macune taken up		2.47	352.14
1926	Macune to Hancock taken up		27.08	325.06
1928	Black Hawk to Central City reduced		.47	324.59
1931	Black Hawk to Central City taken up		3.52	321.07
1934	Morrison line reduction		6.31	314.76
1934	Quartz to Parlin taken up		17.86	296.90
1937	Gunnison to Baldwin sold to D.& R.G.W.		17.82	279.08
1937	Castleton to Kubler sold to D.& R.G.W.		1.56	277.52
1938	Remainder of Morrison line beyond Sheridan Jct. taken up		3.45	274.07
1938	Terminal trackage at Leadville reduced		.65	273.42
1938	Leadville Mineral Belt removed		2.44	270.98
1938	Kokomo to Wilfley's Mill removed		1.10	269.88
1938	Dickey to Keystone removed		6.84	263.04
1938	Como to Climax removed		49.19	213.85

Year	Section	Acquired	Removed	Balance
1938	Leavick to Hill Top Jct. removed		11.33	202.52
1938	Alma to Garos removed		15.41	187.11
1938	Garos to Como removed		16.30	170.81
1938	Como to South Platte removed		58.59	112.22
1939	Idaho Springs to Silver Plume removed		16.88	95.34
1941	Waterton to Silica removed		3.89	91.45
1941	Forks Creek to the Hidden Treasure Mill in Black Hawk removed		7.67	83.78
1941	Idaho Springs to Golden removed		21.95	61.83
1941	Golden to Denver. (Only third narrow gauge rail removed.)		15.81	46.02
1941	Church's Brick Yard to Golden removed		1.70	44.32
1942	South Platte to Chatfield removed		15.61	28.71
1942	Chatfield to Denver. (Third standard gauge rail extended to Sheridan Jct., September, 1938, and to Chatfield in August 1939. See text for details)		14.07	14.64
1943	Climax to Leadville changed to standard gauge		14.64	0

Narrow gauge to
standard gauge 14.83
Main line—Climax to
Leadville 14.64

Apparently additional
side track .... .19

*   *   *   *

THE ABANDONMENT OF THE GAROS-BALDWIN DIVISION

By 1895, Colorado's mining industry began to recover somewhat from the effects of the recent silver panic. New gold discoveries in the Leadville area at this time instilled new life into the ore shipping business. In 1900, the state's production of gold, silver, lead, and other mineral products totaled $50,614,424. This was an all time high figure, and has never been equalled since. Gunnison County and its surrounding area; Chaffee County, including the Chalk Creek region; Summit County and the Breckenridge district; Lake County with its Leadville mines; and Gilpin and Clear Creek Counties covering the entire Clear Creek region; all directly served by the South Park and Clear Creek Divisions, were each enjoying their share of this increased activity. Park County, including the Lon-

A 1938 view of the South Park's roadbed near Bath, the summit of Trout Creek Pass, looking toward the remains of the over-pass used by the Colorado Midland to cross the South Park line.

South Park from Kenosha Pass, showing C.&S. 71 with the dismantling train, backing downgrade in September, 1938.

don and Fairplay districts, was just about holding its own. As a result of the increased activity in these areas, South Park freight drags were plying up and down the mountains 24 hours a day in an effort to handle the great ore shipments. Consequently, when the newly organized Colorado & Southern Railway Company took over the South Park and Clear Creek lines in 1898, it acquired, among other things, a transportation gold mine. The two roads represented a veritable life line between the important mining districts and Denver and the east.

However this temporary boom did not last long. Around the turn of the century, miner's strikes shut down a large number of mines and mills, causing a serious decline in revenue.

The following production figures, for the years 1900 and 1910, were published in a U. S. Government report on mining in the state of Colorado.

	Clear Creek	Gilpin	Park	Lake
1900	$1,580,900.	$1,967,150.	$157,800.	$10,691,900.
1910	1,029,200.	852,700.	465,500.	7,360,700.

	Chaffee	Summit	Gunnison	Entire State
1900	$ 416,500.	$ 865,500.	$256,000.	$50,614,424.
1910	270,600.	973,700.	298,300.	33,671,000.

Meanwhile, traffic over Alpine and Boreas Passes had dropped considerably, but operating expenses continued at their usual high level. To make matters worse, fate entered the picture in the form of a small cave in, which occurred in Alpine Tunnel in October, 1910. The date, as nearly as can be determined, was October 10th. The cave in was not serious and could have been cleaned up; however, the management inferred that the damage was beyond repair. Four days later, The Gunnison News-Champion stated: "We have positive information that the C.& S. has decided to close the railroad to Denver for the winter, perhaps permanently. . . however, the rails will remain in place as this section of the railroad is covered by a mortgage . . ."

The word "permanently" was correct. On October 24, 1910, the South Park management announced that all through service to Gunnison would be discontinued. Immediately afterward, that section of the main line between Hancock and Quartz, a distance of 13.80 miles, was abandoned. And thus came the first important shrinkage in mileage of the South Park system. As a writer in Trains magazine commented, "It was pre-ordained that the Gunnison line would be the first to go, because the operating expenses over Alpine Pass were tremendous, and the Gunnison traffic, like that of Leadville, was subject to D.& R.G. competition. While operating expenses on normal narrow gauge lines are roundly three times as much as on standard gauge, the operating expenses over Alpine Pass were probably five times as great".

Due possibly to some legal stipulation incorporated in a mortgage, the rails between Hancock and Quartz were left intact for 13 years, following the abandonment in 1910. In 1923, all the rail between these two points, with the exception of that between the east portal and a point about one mile beyond the west portal, was removed. The job was completed by September 17, 1923. The C.& S. Engineering Department announced that due to some additional cave ins and a considerable amount of ice which had formed inside the tunnel during the 13-year period of idleness, they found it impossible to salvage any rail inside the bore. This rail, as we have previously explained, is still there spiked to the ties throughout the length of the tunnel. Gilbert A. Lathrop, on January 21, 1939, wrote the author:

"Three years ago I hiked up to Alpine Tunnel from Gunnison. The ties and rails are still through the tunnel and almost a mile down the west side. Although the pike closed down about 30 years ago, a locomotive could still run on the track to a point where a rubble of massive granite chunks came down the mountain just east of the Palisades, blocked the line and kept some scrap iron salesmen from completing their job of total demolishment."

According to records in the railroad's engineering department, the rail removed from the west slope down to Quartz was sold to the Smuggler Mine at Telluride, Colorado.

At the same time the crews at the Gunnison roundhouse were wondering what would happen to them with Alpine Pass abandoned, the boys at the Como yards were passing a few remarks about some ominous looking clouds gathering off to the south in the vicinity of Trout Creek Pass. As usual, they guessed correctly—another flood and washout along Trout Creek.

In October, 1910, floods in Trout Creek washed out a considerable amount of trackage between Bath and Macune. This was nothing new; for some years previous to this time, the stream had been doing much damage to the line, causing constant expense. This last flood was the straw that broke the proverbial camel's back; the management gave up their battle with Trout Creek. Due to continual decreases in revenue, they declined to make further repairs and abandoned the entire main line between Garos and Macune, a distance of 28.73 miles. As an artery of traffic to the Gunnison region the old South Park road was through. These two serious ruptures in the main line ended for all time service between Denver and that area. October, 1910, can be very appropriately termed the beginning of the end for the South Park railroad.

During July and August, 1914, flood waters caused further damage to the remaining track in the canon, washing out additional sections of the line between Bath and Dead Man's Curve. Each succeeding year witnessed the disappearance of more and more trackage and right of way due to these seasonal floods. Dr. Frederick S. McKay, of Colorado Springs, writes:

"For several years, along parts of the old South Park road-bed, sections of rails and ties could be seen hanging together like a ladder in midair across many washed out sections of the right of way between the top of the pass and the lower end of the gulch near Box Canon."

Inasmuch as that part of the line north of Trout Creek Pass remained intact, a freight train would make an occasional run below Garos as far south as Cohen's Spur to pick up a few cars of stock or hay along the line. Finally, in 1922, the Garos-Macune section was completely dismantled and all rails removed. The work began August 7th, and was completed October 21, 1922.[1] Prior to March 1, 1920, railroads were not required to obtain Interstate Commerce Commission authority to abandon any section of their system, therefore, no permission was necessary to abandon either the Hancock-Quartz or Garos-Macune sections.

These two abandonments left the Buena Vista-Hancock segment without any physical connection to the parent system. However, the management continued to operate this section for the convenience of a few communities and mining camps located along Chalk Creek. Inasmuch as the Rio Grande's third narrow gauge rail between Salida and Leadville was not removed until 1925, that road was able to handle any transportation required beyond the South Park's Nathrop or Buena Vista terminals, including shipments of ore from the Chalk Creek mines to Leadville.

The next major dismemberment to occur came about during the year 1911, when the Quartz-Gunnison-Baldwin segment was hacked off. The abandonment of the Hancock-Quartz section the previous year had left all the line beyond Quartz entirely disconnected from the main line. With traffic in the Gunnison area at a low ebb, steps were taken preparatory to abandoning the entire line boynd Quartz. Accordingly, the section between Parlin and Gunnison was abandoned in 1911,[2] although the rails were left in place until 1923, at which time they were removed, the job being completed on September 17, 1923. Side by side the two slim gauge lines had run their trains for 29 years, but now the South Park gave up the struggle, leaving the field to its competitor, the Rio Grande.

The Gunnison-Baldwin segment, being disconnected from the parent Colorado & Southern system, was unprofitable to operate, but in view of its importance the owners knew they would be unable to obtain authority to abandon the line. Accordingly, the Colorado & Southern executed a deal with the Rio Grande on February 15, 1911, whereby the Rio Grande took over the operation of the Quartz-Parlin section, and the Ohio Creek lines between Gunnison and the Baldwin and Kubler mines. In exchange, the Colorado & Southern took over the operation of the Rio Grande's Blue River

1. A. T. Million, Colorado & Southern Engineering Department.
2. Finance Docket No. 9135, 193 I. C. C. 337.

branch between Leadville and Dillon. This arrangement enabled each company to have a transportation monopoly in its own territory. However, with a parallel line of their own through Tenmile Canon, the Colorado & Southern had little use for the Rio Grande trackage. They did not use the Leadville-Frisco section at all. Occasionally a South Park crew would make a run between Frisco and Dillon, but eventually all use of the Rio Grande's Blue River branch ceased and the entire line, consisting of some 36.28 miles of track, was abandoned and the rail removed by its owners in 1924.

The Rio Grande constructed 2,230 feet of connecting track between their line and the Colorado & Southern track at Parlin, and took over operation of the remaining South Park line beween that point and Quartz. This ended all operation of the Quartz-Parlin line, and the Ohio Creek line, by the Colorado & Southern company. The Rio Grande received all revenue and paid all operating expenses, but paid no rent to the Colorado & Southern. The latter, however, paid the taxes.

This arrangement continued for a period of twenty years or more. On February 1, 1932, the Colorado & Southern and the Rio Grande filed a joint request with the I.C.C. for permission to abandon the Quartz-Parlin segment. The usual opposition was presented by the mining, timber, and commercial interests. The Colorado Public Utilities Commission agreed to the dismantling of the Quartz-Pitkin track but recommended that the Pitkin-Parlin section be operated another year to ascertain whether enough traffic to support this remaining segment could be produced. Through efforts of the protestants the case was postponed. On March 27, 1934, the two roads again petitioned the I.C.C. for permission to abandon the Quartz-Parlin segment. Service on the upper end between Pitkin and Quartz had virtually ceased by July, 1933. The railroad's lawyers painted a woeful picture of worn and bent rail, washed and eroded grades, fences, bridges, and buildings in bad need of repair, annual deficits and decreasing traffic. Objections by the protestants and the Public Utilities Commission were presented. On April 8, 1934, the I.C.C. handed down their decision granting the two railroads permission to abandon the line. The order became effective 30 days later. By July 26th, the entire line between Quartz and Parlin was dismantled and the rail removed.

This left only the Baldwin and Kubler branches. From 1911 on, the Rio Grande had been operating the Ohio Creek line as an integral part of its system. They retained all revenues and paid operation and maintenance expense, but the Colorado & Southern paid all the taxes thereon. Around 1934, after abandonment of this line had been seriously considered, additional deposits of coal were found, both in the Baldwin and Kubler areas. Thereupon the Rio Grande concluded that the line should be rehabilitated for continued use. Both the

Baldwin and Kubler mine operators and the railroad anticipated considerable revenue from this source.

On July 9, 1937, the Rio Grande management petitioned the I.C.C. for permission to acquire the Ohio Creek line outright from the Colorado & Southern. The proposal, as outlined in 221-I.C.C.-697, states:

"The Colorado & Southern agrees to furnish the Rio Grande, without cost, sufficient second-hand 70-pound rail to re-lay the entire line, together with the necessary switches and other track material, except ties. The Rio Grande agrees to deliver to the Colorado & Southern the scrap material removed from the line in the course of rehabilitation and to pay taxes on the line for the year 1937, which become due in 1938."

The I.C.C. agreed to the arrangement and on August 13, 1937, the Rio Grande acquired outright all the South Park lines between Gunnison and Baldwin, including the Kubler branch. In other words the Colorado & Southern, through a novel adjustment whereby they gave the Rio Grande enough rail and miscellaneous track material to completely re-lay the Ohio Creek line at a cost of approximately $51,000, finally got rid of their unwanted property. This relieved them of all further taxes and obligations relative to the line in question. With respect to the future of the Ohio Creek line, Mr. Ken Lightburn, Editor of the "Rio Grande Green Light" wrote:

"Rio Grande freight trains still operate regularly on the Baldwin branch, but not on the Kubler branch, as this rail has been removed for some time. At this date, March, 1946, the Baldwin Mine is a steady producer. We run a string of empties up the branch and take out the loaded cars, at least twice a week. Consequently, the future of the Ohio Creek branch looks good as long as the mines produce. There is no reason to believe that they have approached the end of fuel reserves."

The next major operation to be performed on the South Park line was the dismemberment of the 29.55-mile section between Buena Vista and Hancock. By this time the Transportation Act of March 1, 1920, requiring I.C.C. permission to abandon a railroad, or any part thereof, was in effect. Consequently, the Colorado & Southern management was required by law to obtain this body's authority to dismantle the Buena Vista-Hancock segment. The railroad had previously been refused permission by the Colorado Public Utilities Commission to abandon service on this section, so they went over the local state ruling and applied to the I.C.C. In compliance to the law, the railroad filed their first application with the I.C.C. on September 1, 1921, for authority to abandon this section of track. (Finance Docket number 1572.)

In the ensuing arguments the railroad's "legal beagles" submitted records showing that the operation of this particular section of track during the period from January 1, 1916, to November 30, 1921, resulted in a deficit of $357,576, 70% of which was interest and taxes. The applicant further contended that the number of passengers carried decreased from 3,711 in 1916 to 725 in 1922, with the added statement that the population of the entire Chalk Creek Canon (including Buena Vista with 903) was only 993 persons. Intervening petitions protesting against the proposed abandonment were filed by The Flora Bell Mining Co., The Rarus-Warrior Mining Co., The Mary Murphy Gold Mining Co., the town of St. Elmo, the Chaffee County Board of Commissioners, the town of Buena Vista and the Colorado Public Utilities Commission, augmented by local agricultural, lumber and quarry interests. Although mining operations were at a low ebb at this time, the mining interests asserted that the abandonment of the line would result in a loss of their entire investment and the abandonment of the whole district, as no other practical means of transportation was available due to the fact that the wagon road up Chalk Creek was impassable during the winter months. The Colorado Public Utilities Commission filed a motion to dismiss the proceedings on the grounds that the applicant's railroad was located wholly within the state; therefore, the I.C.C. had no jurisdiction to authorize abandonment. The I.C.C. differed with the state commission, contending that they did have jurisdiction.

During the course of the proceedings the railroad company offered to lease the line in question to the protestants for a rental fee of $5.00 per year, providing they would operate it in its present condition and pay expenses and taxes. The offer was declined. After listening to much testimony on the part of various protestants, the I.C.C., on July 28, 1922, stated:

"Upon the facts presented, we are unable to find that the present and future public convenience and necessity permit the abandonment of the line of railroad in question. If the improvement in operating results, confidently anticipated by the protestants, should not materialize within a reasonable period of time, the applicant may renew its application . . . therefore, an order will be entered denying the application."

The anticipated improvement failed to materialize and on May 19, 1923, the Colorado & Southern filed their second application with the I.C.C. for permission to abandon the line. To support their application, the railroad stated that even in the face of a reduced rate on ore to the Leadville smelters, traffic continued to decline and the deficits increased. The protestants argued that railroad strikes, together with abnormal conditions in the mining industry, prevented any increase in traffic. The applicant again renewed their offer to lease the line to the protestants on the same conditions as before, or they would sell it outright to them for its scrap value. The protestants declined the offer.

After listening to the various arguments, the I.C.C., on September 24, 1923, granted the railroad company authority to abandon the line. However, the Colorado Public Utilities Commission, through the State's Attorney General, raised a vigorous protest, claiming the I.C.C. was usurping state's rights and had no jurisdiction over the line of railroad in question, and no right to authorize its abandonment. As a result, the case was reopened on December 1, 1923, for further hearings. After some two months of arguments from both sides, the I.C.C., on February 11, 1924, again granted the Colorado & Southern permission to abandon the line, stating that their orders shall be effective six months from date (August 11). The date was later moved to September 11, 1924.

The Attorney General of the State of Colorado then appealed the case to the U. S. Supreme Court. The details of this move are not known by the writer; however, the state evidently lost its case as the railroad company abandoned the Chalk Creek line and completed the job of pulling up all the rails by November 15, 1926.[1]

THE WATERTON-COMO-LEADVILLE AND ALMA SECTIONS.

Slowly but surely the life blood of the once great South Park railroad was ebbing away and there seemed to be no chance for a blood transfusion. The previously mentioned economic factors were slowly gnawing at the roots of the little road. Up to this point the Colorado & Southern management had been eliminating the system piece by piece as the opportunity presented itself. Of that which remained, the major portion consisted of some 152 miles of main line between Denver, Como, and Leadville, with a few small branches connected thereto. The management was continually on the alert for an opportunity to abandon the line in part or whole. Even as early as November, 1910, they attempted to eliminate the section between Como and Breckenridge, and refused to carry freight and passengers. The Breckenridge Chamber of Commerce appealed to the Courts and forced the road to open up again in January 1913.[2] However, upon resuming operation, the company discontinued Sunday passenger service and reduced their freight trains to three per week in each direction. Two years later, in October, 1915, the Colorado Public Utilities Commission denied the road's application to abandon the entire Denver-Leadville line, requiring them to continue their usual passenger and freight service.

At frequent intervals throughout the '20's, the Colorado & Southern management applied to the Colorado Public Utilities Commission for authority to cut down or eliminate various passenger and freight schedules along the Denver-Leadville line, or on such branch lines as Morrison or Alma, or to close some station. They were allowed to curtail a few train schedules but were refused permission to abandon any of the lines in question.

But the pendulum of economic stress began to swing ever nearer the South Park. For 18 years, from 1910

1. Colorado & Southern Engineering Department.
2. Colorado Public Utilities Commission report, 1913-14.

394

to 1927, the operating revenues of the Denver-Leadville line and branches averaged $330,000 annually; operating expenses averaged $490,000, while the annual deficit, after allowance for taxes, averaged about $240,000. The Colorado & Southern management contended that no railroad in the state of Colorado moved its loaded business over as arduous a route as the Denver-Leadville line. It is a paradoxical fact that in 1928, while the rest of the country was enjoying prosperity, the South Park showed a deficit of $312,174.

The depression of the early '30's presented an excellent opportunity to the management to wipe out the remaining portion of the lines in one final effort. On August 17, 1928, the City and County of Denver, with the blessings and good wishes of the South Park management, filed an application with the I.C.C. (Finance Docket number 7092), asking permission for the Colorado & Southern to abandon that part of the Platte Canon line between Waterton and Buffalo, a distance of 19.14 miles. The City of Denver proposed to erect a dam just below the confluence of the North and South Forks of the Platte River at the station of South Platte, and two smaller dams farther down stream to form three reservoirs for the purpose of providing an increased water supply for the city. At the junction of the two streams where the dam would be constructed, the bottom of the canon is approximately 175 feet wide and the walls are from 500 to 700 feet high. The depth of the main reservoir was estimated to be about 360 feet. The total length of the railroad line to be inundated by the three reservoirs was estimated to be approximately 12 miles.

Due to the protests of the Colorado Public Utilities Commission, together with various other county and commercial organizations, the City amended its application by offering to pay the expense of relocating a new right of way and donating it to the railroad. Surveys for the relocated right of way indicated that such a line would be at least 20 feet above high water level of the main reservoir and that it would be 16.75 miles in length, with a 2% grade for 12 miles. It would entail heavy grading, some high bridges, 16 tunnels, and was estimated to cost about $2,900,000.

Immediately afterward, on September 22, 1928, the Colorado & Southern filed application for abandonment of all the main line trackage from Waterton to Como and Leadville, including the 2.44 mile Leadville Mineral Belt tracks in and around Leadville, all branch lines to Keystone, Wilfley's Mill, the Garos-Fairplay-Alma line, and the Leavick branch. The Colorado & Southern represented that the proposed abandonment of the Platte Canon segment, as sought by Denver, would cut off the entire system west of Buffalo, adding that it would consent to such abandonment (between Waterton and Buffalo) only on condition that it receive authority to abandon the remainder of all main line and branches as previously listed. The railroad company further stated that because of the mountainous character of the country between Waterton and Buffalo it was not practical to relocate and rebuild their railroad around the proposed reservoirs.

Protestants to this petition were composed of the Colorado Public Utilities Commission, various County and commercial organizations, ranchers, stockmen, timber, quarry, and mining interests, and the Maddox Ice Company. The City and County of Denver favored the abandonment. Considerable testimony was offered before the I.C.C. by both sides. The various protestants contended that their business enterprises would be partially or totally destroyed if the railroad were dismantled. They felt that business was surely due for an upturn and they would faithfully patronize the railroad as an incentive to help keep it going. The railroad's lawyers retaliated with a barrage of arguments. Regarding the ranchers, quarrymen, timber interests and others, it was brought out that they could either use their own trucks or ship over regular truck lines that were operating in the territory. In answer to the mining interests, the railroad had much to say. They argued that the high grade non-complex ores in Colorado were virtually exhausted and that the business of metalliferous mining, for which the South Park railroad was originally built, had been almost wholly discontinued. Continuing, they stated that during the mining boom in Colorado, these ores were bulky and furnished much tonnage to the railroads. However, improvements in the manner of processing these crude ores into a greatly reduced concentrated form resulted in the loss of a great amount of ore traffic to the railroad. Furthermore, practically all the mining now carried on in the South Park territory is located on or near the western end of the line. Only two or three mines are producing ore of any great value; the London Mine near Alma and the Tiger and Wellington Mines near Breckenridge. The small amount of concentrates from these and other mines, are and can be easily trucked to the Leadville smelter. Regarding the molybdenum mine at Climax, that ore is now produced in a greatly concentrated form and can be trucked downhill to Leadville for shipment. This highway is closed in winter because of snow; however, if the Climax mine owners, and other mine operators located along Tenmile Creek and in the Breckenridge district need year-round railroad transportation as badly as they contend they do, the Colorado & Southern company offers to turn the Breckenridge-Leadville segment, or even the entire line, including locomotives and rolling stock, over to them, or to any one else interested, to operate as they see fit. In addition, the railroad company promises to make all arrangements for the necessary trackage rights between Waterton and Denver.

Following this session, the railroad company reviewed a host of miscellaneous difficulties they were having in operating the line. They discussed the difficulty and expense of operating the Platte Canon and other mountain sections of the line due to storms, washouts, slides, snow (as much as 114 inches during one winter season) maintenance-of-way expense, that it required two or three of their locomotives to haul 369 gross tons over Kenosha or Boreas Passes, that their annual freight and passenger revenues were constantly decreasing and the deficits increasing, high taxes, high wages of engine and trainmen because of mountain differentials and much overtime. They contended that the South Park division, as a feeder, had furnished only the small amount of $35,000 worth of business to the C. B. & Q. at Denver during the previous fiscal year. In answer to some protestants suggestions that a few new engines might improve the situation they maintained that if the Colorado & Southern purchased new and heavier power, the company would be forced to spend a large sum of money to rebuild the line and lay heavier rail.

For six months the Commissioners sat and listened to the arguments of both factions. On June 2, 1930, the I.C.C. handed down their decision denying both the City of Denver and the railroad's request. They stated:

"The record before us, so far as it relates to existing operations, would justify the issuance of the certificate sought. Although much of the testimony between the railroad and the protestants is conflicting, we, the I. C. C., are sufficiently impressed with the representation of the protestants to afford an opportunity to test their predictions. Accordingly, we will deny the application without prejudice to its renewal by the applicant after the expiration of thirty-six months from the date hereof, if the railroad can show that the situation has not materially improved. The I. C. C. suggests that the road do all it can to reduce expenses. The public must understand that if they desire the railroad to continue, they must appreciate the necessity of providing it with sufficient revenue to enable it to live.

"The application of the City of Denver in Finance Docket number 7092, to have the line between Waterton and Buffalo abandoned, is also denied.

"The state of Colorado has asked that the railroad be saved. If they desire such, let them help by removing some of the tax burden. We have no jurisdiction over this matter. That is up to the State Taxing Commission. We only suggest a fair tax."

As a result of this decision, the old South Park escaped the junkman by a narrow margin, and was assured of at least three more years of life. As matters now stood, the Colorado & Southern management had no other alternative than to wait out the three year period as specified by the Commission and see what would happen. They therefore settled down to the unprofitable job of maintaining service.

In the meantime, pursuant to the offer of the Colorado & Southern to donate the railroad to anyone who might wish to operate it, scores of applicants requested to take it over, but only two corporations were duly organized and filed official requests with the I.C.C. for authority to take over the remainder of the road. The first of these two organizations was known as The Denver Intermountain & Summit Railway Company. This company was incorporated on November 15, 1930, by a group of men headed by W. C. Johnstone. On July 29, 1932, Johnstone applied to the I.C.C. for permission to take over the South Park road, providing it was agreeable with the Colorado & Southern management. After testifying that his group had spent about $67,000 investigating the resources and possibilities of the area between Waterton and Leadville, he submitted some fancy figures as to his proposal for exploiting various resources along the line and making a gross profit of over $329,000 during the ensuing five years. He petitioned a bond firm in Wall Street for a $750,000 loan and submitted a contract to the Colorado & Southern management offering to take over the road and its equipment. He was turned down by both the bond house and the railroad company.

Meanwhile, Victor A. Miller had organized his Denver Leadville & Alma Railroad Company in the hope that the South Park line might be turned over to him. Mr. Miller, a Denver lawyer, had been appointed Receiver, in December 1929, for the Rio Grande Southern, a narrow gauge railroad located in southwestern Colorado. In operating the Rio Grande Southern, Miller made use of a rebuilt motor car for transporting passengers and less-than-carload freight. When necessary to haul additional freight traffic, he used a regular steam locomotive. This converted motor car, referred to by many as "The Galloping Goose", was rebuilt from a seven passenger automobile. It was spread in the body to the width of a narrow gauge car, with the chassis remodeled to fit on two four-wheel trucks, to the rear of which is joined a light metal van supported by a third truck. The entire vehicle is 44 feet long, weighs 14,800 pounds, carries ten passengers and ten tons of commodities, and is operated by one man. It is much faster than a steam locomotive (over poor mountain tracks) and the average cost of operation is said to be 14 cents per mile.[1] His apparent success in operating the R.G.S. properties led him to believe he was fully capable of achieving similar success with the South Park line.

Miller proposed to spend $175,000 on right of way and equipment, to improve service on the line, adjust rates, exploit new developments and resources, etc. He also submitted some figures showing how he proposed to turn deficits into profits. Johnstone criticized Miller, stating that the D. L. & A. plans were fallacious and that his proposed use of motor car equipment was dangerous; that he (Johnstone) had spent $67,000 investigating conditions along the line whereas Miller had spent nothing. Miller denied these accusations, declaring that the D. I. & S. had no financial backing, no right

1. 217 I. C. C. 379.

to do business in Colorado, knew nothing about operating a railroad, and that Johnstone's ideas of building up a large coal and timber business in the South Park territory was chimerical. At the same time other groups of protestants to South Park abandonment criticized the D. I. & S. on the grounds that Johnstone and his associates had not shown any ability to finance or operate a railroad and that the D. I. & S. was purely a promotional enterprise depending mostly on one man of advanced age and without financial means.

On June 14, 1932, Miller submitted a contract to the Colorado & Southern management containing his offer to acquire the road, and on August 11th following, applied to the I.C.C. for their permission to operate it. Apparently Miller stood in better favor with the protestants, the I.C.C. and the Colorado & Southern, but evidently the railroad company felt that neither Miller nor Johnstone had presented satisfactory proof that they could operate the line under existing economic conditions, and rejected their offers.

In view of the unusual interest displayed by many persons in Victor Miller's proposal to take over and operate the South Park line, we quote the Colorado & Southern's reasons for rejecting his contract:

"Mr. Miller introduced considerable evidence regarding his successful operation of the Rio Grande Southern. The Colorado & Southern, as applicant in this case, has no desire to depreciate or disparage what has been done by Mr. Miller in operating the R. G. S. On the other hand, Mr. Miller has enjoyed certain advantages, as Receiver for the R. G. S., with regard to wage scales, etc., which he readily admits. It has been submitted and the record shows that the Denver-Leadville line of the Colorado & Southern has been operated as efficiently as is possible under the existing conditions.

"On the R. G. S., as explained by Mr. Miller, passenger service is handled by a gas motor vehicle. Freight, in car-load lots, is handled by steam locomotives. The Colorado & Southern consider a mixed train better than a motor car. The motor car on the R. G. S. carries some parcel freight, and express, mail, and passengers. The Colorado & Southern could not handle freight traffic in that manner without violating its contract with the Railway Express Agency.

"The R. G. S. at present is borrowing off the fat of previous maintenance, which will have to be repaid someday. The motorized operation unquestionably costs less than a steam train would cost. The motor operation is, however, of doubtful attraction to the passengers. Taking five years prior to this motorized operation on the R. G. S., their passenger train earnings were always greater than on the South Park. In the past five years the reverse has been true. The Colorado & Southern maintains that the motorized vehicle in use on the R. G. S. does not present an attractive mode of passenger travel and does not constitute an attractive passenger vehicle. They lack the usual facilities such as wash rooms, etc. found on steam trains. Records of earnings on the R. G. S. will bear this out, as far as passengers are concerned.

"Attention is also invited to the fact that the mail earnings for this motor car represent 26% of the total operating revenues of the railroad. The R. G. S. is fortunate in having the most generous mail contract with which we are familiar. Under the contract of the Colorado & Southern with the Railway Express Agency, it could not handle freight shipments on a train such as the motor vehicle of the R. G. S. The motor vehicle is operated with one man. Under the Colorado & Southern agreements, it would be required to furnish a conductor and a motorman, and probably a portion of the cost of an express messenger. As regards taxes, the R. G. S. has not paid any taxes since the first half of 1928. At that time the R. G. S. owed $146,692 in back taxes, while its annual report as of December 31, 1934, showed cash on hand of $32,332. There were very heavy expenditures for maintenance on the R. G. S. prior to 1928. The R. G. S. is also fortunate in being able to borrow cars from the Denver & Rio Grande Western during peak periods of freight traffic.

"In short, the difference between independent operation of the R. G. S. and that of the Colorado & Southern operation of the Denver-Leadville line is that the R. G. S. has paid no taxes, is not bound by labor contracts of the standard provision type, has very generous mail pay arrangements, has received very friendly treatment on the part of the D. & R. G. W. with regards to a reservoir of freight cars, is living off the fat of a high maintenance standard, and does not operate a line of railroad similar to the Platte Canon line that is difficult and expensive to operate on account of heavy grades, excessive curvatures, and unfavorable climatic conditions[1]. Trainmen and enginemen are paid a higher rate for a given amount of work on the South Park branch than on other parts of the Colorado & Southern system. These increases run from 10% in through freight service in the case of enginemen, to 18% in the case of firemen. In local freight service the increases are from 2% in case of conductors to 17% in the case of firemen".

In contradiction to certain above statements and in all fairness to Victor Miller, the writer desires to present a little evidence in his behalf. Quoting from Vol. 1, "Pioneers of the San Juan" from the chapter concerning the Rio Grande Southern by Josie Moore Crum, we read:

"On November 30, 1895, the Rio Grande Southern passed under control of the D.&R.G. which eventually came to own 70% of its stock. . . . The D.&R.G. had, considering the service rendered, charged the R.G.S. a huge sum for 'management', 'use of terminals', 'repairs', and 'use of locomotives', (while its own lay idle). . . . The R.G.S. suddenly found itself without a cent of money in its treasury, rolling stock and track badly deteriorated and the Ames Slide down[2]. . . . For rugged mountain country, the Telluride-Ophir-Lizard Head-Rico district cannot be excelled. . . . In fact, over the whole system, the road either ascends or descends a mountain or travels through a tortuous canon. . . . Winter on the R.G.S. is a railroad man's idea of a reversed hell. . . . The Ames Slide which came down in the spring of 1929, carried roadbed and track several hundred feet down the mountain side and was 780 feet long and 50 feet deep where the track had been. . . . A D.&R.G.W. official claimed that it would take several months and $20,000 to remove the debris and restore the railroad. Too much!. . . . This was the beginning of a well-laid plan of the D.&R.G.W. to discontinue all narrow gauge lines and substitute highway transportation. The R.G.S. went into receivership December 16, 1929, and Victor Miller was appointed receiver. . . . On June 1, 1930, work was begun on the Ames Slide and in 19 days the track was clear and ready for operation at a cost of only $1,092.25. . . . Under Mr. Miller the R.G.S. resumed its own supervision saving $15,000 per year, used its own engines saving $10,000 per year, made its own repairs saving $25,000 per year, and built

1. Author's note: This statement would receive little support from anyone who has ridden over both the Platte Canon and Ophir Loop-Lizard Head Pass routes.
2. The Ames Slide was a huge earth and rock slide that occurred on the R.G.S. near Ophir.

its own terminal saving $7,000 per year—a total of $57,000 . . . . Mr. Miller, who took over the R.G.S. when it was in a most deplorable fix, had, by radical changes in the service and saving operational costs, saved it, at least for a time".

Although little is known of the story, there was also organized another group known as The South Park Railroad Company (mentioned in the opening of this chapter) who attempted to acquire control of the road. Concerning this new company, George Trout supplies the following data:

Name: The South Park Railroad Company.
Incorporated: April 12, 1937.
Directors: George Robinson, Benjamin Briscoe, Rodney J. Bardwell, Jr., E. D. Dickerman, and V. C. Herrin.
Object: Acquire by grant, condemnation, etc., construct and operate an intrastate carrier railroad from the City and County of Denver to Leadville, with branches and equipment. Particularly:

  a. From Denver through Waterton and Buffalo to Como to Dickey, southwesterly to Leadville.
  b. Sheridan Junction to Morrison.
  c. Waterton to Silica.
  d. Como to Garos and Alma.
  e. Hill Top Junction to Leavick.
  f. Dickey to Dillon and Keystone.
  g. Kokomo to Wilfley's Mill.
  h. Leadville to Blind Tom Mine, 3-rail.

In the Denver Post of April 13, 1937, we read:

"Judge Luby of Breckenridge, assuming that the Colorado & Southern had given up control of their narrow gauge line, gave the road to The South Park Railroad Co." (This article ended with the statement. . . . "Judge Luby's Court order did not hold".)

Additional material relative to this incident is found in Trains Magazine of November, 1943.

"After the abandonment in 1937, attempts were made to organize a local company to take over; but the offer to give the road away no longer held. The price of junk was too high. The South Park Railroad Company was organized on April 12, 1937, and the District Court of Leadville awarded it temporary possession of the line between Fremont Pass (Climax) and Waterton, almost to Denver. Seven engines at Leadville were supposed to return to Denver on April 14th with most of the cars, but the railroad held them because beyond Climax, they would be in 'no-man's land', and the Summit County sheriff threatened to stop the returning rolling stock".

This was the last ever heard of The South Park Railroad Company.

The passing of the 36-month waiting period, as specified by the I.C.C., found the Colorado & Southern ready with their second petition to that governing body to abandon the South Park railroad. The second application, filed on August 16, 1935, was the same as before, with the exception of an amendment to the effect that the railroad did not at this time choose to abandon the 14.64-mile section between Climax and Leadville. Also, their previous offer to donate the line and its rolling stock to any one interested was withdrawn. With few exceptions, the hearings revolving around this second application contained more or less the same arguments by both the protestants and the railroad, as did the first. Upon opening the case the I.C.C. stated:

"On behalf of the applicant it is contended that—

a. the predictions of the protestants in the previous proceedings as to increased traffic have failed to materialize.

b. traffic as a whole has materially decreased, largely owing to the general use of motor trucks.

c. there is no possibility that traffic will increase in the future.

d. despite all possible economies effected in maintenance and operation of the line, large deficits have recurred year after year, which the applicant is unable to bear.

e. the income of the applicant has been insufficient to pay its operating expenses and fixed charges since 1931.

f. the physical condition of the line is such that large sums for repairs and rehabilitation must be expended if operation be continued.

g. the installation of new and heavier equipment, suggested by the protestants as a means of more efficient and economical operation, would incur an unwarranted expenditure and necessitate strengthening the line to accommodate such equipment.

h. the public has not supported the line in accordance with the suggestions in our previous report."

The railroad estimated that the deferred maintenance over the entire South Park line had, by this time, reached a figure of approximately $85,000. They further contended that although old, the rolling stock had been well maintained during the past period, that operating costs had been reduced, stations closed and agents dismissed at all intervening points except Pine Grove, Como, and Breckenridge, and that taxes had been reduced about 19%. However, in spite of all this, traffic was steadily dropping and the road continued to show an annual deficit. In support of their argument the company produced the following statement showing operating revenue for the Denver-Leadville line and branches:

1910	$707,236.	1923	$423,370.
1911	373,880.	1924	371,779.
1912	342,764.	1925	366,702.
1913	410,925.	1926	388,037.
1914	379,999.	1927	358,438.
1915	386,111.	1928	388,969.
1916	453,362.	1929	328,801.
1917	554,438.	1930	298,102.
1918	489,449.	1931	238,241.
1919	461,559.	1932	276,027.
1920	559,126.	1933	215,409.
1921	475,387.	1934	254,357.
1922	435,676.		

Considerable testimony revolved around the increasing amount of traffic in the South Park area that was being hauled by the trucks and busses. Statistics were produced showing that at this time the truckers were hauling 50% of the ore, 50% of the coal and gasoline, 75% of the hay, and 80% of the general merchandise. It was also brought out that the London Mine was now using trucks exclusively to transport their ore to the Leadville smelter. As an example of the failure of the

protestants to support the railroad, the company introduced the following story:

"In 1934, the Colorado & Southern paid $41,393 in taxes to Park County, of which Fairplay is the County Seat. This was 31.3% of the total amount of taxes received by the County that year. Of this amount, $21,000 was for school taxes. During 1934 a brick addition was built to the Fairplay schoolhouse. The Colorado & Southern freight traffic department, interested in transporting the materials, reduced the rate on brick and tile from 34 cents to 20 cents per hundred pounds from Denver to Fairplay. The Railroad company received only two cars of this business, a weight of 82,000 pounds. The balance of the brick shipments, 20,000 pounds and 340,000 pounds of other building materials were trucked into Fairplay by the Barlow Trucking Company".

In reply to the complaints of the Maddox Ice Company, the railroad contended that the introduction of electric refrigeration had almost terminated that company's existence. They admitted that the ranchers and stockmen in the Garos area would be hard hit by the dismantling of the road. The feldspar interests at South Platte asserted they could guarantee shipments of 8,000 tons yearly, but would have to quit business if the railroad was dismantled.

Relative to this drop in traffic, the I.C.C. stated:

"The general decline in traffic and the losses from operation of the line sought to be abandoned, previously set forth, are not seriously disputed by the protestants, but they do blame the applicant for its alleged *indifference* to the causes precipitating the present plight of the road. They attribute the distressed condition of the line largely to the depression and the action of the railroad officials in persisting in the use of 'antiquated equipment' as a means of combatting modern truck competition. Among other matters of criticism dealt with in their brief, the protestants argue that the applicant has made no bona fide effort to effect such operating economies as were contemplated in our previous report, that the economies effected were mere gestures on the part of the applicant to mislead us, and that excessive rates, poor, slow, and inadequate service, and the general neglect of the ordinary principles of good railroading will not meet truck competition, or even retain existing business.

"Although the applicant's passenger service was reduced in an endeavor to effect economy in operation, as suggested by us in our former report, counsel for the protestants contend, on oral argument, that the present 'dirty, uncomfortable and slow' operation of passenger trains has practically destroyed the passenger, express, and less-than-car load business; that motor trucks are absolutely necessary to transport such traffic as long as the applicant renders such poor service; and that, if the applicant expects to compete with trucks, it must render better service. It is also argued that if busses can be operated on highways they can be operated on rails, and that the applicant should try that method of operation as a solution to its passenger traffic problem".

The protestants still maintained that, in their opinion, some new and heavier locomotives would solve many of the road's troubles; however, the Colorado & Southern answered these remarks as before—rehabilitation of the line would involve the expenditure of too much money. After listening to further miscellaneous testimony by both factions, the I.C.C. handed down their momentous decision, stating:

"The application in the previous proceeding was denied in order to determine whether or not it was possible for the line to make an improved showing during a test period of three years. Nearly six years have now elapsed, and the anticipated improvement has failed to materialize. It has been clearly demonstrated that the line cannot be operated successfully with its present equipment. The record is not convincing that success could be achieved if the applicant would discard its old equipment, in whole or in part, and replace it with new and heavier locomotives, motor cars, etc., as suggested by the protestants. The initial cost of heavier equipment and the cost to strengthen the line for its use would be excessive in view of the traffic possibilities of the territory served. Whether the new methods of operation suggested by the protestants would result in the elimination of truck competition to any great extent is a matter of conjecture. The undertaking would be largely experimental and, if it proved unsuccessful, the sums expended would be an economic waste. The record clearly shows that neither the present nor prospective volume of traffic on the line is sufficient to warrant its retention and that continued maintenance and operation thereof would impose an undue burden upon the applicant and upon interstate commerce.

"THEREFORE—we find that the present and future public convenience and necessity PERMIT ABANDONMENT by The Colorado & Southern Railway Company of its narrow gauge line of railroad and branches . . . . as described in this amended application. . . . Our certificate permitting abandonment, will be issued with the provisions that it shall take effect and be in force from and after 60 days from the date thereof, and that within that period the applicant shall sell said line of railroad, or any portion thereof, to any person, firm, or corporation desiring to purchase the same for continued operation, at a price representing the fair net salvage value thereof. However, no purchaser may operate the line without first securing proper authority from this body".

Thus, December 11, 1936, was scheduled to be the end; however, a reprieve was allowed by the I.C.C. to accommodate such winter business as could not be adjusted to bus and truck travel, and the effective date was moved to April 10, 1937.

As a finale to all the controversy between the Interstate Commerce Commission and the Colorado & Southern, it is indeed interesting to look in on the operating department at the same time the legal staff were expounding their eloquent arguments over mahogany tables in law offices. The irony of the situation is better understood when it is explained that, because of extremely heavy business, the operating department had to borrow three narrow gauge locomotives from the Rio Grande during this particular period, the winter of 1936 and 1937, to keep traffic moving up and down the Platte, while at the very same time the railroad's lawyers were working overtime in their efforts to paint a dreary picture of declining traffic and red figured profit and loss statements for the benefit of the I.C.C. office. In their zeal to kick the old South Park line down in the cellar, the Burlington's lawyers forgot to mention this incident to the Interstate Commerce Commission. This fact came from other sources.[1]

1. Confirmation of this is contained in old train registers found in the Como depot after abandonment; also photographs of the Rio Grande's engines while in service on the South Park line.

THE LAST RUN.

In the Denver Post of Friday, April 9, 1937, we read of the last passenger train to be run from Denver to Leadville and return:

"LAST TRAIN LEAVES DENVER ON FAMOUS LEADVILLE LINE.

"Return on Saturday Will End Traffic on Road Closely Linked With Romantic Period In History of Colorado.

"One coach, one baggage car, and a tiny locomotive stood in the frosty shadows of two big, modern trains at the Union Station early Friday morning, loading a few passengers and some small freight, mostly groceries, for the last trip out of Denver on one of the most romantic railroads in the west.

"The veteran crew of men with more than thirty years of service with the road oiled up the engine, loaded passengers and freight and received orders just as they had for three mornings each week for many years. At 8:15 a.m. the last train to travel out of Denver over the Colorado & Southern narrow gauge South Park road pulled out with no ceremonies other than good wishes to the crew from a small gathering on the platform who had come to hang crepe on the historic old road.

"The road will be abandoned officially after the little train returns to Denver at 4:50 p.m. Saturday. Permission to abandon the South Park narrow gauge line from Waterton to Leadville was granted Oct. 12 by the interstate commerce commission, to become effective at the end of sixty days.

"Before the allotted abandoning date was reached, the commission extended the date to April 10, to accommodate the winter business which could not be adjusted to motor travel.

"Railroad officials have been seeking permission to abandon the road for several years, because of operating losses. After it had been denied the right to abandon it, the Colorado & Southern first offered to give the line away early in 1932. Scores of requests to take over the road as a gift were received from all over the world.

"Only two applications were made to the interstate commerce commission, however, and neither was accepted. It is believed the road will have a higher value for salvage than as an operating unit.

"Officials and old timers standing on the platform at the union station Friday morning recalled many similar occasions on which they had watched the same train pull out, loaded with crowds of happy fishermen, off for a day or two of sport in Platte canon.

"The fish trains, which were inaugurated more than forty years ago, became known all over the country, Platte canon grew famous as a fisherman's paradise and vacation travel grew into the greatest single business enterprise of the line. Often it was necessary to run two and three sections to take care of the crowds.

"Building of the road, begun in 1874 as a trunk line from Denver to the Pacific coast, was at first hampered by financial difficulties. When the Leadville and Breckenridge mining boom broke into full swing three years later, the proposed route was forgotten and the tracks were laid up Platte canon toward Leadville. Traffic was so heavy that the line paid its way during construction and passed out dividends at the same time.

"Rail traffic was connected to the mining camps by stage coach until completion of the line.

"The almost unbelievable speed in construction of as high as two miles a day was reported. Work proceeded twenty-four hours a day, with long processions of torches to light up the work at night.

"E. B. Mitchell, superintendent of the Colorado & Southern, expected many old timers to board the train in the canon and ride to the top of Kenosha pass, in respect to the death of their old friend, the railroad.

Richard B. Jackson.

Engine 9 ready to leave Leadville with Train No. 71 on the last run to Denver, April 10, 1937.

Richard B. Jackson.

The last eastbound train at Como during the stop for lunch.

O. C. Perry.

Locomotives 8 and 69 making the last run from Alma to Como on April 11, 1937.

"Members of the train crew, who were wished well at the station by Gov. Teller Ammons, Superintendent Mitchell and C. J. Shaughnessy, road foreman of engines, were all veterans in service.

"T. St. John, conductor, has been with the railroad fifty years, and on the South Park line forty-five years.

"J. F. Farthing, the engineer, has been with the road thirty years. The fireman on Friday's run is an engineer in his own right, and has seen thirty-five years of service. He is Robert Terrill. Roy F. Hight, the brakeman, is also a veteran in service."

At 8:30 a. m. Saturday, April 10, 1937, the last passenger train left Leadville for Denver. The last Leadville-Denver ticket, number 4356, was sold to Jacob G. Willson; it is now preserved in the State Historical Society museum at Denver. Engine 60 pulled the westbound train from Denver to Como, where it was replaced by the 9; this engine took the train to Leadville and returned to Denver with it the next day.

Ed Haley, of Denver, writes the author:

"I was at the station that Saturday evening, with tears in my eyes, when old number nine wheezed into the Denver depot with the last of the narrow gauge passenger trains".

The writer is most certain that some of the rest of us scattered over the country, could we have been standing there with Ed, would have had a few tears in our eyes also.

William Mathews of Denver, writes in Railroad Magazine:

"There were twenty passengers who finished this last trip, eight men, including myself, six women, and six youngsters".

Although the Colorado & Southern had authority from the I.C.C. to sell the line to anyone interested, there were no offers as far as the writer knows. Preparations to dismantle the line got under way rather slowly and it was not until the following spring that all arrangements were completed and the owners were ready to start work. The following main line and branches were included in this major dismantling job:

Waterton to Como	67.84 miles
Como to Garos	16.30 miles
Garos to Alma	15.41 miles
Hill Top Junction to Leavick	11.33 miles
Como to Climax	49.19 miles
Dickey to Keystone	6.84 miles
Wilfley's Mill Spur	1.10 miles
Leadville Terminal	.65 miles
Leadville Mineral Belt	2.44 miles
	171.10 miles
Less section between Waterton and South Platte that was postponed until 1942	9.25 miles
Total to be dismantled	161.85 miles

In the words of J. C. Wellman: "Once again the section men went to work in the canons and on the passes, but it was a different sort of toil than that which took place 65 years ago, when the cry was "On to Leadville", and the promises of untold wealth lured men to exert every human effort possible to lay steel west. In a pamphlet titled "Abandonment of the South Park Line" issued by the railroad's engineering department, we read:

"Rails, ties, and other track materials on the entire line and the water tank, turntable, and other miscellaneous materials at Como[1], together with the pumping equipment at Garos and Kokomo, were removed by Platt Rogers, Inc. under the direction of Mr. Myron Beswick, under contract dated May 14, 1938. The bridges, buildings and other structures, not mentioned above, being old and in poor condition, were sold on sight to various parties, this being more economical than paying the contractor to dismantle and haul this salvage to Denver.

"The contractor started work on May 17. On account of snow conditions on Boreas Pass and on Fremont Pass, work started on the Leavick branch first. This branch had not been operated since 1922 and had been washed out in many places, making it necessary to use trucks instead of train service to haul the materials to Hill Top Jct. The contractor had to build his own roads, and melting snow and mud caused him much difficulty. The Leavick branch was dismantled by June 14th.

"The contractor used four engines, numbers 71, 58, 69, and 73, along with two cabooses, miscellaneous cars etc., all furnished by the Colorado & Southern. The contractor furnished a small part of the equipment. During July the line between Garos and Como, Dickey and Keystone and Wilfley's Mill branch were dismantled. During August the contractor completed dismantling the line between Climax and Boreas; and in September, Boreas to Grant; finishing up the line between Grant and South Platte in October.

"To speed up the work, a gasoline operated spike puller was used. The removal of bolts in fishplates was done with an acetylene torch by cutting a slot in the top of the nut and knocking the nut off with a sledge hammer. With the use of one-half inch cable operated off a hoisting drum built on a flat car, the rails were pulled up on flat cars and hauled into Denver. All crews on the wrecking train were former Colorado & Southern employees. The Leadville Mineral Belt line was dismantled by the Colorado & Southern and its own employees. The company collected 13,555.678 gross tons of rails from this job. The average mileage made per day in dismantling the complete line was 1.27 miles. The job was completed October 29, 1938."

With the completion of the big 1938 dismantling job, only that section of the original South Park line extending from Denver to South Platte, including the Morrison and Silica branches, and the Climax-Leadville segment remained.

Relative to the Morrison branch, we quote from the I.C.C. Docket number 10107, dated September 21, 1933.

"The Applicant (Colorado & Southern) states that the branch is paralleled throughout its length by good highways, over which substantially all the traffic in the vicinity is transported, as the public has practically discontinued patronizing the railroad. . . . On an average, only a train trip of a few cars once in two weeks is required to haul the little sugar beet business handled by the railroad. . . . No passengers have been carried for more than 15 years". (Author's note: Official Guides show a tri-weekly train as late as 1925).

The railroad submitted figures showing a declining amount of revenue and increased deficits. The I.C.C.

1. The contractor passed up the old Como tank for it was still standing in September of 1945.

R. H. Kindig.

Dismantling the South Park line in Tenmile Canon, near Solitude, in August, 1938.

R. H. Kindig.

Tearing up the rails near the high bridge of the Georgetown Loop on March 1, 1939.

issued the necessary certificate permitting the abandonment of the branch October 26, 1933. Part of the far end of the line, including the Garfield and Soda Lake Spurs, had been abandoned and dismantled in 1919. Following the I.C.C.'s approval, that part of the line extending from milepost 3.45, just beyond Lakeland, to milepost 9.37, just east of Morrison, was removed in 1934, the job being completed on June 6th. The job of dismantling the balance of the line from Sheridan Jct. to near Lakeland was completed on September 30, 1938. Thus, we bid adieu to a large portion of the original "Sunday School Route" that was so popular before the turn of the century·

The next section to feel the axe was the Silica branch. Rail shipments of feldspar and other products along this line had declined to a point where the branch was operated at a loss year after year. Toward the end, an engine and crew would make about two trips per month to bring in a few cars of materials. Most of the little traffic which was left was hauled out by trucks. On October 6, 1941, the Colorado & Southern petitioned the I.C.C. for authority to abandon the Silica branch. There were no protestants. Permission was granted eight days later, and by November 27, all rail and equipment had been removed.

THE ABANDONMENT OF THE CLEAR CREEK LINE.

We have come a long way since that first day of January in 1868, when William A. H. Loveland turned the first shovelful of dirt on the Colorado Central Railroad at Golden. And now, 77 years later, we have the unpleasant task of telling the story of the Clear Creek line's abandonment. It is practically a repetition of the story behind the abandonment of the South Park division; an indifferent management and a declining mining industry, together with the growth of the truck, bus, and private automobile traffic.

The first section to go, on the Clear Creek line, was the four mile segment between a point just beyond Silver Plume and the end-of-track at Graymont. This section was abandoned in 1890, and the rails were pulled up in 1898.[1] No details of the cause have ever come to light and we can only surmise that the line was dismantled because the mines at Graymont gave out. Possibly another important factor that might have entered the picture was that the railroad magnates had, by that time, given up their idea of throwing a ribbon of steel over the mountains to fulfill their dream of a short line railroad connection between Denver and the Leadville region.

After this minor dismemberment, the little trains plied back and forth along Clear Creek, hauling people, and gold, and silver, for 33 years before steps were taken

1. Colorado & Southern Ry. Corporate History.

to sever more of the line. On March 27, 1931, the Colorado & Southern management applied to the I.C.C. for permission to abandon the 3.52-mile segment between Black Hawk and Central City. During the early years the operation of this particular section was profitable. Quoting from I.C.C. Docket number 8748, we read:

"There was then much activity in the mining of high grade ore, which could be cheaply mined because of its close proximity to the surface of the ground. During recent years, however, this ore gradually became depleted and shipments declined to such an extent that the applicant found it necessary to cease operation of the branch between Black Hawk and Central City on February 15, 1925. Operation has not been resumed since that time. The remaining ore, which is of low grade quality, lies at such depth that it cannot be profitably mined. There are no other industries to be served in the tributary area.

"Since the cessation of operation, as noted above, the applicant has made no effort to keep the deserted track in repair. It has now become deteriorated to the extent that it is impossible to operate trains thereover. Reconstruction would be necessary to place the line in safe operating condition at the present time. This would cost approximately $12,000. Central City, the terminus of the branch, is a town of about 600 persons. Its railroad station, situated on the mountain side, is difficult of access. The inhabitants, therefore, find it more convenient to use the applicant's depot at Black Hawk. The main portion of Central City is about 1.25 miles, via streets and highways, from the applicant's western terminus in Black Hawk".

There were no protestants. The hearing before the I.C.C. was of short duration. On May 9, 1931, the railroad was granted permission to cancel their tariffs and dismantle the line. The wrecking crew was put to work, and by July 29th, the job was finished.

This was only a forerunner of what was in store for the rest of Mr. Loveland's pride and joy, the Colorado Central. Five years later, on February 28, 1936, the Colorado & Southern again petitioned the I.C.C. for authority to abandon more of the Clear Creek line. Getting rid of the Black Hawk-Central City section had been easy; this time the railroad's legal staff would not be quite so bashful. So, instead of asking for an OK to chop off a little 3.5-mile piece of track, they frankly requested the Commission's authority to abandon the entire narrow gauge Clear Creek line from Golden to Silver Plume, including the branch between Forks Creek and Black Hawk.

But things were not to go so easy with the lawyers this time. They ran into plenty of opposition. Protestants included the Colorado Public Utilities Commission, various county authorities, miscellaneous mining, livestock, commercial and labor interests; and even the distant towns of Fairplay and Alma intervened.[1] (An odd move on the part of the good burghers of Fairplay after giving the Colorado & Southern a "kick in the pants" in connection with their little school house deal.) During the early '30's a number of towns up and down the canon had increased in population somewhat

1. 221 I.C.C. 330.

because of a small increase in gold mining activity. This was due to the revaluation of gold in 1933. The applicant contended that this was a temporary situation; the protestant maintained otherwise. The applicant submitted figures showing the following annual deficits:

1931	$70,418.	1934	$51,974.
1932	44,892.	1935	51,771.
1933	98,256.		

The railroad contended that these recurring deficits unduly burdened its sytem and interstate commerce. This, the protestants denied. At this point it was brought out that the railroad had relinquished the carrying of the mails up the canon to a bus line back in 1931.[1]

The matter of a greatly reduced ore-concentrate with the subsequent loss of ore traffic to the railroad was brought out. This, the protestants could not deny. Additional arguments followed, revolving around the constantly increasing diversion of traffic to the truck and bus lines and private automobiles over the new highways west of Denver, causing railroad passenger and freight traffic to dwindle to practically nothing. In fact, passenger train service was discontinued altogether as early as 1927. Other arguments revolved around the decrease in silver mining in the Georgetown area, the closing of the mines, men thrown out of work, expense of operating and maintaining the railroad up Clear Creek because of flood damage, etc., and high wages of train crews because of the nature of the territory. The Colorado & Southern contended that, in 1935, the average operating cost per 1,000 net ton-miles of revenue freight handled on the Clear Creek lines was $34.60, compared with $5.57 on the applicant's standard gauge lines.

After listening to considerable testimony by both factions, the I.C.C. stated:

"In earlier years, when mining prospered in the territory and highways had not been improved, the Clear Creek lines obtained sufficient traffic to permit their operation at a profit. Then, during a long period of inactivity in mining, the lines were operated not only unprofitably but at the expense of a serious burden on the applicant's income from other sources. Due to a favorable change in mining economics, this principal industry of the territory had made some progress toward regaining its former prosperity and importance, and this change has already been reflected in a uniformly upward trend in railroad tonnage. There is no present ground for inferring that this progress will cease or recede in the near future, but rather that some further expansion may reasonably be expected. It is possible, if not probable, that with increasing traffic the parts of the lines serving the gold-producing district may be able within a reasonable time to earn revenues at least sufficient to cover the cost of operation.

"All things considered, we think that operation of the railroad from Golden to Idaho Springs and to Black Hawk should continue for a reasonable further period to permit a fair and adequate demonstration, under favoring conditions of this territory's need for railroad service. This is not to say that operation is to be expected to continue indefinitely, irrespective

1. 221 I.C.C. 332.

of the traffic furnished by shippers or the effect of such operation on the applicant's system and interstate commerce. The shippers cannot expect to be continued in business at the applicant's expense. If they divert traffic to the busses and trucks because of service and rate advantages which may suit their interests or convenience, the force of contended need of railroad service will be materially lessened".

The Commission then granted the railroad permission to abandon that section of the road west of Idaho Springs to Silver Plume, the decree to take effect May 30, 1937.

But the protestants raised such a howl that the case was reopened and the date of abandonment was extended by the Commission to December 31, 1938. Both factions went at it again, tooth and nail. The applicant submitted various figures purporting to show huge losses, only to be denied by the protestants. The Chief Engineer of the railroad contended that if the road continued to operate, the company would be forced to spend over $31,000 in deferred maintenance. Meanwhile, more and better highways continued to be built in the area and the trucks and busses went merrily on their way. Finally, the Commission stated:

"We are not persuaded that the prospects of enough traffic to support operation of the segment are sufficiently definite or certain to warrant further postponement of the relief heretofore granted to the applicant in this proceeding but deferred on the protestant's motion. We think that the affected territory has had ample opportunity since 1933 to demonstrate the support upon which the railway may depend, and that with an improved highway permitting relatively short hauls to Idaho Springs, the inconvenience to the mining interests of removal of the segment should be less than the relief which the applicant seeks and needs.

"We affirm our previous finding that the present and future public convenience and necessity permit the abandonment of the Idaho Springs-Silver Plume segment, and the outstanding certificate will not be disturbed".

The date was set for January 31, 1939, and this time, their ruling held. Preparations to dismantle the line beyond Idaho Springs went forward. Through the courtesy of Mr. Henry Comstock, Editor of Railroad Magazine, we are privileged to include Mr. M. L. Hart's interesting story of his trip on the last regular train to operate beyond Idaho Springs.

A GRAVEYARD RUN.
By M. L. Hart.

A few weeks ago when I was doing a routine job of filing tariffs for the Burlington, I suddenly came across a notice that made my heart skip a beat. I learned that the Colorado & Southern was going to abandon a part of its Clear Creek line.

To see part of this line pass into oblivion was like witnessing the death of an old friend; and yet I felt that I should be loyal to the last, and show it by attending the funeral. With that thought in mind, I wrote to E. B. Mitchell, the C.&S. Super at Denver, asking him for permission to ride the graveyard run. Mr. Mitchell replied that I would be welcome, and said that the last freight train would leave Denver on January 30th. So I took a train for Denver.

Crossing the yards on that bleak Monday morning I had no trouble in finding the Clear Creek train. She was all lighted

Engine 70, with Engineer Johannbroer, ready to leave Denver for a run to Black Hawk and Idaho Springs, on May 23, 1939.

With smoke billowing into the chilly dawn, and with headlight and markers aglow, engines 68 and 69 blast through Arvada on the last run to Empire, January 30, 1939.

and waiting and the four-wheeled caboose, No. 1003, was so tiny that her lamps looked oversize. There were two little Baldwin 2-8-0 engines, No. 68 on the point and No. 69 two cars ahead of the caboose. These engines have enormous spark arresters very much like watering cans upside down. A brisk fire burned in the way-car stove and a car inspector sat inside the door waiting for the engines to be coupled on for an air test. He asked abruptly:

"Are you the fellow who was here a few minutes ago?"

I said "No"; and while I was saying it, a tall chap stepped up on the platform and introduced himself as "Bill Gibson from Topeka". We shook hands.

Soon the conductor arrived, a thick-set man named Billy Maas, wearing spectacles, a dark blue sweater and a cap. Maas is the dean of Clear Creek conductors. He seemed gruff and unsmiling, but I had expected that. You don't find much to grin about when you reach the end of a thing to which you'd devoted some of the best years of your life. Silently Maas gave the "high ball", listened for the answering wail of the little peanut whistle, and the trip began.

We all planked down around the old flat-topped stove. It was still dark, and the January nights get cold up there in the Rockies. I asked Maas to tell us about the railroad.

"Oh, the pike made money when the mines first opened", he said. "She brought down ore worth millions and carried back machinery and stuff. They used to call her 'the line that hauls no empties'. We served the boom towns in those days— Black Hawk and Central City and Georgetown—they're practically deserted now".

"At one time the Clear Creek Division had 68 miles of narrow gauge," he pointed out, "and the South Park had 348 miles. Denver had more narrow gauge than standard gauge engines, something like 150 but the 68 and 69 are the only ones that run. Another is in the shops, and there are two or three over at Leadville. The rest are waiting in the dead line for God knows what."

While he was talking, streaks of light showed in a window. Not far off we could see a mound of ruins around a tapering brick chimney. "That used to be a smelter", said Maas. "We've brought thousands of cars of ore down here".

I asked him if mining hadn't picked up some. "Yes", came the answer, "but it's different now. They process the ore up at the mines and send up one car of concentrate where they used to send seven of rocks". He then told us about the first trip to Golden in 1870. All six cars and the locomotive Golden were decked out in flags and wreaths and evergreens. "You'd never guess the engineer's name. Wasn't Vulcan the god of fire? Well, the engineer's name was Vulcan—George Vulcan".

He went on to say that 700 people had crowded aboard that first train, and a brass band from the Grand Army of the Republic had played lively tunes. It had been a great day. Up at Golden, cannon had boomed, and the president of the line had made a great show in honor of the occasion.

I could not escape the feeling that it all must have happened about a thousand years ago. Looking out a window, I could see only a few bleak patches of dead grass. I wondered how many of those noble seven hundred were still living. There was no brass band to mark the last train, I thought sadly; if there had been, it would doubtless be wheezing out a death march. And as for the "thin blue line" of the G.A.R. survivors, I was only too well aware that the gallant old gentlemen were tottering around now with one foot in the grave and the other foot marking time.

There has always been a Maas on the Clear Creek line. Billy's father came to Denver on foot when there wasn't a railroad in the whole city. He was part of the first construction crew of this road, and a brakeman on the first train. One of our brakemen on the last run was Billy's son, F. B. Maas. F. B. was a husky young fellow in a dark zipper jacket. The other brakeman was R. D. Taylor, a young man too, though he'd worked for the line 33 years.

A long toot of the whistle meant that we were coming into Golden. Climbing out, we looked at the 52 pound rails and the odd stub switches, just pieces of track coming together without switch points. The firemen were taking on water. We introduced ourselves to the genial engineer, whose name is John Gottschalk, and to the crew of the helper engine.

It was getting light, so we took a few pictures. Then we saw R. H. Kindig, a well-known railfan, who had come up in his automobile. After we shook hands, Kindig said he'd follow us and bring Gibson and me back to Denver after the run if we so desired. Thanking him for the offer, Gibson and I climbed aboard a car of gravel midway of the train. The cold bit into your skin, but it seemed more like primitive railroading. Here the country got more hilly, with red and brown earth and lots of pine trees. We stayed on the gravel car thirteen miles to Forks Creek, taking pictures of the front or rear of the train as it rounded the many curves.

Forks Creek is where the seven mile branch to Black Hawk begins. We would go up there, caboose in front, followed by the 68, the rest of the train and then No. 69. Maas said the engines were to climb backward. "There's no place to turn around up there", he explained; "no place to run around cars, no nothing".

Part of the train was then set out and the caboose was cut off while one of the engines went around a wye and returned frontward. Gibson and I stood nearby. At a nudge from Gibson I whipped up my camera just in time. Billy Maas was pushing the tiny caboose up against the pilot of the engine with his two big hands. That saved one move of the locomotive, but only a mountain man would have thought of such a stunt. Handling trains in the Rockies is an art. These veterans have solved many sorts of problems; just as in a well-drilled army, each man knows just what to do and the exact time to do it. They remind you of the old song, "Life is like a Mountain Railway", which advises, "Keep your Hand Upon the Throttle and Your Eye Upon the Rail".

Someone told us about the time when this crew was tied up behind a rock slide and an outfit from the main line had to make the Black Hawk trip, which usually took from twelve to fifteen hours. They bungled everything. After sixteen hours they were still in the mountains, so they had to tie up; that's the "hog law". After another sixteen hour spell of work, they still had not returned. Wires crackled: "What the hell you waiting for?" At length the main line men got back to Denver on the morning of the fourth day.

In this narrow canon the State of Colorado is building a highway beside the track, with many bridges and tunnels. Seventy per cent of the track must be removed. The original rails lay close to the rocky walls, twisting and curving to follow the rugged contour. Now they are being laid on a wide fill next to the river. A cynical brakeman said next day in Denver: "That's so the first big flood will wash out the track. Washouts make a swell excuse to abandon a line".

But getting back to the last run. We saw why the Clear Creek branch was called the "Crooked & Slow". Because of the many turns and grades, a train can hardly make more than fifteen miles per hour. At one point the engine seemed to be headed straight for a steel bridge, but we kept on without crossing.

Later we swung in a wide arc around a point of rocks and heard the rat-a-tat-tat of a pneumatic drill, and saw piles of rail. The road was being straightened. Next trip the track would go straight through. Tons of dynamite had been tamped into holes in the rock and copper wires were already strung from one hole to another. Men were ready, as soon as we made our return trip, to blast the whole thing to oblivion, level it off and re-lay the track before the next train was due in four days. I felt a little easier when we were safely past.

There are no tunnels on the Clear Creek line. Pioneer builders liked a mile of track better than three hundred feet of bore. Two highway tunnels have been driven; as we passed the mouth of the first, Conductor Maas pulled out his watch. We rode on and on around the end of a spike of sandstone. At last we came to the far end of the bore. Looking straight through it, we clearly saw the tracks, five hundred feet behind.

"Four and one-half minutes", grunted Maas.

W. A. Gibson.

Conductor Billy Maas at Idaho Springs in 1939.

Just about that time Gibson noticed that a gasoline hand car with two section men was following us. "They follow every train up here", the Conductor said, "on account of rock slides". On the very last trip, in fact, the train had jarred loose a boulder which crashed down just in time to rip the hind step off the caboose. Trains are often delayed by slides and washouts, but apparently there have been no fatal accidents on this line. A few years ago a cow fell into a trestle near Georgetown and it took the crew and the passengers an hour and a half to pull her out. "On the narrow gauge," declared Maas, "anything can happen."

Black Hawk is an almost deserted mining camp in a dent in the mountains. Like Central City nearby, it used to be a great mining town. Not much is left now but a fine station of stone, kept in good repair. After switching and setting out, we picked up four cars of concentrate—not 28 cars of rocks—and headed down grade.

"Everything's gone well," I remarked. And Maas snorted: "Darn well—too darn well!"

At Forks Creek we left the ore and picked up the loads for Idaho Springs. No. 69 was sent back to Denver "light". Again we backed up. We were sorry to learn that our last train

would only go as far as Empire, though the line used to run twelve miles farther to Graymont. At Idaho Springs it was so cold that Engineer Gottschalk had to thaw out the water supply with a steam hose. Then we began our trip over the track that was to be dismantled. We passed Dumont where a famous smelter used to stand; there's little in sight now but a few ruins and the frame station built in 1899.

"The first station here was a box car and the first agent was an old lady," said Maas. "She was a telegraph operator too."

Now the station is also a post office and it's still run by a woman, Mrs. Hunt. That was the last depot in use. At Lawson there had never been any station but an old box car; now there is nothing to see but grass and brown pebbles.

It was late in the afternoon when we arrived at Empire. There's no town, just a notch in the hills with pine trees and red earth, plus a little snow on the mountain sides. Even the depot has been moved away; it's a saw mill now. When we got off, a workman was throwing the last dozen scoops of coal from a box car into a truck. That officially ended the business of unloading freight. The man was bitter. Most of his words were unfit to print.

"I don't get it," he growled, "Empire has been doing a good business with the railroad, why cut off at Idaho Springs?"

He said the region was having a revival and cars had come up under load only the Friday before. But already the shippers had made other arrangements. There were no loads for us and nothing to bring back except fourteen empties. Kindig was already there and we accepted his proffered ride back to Denver, as Gibson had to catch a night train back home to Topeka.

Though it was getting dark we drove on up to Georgetown. At one point the track cut along the shore of a pond, which used to be a race track. Here the valley is half a mile wide and the wind often whips up a gale. The story is told that during the winter of 1885, a train had been hurled over on its side throwing a passenger against a hot stove. This passenger was supposed to have collected $10,000 in damages.[1]

Georgetown today is only a skeleton of what it used to be. Its brick depot gapes windowless and forlorn; the other day I read that it has been sold for $50. When the city had 20,000 people it took care of many freights and four scheduled passenger trains a day. On Saturdays and Sundays there might be seven trains of ten to fourteen cars carrying the sightseers up the canon and over the Georgetown Loop Bridge. Even as late as 1918, they ran fourteen coach trains. Years ago a single passenger train came up in twenty-one sections, bringing 3,500 negroes to work in the mines. Today it would be hard to raise an army of that size in the whole region.

It was dusk when we drove on up to the Georgetown Loop. Without a word we walked out on the high trestle and followed the track around with our eyes.

I recalled what Superintendent Mitchell had said when I asked him why the state didn't buy the Loop and run excursions: "People drive up and marvel at what those engineers built 55 years ago, but they won't ride a train over it any more." A few days ago I read in a Denver paper that the trestle has been sold to a mining company for $450. They will cut it up for mine supports, and the steel will go back into the ground.

But getting back to our trip. Late that night Gibson caught

1. Author's note: The confirmation of this accident is to be found in the 1885 Colorado Railroad Commissioner's Report which states that the accident occurred on February 4, 1885, one-quarter mile east of Georgetown. This report listed thirteen passengers with their names and the injuries each received, however, it did not mention any damage suits. The train was pulled by Colorado Central engine 14, which also overturned.

the Santa Fe for home. I met him at the train, because I had some news for him. On its return trip engine No. 69 had gone aground at Golden and blocked the track. No. 68 would not be able to get through 'till they brought a crane. Later I heard that it arrived at 3:00 AM.

Gibson chuckled mirthlessly. "Maas was right—that last trip was going too darn well."

R. H. Kindig agrees that the last scheduled train to operate beyond Idaho Springs made the run to Empire on January 30, 1939. The next day the wrecking crews moved in and went to work dismantling the line west of Idaho Springs. And sad to relate, the abandonment of this section included the famous "Georgetown Loop Bridge". The wrecking of this famous landmark was of no small consequence. On March 5, 1939, the Rocky Mountain News carried a full-page headline, supported by three large photographs, announcing:

"FAMED 'GEORGETOWN LOOP' GETS NEW JOB
"WORLD WONDER ON DESERTED LINE
SOLD FOR $450.00
"ITS STEEL WILL BE PUT TO WORK IN THE MINES;
TRESTLE ONCE OUTSHOWN THE ROCKIES.

"There is an old saying that what the mountains have, the mountains keep. There is food for romanticists in the fact that the sturdy trestle over which rolled trains carrying millions of dollars in rich ore is actually going back to the mines. The Colorado & Southern has sold the trestle to The Silver Plume Mining & Milling Co. The steel from the dismantled trestle will be used as mine supports in nearby mine properties. The railroad company received $450 for a trestle that cost many times that amount.

"In its hey-day, the Loop and Trestle were known as one of the most remarkable engineering feats of all time. Distinguished European visitors, along with thousands of Americans, looked warily from the windows of the little coaches as the train inched itself along over the serpentine trail. Thousands of pieces of literature went out from Denver describing the 'Miracle of the Loop', which in its hey-day, commanded more attention than any other scenic wonder in the Rocky Mountains.

"Train crews who once rode over the bridge recall winds and blizzards that almost pushed train and all over in the creek. The bridge and loop will long be a memory to pleasure-seekers who rode special excursion trains on week-ends and holidays from Denver to Silver Plume to enjoy the dances that were held at the ornate pavilion operated by the railroad at Silver Plume."

Note: The mining company dismantled the Loop bridge during June, 1939.

By March 21, 1939, all the line beyond Idaho Springs was dismantled and immediately Mother Nature began to cover up and level off man's handiwork. Today, if you will observe closely as you drive along, you might perhaps notice the remains of some of the old bridge abutments, or parts of the old loop grade, especially the big fill over on the west side of the creek.

The railroad had only received permission to abandon that part of their line west of Idaho Springs but they remembered the Scotchman Bruce's proverb; "If at first you don't succeed, try, try again". Exactly one year and one week after removing the Georgetown segment they again petitioned the I.C.C. for permission to aban-

don the balance of the line between Golden, Idaho Springs, and Black Hawk. Once again it was a repetition of the previous proceedings. During this hearing the Commission stated:

"Since it first proposed abandonment of its lines west of Golden, the applicant's contentions consistently have been that, despite the revival of mining activity in the territory with the revaluation of gold in 1933, the traffic offered for shipment on these railroads is too small to support the cost of operating and maintaining them, and that there is no prospect of a sufficient increase in business on the railroads because of truck and bus competition on improved highways to and through the area.

"Operation of the railroad cannot be expected to continue indefinitely, irrespective of the traffic furnished by local shippers . . . and these same shippers cannot expect to be continued in business at the expense of the railroad. If they divert traffic to competing forms of transportation because of service and rate advantages which may suit their interest or convenience, the force of contended need of railroad service will be materially lessened."

The Commission added that the territory was well supplied with good highways, well maintained, kept free of snow and were open and usable throughout the year. The applicant also added that removal of the railroad would permit a saving of between $300,000 and $400,-000 to the State and Federal Government in the construction of another proposed highway to be built directly through the canon. The railroad also brought out that separate passenger service had not been provided on the Clear Creek lines since 1927, and that the use of freight trains for passenger travel had been negligible. A freight train made two round trips a week between Denver and Idaho Springs, with side trips to Black Hawk, from July, 1932, to March 17, 1940. After that, only one trip a week, except for a few extras operated in connection with highway construction, was made. The depot at Black Hawk was closed July 1, 1940.

The railroad's engineers stated that except in a few locations where the lines had been relocated and reconstructed at the request and expense of the State and Federal Governments for their accommodation in the construction of new parallel highways, only urgent repairs had been made; and, for the lines to be continued in operation, expenditures estimated at about $38,500 would be necessary for repairs, tie and rail renewals, reconstruction of bridges, etc., during the next five years. They submitted additional figures showing what the annual deficits had been running since the last hearing, which were as follows:

1936—$53,233.   1937—$47,735. $1938—$54,576.
1939—$48,982.

After listening to all the testimony presented, the Commission handed down their ruling:

"The Clear Creek lines were built more than 60 years ago. They were once profitable but, since the development of modern highway transportation, have been gradually starved. With better prospects of profit, interest in mining was revived in

1933 and there was, for a time, considerable increase in the applicant's ore traffic. Meanwhile Federal and State Governments have collaborated, and are collaborating, in providing excellent roads to and through the territory, with increasing stimulation of highway transportation and decreasing patronage to the railroad. In spite of the possibility of abandonment of the lines, which has existed for five years, the shippers have diverted their freight more and more to the motor trucks, and, despite all possible economies in operation, the applicant has continued to suffer losses which it is not in a position to sustain. The territory has had adequate opportunity to cooperate in the effort to save its railroad, but it is now plainly evident that continued operation of the lines could have no other effect than to impose undue and unnecessary burdens on the applicant.

"We therefore, find that the present and future public convenience and necessity permit abandonment by the Colorado & Southern Railway Company of their lines between Golden and Idaho Springs and Black Hawk. An appropriate certificate will be issued, effective May 4th, 1941. Suitable provision will be made therein for the cancellation of tariffs."

The announcement of this decision brought about the end of the slim-gauge railroad's long struggle for its existence. John W. Maxwell, who was on hand for the last run, writes:

"After the crew spent about two hours switching in Idaho Springs, they headed back toward Forks Creek. Engineer Johannbroer held number 70's whistle cord down all the way out of town—what a sound; it was like a dying wolf. From Forks Creek they went up to Black Hawk for one last switching job. About dark they started for Denver with about 16 cars from Idaho Springs and 11 from Black Hawk."

Thus it is recorded that on May 4, 1941, the flag of the last regularly scheduled train to operate in Clear Creek Canon was whistled in, and the little train returned to Denver from its final run up the canon to Idaho Springs and Black Hawk. Dismantling of the line commenced the next day, and by July 30, 1941, the job was completed. This also included the removal of the narrow gauge rail between Denver and Golden, leaving only the standard gauge rails in place between these two points. Mr. Les Logue states that the dismantling train, consisting of flats, gondolas, and caboose No. 1003, was hauled, at various times, by engine 68, 69, or 70.

So ends the story of the narrow gauge division of the Colorado Central Railroad. William A. H. Loveland's little mountain railroad, which he had so fervently hoped would constitute a section of a great transcontinental railroad route, passed into the pages of history. Its ambitious plans being nipped in the bud very early in life, the little road had no other alternative but to remain in its mountain home. For 69 years its little trains chugged up and down Clear Creek canon, faithfully serving the transportation needs of the communities and mining camps along its route. No more will the shrill whistles of the little engines be heard echoing from the high walls of the canon; the trains are gone and the men who ran them are either gone or fast disappearing.

But you can walk along its abandoned right of way, and as you follow the old grade through the deep canons, you can see the little mountain stream of Clear Creek as it rushes on, turbulent and eternal, unmindful of the troubles of men who live along its banks.

DENVER-SOUTH PLATTE ABANDONMENT

In chronological order, we next come to the abandonment and removal of the remaining narrow gauge lines between Denver and the station of South Platte. Although technically abandoned, the nine and one-quarter mile segment between Waterton and South Platte was not removed in 1938, but was left to accommodate some remaining feldspar shipments from the latter point. A crew made a run up the canon every week or so to pick up a few cars of feldspar at this station.

In the meantime, to accommodate the sugar beet business in the intermediate area, the railroad company made plans to extend the third standard gauge rail from the Denver yards, which had been for years three-rail as far south as milepost 6.18 near the old Griffin Wheel Works. By this time the South Park, especially the few miles left on the eastern end, was living on borrowed time and it was a foregone conclusion that before long the slim-gauge would be eliminated altogether. Accordingly, the third rail was laid from milepost 6.18 to Sheridan Junction by September 30, 1938, and by August 31, 1939, the extra rail was extended to Chatfield.

The Colorado & Southern management did not propose to maintain these few remaining miles of narrow gauge line indefinitely for the accommodation of the feldspar interests at South Platte. Inasmuch as the line had now been standard gauged to Chatfield, no I.C.C. authority was required in order to remove the narrow gauge rail between that point and Denver. As permission to pull up the Waterton-South Platte segment had been granted in 1937, nothing more remained but to secure the usual blessings from the I.C.C. to dismantle the Chatfield-Waterton section. This was a simple matter; in fact, the case was disposed of by the I.C.C. without even a printed report. (Finance Docket No. 13920). The authority to abandon this section was granted on October 15, 1942, and two weeks later, on October 31st, the operation of all freight service on the remainder of the narrow gauge line from Denver to South Platte was discontinued. By November 21st, all rail beyond Chatfield was removed, and by December 5th, all narrow gauge rail between that point and Denver was removed. Only the standard gauge line to Chatfield remained. The job of removing the narrow gauge rail in the Denver Union Terminal and yards commenced the following spring and was completed by April 15, 1943.

With the exception of the Climax-Leadville section, this was the end of the South Park railroad; not one foot of narrow gauge rail remained this side of Climax. Mother Nature and all the elements went to work immediately to cover up man's work where he had labored so hard to lay a steel trail through an unbroken wilderness in order to open up a new region to civilization. Soon the time will come when almost all evidence of a narrow gauge railroad through the canons and over the passes will be no more, and the old right of way will be left to the solitude of the mountains, with only a fading trail and a glorious memory of the once famous and great old South Park.

THE CLIMAX-LEADVILLE CHANGEOVER.

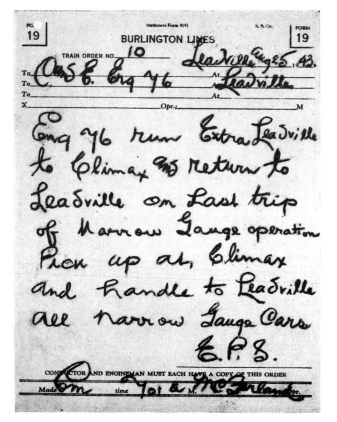

This train order might well be called the "swan song" of the Denver South Park & Pacific Railroad. Officially, it was the end of the narrow gauge line; the end of a great epoch in Colorado railroad history.

As previously stated, the great demand for molybdenum caused the Colorado & Southern to amend their final petition to the I.C.C. for abandonment of the Waterton-Leadville line to exclude the fourteen-mile section between Climax, the site of the molybdenum mine, and Leadville. Due to the growing importance of this mine, it was decided to retain this narrow gauge rail connection with the idea of changing it over to standard gauge sooner or later. In this connection we read in the Leadville Herald Democrat of December 9, 1938, the following item:

"The Colorado & Southern is giving thought to laying a third rail to Climax. It is costing the company about $20,000 a

year to transfer freight in the Leadville terminal. The estimated cost to widen the right of way and lay this third rail is about $80,000. At present two freight trains per day are operated between here and Climax. Complete snow fighting equipment is held in readiness at all times. The survey is already made and some ties are laid by."

However, the war came along and the tremendous need for molybdenum, so vital to the war effort, hastened the decision for the changeover. Changing over to standard gauge improved the transportation facilities, therefore no I.C.C. authority was necessary.

Molybdenum is used in hardening armor plate and in the production of special steels and armor-piercing bullets. As it was, the shipments of molybdenum concentrate, which is packed in sacks or barrels, was hauled in the narrow gauge cars from Climax down to the Leadville terminal where it was then transferred by hand to the Denver & Rio Grande Western's standard gauge cars for shipment to a Pennsylvania smelter. Incoming shipments for the mine, consisting of coal, machinery, food, and other supplies, were also transferred in the same manner. Widening the gauge would eliminate this delay and expense and provide the Climax mine with a direct standard gauge railroad connection to the rest of the country. It would also approximately double the capacity of the line from a tonnage standpoint. For a story of the actual changeover, we quote, in part, from the Railway Age of September 11, 1943:

"Because the output of the Climax mine was so important to the war effort, it was decided that the changeover should be made without interrupting service to the mine for more than 24 hours. The summer season is short at these high altitudes, and for that reason the work was started as early as possible, on May 1st, with an extra gang inserting eight-foot second hand and new ties. Not all of the ties had to be changed out, because the company had been planning for some time to widen the gauge, and during the last several years had made renewals with eight-foot ties. As soon as the remainder of the ties were changed out on about half of the line, a second extra gang started laying rail to standard gauge, with one rail on each side, outside the narrow gauge rails. The rail laid was re-rolled 75 pound, and second hand 70 and 80 pound. The old narrow gauge rail varied from 40 to 56 pounds. As soon as considerable standard gauge rail was laid, a standard gauge locomotive with two steam ditchers, a Jordan spreader and four air-dump cars were shipped to Leadville over the D. & R. G. W. for ditching and bank widening work. In order to get the line widened before winter (which begins about the middle of September at this high altitude), gangs worked ten hours per day, seven days per week, all summer, and the work train and ditchers were operated seven days a week for two months."

Relative to the standard gauge equipment and facilities, Roy Morton writes:

"While visiting in Leadville shortly after the changeover I saw the standard gauge equipment that had been assembled there to operate on the Climax line. Previous to the changeover the Colorado & Southern had kept three narrow gauge engines, numbers 74, 75, and 76 at the Leadville terminal. (Author's note: These were the three old Denver Boulder & Western locomotives obtained back in 1921. See roster for further details.) They were 2-8-0 engines with two pairs of blind drivers. The standard gauge power sent over from

Albert Fenn photo, from Life magazine.

C.&S. 76 drifts down the grade near Birds Eye on the last narrow gauge run from Climax to Leadville on August 25, 1943.

Denver to be used here were also 2-8-0's. One was rated at 450 tons and the other at 500, I believe. This was considerably greater than the 275 ton narrow gauge engine rating. I also saw the rotary snow plow in the roundhouse. It had been equipped with standard gauge trucks, was all painted up and looked to be in good condition. The old roundhouse had been remodeled a bit to accomodate the new standard gauge power. The narrow gauge turntable was not big enough to accommodate the standard gauge engines and had been removed."

August 25th, 1943, is a memorable date in the history of the South Park railroad. From the standpoint of its corporate history, this date marked the end of the railroad's existence. Conceived and born down in Denver town, the great old South Park breathed its last official exhaust high in the Rockies at the old silver camp of Leadville.

By August 25th, the job of standard gauging the line was completed and plans for appropriate ceremonies to mark the changeover had been made. In honor of the occasion, a goodly number of "Brass Hats" and others interested in the event, made their way to Leadville. News photographers, from both the daily press and Life Magazine, and the Burlington's official camera man were on hand to record the event. The story was ballyhooed by newspaper from Canada to the Gulf. They treated it as a gala event that largely tended to remind some of us of a Fourth of July celebration at some poor gent's funeral. A majority of the news stories were rather gushy in reporting the event, carrying such remarks as:

"The old 76 after wheezing, growling, and snorting her way down the hill to Leadville, is now off to war."

"Widen those tracks brother! Make way for the broad gauge of efficiency."

"Seems a shame to junk her," said one reporter.

"Junk her hell," replied another, "the old 76th is going off to war up in Alaska, with many a healthy chug left in her soot-caked sides."

But the payoff comes when we read in a Denver paper that the "Brass Hats" commandeered one of those rolling asphyxiating chambers operated by "The Blue Dog Bus Lines" to transport them to the wake. This news item stated:

"A special bus will leave Denver early this morning carrying Colorado & Southern officials, members of the press, and noted guests to attend the final run of the Climax-Leadville narrow gauge line."

It is a wonder that the ghost of old General William Palmer did not reach out, tap those worthies on the shoulder and say, "Gentlemen, my railroad still runs from Denver to Leadville".

The best news story of the event is found in the Leadville Herald Democrat of Thursday, August 26, 1943, a copy of which was furnished by Lawrence S. Brown. We quote in part:

"Final train order No. 10 ended the narrow gauge career of the Colorado & Southern yesterday—a colorful career which has endured since 1884, (the South Park reached Leadville in 1884) with many ups and downs. And almost at once there will begin a new life for the old railroad, for it has been replaced with standard gauge rails which will mean a great saving of labor and expense in getting the vital molybdenum into war production.

"Appropriate ceremonies to mark the changeover from narrow gauge to standard gauge were held at Climax yesterday when a special bus came up from Denver carrying officials of the Colorado & Southern and noted members of the press who joined officers of The Climax Molybdenum Co. in celebration of the event. All were guests of the Climax company at luncheon. Afterward the whole company gathered at the train where an appropriate talk was made by John Cortellini, Mayor of Leadville. John L. Rice, general attorney for the Colorado & Southern, traced the history of the narrow gauge road.

"At 2:45 the 14-car train, pulled by engine number 76, started its last run, coming into Leadville with all the narrow gauge rolling stock that remained. A motor car carrying photographers preceded the train and stopped it at every vantage point for pictures. Two and one-half hours for the 14-mile run was something of a record, but it gives an idea of the number of pictures that were taken.

Aboard the last train were Dennis F. Haley, of New York, Vice President of the Climax Molybdenum Co.; Wm. J. Coulter, of Denver, General Manager; Lester A. Cowan, of Denver, Purchasing Agent; C. J. Abrams, Mine Superintendent; Ralph Thompson, Chief of Guards. The Colorado & Southern Ry. was represented by Robert Rice, Vice President; John D. Walker, General Manager; John L. Rice, General Attorney; F. P. Stine, General Superintendent; Donald Ashton, Chief Publicity Director for the Chicago Burlington & Quincy system; Fred Lehmann, Burlington photographer; and James Gartside, Roundhouse Foreman at Leadville. Major E. E. McKnight, Military Police, U. S. Army, and Sgt. G. L. Thorpe, also accompanied the party.

"Press representatives included Albert Fenn of Life Magazine; John Vreeland, Railway Age; Ted Metzger, Edward Eisenhand, and John Ward, of the Associated Press; Jack Foster of the Rocky Mountain News; Alexis McKinney of the Denver Post; and Roscoe Fleming of Business Week and the Christian Science Monitor. Mrs. Robert Rice, Mrs. E. P. Stine, and Mrs. Jack Foster also enjoyed the last run.

"The train crew on the historic last run was composed of Oscar Perschbacher, Conductor; Joseph B. Delaney, Engineer; C. L. Dean, Fireman; Milton Ward, Brakeman, and Joseph Perschbacher, Brakeman.

"At the Leadville station the train was met by Station Agent and Operator, A. McFarland, C. & S. employees, and numerous Leadville people.

"The job of changing the line over to standard gauge was in charge of W. S. Broome, Engineer of Maintenance and Ways, and it has been completed more than two months ahead of schedule. November 1st was the date set for the completion of the job. The first regular run on the new rails will be made next Friday. Work of enlarging the round-house began yesterday. Two of the standard gauge engines are already here and the narrow gauge rotary snow plow will soon be equipped with standard gauge trucks. The three old narrow gauge engines are to be shipped back to Denver.

Mr. E. P. Stine and Donald Ashton were largely responsible for the details of the occasion in which they had the close cooperation of The Climax Molybdenum Company."

In commenting on the changeover Mr. Ralph Budd, President of the Chicago Burlington & Quincy stated:

"The last tie to our old narrow gauge railroads of Colorado and the Rocky Mountains is broken. Thirty years ago there were over 400 miles of narrow gauge rails in the Colorado & Southern system. It was gradually abandoned, 160 miles of it at once in 1938. The old west became the new west, and the old railroads that went to the mines became the new railroads that go everywhere. The Climax line was not abandoned—rather it was converted. We're glad we've finally completed the job, but it's nice too, to look back on the narrow gauge days."

For a time it was thought that the three narrow gauge locomotives at Leadville, numbers 74, 75, and 76, along with other narrow gauge rolling stock, would be shipped to Alaska to be used by the Government for military purposes; however, plans were changed and the three engines were returned to Denver and later sold; 74 to the Rio Grande Southern, and 75 and 76 to the Cerro de Pasco Copper Corporation in Peru, South America.

Before taking leave of the Climax narrative it might be well to mention that this particular section of railroad is now the highest standard gauge railroad to be operated in the United States. Prior to its abandonment in 1944, this honor belonged to the Rio Grande's Ibex branch located east of Leadville, whose altitude was 11,522 feet above sea level.

Technically speaking, the 14 miles of narrow gauge line removed between Climax and Leadville was supposed to be the last of the original South Park lines; however, there is still some left, although it is not legally a part of the Colorado & Southern system. This is the 17.82 miles of Ohio Creek line between Gunnison and the Baldwin Mines (the Kubler branch has been abandoned). As previously related, this segment was sold to the D.&R.G.W. in 1937, and is still operated by that company. Consequently, it is not too late (at date of this writing) to enjoy one last ride over a portion of the original South Park railroad.

＊　＊　＊　＊　＊

And now we approach the finale of our story. Among the men who laid the foundations and advanced the superstructure of Colorado's great system of railroads, the names of five great leaders, as our readers will have observed, have appeared conspicuously within these pages. John Evans, William J. Palmer, and William A. H. Loveland, the directors-general; David H. Moffat and Jerome B. Chaffee, the financiers. Today they sleep in honored graves.

Evans and Loveland were strenuous rivals. Loveland was to the Clear Creek Canon roads and those to Boulder, Ft. Collins and various other places to the north of Denver what Evans was to the Denver Pacific, the Denver Georgetown & Utah, the Denver South Park & Pacific, and others south of Denver. All but one of the lines of these rival railroad builders (the Denver Pacific, now Union Pacific) were eventually harmoniously combined in the Colorado & Southern system. But the two men who built them never once thought of such a union, except that it might have resulted from one crippling and exhausting the other and absorbing his roads. John Evans expected to see his South Park road terminate at the Pacific Ocean. Loveland was confident

that his Clear Creek Canon road would become a part of a great transcontinental railway and also reach the Pacific. Neither lived to see his hopes fulfilled. And the irony of it all is that within four decades, their two railroads were both literally uprooted from their very roadbeds and almost completely erased from the face of the land·

These men, builders of Colorado's first railroads, had many trying situations to meet and pass, and many great obstacles to overcome. Physical, financial, and political difficulties dogged their steps while litigation seemed to beset them on every hand. Their courage and struggles were heroic and their victories worthy of the indomitable men who won them.

John Evans envisioned his South Park railroad as a great enterprise. It would extend from Denver across the great Rocky Mountains and the desert wastes—stopping only when it reached the Pacific coast. Truly the South Park would be a mighty artery of transportation. Nature's great bulwarks failed to keep back his determined engineers. They conquered the defiles and clefts in the mountains and scaled their lofty battlements, laying their ribbons of steel as they progressed. But nature did not give up the fight. She hurled avalanches of snow and rock upon their tracks; she sent treacherous streams creeping into their defenses; she reduced her lavish gifts of precious metals thereby depriving them of their life's blood—traffic. Stealthily and steadily she continued in her effort to drive out the intruder, finally succeeding only to have the railroad partially replaced by a concrete highway with its attending traffic. But where she did succeed, the canons and mountain passes are silent and nature's great solitudes are once more her own.

The little railroad had fought a losing battle. The last flag has been whistled in, the trains have ceased to run, and the last engine fire has been banked. Spring water trickles down between the blackened timbers of a tunnel long ago abandoned. Grasses and young saplings grow between ties that once supported busy rails, gaunt bridge piers stand like ghosts who must remain to mourn the road's passing, and the long winding roadbed is fast disappearing in many places, leaving only a few crumbling cedar ties to echo to no sound but the lonely dirge of some mountain stream, or the raucous honk of an automobile horn—all mute evidence of the instability of man's handiwork.

The present day traveler, skimming over improved highways in the open country that once were but mere wagon trails along the old narrow gauge railroad, belongs to a different era. Here and there he might perchance notice landmarks that suggest an earlier day of transportation—the days of the narrow gauge wooden coach and the diamond stacked locomotive. Here and there he may observe the former sites of the little depots that formerly were frequented daily by miners who spent their leisure time discussing the latest "diggings", as they patiently awaited the arrival of the train. And driving on he sees, in the lengthening shadows of the late afternoon sun, the aging figures of an older generation whose dimming eyes gaze wistfully back along the trail to yesteryear—perhaps along the iron trail that is now but a memory of the lusty days of the narrow gauge.

The little railroad is gone, and the mountain sides have echoed to the sound of a laboring South Park engine for the last time—if you wish to see the magnificent scenery along the deep canons, or on the high mountain passes where the ribbons of steel once lay, you will have to plod your way along the fast disappearing old roadbed of crumbling pine and cedar ties, but it can be done if you have the heart, plus a genuine love and admiration for the old South Park.

And yet it is not really gone, for it lives in the hearts and memories of many employees, and it will *always* live in the hearts and memories of hundreds of railfans and historians—many of whom never actually saw a South Park engine, or experienced the thrill of riding the narrow gauge trains as they challenged the Rockies behind a little 2-6-0 twisting and turning and elbowing its way through the mountainous defiles to conquer the steep barriers beyond. In the great tradition of American railroading it will *always* live; and in the hearts of those such as Ed Haley, Jack Thode, Les Logue, Robert Hicks, Dick Kindig, Charlie Squires, John Maxwell, Phil Ronfor, Helen McGraw, Jess Frazier, and many others, including the author, the old South Park will never die. It will live on in thousands of photographic albums, in thrice times thrice told tales of courage and defeat, and in that aura of romance woven in the very name itself — THE DENVER SOUTH PARK & PACIFIC RAILROAD! ! !

George E. Mellen photo,
from Dow Helmers Collection.

In this busy scene, taken at the Como Roundhouse in the 1880's, six Congdon stacked D.S.P.&P. locomotives stand ready for the road. The locomotive at the left is equipped with a gigantic wedge plow for battling the heavy snows on Boreas Pass.

CHAPTER XXII

STATION LIST.

In the following section the writer has made an attempt to list the names of all stations and sidings that ever existed along the lines of both the South Park and Clear Creek roads. Obviously, a few names, along with other pertinent facts, have probably been omitted; however, if such is the case, it is because eight years of research has failed to disclose the information.

Today, it would be difficult, if not impossible, to locate the exact sites of many of these old stations that once flourished along the right of way. Many of these old mining and railroad towns had a merry time of it in their plush days when life, fortune, and shuffling feet coursed through their now silent streets. Some of them, now completely deserted, are derelict ghost towns—deserted monuments to a bonanza period of gold dust and engine smoke. Others have heard the requiem of their various activities, but are still populated by a few of the old guard who persist in hanging on, mainly because they have no other place to go. The mining industry, which nurtured so many of these early places only to desert them later on, continues to furnish a livelihood for a few remaining communities. Others, more fortuitously located, have, with the help of a few filling stations and juke boxes, managed to maintain a hold on some of Colorado's never-ending flow of tourist traffic which practically insures them from passing into oblivion.

As previously explained in this book, the mileage figures varied slightly from time to time; however, those quoted herein, and which coincide with those used in the profile charts, are those which were in effect during the heyday of the railroad. As a matter of fact, a large proportion of the information incorporated in this section shows facilities, etc., which existed prior to 1900.

The question of altitudes proved to be a very perplexing problem. U. S. Government Survey Reports, including those of Henry Gannett; supposedly authentic historical sources; and the railroad's varying figures all failed to agree on the altitude of numerous stations and points along the line. It appears to the author that Trout Creek Pass, where the Colorado Midland crossed over the South Park line at Bath, was the victim of this guessing game more than any other point on the line. Perhaps there will be some disagreement with the altitudes shown in this book, but the figures used were determined upon after much research.

DENVER.
Milepost 0.
Altitude 5,186 feet. (U. S. Geological Survey Bench Mark at Union Station). Station No. 1001. Station call UD (July, 1885). Later calls: DE, GN, DS.
Facilities:
In the early days practically all of the South Park's terminal facilities and shops such as carpenter shop, oil house, paint shop, track scales (Fairbanks, 42 feet long, 80,000 pounds capacity), etc., were located along Lawrence and Sixth.
Located at Lawrence and Fifth were:
Nine stall stone roundhouse 62x202 feet. After standing idle for many years, T. B. Aldridge reports that it was torn down around 1910.
Fifty foot wrought iron "Armstrong" turntable.
Stone machine shop 39x200 feet.
47,500 gal. wood water tank supplied by a well.
Car shop 20x128 feet.
No coal chutes were listed; however, several large size coal bins were located along the yard tracks at various points.
We shall not attempt to give any short historical sketch of Denver in this section.

SOUTH PARK JUNCTION.
Milepost 1.90.
Main line. Altitude 5,208 feet. Location of junction of narrow gauge line to main standard gauge line of the Colorado & Southern. Also known as Canon Junction.

AURARIA.
Milepost 3.00.
Main line. Altitude 5,220 feet. Station No. 1002. 2,193 feet of siding. Auraria, later known as Valverde, became a part of the city of Denver in 1903.

DENVER MILLS.
Milepost 5.10.
Main line. Altitude 5,248 feet. 1,584 feet of siding.

OVERLAND.
Milepost 6.00.
Main line. Altitude 5,272 feet. 2,494 feet of siding.

MOOREVILLE.
Milepost 6.60.
Main line. Station No. 1003. 1,946 feet of siding.

BEAR CREEK JUNCTION.
Milepost 7.55.
Main line. Altitude 5,290 feet. Station No. 1004. Station call BC, JA, SJ.
Facilities:
813 feet of siding, increased later to 2,135. 47,500 gal. wood water tank supplied with water from both creek and well with a 16 foot Eclipse wind mill. Fuel oil, scales, wye. Two story frame section house.
Historical note:

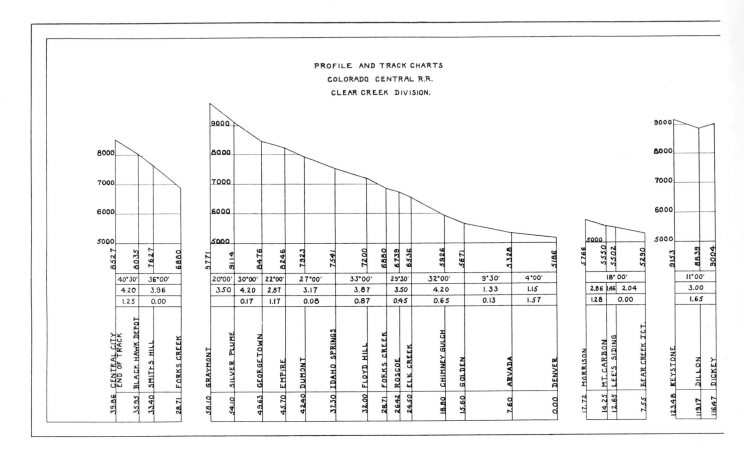

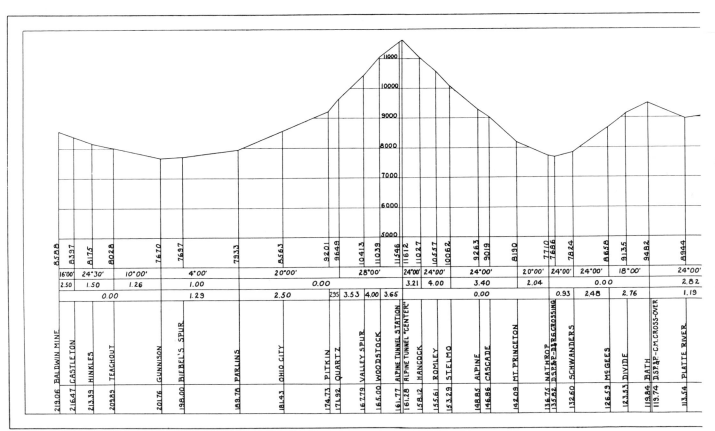

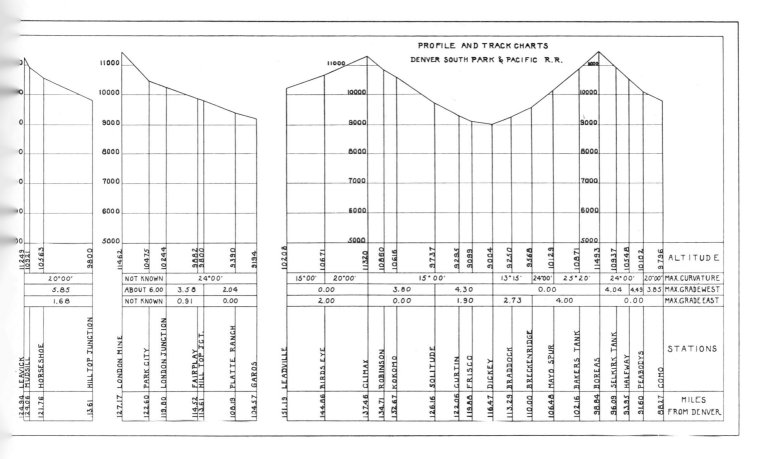

PROFILE AND TRACK CHARTS
DENVER SOUTH PARK & PACIFIC R.R.

Segment 1

Station	Miles from Denver	Altitude
LEAVICK	124.94	11249
MUDSILL	124.06	10921
HORSESHOE	121.76	10563
HILLTOP JUNCTION	113.61	9800

Max. Curvature: 20°00' — Max. Grade West: 5.85 — Max. Grade East: 1.68

Segment 2

Station	Miles from Denver	Altitude
LONDON MINE	127.17	11462
PARK CITY	122.60	10475
LONDON JUNCTION	119.80	10244
FAIRPLAY	114.52	9082
HILL TOP JCT.	113.61	9800
PLATTE RANCH	108.19	9390
GAROS	104.57	9194

Max. Curvature: NOT KNOWN, 24°00' — Max. Grade West: ABOUT 6.00, 3.58, 2.04 — Max. Grade East: NOT KNOWN, 0.91, 0.00

Segment 3

Station	Miles from Denver	Altitude
LEADVILLE	151.19	10208
BIRDS EYE	144.86	10671
CLIMAX	137.46	11320
ROBINSON	134.71	10860
KOKOMO	132.67	10616
SOLITUDE	126.16	9737
CURTIN	122.06	9295
FRISCO	119.86	9099
DICKEY	116.47	9004
BRADDOCK	113.29	9250
BRECKENRIDGE	110.00	9568
MAYO SPUR	106.48	10129
BAKERS TANK	102.16	10371
BOREAS	98.84	11493
SELKIRK TANK	96.09	10937
HALFWAY	93.95	10548
PEABODYS	91.60	10102
COMO	88.27	9796

Max. Curvature: 15°00', 20°00', 15°00', 13°15', 24°00', 25°20', 24°00', 20°00'
Max. Grade West: 0.00, 3.80, 4.30, 0.00, 4.04, 4.49, 3.85
Max. Grade East: 2.00, 0.00, 1.90, 2.73, 4.00, 0.00

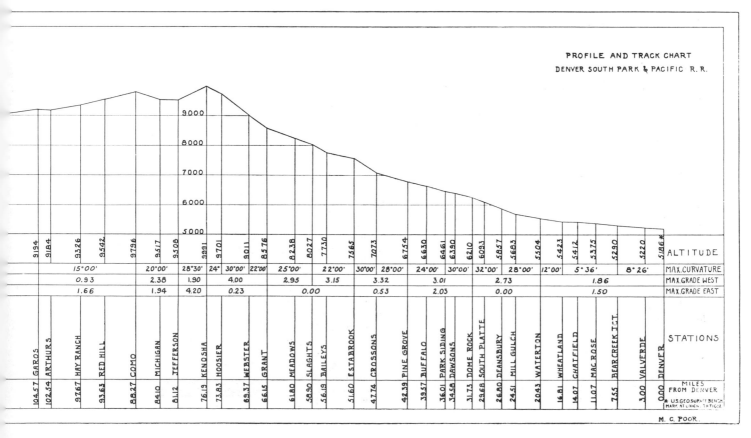

PROFILE AND TRACK CHART
DENVER SOUTH PARK & PACIFIC R.R.

Station	Miles from Denver	Altitude
GAROS	104.57	9194
ARTHURS	102.54	9184
HAY RANCH	97.67	9326
RED HILL	93.63	9542
COMO	88.27	9796
MICHIGAN	84.10	9617
JEFFERSON	81.12	9508
KENOSHA	76.19	9991
HOOSIER	73.83	9701
WEBSTER	69.37	9011
GRANT	66.15	8576
MEADOWS	61.80	8238
SLAGHTS	58.90	8027
BAILEYS	56.19	7730
ESTABROOK	51.60	7565
CROSSONS	47.74	7073
PINE GROVE	42.39	6754
BUFFALO	39.57	6630
PARK SIDING	36.01	6461
DAWSONS	34.58	6390
DOME ROCK	31.73	6210
SOUTH PLATTE	29.68	6093
DEANSBURY	26.80	5857
MILL GULCH	24.51	5683
WATERTON	20.43	5404
WHEATLAND	16.81	5423
CHATFIELD	14.07	5412
MACROSE	11.07	5375
BEAR CREEK JCT.	7.55	5290
VALVERDE	3.00	5220
DENVER	0.00	5186*

Max. Curvature: 15°00', 20°00', 28°30', 24°, 30°00', 22°00', 25°00', 22°00', 30°00', 28°00', 24°00', 30°00', 32°00', 28°00', 12°00', 5°36', 8°26'
Max. Grade West: 0.93, 2.38, 1.90, 4.00, 2.95, 3.15, 3.32, 3.01, 2.73, 1.86
Max. Grade East: 1.66, 1.94, 4.20, 0.23, 0.00, 0.53, 2.03, 0.00, 1.50

* U.S. GEO. SURV'T BENCH MARK AT UNION JCT.

M. C. POOR.

This station was later changed to Sheridan Junction. The Morrison line branched off here. The station was sometimes referred to as Petersburg; however, this point is also located on the nearby Denver & Rio Grande.

FORT LOGAN.
Milepost 8.65.
Morrison branch. 815 feet of siding. A short spur was built south of this point to a U. S. Army camp of this name.

GILMANS.
Milepost 10.55.
Morrison branch. Station No. 1161. 205 feet of siding (later 422 feet). Also known as Balcom and Lakeland.

BEDFORD.
Milepost 11.55.
Morrison branch. Four car spur connected at east end.

LEE'S SIDING.
Milepost 12.65.
Morrison branch. Altitude 5,502 feet. Station No. 1162. 250 feet of siding, increased later to 442 feet.
Historical note:
Ed Haley writes: "The Morrison branch ran just about 30 feet south of Ed Haight's house and the switch east of Lee's Siding was almost opposite it. The depot was a half box car and still stands in Haight's back yard." Ed Haight was an engineer on the South Park.

MT. CARBON.
Milepost 14.25.
Morrison branch. Altitude 5,550 feet. Station No. 1163. 549 feet of siding. Also known as Cowan.

OLD QUARRY SPUR.
Milepost 16.92.
Morrison branch. 11-car siding. A spur was built south from this point to Soda Lakes.

NEW QUARRY SPUR.
Milepost 17.62.
Morrison branch. 35-car siding. A 2¾ mile spur branched off at this point north to the Garfield Quarry and the Satanic Mine.

MORRISON.
Milepost 17.72.
Morrison branch. Altitude 5,766 feet. Station No. 1164. Station call MS. Station agent, July, 1885 was A. C. Lathrop.
Facilities:
Frame depot 20x55 feet. 50-foot gallows type wrought iron turntable. Wye. Bunk house. Hand car house. 17,960 gal. wood water tank. 6,694 feet of siding.

LITTLETON.
Milepost 10.6.
Main line. Station No. 1005. O. W. Judd was agent in July, 1885.
Facilities:
24x40 foot frame depot with living quarters. 987 feet of siding.
Historical note:
This station stop was eliminated from the timetables in later years. The town proper is located on the main line of the Denver & Rio Grande which is nearby.

MAC ROSE.
Milepost 11.07.
Main line. Altitude 5,375 feet. 19-car siding.

WYNETKA.
Milepost 11.50.
Main line. 1,302 feet of siding.

CHATFIELD.
Milepost 14.07.

Main line. Altitude 5,412 feet. Station No. 1006. Ten car spur connected at west end.
Historical note:
It is thought that this station was named after Isaac W. Chatfield, the contractor who built the South Park line here. In 1937, the line from Denver to Sheridan Junction was laid with third-rail to accommodate the sugar beet business in this vicinity. This eliminated the transfer from narrow gauge to standard gauge cars at Denver. This third-rail was extended to Chatfield in 1939. Sometimes called Chatfields.

WHEATLAND.
Milepost 16.81.
Main line. Altitude 5,423 feet. Station No. 1007. Station call WD. 1,302 feet of siding. Stock pens. This station was also known as Willard and Thomas.

CANON SPUR.
Milepost 20.2.
Main line. Altitude 5,497 feet. 31-car spur connected at west end. This station was also known as Lime Switch and Kassler. Station No. 1008.

PLATTE CANON.
Milepost 20.43.
Main line. Altitude 5,504 feet. Station No. 1009. Station call CN. Station agent in July, 1885, was Frank Soper.
Facilities:
Combination frame depot and section house. Four stall frame engine house 58½x60 feet. 47,500 gal. wood water tank. Wye. 3,062 feet of siding.
Historical note:
Charlie Squires writes: "I cut the wires out of the Platte Canon depot on June 25th, 1897, and the telegraph office was discontinued from then on." The Colorado Magazine states: "This station was established in the early 70's. It had a railroad station, water tank, and one store, plus a number of houses. The station was a shipping point for farm produce and fire clay. The depot is now torn down. In 1916 the name was changed to Waterton, account of the nearby Denver water works." Waterton was the railroad's point of entrance to the canon of the South Platte River. The line to Silica branched off from this station.

VINCENT.
Milepost 21.30.
Silica branch. Eight car spur connected at east end.

FRAUENHOFF SPUR.
Milepost 22.90.
Silica branch. Two car spur connected at east end, later extended one-half mile to quarry.

SILICA.
Milepost 24.32.
Silica branch. Ten car siding.

INTAKE.
Milepost 22.90.
Main line. Altitude 5,608 feet. Named from its connection with the Denver water works which uses water from the Platte. Listed in 1925 timetable.

GAYLORS.
Milepost 23.50.
Main line. Station No. 1010. 144 feet of siding. This place was also called Gaylor's Spur.

MILL GULCH.
Milepost 24.51.
Main line. Altitude 5,683 feet. Station No. 1011. 1,059 feet of siding.

STEVENS GULCH.
Milepost 25.90.
Main line. Station No. 1012. 263 feet of siding. Also called Stevens Gulch Spur.

DEANSBURY.

Milepost 26.80.

Main line. Altitude 5,857 feet. Station No. 1013. 551 feet of siding. This station was also known at times as Newberry and later as Strontia Springs.

SOUTH PLATTE.

Milepost 29.68.

Main line. Altitude 6,093 feet. Station No. 1014. Station call SP. Three log and frame section houses. 5,111 feet of siding.

Historical note:

The Night Hawk branch connected with the main line at this station (junction of the North and South Forks of the South Platte). The Colorado Magazine states: "A large saw mill operated by a 300 horsepower water wheel was in operation here in the early days. The population was around 350." Charlie Squires writes: "The telegraph office was in the front end of the general store at South Platte until 1897. During that year a new depot was built on the opposite side of the track (the north side). On the day I cut the wires into the new depot, a Miss Jardine, formerly the Agent at Platte Canon, arrived to take over the duties as the new agent here. The date was June 25, 1897. In those days horse-drawn stages met the passenger trains to carry passengers and mail up the South Fork to the mining camp of Night Hawk."

NIGHT HAWK.

Milepost 33.6.

Night Hawk branch. 12-car siding. The Colorado Magazine states: "This place was an active camp in 1896. The site is practically unknown today."

MULDOON.

Milepost 30.6.

Main line. Altitude 6,127 feet. Station No. 1015.

Historical note:

Miss Anna Vermillion, an elderly lady, is still living (at this writing) in a whitewashed log house built here by her father in the early days. The house is on the north side of the river with the railroad running between the front yard and the river bank. In later years this place was called Vermillion, a name of another station located west of Dome Rock in the very early days of the railroad.

LONGVIEW.

Milepost 31.2.

Main line. Altitude 6,194 feet. No other data known.

EAST DOME ROCK.

Milepost 31.5.

Main line. Station No. 1016. No other data known.

DOME ROCK.

Milepost 31.73.

Main line. Altitude 6,210 feet. Station No. 1017. Station call DO. U. S. Grant was agent here in 1885.

Facilities:

47,500 gal. wood water tank located .4 of a mile west of the depot. 1,549 feet of siding. Combination frame depot and living quarters 18x24 feet. Stock pen.

WEST DOME ROCK.

Milepost 33.0.

Main line. Station No. 1018. No other information known.

DAWSONS.

Milepost 34.58.

Main line. Altitude 6,390 feet. Station No. 1020. 900 feet of siding.

STONE SPUR.

Milepost 35.0.

Main line. Altitude 6,416 feet. 460 feet of siding.

PARK SIDING.

Milepost 36.01.

Main line. Altitude 6,461 feet. Station No. 1021. 759 feet of siding. This station later called Foxton.

GRANITE SPUR.

Milepost 37.0.

Main line. Altitude 6,485 feet. 179 feet of siding. This station was also known at various times as Peterhead, Meyer Switch, and Argyle. Station No. 1022.

FERNDALE.

Milepost 38.0.

Main line. Altitude 6,549 feet. Listed in 1925 timetable.

CLOUDCREST.

Milepost 38.2.

Main line. Altitude 6,565 feet. Listed in 1925 timetable.

BUFFALO TANK.

Milepost 38.8.

Main line. Station No. 1023. 11,700 gal. wood water tank.

RIVERVIEW.

Milepost 39.0.

Main line. Altitude 6,604 feet. 27 car siding. This station was also known as Riverview Spur.

BUFFALO.

Milepost 39.57.

Main line. Altitude 6,630 feet. Station No. 1024. Station call FO. S. S. McDaniels was agent in 1885.

Facilities:

Frame depot 16x40 feet. 2,761 feet of siding.

Historical note:

The Colorado Magazine states: "In the early '80's, the population of this place was about 1,400 persons. For several years they averaged over 30 car loads of lumber shipped to Denver every day. By 1890, almost all the good timber within 15 miles around was gone." Mr. J. W. Green, who still runs the general store he built here at the time the railroad was built, told the writer: "I averaged over $35,000 per month gross business in 1883. During the hey-day of business here, 5 spur tracks were built from the lead back behind my store for unloading merchandise and loading lumber. 25 to 30 cars of lumber were shipped out of here every day for Denver in those days. Later, an average of 5 cars of feldspar was shipped out daily to Denver. The C. & S. people turned a deaf ear to my request for cars and left business standing here when they pulled up their tracks. This forced me to use trucks."

Charlie Squires reports that the depot burned down November 1, 1897. See photo on page 59.

BOWEN.

Milepost 40.0.

Main line. Station No. 1025. No other data known.

BRYN MAWR.

Milepost 42.0.

Main line. Altitude 6,732 feet. Listed in 1925 timetable.

PINE GROVE.

Milepost 42.39.

Main line. Altitude 6,754 feet. Station No. 1026. Station call NI. J. M. Pine was agent in July, 1885.

Facilities:

Combination frame depot and living quarters 24x38 feet. Wye. Coal. 3,015 feet of siding, later increased to 3,652 feet. The 1912 employees timetable lists a telephone at this station.

Historical note:

Mr. G. F. Lewis, who was an agent here at one time, writes the author: "We kept 3 to 5 helper engines here most of the time. There was a coal chute, 3 shovelers, and an engine hostler. Timber was the principal business in the early days."

CRYSTAL LAKE.
Milepost 43.14.
Main line. Altitude 6,765 feet. 541 feet of siding. Also known at times as Morris.

HILDERBRAND.
Milepost 44.7.
Main line. Station No. 1028. No other information.

HAVILAND.
Milepost 45.1.
Main line. Altitude 6,892 feet. 355 feet of siding. Believed also to have been called Mayfield Spur.

GLENMORE.
Milepost 45.70.
Main line. Altitude 6,896 feet. Listed in 1925 timetable.

THOMPSON.
Milepost 46.1.
Main line. Altitude 6,923 feet. Station No. 1029. 1,077 feet of siding. Also called Cliff or Cliffdale.

MOUATS SPUR.
Milepost 47.4.
Main line. 360 feet of siding. No other data known.

CROSSONS.
Milepost 47.74.
Main line. Altitude 7,073 feet. Station No. 1030.
Facilities:
Water at this station was furnished by a standpipe which was in turn supplied by a spring. 687 feet of siding.

SAXONIA.
Milepost 49.0.
Main line. Station No. 1031. Crofutt's 1881 Guide states: "Many rich mineral deposits are found near here, and several hundred locations have been made. The Saxonia Smelting and Refining Works is located here."

ESTABROOK.
Milepost 51.60.
Main line. Altitude 7,565 feet. Station No. 1032. Station call RK. J. H. McFarland was agent in July, 1885.
Facilities:
Combination frame depot and living quarters 18x24 feet. 1,178 feet of siding.
Historical note:
This station was named after Jas. A. Estabrook, and was quite a summer resort. Much game and good fishing were available in the early days.

PINE.
Milepost 53.2.
Main line. Altitude 7,660 feet. Station No. 1033. Six car spur connected at west end. This station was also known as Insmont, and Pinery.

FAIRVIEW.
Milepost 53.7.
Main line. Altitude 7,689 feet. No other data known.

PALMERS.
Milepost 54.0.
Main line. Station No. 1034. No other data known.

BAILEYS.
Milepost 56.19.
Main line. Altitude 7,730 feet. Station No. 1035. Station call BA. F. L. Walther was agent in July, 1885.
Facilities:
Combination frame depot and living quarters 16x40 feet. 728 feet of siding.
Historical note:
The place was named after William Bailey who left Denver and civilization to get away from railroads, by moving up the Platte Canon and settling here in 1864. The South Park

right of way went right up the valley directly between his house and barn.

GLENISLE.
Milepost 56.2.
Main line. Altitude 7,831 feet. Three-car spur connected at east end. Listed in a 1912 employee's timecard.

ROUARKS SPUR.
Milepost 57.5.
Main line. Altitude 7,926 feet. Station No. 1036. 755 feet of siding.
Historical note:
This station was also known as Brookside and Grousemont. There was also a point near this station known as Saw Mill.

MADDOX.
Milepost 58.3.
Main line. Altitude 8,000 feet. 48-car siding here for loading ice for shipment to Denver.
Historical note:
This station was established for the convenience of the Maddox Ice Company, who had two lakes here. During the winter seasons this company shipped great quantities of ice to Denver, storing it for use during the summer months. Upon abandonment of the Colorado & Southern, the Maddox company abandoned all their buildings, equipment, and their ice business.

SLAGHTS.
Milepost 58.90.
Main line. Altitude 8,027 feet. Station No. 1037. 1,171 feet of siding. Combination frame depot and living quarters, 18x24 feet.
Historical note:
The earliest name of this station, built on the site of the old "Slaghts Ranch," was Fairville. Today, an attempt is made by some of the natives to call it Altruria. Lumbering was the principal occupation in the early days.

RICEVILLE.
Milepost 60.0.
Main line. Altitude 8,067 feet. Station No. 1038. 50,000 gal. wood water tank. Two car siding. This station was later called Shawnee.

BOXWOOD SPUR.
Milepost 61.1.
Main line. Seven-car spur connected at east end. Listed in a 1912 employee's timecard.

MEADOWS.
Milepost 61.80.
Main line. Altitude 8,238 feet. Station No. 1039. 896-foot siding. This station was later called Long Meadow.

SINGLETON.
Milepost 62.5.
Main line. Altitude 8,285 feet. A 1907 timecard lists this place as Kline. No other information known.

CHASEVILLE.
Milepost 63.5.
Main line. Altitude 8,353 feet. 450-foot siding. This place was known by a number of names such as Chase, Weller, and Llangollan.

CASSELLS.
Milepost 64.50.
Main line. Altitude 8,419 feet. D. N. Cassell was agent here in 1885. Five-car spur connected at west end. This station later called Santa Maria.

GRANT.
Milepost 66.15.
Main line. Altitude 8,576 feet. Station call US. J. M. Reach was agent here in July, 1885. Station No. 1040.
Facilities:

Como Roundhouse.

Painting by Philip Ronfor.

47,500 gal. wood water tank, removed prior to 1912. Coal bin 13x363 feet. Frame section house, depot, telegraph office, and living quarters. Wye. 2,518 feet of siding. Stock pen. This station was named after Gen. U. S. Grant.

DONAHUES.

Milepost 68.0.

Main line. Station No. 1041. No other data known.

WEBSTER.

Milepost 69.37.

Main line. Altitude 9,011 feet. Station No. 1042. Station call CA. G. D. Lee was agent in July, 1885.

Facilities:

Frame depot and living quarters 20x60 feet. Depot burned in 1903 and rebuilt following year. 13,446 gal. wood water tank. 2,239 feet of siding.

Historical note:

Crofutt's Guide states: "For some time Webster, first known as Hall's Valley, was the jumping off place for the thousands that were headed for the mining camps. Stages left regularly for Montezuma, Leadville, Fairplay, and other mining camps in the southwest. During those early days Webster was a very busy place and the needs of man such as eats and sleep were very high in cost." Thomas St. John states: "There were about 12 to 15 charcoal ovens in operation near Webster around 1892."

SPUR.

Milepost ?.

Main line. The exact location of this place, known as station No. 1043, is not known. It was somewhere between Webster and Hoosier.

HOOSIER.

Milepost 73.83.

Main line. Altitude 9,701 feet. Station No. 1044.

Facilities:

47,500 gal. wood water tank. Records tell us the water supply here was not only bad but that it was also limited. 590-foot siding. The old records also tell us that the railroad company owned three section houses, two barns and a blacksmith shop, all constructed of logs. Probably the barns and blacksmith shop were a hold-over from the early stage coach days.

DAKES.

Milepost 74.2.

Main line. Station No. 1045. 2,094 feet of siding.

Historical note:

Conductor St. John tells that there were 10 to 12 charcoal ovens located at this point. The 1885 Union Pacific Station call sheet lists this station as "Char-Coal-Pits".

KENOSHA.

Milepost 76.19.

Main line. Altitude 9,991 feet. Station No. 1046. Station call KN. F.B. Ross was agent in July, 1885.

Facilities:

Combination frame depot 16x24 feet, with an addition 11x13 feet. Old records disclose that this depot, which originally cost $1,200, was dismantled in January, 1919. There was also a frame car repair shop 12x28 feet. Wye. 3,162 feet of siding.

CASE SPUR.

Milepost 78.78.

Main line. This spur, with a capacity for eleven cars, was listed in a 1912 employee's timecard. The spur connected at the west end.

JEFFERSON.

Milepost 81.12.

Main line. Altitude 9,508 feet. Station No. 1047. Station call JN. U. Vaille was agent in July, 1885.

Facilities:

Combination frame depot and living quarters 20x44 feet. Coal bin. Wye. 47,500 gal. wood water tank. Two-story frame section house. 3,059 feet of siding. Stock pens.

Historical note:

In 1881, the population of Jefferson was 300. Stock raising and hay were the principal industries.

FOX SPUR.

Milepost 84.8.

Main line. Two-car spur connected at west end.

MICHIGAN.

Milepost 84.10.

Main line. Altitude 9,517 feet. Station No. 1048. 540 feet of siding.

COAL BRANCH JUNCTION.

Milepost 87.46.

Main line. Altitude 9,766 feet. Station No. 1049. Sidings at this point varied from time to time from 460 feet to 3,646 feet. Wye.

Facilities:

Coal Branch Junction consisted of a very large wye. The northeast leg connected with the main line to Denver; the southeast leg connected with the King Mines branch, while the west leg connected with the main line west to Como. The peculiar method in which this wye was used to get the Denver-Leadville trains in and out of Como is described in another part of this book.

KING MINES.

Milepost 90.78.

King Coal Mines branch. Station No. 1166.

Facilities:

17,960 gal. wood water tank. Wye. 6,510 feet of siding. Fairbanks track scale, 28 feet long, with a capacity of 69,000 lbs. Second Fairbanks track scale, 30 feet long, with a capacity of 60,000 lbs.

Historical note:

For the benefit of miners and company employees, there were 69 log and frame tenement houses.

9 frame store houses.

4 stables.

2 blacksmith shops.

1 carpenter shop, powder house, company office, school house, etc., etc. For a more detailed history of the King Mines, see the section covering this branch line.

COMO.

Milepost 88.27.

Main line. Altitude 9,796 feet. Station No. 1050. Station calls MO, DE. George A. Koehler was agent in 1885. Al Litchenheld was agent in 1896. J. A. Jamieson was agent and yard-master from 1907 to 1910.

Facilities:

Two and one-half story brick hotel 34x45 feet with two story addition 30x99 feet, and a second two story addition 20x30 feet. This brick building contained three rooms in the basement, 15 rooms and offices on first floor, 24 bedrooms on second floor and 4 bedrooms on third floor. It was built in 1880.[1] The hotel was totally destroyed by fire on November 9, 1896. A new one was built and completed by August of the following year. Combination frame depot 20x60 feet with first addition 14x16 feet and second addition 11x14 feet. Depot contained waiting room, ticket office, baggage room, and a platform containing 2,410 sq. ft. Ice house 16x32 feet. Dispatcher's office 24x50 feet, containing telegraph office, trainmaster's office, reading room, store room, and one bedroom.

Car shop, lumber shed, 6-stall stone roundhouse 125x62 feet, with an additional 6-stall roundhouse 102x30 feet. Fifty-foot wrought iron turntable, blacksmith shop, two-

1. Rocky Mountain News, October 26, 1880.

story section house, hand car house, sand house, four coal bins, 47,500 gal. wood water tank fed by a spring located one mile up on the hillside, nine one- and two-story tenement houses, 11,683 feet of miscellaneous siding. 1897 and 1912 employee's timecards both list a wye, location of which is not known by the writer, unless they were referring to the Coal Branch Junction wye.

Historical note:

The Colorado Magazine of July, 1940 states: "Como was laid out in 1879, on the site of the old Stubbs Ranch. (The original townsite was owned entirely by the South Park railroad company.[1]) The first residents were mostly Italians who worked in the coal mines nearby. They named the town COMO after beautiful Lake Como in Italy, from which they had emigrated." The population was further augmented by the mining camp of Hamilton. In the Colorado Magazine, July, 1940, we also read: "Hamilton, Colorado, a long narrow town with a single street, was established on Tarryall Creek in 1860. Sluice tailings are all that remain today of this once lusty gold camp. It was named for Earl Hamilton, one of the original discoverers of the diggings. The place was quite a town in the 60's, but when the railroad built through the South Park in 1879, all that were left moved to Como." Evidently, there were a few Chinamen living in Como who also worked in the coal mines, for the Denver Daily Times of November 26, 1879, tells of friction between the Chinese and the Italians. Crofutt's Guide gives the place a population of 500 in 1881.

Como, once a bustling and busy division point on the South Park, is rapidly fading into the forgotton limbo of the past. Today, it is almost a ghost town. The few empty stores along the streets stare with vacant eyes. The doors of the old stone roundhouse are boarded up and the building is reduced to the ignominy of serving as a warehouse for a dredge operator who lives in the old hotel building. The same fate happened to the depot. The railroad shops, where scores of men once toiled night and day to keep the engines and cars running, was destroyed by fire in 1909 and never rebuilt. Today the site is a pile of rubble. The old familiar sign "Railroad Crossing—Watch Out for the Cars" still stands but the nearest railroad is 50 miles away. Nell Colligan, widow of "Curley", is faithful to the last; she still lives in their little white house up the hill from the depot.

The writer knows of no more fitting climax to add to this short historical sketch than Charlie Squires' poem—"COMO".

COMO, ON THE D. L. & G.

I knew a little mountain town
   on a railroad long ago,
'Twas where they had headquarters
   in this little town of Como.

It snuggled close against a hill,
   by the famous old South Park;
Its winters were a nightmare,
   but its summertime a lark.

It stood almost 10,000 feet,
   near the base of "Silverheels"
(Named for a generous dance hall girl,
   that gave many a poor man meals).

I've been in that little station,
   with the line all blocked with snow;
The only way to reach that place,
   through their telegraph call "MO".

---

1. McMechen, "Life of Gov. Evans". The proceedings of the Colorado & Southern Corporate History state the division point of Como was laid out and built by the D. S. P. & P. in 1879.

And at that time they'd call just once,
   when Agent Litchenheld would "tap"
"I I, MO", the rotary's called,
   we're still upon the map.

I've spent many pleasant moments
   with the railroad boys up there,
And seen that railroad dining room
   serving meals to every chair.

I think I see Delaney's place,
   and I see Montag's too.
And all the different games on tap,
   with chips red, white and blue.

The men of that division
   on the old D. L. & G.
Back in the middle nineties,
   were honest and carefree.

And like one big family
   all did each other know,
Each man was figured as a friend,
   up there in old Como.

When tied up by a slide or snow,
   to that point all men would ride,
It mattered not your "class" just then
   all labored side by side.

I've face a slide, depth sixty feet
   with hand shovel "number two"
And next to me the Superintendent
   with a shovel did his due.

When I recall the old South Park,
   there's a pain down near my heart,
As I think of each man (most, passed on)
   and the road all torn apart.

Now our old town of Como,
   it is in the "ghost town" row,
Like "Al" its Agent, "passed beyond"
   last answered "I I, MO".

                    Charles C. Squires.
                    March, 1944.

Note: The "Al" referred to in the last verse was agent Al Litchenheld. Mr. Ed Haley writes that the two famous old establishments which Mr. Squires mentions in his poem, Delaneys and Montags, were totally destroyed by fire in April, 1945. Roy Morton writes that Jim Delaney helped string the first telephone wires over Mosquito Pass to Leadville. Sam Montag was a Park man before he established his saloon in Como.

RED HILL.

Milepost 93.63.

Main line. Altitude 9,542 feet. Station No. 1051. 665 feet of siding.

Historical note:

The Denver Daily Times of August 14, 1880, states: "A terrible accident occured at Red Hill, 93 miles from Denver, where passengers leave the train for Fairplay. At 12 o'clock a fire broke out in the D. S. P. & P. depot and exploded 1,000 pounds of black powder. The terrific explosion totally destroyed the entire settlement which consisted of the railroad station and five other buildings. The railroad ticket agent, F. E. Colyer, his wife, and two men were badly injured. His assistant, Chas. Hilton, was killed."

The destroyed depot was replaced by a small station.

The Colorado Magazine tells us that the name "Red Hill", was derived from the rusty color of the soil in the vicinity.

HAY RANCH.
Milepost 97.67.
Main line. Altitude 9,326 feet. Station No. 1052. Five room frame section house. 920 feet of siding.

BURROWS SPUR.
Milepost 100.15.
Main line. Altitude 9,223 feet. Three-car spur connected at east end. This station listed in a 1912 employee's time-table.

ARTHURS.
Milepost 102.54.
Main line. Altitude 9,184 feet. Station No. 1053. 320 feet of siding. Early maps show this place spelled "Arathur".

GAROS.
Milepost 104.57.
Main line. Altitude 9,194 feet. Station No. 1054. Station call GN, GS. J. M. Whittenberger was agent in July, 1885.
Facilities:
Combination frame depot and living quarters. Two-story section house. Coal bin 14x112 feet. 4,512 sq. ft. of stock pens and one loading chute. 35,920 gal. wood water tank supplied from both a well and creek by a 20-foot Eclipse windmill. Wye. 3,055 feet of siding.
Historical note:
Dr. Frederick S. McKay of Colorado Springs writes: "Garos was named after two brothers, Henry and Adolph Guiraud, merchants and sheepmen who established themselves in this locality around 1863.[1] The French "Guiraud" or "Garraud", as it was sometimes spelled, was too much for the South Park people, so they just shortened it to "Garos". Stock raising and hay were the principal lines of business here."
Garos was the junction point for the Fairplay and Alma branch of the railroad.
———

PLATTE RANCH.
Milepost 108.19.
Alma branch. Altitude 9,390 feet. Four-car spur connected at east end. The name "Platte Ranch" was listed in a 1912 employee's timetable. According to mileage figures, this station was apparently known as "Meyers" in the early days of the railroad.

HILL TOP JUNCTION.
Milepost 113.61.
Alma branch. Altitude 9,800 feet. Wye. 12-car siding. This was the junction point for the Leavick branch.
———

PEARTS SPUR.
Milepost 117.76.
Leavick branch. No other information known.

HORSESHOE.
Milepost 121.76.
Leavick branch. Altitude 10,563 feet. Five-car siding. This station was known as East Leadville at times.

MUDSILL.
Milepost 124.06.
Leavick branch. Altitude 10,921 feet. Wye. Four-car siding.

LEAVICK.
Milepost 124.94.
Leavick branch. Altitude 11,249 feet. 20-car siding. Leavick was the end-of-track on this branch.
———

LIME ROCK TANK.
Milepost 114.20.
Alma branch. 1,284 feet of siding. Also called Lime Rock Track.

FAIRPLAY.
Milepost 114.52.

1. When Guiraud's widow died years later, $80,000 in gold was found in some tin cans in her fruit cellar.—Lipsey, "The Brand Book", February, 1947.

Alma branch. Altitude 9,882 feet. Station No. 1168. Station call FP, FY. J. F. Wardell was agent in July, 1885.
Facilities:
Combination frame passenger depot and freight house 20x50 feet. Two log section houses. 2,088 feet of siding. Wye.
Historical note:
This famous Colorado gold camp was established in 1859 by a group of gold seekers who had withdrawn from the "Tarryall Diggings" just northwest of the townsite of Como, because of friction with earlier arrivals. They found rich placer deposits in the bed of the Platte River, established their camp and called it Fairplay.[1] During the camp's early history it was called South Park City for a time.[2] Fairplay was the first mining camp of any importance in the South Park area.[1] Crofutt's Guide of 1881 states: "Population 515. Placer mining was once the sole occupation of the people, but now this is largely replaced by quartz mining and stock raising. Many Chinese are working the placer mines in the vicinity. Most of the mining in this area is now situated west up the Platte."

SNOWSTORM.
Milepost 118.85.
Alma branch. The only facility at this point was a private spur, 156 feet long, owned by The Platte River Placer Co.

LONDON JUNCTION.
Milepost 119.80.
Alma branch. Altitude 10,244 feet. Station No. 1169. Station call B. A. R. Bingham was agent in July, 1885.
Facilities:
Combination frame depot and living quarters 20 x 70 feet. Coal bin. Scale house. (No data on scales) 47,500 gal. wood water tank. Wye. 2,745 feet of siding.
Historical note:
The station of London Junction was the junction point for The London South Park & Leadville line which was built up Mosquito Gulch to the London Mine in 1882. The name London Junction was changed to Alma on September 8, 1895, although the town of Alma proper is located about one mile north. Colorado & Southern engineering files state that a spur built by them in 1908, from the old London Mine track near the depot, south across Mosquito Creek to a new smelter constructed on the site of the old London Mine smelter, cost $313.21. The South Park's depot was located on the London Mine track across the Platte River from their own track. The London Junction (Alma) depot was closed permanently on July 26, 1924. (Colorado Public Utilities Commission, 1925).
———

PARK CITY.
Milepost 122.60.
London Mines branch. Altitude 10,475 feet. No other information known except that the site is marked by a few deserted cabins.

LONDON MINE.
Milepost 127.17.
London Mines branch. Altitude 11,462 feet. No other information known except that which we have included in the section covering the construction of this particular piece of track.
———

COHEN'S SPUR.
Milepost 107.67.
Main line. Station No. 1055. Four car spur connected at east end.
Historical note:
As nearly as can be ascertained, Cohen's Spur was the approximate location of a station known, in the early days of

1. Park County Republican and Fairplay Flume, May 17, 1928.
2. Colorado Magazine, July, 1940.

the railroad, as Weston, mention of which has already been made. Crofutt's 1881 Guide states: "Leaving Garos, the Park widens and after crossing several small tributaries of the Platte, Mill, and High Creeks, we arrive at the deserted town of Weston. For six months Weston was a busy place with a population, mostly floating, of several thousand. It was the 'end-of-track' from whence stages, passengers, mail, express, and all freight for Leadville turned west over the Rockies via 'Weston Pass' (elevation 11,800 feet) and what a villainous pass it was". This station was named after Sam Cohen, a tie contractor who lived in Fairplay.

GRAVEL PIT. Milepost 111.30.
Main line. Station No. 1056. No other data known.

PLATTE RIVER TANK.
Milepost 112.78.
Main line. No other data known.

PLATTE RIVER.
Milepost 113.54.
Main line. Altitude 8,944 feet. Station No. 1057. Station call RN. D. L. Sweet was agent in 1885.
Facilities:
Combination frame depot, telegraph office and living quarters. Frame section and bunk house. 47,500 gal. wood water tank. Coal bin 14 x 26 feet. 3,222 feet of siding. Stock loading pens.
Historical note:
Crofutt's 1881 Guide states: "For miles above and below this station, the grounds were marshy and many salt springs abound. The famous South Park salt works were located nearby".

ROBERTS.
Milepost 117.50.
Main line. Station No. 1058. No other data known.

HILL TOP.
Milepost (Colorado Midland overpass) 119.74.
Milepost (Hill Top station) 119.84.
Main line. Altitude 9,482 feet. Station No. 1059.
Station call HQ. W. Gregory was agent in 1885.
Facilities:
Combination frame section house, depot, telegraph office, living quarters, etc. Three bunk houses. 2,604 feet of siding. Wye.
Historical note:
During the railroad's existence this station was variously known as Hill Top, Bath, Trout Creek Pass, and Summit. The old Colorado Midland overpass was located a few hundred feet north of the South Park's wye and station. Contrary to the belief by some that a spur or branch line was built out from this station, at no time did the South Park railroad ever construct any branch line trackage at this point other than the wye and some siding. For those interested, the South Park's wye lay south of the Colorado Midland's track, and on the west side of their own main line. As far as is known the only local residents were a few railroad employees. Chas. C. Squires writes: "I closed the telegraph office and cut the wire out of the station at Bath on May 5, 1896". Apparently, this was the end of telegraph and agent facilities at this station.

HESS SPUR.
Milepost 121.78.
Main line. 300 feet of side track. No other data known.

DIVIDE.
Milepost 123.53.
Main line. Altitude 9,135 feet. Station No. 1060.
Facilities:
Combination frame depot and living quarters. Section house. 2,200 feet of siding. Wye.

Historical note:
The Colorado Magazine states: "Divide, originally known as Dolomite, was located on the site of the old Chubbs Ranch and was a celebrated stage station long before the railroad was built through". Crofutt's 1881 Guide states: "Divide boasts of a saw mill, a post office, several stores and about 100 people. About one mile below the station, on the north side of the railroad, can be seen the largest and finest spring of cold water in the state of Colorado. It is the head of Trout Creek, and fairly pours out beneath a high cliff close to the track. Just below, on the opposite side, are several other springs but not so large. From these springs down the creek, speckled beauties are very abundant; those fond of fine trout can find them here". Author's note: It isn't that way today; no springs, no fish, no water—unless it rains, and that soon soaks down into the deep sand with the excess running off down the canon into the Arkansas. The name of this station was changed to Newett on August 1, 1900. William Cairns writes: "At one time Newett served as a joint telegraph office for both the South Park and the old Midland".

THOMPSONS.
Milepost 124.8.
Main line. Station No. 1061.
Also referred to as Rankins. No other data known.

McGEES.
Milepost 126.59.
Main line. Altitude 8,658 feet. Station No. 1062. Station call MN. J. W. Soper was agent in July, 1885.
Facilities:
Combination frame depot, section house, and tenement house. 1,585 feet of siding. 17,960 gal. wood water tank.
Historical note:
This place was named after a man who spelled his name McGies. Crofutt's 1881 Guide states there was a post office and a hotel here. William Cairns tells that one of the railroad employees who lived here always had an exceptionally large garden patch. The station has also been referred to as Trout City.

SHIELDS.
Milepost 128.00.
Main line. Station No. 1063. No other data known.

CHARCOAL.
Milepost 131.50.
Main line. Altitude 8,016 feet. Station No. 1064. 1,180 feet of siding.
Historical note:
The writer has been unable to gather much information concerning this point. An old timer in Buena Vista would only say that a few charcoal ovens used to be in operation here in the early days. An 1883 employee's timecard lists the station and shows some side track. Evidently the ovens soon served their purpose and were abandoned shortly thereafter, as an 1897 timecard omits the place. Nothing remains at the site today except the crumbled remains of a few of the old brick and rock ovens.

DEAD MAN'S CURVE.
Milepost 131.75.
Main line. No railroad facilities of any kind here.
Historical note: *How the place got its name.*
Mr. M. S. Goodale in his article "THE GREAT OLD SOUTH PARK", published in Railroad Stories, December, 1933, explains how this point obtained its gruesome name. After further correspondence between Mr. Goodale and the writer, the following account of this story was obtained.
It seems that about 1884, a queer wreck occurred in the lower end of Trout Creek canon just above Box Canon at the point where the old line left the canon and turned north-

425

west across the flats toward Buena Vista. Conductor Carrigan had charge of a freight train consisting of seven cars and two locomotives. The train was traveling west down the canon. Carrigan and his head brakeman were riding with the crew in the head engine.

The vacuum brakes were working satisfactorily, but in going around some sharp curves the pin in the link and pin coupler apparently jogged out and the separation of the train broke the air hose. Since the two engines were running a trifle faster than the cars, the engine crews did not realize their fix until the cars caught up with the engines a little later and gave them a jolt.

By this time they were nearing the lower end of the canon below the charcoal ovens. Control of the train was lost and the whole train jumped the track and piled up on the sharp right curve at the point where the track left the canon. Then came an ear-shattering explosion! There had been a car of dynamite in the train but now neither cars, dynamite, engines, or crews were left.

All except the rear brakeman and a car of hay attached to the rear end of the train were blown up. The "hind shack" had been asleep in this car of hay when the first jolt woke him up. Quickly, he sized things up and even more quickly, he climbed down and pulled the coupling pin. He was then able to slow his car down with the hand brake and was the sole survivor of that awful wreck. Hence the name—Dead Man's Curve.

SCHWANDERS.
Milepost 132.60.
Main Line. Altitude 7,824 feet. Station No. 1065. Station call SC.
Facilities:
No depot was ever built at Schwanders. In its heyday the place boasted of a few section houses where an operator, a man to care for the coal chutes and water, and four to six section men and their families lived. At various times the railroad facilities consisted of a 47,500 gal. wood water tank, an eight-pocket coal chute, a wye, and 2,634 feet of side track. Water for the tank was supplied from Trout Creek.
Historical note:
In 1864 a man by the name of Benjamin Schwanders traveled down the Arkansas Valley looking for a good piece of farm land. The area just below where Trout Creek emerged from the hills looked good to him and here he established himself and his hay ranch. In 1884, the railroad extended their track down Trout Creek through Box Canon and south across the valley to Nathrop. At the same time they built a connecting line between Macune and the new line. The new junction point was named Schwanders, after Benjamin Schwanders.

Later on two brothers, Edwin and Gus Friskey, established themselves on a little place just outside of Trout Creek Gap. On the north side of the stream they built themselves a nice two-story house and, among other things, put in a fine orchard. The little stream of Trout Creek behaved itself in those early days and things went well in the valley. But as the years went by, Trout Creek gradually changed from the innocent little stream it was, into one of destruction. The story of what has occurred on the railroad has been told. The same fate was in store for the farms in the immediate vicinity of the gap, especially the Friskey Brothers' farm and orchard.

Every flood that poured down through the gap brought a new blanket of sand. By 1908, the railroad gave up their battle with the water and sand and abandoned that section of the line that ran down through Box Canon and the Gap to Schwanders. In 1924, when all further service on the South Park through this area was discontinued, the Schwanders-Macune section, including the former station of Schwand-

ers, was abandoned to its fate. Today, no trace can be found of the station site nor any of the right of way between it and the gap; they are buried deep beneath a layer of sand ranging from two to some fifteen feet in depth.

Meanwhile, the great delta of sand, being continually fed by the periodical flood waters of Trout Creek, commenced spreading out like a huge fan, gradually enveloping and covering everything in its path. Mr. J. M. Cuenin, Chaffee County Surveyor, writes that the County, in an attempt to save the farm land in the vicinity, offered to dig a large drainage ditch to carry the flood waters off across the little valley to the Arkansas River, but that Friskey Brothers refused to cooperate. Their folly cost them their farm and orchard. Trout Creek has buried their white farm house in sand up to the second floor, while only the tops of the trees of their once fine orchard protrude above the level of the sand as if gasping for a final breath.

Old Union Pacific records tell that the coal chute at Schwanders was built in 1884 at a cost of $2,796.36. It was removed in May, 1894.

To better understand the trackage layout in this area, the reader is referred to the Buena Vista-Nathrop District map, in the map pocket at rear of book.

MACUNE.
Milepost 133.30.
By way of the main line after 1908. Altitude 7,853 feet.
Wye. Approximately 1,482 feet of siding.
Historical note:
When the end-of-track first reached the east bank of the Arkansas in February of 1880, (the location of Macune) this place was known as Arkansas Station. Upon completion of the line into Buena Vista, the point evidently lost its identity and usefulness, as no further references are found to the station in question until 1908. When the new cutoff was built over the old 1880 grade between Dead Man's Curve and the Schwanders-Buena Vista segment in 1908, the junction point with the latter was thereafter known as Macune. William Coogan states that the only structure here was a small building used at various times by some section hand and his family. There never were any depot facilities at Macune. The old railroad bridge built across the Arkansas River at this point, after being converted into a wagon bridge by the County, survived until 1942 at which time it was abandoned and dismantled. Nothing remains today save the old stone abutments.

BUENA VISTA.
Milepost 135.77.
By way of the main line after 1908. Altitude 7,952 feet. Station calls BV, BU, VA. J. R. DeRemer was agent in July, 1885. C. H. Norris was also agent here at one time.
Facilities:
Combination frame depot, freight house and living quarters 20 x 77 feet. Five room frame section house 22 x 42 feet. 47,500 gal. wood water tank. 12,646 feet of siding. Wye. This wye was listed in an 1889 employees timecard. Its location is not known, unless it was the old wye located south of the town on the west bank of the Arkansas at the junction point of the old Denver & Rio Grande connection in 1880.
Historical note:
Buena Vista means "good view" in Spanish. The town, originally known as Cottonwood, was incorporated November 8, 1879. The South Park Railroad owned one-third of the Townsite Company. Crofutt's 1881 Guide gives the population as 1,075 in 1880. There was a small amount of mining carried on in the vicinity and a smelter for the treatment of low grade ores was in operation here in the early days. From Louisa Ward's book "Chalk Creek", we quote:
"An early physician, Dr. Simmons, says that when he arrived in Buena Vista in April, 1880, neither the Denver &

Rio Grande or the Denver & South Park went beyond the town. Buena Vista was red-hot and boiling over, for it was the terminus of both railroads which were supplying the Leadville and Chalk Creek mines with all their supplies. All transportation beyond Buena Vista to the mining districts was by mule and ox teams. One night was all he could stand. So he packed up his tin cook stove, some flour and other groceries and drove up Chalk Creek, passing Heywood Hot Springs and Alpine to Forest City, later known as St. Elmo".

In the Rocky Mountain News of February 17, 1880, we read where the Denver & Rio Grande pooled their interests in the hotel and depot built by the Buena Vista Townsite Company. Old Colorado & Southern engineering files state that a new South Park depot and some repair shops were built at Buena Vista in 1898.

NATHROP.

Milepost 136.75.

Main line. Alttiude 7,710 feet. Station No. 1066. Station call NR. J. H. Shuckart was agent in July, 1885.

Facilities:

The stone station was used jointly by the Rio Grande and the South Park. The South Park had 1,019 feet of siding of their own.

Historical note:

The Colorado Magazine, Louisa Ward's book, "Chalk Creek", and old files of the Rocky Mountain News disclose some interesting data regarding this station. It seems that one Charles Nachtrieb, who is first heard of as running a little grocery store in old California Gulch (Leadville) around 1868, grew tired of the mining camp and, like Benjamin Schwanders, directed his footsteps south along the Arkansas in search of a suitable location for himself and a ranch. He located near the confluence of Chalk Creek and the Arkansas River. Nachtrieb was a good business man. As a result of his various activities, the place became known as Chalk Creek and was one of the main stations on the old stage line that ran up the Arkansas Valley to Leadville. Later, when the Rio Grande railroad pushed their track up the valley, he moved south, close to where Chalk Creek empties into the Arkansas. Here, on the banks of Chalk Creek, he built new quarters including a flour and grist mill, and a saw mill. By constructing a dam across Chalk Creek and a suitable mill ditch to carry the water, he obtained sufficient water power to run his two mills.

In June, 1880, a townsite was laid out and the place was given the name Nathrop, the spelling of which was an adaptation of his own last name. Crofutt's 1881 Guide states that the population at that time was 200. The site of the new settlement, which grew up around the railroad station, was owned jointly by the Rio Grande and South Park railroads and Nachtrieb himself. They built a two-story frame hotel which contained 6 rooms in the basement, including a bar room, five rooms on the first floor and 13 bedrooms connected by three long halls on the second floor. It was known as the Nachtrieb Hotel. (See photo on page 178.)

Pure water for the little settlement was brought down by gravity from a point on Chalk Creek about a mile upstream by means of a three-inch pipe. This was in 1881. Up to 1904 this same old gravity pipe line was still furnishing water for the Rio Grande's tank at Nathrop. Whether the system still prevails to this day is not known.

Concluding the story of Charles Nachtrieb, Louisa Ward states: "Nachtrieb was a large fellow and of German descent. He was big hearted and gave aid to many a busted pioneer, but he had a hot temper. He was killed in his store on the evening of October 3, 1881, by one Bert Remington, a 20-year-old cowboy, over a difference of twenty-five cents in wages."

HEYWOOD SPRINGS.

Milepost 141.44.

Main line. Station No. 1066. Combination frame passenger and freight depot 16 x 34 feet. See station of Hortense for historical information.

HORTENSE.

Milepost 142.09.

Main line. Altitude 8,190 feet. Station No. 1068.

Facilities:

Combination two-story frame section house. Telegraph office. Coal bin. 47,500 gal. wood water tank—water supplied by gravity from Chalk Creek through 1,380 feet of two-inch pipe. 1,687 feet of side track. Wye. This wye was removed in July, 1912.

Historical note:

This place, originally known as Chalk Creek Hot Springs, lies in the shadow of Mt. Princeton, one of Colorado's highest mountain peaks—14,177 feet. Throughout the history of the railroad this station was variously known as both Hortense and Mt. Princeton. Here, near the mouth of Chalk Creek canon, were located the famous Mt. Princeton Hot Springs, whose waters were supposed to possess some medicinal values. Concerning these hot springs, Louisa Ward writes:

"The earliest inhabitants here were the Ute Indians who came to the Hortense Springs to soak their rheumatic joints in the hot water that flowed from the springs at a temperature of 183 degrees, the hottest spring water found in Colorado".

Located about a half mile below the Hortense Springs was another group of springs known as Heywood (sometimes spelled Haywood) Hot Springs. This second group of springs, which numbered from 35 to 40 springs, and which varied in temperature of from 98 to 150 degrees, probably came from the same source as did the Hortense Springs. In 1920 the rate of flow was estimated at 250 gallons per minute, but this had dropped to about 50 gallons per minute by 1939. This place was also sometimes known as Mt. Princeton Hot Springs.

The Heywood Springs were supposed to have been discovered, about 1870, by a wagon freighter named Romer. The first hotel was built here about 1874-75, by a Mr. D. Heywood, who owned some 820 acres of land upon which the springs were located. The Denver South Park & Pacific Railroad paid Mr. Heywood $3,000 for their right of way through the hotel grounds. In 1881, the population at the springs was given as 50. A new hotel located up the hill, somewhat above the springs, was started around 1877 and completed in 1891. It was four stories high (the fourth floor was never completely finished) and contained 100 rooms. Hotel rates were $10.00 per week and bath tickets were $3.00 per dozen. The old hotel acquired a reputation as a ghostly place and on windy nights the guests reported hearing many eerie and queer noises. The building stood empty many years and changed hands many times. The place enjoyed moderate prosperity for a brief period around 1915, for the first time in its checkered career. After closing down again, it was supposed to have opened up once more in 1921 under the name of the Antero Hotel. At last reports the old green and yellow cracker box, as it was sometimes called, was still standing—a landmark of a bygone era.

RASPBERRY.

Milepost 144.30.

Main line. This station was in existence during the '80's. No other information known.

C.&S. 57 helping at the rear of the Gunnison-Como mixed train near Midway tank, east of Pitkin, about 1905.

The depot at Alpine (later known as Fisher) as it appeared about 1882.

SALEM.

Milepost 145.69.

Main line. 425 feet of siding. This station was in existence around 1910. No other information known.

CASCADE.

Milepost 146.86.

Main line. Altitude 9,019 feet. Station No. 1069. 630 feet of siding. This place was changed to Glencliff around the turn of the century.

ALPINE.

Milepost 148.85.

Main line. Altitude 9,263 feet. Station No. 1070. Station call AN. W. C. Channell was agent in July, 1885.

Facilities:

Combination frame depot, freight room, and living quarters. 47,500 gal. wood water tank fed by gravity through a two and one-quarter inch pipe extending 1,200 feet to a spring. 838 feet of siding.

Historical note:

Alpine, an early mining camp, was founded in 1877. The name of the station was changed to Fisher in June, 1899. Additional historical matter will be found in the notes on St. Elmo.

COAL CAMP.

Milepost 150.98.

Main line. Station No. 1071. No other data known.

IRON CITY.

Milepost 152.55.

Main line. 2,260 feet of siding. This place was later known as Morley's Mill. Additional matter will be found in the St. Elmo notes.

ST. ELMO.

Milepost 153.29.

Main line. Altitude 10,062 feet. Station No. 1072. Station call RS. W. H. Dack was agent in July, 1885. The last agent at this station was one of the Stark brothers, who have lived in St. Elmo all their lives.

Facilities:

Combination frame depot, freight room, and living quarters 16 x 48 feet. Freight platform attached containing 1,176 sq. ft. with an additional platform containing 3,120 sq. ft. Coal. 2,652 feet of siding in 1889. In 1885, a fifty-foot wrought iron turntable was installed here. (St. Elmo Mountaineer, July 11, 1885.) As nearly as can be ascertained, it was removed around the turn of the century.

Historical note:

Along with the St. Elmo story we shall include a short historical sketch of the Chalk Creek district. The greater portion of this information comes from the Colorado Magazine, and Louisa Ward's "Old West Series of Writings".

Chalk Creek, which has its beginning on the east slope of the Saguache Range, flows east between Mt. Princeton and Mt. Antero, two 14,000 foot peaks, and empties into the Arkansas River just below Nathrop. At the base of a southern spur of Mt. Princeton is a mountain called Merriam Mtn. Here are located the great Chalk Cliffs from whence the creek derives its name. These cliffs appear to be made up of chalk but, as truly reported by the Hayden Expedition in 1873, they consist of decomposed feldspar and a clay-like substance.

For a few years Chalk Creek was practically on the road to everywhere. In the latter part of 1880 when Alpine and St. Elmo, were the successive rail-heads, the endless stream of prospectors and travelers rode the cars as far as they could go and then started over the range on foot, horseback or, if financially able, rode the stage coach. Colonel Henry Altman, Eugene Teets, and E. C. Brearley operated their stage line south out of St. Elmo over the old Mays-

ville Toll Road. The Sanderson Stage Lines operated over the Alpine Pass or Williams Pass toll road to Pitkin and the Gunnison country. Traffic to the Tin Cup district went by way of the Chalk Creek & Elk Mountain Toll Road via Tin Cup Pass, while Spotswood & McClellan ran their stage line to the Aspen and Taylor Park country via Tin Cup or Cottonwood Pass. Spotswood's Concord stages were each drawn by six spirited horses. Passengers paid $3.50 for a twelve-mile ride. Sometimes they had to walk, and even help push the coach when the going got tough because of the heavy winter snowdrifts. These toll roads were also utilized by the freighters in hauling merchandise to the various mining camps.

Mining, which was the chief occupation carried on in Chalk Creek Canon, had its beginning in 1872 when rich silver bearing ore was discovered over 12,000 feet up, on the side of Mt. Princeton. Except for the period during the 1893 panic, this mine, known as the Hortense Mine, paid well for years. It finally played out during the 1930's.

Following the discovery of the Hortense Mine, prospectors swarmed into the district. Gold and silver was found in fairly well paying quantities about six miles up the creek and a new mining camp, known as Alpine, was established near where Baldwin Creek flows into Chalk Creek. One of the largest mines in this immediate vicinity was the Tilden Mine, discovered in 1874. 1879-80 were the peak years at Alpine. It was a typical early day, hell-roaring Colorado mining camp. During its heyday the town boasted of a $4,000 dance hall, 23 saloons, 2 hotels, 3 stores, a newspaper called "The True Fissure", and a population of over 500. But Alpine's luck soon ran out. By 1887 the camp's population had dwindled down to a mere 27 persons. Today, Alpine is a shriveled ghost town, long since abandoned and totally forgotten. John C. Ashford writes: "In 1937 all I could find here was a single brick smoke stack of the old smelter hidden in the underbrush down near the creek. The remains of two old log cabins are across the way. The main street of Alpine, once lined with false front saloons and log cabins, is now lined with Aspens".

Just above Alpine two new camps, Iron City and St. Elmo, were established. And, as was usually the case, Alpine's miners, girls, saloon and store keepers, packed up their belongings and moved on up the stream to the new diggings. Iron City is a comparatively little known camp. A smelter was built here in 1880 and did a thriving business for a few years. The remains of this old smelter, which are quite impressive, are all that is left to mark the site of this once busy place.

Meanwhile a new mine, the Mary Murphy, destined to be one of the richest in the district, had been opened up in the vicinity of the north and south forks of Chalk Creek. This brought about the establishment of a new camp above Iron City known as St. Elmo.

Concerning St. Elmo's early history, Louisa Ward writes: "Where the North and South Forks of Chalk Creek join, an early prospector put down a stake, remarking that the site would be a town someday. He was right. In the spring of 1880, a settlement was laid out here and given the name of Forest City". Very soon thereafter the name of the new camp was changed to St. Elmo; however, an 1881 Railway Guide still referred to the place by its former name. History tells us that the Post Office Department rejected the camp's original name and at the suggestion of a lawyer, the name St. Elmo was adopted. The site commanded a very strategic location; it was in the heart of the Chalk Creek mining district, including the Mary Murphy lodes; and it was the distribution or starting point for a number of toll roads that led to four other bonanza districts—Aspen, Tin Cup, Gunnison, and the Maysville or Monarch district.

These toll roads brought plenty of business to St. Elmo. The town's rapidly increasing population was further augmented by railroad laborers, tunnel laborers, miners, prospectors, and a goodly portion of the inhabitants of Alpine and Iron City. By the first of 1881, the population was estimated to be around 500. The town's newspaper was "The St. Elmo Mountaineer". While the South Park railroad was building, Alpine, then St. Elmo, and Hancock were the successive railheads; but St. Elmo, being the largest, drew the Saturday night crowds. During the long months Alpine Tunnel was being bored through the Continental Divide, St. Elmo drew in the money from the hundreds of men who were employed there.

With such prosperity staring the territory in the face, the Chaffee County News attempted to play the role of a prophet and predicted a great future for the new camp but, unfortunately, their predictions went awry. In the issue of January 1, 1881, this paper extolled the wonderful climate around St. Elmo and spoke of the rich mining industry and other potential opportunities that were developing. The editor predicted that thousands would leave the smoky cities and come dwell in one of nature's garden spots, once the South Park railroad was completed. Hundreds of persons did live in St. Elmo at different times during their search for the elusive gold and silver, but they failed to remain.

St. Elmo had a big fire in 1890 which destroyed two entire city blocks, leaving only the fire hydrants standing as ineffectual monuments. Around 1904 there was a second boom at the famous Tin Cup diggings, located on the west slope of the Saguache Range about ten miles northwest of St. Elmo. In view of this a group of men organized THE TAYLOR PARK RAILROAD COMPANY, with the object of building a narrow gauge railway from a connection on the Denver South Park & Pacific at St. Elmo via a tunnel under the Continental Divide to Tin Cup.[1] The project collapsed and no railroad line was ever attempted.

The mainstay of St. Elmo's existence was mining. By 1883 there were about fifty mines in operation in the immediate area. One of the larger mines was the Brittenstein, estimated to be the richest gold mine in the state when first discovered, but which later proved to be a great disappointment to its owners. Other large mines included the Iron Chest, Old Bull, Maple Leaf, Black Hawk, Ballbec, and the Flora Bell. But the largest of these was the celebrated Mary Murphy Mine, located on the South Fork of Chalk Creek, high on the mountainside above Romley.

Dr. A. E. Wright, who was the first person to settle near the site of St. Elmo in 1872, was prospecting with a partner, John Royal; together they discovered the Mary Murphy in September, 1875, naming the mine after a nurse in a Denver Hospital. History tells us that Dr. Wright, who was a colorful and rough frontiersman, wore long hair to cover up a lost ear that had been chewed off by a bear. The Doctor sold his share of the mine in 1878, and moved to Buena Vista where he resumed his practice of medicine.

By 1881 the Mary Murphy was the largest producer in the district. Much eastern capital was invested in the mines, especially the Murphy property. The building of the railroad through the Chalk Creek district in 1881 greatly facilitated the shipment of ore, and enabled the mine operators to improve their property and increase their output. At the Mary Murphy a tramway 4,996 feet long was built from opposite the opening of the number four level down to the railroad at Murphy's Switch at the foot of Pomroy Mtn. This tramway was single endless steel cable with fifty stations located 75 to 100 feet apart. Each of the 96 buckets had a 200-pound capacity which enabled the tramway to deliver 128 tons of ore at the loading switch in a twenty-

1. Tin Cup was originally known as Virginia City.

four hour period. These ore buckets loaded and unloaded automatically and it required forty minutes to make the circuit. Only two men were required to operate it; one at each end to apply the brakes when necessary. The motive power to operate this tram came from the full descending buckets which were heavy enough to bring up, not only the empties, but timber and other supplies attached to the eight pairs of hooks furnished for that purpose. That was efficiency! Later, another similar tramway about a mile long was installed to transport additional ore down the mountain side to a new loading rack. The company erected a mill at Romley and at Buena Vista to handle their ore; however, most of it was shipped to the Leadville smelters.

Normally about 100 men worked at the Mary Murphy. 1914 was the peak year with an average of 250 men on the pay roll. The first world war in 1917 was the beginning of the end. By 1919 the mine was operated only sporadically. Production continued to decrease, and as nearly as can be determined, ceased entirely during the late 1920's. In 1914 the Denver Post estimated that the Mary Murphy had produced a total of over $14,000,000 in gold and silver.

A young miner, in writing of his experiences while working at the old Mary Murphy stated: "It was lonesome as death far up there on the side of the windswept mountain at the fourth level where I was stationed all by myself. My job was sorting ore on the night shift. The only sound to be heard was the almost constant thumping caused by persistent winds on the side of the shaft house. Occasionally I would hear the faint low echo from the whistle of some of the little South Park engines as they laboriously chuffed their way up the far side of the mountain toward Alpine Tunnel. Between the numerous blizzards that swept relentlessly over the mountain side piling up snow in the gulches and ravines to depths of 100 feet or more, the sky, on a clear cold night with a full moon shining, was a sight calculated to inspire awe and excite a feeling of grandeur".

The old St. Elmo depot burned and was replaced by a new one in 1898. The two old box-car bunk houses, which interest a number of South Park fans today and on whose sides of the faded letters, U.P.D.&G., can still be seen under a weathered coat of paint, were set out here in 1908.

Today, one takes the road to Romley up the South Fork on the old railroad grade that rises above St. Elmo. At Romley we wander around the deserted buildings, roam in and about the old Murphy Mill, see the cubbyholes in the old Post Office, stand knee-deep in the paper records of the mine and newspapers scattered about on the floor of the mine office, wonder what was in the old large safe turned face down on the floor, wander over across the abandoned right of way to the little depot and observe names written all over the door and walls and then, perhaps with half-closed eyes, imagine that we can turn back the years and watch a South Park engine switch the gondolas or ore cars here and there, as the never-ending procession of ore buckets came marching down the mountain side to fill more hungry ore cars at the loading racks.

St. Elmo is almost a forgotten town today. A general store, including a Post Office, a few neglected and run-down buildings and houses, along with some tourist cabins run by a surviving member of the Stark family, for wandering fishermen, constitute about all the activity to be found there. The 1937 census lists St. Elmo's population as seven.

GOLF.
Milepost 154.35.
Main line. 2,750 feet of siding at this station around 1910-12. No other data known.

MURPHY TANK.
Milepost 154.78.
Main line. 47,500 gal. wood water tank. This tank was

removed between 1886 and 1889. This station had 1,190 feet of siding and was also known as Lady Murphy. No other data known.

ROMLEY.
Milepost 155.61.

Main line. Altitude 10,557 feet. Station No. 1073. Station call MY.

Facilities:

1,668 feet of siding. A frame depot built sometime after 1886, burned in 1908. In the Colorado & Southern files we read: "A turntable was installed at Romley between August 1st and 18th, 1915. The cost was $1,161.00. This turntable came from Gunnison where it was built in 1888, later overhauled in 1908. It was a fifty-foot lattice girder turntable. The cost new was $1,830.00. It was valued at $150.00 when removed to Romley. The freight via Salida over the D.&R.G. cost $141.00".

Historical note:

In discussing a trip made along the old South Park grade through this vicinity in 1945, Roy Morton writes: "Upon arriving at the Romley Mill site, I found that the old mill had burned some time ago, but the old tramway was still standing. Makes a fellow feel a little sad to see how the place looks now in comparison with the former years of great production when I first knew it. . . . The old Romley boarding house and some of the other buildings are in fair shape. The iron safe is laying over on its side on the floor of the building that used to be the mine office. Above Romley I passed many familiar old mines such as the Flora Bell, the Alie Bell, the Treasury, and the Pittsburgh. Walking along the railroad grade, which is very straight without any curves, one could appreciate the reason why the old South Park engineers feared and hated that stretch of track, as it was the hardest place on the system to hold or check the speed of a loaded train with no curves to pinch them on. They had to use what air they had in their auxiliary tank with the retainers in the proper places and no place or chance to recharge the train line. Sometimes they had to call for the train crew, including the fireman, to tie down a few binders".

In its early days Romley was known as Morley, also as Murphy. In 1897 the name was changed to Romley—why, no one seems to know. Charlie Squires writes: "There was nothing at Romley but the Mary Murphy Mill and office buildings. The freight room in the railroad company's depot was used as a commissary by the mine. The telegraph agent here, who formerly worked as agent at Buena Vista, was paid by the Murphy Mining Company".

FLORA BELL.
Milepost 156.23.

Main line. Three-car spur connected at east end. This spur existed around 1912. No other data known.

ALIE BELL COAL SPUR.
Milepost 156.31.

Main line. 130-foot spur was in here around 1912. No other information known.

ALIE BELL ORE SPUR.
Milepost 156.36.

Main line. 188-foot spur was in here around 1912. No other information known.

COMSTOCK SPUR.
Milepost 157.78.

Main line. One car spur connected at east end. No other information known.

HANCOCK.
Milepost 158.12.

Main line. Altitude 11,027 feet. Station No. 1074. Station call HN.

Facilities:

Combination frame depot, telegraph office, freight room and living quarters. Two story frame section house. Coal bin 10 x 200 feet, 47,500 gal. wood water tank. Various employees timecards list a wye here. A 1904 mileage book shows 2,320 feet of side track at Hancock.

Historical note:

As to the founding of Hancock, the Rocky Mountain News of November 9, 1880 gives the following version: "On the 10th of July last, Mr. Jasen Garlock started to walk across the range to Pitkin, a distance by the only trail at that time of 18 miles. Upon reaching a point three miles east of the South Park railway tunnel, he sat down on the bank of a trout stream to rest. The spot was a pleasant one. Garlock liked it. He lit a fire and cooked a meal. That was four months ago. Today, the site of Garlock's camp fire is now a city of 500 souls. The name is Hancock, where there are five streets, hotels, many saloons, and two sawmills".

In Louisa Ward's book "Chalk Creek", which, from all evidence, seems to be the more truthful version, we read: "When the great exodus started from Alpine (Fisher) in 1880, not all the prospectors stopped at St. Elmo. Some of them moved on up Chalk Creek another five miles and started the town of Hancock. For what or whom the town was named we do not know. It was located on a claim known as the 'Hancock Placer', which had been proved on by James A. Evans, P. F. Barr, L. Dow, and S. E. Land on July 21, 1880. The claim was deeded to the Hancock Town Co. on August 2, 1880. The town was never incorporated. . . . . In 1881, the camp was a thriving place with five stores, many saloons, some restaurants, two sawmills, and a population of some 200. Because Hancock was a boom town, and also because it was the temporary rail-head, serving as headquarters for the Denver South Park & Pacific Railroad while Alpine Tunnel was being built, laborers were in great demand. Wages were around $2.00 per day; miners received $3.00 per day. The Stonewall Mine, discovered in 1879 by Asa Adair, was Hancock's most important mine. It was worked as late as 1915. Other important mines nearby were the Rarus, the Warrior, the Alie Bell, and the Flora Bell. The latter two mines were discovered in 1881".

William Cairns writes: "Prior to around 1893-94, a few cars of ore were shipped out of Hancock now and then, but after that there was nothing much doing at the place".

F. C. Buell writes: "I used to live at Hancock. The town had about 15 houses. About 1902 a snowslide leveled all but four of them". Roy Morton writes that the old depot burned down in the early 90's and was never replaced. (Author's note: The old water tank, sometimes called "Timberline Tank", stood for years but is now gone. Today, nothing remains to identify the station but a big pile of sawdust and a broken string of rotting cedar ties marking the path of the old right of way.) In describing a recent trip through this area Roy Morton writes: "The old impounded water reservoir at Hancock looked just as natural as ever and the drain is still in good operating condition. Plenty of sawdust still scattered about and few signs of decay show after all these years. In the early days when the sawmill was in operation the slender lodge pole pine covered the mountain sides like whiskers".

ATLANTIC.
Milepost 160.99.

Main line. Station No. 1075. Sometimes called Summit. This point, located at the east portal of Alpine Tunnel, served only as a passing track. The length of this passing track varied from time to time. Old Union Pacific records state that it was 530 feet long. 1889-97 employees time-

Looking down on Alpine Tunnel station, on the west side of Alpine Pass, in 1893. The large stone structure is the engine house, and the smaller stone building is the old hotel. Directly across the tracks is the little frame station and telegraph office.

Otto Westerman photo
from E. J. Haley Collection.

cards give the length as 489 feet, while a 1912 timecard describes it as a 16-car spur connected at the west end near the tunnel. This passing track was partially supported by a rock crib 189 feet long.

ALPINE TUNNEL STATION.

Milepost 161.77 at the east face of the telegraph office. Main line. Altitude: the writer has been unable to locate the true altitude of the track at this particular point. By basing our computations on an approximate grade of 2½% between the station proper and the apex of the tunnel, we get an estimated figure of 11,546 feet. Station No. 1076. Station call UH. George H. Colson was an early agent and operator here. Another well-known brass pounder who worked here was Frank Soper. His brother, Wes Soper, was agent on Boreas Pass at the same time.

Facilities:

(In view of the more than ordinary interest in the facilities at this station, we will list them exactly as shown in an old Union Pacific record book of the South Park Division, dated January 1, 1886.)

1. Section house. Stone construction........29½ x 56　feet.
　 Addition. Stone construction...................16　 x 25½ feet.
　　　　1 room　17¾ x 25½ feet.
　　　　1 room　14　 x 25½ feet.
　　　　1 room　 9½ x 13½ feet.
　　　　1 room　10　 x 11¾ feet.
　　　　1 room　 6¾ x 12½ feet.
　　　　1 room　11¾ x 12½ feet.
　　　　1 room　 9½ x 10¾ feet.
　　　　1 room　 3¾ x 9½ feet.
　　　　2 rooms　9　 x 11¾ feet.
2. Engine house. Stone construction.................54 x 153 feet.
3. Coal bin inside engine house.......................14 x 40 feet.
4. Water tank in engine house. Wood tub 5 x 18 feet, capacity 9,516 gal. Fed by 636 feet of four inch pipe to a spring. Self-feeder. Quality and supply of water good.
5. Bunk house. Stone construction.............14 x 16½ feet.
6. Store house. Stone construction.................10 x 16　 feet.
7. Wash house. Stone construction.................10 x 18　 feet.

An 1889 employees timecard shows coal, water, and 660 feet of siding.

An 1897 employees timecard shows same facilities.

A 1912 employees timecard shows only a 13-car siding.

A large scale valuation map, (date not known) shows approximately 1,350 feet of siding, excluding the 212-foot lead to the turntable. This 1,350 feet of track included a 719-foot passing track on the west side of the main line directly in front of the old frame boarding house, and about 630 feet of passing track on the opposite side of the main line, which ran through the stone engine house.

Historical note:

Old Union Pacific records tell that a small section house was built at the tunnel station in 1890. This little building stood on the west side of the tracks opposite the stone section house and shows very plainly in a photograph taken in 1899. From this and other evidence, the little frame building from which the old order board hung so long and upon whose roof rested the two signs reading "ALPINE TUNNEL", is thought to be the same structure which served as the telegraph office in later years and which, at last reports, was still standing.

As nearly as can be accurately determined, a disastrous fire destroyed practically all of the original stone buildings and facilities around the year 1906. The fire ruined them to such an extent that no attempt was ever made to rebuild them. Substitutes were soon in order. Information on the new section and boarding house is found in the Colorado & Southern Annual Report dated June 30, 1907, which

states: "A new two-story frame boarding house was completed at Alpine Tunnel in September, 1906 at a cost of $1,701.58. Additional improvements included a fifty-foot turntable installed during the summer of 1907, on the west side of the main line just outside the west portal of the tunnel. A 212-foot lead connected with the new table." Considerable difficulty was encountered by the writer in determining the exact date this turntable was installed. Roy Morton's findings were later confirmed personally by several old time South Park men including Andy Anderson, Charlie Thomas, and A. C. Anderson. The question as to why this turntable was installed often crops up. Apparently, the only plausible answer is that it was practically an annual occurrence for Alpine Pass to be blocked solidly with snow during the winter seasons. Therefore, in an effort to maintain some semblance of service for the benefit of the localities between the tunnel and Gunnison, an effort was made to keep that part of the line open. In the words of Lewis R. Lathrop, ". . . . passenger coaches were not designed for bucking snow". Therefore the turntable was built to turn engines at Alpine Tunnel.

Relative to the subject of a turntable at Alpine Tunnel Station, considerable discussion has developed over the question of a turntable being located inside the old stone engine house. A number of old time Colorado railroad men contend that a table was built inside this house. Others maintain the opposite. In view of the evidence which has come to light, the writer is forced to agree with the latter group. An assortment of employees timetables, dated prior to 1906, does not list any turntable at Alpine Tunnel Station. Likewise, the 1886 Union Pacific record book of all facilities at South Park stations does not show a turntable here. The question was put to Roy Morton, who wrote:[1]

"There was never a turntable in the old stone engine house at Alpine Tunnel Station. This engine house contained only an old tub water tank, a coal bin, a long tool bench and rack, some wooden lockers, a hose reel and a cinder dump. We operated a long time without any turntable at all, using the wye at Pitkin or Hancock. We worked all kinds of deals with our power. We would run extras west with empties, switch the mines in the St. Elmo and Romley district, set out a train at the tunnel or at Pitkin and return to pick up anything in sight, using the Pitkin or Hancock wye. A turntable was not an absolute necessity at Alpine and even after the table was installed near the west portal of the tunnel in 1907, we didn't always use it."

In 1908 a new water tank was built on the east side of the main line, a few hundred feet beyond the west portal. The Colorado & Southern Annual Report for June 30, 1909, states that the cost was $1,184.09. The foundation for this tank can still be seen very plainly. Some alterations were also made on the two snow sheds at the tunnel at this time. The length of the shed at the east approach was reduced from 150 to 128 feet, while the shed at the west approach was reduced from 650 feet to 527 feet. The reasons for these changes are not known. Today, the scene at Alpine Tunnel Station is one of extreme desolation and loneliness. The original stone buildings are reduced to a pile of rubble, with only a few sections of the walls standing. Only the hand of providence seems to be holding the old wooden buildings in an upright position, as they seem ready to cave in or fall over at any time. In view of the unusual amount of interest in this particular section of the old South Park, additional material pertaining to both the station and the tunnel follows.

ALPINE TUNNEL.

The author is of the firm opinion that if some sort of a vote were taken among the hundreds of South

1. Excavation in 1973 proved existance of a turntable in the engine house.

433

In this multiple flash photo of Alpine Tunnel's interior we see the apex of the tunnel where it begins to descend the east slope of the Continental Divide.

Alpine Tunnel station as it appeared in August, 1944. In the foreground are the ruins of the engine house, and across the right of way are the remains of the coaling platform beside the boarding house, with the little frame station at the end of the platform.

Park followers throughout the country as to the most interesting subject for discussion, Alpine Tunnel would head the list. There is no question but that this great tunnel and the magnificent Palisades, located a short distance beyond the west portal, are the two outstanding pieces of railroad construction on the whole South Park system. As the Arab considers it his sacred duty to visit the Holy City of Mecca, it appears that the ambition of every true South Park enthusiast is to make at lease one pilgrimage to ALPINE PASS and the PALISADES.

If the reader will permit the author to digress from the story for a moment, we might suggest that the best approach is from the east slope. One can enter Chalk Creek Canon at Nathrop and drive up the old grade past St. Elmo as far as Hancock. Here the auto must be parked and the journey continued on foot. From Hancock the right of way, which is a continuous line of decaying cedar and pine ties, can be followed up to the east portal of the tunnel. Roy Morton, accompanied by an acquaintance, hiked up the grade to the tunnel in June, 1945. In writing the author about his trip, Mr. Morton stated:

"The ties along the right of way in the vicinity of Sawmill Curve are in fair condition and appear as if most of them might be able to stand having rails laid after all these years. We found one good link, one good pin, one broken link, two broken pins, one broken bolster, an old battered brakeman's lantern, one broken knuckle, and a portion of an old Jenny type coupler jaw. Of course there are many spikes scattered all along the grade.

"Just beyond Sawmill Curve where the grade really begins to climb, one can observe plenty of cinders, indicative of how the old time engineers back in the years of operation began to gun their hogs along there preparing for the hard climb to the tunnel. As we proceeded up the right of way, I observed a few remaining poles of the old telegraph line. Some were broken off near the ground; some were standing in good shape; a few still had their crossarms intact and occasionally an insulator could be seen. Soon we began to encounter patches of snow which had to be avoided in some places. In many spots the wood culverts were in fairly good shape, others are stopped up and the overflow of water from the melting snow has begun to cut sections of the road bed, making it difficult to travel over. As we advanced farther up the grade the old ties showed more signs of decay because of the heavy snowfall remaining on the ground so long before melting away. Chalk Creek, several thousand feet below, could be seen rushing along the bottom of the canon. As we walked on, the snow became deeper and we encountered more of it. The crest of the mountain was covered with considerable snow and the many clouds obscured the sun at times. We trudged on, resting a little now and then.

The snow became worse and the cut out places in the right of way were practically full of snow. With so much snow on the grade, and above us—clear to the top of the range—we began to wonder just how much farther we would be able to go. We finally reached the last curve just below Atlantic Siding. It was completely white with snow. As the years come and go, this trip will get worse—the washed out and cut through places along the grade will make travel more difficult. The slides have been numerous in the past few years and walking around and over them is difficult at times".

It is reported that up to 1933 one could walk through Alpine Tunnel[1] but now, both portals are filled with fallen rock, snowshed timbers, and other debris; consequently, one cannot walk completely through it. However, as late as the summer of 1944 a daring soul possessed of more zeal and bravery than the vast majority of South Park fans dug his way through the rubble at the west portal and, without any great amount of difficulty, negotiated almost the whole distance of the tunnel to the east portal, which is stopped up completely. We shall read about this expedition later.

To reach the west slope one must climb over Alpine Pass, the altitude of which is 11,940 feet above sea level, and which seldom sheds all its snow, even in the summer. It is a tough climb up that mountain side above Atlantic Siding in the rare mountain air, and will greatly affect one's breathing, especially those not used to living in the higher altitudes. But having once gained the top of the Pass, one is rewarded with a most magnificent view of the abandoned railroad buildings and right of way on the west slope as they lie there, cradled in the stillness and majesty of the surrounding mountain peaks. Here, one can really appreciate the solemn beauty and grandeur of the great Saguache Range.

In descending the slope to the west portal a close observer will note traces of the long-abandoned wagon and toll road where it zigzagged its way to the summit of the pass. Beginning at the west portal and following about a mile and a half of track, one will, in turn, pass the old turntable pit on the right, the water tank foundation on the left, the crumbled stone section and engine houses, the frame telegraph office, and combination two-story wooden boarding house. These wooden structures are still standing—ghosts of a long forgotten past. In its heyday the old boarding house was an imposing wooden structure, but now it leans like the Tower of Pisa and leaks like a sieve. Its doorways are doorless; its open windows stare like vacant eyes; the floors slant; the old dilapilated bunks on the second floor lie in jumbled and haphazard positions; and the winds make eerie noises as they blow through the myriads of cracks and crannies.

1. Louisa A. Ward's "Chalk Creek, Colorado."

One will also find portions of a side track, switches, and an old "harp type" switch still balanced precariously on a rotted cedar tie, bravely defying time and the elements. That is, it may still stand there, provided some overenthusiastic railfan has not carried it away. The two wooden station signs "ALPINE TUNNEL" that, for many years, adorned the top of the little telegraph office are gone; the old order board that used to hang out in front of this little office is also gone. A thirty-inch section of one of the rails in the main line between the tunnel and the depot is missing. In all probability some enterprising individual sawed out this missing section and carried it away to be preserved in his archive of South Park collector's items.

This stretch of main track was laid with 40-pound rail in 1882 and, providing the operators of a few straggling mines in the region have not dragged them away, a considerable portion of the old rails in the immediate section west of the tunnel still lay there, spiked to crumbled cedar ties as they have been for long years past; resisting to the end the blizzards, the winds, and the sun. They have not felt the weight of a South Park engine for nearly 40 years. In places one will find cinders piled up to a depth of some two feet, indicative of the work the little engines used to do. It gives one an eerie feeling to find this rusty piece of main line railroad track, almost 12,000 feet high in the mountains, with the rails laid on ties that will almost crumble in your hands. One listens—in that deep silence so characteristic of the eternal hills—almost expecting to hear the bark of the little engines that stormed the grades so long ago, or hear the shrill scream of their whistles. But the engines and the men who rode them are gone. We shall know them no more; only their memories are with us.

As one follows the track down past the old eating house, a small stream of water will be noted at the right. It is the head of a small stream known as Tunnel Creek. At the point where this stream leaves the right of way, the writer strongly suggests that the reader leave the roadbed and follow a trail beside this stream, down the mountain side for about three quarters of a mile. Here, at the head of Quartz Creek Valley, one will find the South Park grade again. The grade is overgrown in many section with thick bushes and small seedling pine trees, but although the rails have been pulled up long ago, the broken line of ties can be followed quite easily. From this point the old right of way can be followed upgrade, past Woodstock, or Tunnel Gulch Tank, past the old site of Woodstock, around the great Sherrod Curve and back to the Palisades, four or five hundred feet above the lower track level. To anyone interested in Colorado railroads, there are few places in the state that can equal this section of the old South Park, known as the Palisades. To stand there and marvel at what the pioneer Civil Engineers were confronted with, in the construction of this particular section of mountain railroad, is one of the high lights of the trip. One can have nothing but great admiration for the men who surveyed and built that 452 feet of solidly constructed rock work which supports the right of way along the face of this huge granite mountain side, and is still in a remarkable state of preservation.

On a clear day one may face toward the west and look out over a great valley, its vast length dotted by beaver ponds and light green meadows, surrounded by the darker green of the pine clad slopes.

The English language is inadequate to describe this scene—one of the greatest panoramas to be seen in Colorado. Far off on the horizon the noble line of the towering Wasatch Range in Utah penetrates the blue haze, while a little farther south Uncompahgre Peak raises its 14,306-foot head above the range that dwindles into mimic lines in comparison.

And while standing on the Palisades, one might look below and see the old wagon road that twisted its way up the side of the mountain, crossed the track just above the Palisades, and disappeared over the range at Williams Pass (sometimes called Hancock Pass), to drop down the east slope into Hancock. Following a trip over Alpine Pass to Pitkin and Gunnison some years ago, W. E. Mahony of Denver wrote:

"There has been some agitation around Pitkin and Gunnison to convert the old railroad grade into a highway. It would commence at Quartz and follow the grade to a point just beyond the Palisades where it would then take off over Williams Pass by way of the old wagon road and toll road into Hancock, avoiding the tunnel. Such a road would save many miles in driving between the Gunnison region and Denver; however, it would side-track the city of Salida, County Seat of Chaffee County. For that reason, the project would get no support from Chaffee County, therefore nothing has been done about it up to this time".

From the Palisades, the old grade may be followed back to Alpine Tunnel Station. Along here one will observe that a few rusty rails and some sections of the road bed are liberally sprinkled and covered with all shapes and sizes of rock and rubble which have broken off the mountain side, or have been swept down by snow slides. From Alpine Station the route is retraced back over Alpine Pass and down the east slope to Hancock. By following this route, the reader will have a minimum of steep mountain climbing to contend with and will miss none of the sights to be seen along this section of the railroad.

THE INTERIOR OF ALPINE TUNNEL

The writer is greatly indebted to Ed Haley of Denver, a real South Park fan if there ever was one, for information concerning the present day condition and other interesting facts concerning Alpine Tunnel. Many persons have proclaimed that the tunnel was permanently closed and sealed forever to the outside world. During the summer of 1944, Mr. Haley journeyed from

Denver to Alpine Pass on two different occasions and each time made a hazardous trip through a small opening in the west portal to gain entrance to the tunnel; a feat few men would care to attempt at this late date due to the ever present dangerous condition of the supporting timbers. On each of these trips he was fortunate in securing excellent photographs which disclose the true condition of the tunnel at this date. The story of Mr. Haley's findings makes a valuable addition to the history of the South Park railroad. The writer is pleased to present his report, as follows:

"The west portal of Alpine Tunnel, contrary to many reports, is still intact. But the deep snows of many winters have crushed the once sturdy snowshed that guarded the western approach. Rubble, constantly slipping down from the Continental Divide at Alpine Pass, has filled the cut leading to the entrance. Between the level of this debris and the arch of the tunnel is a small opening—not more than three by five feet. The winters at this altitude are so severe that the cut is usually filled with ice and snow until late July. Entrance can be gained only during August and part of September. Once inside, I descended abruptly to the floor of the tunnel. It was cold and very damp in there but the air seemed all right. It is the very blackest hole a person can imagine. Approximately one hundred feet from the entrance, there has occurred a large rock fall from the tunnel's ceiling. Between the entrance and this rock fall, the water is about fifteen to eighteen inches in depth. Through this clear water can be seen the rails rusting on the floor of the tunnel. The smoke-blackened timbering near the entrance is covered in places with vivid green moss.

"The tunnel is lined with California Redwood. All supporting timbers are 12"x12". The lagging or back-up boards are 4"x12". The legs or side timbers that stand upright at the sides of the tunnel are usually four feet center to center. At places throughout the bore they are found to be closer together than this, depending on the amount of support they must give. At a few points they are even placed side by side. The bases of these uprights rest upon a 12"x12" timber running lengthwise along the bottom of the tunnel. Along the tops of these uprights lie the 12"x12" stringers, ten feet above the railhead. The arch itself begins at these stringers and is composed of 7 three-foot, 12"x12" members, so angled at the ends as to form the curve or arch, 16' 5" above the rails. In a few places there are no uprights, but a sill or bench is carved in the rock and the stringer, supporting the overhead arches, is laid along this rock shelf or sill.

"On wading through the water and reaching the rock fall, I found it to be about 100 feet in length and varying in height from one to six feet. This fall occurred in the longest untimbered section of the tunnel. It is the largest fall of debris in the tunnel with the exception of the cave in at the east portal, which is sealed off entirely about twenty feet from the entrance.

"Beyond the rock fall the tunnel floor is extremely wet but there is no water covering the rails. The ground is soggy and the ties gave slightly under each step. Water from the roof constantly pelted down on me as I walked forward. A white fungus growth clings to the timbers and rocks near the apex. In appearance, it resembles ice and snow, but is extremely soft and yielding and in some places, where it has been subjected to train smoke, causes the timbers to look charred. As I approached the apex the roadbed grew more firm and less damp. Here and there were small rocks that had fallen from the top and sides of the bore. There were no footprints found in the mud or any signs of anyone having been inside the tunnel for years. At the apex itself I found the only concrete example I have ever witnessed of water flowing toward two different oceans within the space of inches. At this spot, by stirring up the mud in the bottom of the drainage ditch and watching the action of the particles, I saw the water slowly move toward opposite portals. To the east portal it flowed toward the Atlantic via Chalk Creek, the Arkansas and Mississippi Rivers; and to the west portal it flowed toward the Pacific via Quartz Creek, Tomichi Creek, the Gunnison and Colorado Rivers. Alpine's apex is not in the center but is located about a third of the distance in from the west portal, being approximately 600 feet from the west entrance and 1,205 feet from the east entrance. The grade from the west portal to the apex is slightly over 1%, from the east portal to the apex is slightly under 1%.

"Overhead at the apex I saw the support for a red signal lamp that burned continuously while the tunnel was in use. The old lamp has disappeared. In going through the tunnel, the engineers worked steam right up to this red light where they would then shut off and start using air for the down grade run out of the tunnel. A short distance west of the apex is a small cave in from the north side of the tunnel. Here, one of the supporting timbers was pushed inward and has allowed a pile of debris to cover the rails. Quite some distance east of the apex is another cave in. In this case, it was the arch members that gave way resulting in a large pile of loose rock and timbers on the tunnel floor. On climbing over this pile, which is about four feet high, I again found the track bed extremely wet and soggy. Twenty feet beyond, I was again wading and from there on the water grew deeper gradually until on approaching the curve near the east portal, it was above my knees. Other than this, the entire tunnel, from the west portal to the cave in just inside the east portal, is passable.

"The rails and ties are in place throughout the entire length of the bore. The rails are encrusted with a quarter inch of rust. This rust, which flakes off easily by

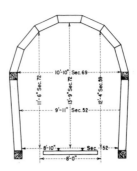

COMPOSITE MINIMUM SECTION

Dimensions shown: 10'-10" Sec.69 · 11'-6" Sec.72 · 13'-9" Sec.72 · 12'-4" Sec.59 · 9'-11" Sec.52 · 8'-10" Sec.Y52 · 8'-0"

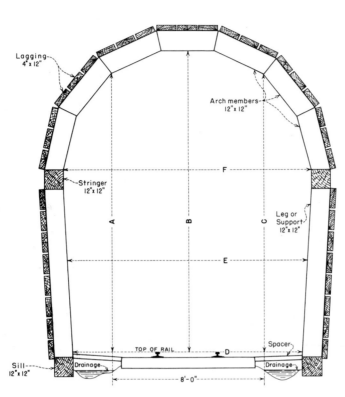

Labels: Lagging 4"x12" · Arch members 12"x12" · Stringer 12"x12" · Leg or Support 12"x12" · Spacer · Sill 12"x12" · Drainage · TOP OF RAIL · A · B · C · D · E · F · 8'-0"

ALPINE TUNNEL DIMENSIONS

MADE IN MARCH, 1900 BY W.T. POWELL, INSPECTOR, B&B DEPT.
REVISED AND REDRAWN IN JAN. 1945 BY E.J.HALEY AND M.E.KNIGHT

Sections 1–40 (dimensions A–F in feet and inches)

SEC.	A	B	C	D	E	F
1	14-0	16-5	14-6	12-2	12-2	13-6
2	13-6	15-5	14-0	12-0	12-6	13-0
3	13-3	15-5	13-11	11-9	12-2	12-7
4 (See Note)		25-0	14-0			
5 (See Note)		23-0	13-11			
6 (See Note)		19-0	13-0			
7 (See Note)		20-0	14-0			
8	14-1	15-5	13-6	11-6	12-2	12-2
9	13-4	15-4	13-3	11-10	12-3	12-8
10	13-4	15-4	13-9	11-9	12-2	12-5
11	13-4	15-2	13-4	11-4	12-0	12-6
12	13-4	15-4	13-0	11-1	12-1	12-8
13	13-2	15-6	13-2	11-2	12-0	12-8
14	13-6	15-5	13-7	12-6	12-7	12-9
15	14-1	15-4	14-2	12-4	12-4	12-9
16	13-4	15-3	13-6	11-0	11-9	12-6
17	12-11	15-7	14-3	12-0	12-4	12-8
18	13-0	15-9	13-9	12-0	12-6	13-0
19	12-9	15-4	13-4	12-0	12-0	12-6
20	13-4	15-2	13-4	11-1	12-5	12-10
21	13-7	15-7	13-7	11-5	12-1	12-10
22	13-8	15-6	13-8	11-0	12-0	12-7
23	13-9	15-8	13-9	11-0	12-6	12-9
24	13-4	15-3	13-2	11-4	12-4	12-5
25	13-8	15-3	13-3	11-0	13-0	13-0
26	13-9	15-10	13-4	12-6	12-6	12-11
27	13-10	15-5	13-9	11-9	12-11	12-11
28	13-4	15-6	13-6	11-9	12-5	13-0
29	13-10	15-5	13-6	11-7	12-3	12-9
30	13-10	14-0	11-0	11-4	11-4	
31	13-7	15-7	13-7	11-9	12-9	
32	13-4	15-7	13-7	11-7	12-7	
33	13-8	15-5	13-3	11-8	12-4	13-0
34	13-9	15-0	13-2	12-8	12-4	12-11
35	13-10	15-4	13-3	11-7	12-4	13-0
36	14-2	15-3	13-2	11-2	12-10	13-0
37	13-4	15-3	13-4	11-6	12-6	13-0
38	13-9	15-6	13-6	11-7	12-8	12-10
39	14-3	15-8	13-7	11-7	13-4	13-0
40	13-6	15-5	13-9	11-5	12-5	13-0

Sections 41–72 (dimensions A–F in feet and inches)

SEC.	A	B	C	D	E	F
41	14-5	15-9	13-6	11-2	12-3	12-6
42	13-10	15-7	13-6	11-3	12-1	12-9
43	14-3	15-9	13-6	11-6	12-4	12-12
44	13-0	15-4	13-11	11-9	12-6	13-0
45	13-7	15-4	13-7	11-9	12-6	13-0
46	13-10	15-1	13-6	10-10	12-0	13-0
47	13-7	15-7	13-7	11-7	12-0	13-0
48	14-4	15-7	13-5	10-11	12-0	13-3
49	14-3	15-10	13-0	10-3	12-0	12-0
50	14-0	14-2	13-0	11-1	12-0	
51	13-3	15-5	13-11	11-0	12-0	
52	12-9	14-7	12-5	8-0	9-11	
53	12-7	14-12	12-10	9-10	12-0	
54	13-6	15-0	12-5	10-10	11-10	
55	12-4	15-6	12-4	11-0	12-4	
56	13-7	15-10	13-0	10-10	11-11	
57	12-11	13-0	10-7	11-7	12-6	
58	12-10	15-0	13-3	9-0	10-11	
59	12-0	14-2	13-0	11-7	12-7	
60	13-9	15-4	10-6	11-6	12-6	
61	13-5	15-0	12-7	10-6	12-5	
62	13-4	15-6	13-6	11-2	12-10	
63	13-0	15-3	13-10	10-6	12-4	
64	13-1	13-0	13-9	10-9	12-6	
65	13-6	15-6	13-4	11-8	12-3	
66	12-0	15-3	13-2	11-5	12-3	
67	12-4	15-4	13-0	11-0	11-0	
68	12-10	15-4	15-9	9-7	11-3	
69	13-0	15-6	12-9	10-0	12-0	
70	13-9	15-7	13-2	12-4	12-0	
71	13-6	15-4	11-6	11-9	9-7	
72	11-6	15-4	11-11	9-0	9-6	

NOTES:
1. Secs. 4-5-6-7 are not timbered.
2. Measurments commence at West end of Tunnel, and run eastward by Sections of 25 ft. each.
3. All Sections are 25 ft. long, except Sec. 72 which is 30 ft.
4. Total length of Tunnel as per these measurments is 1805 ft.
5. All timber used in the tunnel is California Redwood.

CHIEF ENGINEERS OFFICE, C.&S. RY.
DENVER, COLO. MARCH 21, 1900

REDRAWN BY E.J.H.—M.E.K., JAN. 1945

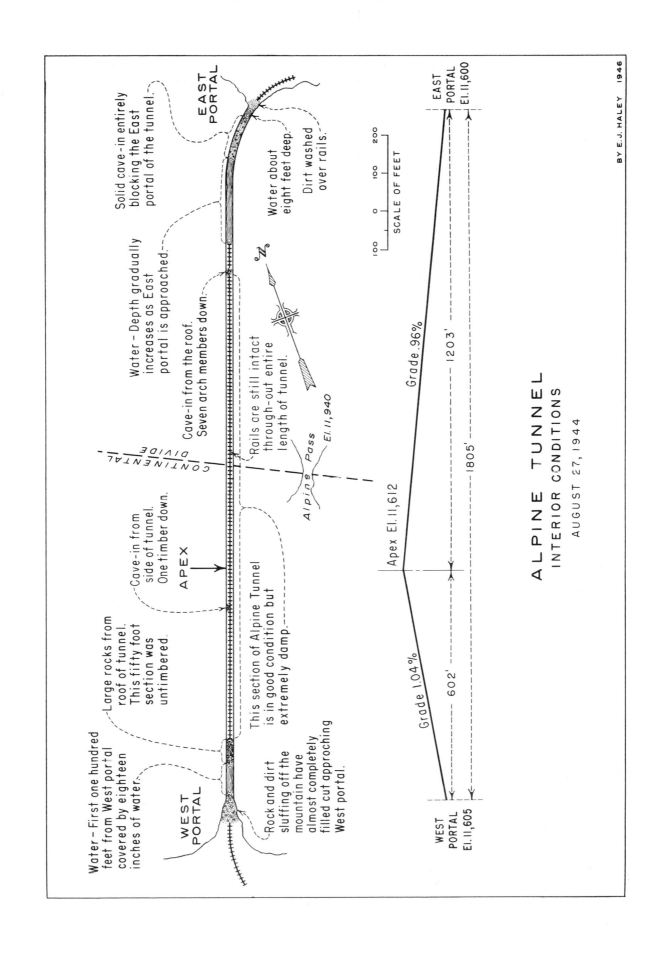

ALPINE TUNNEL
INTERIOR CONDITIONS
AUGUST 27, 1944

BY E.J. HALEY 1946

scraping, reveals a smooth metal surface similar to any well used rail. Every few feet the ties are secured to the walls of the tunnel by means of a crosspiece fastened to the end of the tie and to an upright or to the base timber. At regular intervals along the north wall, about nine or ten feet above the floor, are the insulators that carried the telegraph line through the tunnel.

"Considering the many long years they have been there and the great amount of moisture present, the redwood timbers seem to be in excellent condition except at the immediate entrance. The first two or three arches just inside the west portal are in a cracked and split condition and probably will not hold much longer. When these supports give way, old Alpine Tunnel will be sealed forever and will become but a memory."

* * * *

GRANITE M GOLD MINE SPUR.
Milepost 164.20.
Main line. This station, with a 216 foot siding, was listed in a 1904 mileage book. No other data known.

SHERROD.
Milepost 164.76.
Main line. This station, which was nothing more than a flag stop, was established in October, 1903. It was named after Wm. Sherrod, who operated some mining property in the immediate vicinity around that period. During the early days of the road the curve was known as Woodstock Curve and Woodstock Loop. A 200-foot spur connected at the east end. A small frame waiting room built here was later moved to Ohio City. William Cairns writes that a few cars of ore were shipped from this point now and then.

WOODSTOCK.
Milepost·165.00.
Main line. Altitude 11,039 feet. Station No. 1077. Station operator and agent in 1884 was J. S. Brown. He was killed in the great Woodstock snow slide that occurred in 1884.
Historical note:
Prior to the 1884 slide, this station, which was called a board shack mining town, consisted of the usual frame boarding house, telegraph office, and water tank. A double track spur over 500 feet long connected at the west end. Prior to the slide the population was estimated at about 200. After the slide the railroad company built a small two-room frame bunk house and hand car house. A few years later, in August, 1889, a new water tank, known as Tunnel Gulch Tank, was built about one-half mile west. Further details concerning Woodstock and the great snow slide are to be found elsewhere.

VALLEY SPUR.
Milepost 167.79.
Main line. Altitude 10,413 feet. 287 feet of siding.

MIDWAY TANK.
Milepost 168.66.
Main line. Station No. 1078. The only facility here was a 47,500 gal. wood water tank built during the early days of the railroad. It was fed by gravity from a spring through 257 feet of three-inch pipe.

QUARTZ.
Milepost 171.92.
Main line. Altitude 9,649 feet. Station No. 1079.
Facilities:
Combination eight room frame depot, telegraph office, and living quarters. A 2,413 foot spur, connecting at the west end, ran back up the North Fork of Quartz Creek.

Historical note:
H. L. Curtiss writes: "Quartz was quite a settlement in the early days—a Post Office, stores, saloons, a big log hotel, and a dance hall. Patrick Brogan was the last Postmaster at Quartz". Considerable mining was carried on in this area. Silver ore was discovered in this district in 1878, and the next two years witnessed a general rush of miners into the area, a large number of them coming from Leadville. By 1881, the mining camps in the Gold Brick, Tin Cup, and Quartz Creek district were in full swing. Tin Cup, first known as Virginia City, was located about nine miles north of Quartz. It was one of Colorado's famous boom gold camps in the early 80's. Practically all the Tin Cup ore shipped in the early days came down to the railroad at Quartz. At one time during this period there were 20 stamp mills in operation in the Gold Brick district northwest of Quartz. After the boom died down the region experienced a slight come back around 1905, but it did not last long. Wm. Cairns writes that, in later years, only an occasional car of ore was shipped out of Quartz and sometimes they would pick up a car of logs destined for the pulp mill in Denver. The station gradually developed into merely a passing track for trains.

SPUR.
Milepost 173.98.
Main line. Station No. 1080. No other information.

PITKIN.
Milepost 174.73.
Main line. Altitude 9,201 feet. Station No. 1081. Station call P. H. L. Curtiss writes: "F. W. Juneman was the first ticket agent at Pitkin, and H. M. Funk was the first operator. After 1885, Funk left the South Park for the Utah & Northern at Pocatello. Juneman was ambidextrous; he could copy two train orders at once".

Facilities:
Frame depot and freight house 18 x 50 feet. The freight platform contained 2,208 sq. ft. Coal bin 14 x 157 feet. 47,500 gal. wood water tank supplied with water from Quartz Creek through 2,349 feet of three- and four-inch pipe. Wye. Until about 1900, there was an average of 5,234 feet of siding at Pitkin. In 1901, the railroad built a coal chute at a cost of $2,717.38.

Historical note:
The town of Pitkin was established as a result of numerous mineral discoveries in the nearby Quartz Creek district. In addition to the mines, there was also much lumbering in the area. The settlement, first known as Quartzville, was laid out in April, 1879. Later that year the name was changed to Pitkin in honor of ex-Governor F. W. Pitkin. By 1882 the place boasted of nearly 3,000 population and contained many stores, saloons, hotels, a newspaper, and a bank. George Root, whose father owned a Gunnison newspaper during the early days, furnished the following news item from the Pitkin Mining News of February 10, 1882: "Mr. C. W. Sanborn, who returned from a trip down the Quartz Creek Valley last Wednesday, informs us that the South Park railroad is opening up a stone quarry a mile this side of Parlin in preparation for taking out stone for the building of a handsome stone depot at Pitkin". Evidently the railroad's plans were side-tracked, for the "handsome depot" was never built. John C. Ashford tells that Pitkin still has their old steam fire engine which was purchased in the heyday of the town.

ASHLEY.
Milepost 176.73.
Main line. No other information known except that this station was listed by the D.& R.G. during their control of this section of the Colorado & Southern.

BANK.

Milepost 177.63.

Main line. See Ashley.

OHIO CITY.

Milepost 181.43.

Main line. Altitude 8,563 feet. Station No. 1083. Station call SY.

Facilities:

Six room frame section house. Two ore and freight platforms. 47,500 gal. wood water tank. 1,263 feet of siding.

Historical note:

Ohio City was settled during the discovery of minerals in the Gunnison district. The place was active during the '80's and early '90's, but with the collapse of the silver market in 1893, most of the mines closed down. There was some activity in gold mining around the turn of the century, but it was short-lived.

PARLINS.

Milepost 189.78.

Main line. Altitude 7,933 feet. Station No. 1086. (No information known regarding stations 1084 and 1085.) J. F. Parlin was agent in July, 1885.

Facilites:

Six-room frame section house and two-room bunk house. 47,-500 gal. wood water tank. Wye listed in 1912 employees timecard. 1,146 feet of siding.

Historical note:

The site of Parlins was on the dairy ranch of John Parlin who settled here in 1877. Crofutt's 1881 Guide states: "The place was originally known as Tomichi. It is located at the confluence of Quartz and Tomichi Creeks, and was the junction of the Marshall Pass, Saguache, Pitkin, and Gunnison wagon roads. Some farming, but mostly stock raising in the vicinity". The Denver Daily Times of March 18, 1880 refers to the place as Palmers (probably after General Palmer). The Colorado Magazine tells an interesting anecdote about the place. "About 1880, the Denver South Park & Pacific railroad wanted to buy 1,600 acres of land from John Parlin for the right of way of their railroad. They told Parlin to set his own price. Parlin replied: 'You can have 1,500 acres free if you will build a depot over there by my dairy and make your trains stop for five minutes to permit the train crew, as well as the passengers, time to drink a glass of milk'. The agreement was kept for a time". Wm. Cairns writes that the place was just a Post Office and store for the ranchers.

BIEBLES SPUR.

Milepost 198.00.

Main line. Altitude 7,697 feet. Station No. 1088. 250-foot spur connected at east end around 1895. No other information known.

TOWN SPUR.

Milepost 200.97.

Main line. Listed in 1904 mileage book. No other data known.

D.&R.G. CROSSING.

Milepost 201.23.

Main line.

LA VETA HOTEL.

Milepost 201.32.

Main line. In the early days all passenger trains stopped to discharge and take on passengers at this point.

D.&R.G. CROSSING.

Milepost 201.55.

Main line.

GUNNISON.

Milepost 201.76 at depot.

Main line. Altitude 7,670 feet. Station No. 1089. Station calls SN, GU, DE. Henry Ames was the road's first ticket agent in Gunnison. Ames left the South Park in 1883 and went into the hardware business in Gunnison. D. D. McLaughlin was the first telegraph operator. G. W. Howe was agent in 1885.

Facilites, as of 1886:

Stone depot 20 x 38 feet, containing a waiting room 14 x 17 feet, ticket office 11 x 17 feet, and a bay window 3 x 10 feet. A depot platform containing 1,884 sq. ft. Frame freight house 20 x 60 feet. Two story frame section house. 47,500 gal. wood water tank supplied by a well 12 feet diameter x 14 feet deep. Oil house 12 x 20 feet. Coal bin 14 x 232 feet. Fairbanks track scales 32 feet long with a capacity of 81,000 lbs. Stock pens. Six-stall stone roundhouse 65 x 127½ feet. Wye. Fifty foot wrought iron turntable. Approximately 7,000 feet of miscellaneous siding and yard track.

Historical note:

Inasmuch as a greater portion of the Gunnison story, especially the early details, has already been told, only a few remaining high lights will be included at this point. The first settlement in this immediate vicinity occurred in 1871 when the Government established a cow camp for the benefit of the Ute Indians. In May, 1874 a colony of settlers, headed by Sylvester Richardson, established themselves in a valley lying between the Gunnison River on the north and Tomichi Creek on the south, about a mile or so above the junction of the two streams, and built a group of cabins. Some of the settlers devoted their attention to farming and ranching, while others staked out mining claims. The settlement was called Gunnison, after Captain James W. Gunnison. Sometime later, dissension among the members, together with the attraction of other new camps, caused this settlement to be all but abandoned.

Around 1878 prospectors roaming up and down the Tomichi, Quartz Creek, and surrounding area, found rich carbonates and the rush was on; the camp had survived. In 1879, the Gunnison Town Company was reorganized by Richardson, Governor Evans, Captain Mullen, and others. The townsite of Gunnison was then surveyed, laid out, and in 1880 was incorporated. Between May 15 and August 15, 1880, over 200 houses were erected. Embryo merchants, town-lot speculators, bonanza saloon men, gamblers, and the Jezebels did a flourishing business. The town was wide open and booming. One of the most famous places of amusement in those early days was "The Red Dog Dance Hall".

In addition to the carbonates, rich deposits of iron, coal, and limestone were also found. The processing of the Gunnison ore was more difficult than that required of the Leadville ore; yet, as the mines were frequent and rich, the Gunnison country, because of its extent, was regarded for a time as the treasury of the state. Eastern capitalists erected mills and smelters and referred to Gunnison as "the Pittsburgh of the West". Even Denver was forced to raise her eyebrows and look to her laurels momentarily. Some of the ruins of these early smelters stood for many years to mark the location.

The famous La Veta Hotel, built and furnished at a cost of more than $250,000, was completed in the latter part of 1883. The opening of this famous hostelry was a major event in Gunnison's early history. A manager was imported from St. Louis. On April 9th, shortly before the opening, the gentleman arrived with a retinue of twenty-five employees including clerks, housekeeper, cooks, waiters, bell-boys, and servants. On May 22, 1884, the Masonic Fraternity of Gunnison sponsored the opening with

Gunnison, Colorado in 1881. Looking north on Main Street from New York Avenue.

The famous La Veta Hotel at Gunnison, known far and wide because the management offered a free dinner to every guest in the
house on any day the sun did not shine in Gunnison.

a banquet and grand ball. Both the South Park and the Rio Grande ran excursion rate trips and brought in people from all over the state. It was a gala event. The La Veta enjoyed a more or less successful career until 1925, when it was sold and closed temporarily. In the face of adverse conditions, the new owner found it difficult to keep the old hotel open. Finally, in 1943, the hotel and all its furnishings were sold at public auction. After standing for many years as a monument to the faith of men who dreamed of making millions out of the exploitation of the natural resources of the Gunnison country, the old hotel, with the exception of the first floor, was razed. For a complete story of the La Veta Hotel, the reader is referred to Mrs. Pearle Casey's highly interesting article published in the January, 1944, issue of the Colorado Magazine.

A depression hit Gunnison and the surrounding territory in 1885, and the boom soon wore itself out. With the bursting of the Gunnison mining bubble, the community gradually settled down into a sane, healthy condition, surrounded by a few small mines, including some excellent coal mines, some rich farming and ranching land, good fishing and hunting, and became a town of substantial citizens.

SMELTER.
Milepost 203.74.
Baldwin branch. 2,263 feet of siding. This location, mentioned in an 1889 employee's timetable, was used by one of Gunnison's early smelters. No other information known.

VIDLAS SPUR.
Milepost 204.97.
Baldwin branch. Altitude 7,781 feet. 170 feet of siding. No other information known.

WYLIE'S SPUR.
Milepost 206.80.
Baldwin branch. Altitude 7,917 feet. Three-car siding. No other data known.

TEACHOUT.
Milepost 209.89.
Baldwin branch. Altitude 8,028 feet. Station No. 1115. 11x31 foot coal bin. 237 feet of siding.

LEHMAN.
Milepost 211.88.
Baldwin branch. Altitude 8,114 feet. No other information known.

HINKLES.
Milepost 213.39.
Baldwin branch. Altitude 8,175 feet. Stock pen. 307 feet of siding.

DOLLARD.
Milepost 213.84.
Baldwin branch. Altitude 8,211 feet. This station was evidently established after the D. & R. G. took over the Baldwin branch.

CASTLETON.
Milepost 216.47.
Baldwin branch. Altitude 8,397 feet. Station No. 1116. T. J. Burns was agent and operator in 1885. Station call BN.
Facilities:
Combination frame depot, freight house, and living quarters, 24x58 feet. Platform containing 2,880 sq. ft. Two story frame section house. 37,500 gal. wood water tank. Coal. Wye. Two legs of this wye formed a part of the Baldwin and Kubler Mine branches. 3,307 feet of side track.
Historical note:
This station, the junction of the Baldwin Mine and Kubler Mine branches, was first known as Baldwin. In the latter part of the '80's it was changed to Castleton.

WALLACE SPUR.
Milepost 217.45.
Baldwin Mine branch. Altitude 8,463 feet. Seven-car spur connected at west end.

GREEN CANON.
Milepost 218.27.
Baldwin Mine branch. Altitude 8,503 feet. This station is also known as Laplant. From information found, this station is supposed to have been established by the Rio Grande after they assumed control of the Baldwin branch.

BALDWIN MINE.
Milepost 219.06.
Baldwin Mine branch. Altitude 8,588 feet. Station No. 1117.
Facilities:
Miscellaneous mine buildings such as engine house, shaft house, blacksmith shop, carpenter shop, stables, store houses, powder house, 36 frame and log tenement houses that were the property of the Alpine Coal Company. Scales, coal bin, and approximately 2,682 feet of siding.

END-OF-TRACK.
Milepost 219.27.
Baldwin Mine branch. Altitude 8,597 feet.

COOPER.
Milepost 217.65.
Kubler Mine branch. 305 feet of siding. This siding was sometimes called Gullett's Spur.

END-OF-TRACK.
Milepost 218.03.
Kubler Mine branch. This point was as far as the line of the Colorado & Southern's track extended. The balance of the track north of this point, 1.79 miles, belonged to The Rocky Mountain Fuel Company.

KUBLER MINE.
Milepost 219.66.
Kubler Mine branch. 2,664 feet of miscellaneous side track built at the mine.

END-OF-TRACK.
Milepost 219.82.
Kubler Mine branch. This point was the end of the Rocky Mountain Fuel Company's track.
Historical notes on both the Baldwin and Kubler areas:
The Elk Mountain district proved to be one of Colorado's best coal fields, producing Mesa Verde bituminous and older anthracite coal. Among the better known coal camps were Crested Butte, Anthracite, Mt. Carbon, Floresta, Baldwin, and Kubler. Situated in the heart of a range of snow-crested peaks known as the Elk Mountains, the region was a dense forest of beautiful pines and quaking aspens, whose leaves always seem to be moving. In addition to the valuable coal deposits, the region was also noted as a sportsman's paradise. Racing mountain streams such as East River, Slate Creek, and Anthracite Creek were alive with trout. Elk, black tailed deer, mountain lion, and bear are still common in the territory. Seventy-five years ago, the Ute Indians in the region made this place their summer home.
Concerning the Baldwin and Kubler mining district, we quote in part from a history of the Union Pacific coal mines, published by the Union Pacific Railway:
"From the time of the opening of the Mt. Carbon and Baldwin mines until January 9, 1883, when the Union Coal Company was incorporated in Colorado to operate them, these mines were owned and worked by the railroad's coal department. In 1890 the Union Coal Co. was succeeded by the Union Pacific Coal Company, which took over all the coal properties connected with the railroad, including the Como and King Mines. The most famous mine in the district was the Alpine Mine located near the foot of Mt. Carbon. It

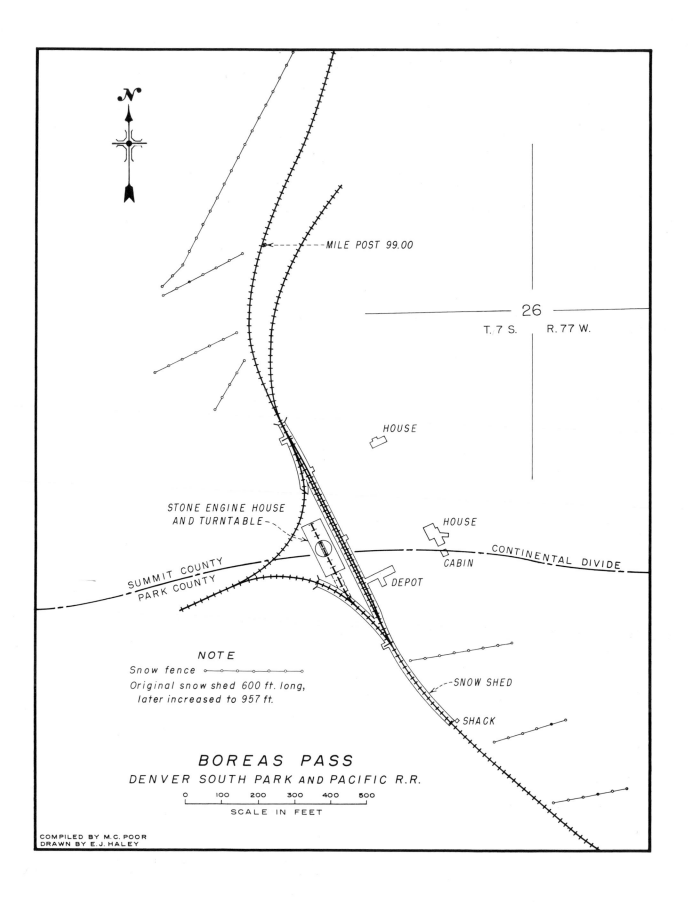

N

MILE POST 99.00

26

T. 7 S.   R. 77 W.

HOUSE

STONE ENGINE HOUSE
AND TURNTABLE

HOUSE

CONTINENTAL DIVIDE

CABIN

SUMMIT COUNTY
PARK COUNTY

DEPOT

NOTE
Snow fence ○○○○○○○
Original snow shed 600 ft. long,
later increased to 957 ft.

SNOW SHED

SHACK

BOREAS PASS
DENVER SOUTH PARK AND PACIFIC R.R.

0   100   200   300   400   500
SCALE IN FEET

COMPILED BY M.C. POOR
DRAWN BY E.J. HALEY

was opened in 1881. The coal in this mine was of bituminous grade and was considered the best domestic coal then mined in Colorado. The vein was five feet thick, with a dip of six degrees and was reached by a slope 134 feet deep. The roof of the mine was soapstone and the floor was fire clay.

"In spite of the high operating costs, Alpine Mine was operated at a profit until 1889. Operations were then curtailed until around 1892, after which time the property was operated by other interests."

The following figures copied from some early statistics show the quantity of coal mined at Baldwin:

1883	12,990 tons.	1888	56,348 tons.
1884	29,034 "	1889	49,183 "
1885	14,175 "	1890	6,619 "
1886	29,845 "	1891	14,339 "
1887	40,904 "	1892	7,936 "

Additional information on the old Baldwin and Kubler district is supplied by Roy Morton:

"Old coke ovens and abandoned coal mine properties are still to be seen around the Mt. Carbon, Baldwin and Kubler district. The present station of Baldwin was formerly Mt. Carbon and was the location of the Alpine Mine, the largest coal mine in the area. It was a slope mine with a five to six-foot vein of clean dry bituminous coal. In its later years it was operated by The Rocky Mountain Fuel Co., and in its heyday it produced around 600 tons of coal per day. In the old days the South Park men working on this branch of the railroad would sometimes allude to this place as Alpine, while at other times they would call it Mt. Carbon.

"The Kubler branch was first known as the Baldwin branch. The old Union Mine, which was a tunnel mine instead of a shaft or slope mine, was the largest mine on this branch and produced a high grade of soft coal. The Kubler Mine, opened around 1895, was located a short distance beyond the Union. It was a slope mine, with its opening in the south wall of Kubler Gulch, and had a seven-foot vein of coal. During my days in Gunnison the Kubler had its periods of operation as well as prolonged shutdowns. Around 1912 it was reopened and equipped with new machinery."

* * * *

COALS.
Milepost 88.70.
High Line to Leadville. 1,734 feet of side track. Sometimes called Coal Spur because of being the junction point of the spur running out to the old Como, or Leckner Mine.

LECKNERS.
This was the name of a coal mine located about one mile northwest of Como. The spur, built in 1880, was partly abandoned thereafter. The name was sometimes spelled Lechners.

PEABODYS.
Milepost 91.60.
High Line. Altitude 10,102 feet. 19-car spur connected at west end. Station No. 1130. This station was also known as Tarryall during the '80's.

HALF WAY.
Milepost 93.95.
High Line. Altitude 10,548 feet. Station No. 1131. Frame section house and bunk house. 47,500 gal. wood water tank. 808 feet of side track.

SELKIRK.
Milepost 96.09.
High Line. Altitude 10,937 feet. Station No. 1132. A 1912 employees timecard shows a water tank at a point called Selkirk Tank, about a mile below the spur. Selkirk Spur included 665 feet of siding.

BOREAS.
Milepost 98.84.
High Line. Altitude 11,493 feet. Station No. 1133. Station call BO. M. J. Trotter was agent and operator during 1885. At a later period Wes Soper was agent and operator here, at the same time his brother, Frank, was holding down a similar job on Alpine Pass.
Facilities:
1886 records show the following: Two-room log telegraph office 16½x24 feet. Log store house 14½x17 feet with dirt roof. One and one-half story log section house containing five rooms. Stone engine house 57¼x155 feet, inside of which was a 49½ foot wrought iron turntable, 16x45 foot coal bin, and a 5x18 foot, 9,516 gal. wood water tank. This water tank was supplied by a spring through 1,830 feet of two-inch pipe. Old records indicate that a snowshed 150 feet long covered the track leading from the main line into this stone engine house. 1,566 feet of side track.
Historical note:
Colorado & Southern engineering records show that a depot was built at Boreas in 1898. The stone engine house, including the turntable, coal bin, and water tank, burned in 1909. A wye was built to replace the turntable; however, the date of its construction is not known by the writer. The original 600-foot snow shed over the main line was later extended in both directions, giving the shed a total length of 957 feet. Only small portions of each of the two legs of the wye were covered by a snow shed. Thomas St. John tells that the big Boreas shed had doors on the Breckenridge end only, adding that "they were harder than hell for a man to open when the snow was piled up against them." Jess Frazier writes that the railroad used an old cave near the depot to store some of their supplies. William Wendell writes that the Post Office at Boreas was the highest in the U. S. at the time. Ed Haley writes: "The Boreas depot was built right into the big snow shed and it was always pitch dark in there when the train would stop in front of the little station. A 632-foot passing track was also under this same shed. The big shed burned down in 1934."

FARNHAM.
Milepost 100.00.
High Line. Station No. 1134. C. H. Pike was agent here during 1885. 480 feet of siding. Sometimes called Farnham Spur, or Flanders.

DWYER.
Milepost 100.80.
High Line. Altitude 11,104 feet. Station No. 1135. 738-foot spur connected at east end. Sometimes called Dwyer Spur. Also thought to be called Belmont in later days.

BAKERS TANK.
Milepost 102.16.
High Line. Altitude 10,871 feet. 9,305 gal. wood water tank. Coal. 350 feet of side track.

ARGENTINE.
Milepost 103.70.
High Line. Altitude 10,604 feet. Station No. 1136. Two-story frame section house 28x34 feet. 814 feet of siding. Sometime after the turn of the century, this station was called Bacon.

WASHINGTON SPUR.
Milepost 105.78.
High Line. Altitude 10,248 feet. 322-foot spur connected at east end.

MAYO SPUR.
Milepost 106.48.
High Line. Altitude 10,129 feet. Station No. 1137. 564-foot spur connected at east end.

445

SUTTONS SPUR.
Milepost 108.20.
High Line. 297-foot spur connected at west end.

SMITH SPUR.
Milepost 108.40.
High Line. 12-car spur.

JACOTT SPUR.
Milepost 108.50.
High line. Eleven-car spur built in 1908 at a cost of $268.27, connected at west end.

LITTLE MOUNTAIN SPUR.
Milepost 108.60.
High line. 212-foot spur connected at west end.

PUZZLE.
Milepost 108.70.
High Line. 13-car spur.

GOLD PAN.
Milepost 109.40.
High line. Altitude 9,669 feet. 31-car spur connected at east end. Sometimes called Tonopah.

BRECKENRIDGE.
Milepost 110.00.
High Line. Altitude 9,568 feet. Station No. 1138. Station call HD, BX. F. W. Juneman, who was the first agent at Pitkin, was agent here in 1885.
Facilities:
Combination frame depot, living quarters, and freight house 24x60 feet. Freight platform with 5,897 sq. ft. Coal bin 12x85 feet. Wye. 3,965 feet of side track, later increased to 4,489 feet. Sometime around 1888, the railroad built a stand-pipe south of town to supply water. The water was piped from Blue River through 782 feet of six-inch pipe.
Historical note:
Breckenridge, originally known as Ft. Mary B, was named after John C. Breckinridge, then vice president of the United States, in an effort to tempt the Congress to create a Post Office in the town. The idea worked and Congress established the Post Office in the new camp. Breckenridge first got under way when some of the horde of prospectors who swarmed into California Gulch, during the summer of 1860, spilled over into the wild and rough Blue River country. The Breckenridge area, including French Gulch which lay just east of the town, proved to be one of the richest placer mining districts in the state. Miles and miles of ditches and flumes were built by the miners to carry the water needed for this type of mining. Almost a million dollars worth of the yellow metal was sluiced out of the diggings in a short period of time. The boom played out around 1864, and the camps were almost deserted. New mining methods, the erection of some smelters, the discovery of silver, lead, and zinc ore, together with the building of the South Park railroad through the Valley of the Blue, acted as a great stimulus to the mining industry in the area, causing a considerable increase in activity between 1880 and 1885. Some of the richest mines, such as the Tiger and the Wellington, are still producing to some extent, even to this day.

BARTHOLOMEWS SPUR.
Milepost 111.70.
High line, 175 feet of side track. No other data known.

BRADDOCKS.
Milepost 113.29.
High line. Altitude 9,250 feet. Station No. 1139. Mrs. F. E. Braddock was agent in 1885. This station was also known as Broncho. 1,072 feet of siding.

446

VALDORA.
Milepost 113.79.
High line. Altitude 9,205 feet. 13-car spur connected east end.

DICKEY.
Milepost 116.47.
High Line. Altitude 9,004 feet. Station No. 1140. Station call HF, JD. C. V. Jackson was agent and operator in 1904.
Facilities:
Combination frame depot, living quarters, and freight house 20x63 feet. Platform containing 5,897 sq. ft. Three-stall frame roundhouse, 45x60 feet. 47,500 gal. wood water tank. Pump house. Coal bin. The Colorado & Southern built a coal chute here in 1902 at a cost of $4,397.82. Wye. 4,383 feet of siding.
Historical note:
Dickey was first known as Placer Junction. It was the junction point for the Dillon and Keystone branch. Charlie Squires writes: "On the night of Dec. 11, 1897, six cars of ore tied up at Breckenridge broke loose and ran away down the line. The switch at Dickey was set for the Leadville track. The six cars were traveling at too high a speed to take the curve, jumped the track and demolished the ticket office, waiting room, and bedroom of the frame depot. After the carpenters made their repairs, I ran in a new telegraph wire."

DILLON.
Milepost 119.17.
Keystone branch. Altitude 8,839 feet. Station No. 1176. Station call ON, DX. W. E. Handy was agent during 1885. Combination frame depot, living quarters, and freight office, 24x80 feet. 2,139 feet of siding.

NICHOLS SPUR.
Milepost 119.67.
Keystone branch. 233-foot spur connected at west end. Around 1897 this station was called Oro Grande, while in 1912 it went by the name of Sterne Spur.

KEYSTONE.
Milepost 123.48.
Keystone branch. Altitude 9,153 feet. Station No. 1177. Station call KY.
Facilities:
Combination frame depot and freight office, 20x30 feet. Coal bin. Ore platform. Wye. 1,900 feet of siding. Considerable ore and timber was shipped from this station, especially in the early days of the railroad.

HATHAWAYS.
Milepost 118.30.
High Line. 669 feet of side track. No other data known.

FRISCO.
Milepost 119.88.
High Line. Altitude 9,099 feet. Station No. 1141. 1,141 feet of siding. (Station No., and length of siding, appear to be a coincidence). The Commercial & Financial Chronicle of Nov. 27, 1880 calls this place San Francisco.

KING SOLOMON SPUR.
Milepost 120.10.
High Line. Six-car spur connected at east end.

SUMMIT SPUR.
Milepost 120.30.
High Line. Three-car spur connected at east end.

CURTIN.
Milepost 122.06.
High Line. Altitude 9,295 feet. Station No. 1142. One and one-half story log section house. 728 feet of side track. Also called Uneva Lake.

WHEELER.

Milepost 126.16.

High Line. Altitude 9,737 feet. Station No. 1143. 47,500 gal. wood water tank supplied by a spring through 1,596 feet of three-inch pipe. 1,355 feet of siding.

Historical note:

This station was later changed to Solitude. The name Wheeler was also used by the Denver & Rio Grande for a nearby station of theirs on the Blue River branch. The Colorado Magazine states: "Wheeler, a ghost town on the Tenmile, was named after John S. Wheeler, who settled there in 1879 and established a ranch."

WOODSIDE.

Milepost 128.90.

High Line. This station was listed in some 1886 records. No other information was given. It is possible that this might be the same place mentioned in an earlier record as station No. 1144, and called "Narrows".

WILDERS SPUR.

Milepost 130.50.

High Line. 281 feet of siding.

DENEEN.

Milepost 131.50.

High Line. No other information known.

KOKOMO TANK.

Milepost 131.97.

High Line. The only facility at this point was a 47,500 gal. wood water tank. 1886 engineering records describe the tank as a wood tub 15x24 feet, supplied by water from Tenmile Creek, by means of a No. 5 Knowles pump and a Shapley vertical steam boiler. The pump house was a frame affair 14x20 feet, the engine room 11x13 feet, and the coal room 7x13 feet. It required 75 feet of three-inch pipe to bring the water from the creek up to the tank. The old tank is still standing today (September, 1945) beside the abandoned right of way. The engine and pump rooms are empty and forlorn, while the sides of the old tub are full of woodpecker holes.

KOKOMO.

Milepost 132.67.

High Line. Altitude 10,616 feet. Station No. 1145. Station call KO. D. C. Mullen was agent during 1885. Frame depot. Wye. 1,214 feet of side track.

Historical note:

Kokomo, a typically derelict Colorado mining camp, had a great past, but its future is a dreary picture. Prospectors appeared in this vicinity as early as 1860, and some modest fortunes were won from placer operations, both gold and silver being found. The real rush came to Kokomo in 1878, during the height of the Leadville boom. The town was founded by one A. C. Smith on July 8, 1878, and was the highest in altitude of any incorporated town in Colorado. The camp was destroyed by fire in 1881, but was soon rebuilt.

With the discovery of rich carbonates, the miners envisioned a second Leadville. Smelters were built capable of processing a huge output of ore; however, the expected ore production failed to materialize to any great extent. Kokomo grew rapidly and declined in the same manner. The abandoned remains of these smelters and mills are to be found there today, monuments to the ambitions of man. Mining camps like Kokomo die hard; a few recalcitrants still hang on doggedly and will never leave until they are carried to their graves.

Kokomo's first depot was built just above the old Rio Grande crossover near the wye formed by the Wilfley Mill branch. Sometime later, the depot was located about three-quarters of a mile downgrade (north), near the junction of a short spur that ran from the main line, across Tenmile Creek to a point near the center of the business district.

BREENE'S SPUR.

Milepost 133.30.

Wilfley's Mill branch. The Wilfley's Mill branch connected with the main line at milepost 132.80. Breene's Spur, built in 1908 at a cost of $714.57, was a 20-car spur, connected at the east end.

WILFLEY'S MILL.

Milepost 133.90.

Wilfley's Mill branch. Altitude 10,831 feet. No other information known except that contained in the section telling of the construction of this spur.

ROBINSON.

Milepost 134.71 .

High Line. Altitude 10,860 feet. Station No. 1146. Station call RB. T. J. Flynn was agent during 1885.

Facilities:

During the '80's there was a freight platform here containing 1,412 sq. ft. 1,175 feet of side track.

Historical note:

Silver was discovered at this camp during the same period that Kokomo sprang into existence. The camp's subsequent history parallels, more or less, the story of Kokomo. The place was named after Lt. Gov. Robinson.[1]

SAND SPUR.

Milepost 135.10.

High line. Two-car siding. No other information known.

BUFFERS SPUR.

Milepost 135.50.

High Line. 21-car spur connected at east end.

CLIMAX.

Milepost 137.46.

High Line. Altitude 11,320 feet. Station No. 1147. Station call AK.

Facilities:

1885-86 records do not list any facilities. 1889-97 records list turntable, coal, telegraph office, and 1,854 feet of side track. 1912 records list a turntable and 38 car siding only. There must have been some sort of an engine house here around the turn of the century, as old records tell that the turntable and engine house burned in 1907.

Historical note:

Climax, highest Post Office in the United States, and Colorado's most prosperous mining town (today), is located on Fremont Pass, named after Lt. John C. Fremont, early Colorado explorer. Climax is the site of the famous Molybdenum Mine. This mine, located at the base of Bartlett Mountain, is the world's largest known deposit, producing 65% or more of the aggregate output of this rare metal. Molybdenum is used chiefly as an alloy for toughening and strengthening steel. This ore is also finding its way into the electronic, ceramic, and chemical industries. According to the Colorado Magazine, an old miner by the name of Senter first discovered this peculiar looking ore in 1879. No one knew anything about it. It looked like graphite. Later it was thought to be galena, but it was not until 1900 that it was properly identified by the Colorado School of Mines. However, little was known about the correct treatment of the ore or its usefulness; consequently there was no market for it. Its great value as an alloy for toughening steel was developed during the first world war. Today, it is one of the state's most important industries, and quite profitable to its owners also; the mine's net income for the year 1942 was over $13,390,000.

1. "The Brand Book" (The Westerners), August, 1947.

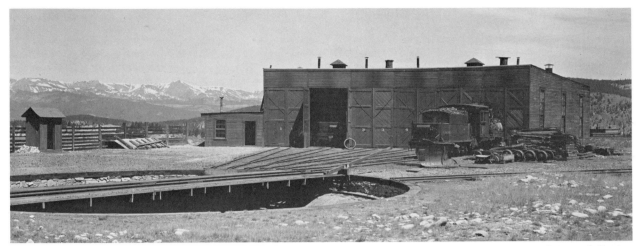

C.&S. 69 at the Leadville roundhouse in June, 1936.

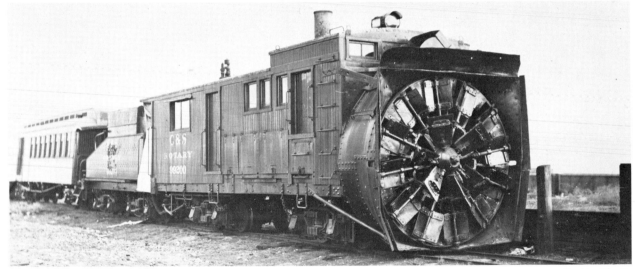

C.&S. narrow gauge rotary 99200 at Leadville on May 16, 1937.

69 and a 4-car train passing the Leadville freight house, on the way to Climax in June, 1938.

WORTMAN'S.

Milepost 138.06.

High Line. Altitude 11,240 feet. Four-car spur connected at east end.

ALICANTE.

Milepost 138.96.

High Line. Station No. 1148. Station call A. S. T. Sheridan was agent during 1885. 733 feet of side track.

FRENCH GULCH.

Milepost 142.36.

High Line. Station No. 1149. 47,500 gal. wood water tank located at milepost 142.00. 297 feet of siding. 1885 records show a station at, or near this point, by the name of Clifton. The station No. (1149) applied to the latter name.

LINDERMAN.

Milepost 142.90.

High Line. Altitude 10,848 feet. No other data known.

ENGLISH GULCH.

Milepost 143.16.

High Line. 217 feet of siding.

BIRDS EYE.

Milepost 144.86.

High Line. Altitude 10,671 feet. Station No. 1150. 532 foot spur connected at east end.

DYES SPUR.

Milepost 145.30.

High Line. No other information known.

THREE MILE TANK.

Milepost 147.56.

High Line. 50,000 gal. wood water tank fed by gravity from a spring through 630 feet of three-inch pipe. 1886 records stated "no water". All records, from 1889 on, list water OK.

LEADVILLE MINERAL BELT JUNCTION.

Milepost 149.96.

High Line. Station No. 1151. Junction point of the Leadville Mineral Belt Railway. See description elsewhere in this book. 530 car capacity side track.

LEADVILLE.

Milepost 151.19.

High Line. Altitude 10,208 feet at depot. U. S. Geological Survey bench mark at Leadville Post Office reads 10,153 feet. Station No. 1152. Station call VI. George W. Cook was agent from August, 1880, through 1885. The end-of-track extended to milepost 152.10.

Facilities, as of 1886:

Frame passenger depot 15x27 feet, with addition 20x28 feet, containing waiting room, office, baggage room, and ticket office. Depot platform containing 4,920 sq. ft. A new brick depot was built in 1893. Frame freight house 42x100 feet. Scale house with Fairbanks scales, 32-foot length and a capacity of 60,000 pounds. Two story frame section house. 50,000 gal. wood water tank. Well. Eight-stall sheet-iron round house 60x126 feet. 50-foot cast iron turntable. Tool house. Coal bin 9x246 feet. Stock pens. Nine frame tenement houses. 1889 records indicate 12,840 feet of yard track. 1897 records indicate 14,628 feet of yard track. Wye.

Sgt. Lawrence S. Brown, formerly of the U. S. Army, writes: "After the narrow gauge trackage in Leadville was changed over to standard gauge, the old narrow gauge turntable was discontinued as it was too small to accommodate the Colorado & Southern's standard gauge engines. The old roundhouse is still used but the doors were enlarged to permit passage of the wide gauge engines."

Historical note:

A considerable portion of the Leadville story has already been told; however, a few miscellaneous notes relative to the camp's later history should not be omitted. In its riotous youth, Leadville proudly called itself the "Magic City"; and well it might. Almost overnight a wild pine flat was seething with some 30,000 excited fortune hunters. Today, much of the old camp and its atmosphere is gone. To the east rises the high Mosquito Range which seems to tumble down in rolling slopes to Carbonate, Iron, and Fryer Hills at the edge of the town. Each of these hills is a treasure house long since stripped of trees and virtually disembowled. Gray and yellow ore dumps from old mines bearing famous names once heard on every tongue, spill down into the town.

The business district that once extended for blocks in all directions is now largely concentrated along Harrison Avenue, the main north and south thoroughfare, lined with low frame and brick structures, many of which are sadly in need of paint and repairs. The residential sections contain many small frame houses whose architecture is definitely of 1880 vintage. Neglected wooden sidewalks still exist along some of Leadville's streets; along one side of Harrison Street the concrete sidewalk is three feet above the street level. The streets along which rolled the glittering carriages of the Carbonate Kings are, for the most part, as rutted and dusty as when ore wagons lurched down them on their way to the smelter.[1]

There were 14 smelters and reduction plants in the Leadville area in 1881. During the intervening years the district had become the smelting center of the Rocky Mountain region. And it was also this same year that Leadville's decline began. Production of silver reached a peak of $11,473,946 in 1880, although the Morning Star, Chrysolite, Catalpa, Little Pittsburgh, Matchless, Iron Silver, and other celebrated mines held production around $10,000,-000 for several years. But some of the largest and richest properties, due to reckless exploitation, were nearing exhaustion. When it was disclosed that several mines had been borrowing heavily to pay dividends, stocks dropped from many dollars to a few cents. Charges were made that stock in many companies had been manipulated by insiders. Investors became panic stricken and unloaded their shares, breaking the market. One by one the banks failed. Tabor and other mining kings abandoned the city for Denver. The sporting gentry and their feminine associates left for more lucrative fields. Fires destroyed the Grant Smelter, a few large hotels, and some of the larger store buildings.

The population dwindled and silver production decreased; but the town itself was as little prepared as Tabor and his associates for the blow that fell in 1893 when the mints in India ceased buying silver for coinage. The Sherman Silver Purchase Act was repealed, and the depression or panic of 1893 pushed the white metal to a new low. In reviewing the events of that year the Leadville Herald Democrat stated: "Those were the days of panic and gloom for Leadville." "Ruin and bankruptcy stared every mining man, every smelting man, and every business man in the face." The fabulous era of silver had ended.

The discovery of some rich gold lodes in Lake County brought about a revival of mining activity around 1900. Another revival occurred around 1915; in fact Lake County's total production of all her mines reached an all time high for the camp's history in 1916 with a production of $16,082,-059 (U. S. Government figures); however, operations decreased rapidly within the next few years. Declining prices, the exhaustion of rich lodes, and the flooding of many shafts subsequently brought about the closing of many mines. During the prohibition era numerous isolated and deserted mine shafts housed whiskey stills, and "Leadville moon" was highly regarded and commanded good prices throughout a wide area.[1]

1. "Colorado", American Guide Series. 1941.

449

Growth of agriculture, ranching, and tourist business has recently contributed to the city's welfare. During the 1930's, the population increased somewhat, largely due to the development of the molybdenum deposits at Climax. Intensive working of some of the old gold, silver, lead, and zinc properties is still carried on, but the chief prop of the camp's economic structure today is the Climax molybdenum mine. Leadville's population follows the curve of employment at Climax; when work is slack there, Leadville takes on almost the same appearance. On Saturday nights the town reminds one of a quiet country town that has known no greater excitement than a good dog fight.

Some writers say that Leadville feels no sorrow for itself, but wears its somewhat tattered and faded purple mantle with an air; others describe the famous old camp as just sitting there—a ghost of its former glory—brooding over its gold and silver past. To this writer, the latter description seems to fit best.

* * * *

ARGO.
Milepost 2.00.
Clear Creek line. Station No. 1300. Station call GO. Combination frame depot and freight house 18x30 feet. This location is now a part of the city of Denver. It was founded in 1878, as a site for the old Boston & Colorado Smelter.

ARGO JUNCTION.
Milepost 3.00.
Clear Creek line. Altitude 5,215 feet. This was the junction point of a new cutoff line, established about 1886, that ran between the original Clear Creek line and the Denver depot.

UTAH JUNCTION.
Milepost 3.60.
Clear Creek line. Altitude 5,232 feet. This point, earlier known as Cutoff Junction, was the junction point of the original cutoff built between the main line and the Denver depot in 1874. It has also been called Clear Creek Junction.

OSAGE.
Milepost 4.80.
Clear Creek line. Altitude 5,215 feet. 245-foot spur connected at east end.

ARVADA.
Milepost 7.60.
Clear Creek line. Altitude 5,328 feet. Station No. 1301. 1,323 feet of passing track and a small depot built here in later years. Arvada, originally known as Ralston Point, or Ralston Station, was founded in 1880.

RIDGE.
Milepost 9.40.
Clear Creek line. Altitude 5,420 feet. 1,532-foot spur connected at west end.

MT. OLIVET.
Milepost 11.50.
Clear Creek line. Altitude 5,495 feet. 390-foot spur connected at west end.

GOLDEN JUNCTION.
Milepost 13.10.
Clear Creek line. This was the old junction point where the original standard gauge Colorado Central line to Longmont and Fort Collins connected with the Clear Creek line. The place was also called Wannamaker Junction at times. The milepost figure is only a close estimate.

WIGGINGTON.
Milepost 13.30.
Clear Creek line. Altitude 5,585 feet. No other data known.

COORS SPUR.
Milepost 15.25.
Clear Creek line. This spur was built over a highway and across Clear Creek to serve the Coors Brewery. As nearly as can be determined, the railroad company removed the old turntable at the Golden roundhouse, turned it upside down and used it as a bridge over the highway.[1] The Colorado & Southern track, 1,377 feet in length, ends on the south side of the creek. Balance of track is owned by the brewery.

CHURCHES BRICK YARD.
Milepost 17.30.
Churches Brick Yard spur. 913 feet of side track. This was originally a section of the old Golden-Ralston line. All trackage except 1.70 miles of narrow gauge track on this line was removed about 1890. See text for further details.

GOLDEN.
Milepost 15.60.
Clear Creek line. Altitude 5,671 feet. Station No. 1302. Station call V. C. J. Fisher was agent during 1885.
Facilities:
Frame depot 17x30 feet, with an addition 10x24 feet, containing waiting rooms, ticket and telegraph offices, and baggage room. 14 stall brick roundhouse. 50 foot wrought iron turntable. Carpenter and paint shop. Brick freight house 30x150 feet with 4,926 sq. ft. platform. 30-foot Fairbanks track scales, capacity 60,000 pounds. Frame ice house 17x51 feet with a capacity for storing 225 tons of ice. 14,534 gal. wood water tank. 1,503 sq. ft. coal platform. Stock pens and section house. 19,979 feet of miscellaneous yard track.
Historical note:
A greater portion of the Golden story has already been told. We might add: During the hard rock mining days of the '70's, Golden was one of the busiest towns in Colorado. They had three flour mills, two breweries, a paper mill, and three brick kilns; five smelters refined gold and silver ores valued in excess of $1,200,000 annually. The Colorado School of Mines and the Coors industries are the town's two principal mainstays today.

CHIMNEY GULCH.
Milepost 18.80.
Clear Creek line. Altitude 5,926 feet. Station No. 1340. 659 feet of siding.

GUY GULCH.
Milepost 21.80.
Clear Creek line. Altitude 6,227 feet. Station No. 1342. 630 feet of siding.

BEAVER BROOK.
Milepost 23.20.
Clear Creek line. Altitude 6,408 feet. Station No. 1343. Station call BC. O. W. Barton was agent in 1885. Two story frame depot. Dancing pavilion, 47 feet in diameter. (Owned by the railroad.) 8,930 gal. wood water tank. Coal shed. 200 feet side track.

ELK CREEK.
Milepost 24.50.
Clear Creek line. Altitude 6,536 feet. Station No. 1344. Two story frame section house. 620 feet of siding.

ROSCOE.
Milepost 26.42.
Clear Creek line. Altitude 6,739 feet. 220 foot spur connected at west end.

BIG HILL.
Milepost 27.70.
Clear Creek line. Altitude 6,832 feet. Station No. 1345.

1. Courtesy Chas. S. Ryland.

Colorado Central 30 on a two-car train below the "Old Roadmaster", one of the famous rock formations in Clear Creek Canon.

FORKS CREEK.

Milepost 28.71.

Clear Creek line. Altitude 6,880 feet. Station No. 1346. Station call FC. W. L. York was agent and telegraph operator during 1885.

Facilities:

Combination two story frame depot and living quarters, 14x24 feet, with an iron roof. 1,943 sq. ft. of platform. Two story frame section house. 8,930 gal. wood water tank supplied with water from Clear Creek. Coal shed 11x13 feet. Wye. 577 feet of siding.

Historical note:

W. L. York, mentioned above, is 80 years old and still living at this date, 1949. Through his good friend Charlie Squires, Mr. York has kindly furnished the 1885 records showing all station numbers, calls, agents and telegraph operators. Roy Morton writes: "Contrary to some thoughts, Forks Creek was never a town from the standpoint of being a community of persons. Throughout the life of the Clear Creek line the station was just a coaling and watering station, and was principally known as being the junction point of the Georgetown and Black Hawk branches".

MC DUFFE SPUR.

Milepost 28.90.

Black Hawk branch. Altitude 6,902 feet. 548 foot passing track. This place also known as Bates.

COTTONWOOD.

Milepost 30.70.

Black Hawk branch. Altitude 7,191 feet. Station No. 1347. 462 feet of passing track was located here in the early '80's.

BRIDGE.

Milepost 31.80.

Black Hawk branch. Altitude 7,374 feet. No other data known.

SMITHS HILL.

Milepost 33.40.

Black Hawk branch. Altitude 7,627 feet. Station No. 1348. 8,930 gal. wood water tank. Water supplied from Clear Creek through 44 feet of two inch pipe. Two story log section house 20x30 feet. 750 feet of siding.

NEW YORK MILL.

Milepost 35.50.

Black Hawk branch. Altitude 7,943 feet. No other data known.

BLACK HAWK.

Milepost 35.95.

Black Hawk branch. Altitude 8,035 feet at depot. Station call B. C. H. Sprague was agent during 1885. Station No. 1349.

Facilities:

Combination stone depot and freight house 38 x 80 feet, with platform attached containing 2,860 sq. ft. Fairbanks scales, 25-foot length with a capacity of 40,000 pounds. Two room log tenement house. Approximately 7,139 feet of miscellaneous track. Fifty-foot turntable.

Historical note:

Black Hawk was one of the first settlements in Gilpin County. The little mining town extends for a mile up the narrow canon of North Clear Creek and around a sharp promontory known as Casey's Point. This "Point" was named for Pat Casey who was among the early arrivals in the vicinity. Pat discovered a rich mining lode and amassed a fortune. Thereafter, the little Irishman wore the finest clothing obtainable in Black Hawk and traveled about the vicinity in an expensive carriage drawn by a team of spirited black horses. Pat had no education to speak of and could not read or write; nevertheless, he carried a little notebook around with him in which he jotted down his various busi-

ness dealings. He often remarked, "I use up tin pincils a day and thin don't even git half through me business".

The first smelter in Colorado, constructed here in 1868 by Nathaniel P. Hill, was removed to Argo, near Denver, ten years later. The boundary line between Black Hawk and Central City is distinguishable only by a highway sign. On this boundary line also stands a granite monument which marks the site of the first gold lode discovery in Colorado made by John H. Gregory on May 6, 1859. After mining $900 from the outcroppings, he sold his claim for $21,000; it proved to be one of the richest in the state.[1]

CENTRAL CITY.

Milepost 39.79.

Black Hawk branch. The end-of-track extended to milepost 39.86. Altitude at end-of-track, 8,527 feet. Altitude at depot, 8,517 feet. Station No. 1350. Station call J. C. W. Sisson was agent during 1885.

Facilities:

The passenger depot was of brick construction with an iron roof. The depot was 20 x 24 feet. Frame freight house 18 x 32 feet with platform 374 sq. ft. Two story brick section house 20 x 26 feet; the only brick section house built along the entire narrow gauge system. The "gandy dancers" around Central City apparently stood in good favor with the management. There was approximately 1,100 feet of miscellaneous yard track.

Historical note:

Central City, one of the best known of all the old Colorado mining camps, is the County Seat of Gilpin County, once known as the richest square mile on earth. The camp stretched out along Gregory Gulch, one of the worst possible sites for a town.

Near the junction of three principal streets are grouped the larger business structures of weathered frame and stone. Many have been abandoned but still flaunt old signs painted there in the golden era when saloons and dance halls were crowded day and night. The surrounding hills, long since stripped of all their timber, are scarred with many old mine shafts and ore dumps.

Within a short time after John Gregory made his rich strike here, this and neighboring gulches swarmed with thousands of gold seekers. Many camps sprang up along the gulch such as Black Hawk, Gregory Point, Mountain City, Missouri City, and Nevadaville. Central City, named for its central location in the gulch, gradually outstripped other camps, absorbing several of them. At first a motley collection of log cabins and shacks, it was substantially rebuilt after a disastrous fire in 1874.

Central City's history has been one of varying fortune. The first miners sought chiefly for rich placer beds and "blossom rock", a gold-bearing decomposed quartz so soft that it could be dug from the hill sides with a pick and shovel. As these quartz veins played out and placer deposits were exhausted, production of the mines dropped, until, by 1864, only a few were being worked. When methods were perfected in the late 1860's for the treatment of refractory ores, the district enjoyed another boom. Mills and smelters were built in Black Hawk, and the Colorado Central railroad was pushed through to Central City in 1878.

Again, as more valuable ore veins were exhausted, the mines became less profitable and a new decline set in. Finally, the mines and mills fell silent and many of the miners departed. Shaft houses collapsed and tunnels became choked with debris; even the herds of burros, once part of the scene, disappeared. Nevadaville became a ghost town, and Central City and Black Hawk languished. The "Kingdom of Gilpin", from which more than $67,000,000 has

1. "Colorado", American Guide Series. 1941.

452

been produced since Gregory's strike, now (1948) mines less than $10,000 in metals annually.

Two other important features in Central City include the famous Central City Opera House, and the Teller House. The Teller House was the last word in frontier hostelries when it was built in 1872. The hotel is still operated in conjunction with the Opera House. Original murals in the hotel's bar were uncovered in 1932, after twelve layers of wall paper had been removed.[1]

As nearly as can be ascertained, the first depot in Central City was a frame affair. Sometime around 1900, a new brick depot was built and the old one was used for a freight house. Today, Colorado & Southern narrow gauge locomotive number 71, combination passenger coach No. 20 and gondola No. 4319, stand as a permanent exhibit on the site of this first Central City depot. The second depot erected by the railroad is today completely buried under the "Chain-O-Mines" tailings dump. This mining company paid $600 for the building.[2]

_____

FLOYD HILL.
Milepost 32.00.
Clear Creek line. Altitude 7,200 feet. Station No. 1355. 566-foot passing track. Three room frame section house.

ARGO MILL.
Milepost 36.70.
Clear Creek line. Altitude 7,491 feet, 1,295 feet of passing track. 375-foot spur connected to east end of passing track.

IDAHO SPRINGS.
Milepost 37.30.
Clear Creek line. Altitude 7,541 feet. Station No. 1357. Station call F. W. L. Bush was agent and operator during 1885.
Facilities:
Frame depot 24 x 75 feet. Five room frame section house 20 x 40 feet. Coal shed. Approximately 5,654 feet of yard track. This included two passing tracks; one 1,194 feet long and another 533 feet in length. A 14,534 gal. wood water tank was located one-half mile east of the depot at milepost 36.8.
Historical note:
Idaho Springs was the scene of some of Colorado's first gold discoveries as well as being noted for its hot and cold mineral springs. The place, being located in a narrow section of Clear Creek Canon, was known as the town that was three blocks wide and three miles long. Colorado & Southern narrow gauge locomotive No. 60 and passenger coach 70 are set up on a short section of track near the center of the town as a permanent exhibit.

FALL RIVER.
Milepost 39.20.
Clear Creek line. Altitude 7,679 feet. Station No. 1358. Two story frame section house. 986 feet of siding.

FREELAND MILL.
Milepost 42.00.
Clear Creek line. 637-foot spur connected at west end.

DUMONT.
Milepost 42.40.
Clear Creek line. Altitude 7,923 feet. Station No. 1359. 581-foot passing track. This place, which was founded as Mill City in 1860, was the location of a number of ore crushing mills. The only facility listed here during the early days of the railroad was a 550 sq. foot platform.

LAWSON.
Milepost 44.10.
Clear Creek line. Altitude 8,126 feet. Station No. 1360.

_____

1. "Colorado", American Guide Series. 1941.
2. Robert Rice, Colorado & Southern Ry.

Station call SN. E. M. Partridge was agent during 1885. Frame depot 20 x 54 feet. 644-foot spur connected at west end.

STEVENS.
Milepost 44.70.
Clear Creek line. No other information known regarding this point.

EMPIRE.
Milepost 45.70.
Clear Creek line. Altitude 8,246 feet. Station No. 1361. Frame depot 12 x 16 feet. Platform attached, 304 sq. ft., 14,534 gal. wood water tank. 715-foot spur connected at west end. Empire was first known as Valley City. The actual town of Empire was located about a mile above Empire Station, on the West Fork of Clear Creek.

ST. GEORGE MINE.
Milepost 47.30.
Clear Creek line. 125-foot spur connected at west end.

GEORGETOWN.
Milepost 49.63.
Clear Creek line. Altitude 8,476 feet at depot. Station No. 1363. Station call G. F. B. McCracken was agent during 1885.
Facilities, (1886):
Brick depot and freight house 25 x 100 feet, with an iron roof. Attached freight platform containing 1,632 sq. ft. 32-foot Howe track scales with a capacity of 60,000 pounds. Stock pens and chute. Frame engine house 18 x 45 feet, number of stalls not stated. Eight 1½- and 2-story frame tenement houses for employees. Wye. 4,889 feet of miscellaneous yard track including a 748-foot passing track (north side of depot) and a 697-foot spur (south side of depot) connected at east end. When the railroad was abandoned, the Georgetown depot was sold for $50.00.
Historical note:
Georgetown, originally known as Elizabeth Town, first came into existence in the early 1860's. The camp prospered until the placer claims gave out. Then came a period of stagnation followed by a boom in the 1870's when lode mining was developed. Prior to the great Leadville strike in 1878, it was the most important silver camp in the state. During its heydey, the town boasted of a population of over 5,000; today, it is around 300. With the decline of silver mining in the early '90's, Georgetown found itself in the grip of a second decline. A few prospectors, some gold mines, and numerous tourists who journeyed up Clear Creek Canon to see and ride the train over the world renowned Georgetown Loop Bridge, did much to keep the town alive. In 1933, higher silver and gold prices brought about the opening of many of the old mines. Activity in the town picked up. Livery stables became garages and filling stations. Many of the old buildings and houses were repaired and painted.

The old fire station, with a tall 70-foot wooden tower supporting a 1,299-pound bell, located near the center of town, still houses an outmoded hose reel and a two-wheeled hose cart pulled by volunteer firemen. Another famous landmark in the little town is Louis du Puy's Hotel de Paris. du Puy, who came from France, was a very peculiar type of individual to be found in a frontier mining camp. He conducted his business in a rather highhanded and arrogant manner; he refused admission to customers whom he disliked, had no use for women, refused to pay taxes—even threatening to shoot any tax collectors that came around and burn his hotel with himself inside. Still, in spite of all these idiosyncrasies, the rank and fashion of east and west continued to register at the Hotel de Paris—if they could get in—to eat du Puy's food, for he was a famous chef, and drink his wine. du Puy died in 1900.[1]

SILVER PLUME.

Milepost 54.10.

Clear Creek line. Altitude 9,114 feet. Station No. 1365. Station call WY. H. J. Whitney was agent in 1885.

Facilities:

Combination frame depot, living quarters, and freight house 20 x 60 feet. Freight platform attached, 1,900 sq. ft. Four-room frame section house. 37,994 gal. wood water tank supported by iron columns, and fed by a spring through 2,431 feet of pipe. 2,516 feet of miscellaneous yard track. The Silver Plume wye track connection with the Argentine Central, was located .3 of a mile west of the depot.

GRAYMONT.

Milepost 58.10.

Clear Creek line. Altitude 9,771 feet. Station No. 1367. Station call RA.

1. "Colorado", American Guide Series. 1941.

Facilities:

Old Union Pacific bridge and building records, dated 1886, indicate that a wye built at this point, necessitated the construction of three wooden trestles, 80, 32, and 16 feet in length respectively. The only information found concerning any buildings here tells that a two-story log house was erected. 1885 agency records state that the station was closed. 1,616 feet of siding.

Historical note:

Graymont, sometimes called Bakerville in the early days, was named after Gray's Peak. The willow and aspen thickets cover the site of this long-forgotten station which was near the confluence of Quayle Creek and Clear Creek. It was the end-of-track, both for the old Georgetown Breckenridge & Leadville and many an ambitious railroad promoter and Civil Engineer who cherished the desire to extend the steel trail over the mountains to Leadville.

State Historical Society of Colorado.

A mixed train, consisting of a boxcar, eight loaded flats, and a passenger car, is prepared to depart from the Morrison depot on a winter day in the 1890's. The track in the foreground leads to the turntable. Originally D.S.P.&P. 40, the locomotive became the 110 in 1885 and is destined to become Colorado & Southern 5 in 1898.

Mason Bogie 28, 2-8-6T, the "Denver," at the Mason Machine Works in 1880.

Mason Bogie 15, 2-6-6T, the "Breckenridge," at the Mason Works in Taunton, Mass., in 1879.

CHAPTER XXIII

THE LOCOMOTIVE ROSTER.

"By their whistles you shall know them—
And you shall never forget them."

In most railroad histories the locomotive roster seems to be of paramount interest; the South Park and Colorado Central rosters are no exception. Throughout the South Park's lifetime, an even hundred different engines ambled up and down the road's slim gauge rails, and over on the Clear Creek Division, 15 different narrow gauge engines carried the name "Colorado Central" into the Georgetown and Central City mining camps. It is interesting to note that all the engines incorporated in the combined rosters of the South Park and Colorado Central roads were built prior to 1899.

The gathering of the material which went into this roster proved to be an arduous task and could have never been achieved without the able assistance of Messrs. Robert R. Hicks, Richard Kindig, S. R. Wood, Jackson C. Thode, Jess Frazier, Miss Ina T. Aulls of the Denver Public Library, Guyon C. Whitley, T. B. Aldridge, John Maxwell, A. T. Million and George Lundberg of the Colorado & Southern Engineering Department, William Cairns, William Wendell, Thomas St. John and others. The writer is greatly appreciative of the valuable assistance given by these persons. Relative to any unanswered questions or possible errors, the author will welcome any additional information or corrections.

Beyond a general discussion of the varied assortment of locomotive power, there is not a great deal to say, as practically all the data collected is incorporated within the roster itself. After getting all the miscellaneous material assembled, a few complex questions arose, some of which we have been unable to solve. Among these missing answers is the disposition of certain engines; for instance, in the Denver Daily Times of October 26, 1899, we read the following:[1]

LOCOMOTIVE NUMBER 1 OF THE SOUTH PARK LINE
SOLD TO A LUMBER CAMP OUTFIT.

"Engine number 1, the pioneer of the South Park line, was loaded for shipment to the lumber region of Wisconsin yesterday. This was the last of the old lot of locomotives first sent to Denver for use on the old mountain line. It has been reported that this engine was built too high and toppled over sometimes."

Upon reading this news item one is inclined to

1. Courtesy D. B. Sandford.

456

wonder just which number 1 does the article refer to—D. S. P. & P. No. 1, or C. & S. No. 1? The Omaha office of the Union Pacific reports that D. S. P. & P. No. 1 was dropped from the roster in 1888, and from the little information that has been uncovered, we are fairly certain that number 57, the "Buena Vista", was renumbered Colorado & Southern 1. Regardless of the peculiar wording of this item, the writer is of the belief that the newspaper was referring to C. & S. number 1.

We have already told the story of the South Park's first new engine, the "Fairplay", its purchase from the builders, Dawson & Bailey (National Locomotive Works), and its subsequent delivery in Denver on May 31, 1874. Mr. F. P. Roesch, Vice President of The Standard Stoker Co., who was General Road Foreman of engines for the Union Pacific Denver & Gulf during the '90's, writes:

"The South Park's first engine, as I recall, was a 2-6-0. The cylinders were quite small, being about 11" x 16". During my first connection with the South Park, in 1881, engine No. 1 was not in general use on the main line but was used mostly on the Morrison branch. As I remember, this engine was still in service as late as 1886. I also recall that No. 2, a 4-4-0, was converted into a switcher and later scrapped."

Joe Plunkett, veteran South Park runner now living in Grand Junction, Colorado, writes that, to the best of his recollection, No. 1 was later used to pump water at the roundhouse in Como but was taken to Denver around 1884. No. 1 was scrapped in 1888. As far as the writer knows, no photograph of this engine exists.

Concerning number 2, Joe Plunkett writes that this engine, a 4-4-0 named the "Platte Canon" was later fixed up as a special to pull the pay car and also the Official's car at times, but because she slipped so badly, especially on 3% and 4% grades, she was removed from this particular service. This was probably the reason this engine was rebuilt as a switcher, as stated by Mr. Roesch. The South Park had acquired these first two engines in the days when finances were none too plentiful, but by 1878, the financial picture had improved and the company standardized on the "Mason Bogie". Old timers often referred to them as "sewing machines" due to their odd motion and valve arrangement. Due to its unique construction this locomotive

D.S.P.&P. 2, the "Platte Canon," a 4-4-0 purchased secondhand from the Kansas Central.

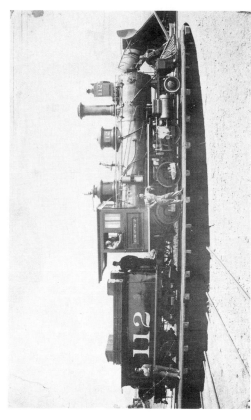

D.S.P.&P. 55, 2-6-6T, (formerly the 22) at Garrison, Montana, on loan to the Utah & Northern in 1886.

D.L.&G. 57, 2-6-6T, (formerly D.S.P.&P. 24) photographed at Garfield Quarry, above Morrison, in 1892.

D.S.P.&P. 112, 2-6-0, (formerly D.S.P.&P. 70 and later C.&S. 7) photographed on the Como turntable about 1888.

was particularly suited for use on a mountain railroad such as the South Park, where plenty of 20- and 30-degree curves were to be found. Conclusive evidence of the adaptability of this little engine to mountain railroading is borne out when it is known that the South Park management, on the recommendation of Col. C. W. Fisher,[1] purchased 23 of Mason's engines between 1878 and 1880. However, due to the demand for larger and heavier power, all subsequent orders for locomotives called for the conventional 2-6-0 and 2-8-0 types. The South Park, in common with other Colorado mountain railroads, found the consolidation an ideal engine for mountain service. Concerning the Mason Bogie type of engine, we quote directly from R. & L. H. S. Bulletin No. 41:

"The Fairlie engine appealed to William Mason but he foresaw difficulties in its use on our American railroads with their sharp curves. Mr. Mason built his driving wheels and cylinders on a truck or 'bogie' frame; consequently they were free to turn around the center pin and thus follow the curvature of the track. The center pin was held by a cast iron saddle attached to the boiler, and others placed the center pin to the main frame of the engine. This plan of Mr. Mason's was satisfactory for the lighter engines but he afterward attached the center pin to a main frame extending from one end to the other, and nearly the whole length of the engine. On his first engines of this type, the tender was carried on a separate frame and was bolted to the sides of the firebox, and this was continued, with some modification, to the last.

"The steam pipe was carried through the front tube sheet in the regular way and then down to the bottom of the smoke box where it was attached to a horizontal pipe which led back to the hollow bed plate casting in the center of which was a vertical pipe connected with a ball and socket joint and stuffing box. Then a vertical pipe went forward and connected with the branch pipes leading to the cylinders. In this way flexibility of the steam pipes was obtained with only one movable joint. The exhaust pipe had to move with the truck and the petticoat pipe was made oblong at its lower end to take care of the transverse movement of the exhaust pipe.

"The first engines were equipped with the plain Stephenson gear but on Mason's later engines (on account of the closeness of the first pair of drivers) he used the Walschaert gear and was the first builder in this country to use this gear to any great extent. The reversing shaft, however, was placed on top of the boiler as clearance did not permit it to be placed underneath as in present practice.

"The early engines did not have leading trucks and the majority were of the 0-4-4 type. Flange wear on the first pair of drivers and increasing size of these engines caused him to use a two wheel truck".

In a letter to the writer, C. E. Fisher states:

"After looking at a profile of the South Park line, I sometimes wonder that the road could operate at all in the winter. Those Mason locomotives must have taken a terrific beating on those grades with any kind of a train. Letters in the files of William Mason show that those bogies had their troubles. Whether this was due to the bogie arrangement, the drivers turning like a truck, with the curvature of the road, or whether it was because the tender frame was attached to the sides of the firebox—we will never know at this late day. The South Park men admitted they were the best steamers of all their engines".

1. F. P. Roesch, Standard Stoker Co.

Further concerning the Mason Bogie, Mr. Roesch writes:

"In my day on the South Park, all of the enginemen preferred the Mason engine. They were good steamers and easy to maintain, particularly the valve gear. At that time none of the locomotives were equipped with driver brakes, but on the contrary, all used the 'LeChatelier' water brake—the customary practice being to operate the locomotive in reverse on descending grades, utilizing the back pressure built up in the cylinders to assist in controlling the speed. This was hard on the valve gear, especially the Stephenson type. The old Eames vacuum brakes eventually gave way to the Westinghouse air-brake".

While on the subject of brakes, we should not fail to mention the auxiliary air tanks that were mounted on practically all South Park engines and their tenders. Back in the days of small motive power and under-size air pumps, this was common practice on almost all mountain railroads. Due to the frequency with which both ascending and descending grades were encountered in mountainous country, the usual air pump equipment found on the average small engine of early day vintage was unable to supply the air needed for the constant charging and recharging of the train line. Therefore, to assist the pump, these auxiliary tanks, which were pumped up at odd times, carried a reserve supply of air which was used by an engineer to recharge his train line and thus maintain proper braking control. Mr. H. L. Curtiss writes that many of the early South Park engines also had independent hand brakes on the tender.

During the writer's search for locomotive material, an interesting incident concerning an old bogie type engine now standing on the grounds of the Iowa State College at Ames, Iowa, came to light. According to statements made in a college engineering publication of this school, this engine was built by Rogers Ketchum & Grosvenor of Paterson, New Jersey, in 1855 for The Mississippi & Missouri Railroad, and was the second railroad locomotive to enter the state of Iowa. This paper further states that later it was sold to the Denver & Rio Grande and still later to the Chicago Burlington & Quincy, following which the engine was retired and given to the college in 1904.

However, a close inspection of this old engine by Mr. Guyon C. Whitley, who lives in Ames, Iowa, discloses some interesting facts. The drive wheel diameters, wheel base, firebox dimensions, gauge and valve gear coincides exactly with the specifications of Mason engines built for the South Park line. The badge plate giving the builder's name and construction number is missing, but on the front of the right cylinder casting are the letters "D.S.P.". Cast in a front wheel truck are the words "Denver Wheel G. W. Co. Denver, Colo. Jan. 14, 1896. U. P. D. & G." On both of the two rear wheels under the tender are the letters "D & S P". In view of this and other evidence, Mr. Whitley and the author contend that this is an original Denver South

R. H. Kindig.

C.&S. 73 at Como in 1938.

R. H. Kindig.

D.&R.G.W. 343, leased to C.&S., at Denver in 1937.

R. H. Kindig.

C.&S. 71 near Jefferson in 1938.

John W. Maxwell.

C.&S. 75 at Leadville in 1941.

Park & Pacific Mason Bogie. How the history of this engine became so confused is not known.

Excluding the earliest engines such as numbers 1 and 2, and the 23 Masons, South Park motive power, which weighed from 27½ to 42½ tons, was rather heavy for a three-foot gauge road. Even with this relatively heavy power it often required from two to four engines to get a ten- to fifteen-car freight drag up Boreas or Alpine Pass. The following chart, from a 1912 employee's timecard, gives the rating in tons which the engines in use at that time could move over various sections of the road.

ENGINE RATING IN TONS OF 2,000 POUNDS

	Engine Classification and Numbers		
	B-3-B 21-22	B-3-C 4-10	
B-3-A 11-13	B-4-A 30	B-4-C 57-62	B-4-E 71-73
	B-4-B 37-55	B-4-D 63-70	
Tons	Tons	Tons	Tons

PLATTE CANON DISTRICT
West Bound

Denver to Platte Canon	340	400	425	475
Platte Canon to Pine Grove	115	150	175	190
Pine Grove to Grant	90	120	140	155
Grant to Kenosha	80	110	125	140
Jefferson to Como	160	210	250	290

East Bound

Jefferson to Kenosha	85	110	130	140

LEADVILLE DISTRICT
West Bound

Como to Boreas	70	95	110	120
Dickey to Climax	75	105	120	135

East Bound

Leadville to Climax	140	185	210	235
Dickey to Breckenridge	110	155	175	195
Breckenridge to Boreas	70	95	110	120

GUNNISON DISTRICT
West Bound

Como to Bath	100	130	150	170
Nathrop to Mt. Princeton	130	160	190	210
Mt. Princeton to Alpine Tunnel	70	95	110	120
Gunnison to Teachout	300	375	430	460
Teachout to Baldwin	130	160	185	200

East Bound

Gunnison to Parlins	275	325	350	400
Parlins to Pitkin	125	160	190	215
Pitkin to Alpine Tunnel	70	95	110	120
Nathrop to Schwanders	325	400	450	500
Schwanders to Bath	90	120	130	140
Platte River to Como	170	200	240	260

With their small drivers, which averaged 37 to 40 inches, the boilers lay very low and extended all the way back through the cab, separating the engineer and fireman. This eliminated the so-called deck as we know it on the modern locomotive. Due to this low boiler construction, the links, when the reverse lever was well down, would drop close to the ties. Roy Morton writes that during sub-zero weather the engine crews would often have to take a steam hose and thaw out the packed and frozen snow in the link blocks before they could reverse.

William Wendell wrote the author:

"The old giant balloon stacks were often called 'Boo-Hoos'. At night the shower of sparks that blew up in the air looked like a fourth of July celebration. Farmer's haystacks along the right of way were often set on fire. The boiler flues were always clean because of the pure mountain water and good Baldwin coal. This coal burned to a white ash, which would blow out the stack if the dampers were opened".

Both balloon and diamond stacks on the South Park began to make their exit around the turn of the century.

Because of the great number of fires started along the railroad by the engines, the company developed a new device known as the cinder catcher. This contrivance resembled a big sausage, hooked to the top of the stack and hung down the side of the smoke box, almost reaching the rails. It was so designed that the cinders, caught by a screen placed above the stack, were deflected into the curved pipe, which was emptied periodically.

Engineer Whitney writes that the old class DJ engines, numbers 29 to 38, were known as "cold-water Brooks" or "ice cream freezers", and because of a shallow firebox with grates which pitched from six inches below the firebox door to below the flue sheet, they were very hard to fire and made poor steamers. He also added the remark that a common gag among engine crews was that if you wanted a cold drink, just open up the blowoff cock of a "cold-water Brooks". Engineer Wendell added that A. L. Humphrey, Sup't. of Motive Power, made a good engine out of number 35 by installing a new type firebox of his own design. According to Wendell, Billy Westall used this engine (later number 162) on passenger service between Denver and Como and it could handle a three-car train on Kenosha Hill with ease.

Engineer Wendell also tells us that around 1883 the following South Park rolling stock was loaned to the Utah & Northern R. R., a narrow gauge Union Pacific controlled road located in Utah and Montana:

Mason engines, numbers 3, 4, 5, 6, 7, 10, 12, 13, 14, 15, 16, 20, 21, 22, Dawson & Bailey engines, numbers 17 and 18, and 200 miscellaneous freight cars. Mr. Wendell added that to the best of his recollection, all this rolling stock was later returned to Colorado. Confirmation of this is apparently to be found in the records of the Pacific Railway Commission Trials wherein an engineer's report dated September 1, 1887, states that three Mason engines, numbers 51, 52, and 55 (original numbers 15, 16, and 22) and two Brooks engines, numbers 156 and 161 (original numbers 29 and 34) were in service on the Utah & Northern on that date.

In addition to the South Park's own power, Thomas St. John states that at various times prior to 1921, three Denver Boulder & Western engines, numbers 1, 25, and 33, were in use on the Colorado & Southern. William Cairns and Jess Frazier both write that the Colorado & Southern was experimenting with number 25, a Shay engine, on Boreas Pass with a view of perhaps buying it. Evidently the Shay's performance did not justify its purchase as this engine was sold to a road in Utah.[1] Also, around 1936, the Denver & Rio Grande Western leased three of their engines, numbers 343, 345, and 346 to the Colorado & Southern. Confirmation of the South Park's use of these various engines from foreign roads is found in Colorado & Southern train registers owned by R. H. Kindig.

Relative to the three Rio Grande engines, Mr. Kindig writes that they were loaded on flat cars at Alamosa and shipped up to Denver. While in use on the South Park they were equipped with the usual Colorado & Southern cinder catcher. In August, 1936, number 346, while running light down the east slope of Kenosha, overturned and suffered considerable damage. The damaged engine was loaded on a flat car and taken to the C. B. & Q. shops in Denver where it was repaired. The three engines were returned to the Rio Grande in the spring of 1937.

Relative to the first two narrow gauge engines owned by the Colorado Central, there seems to be a question

1. Mr. P. H. Graham of Morse Brothers, Denver.

concerning their correct wheel arrangement. Mr. C. C. Rogers of Golden, an old timer who used to work on the Clear Creek line, writes in the Locomotive Engineers Journal of November, 1943. We quote in part:

"The following material was sent to me by the Union Pacific Old Timers Club and should interest the old timers who railroaded on the Clear Creek line.

"The first engines to pull into Georgetown and Central City on passenger were called 'Punch' and 'Judy'.[1] They had two drivers on a side and no pony truck, and pulled two coaches which weighed six tons each. . . . ".

The H. K. Porter Company, successor to Dawson & Bailey and Porter-Bell, report that Colorado Central No. 1 was a saddle tank engine with three pairs of drivers and a four-wheel tender, and that Colorado Central No. 2 had three pair of drivers and a four-wheel tender. On the other hand, a Colorado Central locomotive roster issued by the Union Pacific in 1885 states that No. 1 was a 2-6-0 and that No. 2 was an 0-4-0. Apparently, it is either a case of erroneous information being handed down, or else the two engines in question, especially No. 2, were completely rebuilt.

One or two photographs of these two early engines have come to light, but due to the angle that they were photographed or the age of the print, it has been impossible to accurately determine their correct wheel arrangement. The writer has listed these engines in the roster as described by the 1885 Union Pacific records, with suitable remarks.

1. Evidently, these names were invented by the Clear Creek citizens. As near as can be ascertained, the Union Pacific did not name any narrow-gauge Colorado Central engines.

Jennings and Russell photo, from Francis Rizzari Collection.

Denver South Park & Pacific No. 44, formerly D.S.P.&P. No. 8 "Lake City," stands at the Denver depot with combination car No. 6, ready for a run to Morrison sometime between 1885 and 1889.

"South Park Mogul"

She was dingy, she was humble,
    She was modest in the station;
The rust along her boiler plates
    Proclaimed a poor relation.

Of the proud ones, the mighty ones
    That towered along her side,
She, squatting on the narrow gauge,
    They, strutting on the wide.

But when she cleared the city
    She breathed with lungs of brass,
As proud as any Empress
    She stormed along the pass.

In plumes of black and silver
    She crashed the canon gates,
She labored past mountain cliffs,
    She snorted where hell awaits.

The Courts have taken up her rails,
    She rusts in Denver town;
From tender and from car step
    Her homesick men are down.

Busses now roar between the peaks
    Where once her smokestack swayed,
But still I see the old Gal's ghost
    Go ramming up the grade.

          E. B. Turnbull,
          Railroad Magazine,
          January, 1938.

Just down from the heights of Boreas Pass, D.S.P.&P. engine 54, smoke pouring from its Congdon stack and with its bowler-hatted engineer peering out from the cab window, rounds a curve about a mile east of Breckenridge with a westbound passenger train. With flanges squealing and whistle screaming, engine 54 resumes speed after slowing to allow D.S.P.&P. 67 to back its freight train into Little Mountain Spur. The year is 1884, the line from Como to Leadville, on which this scene takes place, has just been completed.

Painting by Philip Ronfor
"A Meet at Little Mountain Spur"

George E. Mellen photo,
from Morris W. Abbott Collection.

George E. Mellen's special train, headed by D.S.P.&P. 42, halts for one of the great 17-inch by 22-inch glass plate photos in the rocky depths of lower Platte Cañon.

Original C.C. No.*	C.C. No. (1885)	U.P. Class	U.P.D. & G. No. (1890)	C. & S. No. (1899)	C. & S. Class	Type	Cylinders	Drivers	Weight on Drivers	Builders
1(2nd)	284	Odd				2-6-0	12"x16"	33"	39,160	Porter-Bell
2	293	Odd				0-6-0	12"x16"	33"	32,450	Porter-Bell
3	33	AH-1				0-6-0	12"x16"	33"	32,450	Porter-Bell
4	30	AH-1				0-6-0	12"x16"	33"	32,450	Porter-Bell
5	31	AH-1				0-6-0	12"x16"	33"	32,450	Porter-Bell
6	32	AH-1				0-6-0	13"x16"	34"	32,450	Porter-Bell
7	292	Odd				2-6-0	12"x16"	36"	33,180	Porter-Bell
8	150	DJ-1	150,5	15		2-6-0	15"x18"	36"	46,960	Brooks
9	151	DJ-1	151			2-6-0	15"x18"	36"	46,960	Brooks
10	152	DJ-1	152,6	16		2-6-0	15"x18"	36"	46,960	Brooks
11	153	DJ-1	153,2	2		2-6-0	15"x18"	36"	46,960	Brooks
12	154	DJ-1	154,4	3		2-6-0	15"x18"	36"	46,960	Brooks
13	155	DJ-1	155,3	14		2-6-0	15"x18"	36"	46,960	Brooks
14	107	DI-2	107,7	12	B-3-A	2-6-0	14½"x18"	40"	58,300	Cooke
15	108	DI-2	108,8	13	B-3-A	2-6-0	14½"x18"	40"	58,300	Cooke

* Evidence indicates the existence of several earlier locomotives, not included in this roster because of the lack of definite information. According to 1872 newspaper accounts, and other sources, the locomotives bore the following names: *General Sherman, General Sheridan, Punch,* and *Judy.*

Chas. Weitfle photo, from R. A. Ronzio Collection.

Colorado Central 1 arrives at Forks Creek Station with a two-car train from Central City.

Construction No.	Date Built	Disposition	REMARKS
151	4/1874	Scrapped 1889	H. K. Porter Company, successor to Dawson & Baily and Porter-Bell, reports (1st) No. 1 was a saddle tank with three pairs of drivers and a four-wheel tender. Old U. P. records list cylinders as 12"x18" and drivers as 37 inches.
214	3/1875	Scrapped 1889	H. K. Porter Co. reports this engine had three pairs of drivers and a four-wheel tender. Old U. P. records list drivers as 36 inches.
217	6/1875	Unknown	Disappeared from records during 1887-88. Old U. P. records list cylinders as 13"x16" and drivers as 34 inches.
149	3/1873	Scrapped 1889	Old U. P. records list cylinders as 13"x16" and drivers as 34 inches. Engine rebuilt, February, 1884.
150	4/1873	Unknown	Old U. P. records list cylinders as 13"x16" and drivers as 34 inches. Engine rebuilt, September, 1881. Disappeared from records during 1887-88.
Unknown	Unknown	Scrapped 1889	Rebuilt, September, 1882.
Unknown	Unknown	Scrapped 1887	
403	3/1880	Sold by 1902, per C. & S. records	Old U. P. records list drivers as 38 inches.
404	3/1880	Sold 1899	To A. Kent Lumber and Building Company. A report in the Pacific Railway Commission Trials states this engine was rebuilt in December, 1885. From all available evidence, it was renumbered 59. Old U. P. records list drivers as 38 inches.
464	10/1880	Sold by 1902, per C. & S. records	Old U. P. records list drivers as 38 inches.
465	10/1880	Sold by 1902, per C. & S. records	Old U. P. records list drivers as 38 inches.
547	6/1881	Sold by 1902, per C. & S. records	Old U. P. records list drivers as 38 inches.
548	6/1881	Sold by 1902, per C. & S. records	Old U. P. records list drivers as 38 inches.
1558	2/1884	Scrapped August, 1923	Old photographs show this engine as both U. P. D. & G. 107 and as U. P. D. & G. 7. Dates and details unknown.
1559	2/1884	Scrapped August, 1923	Old photographs show this engine as both U. P. D. & G. 108 and as U. P. D. & G. 8. Dates and details unknown.

Reed and McKenney photo,
from R. A. Ronzio Collection.

One of the Colorado Central's 0-4-0 construction engines heads west on brand new track in Clear Creek Canon.

Original DSP&P No.	Name	DSP&P No. (1885)	U.P. Class	DL&G No. (1889)	UPD&G No. (1890)	C&S No. (1899)	C.&S. Class	Type	Cylinders	Drivers	Weight on Drivers
1	Fairplay	4	DF-1					2-6-0	11″x16″	34″	36,180
2	Platte Canon	283	Odd	283				4-4-0	13″x18″	44″	41,450
3	Oro City	40	DH-1	40				2-6-6T	13″x16″	37″	43,850
4	San Juan	41	DH-1	41				2-6-6T	13″x16″	37″	43,850
5	Leadville	291	Odd	291				2-6-6T	12″x16″	34″	42,000
6	Tenmile	42	DH-1	42				2-6-6T	13″x16″	37″	43,850
7	Gunnison	43	DH-1	43				2-6-6T	13″x16″	37″	43,850
8	Lake City	44	DH-1	44				2-6-6T	13″x16″	37″	43,850
9	Kenosha	50	DI-1					2-6-6T	13″x16″	37″	43,850
		101		101				2-6-0	14″x18″	42″	?
10	Granite	45	DH-1	45				2-6-6T	13″x16″	37″	43,850
11	Ouray	46	DH-1	46				2-6-6T	13″x16″	37″	43,850
12	Como	47	DH-1	47				2-6-6T	13″x16″	37″	43,850
13	Ruby	48	DH-1	48				2-6-6T	13″x16″	37″	43,850
14	Twin Lakes	58	DI-1	58				2-6-6T	13″x16″	37″	45,000
15	Breckenridge	51	DI-1	51				2-6-6T	13″x16″	37″	45,000
16	Eureka	52	DI-1	52				2-6-6T	13″x16″	37″	45,000
17		140	DI-3					2-6-0	14″x22″	46″	52,200
18		141	DI-3					2-6-0	14″x22″	46″	52,200
19		142	DI-3					2-6-0	14″x22″	46″	52,200
20	Silverton	53	DI-1	53				2-6-6T	13″x16″	37″	45,000
21	Pitkin City	54	DI-1	54				2-6-6T	13″x16″	37″	45,000
22	Crested Butte	55	DI-1	55				2-6-6T	13″x16″	37″	45,000
23	Grant	56	DI-1	56				2-6-6T	14″x16″	37″	45,000
24	Buena Vista	57	DI-1	57		1		2-6-6T	14″x16″	37″	45,000
25	Alpine	240	EJ-1	240				2-8-6T	15″x20″	36″	55,340
26	Rico	241	EJ-1	241				2-8-6T	15″x20″	36″	55,340
27	Roaring Fork	242	EJ-1	242				2-8-6T	15″x20″	36″	55,340
28	Denver	243	EJ-1	243				2-8-6T	15″x20″	36″	55,340
29		156	DJ-1	156		21	B-3-B	2-6-0	15″x18″	38″	46,960
30	Morrison	157	DJ-1	157				2-6-0	15″x18″	38″	46,960
31	Hill Top	158	DJ-1	158				2-6-0	15″x18″	38″	46,960
32		159	DJ-1					2-6-0	15″x18″	38″	46,960
33	Webster	160	DJ-1	160				2-6-0	15″x18″	38″	46,960

DENVER SOUTH PARK & PACIFIC

Builder	Construction No.	Date Built	Disposition	REMARKS
Dawson & Baily	Unknown	11/1873	Scrapped 1888	Report of Pacific Ry. Commission Trials, Sept., 1887, states No. 4 condemned.
Dawson & Baily	Unknown	6/1874	Unknown	
Mason	591	5/1878	Scrapped 1890	
Mason	597	11/1878	Scrapped 1889	
Mason	589	1/1878	Scrapped 1889	Originally built as Kansas Central No. 4 as an 0-6-6T. Rebuilt by the Mason Works to a 2-6-6T and sold to the D.S.P.&P. on February 4, 1879.
Mason	599	4/1879	Scrapped 1890	
Mason	600	4/1879	Scrapped 1890	
Mason	601	5/1879	Scrapped 1889	
Mason	602	5/1879	Scrapped 1886	C. E. Fisher states this engine was scrapped in 1886 and replaced by the U. P. with Utah & Northern No. 101. The number 101 was retained on the D.S.P.&P. and the D.L.&G.
Brooks	801	10/1882	Sold in 1891	Built as U.&N. 44. Became U.&N. 101 in 1885 and D.S.P.&P. 101 by 1887.
Mason	607	8/1879	Scrapped 1890	
Mason	608	8/1879	Scrapped 1890	
Mason	609	9/1879	Scrapped 1890	
Mason	610	9/1879	Scrapped 1890	
Mason	611	10/1879	Unknown	
Mason	612	10/1879	Unknown	Report of Pac. Ry. Comm. Trials, Sept., 1887, states this engine was rebuilt in 1884, and was in service on the Utah & Northern in Idaho. It was also listed in poor condition.
Mason	613	11/1879	Unknown	Report of Pac. Ry. Comm. Trials, Sept., 1887, states this engine was rebuilt in 1884 and was in service on the Utah & Northern in Idaho.
Dawson & Baily	Unknown	1/1875	Scrapped 1889	Originally Cairo & St. Louis No. 22. Sold to D.S.P.&P. in 1879.
Dawson & Baily	Unknown	2/1875	Scrapped 1889	Originally Cairo & St. Louis No. 23. Sold to D.S.P.&P. in 1879. Rebuilt in May 1884.
Dawson & Baily	Unknown	2/1875	Scrapped 1889	Originally Cairo & St. Louis No. 24. Sold to D.S.P.&P. in 1879.
Mason	614	11/1879	Unknown	
Mason	615	12/1879	Unknown	
Mason	616	12/1879	Unknown	Report of Pac. Ry. Comm. Trials, Sept., 1887, states this engine in service on Utah & Northern in Idaho.
Mason	617	2/1880	Unknown	
Mason	618	2/1880	Sold by 1902, per C. & S. records	C. & S. records indicate this engine rebuilt as 2-6-0 from 2-6-6T prior to 1902.
Mason	623	6/1880	Unknown	
Mason	624	6/1880	Unknown	
Mason	628	8/1880	Unknown	
Mason	632	10/1880	Sold prior to 1899	
Brooks	713	5/1882	Scrapped August, 1923	Report of Pac. Ry. Comm. Trials, Sept., 1887, states this engine in service on Utah & Northern in Idaho. Late C. & S. folio sheets show 41" drivers.
Brooks	714	5/1882	Unknown	Renumbered 61.
Brooks	727	6/1882	Unknown	Renumbered 62.
Brooks	728	6/1882	Unknown	G. M. Best and S. R. Wood report engine rebuilt by U. P. about 1885 with 14"x18" cylinders, and renumbered 60.
Brooks	742	7/1882	Unknown	Renumbered 63.

Original DSP&P No.	Name	DSP&P No. (1885)	U.P. Class	DL&G No. (1889)	UPD&G No. (1890)	C&S No. (1899)	C.&S. Class	Type	Cylinders	Drivers	Weight on Drivers
34	Alma	161	DJ-1	161		17		2-6-0	15″x18″	38″	46,960
35	Dillon	162	DJ-1	162		22	B-3-B	2-6-0	15″x18″	38″	46,960
36		163	DJ-1	163		18		2-6-0	15″x18″	38″	46,960
37		164	DJ-1	164		19		2-6-0	15″x18″	38″	46,960
38	Chihuahua	165	DJ-1	165		20		2-6-0	15″x18″	38″	46,960
39		109	DI-2	109		4	B-3-C	2-6-0	14½″x18″	40″	58,300
40		110	DI-2	110		5	B-3-C	2-6-0	14½″x18″	40″	58,300
41		198	EJ-1	198		37	B-4-B	2-8-0	15″x18″	36″	62,900
42		199	EJ-1	199		38	B-4-B	2-8-0	15″x18″	36″	62,900
43		200	EJ-1	200		39	B-4-B	2-8-0	15″x18″	36″	62,900
44		201	EJ-1	201		40	B-4-B	2-8-0	15″x18″	36″	62,900
45		202	EJ-1	202		41	B-4-B	2-8-0	15″x18″	36″	62,900
46		203	EJ-1	203		42	B-4-B	2-8-0	15″x18″	36″	62,900
47		204	EJ-1	204		43	B-4-B	2-8-0	15″x18″	36″	62,900
48		205	EJ-1	205		44	B-4-B	2-8-0	15″x18″	36″	62,900
49		206	EJ-1	206		45	B-4-B	2-8-0	15″x18″	36″	62,900
50		190	EJ-1	190		30	B-4-A	2-8-0	15″x18″	37″	56,000
51		191	EJ-1	191		31		2-8-0	15″x18″	37″	56,000
52		192	EJ-1	192		32		2-8-0	15″x18″	37″	56,000
53		193	EJ-1	193				2-8-0	15″x18″	37″	56,000
54		194	EJ-1	194		33		2-8-0	15″x18″	37″	56,000
55		195	EJ-1	195		34		2-8-0	15″x18″	37″	56,000
56		196	EJ-1	196		35		2-8-0	15″x18″	37″	56,000
57		197	EJ-1	197		36		2-8-0	15″x18″	37″	56,000
58		207	EJ-1	207		46	B-4-B	2-8-0	15″x18″	36″	62,900
59		208	EJ-1	208		47	B-4-B	2-8-0	15″x18″	36″	62,900
60		209	EJ-1	209		48	B-4-B	2-8-0	15″x18″	36″	62,900
61		210	EJ-1	210		49	B-4-B	2-8-0	15″x18″	36″	62,900

DENVER SOUTH PARK & PACIFIC

Builder	Construction No.	Date Built	Disposition	REMARKS
Brooks	743	7/1882	Scrapped by 1902, per C&S records	Report of Pac. Ry. Comm. Trials, Sept., 1887, states this engine in service on Utah & Northern in Idaho.
Brooks	755	8/1882	Scrapped March, 1927	Rebuilt with new boiler, December, 1894. Late C. & S. folio sheets show 40″ drivers.
Brooks	756	8/1882	Sold by 1902, per C&S records	
Brooks	782	9/1882	Sold about 1902	To Montrose Lumber Company.
Brooks	783	9/1882	Sold by 1902, per C&S records	
Cooke	1550	2/1884	Scrapped May, 1934	Rebuilt with new boiler and 15″x18″ cylinders, June, 1900. New frame, 1917.
Cooke	1551	2/1884	Scrapped December, 1938	Rebuilt with new boiler and 15″x18″ cylinders, August, 1901. New frame, 1917.
Cooke	1478	6/1883	Scrapped December, 1921	
Cooke	1479	6/1883	Scrapped August, 1916	
Cooke	1480	6/1883	Sold June, 1917	Became Hallack & Howard Lumber Company 4.
Cooke	1481	6/1883	Retired February, 1921	Traded to Morse Brothers. See Note 1.
Cooke	1482	6/1883	Scrapped October, 1914	
Cooke	1483	6/1883	Retired February, 1921	Traded to Morse Brothers. See Note 1.
Cooke	1484	7/1883	Retired February, 1921	Traded to Morse Brothers. See Note 1.
Cooke	1485	7/1883	Scrapped October, 1914	
Cooke	1486	7/1883	Sold June, 1918	Tender sold June, 1918 (see engine 67). Engine 49 (with another tender) sold to Hallack & Howard Lumber Company.
Baldwin	4917	1/1880	Retired Feb. 1921	Traded to Morse Brothers. See Note 1.
Baldwin	4919	1/1880	Sold prior to 1902	To Ed Hines Lumber Company; later owned by A. A. Bigelow & Co. and Thunderlake Lumber Co. Dates and details unknown. **On display at Colo. Railroad Museum, Golden, since Feb. 1973**
Baldwin	4926	1/1880	Sold prior to 1902	To J. J. White Company; later owned by Deerfield R. R. Co. (their No. 1). Dates and details unknown.
Baldwin	4930	1/1880	Sold prior to 1902	To Oak Grove & Georgetown R. R. Co., located in Alabama and Mississippi. Dates and details unknown.
Baldwin	4950	2/1880	Sold by 1902, per C&S records	
Baldwin	4951	2/1880	Sold prior to 1902	To B. G. Peters Salt & Lumber Company; later owned by Manistee & Luther R. R. Co., located in Michigan. Dates and details unknown.
Baldwin	4955	2/1880	Sold prior to 1902	To Clarkson Saw Mill Company. One report states this engine later became No. 2 of Deerfield R. R. Co. Dates and details unknown.
Baldwin	4957	2/1880	Sold prior to 1902	To Manistee & Luther R. R. Company. Dates and details unknown.
Cooke	1487	7/1883	Scrapped July, 1916	
Cooke	1494	8/1883	Scrapped February, 1921	
Cooke	1495	8/1883	Sold August, 1920	To Hallack & Howard Lumber Company.
Cooke	1496	8/1883	Retired February, 1921	Traded to Morse Brothers. See Note 1.

Original DSP&P No.	Name	DSP&P No. (1885)	U.P. Class	DL&G No. (1889)	UPD&G No. (1890)	C&S No. (1899)	C.&S. Class	Type	Cylinders	Drivers	Weight on Drivers
62		211	EJ-1	211		50	B-4-B	2-8-0	15"x18"	36"	62,900
63		212	EJ-1	212		51	B-4-B	2-8-0	15"x18"	36"	62,900
64		213	EJ-1	213		52	B-4-B	2-8-0	15"x18"	36"	62,900
65		214	EJ-1	214		53	B-4-B	2-8-0	15"x18"	36"	62,900
66		215	EJ-1	215		54	B-4-B	2-8-0	15"x18"	36"	62,900
67		216	EJ-1	216		55	B-4-B	2-8-0	15"x18"	36"	62,900
68		217	EJ-1	217		56	B-4-B	2-8-0	15"x18"	36"	62,900
69		111	DI-2	111		6	B-3-C	2-6-0	14½"x18"	40"	58,300
70		112	DI-2	112		7	B-3-C	2-6-0	14½"x18"	40"	58,300
71		113	DI-2	113		8	B-3-C	2-6-0	14½"x18"	40"	58,300
72		114	DI-2	114		9	B-3-C	2-6-0	14½"x18"	40"	58,300
73		115	DI-2	115		10	B-3-C	2-6-0	14½"x18"	40"	58,300
74		116	DI-2	116		11	B-3-A	2-6-0	14½"x18"	40"	58,300
				260		57	B-4-C	2-8-0	16"x18"	37"	61,900
				261		58	B-4-C	2-8-0	16"x18"	37"	61,900
				262		59	B-4-C	2-8-0	16"x18"	37"	61,900
				263		60	B-4-C	2-8-0	16"x18"	37"	61,900
				264		61	B-4-C	2-8-0	16"x18"	37"	61,900
				265		62	B-4-C	2-8-0	16"x18"	37"	61,900
				266		63	B-4-D	2-8-0	16"x20"	37"	66,000
				267		64	B-4-D	2-8-0	16"x20"	37"	66,000
				268		65	B-4-D	2-8-0	16"x20"	37"	66,000
				269		66	B-4-D	2-8-0	16"x20"	37"	66,000
				270		67	B-4-D	2-8-0	16"x20"	37"	66,000
				271		68	B-4-D	2-8-0	16"x20"	37"	66,000
				272		69	B-4-D	2-8-0	16"x20"	37"	66,000
				273		70	B-4-D	2-8-0	16"x20"	37"	66,000
					9	71	B-4-E	2-8-0	15½"x20"	37"	70,500

DENVER SOUTH PARK & PACIFIC

Builder	Construction No.	Date Built	Disposition	REMARKS
Cooke	1497	8/1883	Scrapped February, 1921	
Cooke	1498	8/1883	Scrapped October, 1920	
Cooke	1499	8/1883	Scrapped June, 1918	
Cooke	1500	9/1883	Scrapped June, 1918	
Cooke	1501	9/1883	Sold June, 1920	To Hallack & Howard Lumber Company.
Cooke	1502	9/1883	Sold June, 1918	C. & S. 55, with tender from engine 49, sold to the Milwaukee Road and numbered 4; used on their Bellevue & Cascade narrow gauge line.
Cooke	1503	9/1883	Scrapped October, 1914	
Cooke	1552	2/1884	Scrapped December, 1938	Rebuilt with new boiler and 15"x18" cylinders, July, 1900. New frame, 1917.
Cooke	1553	2/1884	Scrapped September, 1929	Rebuilt with new boiler and 15"x18" cylinders, July, 1902. New frame, 1917.
Cooke	1554	2/1884	Scrapped December, 1938	Rebuilt with new boiler and 15"x18" cylinders, June, 1901. New frame, 1917.
Cooke	1555	2/1884	On exhibition	Rebuilt with new boiler and 15"x18" cylinders, April, 1901. New frame, 1917. Exhibited at New York World Fair, 1939-40, with baggage car 13 and coach 76. Engine and cars stored at C. B. & Q., Aurora, Illinois, shops. In service Chicago Railroad Fair, 1948-49. Engine now on display at Hill City, S. Dak.
Cooke	1556	2/1884	Scrapped May, 1934	Rebuilt with new boiler and 15"x18" cylinders, August, 1900. New frame, 1917.
Cooke	1557	2/1884	Scrapped June, 1918	ALCO records state engine was ordered by U. P. for D. S. P. & P., but C. & S. records show Colorado Central as original purchaser. Evidence favors the ALCO records.
Rhode Island	1592	2/1886	Scrapped March, 1923	Received from Utah & Northern R. R. See Note 2.
Rhode Island	1593	2/1886	Scrapped December, 1938	Received from Utah & Northern R. R. See Note 2.
Rhode Island	1594	3/1886	Scrapped April, 1925	Received from Utah & Northern R. R. See Note 2.
Rhode Island	1595	3/1886	On exhibition	Received from Utah & Northern R. R. See Note 2. Now on permanent exhibition at Idaho Springs, Colorado.
Rhode Island	1596	4/1886	Scrapped January, 1930	Received from Utah & Northern R. R. See Note 2.
Rhode Island	1597	4/1886	Scrapped December, 1927	Received from Utah & Northern R. R. See Note 2.
Baldwin	11331	12/1890	Scrapped February, 1929	
Baldwin	11332	12/1890	Sold Sept., 1921	To Sosa & Garcia Company, Mexico City, Mexico.
Baldwin	11340	12/1890	Scrapped December, 1938	
Baldwin	11353	12/1890	Scrapped September, 1923	
Baldwin	11333	12/1890	Scrapped February, 1927	
Baldwin	11352	12/1890	Scrapped December, 1938	
Baldwin	11355	12/1890	Sold April, 1943	To White Pass & Yukon Route; became their No. 20.
Baldwin	11356	12/1890	Sold April, 1943	Converted to oil burner, October, 1931. Became White Pass & Yukon Route 21.
Baldwin	15142	1/1897	On exhibition	Purchased from U. P. D. & G., 1899. Now on permanent exhibition at Central City, Colorado.

Original DSP&P No.	Name	DSP&P No. (1885)	U.P. Class	DL&G No. (1889)	UPD&G No. (1890)	C&S No. (1899)	C.&S. Class	Type	Cylinders	Drivers	Weight on Drivers
					10	72	B-4-E	2-8-0	15½"x20"	37"	70,500
					11	73	B-4-E	2-8-0	15½"x20"	37"	70,500
						74	B-4-F	2-8-0	16"x20"	37"	85,000
						75	B-4-F	2-8-0	16"x20"	37"	85,000
						76	B-4-F	2-8-0	16"x20"	37"	85,000
		C.B.&Q.	537					2-8-0	17"x20"	38"	87,400

Note 1. Colorado & Southern engines 30, 40, 42, 43 and 49 were exchanged for three second-hand Denver Boulder & Western engines, numbers 30, 31 and 32, owned by Morse Brothers Machinery Co., in February, 1921. The D. B. & W. engines became C. & S. 74, 75 and 76, respectively.

Note 2. Union Pacific engines 260-265 were originally ordered for service on the Utah & Northern, a U. P. subsidiary. In September, 1890, they were sold to the Denver Leadville & Gunnison. From information available, these six locomotives retained their original Utah & Northern road numbers after being transferred to Colorado.

R. A. Ronzio Collection.

While descending the Garfield Quarry Branch north of Morrison with a trainload of stone, Union Pacific Denver & Gulf 108 derailed.

DENVER SOUTH PARK & PACIFIC

Builder	Construction No.	Date Built	Disposition	REMARKS
Baldwin	15143	1/1897	Scrapped October, 1940	Purchased from U. P. D. & G., 1899.
Baldwin	15144	1/1897	Scrapped October, 1940	Purchased from U. P. D. & G., 1899.
Brooks	2951	4/1898	Sold March, 1945	To Morse Brothers Machinery Co., Denver (for second time; see Note 1). Built as Colorado & Northwestern 30; became Denver Boulder & Western 30 in March, 1909; sold to Morse Brothers the first time and became C. & S. 74 in February, 1921. The engine was again sold to Morse Brothers in 1945, and held for four years, becoming Rio Grande Southern 74 in March, 1949. Sold to City of Boulder, Colo., in 1952. Placed on display in park as Colorado & Northwestern 30.
Brooks	2969	6/1898	Sold March, 1945	To Morse Brothers Machinery Co., Denver (for second time; see Note 1). Built as Colorado & Northwestern 31; became Denver Boulder & Western 31 in March, 1909; sold to Morse Brothers the first time and became C. & S. 75 in February, 1921. The engine was again sold to Morse Brothers in March, 1945; in 1948 it was sold to the Cerro de Pasco Copper Corp., at Lima, Peru, for use on the Central Railway of Peru. (Converted to standard gauge.)
Brooks	2970	6/1898	Sold March, 1945	To Morse Brothers Machinery Co., Denver (for second time; see Note 1). Built as Colorado & Northwestern 32; became Denver Boulder & Western 32 in March, 1909; sold to Morse Brothers the first time and became C. & S. 76 in February, 1921. The engine was again sold to Morse Brothers in March, 1945; in 1948 it was sold to the Cerro de Pasco Copper Corp., at Lima, Peru, for use on the Central Railway of Peru. (Converted to standard gauge.)
Baldwin	14792	4/1896	Scrapped August, 1939	Built as Deadwood Central No. 5; became B. & M. R. No. 496, 1901; renumbered 537, 1904. Leased to C. & S., September, 1930; returned to C. B. & Q., February, 1939.

C.&S. Rotary Snowplow No. 99200 was built by the Cooke Locomotive & Machine Co. for the Leslie Bros. Mfg. Co., Construction No. 26, in February 1889. Original road number was D.L.&G. 011, later renumbered 064. It became C.&S. 99200 in 1912 and was standard gauged in 1943 for use on the Leadville-Climax line.

C.&S. Rotary Snowplow No. 99201 was built by the Cooke Locomotive & Machine Co. for the Leslie Bros. Mfg. Co., Construction No. 59, in January 1900 as C.&S. No. 0271. Renumbered 99201 in 1912.

H. H. Buckwalter photo,
from R. A. Ronzio Collection.

A group of tourists view the hydraulic mining operations at Roscoe in Clear Creek Canon. Denver Leadville & Gunnison 109 heads the train.

W. H. Jackson photo,
from R. A. Ronzio Collection.

Colorado Central 32, a Porter-Bell 0-6-0, with D.S.P.&P. coach 9, halts just west of Beaver Brook station on its eastbound journey through Clear Creek Canon.

W. H. Jackson photo,
from R. A. Ronzio Collection.

D.S.P.&P. 42 with waycar 72 pauses just west of Webster station while the engineer fills the lubricators with oil. An eastbound 8-car freight descends Kenosha Pass high on the hillside in the background.

The 1885 numbers were assigned by the Union Pacific. The engines which survived until the U.P.D.&G. or D.L.&G. lines were organized usually carried the 1885 number after the change of ownership. For some years after the engines were renumbered, the Union Pacific continued to operate the South Park and Colorado Central lines under their original names; therefore photos may be found showing various inscriptions on the cab sides, depending upon the date the photograph was taken. Inscriptions include "D.S.P.&P.", "Colorado Central", "Union Pacific", "U.P.D.&G.", or "D.L.&G."

The original Colorado Central lettering showed either "C.C. R.R." or "COLORADO CENTRAL" on the tender, with the engine number on the front number plate, the sand dome, and the rear of tender. (See examples on pages 14 and 50.) Early South Park lettering sometimes showed a number only on the front number plate; later the number was shown on the number plate, sand dome, and cab side, with the initials "D.S.P.&P." on the tender (See page 164).

Union Pacific 1885 numbering almost invariably included numbers on the front number plate, the head-light, the sand dome, and large figures on the tender, with the Colorado Central name or South Park initials on the cab sides (photos on pages 88 and 149). After the organization of the U.P.D.&G. and the D.L.&G., while these roads were still associated with the U.P., the same numbers and style of painting were used, but the words "Union Pacific" were applied to the cab sides and the initials of the subsidiary line were painted on the sand dome, below the number. (The top photos on page 262 show this type of lettering.) Engines 266-273 came from the locomotive works with this style of painting.

When the two subsidiary roads were removed from Union Pacific control, the parent road's name was eliminated from the cab and replaced with the initials "U.P.D.&G." or "D.L.&G.", which were at the same time removed from the dome. (Pictures on pages 281 and 283 show engines with this change.)

The earliest C.&S. painting system followed the style introduced by the U.P. in 1885, having the number on the front plate, headlight, and dome, with the large figures on the tender, while the words "COLORADO & SOUTHERN" appeared in a single line on the cab sides. About 1901, the intricate C.&S. monogram was applied to the cab; approximately the same system of applying numbers was used, including the large figures on the tender. (Photos on pages 228 and 315.) Around 1904, the numbers were moved to the cab sides and the railroad's name was applied to the tender; this system of lettering narrow gauge C.&S. engines remained in use until the end. (See page 306.)

PREVIOUS NUMBERS OF COLORADO & SOUTHERN LOCOMOTIVES

Because the roster is arranged according to the first number each engine bore on the railroads covered in this book, the following list is provided to simplify location of Colorado & Southern locomotives in the roster. The column headed "U.P." shows the 1885 number (or the first number, if the engine was built after 1885), regardless of the initials or railroad name carried on the engine.

2-6-0 TYPE

C.&S.	U.P.	D.S.-P.&P.	C.C.	C.&S.	U.P.	D.S.-P.&P.	C.C.
1	57	24		12	107, 7		14
2	153		11	13	108, 8		15
3	154		12	14	155		13
4	109	39		15	150		8
5	110	40		16	152		10
6	111	69		17	161	34	
7	112	70		18	163	36	
8	113	71		19	164	37	
9	114	72		20	165	38	
10	115	73		21	156	29	
11	116	74		22	162	35	

(The numbers 23-29 were not assigned on the C.&S.)

2-8-0 TYPE

C.&S.	U.P.	D.S.P.&P.	C.&S.	U.P.	D.S.P.&P.
30	190	50	55	216	67
31	191	51	56	217	68
32	192	52	57	260	
33	194	54	58	261	
34	195	55	59	262	
35	196	56	60	263	
36	197	57	61	264	
37	198	41	62	265	
38	199	42	63	266	
39	200	43	64	267	
40	201	44	65	268	
41	202	45	66	269	
42	203	46	67	270	
43	204	47	68	271	
44	205	48	69	272	
45	206	49	70	273	
46	207	58	71	9	
47	208	59	72	10	
48	209	60	73	11	
49	210	61			
50	211	62		C.&N.-W.,	
51	212	63		D.B.&W.	
52	213	64	74		30
53	214	65	75		31
54	215	66	76		32

Denver Public Library Western Collection.

Denver Leadville & Gunnison 204 poses in Morrison, Colorado, on a fine summer afternoon in 1893. Built in 1883 as D.S.P.&P. 47, it eventually became C.&S. 43 and was retired in 1921.

Robert M. Davis photo, from G. M. Best Collection.

This early photo shows D.S.P.&P. 70 at Farnham, milepost 100, about a mile north of the summit of 11,493-foot Boreas Pass. Engine 70 bore this number only during 1884 and part of 1885, when it was renumbered D.S.P.&P. 112.

BIBLIOGRAPHY

PRINCIPAL SOURCES

Anderson, George L., General William J. Palmer. A Decade of Railroad Building, 1870-1880. Series 209. Colorado College. Colorado Springs, Colorado. 1936.

Boreas Breckenridge and the Blue. Issued by the Passenger Department of the Denver Leadville & Gunnison Ry. 1896.

Bailey, William F., The Union Pacific R.R. Co. 1906.

Baker, James H., and Hafen, LeRoy R., History of Colorado. 1927.

Bradley, Glenn D., The Story of the Santa Fe. 1920.

Colorado State Bureau of Mines. Miscellaneous Reports.

Colorado Geological Survey Bulletins.

Colorado & Southern Ry. Annual Reports. 1898 to 1938.

Colorado. American Guide Series. The Colorado State Planning Commission. 1941.

Colorado Magazine. Published by the State Historical Society of Colorado. 1924 to 1947.

Colorado Public Utilities Commission. Annual Reports. 1913 to 1940.

Colorado & Southern Ry. Corporate History. January 1, 1916.

Chicago Burlington & Quincy R.R. Annual Reports. 1890, 1909 and 1910.

Commercial & Financial Chronicle. 1879 to 1884.

Crofutt, George A., Grip-Sack Guide to Colorado. Volume I, 1881.

Crofutt, George A., Overland Tours. 1888.

Compressed Air Magazine. July 1941.

Davis, James W., The Union Pacific R.R. Company. 1870.

Dodge, Major General Grenville M., How We Built the Union Pacific. 1910.

Denver & Rio Grande R.R. Annual Reports. 1880, 1881, 1882, 1883 and 1886.

Denver Republican. Denver, Colorado. 1882 to 1913.

Denver Post. Denver, Colorado. 1937.

Denver Tribune. Denver, Colorado. 1878 to 1881.

Denver Daily Times. Denver, Colorado. 1873 to 1909.

Denver South Park & Pacific R.R. Annual Report. 1874.

Engineering News. 1879 to 1881.

Engineering and Mining Journal. 1881 to 1883.

Gannett, Henry, A Dictionary of Altitudes. U.S. Geological Survey. Washington, D.C. 1906.

Gandy, Lewis C., The Tabors. 1934.

Gunnison Daily Review. Gunnison, Colorado. 1880 to 1883.

Gunnison News (Democrat) Champion. Gunnison, Colorado. 1910 to 1947.

Historical Sketches of Early Gunnison. Colorado State Normal School. Vol. V., No. 3. 1916.

History of the Union Pacific Coal Mines. 1868 to 1940. Union Pacific Ry. Co. 1940.

Ingersoll, Ernest, The Crest of the Continent. 1885.

McMechen, Edgar C., The Life of Governor John Evans. 1924.

Mock, Samuel Donald, Railroad Development in the Colorado Region to 1880. (Thesis.) University of Nebraska. 1938.

Moody's Manual of Railroads. 1900 to 1918.

Official Railway Guide. Miscellaneous Issues. 1873 to 1943.

Overton, Richard C., Burlington West. 1941.

Official Railway Equipment Register. 1909 to 1914.

Poor's Manual of Railroads. 1865 to 1943.

Pitkin Mining News. Pitkin, Colorado. 1881 - 1882.

Riegel, Robert E., The Story of the Western Railroads. 1926.

Railway World. 1878 to 1908.

Railroad Gazette. 1872 to 1908.

Railway Review. 1880 to 1888.

Railway Age. 1879 to 1908, 1943.

Railroad Magazine. 1929 to 1943.

Report of the Railroad Commissioner. State of Colorado. 1885.

Rocky Mountain News. Denver, Colorado. 1870 to 1887, 1936.

Smiley, Jerome C., History of Denver. 1901.

South Park and Alpine Pass. Issued by the Passenger Department of the Denver Leadville & Gunnison Ry. 1896.

Trottman, Nelson, History of the Union Pacific. 1923.

Trains Magazine. 1941 to 1946.

U. S. Interstate Commerce Commission. Miscellaneous Reports published between 1924 and 1946.

U. S. Interstate Commerce Commission. Valuation Docket No. 716. March 1926.

U. S. Pacific Railway Commission Trials Reports. 1887.

Union Pacific Railway. Annual Reports. 1879 to 1892.

Vickers, William B., History of the City of Denver, Arapahoe County, and Colorado. 1880.

Ward, Louisa A., Chalk Creek, Colorado. 1940.

Warman, Cy, Tales of an Engineer. 1895.

INDEX

A

B

W

Z